Abnormalities of

Personality

Within and Beyond
the Realm of Treatment

ABNORMALITIES OF PERSONALITY

Within and Beyond
the Realm of Treatment

MICHAEL H. STONE, M.D.

W. W. Norton & Company
New York London

The text of this book was composed in Sabon, with display type in Optima.
Composition by Bytheway Typesetting Services, Inc. Manufacturing by Haddon Craftsmen.

Book design by Justine Burkat Trubey

Library of Congress Cataloging-in-Publication Data

Stone, Michael H., 1933–
    Abnormalities of personality : within and beyond the realm of
treatment / Michael H. Stone.
        p.   cm.
    Includes bibliographical references and indexes.
    ISBN 0-393-70127-1
    1. Personality disorders.   I. Title.
    RC554.S764   1993   93-7704
    616.89—dc20   CIP

W.W. Norton & Company, Inc., 500 Fifth Avenue, New York, N.Y. 10110
W.W. Norton & Company, Ltd., 10 Coptic Street, London WC1A 1PU

2 3 4 5 6 7 8 9 0

For
Henriette Klein

Contents

List of Figures

List of Tables

Preface

THE REALM OF PERSONALITY is becoming increasingly important in contemporary psychiatry and has come to occupy the kind of space—in the minds of practitioners and on the shelves of our libraries—formerly accorded only to schizophrenia or the affective psychoses. The topic is already too vast, its burgeoning literature too extensive, to capsulize even in a long book. Given the great relevance of the topic—the psychoses apply only to a few, after all, whereas *everyone* has a personality—its literature may soon outpace that of rival topics in our field.

Pertinent to any complete presentation of *personality* and its abnormalities are such separate issues as diagnosis, etiology, and ethology (the *which*, the *why*, and the *what is it for* of personality), as well as treatment of the various subtypes and the limitations of our therapeutic interventions. I have tried to touch on all these issues, though cognizant of my own limitations, which compel me to focus on what can and cannot be treated, and to spend relatively little time on matters of personality biometrics, better discussed by Widiger, Spitzer, Millon, Cloninger, Loranger, Skodol, and other experts in this area.

I place considerable emphasis, in the matter of treatment, on the whole vast catalog of personality *traits*, since these are what clinicians first confront in appraising the personalities of their patients and interviewees. The personality *disorders* are abstractions composed of various combinations of these traits; we often need repeated contacts in order to diagnose them with conviction. Furthermore, the catalog of traits describes a domain wider than that of the traditional disorders. Attention to this catalog will, I believe, afford clinicians a more complete grasp of personality in all its ramifications.

ACKNOWLEDGMENTS

My understanding of certain personality disorders—borderline, narcissistic and masochistic, especially—has been greatly broadened through discussions with teachers and colleagues, most notably Arnold Cooper, Allen Frances, John Gunderson, Otto Kernberg, Thomas McGlashan, John Oldham, and Harold Searles. To Hagop Akiskal I am indebted for the clarity of his views on the interrelationship between the affective temperaments and their corresponding personality disturbances. I am indebted to Theodore Millon for his illuminating concept of personality as our first line of defense in the interpersonal world. Thomas Widiger introduced me to the five-factor model, of which I have become a True Believer.

For his encouragement, but most of all for his suggestions concerning the chapter on psychopaths not amenable to therapy, I owe much gratitude to one of the country's most prominent forensic psychiatrists, my cousin Bruce Danto.

Defining normal personality has always been elusive. Yet there are normal personalities out there. I have had the good fortune to number among my colleagues several psychiatrists from other countries, the harmoniousness of whose natures has provided me with a Gold Standard for the measure of what personality should be: Professors Keigo Okonogi of Tokyo, Jean Bergeret of Lyon, Jules Angst of Zürich, and Tove Aarkrog of Copenhagen. The serenity and, in putting up with the long hours I have devoted to this manuscript, forebearance of my wife, Beth, have created a very special Gold Standard.

Susan Barrows Munro, who edited the manuscript, gave me invaluable advice in improving the content and tightening the finished product. Where I heeded her advice, the book is better than it would have been. As for its deficiencies and excesses, the responsibility is mine.

My final thanks go to Ms. Ulrike Henderson. The speed and accuracy with which she typed the revision took the arduousness out of this otherwise forbidding task.

Part One

PERSONALITY: WHAT IS IT?

1

Personality: Definitions and Introductory Remarks

THE WORD "PERSONALITY" is used in a variety of ways and contexts. We speak of personality in an everyday sense and in a technical sense. The term can have positive connotations and negative connotations. In colloquial parlance the word may take on the meaning of charisma ("that actress really has "personality"); more often, we use the term to signify the "exterior," the mode of self-presentation, of the person we are speaking about. The latter connotation comes close to the technical definition of "personality," as used by mental health professionals.

As Millon (1981) has formulated it, "personality" is the outgrowth of the behavioral patterns that develop, in response to the challenges of living, during the first half dozen years of childhood: " . . . the child's initial range of diverse behaviors gradually becomes narrowed, selective, and finally, crystallized into preferred ways of relating to others and [of] coping with the world" (p. 4). The overall pattern is unique for each individual, yet similar enough to patterns observed in many other persons that we can make some meaningful generalizations. Even schoolchildren can, for example, make lists of the people they know who fall into such categories of personality as "mean," "pleasant," "rude," "wild," "kind," etc. These simple terms in fact constitute a first step in the differentiation of "personality" into a number of ingredients — called "traits."

Before we examine the nature of *traits* more closely, there is still much to be said about the umbrella concept: personality. The origin of the word is in the Greek and Roman amphitheaters: the actors (and they were all actors—ladies did not get on the stage until much later) could not easily make themselves heard in the farthermost seats of the amphitheater. They wore masks, and it occurred to somebody to place a little megaphone behind the mouth-opening of the mask, through (*per-*) which the sound (*sona*) could be magnified. *Persona*lity, then, represented the intensification of the individual features of whatever character the actor was attempting to portray.

Personality has come to mean the individual, typical, and enduring manner each of us evolves for conveying our emotions, gestures, and behavior to those around us. "Persona" was actually the Latin word for *mask*, underlining, in effect, the outward or surface aspects of what is ordinarily meant by "personality." The Greek word for personality is *prosopikotes* ($\pi\varrho\sigma\sigma\omega\pi\iota$-$\kappa\acute{o}\tau\eta\varsigma$)—it is a modern coinage; the ancients did not use it—which comes from the ancient word for "mask": *prosopeion* ($\pi\varrho\sigma\sigma\omega\pi\varepsilon\~\iota o\nu$)—only *this* mask stemmed from the word for face (*prosopon*), i.e., what was before (*pros*) the eye (*ops*). Here again, the emphasis is on what one shows of oneself to the external world, though the Greek word stresses what one sees; the Latin word, what one hears. Since our scientific words usually derive from Greek roots (e.g., biology, psychology), the science of personality, were we to construct a word for it, would have to be "prosopikotology." A most cumbersome term; small wonder the Greeks, who have a word for everything, do not use it. Neither will we.

THE WHAT, HOW, WHEN, WHERE, AND WHY OF PERSONALITY

In contemporary usage, "personality," in its technical sense, is customarily subdivided into the discrete attitudinal and behavioral subpatterns we call "traits," but divided conceptually into "compartments" supposedly reflecting the two main sets of causative influences: nature and nurture. Thus, TEMPERAMENT refers to those qualities of personality that may be said to be *innate*: reflections, that is, of genetic and constitutional influences. CHARACTER refers to qualities that one acquires in response to one's early environment, though the term is generally used in a narrower sense, relating to how closely, and how genuinely, we endorse the values and customs of our own society and of all humankind.

I believe the concept of personality ought ideally to be fleshed out with the additional notion of *façade*. Most people some of the time, and some people most of the time, affect to portray to those around them an image or a set of attitudes that differs distinctly from the genuine tendencies and attitudes that are hidden below the surface. This notion overlaps with what Balint meant by the "false self" (1969). The more integrated and comfortable in the world a person is, the smaller the distance between the "true" self and the façade or "false self." Those who exhibit the trait of "frankness" or "straightforwardness" to the greatest degree have very little "façade": what you see is what you get. But in the more severe disturbances of personality, and especially in psychopathic "con artists," the exterior and interior aspects of personality are radically different.*

"Temperament," from the Latin word for the weather, focuses particularly on tendencies of *mood* or "disposition" (Greek: *diathesis*). These dispositions were thought to stem from differing proportions of the "four elements": earth, air, fire, and water, excesses of which might render one sad, irritable, cheery, or sluggish (melancholic, choleric, sanguine, or phlegmatic). Though we now assign the origins of these mood tendencies to differences in neurophysiology rather than in the Aristotelian temperaments (cf. Zilboorg, 1941, p. 89), the concepts have retained their utility 2,500 years later. Manic-depressive patients, in particular, and their close relatives are prone to exhibit temperaments that we would classify as "hypomanic" (sanguine), "irritable" (choleric), or "depressive" (melancholic).

"Character" derives from the ancient Greek *charasso* (χαράσσω) to engrave, to dig in (from an IndoEur. root "*gher," to scratch: cf. Ger. kratzen, Fr. gratter, Eng. scratch), and refers now to qualities that become *etched in* upon the blank slate of infancy—as a result of the myriad interactions of the young child with his caretakers, teachers, and peers. There has been considerable confusion in the literature concerning the boundaries of this term. Among the psychoanalytic pioneers, "character" was routinely used as a designation for all that we now subsume under the rubric of personality. Each of the developmental stages adumbrated by Freud (1905) was associated with a particular "character" (oral, anal, genital). Further subdivisions were created in acknowledgment of the diversity encountered in clinical work. Patients who were particularly clingy might be called "oral-receptive"; those who were notably envious and hypercritical, "oral-sadistic." Likewise, certain passive patients were classified as "anal-receptive"; compulsive persons who were more openly angry as "anal-sadistic," and so

---

*To take an extreme example, serial killer Ted Bundy had an irritable temperament, a vicious character, a charming façade, and a psychopathic or "antisocial" (little-p) personality. The latter is "personality" with a small "p," since the term is used here to distinguish among the dozen or so main personality types in our standard nomenclature. These four components blended together make up Bundy's Personality, in the global, capital-P sense.

forth (cf. Abraham, 1921). In his *Character Analysis*, Wilhelm Reich (1929) also spoke of "phallic-narcissistic" and "masochistic" characters.

Meanwhile, the traditional psychiatrists of that era still spoke of temperament (cf. Kraepelin, 1921); others were already using the term "personality" in referring to the totality of one's self-presentation (cf. Sjöbring, 1914, 1958, 1973; Eysenck, 1967). "Temperament" occurs in Freud's oeuvre in only two passages, actually written by Breuer (1893–5, *SE*, vol. II, pp. 197, 239), alluding to "differences in cerebral excitation" that render some persons "lively" (sanguine) and others "lethargic" (phlegmatic).

Whereas *personality* may be understood as an amalgam of traits, *character type* was understood within the psychoanalytic community as a reflection of particular defense mechanisms. The mechanisms of intellectualization, rationalization and isolation of affect were encountered with regularity in the obsessive-compulsive/"anal" character; repression was a common mechanism of the hysteric/"genital" type, etc. (cf. A. Freud, 1936). Key *traits* were sometimes also mentioned, as, for example, the triad of orderliness, obstinancy, and parsimony in compulsive persons (Freud, 1908). When "character" is used in the special sense of "relative goodness of fit between one's values and those of one's culture," there is a close correspondence between this locution and the psychoanalytic concept of the "superego." Freud, in the Introductory Lectures, speaks of the " . . . strict super-ego, which lays down definite standards for [the ego's] conduct . . . and which punishes [the ego] if those standards are not obeyed—with tense feelings of inferiority and guilt" (1933, *SE*, vol. XXII, p. 78). Freud goes on to illustrate with a diagram the structural relations of the "mental personality" (composed of id, ego, and superego). This, incidentally, is one of the very few references of Freud to the word *personality* (which he uses here in an abstract sense, to denote the whole mental apparatus, not merely the face we show the world).

This abstract usage of Freud's points up another complexity in discussing "personality." We have commented upon the "what" of personality (the traits and, from another perspective, the defenses of character, temperament, and façade), and on the "how" (evolving coping strategies fashioned out of genetic, constitutional, and environmental influences), and the "when" (personality takes shape during the first half-dozen "formative" years and solidifies usually by adolescence). We could even say something about the "why" (the "purpose" of personality is to subserve survival needs, acting as our first line of defense in the interpersonal realm). But what about the "where" of it? Clearly, "personality" is a manifestation of brain function, but are there particular pathways and centers that figure prominently as the mediators of whatever it is that we mean by personality?

We will have more to say in detail about this topic later on; suffice it to say at the moment that, although "personality" can be seen as a reflection of *all* the brain at once, there are regions concerned with the storage of memories and with the on-the-spot comparison of incoming stimuli with this "memory bank" that must figure importantly in shaping the emotional/behavioral patterns whose collectivity we call "personality." Freud's "neurologizing" on this subject was limited to his Project for a Scientific Psychology (1895). There he postulated various types of neurons, some occupied with the task of storing memories, others with inhibiting and modulating the motoric responses, so as to bring these responses more in line with what would be reasonable or adaptive. But in the years that followed, realizing that the science of his day did not permit more accurate "localization" of such diffuse mental phenomena as character (or personality), Freud rested content to speak of mental "agencies" — as in the tripartite theory of 1923 and diagram of 1933 — without committing himself as to the neurological underpinnings of these agencies.

Apropos the *why* of personality, in his 1981 book Millon offered the analogy of personality as the chief "host mechanism," comparable to our immune system as the first line of defense against invading pathogens, in dealing with external, chiefly interpersonal, stressors. The older medical model laid undue emphasis on factors (bacteria, poisons, etc.) external to the body, in the case of physical illness; in the case of emotional illness, there was too much emphasis on the stress factors themselves (a death in the family, the loss of a job) or an organic "brain factors" (genes for schizophrenia, epileptic foci). But just as the occurrence of disease depends on the balance between host immune powers and the strength of the "invading" forces, emotional illness depends on the balance between host defenses and the external stresses. As Millon points out, personality plays the role, in this interactive model, of first line of defense: its strength, or lack of it, determines whether the stresses that impinge upon us can be neatly deflected and rendered harmless, or whether they will pierce through the outer defenses (the shield, that is, of personality) and provoke the maladaptive reactions we recognize as the *symptoms* of mental illness.

Millon's concept of personality as the outer shell of the self — the first line of psychological defense — is reminiscent of Freud's postulate, enunciated in Beyond the Pleasure Principle (1920), of a "stimulus barrier" (p. 26). By means of this barrier, the nervous system offers adequate protection against sensory overload from incoming stimuli. Too "thin" a barrier would predispose to our being swamped by such stimuli and to the outbreak of symptoms. David Rapaport refers to this barrier in his essays on thought and affect (1954, pp. 265, 287), though he does not connect the concept to the realm of personality. In their compendium on schizophrenia Bellak and Loeb (1969, p. 29) include the "stimulus barrier" in their catalog of ego functions—one that is particularly deficient in schizophrenia. This kind of deficiency is mirrored in our lay language, where we speak of certain "oversensitive" persons (including schizotypal and frankly schizophrenic patients) as "thin-skinned." Such thinness is of course metaphorical: the central nervous system of oversensitive people does not lack any cell layers observed in normal people. But the analogy is apt. I find it useful, for didactic purposes, to picture the self, in relation to psychological stresses, as a "radial tire"—kept inflated (i.e., preserving self-esteem) under all but the most adverse circumstances and able to absorb most shocks without its inner layers being breached.

Figure 1 shows a portion of this "radial tire" in cross-section. The threatening incoming stimulus is pictured as a bullet streaking toward the outermost layer, the "façade." In all but the most harmonious persons—persons so genuinely interested in and considerate of others that their hospitable remarks and behavior are genuine reflections from their "true" self—there will be enough of a distinction between the patina of civility and one's innermost feelings as to create a "façade" distinguishable from the underlying personality. In most persons, situations of mild stress can be handled effectively at the façade layer; harm to the self is deflected, symptom outbreak is avoided, and adaptation is successful.

As an example, imagine a boss who yells at an employee, just arrived for work, that he needs a certain report "right away," even though the day before the boss said it could wait till the end of the week. If the employee, though he may not be at all fond of the boss, has a functional *façade* and accepts the fact that the boss sometimes gets hot under the collar for no good reason, he may say, "Gee, Mr. Simpson, I didn't realize you needed it in such a hurry, but it's half done already [really, the employee hadn't started on it] and it'll be on your desk in an hour!" What the employee is thinking, underneath all this good-naturedness, is of course quite different—but he deems those sentiments too dangerous to expose in front of the boss.

If the employee in this example came back with, "You want it right away!? You told me yesterday you didn't need it till the end of the week!" we would say the façade was pierced, exposing some pathological traits in the deeper layers of the personality: in this case, surliness. A still more pathological response: "You said you didn't need it till Friday, so Friday's when you're going to get it!" Here we see *insubordinacy*, which might easily provoke the boss into firing the employee on the spot. A total failure of the personality layer to hold its ground would be exemplified by the emergence of *minor* symptomatic behavior (crying, verbal assault, kicking the wastepaper basket). The layer of *moderately severe* symptoms might include, in the present example, a physical assault upon the boss, sending a poison-pen

Figure 1: *Personality as the Outer Layer of Defense Against Psychic Stressors*

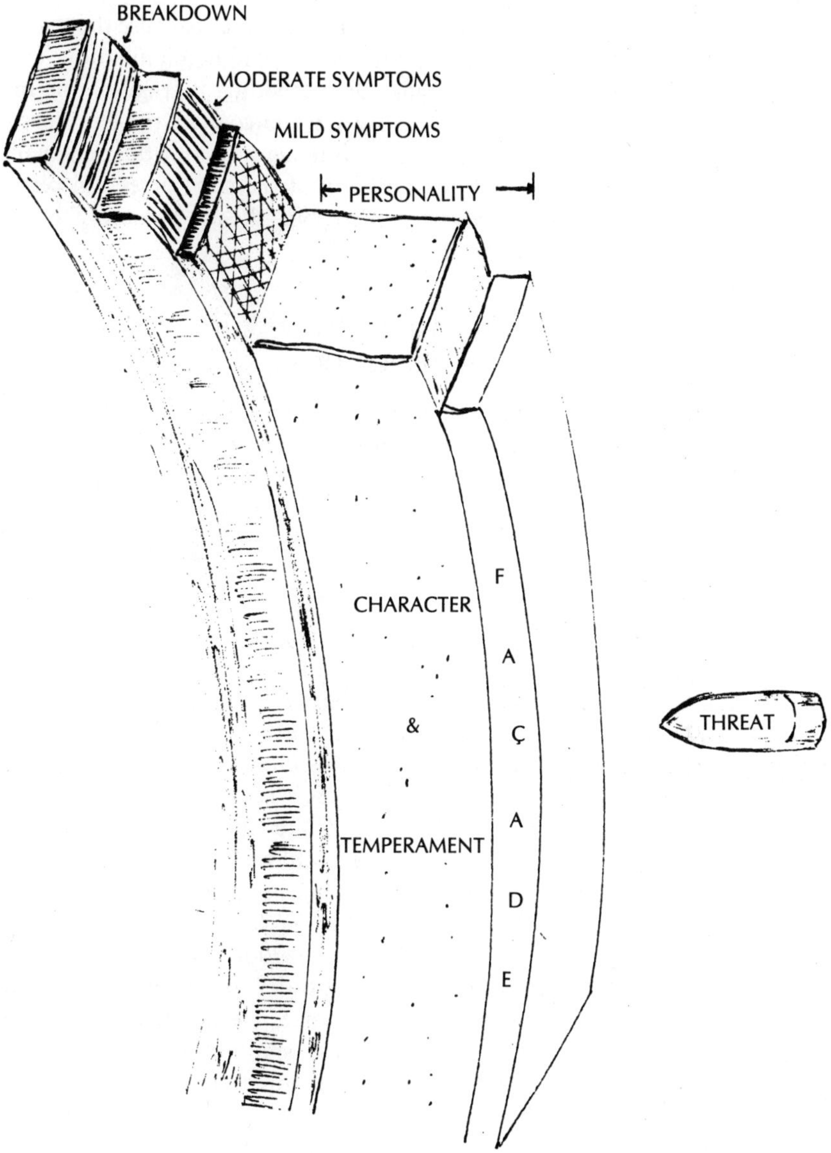

BREAKDOWN

MODERATE SYMPTOMS

MILD SYMPTOMS

PERSONALITY

CHARACTER

&

TEMPERAMENT

FAÇADE

THREAT

letter about the boss to all other coworkers, etc. Many of the disorders enumerated in Axis I of DSM (viz., agoraphobia, anorexia, post-traumatic stress disorder) represent transient or chronic symptoms surfacing after the *failure* of personality to contain various stresses.

If all other layers of the self are overwhelmed — either because the stress is truly overwhelming (concentration camp torture, public humiliation, rage, sudden rejection by a lover) or because the individual is fragile — one may witness psychological collapse. In this state we encounter the extremes of maladaptive reaction: murder, psychosis, fragmentation of the personality (as in "multiple" personality) or annihilation of the self (as seen in certain concentration camp inmates, who become robot-like or "zombies," having lost all dignity and coping ability).

Some Reflections on Façade and Dissociation

A few additional points need to be made concerning the "façade." There is, for example, a developmental aspect. In some persons, what started out in childhood as a "false self," superimposed upon one through parental pressure to behave and think a certain way — a way that at the time went against the grain — may, over the course of years, become endorsed and assimilated to such an extent that the person retains no awareness of ever having had attitudes of a different kind. The graft has taken.

I am thinking in this regard of a fellow-participant in a weekend-long A. K. Rice group workshop I once attended. The workshop was organized for mental health professionals from all the disciplines; the participant in question was a Methodist minister in his mid-fifties who also did pastoral counseling. Throughout the three days of this intense experience groups of eight or nine of us were thrown together for 15 hours a day, with the mission of "relating" to one another and of later on reflecting upon what the experience had meant to us. As one would expect, many situations arose that would stir up angry feelings in almost anyone. But not in the minister. Even when a militant feminist in her last month of pregnancy shoved a chair at him when he "dared" to hold a door open for her, excoriating him for his "antiquated, chauvinist attitudes toward women," he denied feeling so much as a twinge of annoyance. He insisted to us that he was a stranger to the very notion of anger, smiling benevolently at the "defective" creatures around him who felt it often and strongly. He intimated that his faith in the deity had long ago elevated him beyond the susceptibility to that sordid emotion. This revelation of course made us furious at him, which he could no more understand than he could grasp why he should feel ill-used at having the chair pushed against him earlier in the meeting.

Despite 45 hours of group work none of us succeeded in "getting through" to this man's deeper or secret feelings. One could always argue that really he *had* no anger, just as he said he didn't. But I do not believe this. Neither do I think the man was dissimulating, nor a hypocrite. Rather, I think that he had been carefully reared and later trained at seminary to "expunge" anger from his (conscious) soul; he had become so practiced at denying this and other "negative" feelings that "operationally" he was as benevolent as he affected to be. Eventually, as Pryce-Jones (1989) put it, "the mask becomes the face." To admit, after 30 years of maintaining this façade, that he had been blinding himself would have been too shattering to his self-esteem and to his conception of what an "ideal" person should be like. In the case of the minister, one has to be cautious in ascribing "abnormality" to his personality, since in his customary milieu he functioned very well and was a source of comfort and strength to many. But in the no-holds-barred arena of an A. K. Rice workshop, where frankness about one's hostile feelings is the order of the day, this man was handicapped. We saw him as sanctimonious, a hopeless "goody-goody." The more charitable view would be that, his façade having "become" him for too long a time, he was mostly high-functioning but abnormally rigid in contexts foreign to his "ecological niche."

Since most patients strive to instill a modicum of tactfulness in their children, and since most also discourage the too open expression of hostility toward themselves or toward others—even when the parents' behavior would provoke anger or inspire dislike in most children—it is inevitable that a "false self" or façade will develop. For children reared in an atmosphere of kindness, consideration, and patience, this false self will be minimal and not burdensome. Most children do not find it troublesome to say something complimentary about Aunt Sophie's new hat even though the child (and perhaps the parents too) think it funny-looking. Far different is the situation where a cruel or neglectful parent nevertheless demands love and respect. Here the child is forced, usually under threat of punishment, to pretend a love and respect that are either not felt genuinely at all or at best vitiated by simultaneous feelings of an opposite kind.

If the threat of punishment is not too great, the child will still develop a pronounced "false self" but can at least unburden itself, revealing how it really feels, to a confidante, perhaps later to a therapist. If the threat is severe, the child is, in effect, brainwashed—and will have nowhere to turn. Extremes of this situation may, in sensitive children, lead to a fragmentation of the personality. Daughters made to endure the sexual advances of their fathers, for example, especially if they are also subjected to corporal punishment as a warning "not to tell," may actively dissociate — pretending to "be somewhere else" during sex, pretending it didn't happen, etc. — or even develop a "multiple" personality. In this condition the love and hatred toward the parent cannot be integrated and get compartmentalized into two separate personalities, alternating as to which one occupies the center stage of consciousness at any given moment.

Multiple personality, despite the fascination it holds for clinicians and for the public, is an uncommon phenomenon.* Much more common is the creation of an uncomfortable façade via excessive *form consciousness* on the part of the parents and their milieu. Although this can arise in families all across the socioeconomic spectrum, it is seen in its most caricatured extreme in families with aristocratic background or pretensions to such. Children of the wealthy (Stone, 1972) are sometimes raised to be very "proper," by parents who seldom interact with the children or who are rejecting and punitive in what few moments they spend with them. The whole subculture in which these children are reared pressures them to adopt a "sweet" and obedient façade, quite at variance with their true sentiments. Most of the patients with *"as-if" personality*, described by Helene Deutsch (1942), came from aristocratic but neglectful backgrounds of this kind.

The "as-if" person is characterized by " . . . a completely passive attitude to the environment with a highly plastic readiness to pick up signals from the outer world and to mold oneself and one's behavior accordingly" (p. 305). This "passive plasticity" renders the person capable, as Deutsch mentions, " . . . of the greatest fidelity and the basest perfidy." She noted also that aggressive tendencies in as-if persons "are almost completely masked by passivity, lending an air of negative goodness, of mild amiability which, however, is readily convertible to evil" (p. 306).

This ready conversion to evil was also seen in the Nazis (cf. Hannah Arendt's *Eichmann in Jerusalem: The Banality of Evil*), many of whom had been whipped (literally) into obedience and "good form" by parents upholding the imperatives of their culture. When obedience is put ahead of fundamental human values, this strangely juxtaposed niceness and wickedness may develop, creating a personality whose abnormality may surface seldom — or never — unless the capacity for malice is suddenly "switched on" by certain pressures within one's social or political milieu.

---

*Though in an epidemiological study in Winnipeg, Colin Ross (1991) estimates the prevalence of multiple personality disorder to be as high as 1%.

2

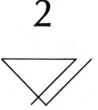

Diagnostic Considerations

THERE HAS BEEN A SHIFT in the last generation away from the predominantly *psychological* formulations concerning the etiology, and by extension the diagnosis, of psychiatric conditions. The shift has been toward the "medical model," i.e., toward *biological* formulations based on abnormalities of neurophysiology and neurochemistry. This shift is not something altogether new: the orientation in psychiatry at the end of the nineteenth century was chiefly biological. It was only when the influence of Freud and the pioneers of psychoanalysis began to outstrip the influence of Kraepelin that the shift toward the psychological/humanistic took place.

Currently, we are in the neo-Kraepelinian era. These changes are cyclical: before Kraepelin (and his teacher, Griesinger), the dominant influences were those of the French school, many of whose members (notably, Itard [1932], who worked with the "Wild Boy of Aveyron," and the followers of Mesmer: Puységur, Déleuze, and later, Liébault) pictured the human condition more along psychological than biological lines. They were the spiritual descendants of the eighteenth-century French humanistic philosophers, Rousseau, Condillac, and Cabanis.

The prevailing views on personality and its origins show this same oscillation over the generations. In our era, the extremes of these views emerge in the theories of Melanie Klein (1975, 1975a) and her followers, who tend

13

to ignore our biological underpinnings—and in the work of Kretschmer (1922) and Sheldon (1954), who, in speaking of the various "somatotypes," paid little attention to the impact of postnatal environment. Because there is something of value on all these disparate accounts, any contemporary model of personality and its origins must be, in relation to biological and the psychological forces, integrative and interactive. The remarks that follow aim at a synthesis of the various factors.

* * * * *

As we have seen, personality in its most general and "everyday" sense refers to the set of behavioral and attitudinal traits that characterize a person—a set of traits that intimates and acquaintances often perceive with greater clarity than the person who possesses these traits. But personality, especially when one is speaking of its "disorders" or severe aberrations, also refers to some complex state of the brain—partly understood, mostly still beyond our ken—that supposedly underlies this personality. In fashioning a meaningful model of personality it is useful to analyze its various "components"—provided we keep in mind that these are for the most part conceptual components (analogous to the mental "agencies" of Freud's tripartite structure); only seldom will any of the components be ascribable to this or that abnormality of neurophysiology.

HUE, INTENSITY, HEALTH/PATHOLOGY

Michels (1989) has found it useful to single out as important variables of personality *hue*, *intensity*, and *degree of pathology or health*. In this schema "hue" corresponds to the collections of traits and to their specific nature that permit us to distinguish one person or group of similar persons from all other persons. The vocabulary of personality "hues" is basically that of the categories of disorders, as outlined in our standard manuals (DSM, ICD). Examples would be "obsessive-compulsive," "passive," "histrionic," "dysthymic," etc. One should confine such a list to pathological types; "easygoing," "intense," and "cautious" could also serve as hue words, but because these are normal variations they are not granted a place in our catalogs of "illness."

Hue words answer to "fuzzy" rather than to sharply boundaried concepts. Few people exhibit the traits of just one "hue." "Pure" paranoid or pure narcissistic persons, etc., are mental constructs, rarely to be encountered in nature. And unlike tuberculosis or measles, which each correspond to one specific pathogen, the hues of personality depend for their recognition upon various traits (vanity, mistrustfulness, etc.). Our ability to recognize traits, however, is fraught with subjectivity and uncertainty; except in the most blatant cases (viz., an abrasive person who is grossly insulting to absolutely everyone), there will not be universal agreement about whether a particular trait is typical of the person in question. Moreover, sociocultural factors will affect whether the trait is perceived as normal or maladaptive. Someone who is intense, assertive and "on the go" may, for example, be seen as "normal" or "just like everybody else" in New York City, but be experienced as rude, overeager, and oppressive in the rural South.

The variable of "intensity" refers to the point along a spectrum of mildness to extremeness that corresponds to the manner in which the particular personality type presents itself. Given that most people, including most patients with personality disorders, show the traits of several different personality types, "intensity" may also be analogized to the heights observable in a chain of "mountain peaks," each named for a different personality type. When we are forced, in certain diagnostic exercises, to label a patient as to his "type," we pay attention to the most intense set of traits (the "tallest peak(s)") and make our diagnosis accordingly (viz., paranoid, with some narcissistic features).

It has been my impression that the presence of an underlying psychosis (manic-depressive, schizophrenic), whether active or quiescent, is associated with an intensification of the key personality traits, often rendering such persons caricatures of their particular personality type. Thus, manic-depressive patients whose personality type is mainly compulsive will tend to be much more compulsive than the general run of obsessive-compulsive patients seen in psychoanalytic practice (Stone, 1978). Whatever personality type develops in the aftermath of severe parental abusiveness also tends to be more intense than corresponding types in nonabused persons.

The degree of health or pathology of the personality is a variable that pertains to what might more simply be called *adaptiveness*. One cannot make broad generalizations about the adaptiveness of the "official" personality types of DSM or ICD. The factor of intensity renders this difficult. Ordinarily, we would group antisocial, schizotypal, borderline, paranoid, schizoid, and passive-aggressive (in descending order of pathology) as the "sicker" personality types. Avoidant and narcissistic might be placed in intermediate bands of the spectrum, leaving obsessive-compulsive, dependent, and histrionic as the least maladaptive.

There are several "provisional" types (sadistic and self-defeating) not yet officially included in DSM, and several types that are recognized by many clinicians, but not included in the manual: e.g., explosive, depressive. Sadistic and explosive would belong to the least adaptive group; depressive and self-defeating to the intermediate group. But clearly, someone with a crippling compulsivity is worse off than someone else with a "touch" of narcissism (who just barely qualifies for the criteria in DSM and exhibits the least pathological of the relevant items). Similarly, someone who has just enough traits to qualify as "paranoid" in DSM but is fairly well integrated in other regards and does not show too many other pathological traits may function better than the most inhibited or pessimistic of "depressives."

Furthermore, many persons with highly maladaptive personalities function unevenly in the various major sectors of life. One commonly encounters rigidly compulsive or embittered depressive patients who, besides being "workaholics," happen to do extremely well at work, but whose "personal" lives, especially in the sphere of intimacy, are meager and painful.

Persons with "antisocial" — or, if one uses the older term, psychopathic — personality are often difficult to place within a single band of the adaptiveness spectrum. The extreme cases are of course dysfunctional in every sphere. But what of the successful con man (such as the fabled Ponzi) who lives in baronial splendor, at least until the law catches up with him? Many of the headlines during the 1980s were taken up with the exploits of Wall Street entrepreneurs whose grandiosity and greed were, shall we say, not obstructed by excess of scruple — and who were lionized in society until the day their fortunes turned (or better, waned). The same could be said of the power-hungry, amoral cabinet members and their operatives who, until the Watergate scandal, ran our country (cf. Colodny & Gettlin, 1992). Only a few of these men, most of whom maintained homes and families, worked assiduously at what they did, etc., could be labeled "antisocial" by DSM criteria. Certainly, many of them were narcissistic, in the sense of being preoccupied with fame, wealth, and power. But many other narcissistic persons, though self-centered, unempathic, etc., would never dream of laundering money or of hiring private investigators to gather "dirt" about their opponents.

We would have to admit, I believe, that the "adaptiveness" variable, though useful in average clinical settings, loses much of its utility, and even its meaning, when we are confronted with the "larger than life" figures of politics, finance, the stage, etc., especially when the abnormalities of their personalities or the disagreeableness of some of their exploits are not exposed during their lifetime. Browse through the biography section of a bookstore and you will have no difficulty in drawing up a list of well-known persons whose accomplishments and peculiarities of personality defy neat categorization. They are not monochromatic in hue nor easy to place along the spectrum of adaptiveness.

A further complication in this task: clinicians tend to estimate health vs.

pathology according to the relative amenability of the personality to some form of therapy. But this gives a distorted picture. Some mildly paranoid persons are difficult to treat because of their tendency to assign all responsibility for their problems to other people, yet in their overall adaptiveness they may function adequately. Some dependent patients, though they form an adequate therapeutic alliance, are extraordinarily clingy and unwilling to meet various challenges—and are therefore "sicker" than certain paranoid patients. In general, externalizing patients are harder to work with than those who are introspective, but there is no one-to-one relationship between this variable (externalize/internalize) and health/pathology.

Michels also makes the excellent point that, in the treatment of personality disorders, "hue" does not change, whereas we will often be able to effect positive changes in intensity and adaptiveness. I would add only one footnote to this comment. To a minor extent, some of the hues are modifiable: one can, in the course of treatment, or of life itself, become less narcissistic, even less antisocial—if the latter is defined mostly by antisocial *actions*. The psychopath, as defined by Cleckley (1972), whether or not he engages in criminal acts, seldom if ever changes for the better. Pessimists rarely switch over to optimists (though certain manic-depressives with cyclothymic personality often alternate between the two polarities). Spontaneous "free spirits" do not become compulsives; the latter seldom become the life of the party. With *hue*, we aim at a softening, or a mellowing, but not a wholesale change.

There is an interrelationship between hue and certain symptom disorders. Sometimes the nature of a personality disorder is so closely related to the underlying symptom disorder as to suggest a common source. *Manic-depressive* patients, for example, are likely to show one of the "temperaments" mentioned by Kraepelin (1921) as either frequent accompaniments or dilute expressions of the disorder. These include the "depressive," the "hypomanic," and the "irritable." The first two tendencies may be combined in a "cyclothymic" temperament, which Kraepelin considered the rarest temperament to accompany manic-depression (noted in perhaps only 3% of manic-depressives). The close relatives of manic-depressives are also apt to show one of these temperaments or a combination of their attributes (viz. depressive plus irritable), even if they do not go on to develop the major condition at any point in their lives.

Similarly, schizotypal and schizoid personalities may be found with unusual frequency either in the premorbid personalities of schizophrenic patients or in the close relatives of schizophrenics. Paranoid personality may be found as an accompanying phenomenon in either manic-depression or schizophrenia, and is thus less "specific" than was once thought (when it was linked in the minds of many clinicians solely with schizophrenia).

Some Traits That are Likely to be
Expressions of Temperament

The personality traits alluded to above are usually considered the manifestations of temperament, specifically, the temperament variations associated with manic-depression or schizophrenia. I outlined some six dozen such traits in an earlier article (Stone, 1978). The following abbreviated list focuses on those related to manic-depression:

- "Depressive temperament": pessimism, joylessness in work, sexual inhibitedness, chronic worrying, shyness
- "Manic temperament": bombastic style, extraversion, intensity, insubordinacy, over-ambitiousness, dilettantism, desultory speech, overconfidence, Wanderlust
- "Irritable temperament": dogmatism, impracticality, tendency to jealousy, irascibility, irritability

These are traits one might find either in adults with manic-depressive illness in one form or another or in certain close relatives of manic-depressive persons. During childhood, even in infancy, "precursor" traits may be apparent that will one day be transformed into the adult traits just mentioned. Such children might show, in infancy, high degrees of intense reactivity or of emotionality. Adolescents with "manic temperament" often are noted to be incessant teasers, or to indulge in scatological humor well beyond the norms for their peers, or to be markedly sensation-seeking. Those with the depressive temperament may show inordinate exam fear. Certain adolescents with explosive tempers will be found to have bipolar first-degree relatives. Consider, for instance, the case of a 14-year-old student expelled from school because he attacked his classmates with a baseball bat: his father, paternal grandfather, and uncle were all on Lithium for bipolar illness (Kestenbaum, 1979).

With respect to evoked potential studies, those with manic temperament tend to be "augmenters"; those with depressive temperament, "reducers." This is in line with the responses to stimuli in general of manic vs. depressive persons: exaggerated or, in the latter, sluggish. Another manifestation of temperamental differences in manic vs. depressive persons lies in their different patterns of marital histories. Kraus (1989) mentions that manic persons are more apt to divorce (by a factor of five) than are depressive persons. Assortative mating also occurs: manic persons affiliating themselves with more high-spirited, sensation-seeking partners; depressives with more introverted, calmer partners.

In their recent compendium on temperament, Strelau and Angleitner (1991) outline a large number of psychometric questionnaires for the assessment of various temperament traits of a general nature (not just those associated with manic-depression). Thus there are instruments for measuring levels of: activity vs. avoidance, approach vs. withdrawal, attention span, boredom susceptibility, distractibility, emotional stability, impulsivity, intensity, persistence, phlegmatic-ness, reducing vs. augmenting, sociability, sensory threshold, venturesomeness, as well as a number of others (pp. 349–351).

As I mention elsewhere (Chapter 3), heritability of temperament traits is usually 50% or even 60 to 70%. But, as these authors mention, the strength of genetic influences varies from trait to trait; studies suggestive of a genetic component (an essential feature of a "temperament" trait) do not prejudge whether the heritability will be high or low (cf. Goldsmith, Buss, et al., 1987). More precise determination requires extensive study of mono- vs. dizygotic twins and, where possible, twins reared apart.

The topic of temperament is addressed again, in connection with the trait-profile and the five-factor model, in Chapters 5 and 6.

* * * * *

There may be an overrepresentation of obsessive-compulsive personalities in patients with obsessive compulsive disorder (OCD), but, as Mavissakalian et al. (1990) point out, obsessive hand-washing and other manifestations of OCD may also be found in conjunction with other personality disorders, such as histrionic, avoidant, and dependent.

In some instances of borderline personality there would appear to be a close linkage with manic-depression, in the sense that (a) several first-degree relatives have one or another form of manic-depression in full-blown form, and (b) the borderline patient, within five or ten years of the personality disorder being diagnosed, develops a clear-cut form of unipolar or bipolar affective disorder (Stone, 1990).

Genetic and constitutional factors may play a role in some cases of antisocial/psychopathic personality (Mednick, Brennan, et al., 1988). There are also some inadvertent experiments in nature that support this argument, as in the case of the serial killer, Gerald Gallego (Biondi & Hecox, 1987), at whose trial it was discovered that his father, whom he had never known, had been executed for murder many years before.

The Category-Based Approach to Diagnosis of Personality

The diagnosis of personality abnormalities according to *categories* with specific criteria is appealing because of its comparative simplicity and its harmony with the "medical" model of illness. Researchers and clinicians with a spiritual affiliation to "hard" science prefer the medical model to, say, the purely descriptive approach (begun by Aristotle's pupil, Theophrastus), since the latter would seem to offer less promise of discovering genetic factors, pharmacological treatments, or other external "validators."

Ideally, there should be a narrow set of criteria (a cluster of traits, for example) for each proposed "personality disorder." Such an approach is called "monothetic." In actual practice, the disorders that clinicians have felt over the years to be classifiable under one heading (for instance, "paranoid") do not, upon closer examination, derive from just one small and repetitive trait-cluster, but rather from a group of overlapping clusters. There may be one or two "main" traits ("mistrustfulness," in the case of paranoid personality), along with half a dozen or more subsidiary traits that are distributed unevenly across samples of patients considered to have the "same" disorder. This leaves the taxonomist with the choice either of creating a large, and probably unwieldy, number of categories, or of drawing up algorithms (specific rules) for arriving at the "same" diagnosis via multiple combinations of interrelated traits. The latter system, called "polythetic," is the system incorporated for the diagnosis of personality disorder in DSM.

In the case of narcissistic personality disorder in DSM-III-R, for example, the manual lists nine descriptors; the presence of any five (or more) will establish the diagnosis. The number of combinations $= [9!/5! \times (9 - 5)!] + [9!/6! \times (9 - 6)!] + \ldots + [1]$, or 256 different ways of being "narcissistic." By the same token, borderline personality disorder (BPD), requiring five or more of eight descriptors, can be established in any of $[56 + 28 + 8 + 1]$ or 93 different ways.

As we shall see when we examine the descriptors (or "items," as they are called in DSM) in greater detail, some of these combinations are quite rare, others probably nonexistent, in clinical practice. Hence the polythetic method is not as chaotic as it would first appear. Few clinicians would be inclined, for example, to diagnose a patient who did *not* exhibit *impulsivity* as having BPD. For all intents and purposes, "non-impulsive borderlines" form a null set. One might hope that, in the future, certain "key" items will be singled out as *necessary* to the (category-based) diagnosis of this or that personality disorder. Each description would include one or more *essential* items, plus some number of accompanying items (all but two or three of which must also be present). As a prelude to any such revision, many clinical trials would have to be carried out, designed to determine the "weights" (relative degrees of importance) of any given item. The resultant descriptions would still be polythetic, but tighter in their construction than are the guidelines offered in DSM-III-R.

THE DSM PERSONALITY CATEGORIES

The latest version of the *Diagnostic and Statistical Manual of Mental Disorders* (DSM-III-R) was published in 1987, though a new revision (DSM-IV) will appear shortly.

In the portion of the manual devoted to personality disorders (Axis II), there are 11 recognized entities, as well as two additional disorders, considered "provisional" at this stage.

The 11 more widely recognized personality disorders (PD's) have been subdivided into three "clusters": the "eccentric cluster" (containing paranoid, schizoid, and schizotypal PDs), the "dramatic cluster" (containing narcissistic, borderline, histrionic, and antisocial PDs), and the "anxious cluster" (containing obsessive-compulsive, dependent, passive-aggressive, and avoidant PDs). The two provisional categories are the "sadistic PD" and the "self-defeating PD." Some of these categories have undergone name changes, but are otherwise clearly derived from previous descriptions under different titles: "histrionic" represents the older "hysterical character"; "self-defeating" was called "masochistic." The earlier terms were in wide use within the psychoanalytic community. "Antisocial" had been known under several headings: "sociopath," "psychopathic," etc.

In Table 1 I have outlined the items relevant to each of the "standard" disorders. Rather than repeat the full descriptions, which can be easily found in DSM-III-R itself or in Oldham and Morris (1990), I have used either abbreviated descriptors or trait-words that summarize the sometimes lengthy wording of the manual.

Under ideal circumstances, the items of a personality catalog would all be true *traits*, i.e., enduring attitudes and behavioral tendencies that fall distinctly short of being cognitive aberrations (viz., illusions) or symptomatic outbreaks of behavior (viz., stealing). One would not describe the *personality* of a thief, for example, as "he steals." One would say, instead, "he is dishonest, unscrupulous, contemptuous of others," etc. Admittedly, the line between trait and symptom is thin and hard to draw. In the matter of *impulsivity* we distinguish between the "spontaneity" of the man who comes home saying, "Hey, the boss just let us have Monday off. Pack up some lunch — we're all going for a picnic right now!" and the no longer appropriate, much less adaptive uncontrolledness of those who shoplift or who are promiscuous. Yet both types are called "impulsive" in everyday speech.

It is evident from Table 1 that three of the "official" personality disorders rely chiefly upon symptoms and states of mind, rather than strictly upon personality traits. Borderline, schizotypal, and antisocial PDs have been placed in Axis II partly out of tradition, partly out of convenience — given

TABLE 1

Characteristics of the DSM-III-R Personality Disorders
(Number of items needed for diagnosis given in parentheses)

A. ECCENTRIC CLUSTER

Paranoid (4 of 7)	Schizoid (4 of 7)	Schizotypal (5 of 9)
fears others will take advantage mistrustful suspicious grudge-holding unable to confide touchy jealous	prefers to be alone prefers solitary activities emotionally constricted indifferent to sex no close friends* aloof indifferent to opinion	referentiality* social anxiety* illusions* magical thinking* no close friends* odd speech* inappropriate affect* eccentric suspicious

B. DRAMATIC CLUSTER

Narcissistic (5 of 9)	Borderline (4 of 8)	Histrionic (4 of 8)
exploitative grandiose feels unique preoccupied with success feels entitled seeks admiration unempathic envious hypersensitive to criticism	impulsive mood lability* irascible self-damaging acts* stormy relations* identity disturbance* boredom* frantic over fear of abandonment*	praise-hungry seductive overdramatic shallow self-centered impressionistic attention-seeking

Antisocial

I. over age 18

II. before age 15, 3 of the following:
   truancy*
   running away from home*
   fights*
   use of weapons*
   forced sex*
   cruelty to persons*
   cruelty to animals*
   destruction of property*
   lying*
   stealing*
   mugging*
   firesetting*

III. (any 4)
   flaunts norms
   no plans
   reckless
   irresponsible
   remorseless
   inconstant
   aggressive*
   conning
   debt default*
   work inconsistency*

TABLE 1

Continued

C. ANXIOUS CLUSTER

Obsessive-compulsive (5 of 9)	*Dependent* (5 of 9)
perfectionism	submissiveness
excessive orderliness	constant approval-seeking
stubbornness	fear of abandonment
"workaholic"	hypersensitivity to criticism
indecisiveness	constant need for reassurance
scrupulosity	intolerance of being alone
reduced display of affect	rejection sensitivity*
parsimony	excessive agreeableness
hoarding	inability to take initiative

Passive-aggressive (5 of 9)	*Avoidant* (4 of 7)
procrastination	no close friends*
argumentativeness	hypersensitivity to criticism
dilatoriness at work	avoids people, out of fear
querulousness	reticence
obstructionistic behavior	overly self-conscious
scornful of authority	avoids tasks with social demands
resentful of suggestions	exaggerates "difficulties"
"forgets" obligations	
unaware of being incompetent	

Sadistic (4 of 8)	*Self-defeating* (4 of 8)
cruel; domineering	overly self-sacrificing
humiliates others	rejecting of those who treat one well
harsh	fails to finish important tasks
sadistic (enjoys the suffering of others)	rejects opportunities for pleasure
lying	incites rejecting responses from others
intimidating	guilt or depression follow positive events*
controlling	rejects help from others
fascinated by violence*	makes self-defeating choices of people and situations

*Designates a descriptor that is not a true personality trait.

the difficulties inherent in situating disorders that are half-trait/half-symptom in nature within a manual that arbitrarily relegates symptom disorders and personality disorders to separate sections.

To scale the taxonomic hurdles imposed by such disorders, we could employ one of two strategies: (1) we could fashion new sets of criteria for these three disorders, composed purely of trait-words; or (2) the DSM could be revised in such a way that "mixed" clinical entities (defined by symptoms + traits) were assigned to a special section. The latter alternative seems but a remote possibility at this time.

The matter of *style* is relevant to personality in general, not just to particular aberrations of personality. Each of us may be seen as "programmed" by early experience to think and feel in certain ways about the important tasks of life (summed up by Freud, succinctly, as "Liebe und Arbeit": love and work). We become enmeshed in certain "core conflicts" (cf. Luborsky, 1984), to cope with which a particular "inner script" evolves (Stone, 1988). Our lives come to center around a key theme, and we develop an image—often enough a "secret self"—whose qualities and ambitions we share with very few people. Our personality is the cloak within which this secret self is wrapped. Usually, the self-image is something positive, even ennobled, a "dream-self" we strive toward, even though we may have little optimism about actualizing the dream. Our personality also contains the elements of attitude and behavior that will, presumably, foster the realization of our most cherished goals.

Oldham and Morris (1990) have affixed a particular self-image and a particular style to each of the DSM-III-R disorders: thus the obsessive-compulsive patient sees himself as "conscientious" and develops a style of "correctness" (the "Right Stuff," as the authors call it); even the antisocial person sees himself as "the adventurer" and develops the style of the "challenger." The person's own labels, in the case of disordered personalities, are, needless to add, self-serving and often much more benign than the words other people would use to characterize that person's image and style. Someone who was victimized by an antisocial person might, for example, label his style the "predator," and speak of his secret self, not as the challenger, but as the "bully." An obsessive-compulsive person might get known as the "Prig"; his style, "self-righteous."

Why do we digress into issues of image and style, inner script and core conflicts? In short, these concepts address the crucial issue of the *organizing principle* of the unfolding personality—the *raison d'être* of the personality, whether it evolves along normal lines or abnormal. The traits we develop along the way may be seen as the tiles of a mosaic, gathered and arranged in a coherent picture—namely, the picture of who we wish to be, and who we are, in our own eyes, and in the eyes of others. It is as though, at some point early in life, we begin to say to ourselves: if only I can be more [*and then pick one of the following*] attractive/sensitive/devoted/creative/superior/cunning/tough/meek/charismatic/dutiful . . . *then* I can get me the mate of my dreams, rise to the top in my job, and live happily ever after.

DIMENSIONAL APPROACH TO THE
EVALUATION OF PERSONALITY

Just as the category-based approach to diagnosis corresponds to the *digital* computer (where quantities are counted one by one), the dimensional approach corresponds to an *analog* computer (where the *degree* to which a certain tendency is present is estimated by the relative position of a dial, by the height of a column as in the thermometer, or by some other device).

The standard categories of personality disorder may be converted themselves into "dimensions," by concentrating upon the *degree* to which a person exhibits each of the 13 recognized "types" of DSM-III-R, each of the types mentioned in ICD-10, etc. I advocated such a method for the fine-tuning of the personality factors that might accompany borderline patients (Stone, 1980a), inasmuch as most patients with BPD show the features of several other PD's, often to such an extent as to warrant two or three "separate" PD diagnoses in addition to BPD. Oldham (1988) has documented this tendency in his study of a hundred BPD inpatients from the New York State Psychiatric Institute. These patients routinely were "positive" for three, four, even five additional disorders—yielding a *profile* that conveyed much more information than just the diagnosis of BPD. The more complex and complete a profile, the closer this profile comes, in effect, to the personality "signature" of that patient—similar in its specificity to the peaks and valleys of a conventional key. Recently, a similar recommendation was made by Juan Mezzich (1988; cf. Figure 2), who showed how the eight main PDs of the ICD could each be used as "prototypes," rather than just as categories: In a diagnostic evaluation, the degree to which a patient exemplified each prototypical dimension could be assessed, yielding an eight-point profile.

These attempts at converting categories into dimensions, to obtain a more complete and accurate assessment of personality, are not new: they draw their inspiration from such instruments as the Minnesota Multiphasic Personality Inventory (MMPI), developed by Hathaway and McKinley in 1940. The dimensions embodied in the MMPI are outlined in Figure 2.

The MMPI attempts to measure personality factors which are, insofar as the subscales can be constructed, nonoverlapping. The ten scales devoted to personality factors *per se* are indicated in Figure 3. A small degree of overlap does exist, however: both the Pd and the Ma subscales, for example, measure "imperturbability," although this trait is mostly a function of blandness and absence of normal social anxiety in the case of the "psychopathic deviate," and mostly an expression of insensitivity to the feelings of others in the case of the "hypomanic." Narcissistic traits, gathered under the separate heading of narcissistic personality disorder (NPD) in DSM,

Figure 2: *The Eight Personality Disorder Categories
of the International Classification of Disease, 9th Edition (ICD-9)
Adapted for Dimensional Assessment: Sample Profile**

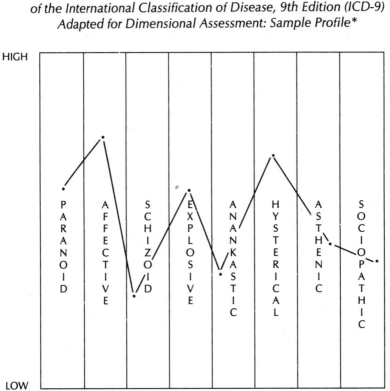

*After J. Mezzich, 1988.

The profile shown should be typical for a patient with borderline personality disorder.

are tapped primarily via the Mf subscale of the MMPI. The Si subscale taps feelings of inferiority, rigidity, distrust, and hypersensitivity. The Ma subscale addresses the areas of amorality and ego inflation (here overlapping conceptually with our picture of the psychopath), as well as of psychomotor acceleration (which belongs conceptually with "hypomania," exclusively).

The 566 questions of the MMPI are applicable to the evaluation of personality in general, not just to comparatively severe *disorders*, upon which DSM and ICD focus. Among these questions, 109 are used for the

Figure 3: *The MMPI Adapted for Dimensional Assessment: Sample Profile*

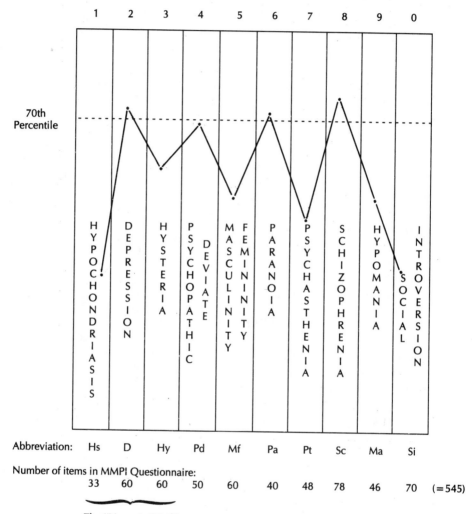

1	2	3	4	5	6	7	8	9	0

70th Percentile

Abbreviation: Hs D Hy Pd Mf Pa Pt Sc Ma Si

Number of items in MMPI Questionnaire:

33 60 60 50 60 40 48 78 46 70 (=545)

The "Neurotic Triad"

The "profile" drawn in on the scale, by way of example, shows high scores on the "8," "6," and "2" subscales and, to a lesser extent, on the "4" subscale. This "8-2-6-4" pattern is common in patients with borderline personality disorder.

assessment of atypicality (the F scale), validity (the K scale), and deliberate falsification (the L or "Lie" scale).

Some of the MMPI subscales are closely related to the "disorders" of DSM: Hy, Pd, Pa, and Sz overlap with histrionic, antisocial, paranoid, and schizoid/schizotypal in the areas of personality upon which they concentrate. But there is no real isomorphism between the MMPI and DSM (or ICD); interviewees meeting the criteria of only one DSM PD would most likely show a complex pattern on the MMPI, with high scores on two or three subscales. A patient positive for only "passive-aggressive PD," for example, would be apt to show a 4–6 (psychopathic deviate/paranoia) pattern on the MMPI—a pattern known to be associated with angry, resentful, argumentative persons (Greene, 1980, p. 132). Because DSM emphasizes acting out rather than merely the ("psychopathic") traits of shallowness and callousness, a diagnosis of antisocial personality will usually be associated with elevations on both the Pd and the Ma subscales of the MMPI.

Review of the personality taxonomy of DSM and ICD* and comparison of these with the more abstract factors of the MMPI point up one of the difficulties in devising a universally acceptable schema for the classification of personality. The recognized disorders have coalesced out of long-standing traditions in diagnosis: entities that are at once severe, easily recognizable, and common in the general population.

Factors represent more elemental tendencies in mood and behavior, often discernible at birth or in early childhood and relevant to normal or to less disturbed personalities as well as to the severe disorders. One might, for example, speak of "other-orientedness" as a factor common to histrionic and hypomanic PDs and to extraverted persons in general. This trend may be observable in the nursery, where one may note in other infants a tendency to withdraw from others. These "molecular" factors may be fractionable in adulthood into more "atomic" traits: assertiveness, joviality, sociability, tolerance (in the case of the other-oriented person); or shyness, timidity, aloofness, intolerance (in those at the opposite end of this spectrum).

Since the *factors* have been abstracted from observations of personality in general, and *disorders* from experience with "exceptional" persons (e.g.,

---

*The ICD system is more widely used in England and in some centers in Europe than is DSM. Efforts are being made to make the personality disorder sections of the two systems compatible. At this time *borderline* and *narcissistic* are not used in ICD. For *obsessive-compulsive* ICD uses the older term *anankastic*. *Borderline* is now used more widely by British psychiatrists than was true in the 1980s; *narcissistic* has yet to be widely accepted in England.

patients, people who are tyrannical, obnoxious, etc., but never seek treatment, criminals being evaluated by experts), we should not be surprised at the lack of congruence between the two sets of variables. Given the multiplicity of "atoms" (traits) and "molecules" (factors), the "compounds" (disorders) are potentially numerous and diverse. But, as in nature, not all combinations that are theoretically possible are encountered and still others are encountered but quite rare. Common to narcissistic, antisocial, and schizoid disorders is the factor of *egocentricity*, since "preoccupation with the self" is noted in all three. The egocentric *traits* are not the same, however: the schizoid person is indifferent to others; the antisocial is contemptuous of others; and the narcissistic is vain, feeling himself "superior" to others.

How Many Dimensions?

In discussing dimensions of personality, the question often arises: how many dimensions are there? The answers are partly dependent upon context. In *clinical* work utilitarian considerations become important: to capture a dozen or so recognized disorders, one could rely on four dimensions (yielding two or sixteen variations) or, if a few disorders could be telescoped into one, on just three dimensions (e.g., if schizoid and schizotypal were seen as differing merely in intensity). The risk in such an exercise is to create a system that is elegant in its simplicity but blurs distinctions clinicians consider important. In *theoretical* work, especially when the focus is on normal personality or on the totality of personality variations, the tendency is to fashion a system that seems complete; however, it may be unwieldly because of the large number of dimensions.

As we shall see, personality theoreticians are becoming increasingly satisfied with a five-dimensional or "five-factor" model, as representing the essential distinctions in human personality variation. But for certain clinical and other tasks, larger numbers of "lower-order" dimensions may prove useful. In the sections that follow we shall review several well-respected systems: some clinical, some applicable to the general population; some composed of a few dimensions, others of quite large numbers. Presentation and discussion of the five-factor model, within which the other systems can be integrated, will be found in Chapter 6.

Three-Dimensional Systems

Because our brains are organized to visualize the world in three dimensions, there is a strong temptation to construct three-dimensional models, built around three "essential" variables. Such models are easy to represent even on the two dimensions of the printed page. Since N dimensions permit 2^N

Figure 4: *Cloninger's Three-dimensional Model
in Diagram Form*

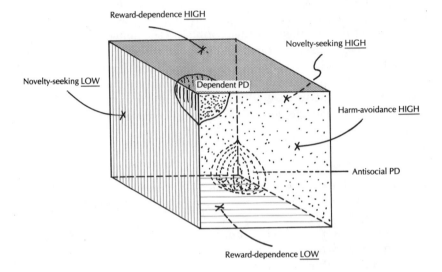

(The back face of the cube represents Harm-avoidance LOW)

combinations, a three-dimensional model of personality yields 2^3 or eight
"types." This would provide enough coverage to encompass the eight main
types of the ICD taxonomy (assuming they could be meaningfully analyzed
according to three underlying attributes), but would fall short of covering
the eleven main types of DSM-III-R. One would have to do some juggling
in order to compress these eleven into eight: choosing *passivity* as a dimension, one might recast passive-aggressive, dependent, and avoidant as the
"same" (*high* in passivity); schizotypal and schizoid might be seen as the
"same" on the dimension of "introversion/extraversion."

Recently, both Torgersen (1988) and Cloninger (1986) have advocated
three-dimensional models. Torgersen utilizes as his dimensions introver-
sion/extraversion, neuroticism, and "obsessivity." But in his efforts to
apply this model to DSM, Torgersen found it less than ideal vis-à-vis paranoid and borderline PDs. He suggests that incorporating a fourth dimension—*reality-weakness*—would make the model applicable even to these
disorders. Still, Torgersen's system would not differentiate easily between
the avoidant, dependent, and passive-aggressive disorders.

Cloninger's system relies on the dimensions of *novelty-seeking, harm-*

avoidance, and *reward-dependence*. These can be either intense or weak, as designated by either a capital or a small letter, respectively (N/n, H/h, R/r).

The biological correlations Cloninger mentions are the following:

CNS Neurotransmitter System   Personality Dimension

1. low basal DOPAMINERGIC activity   Novelty-seeking
2. high SEROTONERGIC activity   Harm-avoidance
3. low basal NORADRENERGIC activity   Reward-dependence

The Cloninger model generates, when the three variables are arranged as the dimensions of a cube (see Figure 4), eight personality types—at the eight edges of the cube (1986, p. 185). These may also be represented in tabular form, as in Table 2.

The tridimensional model of Cloninger is of special interest in that the variables are reflections of behavioral tendencies largely under genetic control. This control is apparently mediated into a significant degree by one or another major neurotransmitter system. The model yields testable hypotheses, thus, the possibility of external validation.

Sjöbring's Personality Dimensions

One of the earliest investigators to propose a multidimensional model of personality diagnosis was Henrik Sjöbring (1914, 1958, 1973). Influenced by the Dutch psychologist Heymans (Millon, 1981, p. 36), and by Janet, Sjöbring actually chose four dimensions, of which one (called "capacity") related to innate factors underlying intelligence. The other three concerned

TABLE 2

Cloninger's Three-dimensional Model of Personality*

	LOCALE ALONG EACH DIMENSION			CORRESPONDING PERSONALITY
	NovSeek	HarmAv	RewDep	
1.	High	Low	Low	antisocial
2.	High	Low	High	histrionic
3.	High	High	High	passive-aggressive
4.	High	High	Low	explosive schizoid
5.	Low	Low	High	cyclothymic
6.	Low	High	High	passive-dependent; avoidant
7.	Low	High	Low	obsessive-compulsive
8.	Low	Low	Low	imperturbable schizoid

*Adapted from Cloninger, 1986, p. 185.

genetic substrates subserving tendencies of the personality: *validity* (the measure of the "energy" available to the nervous system), *stability* (one's maximum potential), and *solidity* (the extent to which experience was necessary to realize this potential). The spectra of traits peculiar to each dimension ranged, as Essen-Möller (1980) explained, from insecurity to forcefulness (in the case of validity), from childish looseness to objectivity (solidity), or from emotional engagement to detachment (stability).

Deficiencies of these attributes were associated with certain traits reminiscent of several of the personality disorders in current usage:

- The traits of "subvalidity": scrupulousness, caution, reserve, precision (similar to the obsessive-compulsive).
- The traits of "substability": sociability, warmth, naïveté (similar to the cyclothymic).
- The traits of "subsolidity": histrionic, unpredictable, impulsive (similar to the histrionic and the borderline).

Because the Sjöbring scales are oriented more toward personality in general than toward the commonly encountered abnormalities, it is not easy to map them onto the disorder schemata currently in vogue (e.g., DSM and ICD).

Millon's Personality Dimensions

The dimensions Millon (1981) considers fundamental to the understanding of personality differences are those mentioned by Freud as the "three polarities that govern all of mental life": active/passive, self/object, and pleasure/pain. The first concerns *initiative*: does the person take primary action in shaping his life, or is he the one upon whom the actions of others impinge? The second relates to reliance on oneself vs. dependence on others. Pleasure/pain is a measure of whether one's actions are primarily *toward* pleasure or are directed *away* from painful or negatively reinforcing interactions. Millon's schema permits correlations with most of the DSM disorders. These are shown, along with their corresponding styles and strategies, in Table 3.

Eysenck's Personality Dimensions

The personality scales developed by Hans Eysenck (1967) in England— extraversion/introversion, neuroticism, psychoticism—take part of their inspiration from the four temperaments of Hippocrates and Galen. The "sanguineous" type, for example, is outgoing and cheerful; the "melancholic"

TABLE 3

Millon's Dimensional System in
Relation to DSM Disorders*

DIMENSIONAL PATTERN	STYLE	DSM PD	STRATEGY
passive dependent	submissive	dependent	lean on others
active dependent	gregarious	histrionic	get approval from others
passive independent	narcissistic	narcissistic	be special
active independent	aggressive	antisocial	be autonomous, get even
passive ambivalent	conforming	compulsive	conform, suppress anger
active ambivalent	negativistic	passive-aggressive	argue, be stubborn
passive detached	asocial	schizoid	keep aloof
active detached	avoidant	avoidant	keep away

*Adapted from Millon, 1981, pp. 62–3. Not readily adaptable within the schema: borderline, paranoid, and schizotypal PDs.

and the "phlegmatic" types are less social, and either dour or sluggish in emotional tone. As Eysenck mentions (Gregory, 1987, p. 246), the terms "extraversion" and "introversion" were used in the 1800s in the popular literature. Jung (1921) brought the terms into the psychoanalytic literature, linking them conceptually both to the earlier notions of temperament and to the then current psychodiagnostic notions of "hypomanic" vs. "schizoid."

Wundt had already made it clear in the nineteenth century that one did not have to belong to this or that temperament-type exclusively (as had long been thought): a person could show elements of more than one type. Emotional reactivity was considered another important variable; this concept overlapped with the emerging notion of "neuroticism" in psychoanalytic parlance. Strong emotional reactions were found in the melancholic and the choleric. Wundt felt "changeableness" constituted another fundamental variable, one that cut across both the sanguine and the choleric. The four temperaments could be collapsed into two "dimensions:" changeableness (= extraversion, with its opposite, introversion), and emotionality (= neuroticism or "anxiety").

When these two orthogonal dimensions are portrayed as in Figure 5, some of the important personality types and disorders can be situated in one or another "quadrant." Schizoid and histrionic, hypomanic and depressed emerge, in line with what we would expect, as pairs of opposites.

Eysenck's third dimension, *psychoticism*, relates to eccentricity and reality-orientedness. In a three-dimensional diagram, one could also situate the more psychotic-like disorders—paranoid, borderline, schizotypal—in their appropriate spaces. Borderline, for example, would map onto the "cho-

Figure 5: *The Dimensional System of Eysenck*

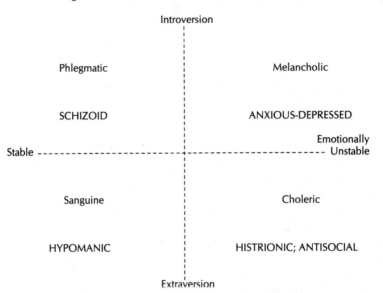

leric" quadrant, in that portion of the now cubic space allocated to high "psychoticism." Paranoid patients would usually show introversion, melancholic temperament and "psychoticism," though some paranoid criminals would inhabit the choleric/extraverted/psychoticism space.

Circumplex Models of Personality

As we have seen from the foregoing, the boundary lines between one personality type and another cannot be drawn with precision. Furthermore, each type seems to blend with a "near-neighboring" type. More accurately, each archtetypal case is reasonably distinct from cases representing other archetypes, but these are the rare "textbook" cases: real people fall to one side or the other of the "pure" types. As a result, it is often difficult to assign a diagnostic case to this category or that.

And how does one refer to a patient who shows as many items of borderline as of narcissistic PD? A "borderline patient with narcissistic features"? "A narcissistic patient with borderline features"? Issues of this sort are usually solved *arbitrarily*, according to which features are causing the greatest problems in therapy at the moment or to which features have caught the interest of the diagnostician—sometimes for frivolous reasons (such as just having read a paper on narcissistic disorders).

Each personality type, as well as most of the standard disorders, also appears to have an opposite type, whose traits are as far removed as possible conceptually from the type in question. Considerations of this sort had led some investigators of personality to propose circular models (called *circumplex*), where two orthogonal dimensions serve to divide a circle into quadrants. Personalities that represent an extreme of one or another dimension are then situated at the ends of the appropriate diameter. Near-neighbor personality types can be placed in between these extremes, according to which type they most closely approximate.

If one is concentrating upon "disorders" of personality, it should be noted that the "opposite" type need not always be pathological. Even here, however, there are unavoidable conceptual problems, having to do with where normalcy ends and some new type of pathology begins. The opposite of "dependent," for example, is presumably "independent." The latter is not a pathological trait. But one can be excessively independent (a hermit, a go-it-alone trailblazer, etc.), so it turns out that most personality types are regions of a spectrum—with a normal mid-region and two contrasting abnormal types on either side.

The circumplex model of Wiggins (1979) utilizes 16 shadings of personality, built around the two axes of activity (or assertiveness) vs. passivity, and movement toward others vs. movement away (basically, love vs. hate). In a subsequent article, Wiggins (1982) discusses at length other circumplex models, as well as the intellectual sources of his own model. Figure 6 demonstrates this model, showing 16 key traits, "A" through "P" (A, J, K, L, M, N, and P are "normal," though "O" can be either the normal "gregariousness" or an abnormal hypomanic kind of extraversion). In addition, eight abnormal personality types are depicted, each spanning two key traits discernible with special intensity in the corresponding type.

Circumplex models have the advantage of underlining the unity of each person and his or her total personality (which the MMPI also does, though in a linear fashion); they also emphasize the "oppositeness" of certain pairs of traits—more clearly than is true of the MMPI.

The Eysenck system described above may be construed as a circumplex model, as was hinted at in Figure 5.

Despite the elegance of Wiggins' model, it still has its shortcomings. Borderline personality disorder, as currently defined, lacks a unifying central tendency (moodiness *and* hostility *and* impulsivity are present in about equal measure), and thus does not fit neatly along any particular arc of the circle.

Perhaps one could claim that all circumplex models and models of only two or three dimensions must fall short of completeness. These models aim at order and neatness. But in the realm of personality and its disorders, one cannot have neatness and completeness at the same time. From the

Figure 6: *Wiggins' Circumplex Model of Personality*

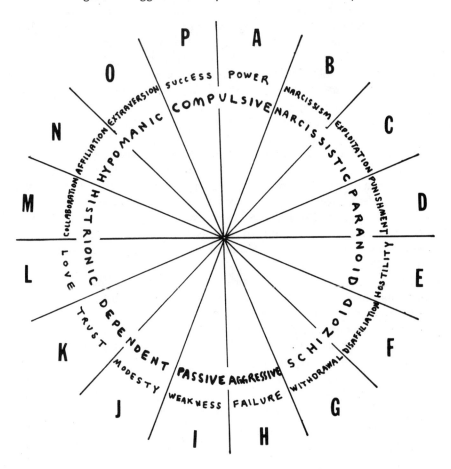

perspective of the researcher, BPD is a "messy" concept because, as we just saw, it cannot be mapped onto a circumplex model built around key traits. From the perspective of the clinician, the circumplex model is "inadequate" because it cannot encompass a disorder that has construct validity (Gunderson, 1980)* and that many clinicians feel is a useful concept. Schizoid and

*Further discussion of the validity of BPD as a diagnosis will be found in Dahl (1985), Tarnopolsky and Berelowitz (1987), Tarnopolsky (1992), and Widiger et al. (1992), the latter showing the greater utility of dimensional over category-based definitions.

schizotypal PDs also do not fit as arcs of a trait circle, because the latter is not so much different in kind from schizoid as different along a dimension not incorporated into the trait circle, namely health/pathology.

Is there a better way, then, to translate into model-form the myriad complexities of personality and its disorders, taking into consideration all relevant dimensions: the multiplicity of traits, the intensity factor, deviance from the "norm," the adaptive as well as the maladaptive aspects, and the cultural relativism that sees what is sick in one place as healthy somewhere else? So inclusive a model must by definition abandon simplicity, and in so doing most of its appeal and probably much of its utility. Still, I believe the exercise is worth carrying out. In the mind of any seasoned clinician there exists just such a multidimensional—or, if you will, megadimensional—model of personality. For heuristic purposes, and I believe for therapeutic purposes as well, it is useful to tease out this megadimensional cerebral model and to get it down on paper. This leads us to the discussion of the many-dimensional (i.e., more than three or five) models, where graphic representation is no longer possible and where the diagram must be replaced by the matrix.

Many-Dimensional Models of Personality

The taxonomist of personality is faced with the same problem that bedevils librarians: a "perfect" system is inherently impossible. (Perhaps this is only a bother to those with marked compulsive propensities!) People of only one personality hue are as uncommon as books of only one subject matter. Where does one shelve *Amelia Ehrhardt, Famed Aviatrix*? In the biography section? In the aviation section? In the section on women's studies? Unable to settle the question on a rational basis, one must settle for convenience. So it is with the nature and even the number of dimensions under which we are to "file" the bewildering array of personalities we are apt to encounter, especially those of us who treat persons with severe disorders of personality.

Among those who, in their effort to capture as much as possible of the *complexity* of personality, have constructed multidimensional systems, there has been disagreement as to the optimal number of dimensions (Frances & Widiger, 1986). As these authors mention, too many dimensions readily become cumbersome (p. 251), while too few ("oligodimensional" systems) fail to address the diversity that is "out there." One cannot speak absolutistically about the "optimal" dimensions, only about a system optimal for this or that set of users. A researcher may need several dozen; a busy clinician may be content to "dimensionalize" the DSM or ICD categories, as we saw with Juan Mezzich's model (see above, p. 25) or with an earlier schema of my own (Stone, 1980) where I used the DSM-III categories (plus "depressive," "explosive," and "hypomanic") as dimensions.

Millon (1981, Chapter 2), in his review of multidimensional systems, noted that the various schemata are based on one of several organizing principles: temperament (e.g., Sjöbring), constitution (e.g., Sheldon), factorial categories (e.g., Cattell), psychiatric syndromes (e.g., Schneider), or psychoanalytic (e.g., W. Reich).

The typology of Schneider (1923/1950) is atheoretic (not tied to a particular theory of personality development and differentiation), derived from clinical experience, and, though usable as a dimensional approach, presented as a list of common categories. Schneider did not emphasize the connection between certain personality types and the various symptom disorders to which they might (as "attenuated" expressions) be related. In this he differed from Kraepelin (1921), for whom extraversion, hypomania, and manic psychosis were different bands of one spectrum. The ten personality types and their key traits, according to Schneider, are shown in Table 4.

The multidimensional system of Raymond Cattell (1957, 1965) was built eventually around 16 "primary factors," from which he could generate seven second-order factors. Actually each factor consisted of a pair of opposites, such as *submissive* vs. *dominant, schizothymic* vs. *cyclothymic, warm* vs. *cold*. This system was itself the outgrowth of earlier work by Cattell (1945), in which he tackled the huge adjective list of Allport and Odbert, abbreviating it (by elimination of redundant and archaic words) to 4500

TABLE 4

The Personality Typology of Kurt Schneider*

PERSONALITY TYPE	KEY TRAITS
1. Hyperthermic	optimistic, shallow, impulsive, undependable
2. Depressive	self-reproachful, with meager pleasure sense
3. Insecure	unselfconfident, disciplined
(a) Sensitive	
(b) Anankastic	
4. Fanatic	combative, aggressive, litigious
5. Attention-seeking	emotional, capricious, sensation-seeking
6. Labile	moody, volatile, immature
7. Explosive	argumentative, violent (often without provocation)
8. Affectionless	callous, cold (like antisocial persons)
9. Weak-willed	docile, gullible, easily (mis-)led
10. Asthenic	hypochondriacal, uninvolved with life

*Adapted from Millon, 1981, p. 42.

traits, then abstracting from these some 171 variables. Later, Cattell reduced these further, to a more manageable list of 35 variables. In some instances Cattell lent a certain scientific cachet to his variables through the use of fanciful names—such as "threctia" vs. "parmia"* for "timidity" vs. "uninhibitedness." This should not blind us to the importance of Cattell's work, since it served as the springboard for the conceptual breakthroughs of Fiske (1949) and later of Tupes and Christal (1961), who detected within Cattell's variables what has come to be accepted in our day as the five key supertraits (see Chapter 6).

Cattell's second-order factors consist of the following: (a) creative vs. conventional, (b) independent vs. dependent, (c) tough vs. sensitive, (d) neurotic vs. stable, (e) leader- vs. followership, (f) high vs. low anxiety, and (g) intro- vs. extraversion. The last two will be seen to overlap with Eysenck's "neuroticism" and "intro-/extraversion."

The Personality Assessment Schedule of Tyrer and Alexander

In the mid '70s British investigators Peter Tyrer and John Alexander developed a multifactorial system for evaluating personality built on the premise that personality disorders differ only quantitatively from normal variations in personality (Tyrer & Alexander, 1988). They aimed at a trait list that was not so long as to preclude thorough data analysis and that did not include traits that were so highly intercorrelated as to be redundant. Cluster analysis of their interviews with many patients clinically diagnosed as having a personality disorder suggested their dividing the domain of all disorders into four major groups. The authors labeled these *sociopathic, passive dependent, anankastic*, and *schizoid*. Most of the individual disorders fit within one of these regions, though "histrionic" overlapped the first two groups, "anxious" overlapped the middle two, and "avoidant" has characteristics of both anankastic and schizoid.

Using a trait list of 24 reasonably separable factors, Tyrer and Alexander then assessed the degree to which each factor was relevant to their subjects. They measured severity (or intensity) on a sliding scale ranging from 0 to 5.0. In Table 5 I have shown the profiles exhibited by *typical* cases of each disorder. For the sake of simplicity, I assigned a number from zero to ten to each rating, according to the length of the severity-bar in their diagrams. This creates a 24 (factor) × 13 (groups and subtypes) matrix.

---

*As Hampson (1988, p. 62) points out, Cattell coined these terms himself.

TABLE 5

Personality Assessment Schedule: Tyrer and Alexander*
(Matrix relating the PAS to various personality disorders)

FACTOR	PERSONALITY GROUP OR SUBTYPE												
	SOC	Exp	Pag	PDP	Hys	Ast	INH	Anx	Dys	Hpc	WDR	Par	Avo
pessimism	2	1	2	2	1	3	2	1	4	2	2	2	4
worthlessness	2	0	2	3	2	4	4	2	7	2	1	2	1
optimism	2	3	1	2	1	1	0	0	0	0	1	1	4
lability	3	4	3	6	7	3	2	3	1	1	2	2	7
anxiousness	5	5	5	6	5	6	6	7	5	7	4	6	7
suspiciousness	3	3	5	2	1	1	2	1	4	1	4	5	0
introspection	2	2	3	2	1	2	4	5	5	3	4	4	8
shyness	2	1	4	3	2	3	5	6	7	3	4	1	9
aloofness	3	3	4	2	1	2	3	2	6	2	4	4	4
sensitivity	3	2	6	5	5	6	4	5	6	2	5	8	1
vulnerability	3	4	0	6	6	5	3	5	3	3	4	4	7
irritability	5	5	6	2	2	1	3	2	2	1	1	2	0
impulsiveness	7	7	4	4	4	1	0	0	1	1	2	1	4
aggression	6	5	7	1	1	1	0	0	0	0	1	2	1
callousness	3	0	3	0	0	0	0	0	1	1	1	1	2
irresponsibility	6	7	3	3	5	0	0	0	1	0	1	0	0
childishness	3	4	2	5	6	3	1	2	1	1	2	2	3
resourcelessness	3	4	1	5	4	5	2	4	2	2	2	3	1
dependence	2	2	1	6	7	4	3	5	3	3	2	4	1
submissiveness	2	1	1	4	4	6	3	8	3	1	2	0	3
conscientiousness	1	1	2	2	2	1	6	6	5	5	3	4	2
rigidity	2	2	2	1	1	1	5	5	4	3	2	3	2
eccentricity	1	2	3	1	1	0	1	1	1	0	2	2	0
hypochondriasis	2	2	1	2	2	4	3	3	1	8	1	1	2

*Adapted from Tyrer and Alexander: Chapter 4 in Tyrer, 1988.

Key (4 major clusters indicated in capitals): SOC—SOCIOPATHIC; Exp—Explosive; Pag—Passive-aggressive; PDP—PASSIVE-DEPENDENT; Hys—Histrionic; Ast—Asthenic; INH—INHIBITED; Anx—Anxious; Dys—Dysthymic; Hpc—Hypochondriacal; WDR—WITHDRAWN; Par—Paranoid; Avo—Avoidant

The factors used by Tyrer and Alexander are the following:

pessimism	worthlessness	optimism	lability
anxiousness	suspiciousness	introspection	shyness
aloofness	sensitivity	vulnerability	irritability
impulsiveness	aggression	callousness	irresponsibility
childishness	resourcelessness	dependence	submissiveness
conscientiousness	rigidity	eccentricity	hypochondriasis

In discussing the advantages and disadvantages of their system, Tyrer and Alexander mention that the diagnostic categories generated by their computer analysis are not the same as those of DSM or ICD and are therefore not immediately translatable into the currently popular "language" of personality disorders. In many areas there is a strong enough similarity among the disorders identified by DSM, ICD, and the PAS to suggest that these particular disorders (viz. sociopathic/antisocial, compulsive/anankastic) have face validity and answer truly to what is there in nature. It is not surprising that there is the least disagreement about the existence and the features of the most disabling disorder, i.e., the antisocial (cf. Blashfield, Sprock et al., 1985).

One of the more important advantages of the PAS lies in its ability to record "trait accentuation" in cases where the full criteria for a particular disorder are not met. This conduces to the maximal preservation of information about *any* abnormalities in personality—information that tends to get swept under the rug in evaluations made by a purely category-based approach. Since there are only about twice as many factors in the PAS as there are disorders in DSM, the use of the PAS dimensions is not burdensome to the clinician.

As for the matrix sketched in Table 5, there is enough diversity of scores, using a 0–10 scale, to highlight the "peak" factors among the various disorders: shyness in the *avoidant* type; feelings of worthlessness in the *dysthymic*, etc. The matrix of Table 5 was derived from assessment of clinic patients. Presumably, the scores on "callousness" would be much higher in a group of psychopathic criminals (few of whom, fortunately, are encountered in clinics) than in the relatively mild "antisocials" who do make their way to outpatient settings. The scores shown are the averages obtained from a number of similar patients; the individual patients would show scores reflecting a gaussian distribution for each factor within their subgroup. In any large sample there will always be "exceptional" cases: the least responsible "compulsive" patient will show less of this trait than the least "irresponsible" histrionic patient, etc. (The smallest giant may be shorter than the tallest dwarf.) A dimensional system of course lends itself well to the task of identifying not only typicality but also the "outliers."

The Multifactorial System of Livesley:
The Search for Prototypicality

Livesley and his colleagues in Vancouver have been interested for a number of years in identifying the most salient characteristics of the personality disorders in the official nomenclature (Livesley, 1986, 1987; Livesley, Reiffer, et al., 1987; Livesley & Schroeder, 1990). Their research led them to believe that the previously low interrater reliability in diagnosis of personality disorders was a function more of inadequate criteria (poor definitions) than of disagreement about their conceptual features. Livesley sought a solution to this lack of clarity via a search for distinguishing qualities of the highest specificity. Attributes emphasizing behavior rather than cognitive or other less visible features seemed to offer the best hope of achieving this "prototypicality." For most of the DSM disorders, Livesely was able, through questionnaires distributed to many experienced clinicians, to identify prototypical *behaviors*, though for several reliance upon prototypical *traits* proved superior.

Among the disorders where behaviors provided the best criteria, "schizoid" showed as its optimal items "does not speak unless spoken to" and "does not initiate social contacts." The two most prototypical behaviors of the "histrionic": "expressed feelings in an exaggerated way" and "considered a minor problem catastrophic." For "compulsive": "has routine schedules and is upset by deviations" and "overreacted to criticism." The most distinctive traits for these disorders achieved lower scores (though only marginally so). For "schizoid": "detached" and "desires minimal personal attachments." For "histrionic": "theatrical" and "labile emotionally." And for "compulsive": "perfectionistic" and "needs to control people and situations" (Livesley, 1986, p. 731).

Livesley's wish to place greater reliance on behavior than on "traits" makes sense from the vantage point of diagnosticians, who must often come to some conclusion even within the space of one or two interviews. It is for similar reasons that DSM's definition of antisocial PD stresses behavior (lying, stealing, acts of violence), since these indices are much more "objective," less easily concealed, than psychopathic traits like shallowness, glibness, etc. But from the standpoint of therapists, the "hues" of personality do not need to be colored with fluorescent paint. What would be undiscoverably "subtle" in a one-shot interview, or in several interviews of a dissembling patient, will become unmistakably clear to a therapist, who usually has months or years of acquaintance in which to ferret out the hidden aspects of personality. Therapists or staff members in a hospital unit may also have access to relatives and friends, who often provide clues to personality traits the patient had just as soon keep out of view.

The distinction between (affective or cognitive) trait and behavioral pattern is, I suspect, not always sharp enough to warrant speaking of them dichotomously. In the case of the hypomanic, for example, the lines between (the traits of) exuberance or joviality and (the behavior of) back-slapping and compulsive joke-telling and (the symptom of) standing intrusively only a few inches from the nose of the person one is talking with can be exceedingly fine.

More recently, Livesley and his coworkers have reorganized the defining features of the official personality disorders in a taxonomic system analogous to the hierarchical system used in biology (species, genus, order, phyllum). Because these features are often portrayed graphically within planes or cubes, the analogy to astronomy is also tempting: individual stars (traits), groups (dimensions), galaxies (disorders), clusters (disorder clusters). The traits making up the totality of DSM-III disorders, for example, could be condensed into 79 dimensions (Livesley, 1987). As an example, the common descriptions of the schizoid—"loner," detached, withdrawn, seclusive—were so close conceptually as to constitute a dimension. Livesley called this dimension "low affiliation."*

This hierarchical vocabulary of personality descriptors can be illustrated diagrammatically, as in Figure 7. The diagram shows regions of overlap, both between the conceptually close traits of near-neighbor dimensions and the similarly close dimensions of near-neighbor "disorders" within the cluster. In the middle of a main dimension is a "signature" trait, i.e., the trait with the most highly rated degree of prototypicality. For example, for *paranoid* PD, "externalization" might be taken as the signature trait. Livesley suggests that for each DSM PD there are prototypical dimensions and that these permit good differentiation of one PD from another. Any revisions in criterion-sets should take these dimensions into account, Livesley argues, in order to reduce the conceptual overlap that currently muddies the boundaries between disorders. (Still, there will be problems: psychopaths are all narcissistic but the reverse is not true.)

CHIMERICAL PERSONALITIES

Problems in Evaluation

As if the diagnosis of severe personality disorders did not present stumbling blocks enough, there will also be many situations where a symptom disor-

---

*Seven other dimensions Livesley felt were pertinent to schizoid PD were: avoidant attachment, defective social skills, generalized hypersensitivity, restricted affective expression, self-absorption and social apprehensiveness (1987, p. 774). His other 71 dimensions cover the remaining DSM personality disorders.

Figure 7: *The "Astronomy" of Personality*

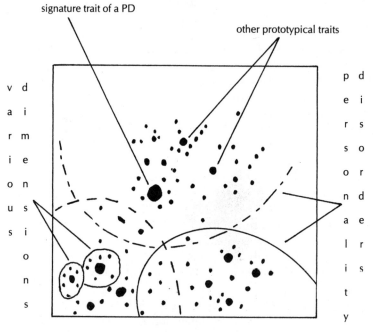

signature trait of a PD

other prototypical traits

A CLUSTER

overlapping traits (of overlapping disorders)

der or drug abuse so alters the personality that what the clinician sees is no longer the "real thing." What one sees instead is a chimera: a "foreign" personality that comes to inhabit the self for varying stretches of time.

The disinhibiting effects of alcohol are well known, and everyone is acquainted with at least one person who becomes aggressive or insulting or seductive or paranoidally angry under the influence of alcohol. Others, to be sure, having been "up tight" all day at the office turn into mellow human beings after the second or third martini. Marijuana, though a euphoriant, can also lead, under circumstances of heavy abuse, to habit deterioration, surliness, "je-m'en-fichisme" (loss of motivation), or a peculiar kind of detachment (often referred to as being "spacey") (cf. Nahas, 1973). Chronic abuse of barbiturates can lead to a condition mimicking paranoid schizophrenia—under which heading I once admitted a woman who had been forging her doctor-husband's prescription pads, giving herself large amounts of secobarbital. She did not admit this while still abusing the drug, but all became clear in the hospital: the inadvertent abstinence made the "paranoid schizophrenia" go away after three days and allowed her underlying (depressive) personality to resurface.

The paranoia and irritability that may overtake the personality during bouts of amphetamine or cocaine abuse have become all too familiar to us in recent years. The point is that, in many cases, the abuse is prolonged, hidden even from coworkers and intimates—such that the opinion they, or a diagnostician, might form of the "personality" may be quite off the mark with respect to the drug-free "real" personality. Sometimes the traits that emerge under the influence of the drug have been there all along: stifled, latent, and hardly ever apparent to others. I recall in this connection a medical student a year ahead of me who used to get drunk on the weekend and would then go down to the women's dorm at 2 or 3 AM, kicking their doors and yelling obscenities. This was his ethanolic personality. Off alcohol, he was overpolite, courtly, deferential.

Chronic alcoholics, marijuana habitués of long-standing, etc., may live for years with a personality that, to those who know them only lately, has "become" the real personality. Unbeknownst to these acquaintances, there is a different person underneath—one who could conceivably reemerge if the drug abuse were curtailed. Whether the more adaptive personality can be teased back into ascendancy is, ironically, dependent upon other personality factors that may or may not coexist. Persons given to denial, rigidity, inability to admit fault, always blaming others, etc., will be (to take the example of alcoholism) far more reluctant to go to Alcoholics Anonymous, to enroll in a rehabilitation program, or to take any other ameliorative steps. The "sick" personality will therefore remain in force. People with equally serious drinking problems who nevertheless can admit fault, are not so disposed to deny illness, etc., can usually commit themselves to a rehabilitative program, conquer their habit, and experience a restoration of their better personality. The treatment of drug abusers is equally dependent upon these personality factors.

Patients with Active Psychosis

Just as mind-altering drugs may render a pleasing personality offensive (and occasionally vice versa), the presence of a psychosis can alter a personality radically, usually in a more offensive direction. Only in *these* situations, a mind-altering drug—one chosen by the psychiatrist—may restore the personality along more harmonious lines.

Many of the personality *disorders* may also be understood as less extreme points of a spectrum: depressive ("dysthymic"), hypomanic, cyclothymic, extraverted, and avoidant personalities are frequently seen in the inter-morbid phases of patients with the different forms of manic-depressive illness. Schizotypal PD may usually be understood as an attenuated form of schizophrenia; schizoid PD as a still more attenuated form. Paranoid personality can develop in patients with schizophrenia, manic-depressive illness, or "delusional" disorder, whether in full-blown or dilute form, and is thus a less clear pointer to any specific psychotic disorder. In some borderline patients there is a close connection between the personality disorder and manic-depressive illness that either coexists already when the personality disorder first declares itself or develops five or ten years later (Stone, 1990).

But here I am focusing on the often flamboyant disturbances of personality seen in active or in chronic psychoses. So long as the psychosis is untreated, the "personality" contains extreme features such as are either not seen at all during quiescent times or are seen in much less noticeable form.

Example   I was once asked to see in an emergency consultation a man in his mid-forties, reportedly in "some kind of crisis." He had flown in that morning, accompanied by his wife and father, from another part of the state. When he entered my office, he proceeded to dump onto my analytic couch the contents of an airline flight bag: a bowling ball and eleven credit cards. I never did learn why he had brought the bowling ball. As for the credit cards, he said, "Mike, pick a card, any card! Charge me anything you want for this visit. Sky's the limit!" I replied, "Charlie" (unaccustomed as I am to using a patient's first name, under the circumstances it seemed right), "I don't take Mastercard or Visa, but this visit isn't gonna cost you anyway, because I can tell in one minute that your trouble is: you've been leaving your Lithium in the drawer! Am I right or am I right?" "Listen, I don't need the shit," he told me, and with that, he charged past his relatives and ran out of the office. It took some hours for the police to track him down and bring him to the hospital. There he was given the Lithium that, as his wife confirmed, her manic husband had been refusing to take over the past two weeks. His premorbid personality, as one could reconstruct it from the wife's story, was exuberant, extraverted, "life-of-the-party," but not out of control, as he had been during our brief interchange. Off Lithium, he became egocentric, contemptuous, irritable, dogmatic, overfamiliar (hence the use of my first name)—"not his usual self."

Example   A man in his thirties, diagnosed as "paranoid schizophrenic" during a hospitalization ten years earlier, had become a "homeless person," sleeping under parked cars in a Greenwich Village garage, eating sporadic meals in soup kitchens, voiding his wastes in the street. Apprehended on numerous occasions by the police for vagrancy, he threatened them with lawsuits if they violated his civil rights by taking him against his will to the municipal hospital. His parents, a well-to-do couple from the suburbs, had spent considerable sums with private investigators in search of their son, whom they had not seen for three years. Having finally located him, they pleaded with him to go to the hospital. He waved them away the first two times they came by, but on the third at last acquiesced. Once in the hospital, he was given neuroleptic medication. Within a few weeks, he had become a "different person," fearful and shy but no longer litigious nor adamantly paranoid about his "rights." Within a few months he was able to return home, enroll in some courses at a local college, and live peaceably, if somewhat standoffishly, with his family. On the medication, he returned to his former, predominantly schizoid, personality; the defiant, paranoid traits receded into the background.

Comment

As these vignettes show (though based on extreme examples), the personality in those whose minds have been altered either by drugs or by psychosis may become distorted in two main ways: the chimerical personality may represent merely an exaggerated version of the underlying "true" personality, or it may represent a marked change (an apparent change in "hue") from the original.

Disinhibiting drugs, in particular (of which alcohol would be the most common offender), may lead to the formation of a Jekyll and Hyde personality. Here, two selves appear to inhabit the same body: a *sociable* self alternating with an outrageously repugnant *hostile* self. Clinically, the situation does not resemble "multiple personality disorder" (MPD) (Bliss, 1986; Kluft, 1985), since the Jekyll and Hyde person is aware of the continuity of "self," whichever side is manifest at the moment, nor does the person spontaneously give different names to the two contrasting self-presentations. But obviously, personalities of this sort are very poorly integrated (simply not as fragmented as in MPD) and not at all easy to diagnose within the confines of a category-based system like DSM or within any other system that relies on *continuity* of self-presentation before a meaningful label can be applied. One should keep in mind that alcohol abuse is not the only catalyst to the emergence of Mr. Hyde. A fair number of *borderline, explosive*, and *psychopathic* persons are prone to sudden shifts from affability to ragefulness, and in the latter state may commit monstrous acts — without necessarily any "help" from alcohol.

3

The Origins and Formation
of Personality: Genetic Factors

> Children memorize parts of stories their parents tell them. They
> want the same story again and again. Don't change a word or they
> get terribly upset. This is the unchanged narrative every culture
> needs in order to survive.
>
> Don DeLillo, *Mao II*, p. 162

To UNDERSTAND THE INGREDIENTS and the formation of normal personality is of considerable help in the understanding and treatment of abnormal personality. In many instances, the disorders of personality severe enough to trigger a diagnosis in DSM or ICD, as well as milder conditions characterized by a few exaggerated traits, have their origins in family patterns, traumatic experiences, and the like, that differ only in degree from what more integrated persons have experienced. Or the interpersonal atmosphere may not have been especially unfavorable, the problem lying more with the fragile constitution of the child who goes on to develop a personality disorder years later.

In the most "normal," best adapted persons — not only adaptable in their original environment, but flexible enough to adapt to new environments if the need arises — genetic predisposition, constitution, physical development, cultural factors, and the home environment are all interwoven so seamlessly and harmoniously that one can no longer tell, in the normal adult, where one influence left off and the next began. What a good mother does, it is hard to remember; what a bad mother does, it is hard to forget. (The same goes for father.) Those who are reasonably bright, reasonably attractive, reasonably even-tempered and who were raised to be well-mannered and respectful of others by sympathetic and reasonable parents can live almost on automatic pilot, getting along pleasantly with friends and family, often without their having any clear understanding of why they are doing so well. They do not know their "secret."

But when we are confronted with abnormalities of personality, we know something has gone wrong *somewhere*. It could be the *"genes,"* as in patients with schizophrenia, manic-depressive illness, or other conditions which sometimes have a primarily hereditary underpinning (e.g., epilepsy, attention deficit disorder), many of whom show aberrations in personality. It could be the *constitution*, as in some cases of "fetal alcohol syndrome" and of babies born to mothers who abused cocaine or took prescribed drugs during sensitive phases of intrauterine life. Some babies with ultra-low birth weight are, and remain, more irritable than normal babies. *Cultural* factors play a strong role in personality formation and can under certain circumstances stack the cards against normal development. Many male homosexuals, for example, became so because of biological predisposition.* If they are raised in families that, for religious/cultural reasons, condemn homosexuality, strong conflicts and, in time, maladaptive personality traits are all but unavoidable. Children born into authoritarian, tyrannical regimes are systematically programmed (by teachers or political authorities) to develop habits of thought and behavior at variance with parental and common human values. Such programming deforms the personality in any of a number of ways: one will become rigid, or mindlessly obedient, or cruel, or rebellious, or dour and bitter, etc. As for the *psychodynamic* factors, they may also involve maladaptive programming (by the parents), but may also center on sibling and other intrafamilial rivalries, etc. In the sections that follow we will examine the various factors in some detail.

Ironically, certain abnormalities of personality that are (by definition) maladaptive for the individual, that cause suffering and serve as the stimulus to psychiatric consultation and treatment, are nevertheless "adaptive" for the society as a whole. From the standpoint of systems theory (cf. von Bertalanffy, 1968), what may be deleterious to survival on the plane of the individual may promote survival on the supra-individual (i.e., societal/ecological) plane. These factors we will also examine, in the closing section dealing with the *ecological* aspects of abnormal personality and with the *evolutionarily stable state* created within any society by the great variety of personality types contained inside its boundaries.

For simplicity's sake I will be discussing the different factors one by one, as though they were quite distinct and not interconnected. Such distinctions are in many instances arbitrary: more "categorical" than the facts warrant.

---

*Quite recently, Bailey et al. (1993) presented evidence of heritable factors in female homosexuals as well.

The risk genes implicated in schizophrenia, for example, are usually spoken of under the heading of a genetic factor. The genes involved in sexual dimorphism, though they too underlie certain shadings of personality, are part of normal variation and are apt to be discussed under the rubric of constitution.

GENETIC FACTORS

Hereditary factors, mediated in some instances by one major gene but more often by a polygenic system, would appear to play a role in the formation of all but a few of the recognized personality disorders and to account for half the variance in personality differentiation.

Eccentric Cluster

Taking the DSM taxonomy cluster by cluster, one can find considerable evidence for genetic contributions to both schizoid and schizotypal PDs. These disorders partake of what Meehl (1962, 1989) called "schizotypy": the inherited tendency to the peculiarities of cognition and eccentricities of thought (and eventually, of behavior) by which we recognize schizophrenia.*

A relationship between schizophrenia (Sz) and schizotypal personality disorder (STPD) is suggested by robust findings from biological and family pedigree studies, as documented by Siever, Bernstein, and Silverman (1989), Siever, Klar, and Coccaro (1985), Baron, Gruen, et al. (1985), and Stone (1985c). There is a higher proportion than would be expected in the general population of STPD in the families of Sz index cases (Baron; Stone). Kety et al. (1968) have found a similar overrepresentation of schizoid and paranoid PDs among the relatives of Sz patients, suggesting that these disorders may (in many but not all instances) be considered as within the "spectrum" of Sz. Evidence from biological studies includes the observation of Holzman et al. (1974, 1984) that impairment of smooth pursuit eye movements (SPEM) occurs not only in 60–80% of Sz patients, but in half of their unaffected or less severely affected relatives, some of whom exhibit STPD.

In trying to assess the presumed linkage between Sz and STPD, it makes a difference if one begins with a sample of Sz patients (and then examines their relatives) or with a sample of STPD patients. When persons are found among relatives of Sz patients who meet DSM criteria for STPD, they are apt to show predominantly the "negative" (Andreasen & Olsen, 1982) or

---

*See also Chapter 10.

"deficit" (Huber, 1966) signs: social isolation, poor rapport, eccentricity (Siever, Bernstein, & Silverman, 1989) as noted in a review of the Danish adoption studies (Gunderson, Siever, & Spaulding, 1983). A clinically selected sample of STPD patients, in contrast, will contain varying numbers of persons notable more for their "positive" symptoms—illusions, ideas of reference, magical thinking. The linkage between positive-symptom STPD and Sz is not as strong as between deficit-symptom STPD and Sz (Frances, 1985). The proportion of these subtypes in any sample of STPD patients will affect the degree to which this disorder appears to be an attenuated form of Sz.

To jump ahead for a moment to cultural factors, the prevalence of illusions and magical thinking is quite striking in certain cultures. This is true in Thailand, for example, where there is no surplus of full-blown Sz—simply many people in whom STPD is *not* a phenotype of Sz genes and whom one should not think of as having mild cases of Sz (Ongkosit, personal communication). DSM, in its effort to make the Axis II definitions "atheoretic" (i.e., free of bias as to this or that etiology), has left STPD in an ambiguous state: the personality disorder is clearly linked to Sz in some cases; in others, the (positive sign) STPD seems more a manifestation of a personality that is for the most part histrionic or superstitious.

Though schizoid personality disorder (SPD) may also be a "spectrum" instance of Sz—an opinion held by psychoanalysts such as Fairbairn (1952) and Rado (1956)—the distinction between SPD and avoidant PD will not always be easy. For this reason the linkage between SPD and Sz will seem either strong or weak. Clinically, the distinction will often hinge on the matter of *why* the shyness? Those who truly want to be alone are more apt to belong in the Sz spectrum as examples of SPD. Those who long for contact with others yet are afraid of hurt, disappointment, etc., are the "avoidantly" shy and belong more properly in the anxious cluster. Such persons would not be expected to have as many Sz relatives as would those with the willed shyness (or true introversion) of the schizoid.

Further evidence from the biologic side linking SPD and STPD to schizophrenia comes from studies, conducted by Siever and his colleagues, on galvanic skin orienting response and on evoked potentials: both STPD patients and college volunteers whose personality profiles (on standardized psychological tests) resembled those of Sz patients showed similar abnormalities (Siever, Coursey, & Alterman, 1984). Later Siever et al. also found, in STPD but not in other PD patients, elevations of plasma and cerebrospinal-fluid homovanillic acid (a metabolite of dopamine): an abnormality characteristic also of Sz patients.

In a long-term follow-up study, Fenton and McGlashan (1989) noted that certain "schizotypal" features—paranoid ideation, social isolation, and magical thinking—detectable during initial interviews of PD patients, were good predictors of eventual schizophrenic decompensation.

Findings in harmony with this follow-up study emerged from the long-term study of children at high risk for schizophrenia carried out by Mednick and Schulsinger in Copenhagen (1968). Of 207 children whose mothers were schizophrenic, 15 became schizophrenic themselves within ten years (the study began in 1962); 29 others had become "borderline schizophrenics" (similar to STPD). All the children had been assessed originally for personality traits that might correlate with the presence of "schizotypy." This judgment was made by Schulsinger, using a 241-adjective list. Important factors that could be condensed from this list included "peculiarity" (via such traits as *peculiar, fatuous, awkward, queer, eccentric*), introversion/schizoid (*dreamy, shy, shut-in, withdrawn*), and paranoid (*hostile, distrustful, guarded*). The children who later developed "spectrum disorders," such as STPD, scored high on peculiarity and paranoia (Parnas & Jorgensen, 1989). Introversion by itself did not discriminate between the children who became ill and those who remained well. Those who developed frank Sz also showed affective/behavioral dyscontrol during the premorbid phase. Parnas and Jorgensen felt that *eccentricity* represented a subtle marker for the schizophrenic genotype.

The recent work of Squires-Wheeler et al. (1989) introduces a note of caution concerning these long-term studies: she and her colleagues found there was not much specificity in the STPD items in DSM-III-R, in the sense that offspring not only of Sz parents but also of affective-disordered (A-D) parents showed a substantial excess (when compared with controls) of "schizotypal" items. This was especially true for the items *inappropriate affect, suspiciousness, referentiality*, and *illusions*. Those with 3, 4, or 5 STPD items constituted 34% of the Sz offspring, but also 34% of the A-D offspring. Conceivably, a revised set of items for defining STPD might yield better specificity: perhaps a list emphasizing the "peculiarity" that figured so prominently in the Danish study, and giving less weight to "social isolation," since this trait was common even in the control group. The measure of "peculiarity" might have to include rather subtle traits, not as yet singled out in DSM, such as *allusive thinking* (McConaghy, 1989). This trait, apparently heritable, is found in about 9% of normals, who may be viewed as situated at one end of a continuum of thought disorder, with STPD- and Sz patients at the other. Allusiveness consists of loosened associations, uncommon associations, and a tendency to assume the listener somehow knows what is in the speaker's mind, as though the latter need give only a mere hint in order to get across a complex idea. (I once treated a schizophrenic woman who would come into my office, cheerily announcing: "It's all a question of ahimsa, Dr. Stone—ahimsa and Ray Milland! Don't you see?!") Someone with more than minimal tendency to allusiveness could easily lead us to suspect "schizotypy," especially if the strange pattern of thought predisposed to eccentric beliefs and eccentric behavior (at which point we might diagnose STPD).

In the light of these studies, the linkage between Sz and STPD is strong; its basis, in large part, reflects genetic influences. This remains valid even when examined from the vantage point of mildly ill persons. The relatives of nonpsychotic psychiatric patients were more apt to have been treated for a schizophrenic illness, for example, if the patients showed schizotypy, than if they did not (Lenzenweger & Loranger, 1989). Even in the negative study of Coryell and Zimmerman (1989), where the relatives of Sz probands did not show a heightened tendency to STPD, the authors speculated (p. 500) that their Sz probands perhaps represented a relatively nonfamilial type of Sz, in contrast to many other Sz samples where, apparently, the familial varieties of schizophrenia predominate.

Even if the current definitions of STPD (as in DSM-III-R) permit inclusion of persons without genetic linkage to Sz, there seems little question that a schizophrenia spectrum exists and that the personalities of schizophrenics and their relatives often show the unusual features we identify as "schizoid," "schizotypal," or (to a lesser extent) "paranoid." The articles cited above reflect research based on family studies, including studies of adoptees, and on biological and psychological correlates. The most convincing demonstration of the connection between Sz and its "attenuated forms" (i.e., certain personality disorders) would come from the study of identical twins reared apart. As Farber (1981) mentions, reared-apart monozygotic (MZ) twins are, as a group, even more alike in personality than are MZ twins brought up in the same home (p. 46). This may have to do with the efforts parents of MZs often make to "differentiate" the twins, by way of enhancing their sense of (separate) identity. But very few sets of reared-apart MZs have been studied (less than 200). Because the base rate of STPD is low (on the order of 2 or 3% in the population), not enough pairs of such twins—where the index case has a Sz spectrum PD—have been gathered to make for valid, statistically supported study. (There were no such pairs, for example, in the 12 pairs examined meticulously and followed over 25 years by Juel-Nielsen [1965]).

As to the possibility of genetic underpinnings for *paranoid PD*, the issue is more complex and less clear-cut than is the case for SPD and STPD. Whereas in the United States, until recently, psychoses with prominent paranoid symptomatology were considered "schizophrenic," the more rigorous standards of current nosology recognize not only a paranoid type of schizophrenia but also a paranoid type of manic psychosis and an apparently separate type (genetically speaking) of "simple delusional disorder"

(Kendler, 1980). The latter is distinguished by delusions in the absence of hallucinations or of other stigmata of Sz or MDP. Similarly, *paranoid personality*, when it is understood as a phenotype, is not always a manifestation of an underlying Sz. The other psychoses just mentioned may also serve as the genetic wellspring from which the personality disorder derives. Organic psychoses and epileptiform conditions may also be associated with paranoid PD. In these conditions (which may overlap with *constitutional* factors; see below), the key element may be a reduction of available association areas in the brain, predisposing to the kind of oversimplified, emergency-based thinking that characterizes paranoid ideation.

In an offshoot of the Danish Adoption Study, a surplus of paranoid PD was noted among the biological relatives of the schizophrenic-spectrum adoptees, when compared with control adoptees (Kendler & Gruenberg, 1982). The paranoid relatives were all male: 4 of 105 schizophrenic spectrum relatives, or 3.8%, as against 1 in 138 (0.7%) control relatives. This study supported the contention of Kety et al. (1975) that paranoid PD, as well as STPD, was part of the Sz spectrum. Because paranoid PD was less common than STPD in the biological relatives of Sz probands, Kendler suggested that the linkage between Sz and paranoid PD is weaker than is the case with STPD.

A subsequent study of psychiatric illness in the close (first-degree) relatives of Sz patients (Kendler, Gruenberg, & Tsuang, 1985) revealed an excess not only of Sz but also of "paranoid disorder" (simple delusional disorder) in the relatives of schizophrenic, as compared with control, patients. This observation ran counter to Kendler's previous observation (Kendler & Gruenberg, 1982) that, if one began with paranoid disorder probands, one did not find an excess of Sz cases among their relatives. One explanation might be, as Kendler offered, that a subgroup of paranoid disorder does indeed have a close linkage with Sz. One could argue, *de fortiori*, that some cases of paranoid PD represent expressions of Sz genotype, though others might have developed as attenuated forms of paranoid disorder or might stem from still other sources. The connection between (some instances of) paranoid personality and paranoid/delusional disorder was reaffirmed in a later study of Kendler's (Kendler, Masterson, & Davis, 1985).

If we can assume for the moment that in a certain proportion of persons with paranoid PD the main causative agent is heightened genetic liability for Sz or for delusional disorder, several questions immediately arise. What is the size of this "genetic" subgroup? And in the (probably larger) group of persons with this personality disorder, what other etiologic factors, singly or in combination, contribute importantly to its evolution?

At present one can say little about the ratio, within the whole domain of paranoid persons, of mainly genetic to mainly environmental cases. Any investigator would be at the mercy of "local variations" in samples of such persons. Social class, social circumstances, cultural and geographic background, etc., would differ from one sample to another in ways that would almost surely create differences in the apparent weights of these and similar contributing factors. In the sections that follow we will see that the paths to paranoid PD are numerous, and no one path has the force of a "necessary-but-not-sufficient" factor. As we saw, one cannot even claim that Sz risk genes have this necessary-but-not-sufficient force within the realm of STPD. Unlike the case with paranoid PD, however, there is in all likelihood a large subset of schizotypal persons in whom eccentricity, cognitive slippage, and bizarre turns of thought are prominent and hardly to be accounted for except by invoking hereditary predisposition.

Dramatic Cluster

In the dramatic cluster of personality disorders, genetic factors are less uniformly discernible than in the eccentric cluster. Histrionic and narcissistic PDs have been studied less extensively in this regard; what data there are concern chiefly the other two disorders: antisocial and borderline.

Antisocial PD (ASP) has received the most attention, as would be expected because of the negative impact persons with ASP exert on those with whom they come in contact. At the extremes of this entity, one encounters violent felons, whose acts have correspondingly serious forensic implications. It should be underlined at the outset that there are obviously no "genes" for antisociality *per se*, any more than there are for "alcoholism." By heritable factors for these conditions, one is referring via a linguistic shorthand to some predisposition to particular aberrations of the central nervous system—whose net effects many steps down the line are (in the case of ASP) various offensive behaviors or (in the case of alcoholism) a type of pervasive social anxiety which can be alleviated by alcohol. The "alcoholic" discovers this through trial and error, sometime during adolescence or young adulthood, and then only in cultures where access to alcoholic beverages is easy. Persons with similar social anxiety living in cultures that actively discourage alcohol use will tend to develop other maladaptive patterns (psychosomatic illness, "hysteria," "phobia," etc.): alcoholism per se becomes less likely as a phenotype. There is another effect of alcohol, besides its anxiolytic effect, that intersects importantly with antisociality. Alcohol promotes the release of inhibition (through counteracting serotonin-mediated CNS inhibitory pathways). Many antisocial persons "prime" themselves with alcohol by way of facilitating their impulse to carry out some antisocial act. One may speak of this under the heading of "willed dyscontrol."

In their efforts to assess genetic vs. environmental factors in ASP,

Cadoret, Troughton et al. (1990) looked at the backgrounds of 286 male adoptees (recruited from two children's agencies in Iowa), of whom 44 met criteria for ASP. Criminality/delinquency and alcoholism were both overrepresented (by a factor of about three or four) in the biological parents. Parental alcoholism predicted alcohol abuse in the adoptee. Antisocial adoptees were in general more likely to have an alcohol problem than were their non-antisocial counterparts. On the *environmental* side, placement into an adoptive home where there was either alcoholism or antisociality also increased the risk of adoptee ASP. This risk was also heightened when adoptees with criminal/delinquent parents were placed with families of lower socioeconomic status (whereas lower-SES adoptive family was not associated with ASP if the adoptee did not have a parent with a criminal or delinquent record). Possibly, the lower-SES parents were less able to impart to their children successful programs for social adaptation than would be true of higher-SES parents. If so, this would be in line with the observation of Gunn (1991) that, in general, successful individuals use aggressivity sparingly, while unsuccessful (less bright in school or otherwise competitively disadvantaged) persons tend, if aggressive, to fail in their attempts, and having failed, to become even more aggressive/antisocial, in a vicious circle.

In a study not designed to tease apart nature from nurture, Huesmann et al. (1984) noted that children judged the most aggressive at age eight (by their classmates) remained the most aggressive, at follow-up, when they were 30. Compared to the less aggressive group, they were two and a half times as likely to commit serious crimes as adults. Once aggressive behavior is established, through whatever combination of factors, the tendency remains stable over the years.

Mednick and his coworkers (1988) examined the nature/nurture question in relation to violent vs. nonviolent (property crimes only) offenders. According to their study, which was based on *adoptees* in Denmark, first-time violent offenders were twice as likely to commit a future violent offense as were those convicted originally only of a property offense. There was a linear relationship between the number of convictions in the male adoptees and the number of convictions in biological parent(s), though fully 70% of adoptees whose parents had three or more convictions had never themselves been convicted. Mednick emphasized the importance of perinatal factors (viz., mild brain damage at birth) and family instability as predisposing to subsequent offender status. The author argued against the notion of hereditary transmission of violent criminal behavior.

As with any Danish study of violence, the chief virtue of Mednick et al.'s study is its chief flaw: the Danish registry made it easy to trace adoptees and their biological families (though this is no longer so) compared with the situation in the U.S., but at the same time the base rate of violent criminal behavior is lower in Denmark by a factor of at least 10 looking at the two countries as a whole (the murder rate in the U.S., for example, is 10 times that of Denmark); by factors of 20 to 60 if one is comparing Copenhagen with New York or Washington. Denmark (to its credit) is not the ideal country in which to study the pathogenesis of violent antisocial behavior.

Occasionally the annals of crime inadvertently offer us a kind of adoption study relevant to the issue of criminality. The California serial killer, Gerald Gallego, for example (Biondi & Hecox, 1987) never knew his biological father, but it emerged at Gerald's trial that, when Gerald was eight, his father had been executed for killing a policeman. But such examples are too few, and the intervening variables (child abuse? neglect? head injury?) usually too sketchily spelled out, to provide us with definitive answers concerning the precise levels of risk (for ASP) attached to genetic vs. environmental factors.

As to the question: what are the heritable traits that may conduce to antisociality (given that there are no genes for truancy, vandalism, etc.), several investigators have concentrated upon CNS abnormalities that may underlie *impulsivity*. This trait is not specific for ASP, since it is also found in persons with histrionic, borderline, and hypomanic configurations; yet it is an important element. Siever et al. (1985), mentioning that impulsivity may reflect a lowered CNS threshold for motoric activity, have shown a correlation between this trait and altered response to challenge by the serotonin agonist, fenfluramine. Subjects with the *least* prolactin response to fenfluramine (who presumably had the least CNS serotonin activity) showed the greatest degree of impulsivity (p. 172).

Low CNS serotonin levels are common in violent antisocial persons, in those who commit suicide,* as well as in other non-violence-prone but impulsive persons. Impulsivity, in the sense of diminished self-control, may not have sufficient explanatory power vis-à-vis antisociality. Psychopaths, criminal and otherwise, also show reduced anxiety in the face of danger, compared with normal people. The same is true of sensation-seeking persons in general and of nonpsychopathic persons who are unusually daring, brave, or adventurous. (A male ballet star who died several years ago from cocaine abuse was noted by his parents to enjoy walking along the edge of the roof of the family home when he was three; fearlessness was his most notable trait.) These traits are also under genetic control to a significant degree.

The traits we associate with the full-blown psychopath also include glib-

---

*Especially in those who commit suicide by violent means, as opposed to nonviolent means such as pill ingestion (Åsberg et al., 1986; Träksman-Bendz et al., 1986).

ness, callousness, and an imperviousness even to shame (let along guilt). Like all extreme traits, they may be understood as the end points of a continuum. Callousness, for example, is the "coldness" that lies beyond the "coolness" of the fearless. Glibness represents an extreme freedom from anxiety in social situations where one is dissimulating, insincere, or lying outright. The glibness of the psychopath may reflect a lack of empathic capacity, originating in a genetic/constitutional defect. It is not likely that this capacity, which when it is present marks us as "human," is localizable in any small region of the brain. There are certain persons, nevertheless, who seem from birth on to lack this human quality to a frightening degree, even if reared in a warm family setting.*

One should also consider the *intensity* of the basic drives as a factor in the complicated equation of antisociality. Someone born with unusual imperiousness of the drives (for hunger, motoric activity, sex, etc.) might not bend the rules of society, if at the same time inner control mechanisms were strong. If the latter were weak, but so were the drives, again perhaps there would be no inducement to antisocial "taking what I want when I want it." The combination of weak control and high drive intensity, in contrast, might indeed predispose to antisociality. This combination is seen in certain sensation-seeking persons with manic tendencies ("hypomanic temperament"). The hypersexuality, overtalkativeness, super-ambition, intensity, willfulness, pacing, etc., of the manic may all be understood as manifestations of a CNS "thermostat" that is set too high (Stone, 1988a). In the biographies of those who have murdered or have attempted murder, several such hypomanic personalities are to be found. These are discussed in detail in Chapter 21 under category 9.

Apropos temperament and its relationship to ASP, Gurrera (1990) speaks of *action-oriented* vs. *inhibited* prototypes. The former is characterized by innate tendencies toward sensation-seeking, extraversion, low harm-avoidance, and augmentation of responses on cortical evoked potential tests. This is the pattern one finds in hypomanics as well as in many persons with histrionic, antisocial, and borderline PDs. Using the Zuckerman Sensation-Seeking Scale, Gurrera found that college students who scored high on this scale tended to report, in comparison to the low scorers, more sex, more smoking, drug and alcohol use, more emotionality and aggressiveness; they also had higher Pd and Hy (psychopathic deviate and hysteric) scores on the MMPI.

Actual psychopaths, in effect, are those who show the extremes of these tendencies; as these traits shade into the normal population one finds (non-antisocial or only mildly antisocial) adventurous persons, overly self-confi-

*Cf. Spungen, 1983.

dent persons, super-salesman types, and a host of other "normal variants" on the extraverted side of the ledger. Those in whom *manic* traits (a) predominate over the antisocial (or where the latter are not present) or (b) turn out to be a forerunner of bipolar illness will show such traits as: active, vivid, strong-willed, imaginative, leadership qualities, early sexual exploration, interest in mystical subjects, and desultoriness (as in not completing courses for which one enrolled).* Further along the continuum toward mania and toward the pathological, one finds: unreliability, irritable temper, unwillingness to compromise, cheeriness, enthusiasm yet with poor empathy, verbal aggressiveness, and a tendency to fall quickly and passionately in love yet without much ability to sustain the relationship (Pössl & von Zerssen, 1990).

Studies of cortical evoked potentials in ASP have yielded somewhat conflicting results. Cleckley's definition of the psychopath mentions, among other attributes, an inability to sustain interest over long periods of time. In their study of ASP adolescents, Raine and Venables (1988) noted, however, that an elevated P3 spike was common in relation to target stimuli. These adolescents showed proficiency in information processing on parietal-lobe-related tasks, suggesting enhanced, rather than diminished, attentional ability. As the authors pointed out, the heightened P3 amplitude might reflect *transiently* enhanced attentional capacity, in very short-term tasks, whereas the time span relevant to Cleckley's definition was much longer: one's ability to remain in school till completion, to stay at one job, etc.

In summary, evidence is accumulating that would support a genetic hypothesis for some of the more prominent traits in a substantial proportion of psychopathic/antisocial persons. What may be inherited are tendencies, operating singly or in combination, such as *high drive urgency, reduced empathic capacity,* and *lowered self-restraint.* Sensation-seeking may be related to the first and third of these tendencies. The traits corresponding to these abnormalities include: possessiveness, ruthlessness, demandingness; callousness, glibness, contemptuousness; impetuousness, impulsivity and recklessness.

The issues concerning *genetic factors in borderline personality disorder (BPD)* are, if anything, less clear-cut and more controversial than those related to antisociality. When I first began writing on the subject, I took the position (Stone, 1977) that genetic factors figured significantly in a

---

*Akiskal (1992) has referred to this group as "hyperthermic," a temperament-type similar to Kraepelin's "manic temperament," consisting of such traits as cheerfulness, versatility, emotional warmth, jocularity, self-assuredness, stimulus-seeking, and indefatigability.

large proportion of borderline conditions. The DSM-III definition was not to be published for another three years, and I based my impressions on work with patients diagnosed by Kernberg's criteria (1967) as having "borderline personality organization." The key features of this definition are an impaired sense of identity, combined with adequate reality-testing (especially in the interpersonal sphere). Associated features are impulsivity, poor capacity for work or avocational activities, and a readiness to experience anxiety in situations other people take in stride. The tighter and less inferential diagnostic criteria of Gunderson and Singer (1975), had I relied upon them at the time, would probably have narrowed the patient sample with which I was working to an even more "genetically determined" subgroup.

Concomitant major affective disorder, usually depressive, less often bipolar II, in nature, was present in two-thirds of the female, and one-third of the male borderline patients on the long-term unit at New York State Psychiatric Institute where my research was carried out. Of the 550 patients admitted to that unit between 1963 and 1976, 299 met Kernberg's criteria for borderline personality organization; of these, 206 met DSM-III criteria for BPD (via chart review following publication of DSM-III). These patients were mostly adolescents or young adults who had passed through only a small portion of the period of risk for manic-depressive illness. At 10-to-25-year follow-up, nine percent of the borderline patients (95% of whom were traced) had gone on to develop recurrent unipolar, bipolar II, or bipolar I affective illness (Stone, 1990). Ten of these 26 patients had one or both parents with a condition in the affective spectrum. In the BPD subgroup, there were 395 biological parents: 32 had a major affective disorder (MAD); 50 had a history of alcoholism. There was no significant difference in the frequency of MAD in the parents of patients with BPD only vs. BPD plus concomitant MAD (the "comorbid" group). Only two of the parents were schizophrenic.

These data, as well as similar findings from Akiskal (1981) and Andrulonis et al. (1981), suggested that BPD and primary affective disorders were often at least fellow travelers and that the affective disorder might in such cases be the preexisting and inciting factor that conduced to the development, some time in late adolescence or early adult life, of the trait and symptom constellation we now identify as BPD. In a number of other studies, however, affective pedigrees were not found in any large number of samples of BPD patients (Kroll, 1988; Loranger et al., 1982). These authors saw the affective component, when it was present, not as a causative element but rather as an overlap phenomenon. Barasch et al. (1985) noted that depressive conditions were common in the families of BPD probands, but also in the families of patients with other PDs.

The one twin study of BPD, carried out in Norway, was based on ten pairs, of which only three were MZs: none of the MZ cotwins had BPD, though two of the seven DZ cotwins did (Torgersen, 1984). The sample size is very small, preventing the data from shedding much light on the question of a genetic factor. I have come across only one MZ pair where the index case had BPD: this pair happened to be concordant—but this positive finding is no more instructive than Torgersen's negative finding. Unfortunately, it will not be easy to accumulate series of BPD twins large enough to support meaningful statistical analysis: standardization of the diagnosis is relatively recent, so one cannot go into the old records (as in the Scandinavian adoption studies) in order to locate hundreds of BPD twin probands. Extensive search at several large psychiatric centers working in tandem will be necessary to create a sample of adequate size. In the meantime, it is of interest that in a small but carefully conducted study of first-degree relatives, STPD appeared to breed true, and the relatives of BPD patients were at greater risk for BPD than were the relatives of STPD or control probands (Baron, Gruen et al., 1985).

What is the proper course to navigate through such an array of conflicting data? Gunderson has said: "I find it difficult to conceive of any adult personality that would not have important genetic determinants" (1987, p. 43). While most of us find this eminently reasonable, the question is still open, as Gunderson also mentions, as to *what* precisely is inherited? And if this elusive entity is found, how specific is it to the genesis and nature of BPD? Matters of definition and culture come into play. As has become clearer than ever in recent years, BPD is best understood as the final common pathway of many etiological factors (Stone, 1993), sometimes acting almost alone, more often acting in concert. The abuse of children—physical or sexual—is now seen as an important factor, exerting far greater influence in some series than heredo-familial factors for manic-depression. Further, alcoholism is common in the parents of BPD patients, which may be implicated both as a heritable factor and as a catalyst to the abuse factor (since alcoholic parents tend to be more abusive, physically and/or sexually).

If we conclude that *irritability* is the key heritable factor in BPD (similar to the *aggressiveness* of which Kernberg speaks [1967]), we would need to trace its neurophysiological antecedents. Lowered serotonin activity in the CNS may be one mediator of this aggressiveness (cf. Coccaro, 1989), but other transmitter systems may also be involved. Are any of these abnormalities *specific* for BPD? Probably not. The central features of BPD are impulsivity, anger, and moodiness (cf. the "affective dysregulation," postulated by Klein, 1977). There may be different neurophysiological/neuroendocrine mechanisms subserving these attributes. BPD may thus represent the confluence of several such abnormalities, each under at least partial genetic control and no one of which is unique to BPD. In "moodiness" BPD overlaps with depressive and histrionic PDs; in "aggressiveness" with ASP; in impulsivity with ASP, hypomanic temperament, "explosive" PD, and certain instances of histrionic and narcissistic PDs. BPD can only be understood, as it were, in the aggregate: it is not nearly so "unitary" in its component traits as is, say, schizoid PD.

The earlier psychoanalytic definition of "borderline" centered on "identity diffusion" (an impaired or insecure sense of identity), which is not a personality trait and also does not point to any specific etiological source, biological or otherwise. The newer definitions (Gunderson & Singer, 1975; DSM-III and III-R) are polythetic and do not insist on any one feature as the key item. This leaves clinicians more likely to be influenced by personal experience, i.e., by whatever most typifies the cases with which they are familiar in their daily work. At some centers the typical BPD patient is someone with inordinate anger/irritability, based on an abuse history. At others, moodiness, based on genetic influences, is seen as predominant. All these considerations will affect one's impressions as to what genetic factors to look for—or whether one should be searching for them at all. Another factor complicating the study of family patterns in BPD is the likelihood of BPD, diagnosed usually before age 25, to "mellow" into some more benign pattern after age 30 or 35 (into histrionic or narcissistic PD, for example). Starting with BPD probands, an investigator is not apt to find many parents with currently diagnosable BPD. This may help account for why Reich (1989) found no evidence of familiality in BPD: he began with a small N and examined only the parents.

There is no reason to think a clinical entity as heterogeneous as BPD would "breed true" in the first place, if by "breed true" one restricted one's gaze only to relatives with BPD. In the variety of BPD where mood disorder seems primary, it might be relevant, for example, to count those relatives with major depression, bipolar conditions, or the four Kraepelinian temperaments (depressive, manic, irritable, cyclothymic) as "positive" cases. In the variety of BPD where the average case seems like an instance of posttraumatic stress disorder (stemming from abuse), pedigree analysis may turn up little in the way of psychiatrically ill relatives, except for those with alcoholism or antisociality.

In contrast to the situation with ASP and BPD, the other disorders in the "dramatic cluster" have been much less studied from a genetic standpoint. Psychogeneticist John Rainer (1978), drawing on Irving Gottesman's work with the MMPI, mentioned that the heritability of "hysteria" was the lowest (comparing the various MMPI dimensions), while that of introversion and of depression was the highest. Reznikoff and Honeyman (1967), however, in their study of 18 MZ and 16 DZ twins did find evidence, from the MMPIs, of a genetic contribution to hysteria. Similarly, Vandenberg (1967) found a probable genetic linkage in certain key traits of both hysteric (as the current term "histrionic" was then called) and sociopathic PDs—namely, impulsivity and delinquency. In the latter study aggressiveness and dependency seemed much more related to sociocultural factors than to genetic factors.

As for sociopathy and hysteria, Cloninger (1978) has presented findings from pedigree analysis that support a multifactorial model of inheritance, where, in effect, "hysteria is a more prevalent and less deviant manifestation of the same process which causes sociopathy" (p. 199). Sociopathy is predominantly a male condition; hysteria, a female condition. However, if one begins with a sample of probands of either type (sociopathic men or women; hysteric women), the prevalence of sociopathic persons and of hysteric women is greater than expected among their first-degree relatives (Cloninger, 1978, p. 199).

It should be emphasized that the heritable factor(s) Cloninger speaks of as conducing to hysteria relate to the severe end of the histrionic personality spectrum. At this end of the spectrum one finds persons (predominantly women) who are self-dramatizing, sensation-seeking, shallow, impulsive, distractible, irresponsible, demanding, and immature, all to a marked degree. In this way, they resemble the "infantile" type of borderline patient described by Kernberg (1967) or the "hysteroid" patients described by Easser and Lesser (1965). Obviously, there are great numbers of people with milder degrees of some of these traits, who might also be diagnosed "histrionic"—or as just having some histrionic features—but who are never in trouble with the law and who show not even a hint of sociopathy. One would not expect to find in these milder cases the various neurophysiological correlates (expressions, as would seem likely, of the relevant genes) common to sociopaths, (severe) "hysterics," and also hyperactive children (Satterfield et al., 1974). These correlates include slow recovery of evoked responses to auditory stimuli and low cortical arousal. The latter, as mentioned earlier, has been implicated in the characteristic *sensation-seeking* of persons with these disorders (analogous, perhaps, to the drowsy concertgoer's need for loud music at an exciting tempo, if he is to stay awake).

A genetic base for "narcissistic personality disorder" (NPD) is no more apparent than for histrionic PD, probably for similar reasons. The total domain of narcissism—NPD itself, plus the more numerous, usually milder disturbances of personality where there are a few "narcissistic" features (vanity, haughtiness, self-centeredness, preoccupation with fame, etc.)—is too vast for us to expect there would be one readily identifiable genetic abnormality. There is no common, unifying "phenotype," pointing the way where we should look, say, for neurophysiologic correlates. As with HPD, it would be only at the extremes of NPD that such correlates might be discoverable. Among the "outliers" on the bell curve of narcissism, one finds persons who are ruthlessly exploitative, unempathic, and callous. Kernberg has aptly called such persons "malignant narcissists" (1989a). Precisely because of these qualities, such persons are in the region where ASP and NPD overlap. Some of the genetic factors said to underlie psychopathy (such as we have outlined above) might therefore be contributory to these extreme varieties of narcissistic personality.

Anxious Cluster

Persons manifesting any of the "anxious cluster" PDs or milder disturbances of personality with similar traits share the common feature (besides the definitional one of anxiety) of "high harm-avoidance" (Cloninger, 1986). The opposite state—low harm-avoidance—is associated, as noted above in the case of BPD, with low serotonergic activity and low prolactin response to fenfluramine (cf. also Steiner et al., 1988). In the CNS, serotonergic systems are involved with the suppression of "punishable" behaviors (Gray, 1982; Siever, Klar, Coccaro, 1985). Low activity in these systems has, in animal studies, been correlated with heightened aggressiveness (Valzelli, 1981). As for studies of serotonin metabolites (viz., 5-hydroxyindoleacetic acid: 5-HIAA), more attention has been paid, understandably, to BPD and ASP. Patients with these disorders are more apt to be found in institutional settings, where research is more feasible, than are dependent, avoidant, or other "anxious" persons.

Family studies of obsessive-compulsive disorder (OCD) shed some light on possible genetic factors both in OCD itself and in obsessive-compulsive personality (OCPD). As Rasmussen and Eisen (1990) mention, a report in the 1940s noted that "obsessive neurosis" (roughly equivalent to OCPD) was found in about 6% of patients or siblings of patients with OCD, but in none of the first-degree relatives of patients with anxiety or hysterical neurosis (p. 18). If one began with OCPD patients as the probands, OCD was uncommon in their parents, but obsessive traits *were* common. Since two-thirds or more of OCD patients do not show an underlying OCPD premorbidly, the earlier psychoanalytic theory positing a connection between the two may have to be modified (Rasmussen & Eisen, 1990, p. 24). Still, in some families, obsessive traits (and OCPD itself) are overrepresented in a manner suggesting a hereditary factor. As for OCD, the accumulated twin studies show about double the number of concordant monozygotic pairs to discordant pairs. This suggests a genetic factor for OCD; unfortunately, there are as yet no reports of MZ twins reared apart where both had OCD, which would be a more convincing demonstration of genetic predisposition.

A NOTE ON ORGANIC CONTRIBUTORS TO
ABNORMALITIES OF PERSONALITY

Organic conditions of many different kinds can bring about either transitory or lasting changes in personality. When the changes are abrupt, the clinician's suspicions are more readily heightened as to the likelihood of some underlying illness. Diseases with a slower course, which induce insidious changes over long stretches of time, may pose severe challenges to the diagnostician.

The paranoid personality changes that overtook George Gershwin toward the end of his life were occasioned by a slow-growing meningioma—not suspected by the psychiatrist who had been treating him at the time. Belfer and d'Autremont (1971) reported schizophrenic-like withdrawal in a 14-year-old boy, which had also been brought about by a meningioma. The tumor was fortunately resectable and postoperatively the boy's personality reverted to normal.

Abuse of anabolic steroids by athletes or by men hoping to become super-strong for other reasons may induce radical changes, usually in the direction of paranoid ideation and irritability. Cerebritis in the course of disseminated lupus erythematosus may provoke extreme paranoid changes as well as general deterioration of habits. Prolonged abuse of amphetamines may induce similar changes. Chronic marijuana abuse may lead at first to euphoria, then to surliness, loss of motivation, and habit-deterioration (Nahas, 1973).

Many endocrine disorders are accompanied by marked personality alterations: sluggishness, in the case of hypothyroidism; nervousness in the case of hyperthyroidism; paranoid traits in the wake of hyperadrenalism, etc. Impending insulin coma in poorly regulated diabetics may be preceded by extremes of irritability and paranoia—rather abrupt ordinarily, capable of taking coworkers and friends by surprise if they are unaware of the person's underlying condition. Strange, inexplicable changes in personality are at times the premonitory, rather than end-stage, sign of bronchogenic carcinoma.

In general, conditions that lead to insidious, disturbing personality changes are the most worrisome, since they are more likely to come first to the attention of a psychiatrist rather than a neurologist or internist. Psychiatrists, unless they are unusually well-versed in the organic aspects of our field, may miss the underlying diagnosis. This will be the more likely to happen if clear-cut accompanying physical signs are absent. In multiple sclerosis, one may see a personality change in the direction of euphoria or the "belle indifférance" reminiscent of the hysteric. But usually there will also be some neurologic abnormalities as well, even if these are transitory and shifting. I have seen Lyme disease present as an otherwise unaccountable change in the personality.

Head trauma is an important factor. A fair percentage of murderers had sustained serious, often multiple, head injuries during childhood or adolescence—injuries that combined synergistically with other adverse factors to lower frustration tolerance and propel the injured person toward violent acts. Benton (1991) offers an interesting example from the nineteenth century literature: A man of 37 had survived a fall from a fourth-storey window, enduring a penetrating wound in the frontal area. Several days after recovering from the skull fracture, he began to show marked changes in personality. Having always been industrious, cheerful, and honest, he now became aggressive, malicious, paranoid, and given to playing pranks or making obscene remarks. Gradually, he became less quarrelsome and even felt remorseful for his previous behavior. He died several months after his accident; at autopsy there was destruction of the gyrus rectus bilaterally and, on the right side, of the medial portion of the inferior frontal gyrus. According to Feuchtwanger (1923) frontal lobe injuries are apt to be associated with mood disorders, loss of impulse control and compulsive punning or joke-making (Witzelsucht).

Though we can only touch briefly here on this broad topic of organic factors in personality change, we should not omit mention of the many abnormalities—some gross, others subtle—brought about by psychotropic medications. None of the many recent textbooks on psychopharmacology (Baldessarini, 1985; Yudofsky et al., 1991) is so complete in describing side-effects as to permit complacency on the part of psychiatrists utilizing these medications. Hypomanic behavior can be brought to the surface in susceptible depressed patients given any of a variety of antidepressants. Even drugs in the new generation of serotonergic antidepressants, reputed to be relatively free of side-effects, do not always live up to their claims. I have worked with depressed patients taking fluoxetine (Prozac) who became either highly and uncharacteristically irritable or else hypomanic. In the latter state, they became euphoric and went on gigantic spending sprees. Paradoxical effects of anxiolytic medications have also been described: for example, patients with borderline personality disorder becoming more, rather than less, anxious and irritable when taking benzodiazepines (Cowdry & Gardner, 1988).

Rapid-cycling manic-depressive patients seem especially vulnerable to the side effects of psychotropic medications. This becomes a vexatious problem in therapy, since these patients are prone to undergo frequent shifts in certain personality qualities just from their underlying condition. Distinguishing between the roller-coaster mood shifts from the latter and the side effects of concurrent medications can at times be extremely difficult.

4

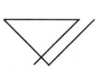

Ethological and Ecological Considerations in the Formation of Personality

WE HAD EARLIER STRESSED the notion, promulgated by Millon, that *personality* constitutes a first line of defense in coping with the challenges of the interpersonal field. Millon's idea is valuable in understanding psychopathology, insofar as it helps us to understand the gradations along the path from smooth function to poor function but with minimal distress to the individual (because of egosyntonic traits that are annoying to others), and on to very poor function (where even dystonic qualities make their appearance).

If we are to understand the origins and the purposefulness of personality, however, we will need to look beyond the horizons of psychiatry and psychology as they are customarily pictured, and cast our glance into other fields. The most fertile in this respect would seem to be that of ethology. In the case of humans, this subject, as set forth in the comprehensive treatise of Eibl-Eibesfeldt (1989), embraces the biology of human behavior and seeks to answer the question: why do we behave as we do? Many clues to the riddle are to be found in the literature devoted to the ethology of our primate near-cousins (Byrne & Whiten, 1988), as well as in the neo-Darwinian literature concerning mammalian genetics, in general (Dawkins, 1976), and the genetics of the human brain, in particular (Changeux, 1985).

WHAT WE CAN LEARN FROM
OUR PRIMATE COUSINS

Though we might be accused of anthropomorphizing, it does not seem too far off the mark to speak of "personality" in relation to many animal species. Often we mean little else besides temperament or disposition, as when we refer to the platypus as "shy" or a puppy as "playful." Among the larger mammals with whom we interact frequently, we are able to discern fairly subtle differences in "personality": some that help distinguish one animal from another; others that become manifest in accordance with moment-to-moment changes in the environment.

Each species has its own range of traits and its own pattern of flexibility (or lack of it) in the display of these traits. The relative fixity of species-specific patterns has led us to postulate genetic underpinnings operative within in each species, as though the typical personality of each is in some sense "hard-wired" into place during fetal life, waiting to express itself in these characteristic ways throughout the course of life.

The emergent personality is presumably in harmony with the adaptive repertoire pertinent to any given species. The repertoire will include strategies for basic tasks such as competition for necessary supplies, cooperation, defense against aggression, and awareness of dominance hierarchy. Cooperation can be further subdivided into "subroutines" for mating, child-rearing, and, in the case of social species like lions and chimpanzees, getting along with the conspecifics within one's group. Defense consists of both intra- and interspecies behavior patterns, since most animals must cope not only with predators but also with stronger, more dominant members of their own species.

Humans, whose genome differs only slightly from that of the chimpanzee, are clearly descended from social primates. As Byrne and Whiten mention (p. 7), the life of a social animal is problematical: its tasks are more complex and more subtle than those of, say, a solitary predator like the leopard. The leopard has only to distinguish friends (a potential mate, a few close relatives) from enemies (every other creature it will encounter), and does not have to size up its position in a dominance hierarchy relative to other leopards in a "group." Social apes, in contrast, must monitor subtle gradations in status among relatively large numbers of conspecifics within the troupe, relying on an extensive memory as to who outranks whom. The daughter of a chimpanzee, for example, occupies a rank just beneath that of her mother; a subordinate chimp would thus not challenge a much smaller troupe member if the latter happened to be the offspring of a high-ranking chimp—even if the higher-ranking parent were nowhere in sight.

Primatologists have observed a kind of political in-fighting in monkeys and apes, where a hitherto leader-male is deposed by two or more erstwhile subordinate males, one of whom becomes the new "alpha" male in the troupe. As Harcourt (1988) points out, "Alliances are far more complex social interactions than are two-animal contests, requiring more information and more complex information for their successful outcome" (p. 132). The evolution of species that could form alliances for the acquisition of goods necessary to survival seems itself to have been fostered, as this author explains, by life in an ecological niche where the most valuable resources are not very abundant (hence worth defending) and concentrated in small areas (hence capable of being defended by a group of animals).

Whereas the large cats depend upon moving (hence nondefensible) targets (zebras, gazelles, etc.), primates are mostly frugivores whose food comes from stationary, defensible objects, namely trees. Once a large cat has made a kill, it usually does not have to compete for its food amongst others of its species: there are none in the neighborhood. But many apes can gather around a tree, there to compete for the fruit. In the ensuing contests, the ability to form alliances or to outmaneuver others is a distinct advantage.

In the matter of defense, social nonprimates, such as lions, who live in prides of a dozen or more interrelated members, threatened kin will receive support from other relatives. Primates go beyond this level of cooperation, in supporting even nonconsanguinous troupe members under circumstances which make such alliances advantageous (viz. supporting a dominant non-relative male, grooming the offspring of the dominant female, etc.). Such tactics require an ability to second-guess the intentions of other troupe members, to make accurate assessments of dominance, and to read facial expressions for subtle signs of others' intentions. More cortex is needed to effect these operations.

In keeping with this, it is noteworthy that the ratio of brain-weight to body-weight remains similar in nonprimate mammals, only to be tilted in favor of brain-weight in the case of primates and man. Formerly, it had been thought that this "encephalization" was, in the case of man, spurred on by better tool-making. But Wynn has recently exploded this theory, showing that the brain-size of *Homo sapiens* is not much greater than that of our predecessor, *Homo erectus*; two million years ago the latter had a much more encephalized brain—yet had tools scarcely more sophisticated than those used by modern apes (1988, p. 283). Wynn's observations led him to revise the hypothesis about technology stimulating the evolution of our intellectual capacities, in favor of what Jolly (1988) has called "Machiavellian" intelligence—intelligence, that is, suited to the complexities of social problem-solving.

The computer analogy is useful in this context, though let it be understood that computers are not nourished and protected by a mother, have no consciousness, and no awareness of inevitable death—and therefore can never be "human." That aside, it would appear that social intelligence requires a large "working" memory for processing recent social data and a large long-term memory bank for storing past relationships, social events, etc. (Whiten & Byrne, 1988, p. 58). Our brains would appear also to be hard-wired genetically for the tasks of recognizing faces and facial expressions—to a degree far surpassing our endowment for grasping large numbers of objects at a glance. The survival value to our ancestors of face recognition was, we can assume, far greater than the value attached to distinguishing between, say, 17 and 19 animals or objects. (The next time a car-delivery truck speeds past you on the highway, try to tell whether it is carrying seven or eight or nine cars! You will make many more mistakes than you will in recognizing college acquaintances from twenty years ago.) The acquisition of superior social intelligence probably preceded, in any event, the ability to fashion sophisticated tools.

The interconnectedness of social intelligence, optimal survival strategies, and personality shows itself in all the important facets of primate society, including that of breeding patterns. Males who would bid successfully for the attraction of estrous females must, among other things, be able to deal appropriately with conflicts that may arise from more mature and more dominant males (Chance & Mead, 1988). Success depends upon the ability to suppress aggressive responses until such time as the likelihood of winning increases. An adolescent "contender" would do better, for example, to hold back from competing directly with an older, stronger male, until he had proven himself via successful encounters with less formidable opponents.

The social competence that fosters this ability to "work one's way up the ladder," postponing major challenges until success is likely, is what allows certain primate males eventually to enter the charmed circle where breeding opportunities await. Their genes will pass on into the next generation, while those of their too impatient and less "savvy" competitors will not. Chance and Mead refer to this ability to withstand conflict as reflecting an "equilibration" component in one's behavioral repertoire (1988, p. 46). Enlargement of the neocortex is the evolutionary development that, in their view, subserved this equilibrational fine-tuning of behavior.

Another manifestation of social adaptation facilitated by the large neocortex is the tempering of ordinary animal "selfishness" by the ability to identify with the needs of even nonconsanguinous troupe mates and to suppress momentarily the fulfillment of one's own ends in favor of helping another. The behavioral repertoire comes to include *sympathy* as well as self-centeredness (Humphrey, 1988, p. 23).

Experiments with monkeys have shown, in this regard, that resection of the rostral cingular gyrus leads to a profound change in the animal's personality: it no longer shows affection toward its companions, no longer grooms them, snatches food from them unceremoniously, and seems surprised when they retaliate (Change & Mead, 1988, p. 47). Loss of the anterior limbic area led to a diminution of the social fears that normally govern the monkey's behavior, as well as to an impaired ability to forecast the social consequences of its actions. The neuroanatomical change brought about a "loss of social conscience," though it was also accompanied by a lessening of aggression. Apart from the latter change, there are many similarities between the behavior of the monkey minus its anterior limbic area and the human "psychopath," who also lacks a social conscience and is indifferent to the feelings of others.

The larger neocortex of primates permits what Dennett (1988) calls higher levels of "intentionality" than can be inferred from the behavior of most nonprimates. First-level intentions relate to what an animal wants at any given moment. An animal shows second-level intentionality when it behaves as though it understands what another animal wants; viz. when animal A "believes" animal B wants such-and-such. Humans certainly, and higher primates probably, exhibit third-level intentionality, as would occur if "I believe that you think that I'm planning to. . . . "

Dennett gives as an example of higher-level intentionality, offered to him by a primatologist, an incident when two groups of vervet monkeys were contesting a certain territory. One temporarily sidelined member of the losing side suddenly uttered the "leopard alarm" (this species has three different alarm-cries for each of its chief predators: leopard, snake, and eagle). At once, all the monkeys disbanded, establishing a kind of truce. (This would be like a Team B player yelling "Fire!" when, in a basketball sudden-death overtime, a Team A player was poised at the foul line.) The clever monkey behaved as though he *wanted* the rivals to *think* they were overhearing a command *intended* just for his own group (p. 190).

A brain capable of second- and higher-levels of intentionality is clearly better adapted to the task of *deceiving* an opponent in a contest for some desired object (including a potential mate). LaFrenière (1988) accepts the views of social psychologists who claim, in relation to the human situation, that " . . . all social interaction [involves] an element of deception, in the sense that participants are engaged in a dramatic performance to control the impressions of themselves that are presented to others" (p. 239). Optimal function in social animals—and this is most visible on the human level—depends on a judicious balancing of openness and deception, adapted both to the needs of the moment and to long-range goals. In courtship, for example, people "put their best foot forward," omitting mention of failures, covering up flaws, etc., but they are usually careful not to lie so outrageously as to be found out easily and then rejected (as an unreliable partner for a long-term relationship).

We are capable of such subtlety as to weave openness and deception into the same utterance, as when a college baseball player tells a new girlfriend, "Yeah, I did OK last year: hit over .300," when his average was in fact .301. He is being *honest*—technically—and is appearing *modest* (both nice qualities), but he is being deceptively boastful in leading her to think he hit way over .300 (and out of modesty is just claiming "over .300"), in hopes of impressing her more. But the deception is not outrageous (even if she finds out the real average, ".301" is still pretty good). This type of behavior is, in fact, so acceptable and common as not to be experienced as "deceptive" by most people, who reserve that term for the more harmful, or poorly disguised, or absurdly exaggerated deceptions of the con man or the cheating spouse, etc.

LaFrenière's study of children suggested to him a developmentally related taxonomy of deceptive behavior, beginning with *playful* deception at about 1½ years of age (viz., pulling a toy away from mother as she is about to reach for it); *defensive* (about age 2), as when a child blames his brother for something naughty he did; *aggressive*, (age 2½), as exemplified by a child who bites himself on purpose and then says another child (whom he is trying to get back at) "bit" him; *competitive* (age 4), manifest in cheating at marbles or other games; and finally, *protective* deception (beginning at around 8), as when a child compliments his aunt's hat that he actually thinks is unattractive (p. 251).

Much of what we distinguish on the human plane as relating to *personality* concerns the subtlety—or lack of it—with which each person negotiates and balances the competitive and cooperative "game plan" (including both tactics for immediate problems and strategies for the long-term) for successful life. What constitutes "success" is itself dependent on a host of variables reflecting both one's culture and one's individual niche within that culture. Though our generation is disposed to pride itself on technological prowess, as Cheney and Seyfarth underline (1988, p. 270), we are the inheritors of a primate evolutionary predisposition to understand relationships between conspecifics better than we comprehend relationships among things.

LaFrenière's developmental outline reinforces Cheney's point that up to a certain age, children demonstrate this heritage in clear-cut form. Later on, some transform themselves into *Homo technologicus* (certain obsessive-compulsives, in particular, who carry on lifelong love affairs with machines), shifting the balance from people- to thing-orientedness.

Over 90% of our personality-trait vocabulary is devoted to social contexts and interpersonal situations. Quite a few of these words concern nuances pertaining to acceptable vs. unacceptable forms of deception (coy, coquettish, diplomatic, cunning, deceitful, treacherous, smooth, glib, etc.). The greater size and complexity of the human brain and of human society, compared to what we observe in nonhuman primates, is reflected in the greater heterogeneity of subtypes within the major categories of interaction patterns pertinent to human society. Partly, this may be a function of the much greater number of people who impinge upon the lives of any one of us, than of, say, other chimpanzees who will cross paths with any given chimpanzee during its lifetime.

But more importantly, our neocortex is large enough and has developed in such a way as to conduce to the emergence of *language*. The diversity of "calls" among primate populations does not begin to compare with the number of categories, and words for these categories, that humans routinely fashion. Language evolved out of the larger neocortex, and societal diversity has been facilitated by language. In the process, human society has come to depend upon an immense variety of personality types—some common, some rare, some advantageous to the individual as well as to society as a whole, others disadvantageous to the individual while still necessary to the larger group, and still others advantageous to the self but disadvantageous, or even disastrous, to the group. Structurally, human society divides into specialists, the way the body divides its main functions via its organs, and the cells of those organs, via their organelles.

PERSONALITY IN RELATION TO
TASK SPECIALIZATION

The simpler societies of bees, ants, lions, primates, and of other social animals divide into relatively small numbers of basic subgroups (queens, drones, workers . . . ; alpha males and females, breeders, followers . . .). Corresponding to such subdivisions, there may be a similar number of personality types that one might meaningfully identify, at least among the higher mammals: "aggressive" leaders, "subservient" followers, and the like.

In human society, one may distinguish smaller or larger numbers of subtypes, answering to various levels of generalization. Bion (1961) noted, for example, that in groups led by a maximally non-intrusive leader, the group members began to organize themselves over time into different roles, much as might a collection of shipwreck survivors stranded on an island. Differentiation into leaders and followers occurs; couples begin to form, unified by sexual interest in one another; over longer periods, an "aristocracy" develops, which may include the leaders and some "archivists" who record the important events in the group's history. This inner group may set the tone for what is considered good behavior. In short, a group *culture* develops, with its own ethos, mores, rules for assigning tasks, etc. Further division of function takes place, in accordance with subtle differences in personality and ability among the group members.

As for the differences in personality, we might organize them in relation to overarching themes. The following schemata are illustrative:

THEME	SOME RELEVANT TRAITS
Dominance/submission	aggressive, authoritarian, courageous, meek, slavish
Competition	ruthless, greedy, ambitious, defiant
Cooperation	altruistic, generous, tactful, cooperative, fawning
Sexuality	prissy, inhibited, coy, respectful, flirtatious, seductive, licentious

We could also think of the common personality disorders as the names of personality dimensions, to most of which we could assign various roles and occupations best carried out by persons of the corresponding type:

PREDOMINANT PERSONALITY TYPE	SUITABLE ROLES and OCCUPATIONS
Hypomanic	entrepreneur, talk-show host
Obsessive-compulsive	computer specialist, accountant, banker, researcher
Paranoid	secret service agent, spy, detective
Schizoid	night-watchman, darkroom technician
Histrionic	actor/actress, choreographer

Not all the roles are flattering. Narcissistic traits, for example, sometimes confer an advantage in tennis: those who play "to kill," without the slightest hesitation in humiliating an opponent, often win. Psychopathic traits may be associated with a number of at least temporary advantages, as spelled out in greater detail in Chapter 13 (Table 18). From the standpoint of the gene, philandering (as indulged by psychopathic males) and promiscuity (to which a proportion of borderline women are prone) represent "successful" strategies for the survival of one's genes into the next generation. (In discussing Dawkins' work a little further on we will return to this point.) Perhaps even passive-aggressive traits are at times advantageous, to the extent that these traits may underlie "whistle-blowing" by disgruntled employees, who at times may have quite justified complaints about corrupt practices, shoddy work, etc. These complainers may have an admixture of paranoid traits as well.

Persons with traits belonging to the eccentric cluster (paranoid/schizoid/schizotypal) tend to stand apart from the main, conventional group in society, and to this extent they may have an objectivity about certain things going awry in the main group. And because of their lesser degree of dependency upon the good opinion of others, they do not hesitate to voice their opinions, where more conventional people would keep silent. The outspokenness of the prophet Jeremiah might be viewed in this context as a kind of early warning device within the body social.

Dawkins' Model of the "Battle of the Sexes": Implications for Personality Development, Normal and Abnormal

The interplay between competitive and cooperative strategies, demonstrable in all fundamental aspects of social life, is clearly visible in the two domains mentioned by Freud, into which most of life can be compartmentalized: love and work. In "work"—here used as a catchall for survival-oriented tasks like food-gathering—the short-term desire to "have it all" is tempered by the long-term, optimal strategy of sharing.

Dawkins (1976), writing from the perspective of a neo-Darwinian ethologist, invites us to focus our view not so much upon our adult (and comparatively bulky) selves as upon the genes struggling within us to replicate themselves. From "their" standpoint, we are but fruit soon to topple to the ground, there to disintegrate, leaving the valuable seeds to create a new generation. Nonsocial creatures like the leopard do not walk a tightrope between selfish vs. altruistic strategies (except where their young are concerned): in the matter of food supply, they may be said to play Monopoly (I have no doubt that the lasting fascination with this game is an expression of our lurking desire, as inescapably socially interdependent creatures, to enjoy a few precious moments of *having it all*).

Humans, on the other hand, are saddled with the complicated task of discovering the optimal balance between altruistic and selfish impulses. A family led by parents who hogged all the food for themselves, sharing none of it with their children, would not be a family for long: lacking survivors, they would experience genetic death with their own passing. The better to minimize such selfishness, we make it a criminal offense and regard miscreants of this sort as having outrageously abnormal, narcissistic personalities.*

Turning our attention to the "Battle Between the Sexes," we become aware, from Dawkin's exposition (p. 151ff), that there exist at any one

---

*There is a long history to such behavior. An example: John Cornish and his second wife, Eliza, killed his 11-year-old son by his first wife via slow starvation. This became a celebrated case in Gloucestershire, England in 1853 (Boyle, 1989, p. 27ff).

time several competing "unconscious behavior programs" (strategies), some employed by males, others by females, for ensuring the continuity of their genes. In humans, as in most mammals, females have more at stake in the "game" of reproduction, not only because of their greater investment of time and energy in the rearing of their young, but because they have a limited number of eggs (women have about 350 chances to become pregnant during their menstrual life), whereas men, besides investing less energy in the direct care of their offspring, could theoretically impregnate several thousands of women over the course of their reproductive life. (This kind of potential was, to an extent, actualized by the Turkish sultans with their harems, so as to maximize the likelihood of generating at least one princeling.)

Because of their greater stake in child-rearing, females will incline toward what J. Maynard-Smith (1988), writing from the perspective of game-theory, characterized as the *coy* strategy. The coy program dictates a long courtship before sex is permitted. The patience required to mate with a coy female will be found in those males who pursue the *faithful* strategy; such males are better risks for remaining with the female after she gives birth and for helping her with child-rearing. But in nature, the bell-curve of variation is such that males below a certain threshold of patience will lose interest in the coy female.

If there were only coy females, these *philanderer* males would have nowhere to turn: they would have either to learn patience or do without a mate (and without offspring). Some females, however, are inclined to the *fast* strategy and impose no such time requirements upon their suitors as do their coy sisters. They will allow males of either type to mate with them very readily, thus insuring that (to the extent there is a genetic underpinning) their "fast" genes survive into the next generation. Given the ease with which the fast females accommodate males, and the readiness of philanderers to mate with them, it could come about rather quickly that fast and philanderer genes spread, while those of the other two strategies died out.

But in this scenario, as Dawkins points out, large numbers of "fast" females would end up "stuck" with the whole burden of child-rearing, since their philanderer mates would soon abandon them. At such a moment, the first faithful mate to appear on the scene would become very desirable, because of his willingness to assist in the tasks of parenthood. "Faithful" genes would now begin to replace the philanderer genes; coyness would emerge as a better strategy than fastness, and the corresponding genes would dominate. In a word, the whole process would recycle.

If matters were as simple as this, we might expect to see wild oscillations, within any given society, from one preferred set of strategies to the other, viz. a pattern of mostly coy/faithful matings in one generation giving way to mostly fast/philanderer matings in the next. What we find instead is an equilibrium, or "evolutionarily stable state," in which all the strategies coexist, but do so in just such a numerically balanced way that the ratios scarcely change from one generation to the next. Dawkins gives an illustration (p. 164) where the advantages (in economic terms, the respective "payoffs") of each adaptation are such that coyness would be found in five-sixths of the female population and fidelity in five-eighths of the males.

What the precise ratios are in a particular society will depend upon many factors, including climatic ones. In a hot climate with abundant food there might, for example, be less need for paternal care, conducing to a somewhat smaller proportion of males pursuing the "faithful" strategy. In the cold climate/scarce food areas, paternal care might be more necessary to the survival of offspring, such that the evolutionarily stable state would be achieved with a somewhat higher proportion of such males. What would hold the ratios in place in any one region is a "feedback mechanism" such that any tendency for members of either sex to deviate from their optimal ratios will bring about changes in the ratios of the remaining strategies — to the ultimate disadvantage of those who first strayed. In this way the stable state is preserved.

What are the implications of Dawkins' argument for *personality*? From the very descriptions of the different strategies it is apparent that a different personality pattern underlies each one. Coy/fast/faithful/philanderer are all personality trait-words. Since our culture, like most cultures, thrives best with more fidelity and less promiscuity, pejorative connotations attach to "fast" and "philanderer." With regard to the official personality "disorders," there is probably a correlation between antisocial/psychopathic and the philanderer strategy, since many psychopathic males are notoriously unfaithful. There may be a (weaker) correlation between borderline personality disorder and the "fast" strategy, if only because many borderline women have been sexually overstimulated in their early years via incest experiences, which may "reprogram" them so as to favor the "fast" behavioral style during adult life. Sensation-seeking — as noted in the dramatic cluster personality types and in hypomanic persons — would be associated with fast/philanderer styles; anxious cluster types, characterized by high "harm-avoidance," with coy/faithful styles.

The strategy one pursues represents the cumulative influence of genetic predisposition plus early rearing. In computer-model terms, the former would be analogous to "hard-wiring"; early rearing to a software program engrafted onto the original "hard disc." The human brain allows for greater flexibility in behavior than is customarily found even in nonhuman primates. Parental programming (accomplished both by what the parents *say*, and perhaps more importantly, by how they themselves *behave*) does not always fix for all time which strategy their children will follow. Indeed, some women switch from "fast" to "coy" at a certain point, just as some men switch from "philanderer" to "faithful." This, by the way, does not affect the constraints of the evolutionarily stable state, since a population where five-sixths of the women were coy, and one-sixth fast, etc., would lead to the same stable state as one where each women was fast one-sixth of the time and coy the remaining five-sixths (Dawkins, p. 165).

One impressive aspect of the theory concerning an evolutionary stable state is its ability to make sense of some otherwise paradoxical observations about the way human society organizes itself. Why, for example, would some women put up with philandering men? Unattractiveness (either in personality or appearance) might force some to make do with men who offer at least (but no more than) a brief spell of sexual gratification, plus the opportunity to have a child. The child, in turn, might have a value great enough to her to outweigh the unpleasantness of having no partner to help care for it.

However, as Sheila Isenberg (1991) makes clear in her book, *Women Who Love Men Who Kill*, certain misfortunes make even lethal philanderers — serial killers — attractive. A number of women who have been sexually abused by relatives, physically abused by former mates, etc., have become infatuated with notorious, and incarcerated, serial killers. Several of the latter have been allowed to marry while in prison, including both the "Hillside Stranglers," Ken Bianchi and Angelo Buono, and also Ted Bundy (whose wife, Carole Ann Boone, thanks to conjugal visits, actually bore Bundy a son). Another woman, Sue Terry, became enamored of the imprisoned serial killer, John Wayne Gacy. Battered and tortured by her former husband, Terry harbored homicidal wishes toward him, understandably enough, and seemed to regard Gacy as the kind of man who would have "taken care" of her ex in a way she was unable to do: she saw Gacy as a macho and, in her eyes, innocent "protector" — a view she clung to for over a year, until his braggadoccio about murdering 33 boys finally shook her faith in his innocence. These examples are, of course, rare and extreme but they do demonstrate how unusual histories of life and circumstances may conspire to heighten the attractiveness of persons whom one would suppose could only be "losers" in the battle of the sexes.

BALANCED POLYMORPHISM
AMONG PERSONALITY STYLES

Though we concentrated in the preceding section on strategies involving sexuality, similar comments and a similar type of mathematical analysis are applicable in the realm of *work*, in all of its manifestations. Here again, genetic, constitutional, and environmental factors collude in predisposing some persons to becoming "leaders," and others, followers. As mentioned earlier, hypomanic traits are noted in many entrepreneurs, as well as in many successful comedians and other entertainers and in many politicians. The "charisma" that elevates certain orators to high places in the public arena can often be seen as stemming from an amalgam of "dramatic" traits, such as high emotionality, supreme self-confidence that may border on grandiosity, etc. The detail-oriented persons who dot the i's and cross the t's of the leader's plans often show compulsive traits. The followers who carry out the plans may be persons who are loathe to take risks (i.e., are high in "harm-avoidance"); at the extremes, they may even show dependent, avoidant, masochistic, or depressive qualities enough to satisfy the criteria for the corresponding personality disorder categories.

Presumably, there are optima within any given culture for ratios of these attributes. A society of all leaders could not agree on any one plan, nor would anyone be contented merely to implement the plan; a society of all followers would be doomed for equal and opposite reasons. It is not so easy to agree on some objective criteria for having "leadership"—partly because of the multiple layering within a large complex society. An army sergeant, for example, is a leader to some 40 men, but a follower to his lieutenant. "Middle" executives in corporations play these dual roles. Still, there are some who rise to the top in their respective areas and who remain there—helped along by various personality traits in addition to their intelligence and vision. Empathy, forcefulness, ambition, consideration, trustingness (and therefore an ability to delegate responsibility), steadiness, integrity, and courage are some of the important traits of leadership. Besides these virtues, leaders must have better-than-average skills at second-guessing competitors, at skillful deceptiveness, diplomatic evasiveness, and the like, by way of maximizing their own and their subordinates' interests within a competitive field. Persons with similar ambitions—to lead, to dominate—but who lack the personality traits that allow leadership to be exercised with finesse, may resort, thanks to various *abnormal* traits, to intimidation, brain-washing, and other forms of crude manipulation.

There is good reason to suppose that in any society a stable state would develop between leaders who play fair and those who are corrupt or who intimidate; universal unfairness, needless to say, brings chaos, weakens the solidity of the social structure, and invites invasion from outside. If all pursued the "fair" strategy, however, the first devious or tyrannical leader would enjoy a tremendous advantage. History is chock-a-block with examples. Hitler's rise to power via intimidation of his (fair-playing) opponents, his orchestration of the Reichstag fire (then blamed on the "Communists") is one of the more dramatic (and temporarily successful) instances.

There is hardly a daily newspaper that lacks examples concerning the equilibrium between "fair" and "unfair" strategies in the domain of leadership. As in the sexual domain, an evolutionarily stable state will be established—in all but the most corrupt states—where fair and unfair strategies coexist, but where those employing the fair strategy substantially outnumber those pursuing the unfair. Similar equilibria will develop between those who are honest vs. those who cheat (in effect, between the "cops" and the "robbers"), and between all other sets of opposing groups in their struggle to garner for themselves the greatest amount of some survival-oriented or otherwise highly desirable good—whether that "good" be a scarce and valuable commodity, political power, a sexual partner, notoriety, or whatever.

If we were to examine society the way an epidemiologist might go about it, determining as precisely as possible the range and prevalence of all the competing strategies and of the personality traits (or styles) common to each, what we would see would be a *balanced polymorphism*—each type and style existing side by side with all the others in ratios that are "just right" for that society during the particular phase of its evolution when we chanced to study it. The epidemiological work of Lee Robins and her coworkers (1991) has helped establish more reliably the percentage of Americans exhibiting antisocial personality disorder (ASP), depending on age, race, socioeconomic status, etc. Similarly, Regier and his coworkers at the NIMH reported (1988) a lifetime prevalence of ASP of 2½%. Merikangas and Weissman (1986) provide statistics covering a wider array of personality types and disorders. Their report alludes both to studies concentrating on DSM-III personality disorders and to others, such as the Midtown Manhattan study, whose data represented subclinical manifestations as well: viz., the presence of hostile, suspicious traits, not just the presence of a full-blown paranoid PD) (Langer & Michael, 1963).

Personality disorders may be found in approximately 10% of the population, according to the authors Merikangas and Weissman cited. For our purposes here, we are more interested in the proportions of certain widespread traits relevant to a hypothesis about balanced polymorphism. Some studies have addressed this issue, such as that of Leighton, Harding, and Macklin (1963), who noted that in their Canadian sample *dependent, passive-aggressive,* and *compulsive* traits were found in 2½%, 0.9%, and 0.4%; *histrionic* and *borderline* traits in 2.2% and 1.7%, respectively. The latter study predated DSM-III, and the rates for dependent and compulsive traits seem unrealistically low. I mention their work simply to reinforce the idea that, were a contemporary and more methodical study conducted, some set of ratios would emerge for the various important trait-combinations; these ratios would probably remain stable, or change but slightly, over long periods of time within any one culture, and to this extent they would provide a clue as to the "correct" balance of the polymorphism in personality styles that "worked" best for that culture.

Looked at from the perspective of a whole culture, certain personality styles considered abnormal from the point of view of interpersonal relations may not, as adumbrated above, be so considered in relation to certain tasks necessary to the survival of that culture. *Paranoid* traits are abysmal in the interpersonal context, impose terrible strains within a marriage (especially if they take the form of pathological jealousy), yet are an advantage in the context of security operations (spies, private investigators, narcotics agents, etc.). *Submissiveness* (including the more extreme forms of dependent PD and masochistic/"self-defeating" PD) is an advantageous trait for women from many cultures (and from many subcultures within our own society), in that many men prefer women with these qualities to those who are markedly assertive. Yet, in a society where the likelihood of divorce has become substantially greater over the past generation, submissiveness has become a much less successful strategy for women, who may find themselves handicapped in the workplace, where they must now compete effectively in order to secure their own economic survival (especially if they had originally picked a "philanderer" who ducks out of child support).

Eibl-Eibesfeldt (1989) provides an interesting sidelight on the role of submissiveness: he speaks of " . . . two biological strata determining human sexual behavior, the oldest being the archaic layer of agonistic sexuality, characterized by male dominance and female submissiveness. This 'reptilian heritage' still determines certain aspects of human sexual behavior. It is controlled by affiliative sexuality . . . a mammalian heritage, and by individual bonding" (p. 238). As this author tactfully suggests, "A predominance of the archaic agonistic sexuality gives rise to certain pathologies." Presumably, these pathologies would include the cult of "machismo" as well as all that Freud meant by "feminine masochism."

As mentioned earlier, some of the more dysfunctional personality types may maintain themselves within fairly predictable limits in society, because they happen to represent the extremes of tendencies that are under a high degree of genetic control and that in their more moderate forms have high survival value. Here the situation is analogous to that of sickle-cell anemia, where the (much more common) heterozygous person is not ill (and has better protection against malaria), whereas the rare homozygous carrier has a fatal illness. Persons with *mild* genetic loading for schizophrenia may, for example, show superior creativity or, in the case of mildly paranoid schizotypes, greater scientific objectivity. Schizophrenic psychosis is in a sense the societal price paid for the advantages of the mild carrier. The same is true with respect to genetic liability for manic-depression: the mildly affected person may be more extraverted, more entrepreneurial, more self-confident, etc., while the (less common) manic-depressive psychotic person has a tumultuous and difficult life.

In general, the concepts of evolutionarily stable state and balanced poly-morphism have greater relevance in spheres of personality variation where (1) genetic/constitutional influences are strong, or (2) parental "program-ming" during the formative years (up through age 6, especially) is intense. The personality traits that evolve from these sources would be relatively inflexible. Thus, the callous, unempathic type of psychopath, who would also be expected to pursue the "philanderer" sexual strategy, may represent an abnormality sufficiently rooted in genetic influences that one would not expect much mellowing to occur with age. Such mellowing often does occur with men whose intrinsic character is less predatory, who turned to antiso-ciality chiefly out of early social deprivation, and who are capable of genu-ine feeling at least for close kin. Certain members of organized crime fami-lies are of the latter sort, as are certain nonviolent persons who commit misdemeanors or petty crimes in the face of economic duress, but who are able to put their antisocial tendencies behind them when circumstances im-prove.

The first English settlers in Australia in 1789 constituted an unplanned natural experiment of this sort. About four-fifths of the 700 people who landed in Botany Bay had been "transported" (i.e., sentenced) to Australia for petty theft and other small-scale crimes (Hughes, 1987). The remainder were the sailors, officers, ships' doctors, etc. Almost all of the "criminals" immediately pitched in and worked for their own and the common good, spurred by the exigencies of survival in a wild and unfamiliar place ten thousand miles from home. A small number of the transportees seemed more "hard-wired" for bad behavior, and would steal chickens or commit other acts of unequivocal threat to the emerging society. They were dealt with summarily within days of being caught (thus also eliminating their genes from the gene pool of the developing country). Within a short time, what might have seemed a skewed population, whose "stable state" would include an uncomfortably high proportion of undesirable persons, turned into a population much like that of any other country—where the antisocial subgroup was acceptably small.

Other personality styles that derive importantly from genetic predisposi-tion include the *schizoid, schizotypal, hypomanic, cyclothymic*, and to a lesser extent, paranoid and depressive (cf. Chapter 3). I would anticipate that their proportions in the culture vary less from one generation to the next, compared with the ratios of narcissistic or even borderline personali-ties. Though genetic liability for affective illness seems of etiological signifi-cance in some borderline patients (Stone, 1990), in others physical and sexual abuse during childhood or adolescence figures more prominently.

Leadership in nonhuman primates seems to depend more on genetic and constitutional than on early-rearing factors. Size and testosterone levels may help determine which monkey becomes the alpha male, more so than what its parents taught him. Even so, in chimpanzee troupes there is considerable flexibility; shifts of leadership can take place under certain circumstances, such that erstwhile subordinate chimps assume the leadership role (Ghiglieri, 1985). Leadership is a more complex affair in humans, relying as it does on a large number of personality factors, some of which derive largely from innate sources, others more from parental influences. Chance factors like birth order (being the firstborn of either sex, being a singleton) also figure in the equation. Simonton (1990), in his assessment of factors associated with political power, mentions such traits as authoritarianism, extraversion, need for power, affiliation-orientedness, charisma, and deliberateness (akin to decisiveness and determination to see one's plans through to completion). Other qualities, like intelligence and creativity, may also reflect both hereditary and environmental influences, but are on separate tracks from personality.

Leaders with good legislative capabilities excel at "Machiavellianism," forcefulness, moderation, and poise. It may be that the kinds of leadership important to the military and political sectors are more closely related to the primate alpha male phenomenon and would not develop without the proper genetic predisposition (though the tendencies, if present at birth, could, in humans, be squashed by destructive parenting). The same might be said of the combination of toughness, low "harm-avoidance," and machismo found in men who rise to the top in organized crime, though deceptiveness would also be a necessary quality—one that may relate more to high intelligence than to mere bravado. Dawkins speaks, in this regard, of the "poker face" as evolutionarily stable, inasmuch as reflexively honest persons and habitual liars are both easier to outsmart in a contest of wills. Machiavellianism contributes to success in personalities of whatever type, though in normal/socially admired types we are apt to use trait-words like "wily, shrewd, cool or clever," whereas in abnormal types (viz. certain borderline or antisocial persons) we speak of "manipulative" or "treacherous."

Among the other qualities associated with leadership, some might be viewed as almost essential (forcefulness, self-confidence); others as common only to particular kinds of leaders (extraversion, affiliativeness—as in sales executives, masters of ceremonies, etc.; integrity—in judges, medical researchers, etc.). Probably there is a continuum, with respect to nature vs. nurture: some attributes (like extraversion) being manifestations of temperament and thus largely innate; others (like integrity) being manifestations of character and thus largely the product of early rearing.

The interplay of personality attributes that make for the most effective leadership—some of which we now see as mostly inborn, others imprinted by caretakers, some admirable, others seemingly abnormal or wicked—was well appreciated by the fifteenth-century author (Machiavelli, 1977, 1983) from whom ethologists have coined the term Machiavellian. Adams, in his commentary on *The Prince* (1977, p. 243), summarizes Machiavelli's precepts in this way: Do good when you can, do evil if you must; do both unhesitatingly, and don't lie to yourself about which is which. A personality, which at one stage in the evolution of its possessor is integrated in such a way as to promote the greatest success, later may—partly thanks to the corrupting impact of that success—be transformed in certain key aspects so as to ensure a downfall. It was when, after a string of brilliant victories, Napoleon became, in Adams' words (1977, p. 246), a reactionary, self-aggrandizing tyrant, that his fate was sealed. Only Napoleon could defeat Napoleon—and eventually he did.

Hitler was carried away with the same grandiose notion that he could conquer Russia. But his narcissism, paranoia (viz., mistrust of his generals), and psychopathy (which led him to waste valuable resources on non-military killing expeditions) were as much a factor in his defeat as the combined forces of the Allies. The author of *Mein Kampf* would have done better to have read *The Prince*, where, on the subject of cruelty, Machiavelli cautions us that, although " . . . every prince [= "leader"] should prefer to be considered merciful rather than cruel," at the same time, " . . . no prince should mind being called cruel for what he does to keep his subjects united and loyal; he may make examples of a *very few*, but he will be more merciful in reality than those who, in their tenderheartedness, allow disorders to occur, with the attendant murders and lootings" (p. 47, emphasis added). It is most unfortunate that Machiavelli has been misunderstood by many as a cunning practitioner of treachery, when in fact he is an exponent of benign deception where necessary for the common good, and of striking an optimum balance between the (primary) need for wisdom and human values and a (secondary) need for less pleasant traits (severity, monetary tightfistedness) when these are necessary for the preservation of order and the attainment of long-range goals.

Consider how different a set of rules for the "Prince" a gangster-leader, such as Stalin, might have written if *he* had expatiated on the "ideal" leader. Composed of the same amalgam of narcissism, paranoia, and psychopathy as Hitler, Stalin's main interest was not the long-term good of the State, but rather the long-term good of Stalin—whose rules for How to Stay on Top & Die in Bed might have included the following:

- Pick as your immediate subordinates strong followers, capable of dominating others, but not quite capable of overthrowing the Leader.
- Reward these men enough to ensure loyalty, but not so much as to permit the creation of alliances more powerful than the Leader and

those still loyal to him; pay the soldiers handsomely and everyone else poorly.

- As for those with real leadership ability, either kill them or exile them.

- Sacrifice the few to the many, to placate the majority.

- Favor relatives over nonrelatives except where the latter are (as in the case of rocket scientists) indispensable.

- Use cunning to keep everyone guessing; turn son against father, neighbor against neighbor.

- When in doubt, purge.

CULTURE AND ERA AFFECT WHAT IS "ABNORMAL" IN PERSONALITY

Despite the laudable efforts of DSM and ICD to create a "lingua franca" of abnormal personality, valid not only in their countries of origin but elsewhere as well, such an ambition is ultimately quixotic. The abnormal types and their descriptors work well in cultures closely resembling America and England, but less well in cultures whose values are quite different. In a similar way, what is abnormal in a given society now would probably be so viewed a decade earlier (or later), but not necessarily a century—let alone a millennium—ago.

The survival needs of the Scandinavian countries in the ninth century were apparently best served by a personality "profile" that stressed daring, bravery, and indifference to the feelings of nonkinsmen. As the Vikings expanded southward, they sought to bring home the beauty, riches, and culture of the lands they invaded. The historian Nilsson (1899) mentions: "They were not delicate as to means. Violence was as natural to them as their freedom of individuality was indispensable" (p. 45). Their success over the centuries was accompanied by elevation to aristocratic status in the lands they conquered (Russia, England, etc.), by a shift away from violence toward negotiation and diplomacy, and by a transition from rural to urban life, necessitating changes from the rough-and-ready manners and habits of marauders to the civilities and tact of a citified ruling class. Twelve centuries pass, and we find the Northmen (now the Danes, Norwegians, and Swedes) a particularly nonviolent people, whose personalities have little in common with their remote ancestors.

Dramatic changes of a corresponding sort have been taking place in Australia within a much shorter time-span: just the few decades since World War II, during which time the autocratic, rough-and-ready outbacksmen, "kings" on their own enormous land-tracts, have largely moved to the seven large cities, where 80% of the population now resides. Their grandchildren might regard some of them as "sociopathic" or "male chauvinist" or violent, whereas in their day they were the paragons of "normal manhood."

Long periods of peace and progressive urbanization and cosmopolitanism favor the flourishing of personality types adapted to "getting along" with others (via tolerance, affiliativeness, tenderness, suppression of aggressivity, etc.). Perpetual war conduces to a different "ideal" personality, as one sees in modern Israel, whose native-born sons ("Sabras") have to be tougher and more combat-ready than their comparatively bookish and non-aggressive fathers. The latter had to struggle in Europe as an oppressed minority; for them ingratiation of the oppressors, indirect means of expressing anger, and various other "passive" attitudes were more compatible with survival.

In the heterogeneous society of America we can see an immense number of competing "life-programs," each one adaptive within the context of a particular country of origin, a particular religion, or a particular racial background. While certain forms of antisociality (especially the propensity to commit felonious assaults against other persons) are regarded as highly abnormal in all these diverse groups, what constitutes "normal" behavior for men and women, what is considered "rude" vs. "tactful," etc., depend upon values that differ to varying extents within these different groups.

This cultural "relativism" is itself a reflection of the subtle differences in behavioral norms, according to one's background, that go to make up national, religious, or racial stereotypes. As with most such stereotypes, there is just enough validity to warrant their retention—as a useful first guess about expectable behavior, and more than enough exceptions to the rule to warrant the label of "prejudiced" to persons who subscribe too heartily to the stereotypes. It is differences of this sort that contribute to Americans' experiencing the Japanese, who place great value on "wa" (harmony between people), as "overly conformist" or overly "dependent," while the Japanese experience Americans, with our championing of assertiveness and of the individual and his rights, as "inconsiderate" or "aggressive" or, in their own word, "dokuritsushin-ga-tsuyoi" ("too independent of spirit"). Similarly, we see the Russians as "xenophobic"; they see us as "gullible," etc. Many people from Thailand or the Caribbean who are quite normal within their culture are seen, if evaluated by an American psychologist, as given to illusions and magical thinking, which might make them appear as "schizotypal personalities" until these cultural distinctions are taken into account.

For all these reasons I do not think it rash to assert that, in the realm of personality assessment, no universally applicable standards can be drawn up, and no diagnostician can evaluate someone from a culture that is more than a little divergent from his or her own—in a way that is in perfect agreement with the impressions of a diagnostician raised in that culture. In other words, the diagnosis of symptomatic conditions is much less culture-dependent than is the assessment of personality disorders.

Cultural factors also affect the proportionality of the personality disorders that one might encounter in various regions. The open expression of anger is strongly discouraged in Japan, for example, such that the base rate of "borderline PD" would be (and I believe actually is) lower in that country than in ours. Rebelliousness and angry outbursts in women are strongly suppressed in traditional Moslem countries—where the women whose constitutional and family factors might have led to the development of borderline PD in a Western country instead develop phobia or hysteria or a psychosomatic condition (Al Tariq, personal communication, 1990).

The complexities involved in bridging cultural gaps are enormous. I am currently working with several Japanese colleagues (Drs. M. Shimada, Y. Oto, M. Katoh, T. Maruta, K. Okonogi) on the translation into Japanese of my Personality Trait list. Over and above the difficulties already mentioned, there are whole realms of personality abnormality that the Japanese would consider crucial to evaluate that we would look at only with peripheral vision, and vice versa. My list, for instance, has no specific word for "undutiful to one's parents" ("fukohna") or "having no sense of duty" ("giri-o-shiranai"). The Japanese, on the other hand, have no simple word for "inhospitable," no pejorative word for "macho," and do not make the same distinction we do between "jealousy" (which implies a triangular situation) and "envy" (a two-person situation).

Once translated, this instrument will permit my Japanese colleagues to describe in greater detail (than would be possible with just DSM-III-R) *their* borderline or *their* narcissistic patients, according to the standards of their culture. We might be able to piece together a better picture of how their typical borderline and narcissistic patients resemble and differ from ours. But the instrument would not permit me, even if I became fluent in their language, to diagnose their patients in the same way they would, because I am not, and could never truly become, "fluent" in their culture. The line I might draw between narcissism and mere "enlightened self-interest" would not be made at the same place my Japanese colleagues would put it; their threshold for the borderline person's "inordinate anger" would not be the same as their American colleague's, etc.

A COMMENT ON SOCIAL INTELLIGENCE, NEURAL CIRCUITRY, AND THE LIMITATIONS OF THE COMPUTER ANALOGY

The marked encephalization noted in the brains of primates (including man) correlates, as mentioned above, with the special adaptations necessary to the survival of social, as opposed to nonsocial, animals—especially those adaptations having to do with figuring out what is in the minds of other members of one's group and with concealing one's own intentions in order to gain some advantage.

Since social adaptation depends upon processing huge amounts of information (pertaining to language, bodily gestures, the whole history of relationships with important other persons, etc.), we find it tempting to look for what resemblances there might be between our information-processing organ and the latest and best information-processing machines we have thus far constructed, namely, computers. It helps us preserve some perspective, in discussing this analogy, to remember that the capacity (in bits) and the power (bits processed per second) of elephants, whales, and humans are in the range of 10^{15} (a quadrillion). Our biggest supercomputer (of the Cray-2 type), in contrast, has a capacity on the order of 10^{10}—like that of a 1-gram mouse brain (Moravec, 1992).

The computer consists, in its most basic constituents, of an input unit, an output unit, in between which is a processing unit; connected to the latter (with the potential for exchange of information in either direction) is a memory unit. A "program," often in the form of a "floppy disc," is a long sequence of instructions in a binary code; this makes up the "software" to be utilized (and perhaps absorbed) by the just-described "hardware." Depending on the size of the memory-unit, one or several programs could be "fed in," for such functions as word-processing, playing chess, doing statistical calculations, and the like. Under the heading of "memory," there will be a "Read-Only Memory" chip that encodes permanent instructions allowing the processing unit to control the input in an appropriate way. Besides this "ROM" chip there will be a "Random-Access Memory" (RAM) chip, for storing temporarily data currently in use and the codes that designate what material is flashed on the monitor screen (Macaulay, 1988, pp. 330–338). The hardware is concealed within a metal box (or series of boxes) containing keys for producing input, and a TV-type monitor for showing output.

Points of similarity and difference with a human being include the following: the brain may be seen as a processing unit plus memory (both ROM and RAM) combined. Input enters the brain's "processing units" via the five senses, but also via previously recorded memories of various experiences, commands, etc. Output will generally be in the form of language or actions, involving the corresponding musculature. The programming of a person involves learning, which (one hopes) goes on throughout life, but most especially concerns the many survival-oriented subprograms that make up one's identity (as to gender, nationality, subculture, social class, religion, morality, social habits and manners, sexual aims and partner-preferences, etc.).

The distinction between hard-wiring and soft-wiring is not as sharp in a person as in a computer. The brain is "hard-wired" to respond to certain stimuli (e.g., a mother's smiling face), to acquire language, and to process information in particular ways (viz., to recognize faces, to solve various problems). The subprograms fed into one by primary caretakers during the first five or six years of life—identity and language—take on the qualities of "hard-wiring," in the sense that they are often well-nigh immutable. Yet some persons develop unskakeably high morals despite abysmal caretaking (see Chapter 17), others become amoral psychopaths despite an excellent upbringing (viz., Nancy Spungen: cf. D. Spungen, 1983).

Feedback mechanisms operate between early programming and later experience to permit some alteration of early beliefs, prejudices, "gameplans," etc. Still, it is extremely difficult to overturn, say, one's original religion so thoroughly as to feel "genuinely" a Buddhist, having acquired that religion in adult life, if one had been raised a Moslem. As social creatures, we are far more susceptible than are computers to "viruses" that instruct via group pressure all but the most unwaveringly moral people to begin picking on or exterminating the Blacks, Ibos, Jews, Mensheviks, Incas, or whatever competing group is suddenly seen as "in the way."

Most of what we understand under the rubric of *personality* may be seen as the set of all subprograms serving social interaction as well as one's personal "philosophy." The latter informs one's day-to-day interactions with others, as to whether deception is appropriate, whether outright cheating is ever permissible, and if so, under what circumstances. Whether one has the strength of character, like von Stauffenberg, to risk one's life in order to overthrow a Hitler, or whether one has the moral flabbiness of a Qvisling relates to the solidity (or lack thereof) of one's personal philosophy. Whereas a computer, if programmed for "WordPerfect" is exactly that—no more, no less—there is no way of knowing whether a particular child will emerge as a von Stauffenberg or a Qvisling, since the result depends upon experiences occurring *beyond* the period of initial (first six years of life) "programming," and rarely gets tested in ordinary life anyway.

There are other peculiarities to personality for which no ready counterparts exist in the "society" of computers: personality may be capable of at least mild alteration throughout life, and at times of sweeping transformation (as in the case of certain mendacious politicians who, once held up to public scorn, become "born again," thereafter to remain respectable and honest citizens). Also, personality has an inner and an outer aspect: some people are abrasive, even downright nasty, socially, but loyal and ethical underneath; others are outwardly sociable, even charming, but unscrupulous or even vicious underneath. Most people see only the outward personality of all but their close friends, intimates, and closest coworkers. The *total* personality of any given person is *not* known by the person in question and is really only "known" to the *collective* comprised of all the people with whom that person has ever interacted.

With most ordinary people, the discrepancies between the superficial self and the "real" self are not so glaring as to cause consternation. But in the case of "borderline" personalities, wildly inconsistent facets of the "total" personality are exposed, some to this, some to that group of persons, who seldom have the chance (unless they are staff members of a psychiatric facility) to compare notes.

Psychopaths represent a more extreme example. I had the chance (February 14, 1992) to share the discussion about Jeffrey Dahmer, on a television program, with the woman Dahmer escorted to his high-school senior prom some 13 years before his capture. She experienced her "date" (whom she had known only on this one occasion) as "friendly enough" though rather aloof and "nerdy." It would have come as a great surprise to her to learn about his habit of decapitating dogs and planting their heads on sticks in his backyard; likewise, to learn that he murdered his first victim some two weeks after their prom date. The people who knew Dahmer best were the 17 victims, none of whom, of course, was able to impart these crucial observations about Dahmer's real self to the outside world.

Conceivably, Dahmer's "nerdiness" stemmed from a genetic abnormality (akin to a computer with a "hard-wiring" defect) of the sort Semrud-Clikeman and Hynd (1990) and Voeller (1991) have written about under the heading of social-emotional learning disability (S.E.L.D.). Children born with the right-hemispheric malfunctioning underlying S.E.L.D. " . . . do not interpret the emotional responses of others accurately, or make correct inferences about affective behaviors. They remain isolated, on the periphery of their social group, rejected by their peers" (p. 735). Such persons do poorly at interpreting emotional utterances and may show peculiarities of prosody (vocal intonational patterns). A computer with this gross a defect of hard-wiring would be a "factory reject." Persons with comparable abnormalities must survive as best they can, condemned to a severe disorder of personality, showing up as eccentricity or "weirdness" (as noted also in schizoid and schizotypal persons).

Another dissimilarity concerns "packaging." Were my NEC lap-top connected via a modem to somebody's IBM PC, the $2'' \times 12''$ black box in which my machine is housed would signify nothing to my friend's beige, $18''$-high counterpart. But *our* "packaging" — skin color, facial appearance, build — conveys a great deal of information to others, and helps shape the developing self-image, and hence the personality, of each of us. Parents, schoolchildren, teachers, and others tend to equate physical attractiveness with being "nice"; unattractiveness with being "not nice." We prejudge fat people as "jolly"; thin people, like Shakespeare's Cassius, as too clever by half, or else as aloof or intellectual.

As a final comment, computers can under certain circumstances be re-programmed, or even programmed so as to make various modifications in their software as dictated by "past experience" (as in chess-playing machines), a human being must first build into the program this feedback mechanism. We make changes of this sort quite by ourselves throughout life—some major, some minor, depending upon our plasticity, our age, our determination, the strength with which parental commands were rein-forced. The more intense the parental reinforcements—the harsher the superego in Freudian terms—the more difficult we would find it to replace such programs with more adaptive ones.

Much of our psychotherapy involves just such attempts to modify mal-adaptive programs. People with the healthiest personalities are those with rock-solid humanistic and ethical values, but with maximal capacity to adapt, where prudent and not harmful to others, in ways that might violate some of the survival instructions inculcated by parents and other caretakers. The interconnections in the brain themselves undergo modifications through-out life, but especially in the early, "formative" years. Those neuronal connections associated with a high survival or social value tend to be retained,* while those no longer deemed necessary undergo "pruning" and are lost or weakened (Hoffman, 1987).

Presumably, it is this change in interconnectivity that accounts for the transformation of the infant—who has "omnipotential" for the pronunciation and syntax acquisition of any language—into a speaker, several years later, of just the "mother tongue." Past age 12 or so, most persons can no longer learn a new language without showing some trace of an accent. I suspect matters pertaining to our identity—our values, our prejudices, our preconceptions about new situations and persons, and most importantly for our purposes, our personalities—also become relatively fixed, via this kind of neuronal pruning and subsequent streamlining of our response

---

*Edelman (1992) offers a most convincing argument about the inadequacy of the computer as an analogy for the brain. As he explains, the digital computer is, in effect, " . . . marked unambiguously with symbols chosen from a finite set; in contrast, the sensory signals available to nervous systems are truly analogue in na-ture and are therefore neither unambiguous nor finite in number." Further on, he adds that the transitions from one state to another are deterministic in the com-puter but in humans " . . . give ample evidence of indeterminacy." Human experi-ence—and by extension, the personalities that take shape in us partly in response to this experience—is not based, as Edelman reminds us, " . . . on so simple an abstraction as a Turing machine; to get our 'meanings' we have to grow and communicate in a society" (p. 225). Our nervous systems select appropriate re-sponse patterns (or the maladaptive and at times horribly inappropriate responses that underlie a text such as this one, on personality disorders) "only *through interactions with the world*" (p. 226).

mechanisms, such that great effort is often required to effect even little changes as we grow older.

Readers who wish to become better acquainted with contemporary models of brain function, including those that have explanatory value in the domain of personality, would do well to consult the works of Rumelhart and McClelland (1986), McClelland and Rumelhart (1986), Edelman (1987, 1989), Changeux (1985), and Dennett (1991). Other articles dealing with memory storage and with the computer analogy to brain function include those of Alkon (1989) and Searle (1990).

CONCLUDING REMARKS

Personality is a construct relating to a complex set of stable mental states and corresponding behavioral patterns that perform, in the domain of social relationships, both actively and reactively. "Actively" refers to the mental "programs" we utilize in seeking to satisfy physical and sexual needs, by way of ensuring our survival and the survival of our genes. "Reactively" refers to the defensive strategies, as emphasized by Millon, that we characteristically employ when confronted with challenges from other persons to our welfare.

Many of these survival programs are taught us by our parents, other important caretakers, and the surrounding culture in such a way as to create a kind of software program for *involuntary* immediate responses, not necessarily accompanied by thought (at least not in the heat of the moment), which we often speak of as *conditioning* (Premack, 1988). This is in contrast to *cognition*, which relates more to voluntary behavior preceded by reflective thought. Personality partakes of both mechanisms. Either tendency may be deficient or excessive: we apply the trait-label "unspontaneous" to those whose behavior is not immediate enough; "impulsive" to those whose behavior shows an excess of involuntary responses and an insufficiency of reflective mechanisms.

The evolution of these mechanisms may be said to have begun with the awareness of membership in a group of other individuals similar to oneself, followed by the emergence of "cooperative competition." These steps Crook (1988) refers to under the heading of *ecological* selection. Next in his schema comes *social* selection, with the development of complex social relationships, and eventually the emergence of intellectual capacities. The latter would include advances in the ability to *imagine*, i.e., to flash upon the screen of consciousness, as it were, a variety of plans of action—without at first acting upon any of them—then to be weighed as to their merits and demerits, till the optimal plan is chosen. Crook then speaks of a further evolutionary stage: *cultural transmission*, characterized by the transfer, via teaching, admonition, etc., of successful traditions to members of the new generation, especially one's own kin. The ability of each person to recognize a "self" as the agent of social experience also develops. Introspective reflection is the next evolutionary step, followed by "linguistical intentional sharing" (Crook, 1988, p. 348). Jolly (1988, p. 377) underscores the hypothesis that human consciousness evolved in large part as a model to predict the actions of others. This "social intelligence" is intricately interwoven with what we mean by *personality*, which, in a manner of speaking, is the suit our social intelligence wears in the company of others.

5

The Profile of Personality Traits

出る金丁は、打たれる.

deru kugi wa, utareru
(The protruding nail gets hammered.)

Japanese proverb

IN ASSESSING THE PERSONALITY of a patient, clinicians instinctively make categorical as well as dimensional assessments simultaneously. This "parallel processing" must nevertheless be described in a purely linear fashion, because speech and, to an even greater extent, writing must emerge in a linear, sequential, one-word-at-a-time, one-topic-at-a-time manner. This may help explain why the diagnostic manuals and introductory texts on personality focus on categories—the simpler of the two approaches—while seasoned mental health professionals have moved on to more complex and inclusive ways of evaluating their patients.

It is a reasonable assumption, I believe, that all people, whether lay or professional, appraise the people they get to know by making, in an automatic and scarcely conscious way, measurements of the degree to which the person in question conforms to or deviates from the "norm" for various traits. The norm will depend on one's experience and cultural background. The need for a thesaurus of trait-words seems compelling in any case, and has been emphasized recently by Tellegen (1991).

As for the mental list of the various traits, it seems almost numberless in length. In an effort to get a handle on just how many monikers we might possibly apply to other people, Allport and Odbert (1936) combed the unabridged dictionary and came up with 18,000 words. Happily, we all get by with a much shorter list than that: many of those words are archaic;

others are unnecessary because they overlap almost perfectly with other simpler words. Goldberg (1982) was able to select some 600 descriptors that gave a fairly complete coverage of the personality traits a clinician might encounter. My own list of negative traits (1990e), drawn up before I became aware of the two preceding investigators, includes 530 words for maladaptive traits. This list I later amplified with 100 more negative traits and 100 positive traits. The resultant list can be abridged to about 600 descriptors, owing to a peculiarity of English—in that it is basically a double language. Our Anglo-Saxon vocabulary became overlain with a latinate vocabulary of equal richness. Thus we have "shy" but also "self-effacing"; "stuck-up" but also "supercilious."

Suppose for the moment, however, that our internal yardstick for measuring personality has about 600 notches, give or take. (It is of interest to note that a recent and independently created trait-list in the Chinese language contains 557 adjectives; see Yang and Lee, 1989.) We may envision a long vertical line within our brain that represents "normality" or "averageness" or "typicality." So long as the personality of someone we know remains in all its facets close to this imaginary line, we register very little about that person. He or she, being ordinarily honest, polite, considerate, unintrusive, etc., is an "ordinary" person—not easy to describe, actually, if we were asked to give a picture of that person to a third party. But if the person were cheap, rude, and tactless, then on those points on our normality-line he would be off-center. Those are the adjectives we could make readily available to someone asking us for a description.

We might pictorialize this internal mechanism as a "normal" line, containing a list of average or ideal traits, most of which would be associated with other trait-words representing "too much" or "too little" of each given trait, or else excesses in either a "good" or a "bad" direction of the given trait. Figures 8 and 9 are illustrative.

Figure 8 is built around 24 normal or ideal traits, located vertically in the center line. For each, a pair of traits representing socially irritating degrees of the main quality is placed to the left. Usually, but not always, these traits involve "too little" of the trait in question. To the right is an opposite pair of traits. At the extreme right, it will be noted, some of the qualities are disadvantageous to their possessor ("obsequious," as the extreme of "polite"); others are advantageous ("altruistic," "charismatic"). The list does not aim at completeness. In actual practice, some of the more extreme traits diverge along different paths. There is, for example, another possible path for *assertive*, having to do with facing adversity. This might read (moving from one edge to the other) "cowardly–timid–*assertive*–brave–heroic/rash" (the latter depending upon whether the behavior were appropriate or foolish).

Figure 8: *Personality Trait Schema:*
Average/Typical Traits and Extremes

abrasive	tactless	polite	courtly	obsequious
stingy	tight	thrifty	generous	prodigal
irresponsible	procrastinating	punctual	compulsive	punctilious
unfeeling	cold	sympathetic	oversensitive	maudlin
vampish	seductive	receptive	coy	prudish
randy	pushy	(sex-)assertive	reserved	inhibited
domineering	bossy	(work-)assertive	unassertive	submissive
paranoid	suspicious	trusting	naïve	gullible
abusive	irritable	calm	phlegmatic	spineless
ruthless	exploitative	fair	deferential	meek
chaotic	sloppy	neat	meticulous	fussbudget
vengeful	bitter	forgiving	philosophic	altruistic
brittle	rigid	flexible	yielding	flabby
aggressive	hostile	agreeable	friendly	overfriendly
defiant	uncooperative	cooperative	super-accommodating.	
bigoted	dogmatic	openminded	easily swayed	"as-if"
unscrupulous	devious	honest	scrupulous	overscrupulous
garrulous	talkative	communicative	laconic	taciturn
extraverted	outgoing	at ease	shy	reclusive
disloyal	uncommitted	faithful	fawning	clingy
pretentious	affected	modest	humble	self-effacing
reckless	impulsive	spontaneous	hesitant	fearful
obnoxious	disagreeable	likeable	charming	charismatic
boorish	philistine	cultured	mannered	precious

  In Figure 9 I show, by way of example, how this ideal-line is bent in the case of a former patient: an obsessional man who, in relation to his wife in particular, was remarkably stingy and controlling.

  If one thinks of the middle line as a log, and the protruding parts as nails that stick out at varying lengths from the surface of the log, then one can appreciate the meaning of the epigraph for this chapter: Where the "nails" of personality "stick out," we as therapists endeavor to hammer them down—toward the middle line of adaptability and harmoniousness.

  Though I believe there is much utility in this linear approach to traits for didactic purposes, I suspect that traits become encoded in our brains in a different way. Children learn gross before subtle, category before dimension. Probably the neuronal assemblies that subserve the various key concepts (cf. Edelman, 1987, 1989) are organized as nodal points within the grey matter. Branching out from them, and feeding into them, are, we may suppose, the relevant "species" of these nodal "genera." As we grow older, some of the species-concepts become minor nodal points to which even more "special cases," single instances, etc. become enregistered in memory. This mode of organization, becoming ever more complex throughout life, might be represented by a branching diagram, wherein the main concepts, laid down in childhood, act as the trunks of an endlessly branching and ever more finely branching tree.

In Figure 10 I have shown how such a "dendrogram" might be constructed in relation to personality traits. As for the nature of the trunks and main branches, it requires no feat of memory to recall that as children we learned first about "good guys" and "bad guys," cops and robbers, good fairies and witches, angels and devils.

The interplay between *category* and *dimension*, to do it justice diagrammatically, would need at least a third (spatial) dimension: we distinguish not only the species words of each genus word, but also the *intensity* of any given trait-word (not very mean, mean, very mean, . . .). The situation is

Figure 9: *Personality Trait Schema for Obsessional Man*

abrasive	tactless	polite	courtly	obsequious
stingy	tight	thrifty	generous	prodigal
irresponsible	procrastinating	punctual	compulsive	punctilious
unfeeling	cold	sympathetic	oversensitive	maudlin
vampish	seductive	receptive	coy	prudish
randy	pushy	(sex-)assertive	reserved	inhibited
domineering	bossy	(work-) assertive	unassertive	submissive
paranoid	suspicious	trusting	naïve	gullible
abusive	irritable	calm	phlegmatic	spineless
ruthless	exploitative	fair	deferential	meek
chaotic	sloppy	neat	meticulous	fussbudget
vengeful	bitter	forgiving	philosophic	altruistic
brittle	rigid	flexible	yielding	flabby
aggressive	hostile	agreeable	friendly	overfriendly
defiant	uncooperative	cooperative	super-accommodating.	
bigoted	dogmatic	openminded	easily swayed	"as-if"
unscrupulous	devious	honest	scrupulous	overscrupulous
garrulous	talkative	communicative	laconic	taciturn
extraverted	outgoing	at ease	shy	reclusive
disloyal	uncommitted	faithful	fawning	clingy
pretentious	affected	modest	humble	self-effacing
reckless	impulsive	spontaneous	hesitant	fearful
obnoxious	disagreeable	likeable	charming	charismatic
boorish	philistine	cultured	mannered	precious

Figure 10: *Dendrogram Showing How Personality Concepts Might be Encoded in Memory in the Course of Ontogenesis*

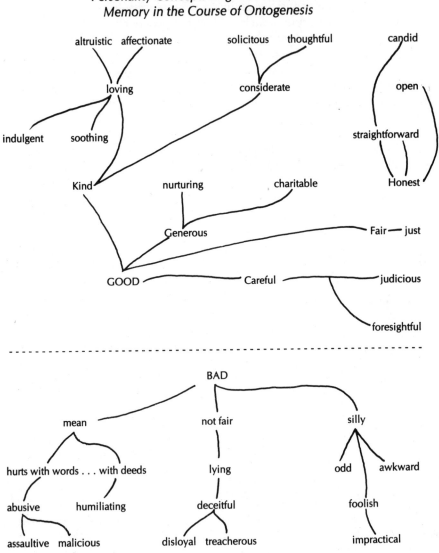

really more complex, since we often create a new trait-word that in itself signifies a particular intensity. "Meanness," for example, when it crosses a certain threshold of intensity, becomes "maliciousness."

It is my impression that in most languages people invent more words to highlight various gradations and subtle differences among "bad" traits than among "good" traits, if for no other reason than bad traits irritate or threaten us (and hence need greater attention and more specific remedies). We are cognizant, to be sure, of gradations of honesty, loyalty, kindness, etc., but we are usually content to designate these gradations with modifiers like "very," "extremely," etc. I think it is no accident that my trait list of negative words is much longer than the vocabulary of positive words, and does not merely represent exhaustion on my part (after having spent a year thinking up the 600 + negative traits).

Tables 6 and 7 contain the negative (maladaptive) trait words and the positive trait-words, respectively. These lists concentrate on descriptors that have particular relevance to a person's life-trajectory in general, as well as to long-range outcome in psychotherapy. Certain words that describe a person's style, but which may not have great significance vis-à-vis the life-course, I have omitted. "Earthy," "witty," etc., refer mostly to style — the overall impression a personality creates — rather than to specific traits.

I believe that comprehensive lists that include the positive as well as the negative can account for a larger portion of the variance in outcome of persons treated for or observed with various personality disorders and disturbances than can be captured by the briefer item-list embodied in the 11 disorders of DSM-III-R. The standard psychiatric manuals pay little attention to positive traits, which of course exert great influence on outcome, offsetting in many instances the impact of certain maladaptive traits. Needless to say, there are a number of characteristics of the (inner) self, as opposed to the outer self of "personality," that shape a person's life — intelligence and talent, for example — that also figure in the final equation.

The lengthy list of negative traits requires some explanation. There are still a number of words no longer in common use that convey a slightly different shade of meaning than their more common equivalents. Thus "double-tongued" is roughly the same as "duplicitous" or "hypocritical," though it carries a sense of *consciously* and purposely saying one thing and meaning another, whereas many "hypocritical" persons are scarcely aware of their disingenuousness. I have also left in some colloquialisms and slangy words like "nerdy" and even "nebbich" and "wimp," though I realize that not all speakers of English would know their meaning. Some of these words will no longer be in use at all a generation from now. But they paint a complex picture with just a brief stroke, and in a most piquant manner. For the time being, they are useful words.

TABLE 6

Preliminary List of Negative
(Maladaptive) Personality Traits

1. abandoned	51. bumptious	104. demanding	154. faithless
2. abrasive	52. busybody	105. dependent	155. fastidious
3. absent-minded	53. cad	106. depraved	156. fault-finding
4. abusive	54. calculating	107. depreciatory	157. fawning
5. adventurous, overly	55. callous	108. despotic	158. feckless
6. affected	56. cantankerous	109. desultory	159. fee
7. aggressive	57. captious	110. devious	160. feud-loving
8. agitated	58. careless	111. diabolical	161. fickle
9. aimless	59. catty	112. dilatory	162. fiery
10. aloof	60. censorious	113. dilettantish	163. finicky
11. ambitious, overly	61. chaotic	114. disconsolate	164. flaccid
12. amoral	62. "chauvinistic"	115. discourteous	165. flaky
13. angry	63. cheap	116. disdainful	166. flatterer
14. apathetic	64. cheating	117. dishonest	167. flighty
15. arbitrary	65. cheeky	118. disingenuous	168. flinty
16. argumentative	66. childish	119. disloyal	169. flippant
17. "arriviste"	67. churlish	120. disobedient	170. foolish
18. arrogant	68. clinging	121. disorderly	171. foppish
19. attention-seeking	69. coarse	122. disorganized	172. form-conscious, excessively
20. authoritarian	70. coercive	123. disputatious	173. forward, too
21. avoidant	71. cold	124. disrespectful	174. foul-mouthed
22. awkward	72. combative	125. dissembling	175. fractious
23. babbler	73. competitive	126. dissident	176. fragile
24. backbiting	74. compulsive	127. dissolute	177. frenzied
25. bashful	75. conceited	128. distractible	178. fresh
26. bawdy	76. condescending	129. dogmatic	179. frumpy
27. beastlike	77. confrontational	130. domineering	180. fussy
28. bellicose	78. contemptuous	131. don juan	181. garrulous
29. bigoted	79. contentious	132. double-minded	182. giddy
30. bitchy	80. contrary	133. double-tongued	183. glib
31. bitter	81. controlled, overly	134. dour	184. gloomy
32. blaming others, always	82. controlling	135. dramatic, overly: melo-dramatic	185. glory-hunter
33. blase	83. contumacious		186. glutton
34. blunt	84. contumelious	136. dull	187. goody-goody
35. bluster, given to	85. coquettish	137. duplicitous	188. gossipy
36. boastful	86. corrupt	138. easily led	189. grandiose
37. bombastic	87. covetous	139. eccentric	190. greedy
38. boorish	88. cowardly	140. egocentric	191. gross
39. bored	89. coy	141. empty	192. grudge-holding
40. boring	90. crabby	142. ennuied	193. gruff
41. bossy	91. crafty	143. entitled	194. guarded
42. braggart	92. cranky	144. envious	195. gullible
43. brassy	93. crass	145. evasive	196. gushy
44. brazen	94. "creep"	146. evil-minded	197. hardhearted
45. brittle	95. cross-tempered	147. evil-planning	198. harsh
46. brooding	96. cruel	148. exclusive	199. hateful
47. brusque	97. cunning	149. exhibitionistic	200. haughty
48. brutal	98. cynical	150. exploitative	201. headstrong
49. buffoon	99. dandy-ish	151. explosive	202. heartless
50. bullying	100. dawdling	152. extravagant	203. hedonistic
	101. daydreaming	153. failure at everything	204. highstrung
	102. decadent		205. histrionic
	103. deceitful		206. hostile

TABLE 6

Continued

207. hot-tempered	260. interrupting,	312. mistrustful	365. persecuting
208. humiliating	chronically	313. moody	366. persistent,
209. humorless	261. intimidating	314. moralistic	overly
210. hypercritical	262. intolerant	315. morose	367. pessimistic
211. hypocritical	263. intractable	316. mournful	368. petty
212. idler	264. intrusive	317. mousy	369. petulant
213. ill to live with	265. invidious	318. murder-stained	370. philandering
214. illiberal	266. irascible	319. nagging	371. philistine
215. ill-mannered	267. irksome	320. name-dropping	372. phlegmatic
216. ill-reputed	268. irreconcilable	321. narcissistic	373. phony
217. immoderate	269. irresponsible	322. narrow-minded	374. pitiless
218. immodest	270. irritable	323. "nebbich"	375. plastic
219. impassive	271. jaded	324. negativistic	376. pliable
220. impatient	272. jealous	325. negligent	377. plot-hatching
221. imperious	273. jekyll & hyde	326. "nerdy"	378. pompous
222. impertinent	274. joyless	327. niggardly	379. pontificating
223. impetuous	275. judgmental	328. nitpicking	380. poseur
224. impious	276. know-it-all	329. nonconformist,	381. possessive
225. impish	277. labile	aggressively	382. pouty
226. implacable	278. lachrymose	330. nosey	383. prating
227. importunate	279. lacking ini-	331. obnoxious	384. preachy
228. impractical	tiative	332. obsequious	385. precious
229. improvident	280. laconic	333. obstinate	386. predatory
230. impudent	281. lawless	334. obstreporous	387. prejudiced
231. impulsive	282. lazy	335. obstructionistic	388. pressuring
232. inappropriate	283. lecherous	336. offensive	389. pretentious
233. inarticulate	284. licentious	337. officious	390. priggish
234. inattentive	285. litigious	338. oily	391. prissy
235. inauthentic	286. low-minded	339. opinionated	392. procrastinating
236. incautious	287. lubricious	340. opportunistic	393. prodigal
237. incompetent	288. luckless	341. oppositional	394. profane
238. inconsiderate	289. lugubrious	342. oppressive	395. profligate
239. inconstant	290. macho, offen-	343. ostentatious	396. promiscuous
240. incontinent	sively	344. overanxious	397. provocative
241. incorrigible	291. malicious	345. overbearing	398. prudish
242. indecisive	292. malignant	346. overcheerful	399. pugnacious
243. indifferent	293. maniacal	347. overeager	400. punctilious
244. indiscreet	294. manipulative	348. overfamiliar	401. puritanical
245. ineducable	295. mannered	349. overinquisitive	402. pushy
246. ineffectual	296. martinet	350. overmeticulous	403. pusillanious
247. inequitable	297. masochistic	351. overoptimistic	404. quarrelsome
248. inflexible	298. maudlin	352. overpolite	405. querulous
249. ingratiating,	299. mawkish	353. overscrupulous	406. quibbling
overly	300. mean	354. oversentimental	407. quitter
250. inhibited	301. meddlesome	355. paranoid	408. rageful
251. inhospitable	302. meek	356. parsimonious	409. randy
252. insatiable	303. megalomanic	357. passionless	410. rascally
253. insecure,	304. melancholy	358. passive	411. rash
always	305. mendacious	359. passive-	412. raucous
254. insensitive	306. mercenary	aggressive	413. rebellious
255. insincere	307. mercurial	360. patronizing	414. recalcitrant
256. insolent	308. messy	361. pedantic	415. reckless
257. insubordinate	309. mischievious	362. peevish	416. rejecting
258. intemperate	310. miserly	363. penny-pinching	417. remote
259. intense, overly	311. misfit	364. perfectionistic	418. reproachful

(continued)

101

TABLE 6

Continued

419. resentful	469. skulking	524. toady	573. unregulated
420. reserved, overly	470. slanderous	525. tormenting	574. unreliable
421. restless	471. slavish	526. touchy	575. unrestrained
422. rigid	472. sleazy	527. tough-as-nails	576. unruly
423. risqué	473. slick (operator)	528. treacherous	577. unscrupulous
424. robot-like	474. slippery	529. tricky	578. unseemly
425. roguish	475. slob	530. troublesome	579. unselfconfident
426. rowdy	476. slothful	531. truckling to the mob	580. unsettled
427. rude	477. slovenly	532. truculent	581. unsociable
428. ruthless	478. smart alec	533. tyrannical	582. unspontaneous
429. saccharine	479. smarmy	534. unaccommo- dating	583. unstable
430. sadistic	480. smelly	535. unaffectionate	584. unstudious
431. sanctimonious	481. smooth-talker	536. unapologetic	585. unsympathetic
432. sarcastic	482. smug	537. unappreciative	586. untameable
433. sassy	483. snobbish	538. unapproach- able	587. unthoughtful
434. saturnine	484. sneaky	539. unassertive	588. untidy
435. saucy	485. sniveler	540. unblushing	589. untrustworthy
436. scatterbrained	486. snoop	541. uncivil	590. "up-tight"
437. scheming	487. spendthrift	542. uncommitted	591. vacillating
438. scoffer	488. spineless	543. uncompassion- ate	592. vacuous
439. scornful	489. spiteful	544. unconscien- tious	593. vagrant
440. "scrounge"	490. spoiled	545. unconsidering	594. vain
441. scruffy	491. sour-puss	546. uncooperative	595. vainglorious
442. secretive	492. "square"	547. uncordial	596. values, lacking in any firm
443. seditious	493. squeamish	548. uncouth	597. vampish
444. seductive	494. standoffish	549. uncultivated	598. vapid
445. seedy	495. stiff	550. undemon- strative	599. vehement
446. seething with hatred	496. stilted	551. undependable	600. vengeful
447. self-conscious, excessively	497. stingy	552. underhanded	601. vicious
448. self-defeating	498. stodgy	553. undiplomatic	602. victim, an easy
449. self-effacing	499. stubborn	554. undisciplined	603. vindictive
450. self-important	500. stuffy	555. unemotional	604. violent
451. self-indulgent	501. submissive	556. unempathic	605. violent- tempered
452. selfish	502. sulky	557. unfair	606. vituperative
453. self-pitying	503. sullen	558. unfeeling	607. volatile
454. self-righteous	504. supercilious	559. unfeminine	608. vulgar
455. sensation- seeking	505. superficial	560. unforeseeing	609. waspish
456. sensitive, overly	506. superstitious	561. unforgiving	610. wavering
457. shallow	507. surly	562. unfriendly	611. weak-willed
458. shameless	508. suspicious	563. ungrateful	612. whiny
459. shameworking	509. swindler	564. uninsightful	613. whorish
460. shifty	510. sycophantic	565. unjust	614. wild
461. shirker	511. taciturn	566. unkind	615. willful
462. short-fused	512. tactless	567. unmasculine	616. wimp
463. show-off	513. tantrumy	568. unobliging	617. windy-worded
464. shrewish	514. tardy	569. unpredictable	618. wiseacre
465. shy	515. tasteless	570. unpreparing	619. witchy
466. side-stepper	516. tattler	571. unprincipled	620. withdrawn
467. simpering	517. taunting	572. unreasonable	621. "workaholic"
468. skinflint	518. teasing		622. worry-wort
	519. temperamental		623. "yes-man"
	520. tempestuous		624. zany
	521. temptress		625. "zombie"
	522. theatrical		
	523. timorous		

TABLE 7

Positive Personality Traits

1. adaptive	26. diplomatic	52. kind	77. responsive,
2. affectionate	27. discerning	53. listens well	emotionally
3. assertive	28. discretion	54. loyal	78. self-confident
4. attentive	29. docile	55. merciful	79. self-controlled
5. benevolent	30. earnest	56. modest	80. self-disciplined
6. calm	31. empathic	57. moral	81. self-reliant
7. candid	32. even-tempered	58. neat	82. self-respecting
8. careful	33. fair	59. obedient	83. sensitivity
9. charming	34. faithful	60. optimistic	85. serene
10. cheerful	35. flexible	61. orderly	86. simplicity
11. committed	36. focused	62. passionate	87. sincere
12. compassionate	37. forgiving	63. patient	88. sociable
13. compliant	38. friendly	64. perseverant	89. spontaneous
14. conscientious	39. generous	65. polite	90. straightforward
15. considerate	40. good-natured	66. prudent	91. sweet
16. contented	41. gracious	67. punctual	92. sympathetic
17. cooperative	42. gratefulness	68. reasonable	93. tactful
18. courageous	43. helpful	69. receptive	94. thrifty
19. courteous	44. honest	70. reflective	95. tolerant
20. cultivated	45. hospitable	71. reliable	96. tranquil
21. curious (eager	46. humor, sense of	72. resilient	97. trusting
to learn)	47. independent	73. resolute	98. trustworthy
22. dedicated	48. industrious	74. resourceful	99. unaffected
23. deferential	49. integrity	75. respectful	100. unflappable
24. determined	50. jovial	76. responsible	101. well-mannered
25. dignified	51. just		

Each language has its own genius, its own storehouse of personality descriptors that are, if not untranslatable, certainly hard to reduce to one word in a foreign language. One might hazard a guess that each language covers the same total domain of personality, with a large though not equally extensive vocabulary. The small regions of meaning created by each word in one language cannot be made to overlap perfectly with the (only approximately) corresponding words in another language. This non-superimposability of trait-words means that, beyond the most common concepts ("honest," "cruel," etc.), there will be too many subtle differences among languages and cultures to allow any one of them to serve as a "standard."

It has already proven difficult to translate the relatively few trait-words of DSM's Axis II into the languages of cultures (e.g., Japanese, Thai) quite different from American culture. The "disorders," as well as the milder disturbances, of personality will remain inherently less sharply bordered concepts than those of, say, mania or schizophrenia—and will become all the "fuzzier" in cross-cultural comparisons. Yang and Bond (1990) have demonstrated that, although there is much congruence between "imported" trait-lists (from English-speaking investigators) and "local" lists developed for Chinese speakers, there are also areas of non-overlap, raising the question as to whether an already developed list from another culture will or will not suffice as a personality instrument in a very different culture.

Trait-lists of 600 or 700 words, while far more wieldy than Allport's 18,000-entry list, are, in their raw form, unwieldy in clinical practice. As a first practical step it seems prudent and, because of the redundancy in a 630-word list of negative adjectives, justified to reduce the list in Table 6 to 500 words. The resultant, simplified list is shown in Table 8.

TABLE 8

Five Hundred Negative Traits

1. abandoned	30. boastful	65. contentious	98. disdainful
2. abrasive	31. bombastic	66. contrary	99. disingenuous
3. abusive	32. boorish	67. controlled,	100. disloyal
4. adventurous,	33. bored	overly	101. disobedient
overly	34. boring	68. controlling	102. disorderly
5. affected	35. braggart	69. coquettish	103. disorganized
6. agitated	36. brassy	70. corrupt	104. disputatious
7. aggressive	37. brazen	71. covetous	105. disrespectful
8. aimless	38. brittle	72. cowardly	106. dissembling
9. aloof	39. brooding	73. coy	107. dissolute
10. ambitious,	40. brusque	74. crafty	108. distractible
overly	41. brutal	75. cranky	109. dogmatic
11. amoral	42. bullying	76. crass	110. domineering
12. angry	43. busybody	77. cross-tempered	111. dour
13. apathetic	44. cad	78. cruel	112. dramatic,
14. arbitrary	45. calculating	79. cunning	overly
15. argumentative	46. callous	80. cynical	113. dull
16. "arriviste"	47. cantankerous	81. dandyish	114. duplicitous
17. arrogant	48. careless	82. dawdling	115. easily lead
18. attention-	49. censorious	83. decadent	116. eccentric
seeking	50. chaotic	84. deceitful	117. egocentric
19. authoritarian	51. chauvinistic	85. defiant	118. entitled
20. avoidant	52. cheating	86. demanding	119. envious
21. awkward	53. cheeky	87. dependent,	120. evasive
22. backbiting	54. childish	overly	121. evil-minded
23. bellicose	55. clinging	88. depraved	122. exhibitionistic
24. bigoted	56. clownish	89. depreciatory	123. exploitative
25. bitchy	57. coarse	90. despotic	124. explosive
26. bitter	58. cold	91. desultory	125. extravagant
27. blaming	59. combative	92. devious	126. fastidious
others,	60. competitive	93. diabolical	127. fault-finding
always	61. compulsive	94. dilatory	128. fawning
28. blunt	62. conceited	95. dilettantish	129. feckless
29. bluster,	63. confrontational	96. disconsolate	130. fee
given to	64. contemptuous	97. discourteous	131. fickle

TABLE 8

Continued

132. flaky	180. impractical	227. lawless	276. overcheerful
133. flatterer	181. improvident	228. lazy	277. overeager
134. flighty	182. impudent	229. lecherous	278. overfamiliar
135. flinty	183. impulsive	230. licentious	279. overinquisitive
136. foolish	184. inappropriate	231. litigious	280. overmetic-
137. form-	185. inarticulate	232. low-minded	ulous
conscious,	186. inattentive	233. macho, too	281. overoptimistic
excessively	187. incautious	234. malicious	282. overpolite
138. forward, too	188. incompetent	235. malignant	283. overscrupu-
139. foul-mouthed	189. inconsiderate	236. manipulative	lous
140. fragile	190. inconstant	237. mannered	284. oversenti-
141. frenzied	191. incorrigible	238. masochistic	mental
142. frumpy	192. indecisive	239. maudlin	285. paranoid
143. fussy	193. indifferent	240. mean	286. parsimonious
144. garrulous	194. indiscreet	241. meddlesome	287. passionless
145. giddy	195. ineducable	242. meek	288. passive
146. glib	196. ineffectual	243. megalomanic	289. passive-
147. gloomy	197. inflexible	244. melancholy	aggressive
148. glory-hunter	198. ingratiating,	245. mendacious	290. patronizing
149. goody-goody	overly	246. mercenary	291. pedantic
150. gossipy	199. inhibited	247. mercurial	292. peevish
151. grandiose	200. inhospitable	248. messy	293. perfectionistic
152. greedy	201. insatiable	249. mischievous	294. pessimistic
153. gross	202. insecure	250. miserly	295. petulant
154. grudge-holding	203. insensitive	251. "misfit"	296. philandering
155. gruff	204. insincere	252. mistrustful	297. philistine
156. guarded	205. insolent	253. moody	298. phlegmatic
157. gullible	206. insubordinate	254. moralistic	299. pitiless
158. hard-hearted	207. intemperate	255. morose	300. plastic
159. harsh	208. intense, too	256. mousy	301. pliable
160. haughty	209. interrupting,	257. nagging	302. pompous
161. headstrong	always	258. name dropping	303. "poseur"
162. heartless	210. intimidating	259. negligent	304. possessive
163. hedonistic	211. intrusive	260. "nerdy"	305. pouty
164. highstrung	212. invidious	261. nitpicking	306. preachy
165. histrionic	213. irascible	262. nonconformist	307. precious
166. hostile	214. irksome	263. nosey	308. predatory
167. humiliating	215. irresponsible	264. obnoxious	309. prejudiced
168. humorless	216. irritable	265. obsequious	310. pressuring
169. hypercritical	217. jaded	266. obstinate	311. pretentious
170. hypocritical	218. jealous	267. obstreperous	312. prima donna
171. ill to live with	219. jekyll & hyde	268. obstruction-	313. prissy
172. illiberal	220. joyless	istic	314. procrastinating
173. ill-mannered	221. judgmental	269. offensive	315. prodigal
174. immoderate	222. know-it-all	270. oily	316. profane
175. immodest	223. labile	271. opinionated	317. profligate
176. impassive	224. lachrymose	272. opportunistic	318. promiscuous
177. impatient	225. lacking	273. oppressive	319. provocative
178. impetuous	initiative	274. overanxious	320. prudish
179. importunate	226. laconic	275. overbearing	321. pugnacious

(continued)

TABLE 8

Continued

322. punctilious	368. self-righteous	414. temperamental	456. unjust
323. puritanical	369. sensation-	415. tempestuous	457. unmasculine
324. pushy	seeking	416. theatrical	458. unobliging
325. pusillanimous	370. sensitive, too	417. timorous	459. unpredictable
326. quarrelsome	371. shallow	418. tormenting	460. unprincipled
327. querulous	372. shameless	419. touchy	461. unreasonable
328. a "quitter"	373. shiftless	420. tough-as-nails	462. unreliable
329. rageful	374. short-fused	421. treacherous	463. unrestrained
330. randy	375. show-off	422. tricky	464. unruly
331. rascally	376. shrewish	423. troublesome	465. unscrupulous
332. rash	377. shy	424. truculent	466. unselfcon-
333. raucous	378. slanderous	425. tyrannical	fident
334. rebellious	379. slavish	426. unaccommo-	467. unsociable
335. reckless	380. sleazy	dating	468. unspontaneous
336. rejecting	381. slothful	427. unaffectionate	469. unstable
337. remorseless	382. slovenly	428. unapologetic	470. unsympathetic
338. remote	383. smarmy	429. unappreciative	471. untrustworthy
339. reproachful	384. smug	430. unapproach-	472. "up-tight"
340. resentful	385. sneaky	able	473. vacillating
341. reserved, too	386. snobbish	431. unassertive	474. vain
342. restless	387. snoop	432. uncivil	475. values, lacking
343. rigid	388. spendthrift	433. uncommitted	in any firm
344. risqué	389. spineless	434. uncompas-	476. vampish
345. robot-like	390. spiteful	sionate	477. vapid
346. rude	391. spoiled	435. unconscien-	478. vehement
347. ruthless	392. squeamish	tious	479. vicious
348. saccharine	393. stiff	436. unconsidering	480. victim, an easy
349. sadistic	394. stilted	437. uncooperative	481. vindictive
350. sanctimonious	395. stingy	438. uncordial	482. violent
351. sarcastic	396. stodgy	439. uncouth	483. vituperative
352. saturnine	397. stubborn	440. uncultivated	484. volatile
353. scatterbrained	398. stuffy	441. undemon-	485. vulgar
354. scheming	399. submissive	strative	486. waspish
355. scoffer	400. sullen	442. undependable	487. wavering
356. scornful	401. supercilious	443. undiplomatic	488. weak-willed
357. scruffy	402. superficial	444. undisciplined	489. whiny
358. secretive	403. superstitious	445. unemotional	490. whorish
359. seductive	404. surly	446. unempathic	491. wild
360. seething with	405. suspicious	447. unfair	492. willful
hatred	406. swindler	448. unfaithful	493. "wimp"
361. self-conscious,	407. sycophantic	449. unfeeling	494. "wiseacre"
overly	408. taciturn	450. unfeminine	495. witchy
362. self-defeating	409. tactless	451. unforeseeing	496. withdrawn
363. self-effacing	410. tantrumy	452. unforgiving	497. "workaholic"
364. self-important	411. tasteless	453. unfriendly	498. worry-wort
365. self-indulgent	412. tattler	454. ungrateful	499. "yes-man"
366. selfish	413. teasing	455. uninsightful	500. zany
367. self-pitying			

It then becomes necessary to condense these many trait-words into a more convenient number of *factors* (based on synonyms). Thus the traits *covetous, greedy, illiberal, mercenary, miserly, parsimonious, selfish,* and *stingy* all relate to the general idea of wanting to retain more than you have a right to or of being discomfited at the thought of having to spend money. The red thread that runs through these trait-words means they have a "factor" in common. It will not always be clear what is the best name for these factors. The choice is often arbitrary and not very important in any case. For the abovementioned words, I have chosen to call the factor "greedy": it is as convenient as any other I might have picked. There is no absolutely rational and non-overlapping way to reduce 500 trait-words to a smaller number of factors. The number of factors is to a certain extent a matter of clinical utility. In my attempt to compartmentalize the words, for example, I came up with some 50 factors. One of the larger factors (to judge by the number of words covered) is "offensive." Another factor I called "superior/haughty: thinking one is better than others." The trait "abrasive" belongs pretty clearly with "offensive." I placed "snobbish" and "scornful" under the latter heading. But people at the receiving end of someone's snobbishness or scorn certainly feel offended. Still, it seemed more reasonable to assign "snobbish" and "scornful" to a word-group of conceptual near-neighbors (egocentric, disdainful, patronizing) that share a feature over and above offensiveness, namely, thinking one is better than others.

In Table 9 I have shown the 50 factors that emerged from fractionation of the negative trait-words. This can be taken only as a first step in the complicated process of creating the "optimal" partitions. One would have to examine a large number (several thousand) of persons via the trait list, and then perform a factor analysis to see which descriptions truly hung together the most often. The optimal number and nature of a factor list would also depend upon the most commonly occurring personality types in a given culture during a given era. (There were probably more "Uriah Heeps"—fawning, ingratiating schemers—in Dickens' time than now; more "plastic" middle-management types currently than in his day.)

The 50 negative factors are broken down into two large subgroups: those pertaining to traits bothersome to other people (much the larger group), and those pertaining to personality qualities bothersome mostly to the person who exhibits the trait in question. "Meddlesome" is bothersome to others; "overly sensitive" is a burden mostly to oneself.

The cataloging and factoring of personality traits, however tedious, is a useful clinical exercise, since it facilitates the testing of certain hypotheses related to treatment. We might expect, for example, that a number of traits would crop up repeatedly in the personality profiles of persons whom

TABLE 9

Fifty Factors Abstracted from the Negative Trait List

A. Factors Representing Traits Troublesome to Others

1. aggressive	19. ingratiating
2. angry/irritable	20. mistrustful
3. antisocial/psychopathic	21. narcissistic
4. argumentative	22. offensive
5. bitter	23. overinquisitive
6. bossy	24. philistine
7. coquettish	25. possessive
8. decadent	26. preciosity
9. defiant	27. procrastinating
10. devious	28. sensation-seeking
11. dogmatic	29. sexually offensive
12. envious	30. sloppy
13. garrulous	31. spendthrift
14. greedy	32. superior/haughty
15. histrionic	33. unemotional
16. hypomanic	34. unfair
17. impulsive	35. unregulated in mood
18. indiscreet	36. unsympathetic

B. Factors Representing Traits Troublesome to the Self

1. ambivalent	8. odd/eccentric
2. anxious	9. oversensitive
3. careless	10. overscrupulous
4. dilettantish	11. passive
5. distractible	12. plastic
6. dull	13. shallow
7. moody	14. shy

Traits not readily classified: ambitious (overly), attention-seeking, overly controlled, jaded, inarticulate, ineducable, laconic, poseur, superstitious, tough-as-nails, unfeminine, unspontaneous.

therapists found easy to work with and who had favorable outcomes; a number of other traits would be overrepresented in the profiles of their most difficult or most unsuccessful patients. A few traits might be associated with persons who were completely unmotivated for therapy or who were beyond the scope of all contemporary methods of treatment. The latter groups would presumably include persons of whom it is often said, "He should have been in treatment!" even though in the cold light of reality no effective treatment exists, nor would the person in question ever accept "patienthood." Hardened criminals, serial killers, and political tyrants come readily to mind as instances of untreatable personality disorders.

We will expand on this topic in Chapter 21. Just to cite one example here: there was during Operation Desert Storm a naive article in the *New York Times* about Saddam Hussein, to the effect that he "suffers from malignant narcissism," the implication being that "appropriate help" at the right time might have made him a better person. But supreme narcissists at the height of power do not "suffer" a personality disorder: *we* suffer (from) their disorder. And what form of therapy might we propose to humanize a Saddam Hussein, or the Ceaucescus, or Abu Nidal (to scoop but a few off the top of this dreary list)?

To return to the reality of clinical practice: the trait words and the resultant factors can be established toward the beginning of treatment, when the therapist knows the patient well enough to check off the pertinent items, or retrospectively, when, some years later, the therapist learns of a particular patient's outcome. The former exercise is better, since there would be less bias. Knowledge that the outcome was bad might incline one to circle more of the "bad" items than might have been recorded at the outset. But even retrospective information is useful. In a recent survey, for example, a dozen colleagues were asked to fill out the trait lists for two patients with borderline personality disorder: one whom the therapist knew had a good outcome ten years after treatment; one whose outcome was poor. For the first patient 23 items were checked off, most of which were clumped within four factors: superior/haughty, dogmatic, overscrupulous, and passive. To the patient with the poor outcome, 55 items seemed to apply. These were grouped chiefly within the following factors: aggressive, angry, defiant, devious, dogmatic, mistrustful, offensive, superior/haughty, and unsympathetic. The traits of the more successful patient were, at worst, merely annoying. Those of the poor-outcome patient were of a much more serious nature and far more prejudicial (especially, deviousness, mistrustfulness, and anger) to the development of a therapeutic alliance. In general, the poor-outcome borderline patients differed from those with good outcomes in manifesting traits belonging to the factors: angry, mistrustful, devious, bitter, and unfair.

A COMMENT ON THE POSITIVE TRAIT LIST

Psychiatry, by virtue of its concentrating on the pathological, has not paid sufficient attention to normal aspects of personality. The field of psychology has been much more evenhanded in this respect. Yet it makes good clinical sense that, of two patients with approximately similar personality

TABLE 10

Positive Categories of Personality: The Inverse of DSM

DSM CATEGORY	CORRESPONDING POSITIVE CATEGORIES
schizoid	gregarious
schizotypal	conventional
paranoid	trusting
histrionic	modulated, orderly
narcissistic	modest, altruistic, generous
borderline	self-controlled, even-tempered
antisocial	honest, kind, merciful, empathic
obsessive compulsive	spontaneous, emotionally responsive
dependent	self-reliant
passive-aggressive	straightforward
avoidant	self-confident, sociable
sadistic	compassionate
masochistic	assertive*
depressive	optimistic, self-respecting

*Perhaps a truer opposite would be "non-self-sabotaging," but there seems to be no simple word that conveys this.

disorders, or even similar sets of maladaptive traits, the one with more positive traits ought eventually to have a smoother life-course than the other. Certain positive traits—reflectiveness ("introspectiveness," "intraception"), patience, consideration—facilitate psychotherapeutic work, and thus conduce to a better outcome.

In the same way we have fractionated the negative traits into various synonym-groups, from which factors and dimensions can be abstracted, we can also classify the positive traits into meaningful categories. There are several approaches we could take. If we focus on the existing personality disorders of DSM-III-R, for example, we can at once create an *inverse* taxonomy of *positive* features. Table 10 shows one possible schema of this sort. For sake of completeness, I have included the provisional disorders, as well as "depressive" personality.

An alternative approach might consist of taking the 100 words from the preceding positive trait list and dividing them as best one can into synonym-groups—groups that could serve as a "first draft" of a factor list. Table 11 represents one such effort on my part to compartmentalize these traits. It will readily be appreciated that some words fit neatly into their respective niches; others had to be shoehorned in—because it made as much sense to insert them into one category as another (e.g., "good-natured" goes as well with "jovial" as with "kind"), or else because the trait word was only distantly related to any of the emerging factors ("modest" fits not very precisely with "serene," but even less so with the other categories).

TABLE 11

Factors Emerging from the Hundred Positive Personality Traits

I. JOVIAL: charming, cheerful, friendly, good-natured, having a sense of humor, jovial, optimistic, sociable

II. ATTENTIVE: attentive, dedicated, earnest, focused, industrious, listens well, perseverant, responsive emotionally, responsible

III. SERENE: calm, contented, dignified, modest, serene, simplicity, tranquil, unaffected

IV. SELF-ASSURED: adaptive, independent, resilient, resourceful, self-reliant, self-respecting, unflappable

V. KIND: affectionate, benevolent, compassionate, considerate, courteous, forgiving, generous, gracious, helpful, kind, merciful, sweet, sympathetic, tactful

VI. RESPECTFUL: cooperative, deferential, diplomatic, discreet, fair, hospitable, just, reasonable, polite, respectful, tolerant, well-mannered

VII. ASSERTIVE: assertive, courageous, determined, resolute, self-confident, spontaneous, straightforward

VIII. DOCILE: compliant, docile, obedient, patient

IX. CONSCIENTIOUS: careful, committed, conscientious, neat, orderly, prudent, punctual, reliable, self-controlled, self-disciplined, thrifty, trustworthy

X. HONEST: candid, honest, (having-) integrity, moral, sincere

XI. OPEN: cultivated, curious, discerning, receptive, reflective, sensitive artistically

XII. AFFILIATIVE: empathic, faithful, flexible, grateful, loyal, passionate, trusting

In my first effort, it seemed possible to compress the 100 terms into a dozen preliminary factors. In the chapter that follows we make the case that personality traits in general can be understood as belonging to *five* supertraits: *extraversion* (E), *agreeableness* (A), *non-neuroticism* (= *emotional stability* (−N), *conscientiousness* (C), and *openness* (O). Viewed from this perspective, "E" embraces factor I of Table 11; "A" covers factors V, VI, VIII, and XII; "−N" covers IV and VII; "C" takes in II, IX, and X; and "O" covers III and XI.

6

The Five-Factor Models:
An Integration

THUS FAR WE HAVE PASSED in review a fair number of personality theories and models: some based on a few factors or dimensions; some based on a multiplicity of dimensions; some consisting of complications of traits, presented either as an immense alphabetic list or as a smaller set of factors; others consisting of small collections of "items" (a half-dozen or a dozen) said to comprise one or another "personality type." The material, taken as a whole, tends to appear chaotic, random, arbitrary, parochial, wedded to this theory or to that clinical application—and to this extent not very scientific or durable. It is as though the reader is left to choose, and to utilize, a particular schema according merely to personal preference or to such accidental matters as where one trained. One wonders: is there a way out of the maze?

In recent years several investigators in the field of personality have elaborated models constructed of what their authors believe to be the fundamental factors or dimensions. Their work also suggests that there is an irreducible number of these factors—five—hence the promulgation of "five-factor models," such as those of Tupes and Christal (1961/1992), Norman (1963), Zuckerman (1991), and McCrae and John (1992). Figure 11 provides the names for these factors, which differ slightly from author to author, and which sometimes reflect the negative or antonym of one of the basic factors.

Figure 11: *Integrated Model of Personality Traits and Factors, Affects, and Temperament*

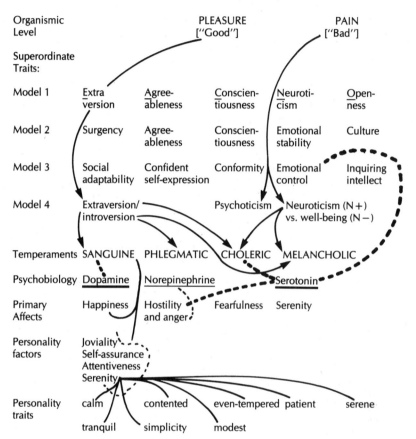

| | | PLEASURE ["Good"] | | PAIN ["Bad"] | |

Organismic Level

Superordinate Traits:

		PLEASURE ["Good"]		PAIN ["Bad"]	
Model 1	Extraversion	Agreeableness	Conscientiousness	Neuroticism	Openness
Model 2	Surgency	Agreeableness	Conscientiousness	Emotional stability	Culture
Model 3	Social adaptability	Confident self-expression	Conformity	Emotional control	Inquiring intellect
Model 4	Extraversion/introversion		Psychoticism	Neuroticism (N+) vs. well-being (N−)	

| Temperaments | SANGUINE | PHLEGMATIC | CHOLERIC | MELANCHOLIC |

| Psychobiology | Dopamine | Norepinephrine | Serotonin |

| Primary Affects | Happiness | Hostility and anger | Fearfulness | Serenity |

Personality factors:
Joviality
Self-assurance
Attentiveness
Serenity

| Personality traits | calm | contented | even-tempered patient | serene |
| | tranquil | simplicity | modest | |

Model 1: McRae & John, 1992; Model 2: Norman, 1963;
Model 3: Zuckerman, 1991; Model 4: Eysenck, 1967

Figure 11 presents an integrated schema of personality traits, factors, superfactors, affects, and temperaments. In the hierarchy of this schema, one first attends (as does the infant) to gross organismic matters of pleasure vs. pain. During ontogenesis, we learn to make finer and finer distinctions about the good and bad, pleasurable and painful attributes of those who impinge upon our lives. The FFM answers to the five next most important set of distinctions and their opposites. Each such "superordinate trait" may then be said to differentiate into a small number of lower-order, but still rather general, traits. For reasons of space, only one of these sets is shown in Figure 10, namely, a set of four factors pertaining to +E (joviality, self-assurance, etc.). The further differentiation and linguistical branching of this set are suggested by the grouping of roughly synonymous traits pertaining to one of the lower-order traits: eight terms belonging to the concept of serenity. A more detailed picture of such branching is offered in Figure 12. Correspondences between the FFM and several temperament, affect, and biological factors are also shown.

McCrae and John, for example, refer to *extraversion, aggreeableness, conscientiousness, neuroticism*, and *openness*.* These may be abbreviated: E, A, C, N, and, O. Zuckerman speaks of "N" in the positive—"emotional control"—rather than in the negative, but N is used widely, owing to the tradition established by the influential system of Eysenck (q.v., 1967).

LEXICAL AND STRUCTURAL SOURCES OF FIVE-FACTOR MODELS

The five-factor models (FFMs) derive from the two main sources alluded to in the preceding chapter, namely, the *lexical* and the *structural* (based on theories and the questionnaires developed to test these theories). The lexical approach, as McCrae and John mention (p. 201), represents the codification of laypeople's perceptions, i.e., the combing of a whole language for the treasure of trait-words contained within it. As we saw with the lists of Allport and Odbert, Goldberg, and my own 600-trait contribution, this approach aims at *completeness*—such that, even if the list is bereft of any organizing principle, one can sift through it and describe a person in every relevant detail without omitting anything of even minor significance. The 300-trait list of Gough and Heilbrun (1983), containing both positive and negative (maladaptive) traits, also aims at comprehensiveness of this sort.

In the related domain of affect, similar exercises have been carried out, in this century by de Rivera (1977) and Hartvig Dahl (1978), but much earlier (and with dramatically similar results!) by Descartes in 1650 (Stone, 1980). Descartes spoke of six basic emotions; Dahl of eight, the latter derived in part from his preliminary task of enumerating all the emotion-words in English: about 350 in all.

There is an analogy here, both in the realms of personality and affect, to chemistry—where 92 elements (corresponding to traits or emotion-words) are found in nature; these elements then susceptible of organization into rows of similar valence (corresponding to factors). One can speak of elemental traits or affects (attentiveness, sadness), or of "compounds" made up of several ingredients (cowardliness: excess harm-avoidance + too little concern for others; jealousy [here as an emotion]: love for the object, hatred of the rival, sadness at the loss of the object).

---

*These five superfactor labels are among the currently most widely accepted, and are used in Figure 11 as labels pertinent to Model 1. Somewhat different sets of labels are included for the sake of completeness (Models 2 and 3). Some of the names derive from Eysenck's older three-dimentional model (Model 4 of Figure 11).

As an example of how the FFM could have been derived from the lexical approach, McCrae and John showed how independent judges were able to assign Gough's 300 traits to the five factors, with high coefficients of reliability on each. Questionnaires based on various theories, each of which is assumed to embrace whatever is relevant about personality, may be used, in other words, to cross-check the validity of the lexical compilation. If the two methods are in harmony, the trait-vocabulary can be analyzed into just the right number of fundamental factors predicted by the theory, without "leftover" traits that beg for compartmentalization in some hitherto neglected or undiscovered factor. As a first step in the integration of the two approaches, one places the lexical *synonyms* together, as Cattell did with Allport's list—a process that yields a fairly large and rough-hewn set of factors. The five superordinate factors of the FFMs represent a further distillation, down to non- or scarcely overlapping abstractions.

The structurally oriented investigators, having begun with varying numbers (less than five usually) of abstractions, have converged toward the FFM from the other, theoretical, side. Eysenck began with "E" and "N" but later added "P"—psychoticism, comprising traits bespeaking asociality and eccentricity. The asociality in particular maps onto the superfactor, aggreeableness, as its opposite (just as introversion = "−E" and emotional stability = "−N") "Openness" (to absorbing experiences) was added by Tellegen and Atkinson (1974). In the '80s several investigators suggested the need for another dimension (or supertrait), one related to self-control or "conscientiousness" (Costa & McCrae, 1985). Analysis of competing models of personality has shown that, again, only five superordinate factors emerge—not as exhaustive descriptors of personality (for that one needs the trait lists), but, as McCrae and John mention (1992, p. 190), as the " . . . highest hierarchical level of trait description."

Cross-cultural research, based on near-neighbor languages like German, but also on languages quite different from English (Chinese and Japanese), also conduces to the same FFM—an indication that the FFM reflects something enduring and deep about human nature. This may be analogous to the linguistical theory of Chomsky (1965), which suggests a common, "hard-wired" grammar for members of our species, independent of locale and of the language actually spoken.

The stability of human nature, across cultures and across the millenia, would itself seem to ensure that, once the basic human tasks are delineated, the resultant catalog would be valid for all time and places; the personality traits that subserve these tasks would likewise be confronted in every society and in every era, with only minimal and superficial differences (viz. the sycophancy of courtiers during the days of kings vs. the fawning of middle executives during our era of big corporations). McCrae and John outline the basic human tasks (1992, p. 199), which, curiously, also were five in number in their model: (a) to respond to danger or loss, (b) to interact with others, (c) to make choices between exploration and its attendant risks vs. familiarity and its limitations, (d) to weigh self- vs. social interest, and (e) to balance work and play. There does not seem to be a one-to-one isomorphism between these tasks and the five factors, but there are close relationships: response to danger is mediated by well-being ("−N"); inter/action by "A" and "E"; exploration partly by "O" (which is related to sensation-seeking); self vs. social interest by "C"; and work vs. play by "C" and, to an extent, "O."

At present there is, in sum, much to suggest that these five factors carve nature at her joints, just as "six" is the right number for the continents and "92" for the elements.

THE TRAIT TREE WITH ITS MANY BRANCHES

Ideally, there should be an equilibrium between the five-factor model, as derived from preexisting abstractions and theories about personality, and the catalog of *traits* generated by the lexical approach, as sketched out by wordsmiths with neither a theoretical axe to grind nor any preconception as to how many natural groupings (dimensions, factors) these traits might form. The FFM should be the middle-ground where the two approaches meet. It might be too much to expect that *every* trait-adjective could fit neatly into one or another of the five factors, but the "leftovers" should be few in number, probably non-evaluative, and not susceptible of forming a supertrait (i.e., a new higher-order factor) of their own.

It is of interest, then, to see what emerges when we follow the trait-tree past its five large branches onto the "lower-order traits" that constitute the next level of branching—beyond which are the finer and finer "twigs" of very specific adjectives that admit (apart of archaicisms and slang-words) of no further bifurcations. These twigs should resemble very closely the catalog created by the lexicographers.

A number of personality specialists have begun such an exercise, offering several examples of positive and negative traits, lower in order but still fairly general, relevant to each of the five higher-order "supertraits." Buss and Finn (1987), for example, recreated the next-finer branches suggested by Norman (1963), one of the earliest of the FFM theoreticians.

Using Norman's schema as a springboard, one can demonstrate still finer branches and terminal twigs, as an exercise in comparing the resulting trait-list with the atheoretical lists of Goldberg or Gough or myself. In

Figure 12 I have shown how the Norman/Buss schema can be expanded in this fashion.

The tree contains some hundred fifty small branches and twigs. Considerations of space limited these more narrowly defined traits to this number. One could situate just about all the 500 negative and 100 positive traits from my trait-list *somewhere* on this five-factor tree.

Certain traits, like "charismatic," are combinations of qualities belonging to several of the supertraits: E, A, and O (in the case of Churchill), but −E, O, and extreme −A (in the case of Hitler). A number of other traits are either non-evaluative or ambiguous in the language, their valence depending upon context. Thus "absent-mindedness" can be an endearing or at least amusing trait in one person; an irksome trait in someone else. "Sophisticated" is another such "bivalent" trait. Perhaps "witty" is also: obviously a positive trait in Oscar Wilde, but a negative trait in Truman Capote, who used his wittiness to put others down. "Exhibitionistic," similarly, can be understood in two ways: offensively showy, but also vivacious and at ease in revealing oneself—qualities that are often found and much admired in public performers. The main point is: the trait catalog can be mapped quite well onto the FFM model, if we allow for a few traits that (as do the DSM personality disorders themselves) span more than one factor, and just a few traits that cannot easily be made to conform to the model.

There are other conceptual subdivisions one can make in the taxonomy of traits for didactic purposes: Buss and Finn speak, for example, of *instrumental, affective,* and *cognitive* traits. They distinguish, among the instrumental traits, between those that are power-oriented (aggressiveness, rebelliousness) and those that are prosocial (altruistic, sociable); among the "affective," those that are self- (shy) vs. "nonself-oriented (empathic); and among the "cognitive," self- (viz., moral) vs. non-self-oriented (trusting, sensitive).

As for our tree (Figure 12), it should also be noted that one runs into special difficulties in trying to assign certain traits to the "+" or "−" branches off the five main factors: some traits switch valence at their furthermost extensions. Thus, "+A" shades into "trusting"—clearly a positive trait—but the twig at furthest remove is "gullible" (i.e., too trusting), which is no longer a positive trait. Still, this is only a minor complication to what is otherwise a highly successful and useful model.

Those interested in a comprehensive review of the FFM and its evolution from the time of Cattell and Fiske in the 1940s (themselves influenced by German characterology of the 1920s) would do well to read Oliver John's excellent chapter (1990) on the "Big Five" factor taxonomy.

Figure 12: *Five-Factor Personality-Trait Tree*

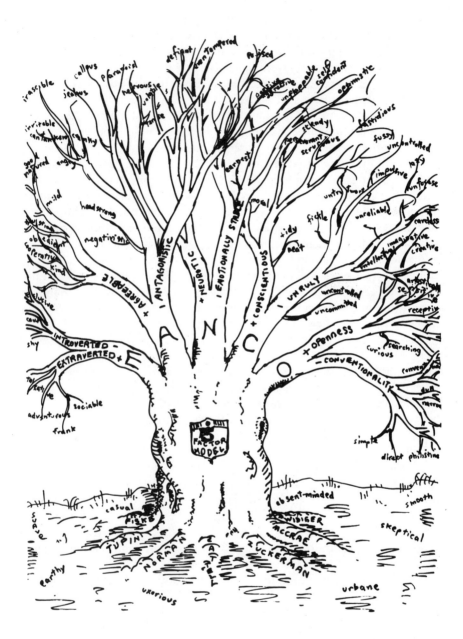

DSM Personality Types and
the Five-Factor Model

It would be encouraging, as an index of the validity of the FFM—or at least of its utility—if the standard personality types of DSM-III/III-R could be encompassed within the five factors. Three-factor models, as we saw in Chapter 2, generate 2^3 or 8 subtypes, which at best orphans three out of the 11 recognized types.

Widiger and Trull (1992), in their excellent review of the FFM's application to the domain of personality type, cite the work of Wiggins and Pincus (1989), who demonstrated that much of the variance in our current typology could be accounted for via a five-factor model. Using the factors of McCrae and John, we can illustrate this point by means of Table 12, where the 11 standard types, plus the provisional "sadistic PD," are all mappable onto the FFM. Widiger and Trull reproduced the precise factor loadings; for sake of brevity, I have indicated weak loadings (.35 to .49) with a "w"; strong but negative correlations with a "−"; and extreme situations with an "e." In this schema borderline PD represents the extreme of neuroticism, lending support, as Widiger mentions, to Kernberg's advocacy of "borderline" as a level of function (rather than as simply the name of a personality type).

Widiger and Trull also comment on an interesting point, raised recently

TABLE 12

Correlations between Personality Types and the Five-Factor Model*

Factors:	E	N	A	C	O
P	histrionic			compulsive	
E	(−) avoidant			(w-) antisocial	
R	(−) schizoid			(w-) passive-aggressive	
S	(w) psychopath				
O		dependent			(w) schizotypal
N		avoidant			
A		passive-aggressive			
L		borderline (e)			
I					
T			dependent		
Y			(−) antisocial		
			(−) narcissistic		
T			(w-) paranoid		
Y			(−) passive-aggressive		
P			(e-) sadistic		
E					

Key: − —negative; w—weakly correlated; e—extreme example
*Adapted from Widiger & Trull, 1992.

by Tellegen, that the FFM may not be adequate to deal with *evaluative* personality terms, such as become important in trying to describe severely abnormal personalities. I have added my own thoughts on this subject, in some detail, in Chapter 21. "Positive Evaluation" might include such terms as "lofty," "exceptional," "special"—and thus have some applicability to the domain of narcissism. "Negative Evaluation" could include "evil," "depraved," "detestable," "immoral," etc. Widiger suggests a way around the stumbling block (thus obviating the need to expand the five-factor model into a seven-factor model), by picturing Positive Evaluation as an extreme form of −N (very unneurotic). I suspect certain aspects of Positive Evaluation may also be seen as extreme forms of "A" (agreeableness). If we envision the extreme of "−A," the most antagonistic traits may be situated there, and could thus include sadistic and ruthlessly psychopathic persons: the least "agreeable" or most antagonistic persons.

Schizotypal PD does not fit very well into the FFM: it has to be hammered a bit to conform to the "O" factor. I see this, however, less as a criticism of the FFM than a reflection of the conceptual muddle that places a largely symptom-based disorder into Axis II (a criticism I have mentioned in other chapters, relevant also to borderline PD and antisocial PD, though not to the concept of psychopathy, which is based, as it should be, upon personality *traits*).

PSYCHOBIOLOGICAL CORRELATES

As Zuckerman (1991) aptly remarks, there has been an " . . . explosion of research in the neurosciences and in the cross-disciplinary interests . . . that one can expect that progress in the psychobiology of personality will be rapid" (p. 427). One sign of this progress would be the discovery of more and more linkages between various brain mechanisms and neuroactive substances—and corresponding facets of the major personality factors. This will happily shrink the hitherto large territory within which casuistical discussions take place regarding the "correct" number and kind of relevant dimensions. Cloninger's model (1986) is an important step in the proper direction, establishing linkages between low basal dopaminergic activity and novelty-seeking; high serotoninergic activity and harm-avoidance; and low basal noradrenergic activity and reward dependence.

Some of the CNS pathways mediating these response patterns are shown in Figure 13. The diagram, derived from rat-brain studies, is schematic and simplified (cf. Zuckerman, 1991, p. 178), but analogous to the pathways in the human brain subserved by the same neuroregulators. With respect to the five-factor model, dopamine may be linked with positive affects, sociability, and extraversion: the E factor. Serotonin enhances CNS inhibi-

Figure 13: *Major CNS Pathways Involving the Neurotransmitters Serotonin, Dopamine, and Norepinephrine*

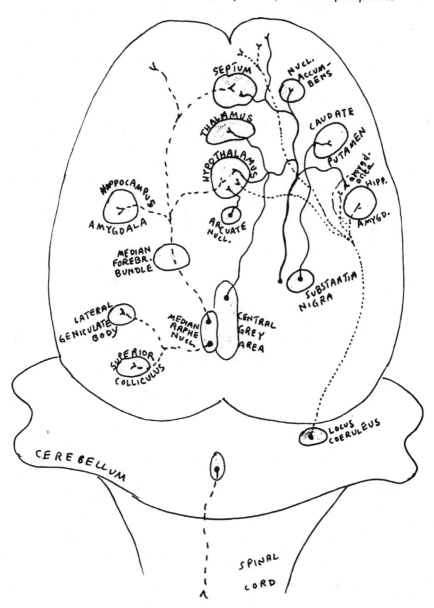

Serotinin (---); dopamine (——); norepinephrine (· · · ·)

tion, and may thus be linked with self-control (as opposed to impulsivity): the C factor, and also the N factor (emotional control as the opposite of neuroticism). Norepinephrine, via adrenergic arousal, fosters aggressive/ angry responses, in the surplus, and reward-dependence, at the low-basal level: these may have correlations with both the N and the A factors.

Figure 14 adapted from Zuckerman, p. 407, shows these interrelationships, along with those pertaining to several other neuroregulators, including gonadal hormones.* In a parallel finding, Scaramella and Brown (1978) reported heightened testosterone levels in the most aggressive hockey players, when compared with levels in the least aggressive members of this already quite aggressive group. These hormonal interconnections are discussed in greater detail in Valzelli (1981) and Stone (1992a). The benzodiazepine receptor agonists and inverse agonists have effects on anxiety levels and may therefore also be implicated in the N factor. Whether neuroregulatory substances play any role in the O factor is as yet unclear; however, if there is a significant linkage between schizotypy and "O", then the related genes and their products may exert at least some influence on this more elusive factor.

The innate, primordial tendencies outlined by Cloninger along with the three important neurotransmitters that help shape these tendencies, put us in mind of another major aspect of personality: *temperament*. Of the four temperaments mentioned by the Greeks, three relate to manic-depressive illness: *sanguine, choleric,* and *melancholic,* which in turn may be mapped onto extraversion, irritability, and depressive "neurosis," respectively. These are related to several of the five main factors: E (sanguine), N and A (choleric), and N and C, perhaps also −E (melancholic). Not shown in Figure 11 is the non-gregarious "schizoid" temperament: this temperament had not been singled out by the ancient Greeks but merits a place alongside the more commonly recognized types.

Temperament has not as yet been well integrated into theories of adult personality (McCrae & John, 1992, p. 204), owing in part to the greater attention given this topic by specialists in child-, as opposed to adult-, psychology/psychiatry—and to the dearth of long-term follow-up studies where adults who had been studied during childhood are then reevaluated

---

*Gonadal hormones (especially, androgens), along with neurotransmitters subserving anxiety and harm-avoidance, may also influence the degree to which people exhibit what M. Balint (1969) called *philobatic* vs. *ocnophilic* tendencies. The "philobat" (from the Greek: loving to walk) is someone who likes to be independent, to roam far away from security objects, etc. (as noted in young boys more so than in young girls). The "ocnophile" (loving to hang onto) prefers to cling to security-objects and to assume a more dependent role—a tendency noted more often in girls than in boys.

Figure 14: *Psychobiology of Personality**

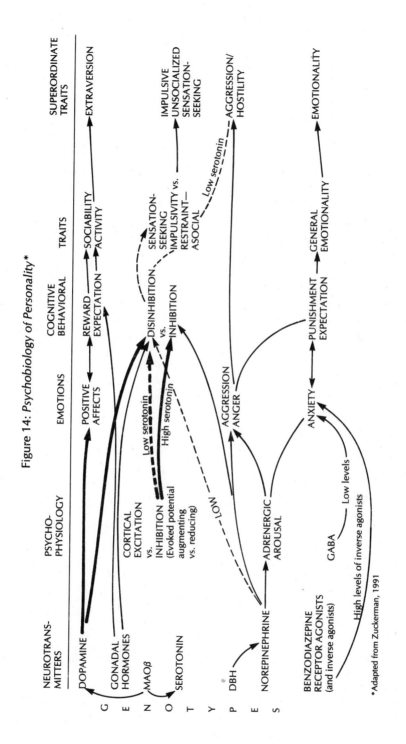

during their twenties and thirties. The durability of schizoid temperament, evolving into schizoid or schizotypal PD twenty years later, has been documented by Wolff et al. (1991; see Chapter 9).

GENETIC CORRELATES

In an effort to assess the contribution of heredity to temperament, and by extension to those aspects of adult personality that are most likely to be continuing manifestations of innate predisposition, a number of investigators have carried out studies comparing identical vs. fraternal twins. This method permits the calculation of "heritability"—the proportion of total phenotypic variance that is related to (additive) genetic variance (Falconer, 1967). Heritability offers an estimate of whether the role of genes in determining a given phenotype is large or small (Thompson & Thompson, 1980), though the resulting percentage reflects the average within a group and does not reveal the level of genetic influence in a particular individual.

As for temperament attributes pertinent to infants (as outlined by Thomas and Chess, 1977), Torgersen (1985) contrasted 34 pairs of identical twins (IT) with 15 pairs of fraternal twins (FT)—evaluated at two months, nine months, and six years. Greater similarity (hence higher heritability ratios) were noted in the identicals in relation to all nine temperament factors studied at nine months (only three had begun to show significant differences at two months); these differences persisted (though not in the same proportions) in the children at six. The factors showing the highest IT > FT ratios at age six were "activity," "approach/withdrawal," and "intensity."

Zuckerman (1991, p. 97) reviewed a number of studies of IT/FT differences in relation to Eysenck's supertraits, E, N, and P (here corresponding to sociability, emotionality, and impulsive-unsocialized-sensation-seeking). The mean correlations among the ITs as compared with the FTs across all studies were: for E .54 vs. .19; for N .46 vs. .22; and for P .56 vs. .27, all suggestive of the importance of additive genetic factors in the development of these supertraits. These results point to significant heritabilities for the E and N moieties of the FFM; recent work also supports the notion of substantial heritability for the O and C factors (Plomin & McClearn, 1990).

Support for the hypothesis of strong genetic underpinning in the remaining factor, A, comes from the twin study of Rushton et al. (1986), who measured five attributes—aggression, altruism, empathy, nurturance, and assertiveness—that may all be seen as contrasting aspects of A. Rushton's group found gender and age differences: women had higher mean scores on empathy and nurturance; men on assertiveness and aggressiveness. With increasing age, aggressiveness decreased; all the other attributes increased (changes that, in males, would correlate with diminishing testosterone levels with advancing age). As in many twin-based personality studies (cf. Plomin & Rende, 1991), 50% of the variance could be accounted for by additive genetic factors, 47% by the twins' non-shared environment, and only 3% by shared environment. For further discussion of the important topic of non-shared environment as a determinant in personality differences, the paper of Plomin and Daniels (1987) is an invaluable source. The 20 + year follow-up study of Huesmann, Eron et al. (1984) is also relevant to the "A" factor: aggression at age 8 correlated 0.46 with aggression at age 30, and was actually stable over three generations.

AN EVOLUTIONARY PERSPECTIVE

Consensus concerning the basic human tasks, such as those enumerated above by Costa and McCrae, leads us to contemplate the "why" of personality from an evolutionary perspective. I addressed some of the relevant questions in Chapter 4: there the focus was on correspondences between the division of labor in any functioning society and the proliferation of different personality types, each of which might bring certain advantages to the various basic tasks.

Costa and McCrae's comprehensive list included certain tasks that concern all animal species, such as the need to sense and to ward off external danger. It will be useful to narrow our focus here to the tasks that particularly characterize our species, namely, social tasks. Admittedly, there is some overlap here, since for humans the main source of external danger is no longer cold, floods, and lightning, but other humans.

Buss (1991) makes this point in his excellent review of personality as it relates to social tasks. Buss outlines five types of relationships as most important to our individual and species survival; these identify, in effect, the kinds of persons with whom people "strive to maintain relatedness" (p. 468). Such persons include these who (a) make good reciprocal allies, (b) can become mates of high reproductive value, (c) occupy elevated places in the social hierarchy, (d) are genetically related, and (e) will make good members of one's coalition. It is our ability to attend to and to act upon our observations of others as either enhancing or thwarting our survival and reproductive needs that determines in large measure whether we succeed or fail at the "game" of life.

In line with this, most (all but 3%, according to Peabody, 1985) personality trait-words are, as Buss underlines, *evaluative*: how "good" or "bad" is this person I am thinking about for my various survival/social/sexual needs? In drawing my own trait list I also began to realize there were few words that could not readily be assigned to either the negative (maladaptive) or the positive category ("worldly," "skeptical," and "urbane" are three such words).* As for the advantage, evolutionarily speaking, of having an optimal set of traits pertaining, specifically, to the tasks of reproduction (viz., eliciting the interest of a potential mate, etc.), those so possessed are more likely, as Buss put it, to be our ancestors and become our heirs. Their genes will, so to say, be overrepresented in the next generation, in comparison to the genes belonging to those who are maladapted to these tasks.

If we examine these issues against the backdrop of the five-factor model, we can make the case that extraversion and agreeableness—E and A—confer advantages (to those who would score higher on scales for these factors) in forming harmonious relationships and in discerning (via empathy) similar traits in potential friends, coworkers, and mates, such as would further our own aims and, as a not so trivial side-benefit, ensure the continuity of our genes. Conscientiousness and emotional stability—C and —N—conduce to the steadiness and dedication that foster the durability of relationships in work, friendship, and intimacy. The O factor might be seen as having more to do with the embellishment than the perpetuation of life, and thus as conferring less in the way of evolutionary advantage than the other four. Even so, it is of interest that, in my long-term follow-up of borderline patients, those with the most marked artistic sensibilities and the greatest capacity to become absorbed in some type of artistic pursuit tended to lead more successful lives, eventually, than those who were less endowed with these "O-factor" traits.

Buss summarizes the evolutionary implications in this way: The five-factor model " . . . represents important dimensions of the social terrain that humans were selected to attend to and to act upon" (1991, p. 91).

REEXAMINING THE FREUDIAN DEVELOPMENTAL MODEL

In the traditional psychoanalytic characterology, distinctions in "character" type (akin to our contemporary term, personality type) arose in reaction to abnormal patterns of parental behavior during the succession of developmental stages in early childhood. Though, in the domain of character typology, Freud gave considerable weight to innate or constitutional factors, many of his followers gave less so; some (Melanie Klein and her disciples,

---

*Pride is another example. Too much pride is, in our culture, one of the 7 Deadly Sins. Too little is equated with self-disparagement. There is no simple word for just-enough-pride, though "self-respecting" comes close.

for example) emphasized psychological factors to the near exclusion of the biological. According to the linear, developmental track, the infant progressed from the passive to sadistic oral stages, through the passive and later sadistic anal stages, on to the (less dwelt upon urethral, and) genital stages—the latter asserting itself between roughly ages 3½ and 5. Deprivations or improper handling during these stages were said to give rise to: dependent, depressive, envious, passive-homosexual, obsessive-compulsive, aggressive, narcissistic ("aristocratic," in W. Reich's terminology), and finally, hysteric character types.

But as we have seen in the preceding sections, the forces influencing the differentiation of personality into various types are primarily genetic (including those determining gender), accounting for half the variance, and non-shared environment, accounting for most of the remainder. Independent of parental interactions during the main stages, histrionic and dependent personalities are more apt to be diagnosed in women; compulsive, antisocial, and probably schizoid personalities in men. Depressive personality, or "dysthymia," may arise from severe neglect during the first few years of life, but aside from that will more often be a reflection of risk genes for unipolar depression. Psychoanalytic theoreticians were drawn to their conclusions by the *analogies* between certain key life tasks and the stages in childhood when the *Anlagen* of these tasks first seemed to manifest themselves. These correlations have more to do, however, with neurophysiological maturation (myelination of nerves in the oral mucosa proceeds ahead of myelination in the anal and genital mucosa), and with the critical times certain genes, already present at birth, "switch on" and activate key physiological processes. "Genital"/histrionic personality should therefore not be regarded as "healthier" than obsessive-compulsive simply because the latter bears similarity to the earlier, more "primitive" anal stage (Stone, 1980b).

Contemporary theory about the evolution of personality types—no longer linear and purely psychological, but cognizant of genetic/constitutional factors, cognizant also of the impact of early habit-formation (in the firming up of prejudice and other "fixed" attitudes)—has important ramifications in the arena of therapy. Psychoanalysis deals mainly in the resolution of conflict, especially of conflictual attitudes toward one's primary caretakers. But, in the aberrations of personality, there is much that belongs to temperament, to other innate factors, and to nonconflictual patterns of thought and behavior inculcated very early in life. It would be too much to expect that analysis alone could effect all the ameliorative changes one might like to see in someone with maladaptive traits or with a severely disordered personality. Rather, behavioral/cognitive interventions take on a special importance. About these and other treatment modalities we will have more to say in the chapters that follow.

SUMMARY

In Figure 11 we focused on the five superfactors and their relationship to temperament and to certain personality traits. In Table 12 we looked at the relationship between the five factors and the personality disorders of DSM. There are some further points to be made that tie together, and focus more closely, on connections between these aspects of personality and other aspects relating to temperament, character, and the amine neurotransmitters. It is once again to the seminal work of Cloninger (1993) that we turn in setting forth this, as we may call it, *grand unified theory* of personality.

In drawing attention to the allure of the four temperaments—not many topics in our field retain their fascination for 2,500 years—Cloninger mentions that Pavlov himself struggled to find a unique place for the temperaments within his three-dimensional model. Pavlov spoke of *strength of excitation* (the melancholics were weak in this), *strength of inhibition* (here the cholerics were weak), and *capacity for mobility* (high in the sanguines; low in the phlegmatics).

The Pavlovian dimensions are reminiscent of Cloninger's interesting point that, as for behavior, it has only three ways to go: it can be turned on; it can be inhibited; or it can be kept going. But it is precisely here that the three amine systems have their parallel: dopamine is associated with turning behavior on (novelty-seeking); serotonin with turning it off or down (harm-avoidance); noradrenalin with keeping it going (reward-dependence).

These three overarching behavior patterns (novelty-seeking/harm-avoidance/reward-dependence) account for a good portion of what we mean by personality, particularly the portion having to do with innate biological influences (i.e., temperament). Cloninger found that one needed to add a fourth: *persistence*. All these factors have high heritabilities, in the range of 50%. But beyond these factors is another group of factors. Cloninger refers to these as *self-directedness, cooperativeness, and self-transcendence*. The latter has to do with the ease with which one can become self-absorbed or feel at one with nature. This factor is thus similar to the openness of the five-factor model. It turns out that heritability is high for these factors as well.

What is different about these factors is the degree to which shared parental influences contribute to them. As we have seen, with the five superfactors these influences accounted for very little, in comparison to nonshared environment and to genetic factors. But self-directedness and cooperativeness are best understood as aspects of *character*. There is an interplay between genetic and parental influences determining character. One might say, for example, that parents (ideally) shape character (being honest when one could cheat and not get caught, being considerate of others, etc.) via operant *conditioning* in the early years of a child's life, mediated by the "habit" (or "procedural") memory system. This memory system has its own pathways (Mishkin et al., 1984) and is not accompanied by thought, as is "cognitive" memory.

But the child's susceptibility to this socialization process is itself to no mean extent dependent upon the balance between the inherited levels of harm-avoidance, reward-dependence, and novelty-seeking. There are, after all, some intractable or incorrigible children, alongside the majority of compliant and socializable children. Probably sex hormones affect this balance as well, given the fact that incorrigible children are more apt to be boys.

If, in any event, a child is not burdened with an adverse balance of the amine-related factors, and if the child has parents who are themselves well-socialized, good character ought to result (and usually does). Mendacious, abusive, corrupt, or wicked parents can spoil character—but not always. As we shall see in Chapter 17, some children emerge whole, with sterling character, even though raised by the worst of parents.

The character factors, especially self-directedness and cooperativeness, act, as Cloninger suggests, as nonspecific agents relative to DSM's catalog of personality disorders. Persons low in these two factors have an inordinately high likelihood of having a personality disorder—but it can be any one at all from the catalog. Personality-disordered patients tend, for example, to blame others, to react in a stimulus-bound way, and to fight against the idea of having to accept limitations; they may also be less empathic, helpful, or compassionate than average people.

Beyond these abnormalities in the realm of *character*, personality-disordered patients will tend to show more specific abnormalities that we, in the gross, compartmentalize into one of the three DSM clusters. Here Cloninger's amine-related factors come into play once again: cluster A patients behave as though low in reward-dependence; cluster B patients as though high in novelty-seeking; and those in cluster C may be viewed as high in harm-avoidance. The correlation between these clusters and the four temperaments is only moderately strong: some paranoid, schizoid, and schizotypal patients (cluster A) are phlegmatic, but many paranoid patients are more choleric (angry, explosive). Many histrionic, narcissistic, and antisocial patients (cluster B) are sanguine in temperament, though borderline patients usually have a stronger choleric (and often, melancholic) component. Melancholic and choleric temperaments are common among avoidant, compulsive, dependent, and passive-aggressive patients (also among depressive/dysthymic and pain-dependent patients).

This unified model and the distinctions we have drawn here will be useful as we progress through the individual personality disorders and the various trait-abnormalities in the chapters that follow. Freud's emphasis on the need for good character as a precondition for psychoanalytic treatment (of what are essentially milder troubles of personality) and the modern emphasis on behavioral techniques (for the more serious personality disorders) become more comprehensible in the light of this unified model.

7

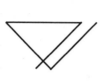

Long-Term Outcome in
Personality Disorders

LONG-TERM FOLLOW-UP HAS BEEN considered the psychiatrist's "micro-scope" (Heller, 1987). As with real microscopy, we must familiarize our-selves with a number of special factors in order to make sense out of what we are viewing. In the domain of chronic conditions such as personality disorders, short-term follow-up is of little value in providing clues as to the most likely life-trajectory. But long-term studies, besides being arduous, are fraught with problems affecting validity. Diagnostic criteria change from one generation to another. Patterns of illness also shift, such that long-term results, even if accurately assessed, may begin to lose relevance. Conditions of similar diagnosis confronting clinicians 15 to 25 years later may no longer resemble their earlier conditions so closely. Also, the longer the interval, the greater the multiplication of intervening variables. Data about outcome are more secure, but inferences about the efficacy of the initial treatment become riskier.

Retrospective study design is burdened not only by the evanescence of memory but also by the spottiness of the old records with respect to vari-ables whose importance was not suspected a quarter century ago. Prospec-tive design reduces the memory problem, but forces the investigators to rely only on the variables they assumed were important at the outset; they cannot inquire systematically about factors whose significance will have hit home only in the distant future.

In the realm of personality disorders, there is a unique problem affecting the clinician observer: patients exhibiting severe and socially offensive traits are often at pains to hide these traits from the diagnostician or, at follow-up time, from the interviewer. The existence and long-term fate of *psycho-pathic* tendencies, in particular, present great difficulties to the investigator.

Personality disorders exist within a bell-curve of variation. The readily diagnosed conditions represent "outliers." The fatter mid portions of the curve contain, depending on the disorder in question, mildly shy or extra-verted persons, mildly mistrustful or mildly gullible persons, etc., who would not be identified within psychiatry as "cases."

The personality disorders defined in DSM or ICD may thus be seen as extreme examples of tendencies observable in the general population. Sev-eral of the standard personality disorders bear a close relationship to the symptom disorders enumerated in DSM's "Axis I." In many agoraphobics, for example, there is a residue of "avoidant personality." The lines between "depressive personality" (Phillips, Gunderson et al., 1990) and "major de-pressive disorder" are often indistinct. Many patients with obsessive-compulsive *disorder* do not have an underlying obsessive-compulsive *per-sonality*, but in those that do the two conditions seem like different degrees of the same tendency.

Another problem arises in regard to personality disorders stemming from the narrowness of the personality-domain in DSM/ICD compared with the larger realm of maladaptive personalities recognizable within society as a whole. Many persons exhibit one or a few irritating traits (stinginess, indiscretion, intrusiveness, abrasiveness) with adverse social effects. Yet these traits need not "add up" to an officially defined personality disorder. As we review the long-term outcome of personality disorders, we have little choice but to concentrate upon disorders within the standard nomenclature, since the studies thus far published chiefly rely upon this common language.

Also complicating the analysis of outcome (besides the frequent admix-ture, in clinical practice, of *personality* disorders with well-defined *symp-tom* disorders) is the even more frequent admixture of personality disorders as currently defined. The latter situation is often called "comorbidity." This is not an ideal term, since it suggests the accidental coexistence of two or more unrelated conditions (like measles and tuberculosis), and blurs our recognition of how arbitrary our personality labels really are.

Since psychopathic persons are, for example, self-seeking and contemp-tuous of others, they are therefore also "narcissistic." As Oldham has docu-mented (1988), "borderline" patients almost invariably have enough other traits to warrant a "comorbid" personality diagnosis. As a result, BPD needs, even more than the other categorically-defined personality disorders, to be understood also in *dimensional* terms (Stone, 1980a)—specifically, as part of a personality *profile*, as discussed in Chapter 2.

Most of the personality disorders under discussion here are "true" personality disorders, defined solely by traits. A few are admixtures of traits and symptoms: borderline, schizotypal, and antisocial PDs (cf. DSM) and ICD's "affective" (similar to dysthymic/depressive) and "explosive" (similar to irritable temperament as defined by Kraepelin).

As noted, the domain of traits is more extensive than the domain of personality *disorders*. The diagnosis of a "disorder" is reserved for more serious conditions that would awaken the interest of a therapist or a forensic specialist. Some traits (e.g., frivolousness, silliness) remain, even in their extreme form, beyond the fringe, psychiatrically speaking. Still other traits, though clearly pathological, inhabit a disputed territory where there is insufficient agreement among clinicians, or insufficient interest, to situate them within or outside the domain of obvious disorders. Traits such as lascivious, vampish, dandified, bigoted, and witchy are reminiscent of certain disorders (histrionic, narcissistic, passive-aggressive) but are not among their itemized descriptors. Cultural factors also enter the equation—so much so as to render the establishment of universal standards for the diagnosis of personality disorders extremely difficult.

The foregoing remarks should help one understand that the literature on outcome in personality disorders is confined to a small region within the totality of abnormal or "disordered" personality. Even that region will have indistinct boundaries because interrater reliability for personality disorders is less than that for conditions marked by severe symptoms. In Figure 15 the relative size (region A: the tip of the iceberg) and unrepresentativeness of the disorders captured in this literature are shown in relation to the domain of *all* personality problems (regions A through E of the "iceberg").

OUTCOME STUDIES AND THEIR RESULTS

The outcome studies thus far reported have concentrated on personality disorders associated with good reliability and with greatest interest to clinical and forensic specialists. These happen to be the "mixed" (symptom and trait) disorders: borderline, antisocial, and schizotypal. Partly this relates to the ease with which symptoms (viz., self-damaging acts) can be reliably rated, in comparison to traits (viz., vanity, indecisiveness). A search of the literature spanning 1980–1989 revealed some 61 outcome studies in this area, mostly devoted to borderline (24), antisocial (13), or schizotypal (9) personalities. Among the remainder, only narcissistic, obsessive-compulsive, and schizoid received attention, apart from a few articles on "mixed" disor-

Figure 15: *Compartments within the Domain of Personality*

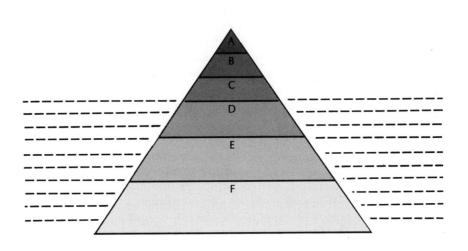

A Personality disorder (PD) correctly identified via DSM/ICD criteria; cases followed-up long-term via reliable methods
B Persons seeking therapy; diagnosed correctly as examples of personality disorder via standardized criteria
C Persons seeking treatment for personality problems not meeting standardized criteria for a "personality disorder"
D Persons with severe personality problems warranting a personality disorder diagnosis, but not seeking help or becoming identified as "cases"
E Persons with several bothersome traits, short of meeting PD criteria
F Remainder of the general population

Compartments A, B, and C represent the portion of the "iceberg" exposed to the mental health professions. The larger compartments, D and E, of personality pathology remain below the surface, apart from notorious figures in forensic, political, and other realms whose abnormal personalities suddenly come into public view.

ders, that is, disorders that are admixtures of the various PDs. Because of the greater ease in conducting follow-up studies with hospitalized rather than with ambulatory patients, almost all the data available concern a population skewed toward greater severity of illness, namely, patients who were originally in residential treatment centers.

Borderline Personality Disorder

The first follow-up studies of borderline patients, stemming from the 1970s, were of brief duration (three to five years) and used a variety of diagnostic criteria, mostly broad and unsystematic. Their results are reviewed elsewhere (Stone, 1989g). The life-course appeared unfavorable, scarcely distinguishable from that of schizophrenics, except for the better socialization noted among the borderline patients.

During the 1980s a number of studies based on larger Ns and longer intervals were reported, beginning with that of Plakun and his colleagues (1985) at Austin Riggs. Plakun's and the subsequently reported studies of McGlashan (1986), Stone et al. (1987), Paris et al. (1987), and Kroll et al. (1985) were more homogeneous with respect to diagnosis, all utilizing DSM-III or the closely related Gunderson (cf. Gunderson et al., 1981) criteria. The DSM criteria utilized in these studies were those of the 1980 edition.

Of these studies, ours (Stone et al., 1987; Stone, 1990) had been based on the largest N (550, of which the BPD patients comprised the largest subgroup: 206), with the highest trace-rate (currently: 95%). We refer to this study as the *P.I.-500* (for New York State *P*sychiatric *I*nstitute). The patients were predominantly middle- to upper-middle class, socioeconomically: 87% came from families in Hollingshead and Redlich's (1958) S.E.S. I, II, or III. Half the patients came from New York City; the remainder from the rest of New York State. Their religious affiliations were largely Jewish (52%) or Protestant (22%). Almost all were single (91%); their average age when hospitalized, 22. Average length of stay was 12½ months. A fourth of the patients had never been hospitalized before. Most had completed at least some college; average IQ was 118. Though the levels of parental abusiveness, physical or sexual, had not been negligible, their homes, and the patients themselves, had been less violence-prone than is the case with many samples of BPD patients in the recent literature (Stone, Unwin et al., 1988).

In the combined studies all socioeconomic groups are represented: the patients traced by McGlashan and by Plakun were predominantly of S.E.S. I, II, and III; those of Paris and of Kroll, of S.E.S. III, IV, and V. All these studies (including the P.I.-500) are in agreement that when the original borderline patients of the 1960s and 1970s have been traced at intervals of 10–30 years, outcome has in general been favorable. Two-thirds of the patients in each study were clinically well at follow-up. Many had residual mild symptoms. About 20% were asymptomatic, working well, and involved in a gratifying long-term sexual partnership. This was more apt to be true of women than of men.

In our study, the marriage rate was half the national average for persons from their respective culture and era. The percent of the former BPD women who now had children was about a fourth of the general population average. Only about one patient in four, as the group entered the fourth or fifth decade of life, still retained enough clinical features of BPD to justify its diagnosis by DSM-III criteria. The majority would currently be diagnosed as manifesting one of the milder personality disorders (viz., histrionic, avoidant, obsessive-compulsive).

McGlashan has reported (1986) that some BPD patients, as they enter their forties, become symptomatic again (usually depressed), owing to the loss of a sustaining relationship. Death of a spouse was the precipitant in some cases, but more often it was separation or divorce, prompted by the irascibility of the borderline spouse.

Subsequent rehospitalization during the follow-up years was, in our series, only a *third* as likely for a borderline patient as for a schizophrenic one (28% vs. 77%). Similarly, BPD patients were much more likely to have worked during half or more of the follow-up period than were the schizophrenics (66% vs. 18%), and to have worked at higher levels of complexity (executive/professional). Among the borderline patients at follow-up, we found ten who had become psychologists, six lawyers, five physicians, three clergymen, ten teachers, two manufacturers, and a television executive. The 99 schizophrenic patients (all but two of whom have been traced), apart from one lawyer and one accountant, were either still unemployed or else working at jobs of less complexity than was characteristic of their families of origin.

One of the factors implicated in delayed recovery or in poor outcome is substance abuse, a common accompaniment of BPD (ever since the drug epidemic began in earnest, in 1962), especially in patients under 30 years of age. As they approached 30, many of the patients lost their enthusiasm for marijuana, amphetamines, etc., or, if alcohol had been their main addiction, they conquered their habit with the help of Alcoholics Anonymous (AA).

In our series (Stone, 1990, p. 162), 37 of the BPD patients had, concomitantly, serious problems with alcohol. Of these, 10 were able to maintain a lasting relationship with AA and all are now well. But the suicide rate—7 of 37, or 19%—was over twice the level in the BPD group as a whole. Among the AA refusers, the rate jumps to 7 of 27 or 26%. More striking still: of the 13 BPD females comorbid for both alcoholism and major affective disorder (MAD), there were five suicides (38%). This combination— BPD × MAD × Alc.—constituted one of the most fatal subgroups within the entire P.I.-500, matched only by the suicide rate among BPD patients exhibiting all 8 DSM-III items. In this group of 15, there were six suicides (40%) (p. 208). Our findings are in line with those of Zilber et al. (1989), who noted that in psychiatric patients of all diagnostic groups, the suicide risk was substantially greater than in the general population and that the standard mortality rate (SMR) in those with a personality disorder who also abused alcohol or drugs was *three times* that of those who did not abuse substances (21% vs. 7%).

The third of the BPD patients who did not do well belonged to two broad categories: suicides and the chronically impaired. In the patients of our series, traced after an average of 16½ years, the suicide rate was 9% (the 17 reported by Stone et al., 1987, plus an additional suicide discovered subsequently), a rate similar to that noted by Paris et al. (1988)—of 8%. In McGlashan's series (1987) only the BPD patients with concomitant unipolar depression showed suicide rates in this range. In the large remainder the rate was 3%. The lower suicide rate in McGlashan's series is partly a reflection of the older average age (26) of the patients when first hospitalized at Chestnut Lodge, compared with that of the P.I.-500 series: the Chestnut Lodge patients had, in effect, passed through more of what is now the main age of risk (20–29) in the United States for suicide (Solomon & Murphy, 1984).

In addition to the 18 suicides within the traced BPD patients of the P.I.-500, we could identify five patients who had made suicide attempts of such lethality that their survival seemed miraculous. Two had hanged themselves in the shower-room of the hospital ward and were cut down by the nursing staff seconds before the effects would have been irreversible. One hurled himself under an oncoming subway, only to have the entire train pass over him without inflicting injury. Another, trying to die by oven-gas, was saved when the ensuing explosion blew him out of a room that was otherwise engulfed in flames. The last, having taken an overdose of heroin, was rescued in a hospital emergency room with only a minute to go before brain-death. Each of these patients responded in a manner reminiscent of Gloucester, who, when fooled by his son into thinking he had jumped off a cliff, promised, on discovering himself still alive: "Henceforth I'll bear affliction till it do cry out itself 'enough, enough,' and die" (*King Lear*, IV, vi). For each of these suicide-*manqués* the near-fatal attempt was the last: each has gone on to clinical recovery. The man who nearly died from heroin, for example, is now on the lecture-circuit for Narcotics Anonymous, speaking to groups of young people about the dangers of drug abuse.

The opposite situation also occurs: a depressed person, not intending to die, makes a suicide gesture that turns out to be fatal. Two patients in the P.I.-500 took overdoses of a sleeping compound, expecting to be rescued by the return of a roommate—who never showed up.

Factors contributing importantly to suicide in BPD patients include continuing alcohol abuse, chaotic impulsivity, and a history of parental brutality or sexual molestation (Stone, 1990a). The alcoholic BPD patients who refused AA tended to show more impatience, denial of illness, uncoopera-

tiveness, and disdain of authority. These "hidden" personality factors interacted synergistically with the traits of BPD to drive the life-trajectory downwards toward either chronic impairment or early death. In the P.I.-500
the violence commonly associated with alcohol abuse was directed mostly
against the self, though one of the alcoholic BPD females who eventually
suicided had been arrested for molesting children, and a second had torched
her apartment. One of the BPD male suicides had been jailed for arson,
and another had been violent toward his parents. The only *non*-suicided
alcoholic BPD patient with a history of violence was a woman arrested for
abusing her own child. In general, the connection between alcohol abuse
and violence is strong, as underlined in the study of Norton and Morgan
(1989): high percentages of persons exposed to alcohol have been involved
in violence (3% to 92%, depending on the series).

Table 13 shows the frequency of affective disorder, alcohol abuse, and
other variables, in relation to the 20 suicides of the P.I.-500 series who
were "borderline" by *any* criteria. Fifteen of these suicides occurred within
five years of leaving the hospital.

The chronically-impaired group consisted in addition of persistently hostile persons who undermined otherwise sustaining relationships (and often
signed out of hospital "against medical advice": McGlashan and Heinssen,
1988); of those whose self-esteem had been shattered by severe sexual or
physical abuse; of persons, many of whom were chaotically impulsive, who
never developed hobbies or work skills; and of "comorbidly" affectively-ill
(BPD × MAD) patients whose condition evolved during the follow-up

TABLE 13

The P.I.-500 Series[a]: Nineteen Suicides
in Borderline Patients

Diagnosis	N	History of affective disorder[c]	History of alcohol abuse	History of incest[d]	At least one psychiatrically ill relative[e]
BPD	18	14	7	5	8
BP Organization[b]	2	2	1	0	0

[a]Stone, M.H., 1990
[b]Kernberg, O.F., 1967
[c]consisting of atypical depression (2), unipolar recurrent depression (5), bipolar illness during follow-up
interval (1), bipolar II illness during follow-up interval (1), and solitary episodes of major affective disorder
(MAD) (4)
[d]as defined by D. Russell, 1986
[e]both parents alcoholic (2), both parents depressed, alcoholic and suicided (1), one parent depressed and
suicided (1), one parent with MAD (4)

years into uni- or bipolar affective disorders. The latter accounted for 8% of the BPD patients in the P.I.-500 series. Among the males in this series, though not among the females, BPD × MAD was associated with a doubling of the suicide risk as compared with BPD alone (18% vs. 8%). Many of the BPD × MAD males showed the personality characteristics mentioned by Benjaminsen et al. (1990) that are considered a predisposition to suicidal behavior: moodiness, pessimism, introversion, and dependency.

Evolution into schizophrenia was rare in the American series (Akiskal, 1981; Fenton & McGlashan, 1989; Stone, 1990), but reaches 20% in Scandinavia (Dahl, 1986), where admixture with schizotypal traits is more common in samples of BPD patients than is the case in the United States.

The presence of strong antisocial traits also predicted chronic impairment in BPD (Gabbard & Coyne, 1987; Stone, 1989g; Woolcott, 1985). Males are more likely to show this combined picture than are females. In the P.I.-500 series, the suicide rate among those with BPD × ASP (antisocial personality) was nearly three times that of the BPD group as a whole: 3 of 13 or 23%.

Chronic impairment was also noted when schizotypal traits were prominent in a BPD patient (McGlashan, 1986a), presumably because the key schizotypal traits (odd communication, suspiciousness, social isolation: McGlashan, 1987) interfere grossly with the creation of sustaining intimate and other relationships.

Because outcomes at long-term follow-up of BPD spanned the entire range from suicide to recovery with success in all areas of life, it becomes important to ascertain what factors might contribute to the extremes of this wide range. In the P.I.-500 series, BPD patients whose outcomes were distinctly better than the average tended to show one or more of the following attributes: (a) high intelligence, (b) unusual talent in music, art, writing, etc., (c) in the female patients: unusual attractiveness, (d) concomitant obsessive-compulsive traits, or (e) in the case of alcoholics, adherence to AA. Woolcott (1985) also includes the quality of *likeability* (similar to "+A"—*agreeableness*, in the five-factor model; cf. Chapter 6).

The value of the obsessive-compulsive traits probably lay in the self-discipline, work-orientedness, and ability to structure leisure-time constructively (similar to the "+C"—conscientiousness—factor) that are typical ingredients of the compulsive personality type. In contrast, BPD patients who are particularly sensation-seeking and dependent on other people become disorganized and anxious when alone; unless treatment succeeds in fostering self-discipline, their extramural life is a succession of calamities.

Outcomes distinctly worse than the average were noted in BPD patients with (a) a history of parental brutality, (b) a history of father-daughter incest (Stone, Unwin, et al., 1988), (c) concomitant schizotypal features, or

(d) antisocial features. The observation of Links et al. (1990) that marked impulsivity and poor premorbid functioning correlated with (continuing) poor function at two-year follow-up remains valid, in the light of long-term studies, at 10 and 20 years after initial treatment.

The correlations between outcome in borderline patients and *negative* factors, as well as some additional factors, are shown in Table 14, derived from the P.I.-500 series. Most of the correlations concern a given variable in relation to "BPD" as the standard condition, but in some instances the broader Kernberg definition of "borderline" is used. The latter definition encompasses BPD, plus a number of other nonpsychotic clinical states of intermediate severity (e.g., anorexia/bulimia; agoraphobia). In the P.I.-500 series there were an additional 93 patients who were borderline only by Kernberg, and not by DSM, criteria.

The impact of many variables is difficult to assess owing to their sheer number and also to sample differences. The coexistence of major affective illness led, for example, to a worsening of outcome in Plakun et al.'s series (1985), whereas Stone (1990) noted that, in males with BPD, affective illness was associated with a generally better outcome (though a higher suicide rate)—because in the remainder of the male patients there was an overrepresentation of antisocial comorbidity. The counterintuitive finding of Modestin and Villiger (1989) that outcome at 4½ years was similar in BPD and in other personality disorder may also be a reflection of sample peculiarities.

In the P.I.-500 series, *parental brutality* emerged, in analysis of variance, as the most important *negative* factor, i.e., as the factor with the greatest power to divert the life-trajectory downwards toward a "worse than average" outcome. This makes sense clinically. Being reared in an atmosphere of withering rejection and cruelty is likely to have more damaging effects upon the humanization of children—upon their ability to trust, love, and feel compassionate towards others—than most other traumata. Even father-daughter incest is not as uniformly shattering as parental brutality, since in some cases the daughter is the victim "merely" of betrayal and perverted love, whereas in the worst cases parental love was absent and in its place there was only sadistic exploitation.

The consistently poor outcomes noted in borderline patients who had ever been jailed (even for one day, after being caught "joyriding" in a stolen car) were related in some cases to a lifelong pattern of impulsivity and flaunting the law; in other cases, to antecedent parental cruelty, which had led to demoralization and counter-aggressivity, culminating in a persistent pattern of antisociality.

More so than most other personality-disordered patients, those with BPD are exquisitely sensitive to initial conditions (Stone, 1988a). Minor

TABLE 14

Borderline Patients of the P.I.-500: Impact of
Certain Variables upon Outcome

FACTOR	FOLLOW-UP G.A.S. Scores >60			
	N Traced	N	%	
Borderline × alcoholism × AA	10	10	100.0	More than 1½ G.A.S. deciles above average
Borderline × artistic talent	9	8	88.9	
BPD × obsessive-compulsive personality	17	15	88.2	
Borderline × attractiveness (1 SD above group mean)	25	22	88.0	
Borderline × IQ (2 SD above group mean)	18	15	83.3	
BPD female, no MAD	37	28	75.7	
Dysthymic borderlines	34	25	73.5	
Borderline × male homosexuality	13	9	69.2	
BPD × anorexia nervosa/bulimia nervosa	22	15	68.2	
BPD × MAD female	100	66	66.0	
All BPD	185	118	63.8	
Borderline females who eloped	33	21	63.6	
BPD × MAD male	27	17	63.0	
Borderline female × incest	35	22	62.9	
BPD × MDP	26	15	57.7	
BPD × alcoholism	35	19	54.3	
BPD female × incest	28	15	53.6	
Borderline × male/female homosexuality/bisexuality	23	12	52.2	
Borderline × parental brutality	30	15	50.0	
BPD female × incest with father/stepfather	22	10	45.5	More than 1½ G.A.S. deciles below average
Borderline × STP	14	6	42.8	
BPD × parental brutality	22	9	40.9	
BPD with all eight DSM items	15	6	40.0	
Borderline × firesetting	8	3	37.5	
BPD male; no MAD	24	9	37.5	
Borderline males who eloped	9	2	22.2	
BPD × ever raped	7	1	14.3	
BPD × ever jailed	8	1	12.5	
(Schizophrenia)	95	8	8.4	
BPD × ASP	13	1	7.4	

Key: G.A.S. = Global Assessment Score (Endicott et al., 1976)—an anchored rating scale (0 to 100) of overall function. Scores of 1–30 indicate clinical incapacitation; 31–50, marginal function; 51–60, "fair" (persistence of moderate symptoms and social handicaps; 61–70, "good" (mild symptoms, generally functioning pretty well); >70 clinically recovered.
Group-scores *exceeding* 1½ G.A.S. deciles (i.e., 15 points) represent statistically significant deviations from the average of the whole population.

events lead to major upsets; major events that most people take in stride lead to catastrophe. In the pathway analysis of the man who almost died of heroin overdose, we saw that he was developing normally until his mother died of cancer when he was 11. His father remarried. The stepmother was abusive and rejecting. The patient ran away from home, lived with a delinquent gang, became addicted, stole, was jailed, remanded to our unit, eloped, resumed his heroin habit, overdosed, and almost died. The near-death set in motion a favorable trend (perhaps galvanizing long-buried positive qualities into reemergence), just as the stepmother's behavior had sparked the destructive trend. If the mother had not died, his life-course might never have passed through such a turbulent phase to begin with.

Antisocial Personality

The current DSM criteria for antisocial personality (ASP) emphasize *acts* (e.g., stealing, aggressive behavior) rather than *traits*. The corresponding ICD category (301.7) lays more stress upon traits, viz., irresponsibility, callousness, affective coldness. This difference in approach may account for the poor correlation between DSM-III-R ASP and ICD-10's Dyssocial Personality (Blashfield, 1990).

In the discussion of outcome, antisocial *acts* are much easier to record in the anamnesis and to agree upon between raters than the "psychopathic" traits outlined by Cleckley (1972), viz., insincerity, mendacity, and irresponsibility. Registering these requires long personal experience with whomever the diagnostician is evaluating. The outcome studies that exist have relied almost exclusively upon the recent DSM criteria and are thus largely uniformative concerning the fate of persons exhibiting the Cleckleyan *traits* (cf. also Chapter 13).

The presence of ASP generally betokens a pessimistic prognosis and an unfavorable life-trajectory as tracked in the various outcome studies. This is no more than one would expect. Occasionally, there are reports of improvement or recovery and it is in these instances we would most want to know: had these persons originally manifested the callousness, glibness, etc., of which Cleckley spoke? Or were they persons of a more sympathetic character who got caught up transitorily in antisocial *acts*?

As for DSM-III, ASP, Gabbard and Coyne (1987) noted that of 33 patients at Menninger's so diagnosed in their survey, 19 were "completely unresponsive to treatment" (p. 1183); 21 left the hospital prematurely, and only five met initial treatment goals. Predictors of a negative response included a history of a felony arrest or of repeated lying and "conning." An *early* onset of dyssocial behavior during childhood was a worse prognostic sign than later onset (Offord & Reitsma-Street, 1983). Patients with opioid dependency did worse if they also met ASP criteria than those free of such signs (Woody et al., 1985); the case was similar with alcoholic patients (Rounsaville et al., 1987). Incarcerated rapists who did not meet ASP criteria showed less recidivism 4 years after release than did their ASP counterparts (Rice et al., 1990). In the Chestnut Lodge study, McGlashan (1986) noted that patients with BPD, BPD plus ASP traits, and BPD plus narcissistic PD traits showed similar life-trajectories. But in the ASP group, there were not sufficient antisocial traits to make an independent ASP diagnosis; the traits that were present were milder and well short of felonious acts, ruthless exploitativeness, etc.

McGlashan's findings are in accord with the outcome-patterns noted in the P.I.-500 study—namely, that a history of antisocial *acts* prior to a psychiatric hospitalization was not always indicative of a bad prognosis or of "psychopathic" personality. Many of the ASP patients in the P.I.-500 were adolescent males remanded to the unit because of violent acts or serious nonviolent crimes, alongside depression or other symptoms suggestive of psychiatric disturbance. These patients, almost all of whom were male, did uniformly poorly. But several of the males and most of the adolescent females whose antisocial acts had been less serious (truancy, shoplifting, running away from home) eventually made good adjustments. Almost invariably, these patients came from abysmal environments. They had been young persons of fundamentally decent character, forced by parental rejection or cruelty to take to the streets and survive by their wits. Some had become rebellious and while on the treatment-unit were arrogant and indifferent. They left the unit (usually against advice) as treatment failures, yet were amenable to rescue by some other agency: most often, an Anonymous group or a nonstandard church. Some simply outgrew their wildness as they rounded the turn of 30, settling down into respectable jobs and conventional lives. One such patient, 20 years later, became the mayor of a town in the Midwest; another, a manufacturer; a third, a counselor in AA.

The tendency toward spontaneous remission, such that few persons diagnosed "ASP" in adolescence would still be so diagnosed in their thirties, has also been noted in the large series of Robins and Regier (1991). In their epidemiological study, only 47% of persons diagnosed ASP had arrest records, and only 37% of a group of arrestees met DSM-III criteria for ASP.

One reason for the equivocal findings in outcome studies of ASP is the conflation, within this diagnostic heading, of both *transitory delinquents* and *continuous antisocials*. As Dilalla and Gottesman (1989) point out, there are many delinquent young persons who do *not* go on to commit criminal acts during adulthood. In contrast, the "continuous antisocials," who probably have a "higher loading of either genetic or environmental influences or both" (p. 346), show criminal activity at a younger age and persist in this pattern. ASP patients in the follow-up studies conducted by McGlashan and by our group were predominantly of the transitory delinquent type, hence the tendency toward "mellowing" as they entered their late twenties or earlier thirties.

Schizotypal Personality Disorder

Patients with schizotypal personality (STP) are rarely admitted to hospitals in the United States and have thus received less comment in American follow-up studies than have borderline or antisocial patients. In Scandinavia, where this personality type is more common, a different designation is sometimes used. Many of the adolescent inpatients who formed the basis of Aarkrog's monograph on 50 consecutively admitted "borderlines" (1981) would be schizotypal by DSM III/III-R criteria (cf. Chapter 9). In the Norwegian study of Mehlum et al. (1991), STP inpatients, when followed up three years later, were the *least* socially adjusted, employed, or self-supporting of all their diagnostic subgroups, whereas "cluster C" patients showed good global outcome and marked symptom reduction.

Among the American studies, that of McGlashan (1986a) compared 10 patients with STP with 18 in whom the traits of STP and BPD were combined. Outcomes were less favorable in the "pure" STP group than in those with BPD as well. The latter did not fare quite as well as those with BPD who were not "comorbid" for STP, whereas the pure STP patients had outcomes only slightly better than those with frank schizophrenia. STP patients showed considerable residual impairment socially and usually worked at occupations considered below their "potential" as this had been estimated during their youth. Few achieved closeness with a sexual partner and most lived as marginal "loners." Less tempestuous than affectively ill patients, the schizotypal patients seemed to have a suicide rate lower than that of patients with BPD or either schizophrenia or manic-depression (Stone, 1990), though their small number makes comparison with the more populous diagnostic groups hazardous.

Minichiello et al. (1987) reported a downward drag on the life-trajectory in patients with obsessive-compulsive disorder (OCD) *if* STP was also present: behavior and pharmacotherapy led to improvement in 16 of 19 patients with OCD alone, but in only one of 10 with OCD × STP in the original article; one in 14 (Jenike et al., 1986) in a later paper.

Evidence for viewing STP as a condition within the spectrum of schizophrenia has been presented from many sources. A schizophrenic *dénouement* is common in patients first diagnosed "STP," who showed magical thinking, suspiciousness, and social isolation (Fenton & McGlashan, 1989). In the P.I.-500 only one of 196 traced BPD patients went on to develop schizophrenia, and only one other developed a schizoaffective psychosis (Stone, 1990).

Of the 12 patients with STP × BPD in the P.I.-500, the 10 thus far traced include three recovered persons who are self-supporting and raising families, a murderer currently imprisoned, a suicide, and two chronically incapacitated persons receiving public assistance. Three others are working but severely constricted socially (one took holy orders and lives in a monastery). Those with the worst outcomes usually showed strong paranoid features as well.

Narcissistic Personality Disorder

Hospitalized patients with narcissistic personality disorder (NPD) represent a highly skewed sample, since most persons with NPD come to the attention of neither psychiatric or forensic authorities. Psychoanalysts who specialize in the treatment of narcissistic patients, such as Kohut (1971) and his colleagues, have used different and less well-defined diagnostic criteria, making comparisons with DSM-defined patients difficult. Follow-up studies by psychoanalysts working with narcissistic patients have not been carried out.

In his comparison of 17 inpatients with NPD and 33 with BPD, Plakun (1989) found that the NPD group showed a higher rate of rehospitalization at long-term follow-up than did the BPD patients, and also a poorer overall level of function and sexual satisfaction. McGlashan and Heinssen (1989) and Stone (1989b) in their series found no appreciable differences in long-term outcome in BPD patients with or without concomitant NPD, unless to the BPD × NPD combination ASP was superadded (Stone, 1989b). Of the 13 patients meeting all three criteria 12 were male; two of the 11 traced were suicides, one has been jailed for the past 20 years for multiple murder, six others are living marginal existences, and only two are now well (Stone, 1990).

As with BPD patients, those with NPD spanned the whole range of outcomes, from suicide to total recovery. One might suspect that, in this generation, young males with prominent narcissistic features (especially overweening ambition and preoccupation with wealth and power) would be particularly prone to suicide. In the currently available studies the sample sizes were too small to permit testing of this hypothesis. BPD males with depressive illness in the P.I.-500 did have a suicide rate of 18%: three times that of the males without depressive illness, and two and a half times that of BPD females (with or without concomitant depressive disorder). Narcissistic features appear to have played a role in the excess mortality: many of these males were acutely distressed over their inability, because of the underlying depressive illness, to "live up to their potential," become self-supporting, etc. — narcissistic injuries to which males in our society are especially sensitive.

Other Personality Disorders

The literature is sparse on outcome in personality disorders other than those just mentioned. The very nature of *paranoid* personality militates against the cooperation of patients with this disorder in long-term follow-up work. Patients in whom paranoid elements predominate lack the "feedback" mechanism upon which successful therapy of personality disorders depends. This mechanism consists of a collective of positive traits: introspection, humility, candor, and a willingness to acknowledge imperfections. Paranoid persons, in contrast, tend to externalize and to relate with evasiveness rather than candor.

Schizoid persons seldom seek help from the psychiatric profession; those who do seldom remain long in treatment (Stone, 1989e). The 10-year follow-up by Wolff and Chick (1981) of 22 boys, aged 5–14, with schizoid personality did not address the issue of change in function, mentioning merely that 18 still met the criteria for this disorder 10 years after initial evaluation (cf. also, Chapter 9).

The four disorders of DSM cluster C — obsessive-compulsive (anankastic), passive-dependent, avoidant, and passive-aggressive — seldom lead in and of themselves to residential treatment, let alone to incarceration. Because of the ambulatory status of most such patients, they are glimpsed with but peripheral vision by investigators pursuing long-term follow-up work. These disorders are often found in conjunction with the symptom neuroses. Tyrer et al. (1983) has demonstrated the kind of dynamic equilibrium that exists between anxiety disorders and passive-dependent personality and between obsessional neurosis and anankastic personality. Anxious, including agoraphobic (Stone, 1991), persons may, when not under stress, emerge as passive-dependent or as avoidant; forced into uncomfortable social and other situations, the anxiety symptoms resurface.

Patients in whom *avoidant* personality had been preceded by severe agoraphobia represent, as their long-term life-trajectory suggests, the severe end of the avoidant spectrum. Only two of the ten hospitalized agoraphobes in the P.I.-500 have recovered; two are still house-bound 25 years later, and the remainder lead markedly constricted lives (Stone, 1991). Patients with milder forms of phobia/avoidant personality often respond favorably to the behavioral methods pioneered by Marks (1987), such that they become less phobic and less socially withdrawn.

About the long-term fate of patients with *passive-aggressive* personality there are only anecdotal reports. Such patients often develop their personality style in response to parental intrusiveness and pressure to conform —

the response being one of covert hostility, defiance, sabotage, and general noncompliance. In the course of therapy these attitudes quickly become apparent, manifesting themselves typically as a need to prove the therapist incompetent. Given time enough, and a commitment to the process of change, the passive-aggressive patient might eventually overcome these maladaptive patterns. But many quit treatment (a passive-aggressive act in itself) before any positive changes can occur. Hence passive-aggressive personality has the reputation of being particularly resistant to treatment (Liebowitz et al., 1986).

Ironically, follow-up data are the least available on personality disorders that are the most common. For the most part, *histrionic, obsessive-compulsive, masochistic* ("self-defeating"), and *depressive* patients are ambulatory. These are the patients who have formed the bulk of the caseloads for three generations of psychoanalysts and, more recently, for therapists of psychoanalytic, behavioral, cognitive, and other orientations. Most of the literature of the short- and long-term fate of these patients is anecdotal (cf. Pfeffer, 1961; Schlesinger & Robbins, 1974). The focus is seldom on personality or "character" disorders per se, but rather on transference responses and related variables (cf. Kantrowitz et al., 1990), from which inferences about personality types and their differential outcomes cannot be drawn.

The few follow-up studies that exist of patients treated with psychoanalysis either lack systematic diagnoses of personality (or "character") or else do not present outcome data with precision. The review by Knapp et al. (1960) of 100 cases mentioned that of 27 patients considered least suitable initially, nine had obsessive and 13 had hysteric characteristics. All but one of these obsessives improved, whereas the hysterics showed wider variation in outcome—some doing very well, others poorly. In the five-to-ten-year follow-up of 183 analytic patients studied by Sashin et al. (1975), no significant differences were observed among the various diagnostic groups (predominantly hysteric, obsessive-compulsive, and depressive), but "outcome" was reported as a measure not of current function, but of whether treatment had ended (as in six out of seven cases it did) by mutual consent. The report of Weber and his colleagues at Columbia Psychoanalytic Center, though more extensive in scope than the preceding, did not analyze their results in relation to personality/character diagnosis at the outset and did not use the more common outcome scales (Bachrach et al., 1985; Weber, Solomon, & Bachrach, 1985).

With regard to *treatability*, there is considerable *indirect* evidence for positive response to therapy, within the realm of mild character and personality disorders. In Mavissakalian et al.'s study (1990a), for example, patients with obsessive-compulsive disorder showed any of a number of concomitant personality disorders. Those who responded favorably to treatment became measurably less histrionic, avoidant, dependent, and compulsive, according to standardized rating scales. Still, suicide risk is greater in those with any "personality disorder" by a factor of 3, and in those showing "neuroticism," by a factor of 2, when compared with the general population (Allebeck et al., 1988). Similarly, patients with depression alone fare better than those with concomitant personality disorders (Andreoli et al., 1989; Duggan et al., 1990).

The most persuasive evidence comes from the elegant study of Mary Smith and her colleagues (1980). They concluded, from statistical analysis of 475 studies, "Psychotherapy is beneficial, consistently so and in many different ways" (p. 183). Though their focus was on the different types of psychotherapy, the articles they reviewed included many devoted to patients with hysterical, obsessive-compulsive, passive-aggressive, "as-if" and other personality disorders. It is an inference, admittedly, but not a rash inference, to claim that patients with these personality disorders are often capable of sustained improvement. This was the general conclusion of the psychoanalytic studies of Weber and Sashin cited above.

Smith and her colleagues noted, however, that the various and competing forms of therapy they reviewed appeared *equally effective* (p. 185). Efficacy seemed to depend at least as much on certain key patient variables as on the length and variety of therapy. The key variables are, in effect, the *positive* personality traits of motivation, the strength to face weakness, the confidence to trust another person, and the flexibility to weigh and select among contingencies. These qualities, when present, can offset many of the maladaptive traits that make up the item-lists of the standard personality disorders. Paranoid, antisocial, schizoid, and sadistic, along with some borderline, narcissistic, and passive-aggressive persons are deficient in one or several of these key traits.

One could argue that, *de fortiori*, persons exhibiting the *other* disorders ought to show long-term outcomes at least as favorable as those of, say, the borderline and narcissistic patients mentioned above—if not more favorable. Indeed, one of the chief stumbling blocks to the follow-up study of the milder personality disorders is the patients' relatively good occupations and interpersonal function at the outset. What researchers are left to evaluate, years later, are *subtle* measures of satisfaction with life, quality of friendships, and the like, rather than such easily measured variables as to whether one has a job or is on public assistance, etc.

GENERAL ISSUES

Existing follow-up studies have been devoted almost entirely to the severe end of the personality disorder spectrum. In this region of the spectrum, admixture of traits with symptoms (including, in the case of ASP, unlawful acts) is routinely found. The interaction between traits and symptoms is such that the prognosis of a symptom disorder (such as an affective disorder) is worse in the presence of a personality disorder, and vice versa. Paradoxically, alleviation of certain symptoms (viz., antidepressants in a unipolar patient) often reduces the intensity of accompanying traits (such as low self-esteem, pessimism), sometimes even in the absence of supportive or other psychotherapies. Similarly, successful therapeutic work with certain traits may bring about reduction of symptoms. Depressive patients who learn to become less self-critical may, for example, become less anxious henceforth in social situations.

Outcome in all personality disorders depends in part upon the balance between maladaptive and adaptive traits, but the effects of this balance can be seen more clearly when the clinical picture is not clouded by the presence of disabling symptoms. Candor and introspectiveness were mentioned earlier as examples of positive traits. Related to introspectiveness is the willingness to accept responsibility for contributing—perhaps heavily—to the creation of one's interpersonal difficulties.

The opposite trait is *externalization*, where all blame is localized in persons other than oneself—a trait especially prominent in paranoid patients, but common as well in the antisocial/psychopathic, narcissistic, borderline, passive-aggressive, and sadistic disorders. While psychotherapy can succeed in reversing the tendency to externalize in patients with the mild forms of these disorders, the task becomes insuperable in the face of massive externalization. Premature rupture of the treatment contract is the customary "outcome" in the latter case.

There is a parallel between the concepts of externalization vs. introspectiveness and the no-longer-popular psychoanalytic terms, "alloplastic" vs. "autoplastic." Those who would mould the external world so as to suit their wishes (the "alloplastic" strategy) tend to blame, as well as to manipulate and coerce, others. Personality disorders characterized chiefly by alloplastic maneuvers are many times more resistant to treatment than are those whose approach (blaming oneself, changing oneself) is autoplastic.

The "classical" psychoneuroses that served as the inspiration for the development of psychoanalysis involve chiefly autoplastic patterns. The hysteric, obsessional, phobic, depressive, masochistic, and dependent neurotics of Freud's day suffered mainly from inhibitions that interfered with normal sexual life. Psychoanalytic therapy helped lift these inhibitions. To the extent similar patients nowadays can be diagnosed with a personality disorder, the disorder will usually be within DSM's "anxious cluster," with the exception of histrionic PD. Psychoanalytic and related methods are less well suited to the treatment of alloplastic disorders, including those personality disorders where externalization is an identifying feature. Persons whom others consider offensive or obnoxious, whether diagnosable in standard terms or not, make heavy use of alloplastic defenses, though certain clingingly dependent patients manage to be simultaneously offensive yet autoplastic and self-reproachful.

Most of the standard personality disorders may be understood as midway points along spectra at whose extremes one finds either mild traits or, at the opposite end, severe symptom disorders. This situation is illustrated in Figure 16. In this diagram, the personality disorders are presented dimensionally, in keeping with Millon's remark (1988) (cf. Chapter 1) that *personality* is our first line of (interpersonal) defense—a line which, when breached, leads to less adaptive "breakdown" symptoms. Some personality disorders are not easily visualized as belonging only to one spectrum. *Anger* and *moodiness* are both central to our current concept of BPD, for which reason this personality disorder is placed between those two spectra. Cyclothymic personality, as Kraepelin (1921) mentioned, is a blend of depressive and hypomanic attributes.

This dimensional view of personality disorders highlights the *severity* factor alluded to earlier: outcome depends on severity (i.e., how *pervasive* and how *ingrained* the maladaptive traits are) in such a way that persons with mild paranoid traits may fare better in treatment, and in life, than will persons with extremely dependent traits, despite the aura of ominousness that ordinarily surrounds the paranoid label.

As one moves toward milder expressions of personality aberrations, one departs from the medical model of illness and also from DSM and ICD. Many persons, for example, have integrated and reasonably tolerable personalities except for one or two offensive or obnoxious traits. Included here would be persons who are markedly jealous, smug, stingy, abrasive, garrulous, aimless, bigoted, boring, risqué, cynical, or vacuous (to mention but a few). Such persons do not fit comfortably into our standard nomenclature. Their traits, nevertheless, may render them just as handicapped, or more so, than some persons with diagnosable personality disorders whose overall personalities are more pleasing.

It is for this reason Woolcott (1985) stressed the prognostic importance of *likeability* (cf. the supertrait "agreeableness," Chapter 6). Opposite to *likeability* is of course *unlikeability*, which immediately invokes the thorny issues of moral judgment, raised by Blackburn (1988), and of countertransference feelings in therapists confronted by psychopathic or obnoxious persons (cf. Winnicott, 1949). Among the latter are persons who display anger more often and more intensely than other persons in similar life situations. Highly irascible persons offend coworkers and superiors, destroy intimate relationships, alienate their children, and undermine any attempts at treatment. They appear to have what Weyer (1577) called the "disease of anger." The impact of "inordinate anger" (BPD diagnostic "item") upon

Figure 16: *Spectrum Aspects of Personality Disorders*

MILD TRAIT	MORE PRONOUNCED TRAIT	PERSONALITY DISORDER			SEVERE SYMPTOM-DISORDER
shy	aloof	**SCHIZOID**	**SCHIZOTYPAL**		schizophrenic
skeptical	mistrustful	**PARANOID**			delusional disorder
restrained orderly	over-meticulous	**OBSESSIVE-COMPULSIVE** (anankastic)			obsessive-compulsive disorder
		PASSIVE-DEPENDENT			
unself-confident socially		**AVOIDANT**			phobic
		PASSIVE-AGGRESSIVE			
cranky	irritable angry	abrasive	verbally abusive	**SADISTIC**	violent; explosive
			BORDERLINE		
overreactive impulsive	unreasonable very impulsive	mercurial stormy	"impulse-ridden character"		
moody	pessimistic	**DEPRESSIVE**			unipolar depression
			CYCLOTHYMIC		
outgoing	extraverted	**HYPOMANIC**			bipolar mania
dramatic flirtatious		**HISTRIONIC**	infantile (BPD × Histrionic PD)		"hysterical psychosis"
irresponsible glib amoral	socio-pathic dyssocial		**ANTISOCIAL**	psycho-pathic	career crimnal with ASP
self-centered ambitious vain	conde-scending	**NARCISSISTIC**			manic or schizophrenic, with grandiose or Messianic delusions

outcome is great enough to cause a downward shift in the life-trajectory of BPD patients who are relatively asymptomatic—in comparison with BPD patients comorbid for eating disorders and depression—but whose anger threshold is not high.

Personality disorders (including the single-trait disturbances mentioned above) derive in part from patterns of thought and behavior that appear to be "hard-wired" into the central nervous system (in pathways that probably involve the basal ganglia "habit-memory" system: Mishkin et al., 1984) during the first five or six years of life. Heredofamilial factors play a role in many of the standard disorders (cf. schizoid PD, schizotypal PD, and some instances of paranoid PD as "spectrum" cases of the schizophrenic genotype; depressive and hypomanic personalities as attenuated forms of manic-depression: Pössl & von Zerssen, 1990). Deeply etched as these disorders are in the neurophysiological framework of our minds, it is small wonder that personality disorders are hard to modify and slow to change. The follow-up studies outlined here, even though centered on the more severe disorders, suggest nonetheless that beneficial changes can often occur, and that current treatment approaches can often be instrumental in effecting these positive changes. All methods of treatment aim at the same goal: the gradual conquest by new, more adaptive habits of thought and behavior over the preexisting, maladaptive habits—in effect, the conquest of Reason over Habit.

Part Two

THE PERSONALITY DISORDERS OF DSM

8

General Remarks on the Treatment of Personality

IN THE CHAPTERS DEVOTED TO the personality disorders of DSM (III/III-R), I have followed the schema utilized by the manual: division into clusters (A = "eccentric," B = "dramatic," and C = "anxious"). I have also included a separate chapter on pain-dependent (masochistic/self-defeating) personality disorder, given its importance in the clinical realm.

Clinicians are well aware of the fact that their personality-disordered patients rarely, if ever, present a collection of traits belonging to only one "disorder." This is especially true of borderline patients, whose personalities often appear as an amalgam of three or four or more of the standard disorders. Considerable prognostic significance attaches to the mixture of traits discernible in any given patient. Viewed against the backdrop of the five-factor model, supertrait "A" (agreeableness, or its opposite, antagonism) accounts for a large share of the variance in treatability and outcome: Patients high in agreeableness generally do better; those high in antagonism (chronically angry, bitter, hostile, contemptuous, etc.) do worse—if indeed they remain in treatment at all. Supertrait "C"—conscientiousness—is also important. To this factor belongs such traits as perseverance, earnestness, and the absence of impulsivity (a " −C" trait), all of which conduce to the success of any therapeutic venture.

THE PERSONALITY MATRIX

It may be useful to pictorialize the associations between any one personality disorder and the remaining disorders: how likely is it, having diagnosed a particular disorder, that disorders X, Y, and Z (or enough of their traits to deserve mention, even if they do not constitute enough items to establish another diagnosed disorder by DSM criteria) are simultaneously present?

In Table 15, the Personality-Type Matrix, I have shown the relative likelihoods of association (or "comorbidity"), starting with any of the standard disorders. I have added depressive, hypomanic, and self-defeating, because of their clinical importance, even though they are not among the standard 11 disorders. The numbers (from 1 to 5) are based on my clinical experience and perusal of the literature. They are therefore approximate. The research that has been done in this area has concentrated mostly on borderline and antisocial disorders. Based on their own review of the relevant literature, Widiger and Rogers (1989) were able to create a co-occurrence matrix (p. 134), focusing on the 11 standard disorders. Their results are similar to those of the matrix presented here.

GENERAL REMARKS ON THERAPEUTIC WORK
WITH PERSONALITY

Personality, especially as it begins to crystallize in its final shape at around age 30, both in its normal and abnormal characteristics, is highly resistant to change. Costa and McCrae (1986) make this point compellingly in their important paper on the stability of personality. As these authors mention, this stability is not a matter of inertia (nor, one could add, of persnicketiness or uncooperativeness). The sameness of personality is inextricably bound up with one's sense of identity, and helps " . . . provide a basis for planning a future life" (p. 415). Undesirable, especially socially obnoxious traits (abrasiveness, pomposity, callousness, deceitfulness, jealousy, etc.) contribute to the misery of those intimately connected with persons exhibiting such traits and to the discomfiture of therapists who struggle to work with them.

As time goes on, in the life of someone with highly maladaptive personality traits (or a full-fledged disorder), that person begins to reshape the world around him so as to be in greater conformity with the disorder, so as to "justify" the disorder. Avoidant persons, for example, choose as mates "phobic partners" who, for needs of their own, do not challenge them to confront hitherto anxiety-provoking situations. A woman who is afraid to drive will marry a man who doesn't think women belong behind the wheel. A pathologically jealous man may marry a mousy woman whom other men

TABLE 15

Personality-Type Matrix

Primary Type	Secondary Type													
	SZD a	STP b	PAR c	HYS d	BOR e	ASP f	NAR g	PAG h	OBC i	DEP j	AVO k	SDF l	DPR m	HPM n
SZD	X	3	3	1	1	3	3	2	3	2	2	2	2	1
STP	3	X	3	2	2	2	3	2	2	3	3	3	3	1
PAR	3	3	X	1	2	2	4	4	4	2	3	3	2	1
HYS	1	2	1	X	2	2	4	2	2	4	1	3	4	3
BOR	1	2	3	4	X	3	4	3	2	3	3	4	4	3
ASP	2	1	3	3	2	X	5	3	2	2	1	2	2	3
NAR	2	2	3	1	2	2	X	3	3	3	2	3	3	3
PAG	2	2	4	2	2	3	3	X	4	3	3	2	3	2
OBC	2	2	3	3	2	2	3	3	X	2	3	3	3	2
DEP	2	2	2	2	2	1	3	3	4	X	4	2	4	1
AVO	3	2	3	3	2	1	3	3	3	4	X	3	4	1
SDF	1	1	3	3	2	2	3	3	3	3	3	X	4	2
DPR	3	2	3	3	2	1	3	3	3	4	4	3	X	2
HPM	1	1	3	3	2	3	4	3	2	2	1	2	2	X

Note: The pattern of secondary traits for borderline PD pertains to female patients; among males, antisocial traits would be common, hysteric traits rare. The patterns outlined for depressive and hypomanic are for those with "pure" forms of these disorders; cyclothymic persons exhibit both sets of traits, in an alternating fashion.

Key: The numbers within the matrix represent the following: 1—rarely or never comorbid; 2—uncommonly comorbid; 3—occasionally to commonly comorbid; 4—quite commonly or usually comorbid; 5—if one is present, the other is almost always present also.

Abbreviations: SZD—schizoid; STP—schizotypal; PAR—paranoid; HYS—hysteric; BOR—borderline; ASP—antisocial; NAR—narcissistic; PAG—passive-aggressive; OBC—obsessive-compulsive; DEP—dependent; AVO—avoidant; SDF—self-defeating; DPR—depressive; HPM—hypomanic

don't find especially attractive. Or the same sort of jealous man may so
mistreat his wife as to drive her into the arms of another man, thus "proving," within his warped, solipsistic world, that "all women are cheats"—
thus justifying his hypervigilance and suspiciousness.

Up to a point these assortative matings work out. But if there is strong
inner *conflict*, the situation may deteriorate seriously and someone may
seek treatment: either the *agent provocateur* or the victim. For example, a
woman who is controlling and highly competitive but who at the same time
claims to want a highly assertive mate is in a difficult spot. The more
"manly" the mate, the more open conflict with her own demands. The
more controllable and passive the mate, the more her controlling side is
gratified and the more contempt she may feel toward his lack of ambition
or lack of assertiveness. Something has to give: it is the business of therapy
to help the person in this "trap" to decide whether a change in personality
(to become more accepting) or a change of mate is the more realizable goal.

Dependent persons are notorious for choosing partners who act as "en-
ablers" (in the language of the 12-step programs); once the dependent person (who is often unusually sweet and accommodating, in order to ensure
the loyalty of the partner) chooses the take-charge mate, emotional growth
screeches to a halt. Whatever the dependent person is afraid to do, the
partner does instead—thus extinguishing further impulses toward autonomy.

Left to our own devices, we fit ourselves into the world in such a way
that our personality seems more and more "right"—whether it is or not.
The already hard carborundum of personality changes slowly into diamond. One of the more extreme, though common, examples: the psychopath who commits violent acts, leading society to imprison him, where he
becomes exposed to similar antisocial persons, the next effect of which is
to produce a "hardened" criminal.

Much of personality is the latter-day manifestation of innate factors such
as temperament, constitution, and gender. The determinants of personality are, in general, "deep-seated," as Costa and McCrae phrased it:
" . . . given an opportunity, individuals revert to their 'natural' selves"
(1986, p. 418).Therapists who aim at the amelioration of those with serious problems in the realm of personality come to realize that there is a
layering to psychopathology: first we see symptoms (if any are present);
when symptoms are dispelled, we confront the personality layer. This layer
itself divides into two skeins: one that is more *environment*-related and
more modifiable. Underneath this we encounter a skein relating primarily
to *innate* sources (but which also includes certain aspects of *character*, e.g.,
firm or else slippery moral values). This latter group of traits is the least
modifiable therapeutically.

The Symptom Layer

As for the symptom layer, patients with a personality disorder involving mostly one of the DSM clusters will tend, under stress, to show symptoms related to that cluster: cognitive aberrations (suspiciousness, eccentric or allusive thought, etc.) in the case of a cluster A disorder; impulsivity in the cluster B disorders; and one or another form of anxiety in those with a cluster C disorder.

One could add that patients with one of the temperaments associated with manic-depression may at times show depressive, irritable, or hypomanic symptoms (or any combination of the three). There would appear to be a dynamic equilibrium between certain constellations of personality traits and corresponding forms of manic-depressive illness. As Akiskal et al. (1983) underline, bipolar illness often " . . . arise[s] from the soil of extraverted, cyclothymic and related dysthymic temperamental disorders" (p. 808). Many such persons are driven "workaholics." Similarly, unipolar depression is often linked with preexisting introversion.

Alnaes and Torgersen (1990) make a still finer distinction, having found that patients with pure major depression or pure anxiety disorders showed certain neurotic traits — self-doubt, introversion, oversensitivity — but less so than patients suffering from major depression *and* non-panic/anxiety disorders. Those with the latter combination scored particularly high on scales of dependence and emotional instability as well; they were the most apt to show "oral" and obsessive traits. Meanwhile, a number of investigators have shown that in patients with depression, high scores on "neuroticism" and obsessionality correlate with overall outcome and chronicity (cf. Duggan et al., 1990).

Personality-disordered patients who show target symptoms amenable to medication are apt to benefit from a drug known to be effective within their corresponding DSM cluster. Those with severe cognitive dysfunction (schizotypals, a few paranoid patients) may benefit from neuroleptics, usually in low dosage. Borderline patients are apt to show a combination of depression, anger, and impulsivity: depending on the relative weights of these features, antidepressants and mood regulators (viz., lithium, carbamazepine, valproate) may be useful. (This is discussed in greater detail in Chapter 11.)

For those in cluster C with disabling symptoms, anxiolytics and antidepressants are often useful not only in alleviating the symptoms but also in helping to correct the underlying personality traits. For example, an avoidant patient whose self-confidence is so low as to render ordinary social gatherings intensely anxiety-provoking may feel much more comfortable on a regimen of alprazolam — so much so, as to be able to engage in conversations with persons he might have shied away from before. This in itself does not automatically heighten self-confidence, but it clearly paves the way for positive interactions with others (something that was hitherto impossible). These positive experiences, in turn, can eventually bolster self-confidence, in effect setting up a positive feedback system; this gradually reverses the vicious circle in which the patient had previously spun.

Similarly, some patients with cyclothymic or hypomanic personalities, prone to overspending, sensation-seeking activities that threaten to get out of control (promiscuity, substance abuse, etc.), and the like, respond well to lithium. Their thermostat is lowered, so to say, such that these tendencies are curbed, even without any examination of childhood antecedents or dynamics. Actually, discussion along those lines might not be germane to the issue anyway, since the abnormal personality traits are mobilized much more by "biology" than by conflicts in early life. This brings us to the topic of the personality/temperament layer.

The Personality/Temperament Layer

Once symptoms are brought under control, therapy shifts its focus to personality. There are often two skeins to this layer: one relating to traits that do *not* seem to be the latter-day expressions of innate tendencies; the other relating to just such tendencies. If a patient were self-effacing, for example, this might link up with having been humiliated repeatedly as a child. This might have more to do with the early environment than with temperament. But being phlegmatic, or intense, or pessimistic, or super-vivacious, or irritable—these traits might very well be derivatives of temperament and as such not likely to change much at all, no matter what conflicts are unearthed and eventually resolved. If the temperament aspects are not only clearly present but also offensive, they cry out to be brought under better control during the course of treatment. (*Example:* the boyfriend of a patient of mine was a man with a highly irritable temperament. In a fury because she didn't have supper on the table "on time" one evening, he threw a coffee mug at her, breaking a finger. He was in treatment with someone else at the time, and, as I heard from my patient, his therapist then dropped all talk of the man's "father-complex," dwelling instead on his outrageous behavior.)

Once therapists and patients accept that there is no quick cure for problems in personality or temperament, both will be operating on a more realistic plane. As Costa and McCrae mention: human nature is by no means easily changed; therapists would do better to think of effecting modest improvements rather than a "cure" (1986, p. 421). The therapist who works with personality disorders is more cabinetmaker than carpenter. We do not build and reshape so much as polish and sand down with #600 paper: with luck and elbow-grease we can smooth the surface. The shape stays as it was.

Still, this sanding down can accomplish a great deal. So long as the personality is more than half acceptable to others (something hard to measure precisely), treatment can bring about modifications that render someone much easier to live with or to work with. This can occur with just *minor* changes, which scarcely affect the basic personality profile. It is a question of thresholds: the fundamental nature of the personality will remain unaltered, but the intensity of the more bothersome attributes may lessen. One can become less pessimistic, less disdainful, less reckless, less irascible, more accepting (and therefore less impatient) with one's mate, etc. One could plot the final result as one does the MMPI: similar peaks and valleys, but each one lower in amplitude. Figure 17 shows how this might look for a hypothetical case.

One can envision the patient of Figure 17 as someone with borderline PD, whose most striking features at the outset were depressive, avoidant, and irritable; less noticeable but still bothersome traits were in the hysteric, paranoid, dependent, and narcissistic dimensions. At the end of treatment, the personality profile was, in its contours, just the same as it was at the beginning, but the amplitudes of the negative traits were lower. In particular, the patient was less irritable and thus less likely to alienate others; also, less avoidant and dependent, and for those reasons less frustrated. Under ideal treatment circumstances, modest quantitative changes can spell impressive qualitative changes for the better, even while the basic personality tendencies remain pretty much as they were.

A PRAGMATIC APPROACH TO THE TREATMENT OF PERSONALITY ABNORMALITIES: THE PLACE OF ECLECTICISM

Therapists conducting classical psychoanalysis or analytically oriented psychotherapy have the task of fostering a therapeutic alliance. Absent this alliance, therapeutic work will tend to run aground. We owe the concept of therapeutic alliance to a number of analytic writers, especially Zetzel (1956) and Leo Stone (1961) (the latter using the term "physicianly commitment"). Ralph Greenson (1967) emphasized the real or rational aspects of the therapist-patient relationship under the heading of the "working alliance." The evolution of the concept is well presented by M. and E. Shane (1992). The real (as opposed to transference) relationship has been defined recently by Kernberg (1988a) in this way:

Figure 17: *Personality Trait Schema Showing Treatment Effects*

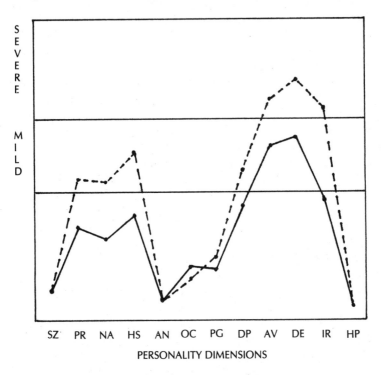

PERSONALITY DIMENSIONS

- - - - - - - -Personality Profile at the Beginning of Treatment

————— Personality Profile at the End of Treatment

Key: SZ—schizoid; PR—paranoid; NA—narcissistic; HS—hysteric; AN—antisocial; OC—obsessive-compulsive; PG—passive-aggressive; DP—dependent; AV—avoid-ant; DE—depressive; IR—irritable; HP—hypomanic

. . . the analyst as an interested, objective, but concerned and sympa-thetic listener who respects the patient's autonomy, and the patient as one who expects to be helped to increase his own understanding of his unconscious conflicts. (p. 483)

Patients seeking help because of painful symptoms or other forms of neurotic suffering are perhaps predisposed to enter into a working alliance, since they are apt to be highly motivated to overcome their distress. They may give their therapist the "benefit of the doubt" in the beginning, even before they have had the time to assess the therapist's trustworthiness and efficacy. When the focus is on areas of personality or temperament, the situation may be very different. This is especially true when a patient who has little in the way of "neurotic suffering" is coaxed (by a relative, for example) to seek treatment for problems in personality that bother the relative a great deal but affect the patient hardly at all. (I recall in this connection working—briefly—with a man referred by a colleague who was treating his wife, who complained of his philandering. He liked his philandering just fine and any hopes of "treatment" died aborning.)

When the personality/temperament layer is reached, at all events, the therapist is now dealing with (largely) ego-syntonic aspects of the self, which the patient will defend mightily. The efficacy of interpretation and clarification, in this context, may be seriously compromised. Therapists will have to rely upon compassionate persuasion (that there is a need for change). This will not work unless there is a positive attitude toward the therapist. In order to effect this positive attitude, the therapist will need wisdom, objectivity, but above all, a mixture of sympathy and empathic accuracy. Perhaps this helps explain why therapeutic work with unremittingly hostile or psychopathic persons succeeds so seldom: patients of this sort destroy the therapist's sympathy, and with it, the working alliance.

Fashioning a therapeutic alliance with patients whose clinical picture involves personality or temperament only, without accompanying ego-dystonic systems, will probably require supportive techniques, as the first step. Of these the compassionate persuasion mentioned above is the most important. This is similar to what Spillane (1987) meant by "noble rhetoric." With some patients, analytic interpretations may serve adjunctively in this endeavor, since they may help resolve certain resistances or conflicts that had initially blocked receptivity to the need for behavioral changes. I refer here to behavior that either offends others or that clearly defeats the patient's own stated goals.

Problems in personality (including those based on temperament) await, for their resolution, the formation of more adaptive attitudes and behavioral patterns: new habits conquering old ones. This can seldom be rushed and requires that the patient, via exercise of will, gain cognitive control over hitherto maladaptive tendencies. It is no surprise that, in an era when psychiatry is paying more attention to personality—and when there is probably more action-oriented psychopathology than a generation ago—*cognitive* and *behavioral* techniques are being developed and warmly accepted by the therapeutic community. Even so-called classical psychoanalysts have always, and unconsciously, interacted from time to time in ways that partake of what behaviorists do on purpose. One has only to consider the differences in voice intonation on the part of an analyst hearing a patient talk about meeting " . . . this great-looking girl, in a singles bar; she used to be a call-girl, but now she just has a regular job . . . " (Analyst: "OOOOoooh") vs. meeting " . . . this great-looking girl in my law-school class: her dad's the dean . . . " (Analyst: "AAAAaaah!). And of course there are much less subtle interventions, as described in the chapter on avoidant PD—where at a certain stage in the therapy, analysts have always found themselves *urging* such patients to confront the situations they had been at pains to sidestep before—or else the analysis will bog down.

The eclectic approach that is usually necessary in treating problems in personality (single maladaptive traits as well as full-fledged disorders) consists, then, of supportive interventions (useful in fostering a therapeutic alliance), psychoanalytically informed interventions (useful in resolving negative transferences at the outset), and cognitive-behavioral interventions (useful in development of new habits and attitudes). Special interventions, such as the use of medications or of group therapy, will often be necessary as well.

The approach I have just sketched is not the only combination that might prove effective. It is an approach I recommend simply because, as a reflection of my own background (which happens to include psychoanalytic training), I am most familiar with it. Others will fashion an eclectic therapy derived from similar sources, but with a different emphasis. For instance, Aaron Beck, his colleagues, and therapists they have trained emphasize cognitive/behavioral techniques and have an impressive record in this domain of treatment. Bypassing detailed exploration of childhood experiences, adherents of this school focus on current life and urge their patients, in a very practical manner, to weigh the consequences of handling stressful situations in the "old" way vs. any one of several more adaptive ways that emerge from discussion between therapist and patient.

There are many personality constellations whose early psychodynamics are easily reconstructed by psychoanalysis, which yet remain irremediable by analytic treatment alone. Personalities permeated by *envy* are a good example. Perhaps the envy arose out of parental preference for a sibling, perhaps out of severe deprivation. Talking about the rivalry or the deprivation will, by itself, lead nowhere. Supportive and behavioral interventions directed at helping the patient achieve or obtain (by rightful means such as hard work) what he earlier envied can reduce this envy to manageable proportions. It is of interest that, as Angus Wilson (1962) reminds us, envy is the only one of the "morbid appetites" that " . . . knows no gratification save endless self-torment" (p. 11). As for the trait of pessimism—often enough an expression of depressive temperament but sometimes the derivative of a crushing environment—I have seldom seen improvement except in the similarly roundabout way of helping the patient to succeed again and again and again, both in the areas of life where discouragement was the greatest and in other areas—until the patient's cognitive powers at last overwhelm the old pessimistic way of thinking.

It is important to remember that, with personality disorders and their related but less serious conditions, patients with mostly *likeable* personalities, irrespective of the particularities of their trait-profile, will tend ultimately to do well. Lamentably, the reverse is also true: those with unlikeable personalities will tend to do poorly. In the grey zone in between are patients whom some therapists find likeable and easy to work with, while other therapists have the opposite reaction. Such patients will, and by all means should, switch and change until they find someone whom they like and who likes them. To remain in an unhappy combination (out of inertia or misplaced loyalty) is self-defeating, and only adds one more maladaptive trait to those which prompted the quest for treatment in the first place.

Costa and McCrae's cautionary note is well-taken: "The long-term success of therapy may prove to be more a function of the person than of either the presenting problem or the therapy" (1986, p. 419). As a corollary, we can add that successful treatment of personality will also include the attribute of the ability to change (for the better) what *can* be changed and to *accept* what cannot be changed—not only in oneself but also in those with whom one's intimate life is lived. The treatment of personality should always aim at that most important, ultimate goal—best captured by the Japanese concept of "wa"—*harmony.*

Cluster A

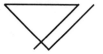

Eccentric Disorders

9

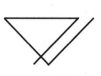

Schizoid and Schizotypal
Personality Disorders

ALTHOUGH THEY ARE DEPICTED as separate entities in DSM, *schizoid* and, *schizotypal* personality disorders may with some justification be described here within the same chapter. We need not impose upon ourselves, as does DSM, the constraint of being "atheoretical." There is evidence from various family studies (cf. Chapter 3) of an overrepresentation, in the close relatives of schizophrenics, of persons with either schizoid or schizotypal personalities. These disorders, that is, appear to be valid members of the schizophrenia "spectrum." Fairbairn (1952) envisioned this spectrum as harboring schizoid PD at the least severe end; frank schizophrenia at the most severe end.

The salient characteristic of schizoid PD is *aloofness*: a shyness in which there is neither the desire for nor enjoyment in close relationships (the first item of the DSM description). This type of shyness is distinct from that of the *avoidant* person—who wishes for closeness but is too afraid of the possible adverse consequences of intimacy to become involved with other people. Schizoid persons tend to function in a stable manner, albeit marginally, choosing solitary occupations (like that of night-watchman or key-punch operator during the "graveyard" shift), navigating a zigzag course through life, such that there is neither joy nor catastrophe. Greta Garbo

169

may, or may not, have exemplified this condition, but she certainly gave it its slogan: "I vant to be alone."

Schizotypal persons tend to be shy or at least ill at ease with others, and thus have some "schizoid" qualities, but in addition they are *eccentric*, which is the most distinguishing characteristic of this personality type. Schizotypal persons are more susceptible to psychotic episodes and to peculiarities of thought and behavior (manneristic, superstitious beyond what is typical for their subculture, etc.) of a sort that may interfere with their life goals and occupational ambitions. Consequently, they are much more apt to seek psychotherapeutic help than are schizoid persons. The latter are seldom seen in any "portal of entry" of the mental health system, whether clinic, hospital or private office.

Another reason for discussing these two personality types under the same heading—besides the likelihood of their being phenotypes of (mild) genetic loading for schizophrenia—is their frequent interrelatedness and conceptual overlap. Wolff, Townshend et al. (1991), for example, noted that, in their follow-up study (approximately 18 years later) of 32 "schizoid" children, three-fourths later met DSM-III criteria for schizotypal PD, and two had gone on to develop schizophrenia.

Diagnoses of personality disorders in children often rely on criteria different from those of adult disorders, since their elements may not yet have crystallized or taken their (adult) recognizable form. Wolff and Cull (1986) regarded as core features at the outset (when the children in their sample were about 9 years old): *solitariness, impaired empathy and emotional detachment, increased sensitivity (approaching paranoid suspiciousness), unusual or odd styles of communicating, and rigidity of mental set (viz. single-minded pursuit of special interest)* (p. 677). The "odd communication" item is currently associated with schizotypal PD, so it is perhaps not surprising that so many of their "schizoid" children were seen as schizotypal as adults. It would be of interest to know how many of these "schizoid" children did *not* manifest odd communication or other eccentric attributes, yet still emerged as schizotypal at follow-up.

Many of the "borderline" children and adolescents treated by Tove Aarkrog (1981) and her colleagues in a long-term residential unit in Copenhagen also had schizoid and schizotypal features. Nine of their 50 patients showed evidence, either on neurological or psychological testing, of brain damage, raising three questions: what percentage were only pheno*copies* (i.e., showed "schizotypy" that really stemmed from organic sources), how many owed their abnormalities to genetic factors alone, and in how many cases was a "silent" predisposition to schizotypy nudged into clinical recognizability by perinatal damage?

Before turning our attention to clinical and treatment aspects of schizoid and schizotypal personalities, it may be useful to view them in relation to the whole terrain of abnormal personality. If schizotypal PD can be seen as an intermediate condition between schizoid PD and schizophrenia, schizoid PD can itself be seen as a more intense expression of the still wider phenomenon of "introversion," of which Jung (1921) spoke, or of the "schizoid temperament" sketched in great detail by Kretschmer (1922), or of "ectomorphy" as conceived by Kretschmer's disciple, the constitutional psychologist, Sheldon (1940, 1954). Sheldon felt there was an association between thin body build and tendencies to inwardness, self-consciousness, social awkwardness, and aloofness; i.e., to introversion and schizoid personality.

Kretschmer's "Schizoid Temperament"

In his *Körperbau und Charakter* (Body-build and Character) Kretschmer classified people according to three broad types: asthenic, athletic, and pyknic, similar to the concepts of thin, muscular, and fat, respectively, or, in Sheldon's language, ectomorphic, mesomorphic, and endomorphic. Noting that schizoid persons were often thin and not very muscular, he felt that whatever genetic forces led to this "asthenic" constitution also predisposed one to develop the "schizoid" constellation of personality traits. He described this constellation in the following way:

> "Cycloid" [i.e., manic-depressive-like] persons are straightforward and of an uncomplicated nature, direct in their expression of feelings, natural and undisguised on the surface, such that they can be correctly evaluated by just about everyone. Schizoid persons have a surface, but also a deeper layer. On the surface, they may be brutally frank, or grumpy and vague, or sarcastically ironic, or shy as a mollusk, silent and withdrawn. What is the layer underneath this mask? It can be a nothingness, the black, hollow nothingness of an emotional zombie . . . or there may be a cold soul-lessness. Some schizoid people are like the seemingly barren Roman villas that have their shutters closed to the blazing sun, yet where celebrations go on, in their muted inner lights. . . . There are schizoid persons we can live with for ten years, and still we cannot say that we *know* them. (p. 113, my translation.)

As for the actual traits shown by schizoid people, Kretschmer's list mostly resembles that of DSM's definition: unsociable, reserved, quiet, humorless, bashful, shy, overly sensitive, tractable, and easily startled. He also includes the trait of eccentricity that we currently categorize with "schizotypal."

Figure 18 portrays Kretschmer's views of the schizoid and cycloid temperaments as polar opposite tendencies, which one might place toward the extremes of a bell-curve having to do with relatedness-to-others. In reality, one might want to modify this oversimplified picture. The temperaments associated with manic-depression—as outlined by Kraepelin around the same time Kretschmer wrote his monograph—are not all "opposite" to schizoid. Hypomanic and cyclothymic persons do tend to be outgoing or "extraverted," but those with "depressive" temperament (cf. dysthymics, depressive personality in the current nomenclature) are more apt to be introverted. People who do not know them well often mistake the painful shyness and self-consciousness of the "depressive" for the aloofness of the true schizoid. As depicted in Figure 18 "pure" schizoid persons are seldom depressive; in reality, however, one may encounter schizotypal patients who have a marked depressive component.

Mixed schizoid/schizotypal pictures are common in any group of patients identified as schizoid (see Figure 19). Obsessive-compulsive features are common in either, as are paranoid traits. In forensic work, one may encounter schizoid and antisocial traits in common (cf. Wolff & Cull, 1986), as in the "schizoid psychopaths" mentioned by Gallwey (1985). In the biographies of serial killers alluded to in Chapter 21 about one in four are schizoid psychopaths: unempathic, cold, detached, as well as psychopathic. Several, but by no means all, have the "asthenic" build Kretschmer (1922) emphasized, though none is as thin as the "schizoid psychopath" photographed in Kretschmer's first illustration (see Figure 20).

Figure 18: *Distribution of Temperamental Types Based on Kretschmer's* Körperbau and Charakter

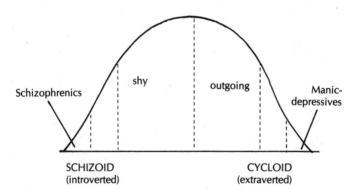

Figure 19: *Areas of Overlap Related to Schizoid Personality*

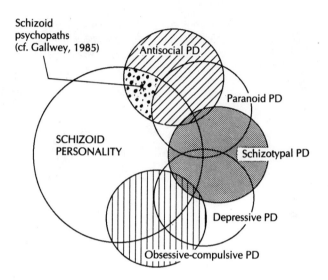

EPIDEMIOLOGY

Schizoid PD, in epidemiological studies of prevalence, is usually the least commonly diagnosed personality disorder. In 200 randomly selected subjects from the general population in Britain, for example, only one (0.5%) was so diagnosed, according to the Personality Assessment Schedule of Tyrer, Alexander, and Ferguson (Casey, 1988). Even in their review of eight studies based on assessments of outpatients and inpatients, Widiger and Rogers (1989) did not find prevalence rates much higher than this: rates varied from 0 to 8%, but most often were 1%.

Shifting standards in category-based diagnosis help explain the low incidence of schizoid PD, as Widiger and Rogers point out: [many] "patients previously diagnosed as schizoid by DSM-II criteria are now diagnosed by DSM-III criteria with avoidant or schizotypal PD" (p. 134). These authors also mention that the newer criteria are prejudicial to the diagnosis of schizoid PD, since few people are as completely lacking in warm, tender feelings, or as indifferent to others, as the contemporary criteria seem to

Figure 20: *Photographs of Two Men Exemplifying the*
*"Asthenic" (Schizoid) Somatotype**

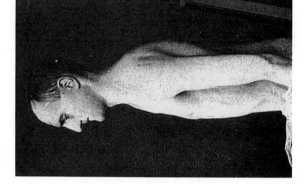

Abb. 2. Asthenischer Typus. Profil.
(Schizophrenie.)

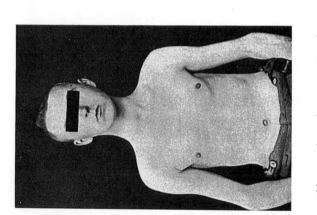

Abb. 1. Asthenischer Typus, Frontal.
(Schizoider Psychopath.)

*From Kretschmer, *Körperbau und Charakter*, 1922

insist on. Perhaps for reasons of this sort, *schizotypal* personality is more commonly diagnosed—about as commonly, in Widiger and Rodgers' survey, as histrionic or avoidant personality.

Cultural factors enter fairly prominently into the equation: the patients whom clinicians in the Scandinavian countries are currently calling "borderline," using DSM-III as their guide, are more prone to show admixture of schizoid/schizotypal traits than would be noticeable in American samples of borderline patients. Pronounced shyness, reserve, and muted expressions of emotion are more culturally "syntonic" than these qualities are in the U.S., where borderline patients are, on average, more tempestuous. Schizoid comorbidity in cases of BPD was rare (only 2%) in the (American) samples surveyed by Widiger and Rogers, though schizotypal comorbidity was not: 24% (1989, p. 134). In my experience in Sweden and Denmark, however, schizotypal comorbidity in BPD was considerably more frequent.

To some extent any such epidemiological investigations of personality disorders in this domain become further complicated by issues concerning etiology. Precisely because DSM is atheoretical, "schizotypal" PD should, for example, be diagnosed if the criteria are met, irrespective of whether the clinician believes a given patient developed this personality type via the more customary route of "risk genes for schizophrenia" or through unrelated factors. If the latter happened to be severe traumata in early life, certain clinicians will diagnose post-traumatic stress disorder, omitting mention of the schizotypal PD (such as would be picked up if a standardized personality instrument had been utilized). Since the etiological underpinnings of these disorders have implications for optimal therapy, a comment on these underlying factors is in order.

PHENOTYPE VS. PHENOCOPY
VS. GENOPHENOCOPY

In a recent comprehensive essay on schizophrenia, Paul Meehl (1990) raises an intriguing question regarding this disorder, for which, ordinarily, a genetic factor is a necessary, though not always sufficient, precondition. He speaks of this specific factor as the "schizogene"; for the moment whether this will turn out to be a single dominant gene or a polygenic system need not concern us. The common phenotype stemming from this "schizogene," from the standpoint of personality, consists of reduced pleasure capacity ("hypohedonia") and introversion. "Suppose," Meehl argues, "someone lacking the schizogene has a heavy loading of polygenes for submissiveness, hypohedonia, anxiety, and introversion; is traumatized as a child; and has a run of bad luck as an adult." Such a person, Meehl contends, " . . . has a good chance to present a clinical syndrome sufficiently close to true schizophrenia . . . to be so diagnosed" (p. 53). Meehl calls cases of this sort "genophenocopies" because the end result is not only a phenocopy (i.e., imitation schizophrenia), but comes about partly under the influence of genes (rather than just from environmental factors) that are *not* those predisposing to *true* schizophrenia.

These complexities are illustrated in Figure 21. In the domain of true schizophrenia, schizotypal PD, schizoid PD, and many instances of marked introversion may be understood as occupying orbits at correspondingly greater distances from the schizophrenic "epicenter." In a neighboring domain, a confluence of factors conduces to the development of a certain number of schizotypal personalities—some phenocopies, stemming from adverse environment (viz., sexual abuse, extreme neglect), and some genophenocopies, as in Meehl's description. Probably there is even some intersection of these worlds, in the sense that some unfortunate persons harbor both genetic liability to true Sz *and* combined genetic/environmental liability of the kind that creates copies of schizotypal PD. A proportion of patients with "genetic" schizotypal PD have, for example, also been incest victims, been crushingly humiliated by caretakers, etc.—and thus are bur-

Figure 21: *Clinically Diagnosable Schizotypal Personality Disorder as the Amalgam of SZ-Phenotype + [Phenocopies and "Genophenocopies"]*

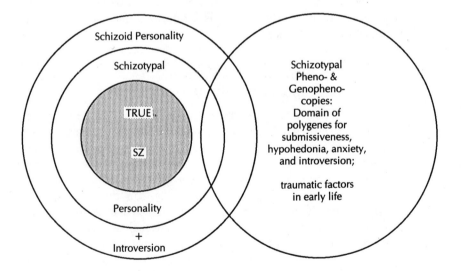

dened with a "double dose" of the factors capable of engendering this personality disorder.

The two circles in the Venn diagram of Figure 21 also answer to Kendler's observation (1985) that, as for *schizotypal* PD, the current concept is a blend of two traditions: one emphasizing genetics, where the disorder is seen as a nonpsychotic condition showing up in family studies of schizophrenic index cases; the other reflecting descriptive, clinical traditions, where certain patients with cognitive slippage, introversion, etc., are diagnosed "pseudoneurotic" or "borderline" schizophrenic, without much attention being paid to whether these patients happen to have clear-cut schizophrenic relatives (cf. Meijer & Treffers, 1991).

Meanwhile, Kendler, Ochs et al. (1991) present evidence from twin studies that inherited factors are important in the whole domain of schizotypy, both in the predominantly "positive symptom" and in the predominantly "negative symptom" variants. "Negative symptom" schizotypy was correlated with anhedonia and with attentional and eye-tracking dysfunction. Neurophysiological testing for eye-tracking dysfunction might presumably be helpful in discriminating between those cases of schizotypal PD stemming from genes specific for schizophrenia and those representing phenocopies.

CLINICAL EXAMPLES OF SCHIZOID AND SCHIZOTYPAL PATIENTS

A "Phenotypic" Schizoid Patient

Samuel* was 26 when he came for consultation at the urging of his father. Concerned that his son had done little with his life since graduating college, the father was worried that Samuel would end up like his mother—a schizophrenic woman who had been in and out of hospitals, and whom the father had divorced when Samuel was about 15. Samuel was now living with his father, working as a messenger for a company where, before his retirement, the father had been an executive. Samuel had no friends, no social activities, and no real interests or hobbies apart from collecting old magazines. He had never dated. On rare occasions he would go to a movie with one or another messenger-boy from the company—the only pretense he made at being with other people.

*Names and initials have been changed in all cases.

Samuel came dutifully to the consultation but saw little point in the idea of therapy. He was not happy, by any means, but neither was he significantly depressed. His life was routinized and boring, but manageable; the idea of working in therapy in order to get more comfortable with, or closer to, people seemed an insuperable task, and not one for which he had any real motivation.

In the four months I worked with this man I learned some things about his past that made it clear that there was an overlay of avoidance superimposed on his schizoid nature. His father was a mild-mannered, placid person, but his mother was irascible and argued constantly with her husband up through the time of their divorce. Occasionally she would turn her wrath against Samuel, once locking him in a closet for 10 hours as a punishment for some childhood peccadillo.

In one of the earlier sessions he reported the following dream: "I am in some hospital. My mother had done something 'crazy' to me, and I did something back to her: I gave her a shove. A nurse then tells me I must go to the basement floor where the craziest patients were. A doctor said I didn't have to be there, so I tell the elevator guy to let me off on the correct floor. I was in my underwear. The ground was littered with pieces of glass."

He associated the "basement floor" to "getting to the bottom of my mind." A scary process (area littered with glass)—all the more so, since his mother wound up several times in mental hospitals: would he end up like her?

In another dream, he saw himself as " . . . Superman being chased by some guys: they grab me but I escape. I take a short-cut through some school where there are picture of kids with V.D., like maybe part of a sex-education course."

He said that in that dream he had wanted to hitchhike in order to get away from his pursuers. But this was uncomfortable "because I hate to have to get to know people, to strike up conversations with people." He felt part of his difficulty in connecting up with people emotionally was a "learned thing," stemming from his parents, who as he put it, never expected any fun in life, never enjoyed life. I was also a "pursuer," in the sense that I was trying to get to know him, which he experienced as an unwelcome intrusion. In the last dream he reported, shortly before he interrupted treatment, he was " . . . running toward my grandmother's house, dressed only in pajama bottoms, and not having the key, as I was being chased by madmen. But they were weak and I was able to subdue them." Again, the theme of exposure and the threat of being controlled by others— here, his father and myself, who "force" him into therapy. Sex was seen as dirty (as the "kids with V.D." dream) and to be avoided.

A "Phenotypic" Schizotypal Patient

Sandra, when she first came for treatment at the age of 27, presented with referentiality, marked anxiety in social situations and in getting along with coworkers, eccentric behavior, and paranoid ideation. She had no close female friends and only one male friend, and though the latter was a sexual relationship, she revealed almost nothing to him about her past. She had many strange beliefs involving astrology, foods, and medicines.

Her mother and a maternal uncle were both hospitalized at various times for schizophrenia; her one sibling (a brother) was paranoid, eccentric, and had never been able to work; when Sandra was 30, he too was hospitalized.

During their early years, their mother was neglectful to both her children, at times thoughtlessly cruel—wandering away from them in crowded department stores, forgetting about their lunch-pails as they were going off to school, etc.

Sandra had only one friend during her adolescence: someone who shared her faddishness about foods and her beliefs in astrology. Girls excluded her from their school clubs. She never understood why they rejected her, though it is probable that they considered her "weird" because of her inability to make small talk and her voice-pattern: a flat, high-pitched, stilted-sounding monotone that made her come across as mannered and insincere. Added to this peculiarity of speech was her tendency to skip from topic to topic abruptly, giving equal emphasis to each, such that it was difficult to distinguish the trivial from the important. From a therapeutic standpoint, this was particularly bedeviling, since it strained one's intuitive capacities to the uttermost just to figure out what was really bothering her or what was the "main theme" on any particular day.

Her empathic skills were very limited, leading her to comment at times that she found people and their motives completely puzzling: "I can't connect up with them. If they invite me to lunch with them, I can't seem to join in the conversation or else I say the wrong thing, so after a while they don't invite me anymore and I eat by myself." If a teaching supervisor wore a dour expression walking down the hall, Sandra assumed the supervisor was dissatisfied with her work, even though it might be a person who was not even assigned to her department. She tended to be surly and "superior" sounding when asking for vacation requests and the like—and often didn't get what she wanted because of having alienated the people whose favor she needed. This reinforced her notion that the world was pretty much against her.

Though considered a knowledgeable teacher, she had no charm or patience with the children (who often made fun of her schoolmarmishness and mannerisms) and was eventually given a semi-administrative job where little interaction with others was necessary. With boyfriends, she was comfortable about having sex, but made such fussy and endless-seeming preparations (doing her fingernails in the bathroom for half an hour, etc.) that the men lost the mood and usually ended the relationship after a few months.

More striking than her empathic difficulties was a curious inability to grasp what one might call the statistics of everyday life. Travel was a great burden, since she felt it necessary to plan for all possible contingencies. She once went to Nice on an August vacation packing her winter overcoat, because, as she reminded me, "There was a cold spell there in the '50s and it could happen again." Furthermore, she sent a packet of clothes on ahead to the hotel because, "What if my baggage got stolen?" She had great difficulty, in other words, aligning her behavior in harmony with the expectable, in contrast with the remotely possible—all thinkable events being in her mind equally probable.

This tendency asserted itself with a man she had once been dating, in a way that also told something about her suspiciousness. As she returned from a movie they had seen, she noticed that one of her slippers was missing. During her session the next day she was in a fury about the slipper, claiming that her boyfriend had stolen it and that she was going to give him hell. I said, "You best not do that or he'll think you've gone over the edge!" "Well, I looked *everywhere*," she told me. I asked her to think what on earth a man would do with one lady's slipper? Two, you could sell for a few pennies. But *one*? Unless he's a shoe fetishist, I said, there's nothing in it for a man to swipe a girlfriend's slipper, since he'd risk losing her if she found out. I suspected the slipper would turn up, and warned her again not to alienate her friend by accusing him of something so unlikely. A few days later she sheepishly informed me that the slipper had indeed turned up, underneath a sofa, where it had apparently been dragged by her cat, whose teeth marks were still plainly visible.

Another manifestation of her cognitive peculiarities, of a sort that one encounters with some regularity in schizotypal patients, was the impairment in "lateral learning"—the difficulty in applying a lesson learned in one situation to future situations that were comparable. One example of this concretism showed itself when she would enter my waiting room and plop a wet umbrella onto the persian rug, even though there was a large umbrella rack perched prominently nearby. I finally said something about this one day, asking her, could she please use the rack so as not to muss the rug. A week or so later, during another rainstorm, she came for her session, this time setting her rubbers on the rug (though careful to place the umbrella in the rack)—despite there being a receptacle clearly in sight for people's galoshes and rubbers. When I told her, "Gee, I remember asking you the other day to be careful about that rug so as not to get it all mussed," she retorted, "You didn't say anything about rubbers!"

A Schizoid "Phenocopy"

Paul, the patient whose background I describe in two sections of Chapter 10, may also be seen as an example of a phenocopy vis-à-vis Meehl's concept of schizotypy. Five of the seven items in the DSM-III-R description of schizoid PD were applicable: no desire for close relationships, chooses solitary activities (jogging, reading, working a night shift), no desire for sexual relations, no close friends, and cold or aloof affect. When he was growing up, his only "friends" were his dog and his pet rabbit. He was often angry, though in a smoldering, rigidly contained way, and was overly sensitive to criticism. He was, underneath his intense bitterness, a person of unusual honesty and probity of character. His speech betrayed no eccentricities, and apart from his paranoid reactions to strangers and coworkers, was always coherent and reality-based in his thinking.

Because there were no persons in his extended family with schizophrenia-spectrum disorders, Paul's "genogram" was in this respect uninformative. That is, either he had inherited a surplus of schizophrenia-related genes from his family—no members of which showed any distinct signs themselves—or there was no such surplus. One could not state with conviction which was more likely, nor was it possible to subject his relatives to eye-tracking or other measures of possible physiological markers for schizophrenia. It did seem that one could make a compelling argument for "phenocopying"—on the basis of the extremely adverse early home environment (which included being sodomized by his father and repetitively brutalized by his older brother). While it may be true that a few persons manage to rise above such abusive childhoods, becoming at least moderately sociable and trusting adults, the *usual* response is to become aloof, solitary, untrusting, joyless, and cold—most of which attributes belong to our notion of "schizoid" personality.

A Schizotypal "Phenocopy"

Susan, a divorced woman of 35, came for treatment in hopes of becoming less timid with people. As she put it: "Other people own the earth, and I don't." A successful illustrator of children's books, she worked freelance, supporting herself and her nine-year-old daughter. She had had a number of love affairs since her divorce six years before, but as each relationship became closer, she would feel "victimized and frightened." At any one time, she had no more than one female friend (her confidante) and one male friend (her lover).

Besides these qualities, which amounted to three "schizotypal items" (social anxiety, paucity of close friends, suspiciousness), Susan also gave evidence of odd beliefs and unusual perceptions. She announced with some pride, for example, that she could see right through my head and glimpse the titles of the books in back of me, whose titles would ordinarily have been obscured by that part of my anatomy. She had an intense way of speaking and peppered her conversation with words used in novel ways, conveying most often a sense of foreboding or ominousness, at other times an air of loftiness or else of clairvoyance. Looking around my office, which at that time consisted of a walnut-paneled library and an assortment of sepia-toned furnishings, inspired her to comment: "I get a feeling of Australia here . . . a combination of 'austere' and 'ail' . . . your dark suit . . . forbidding, Dracula-like . . . you *chose* these colors because of some forbidding aspect of your character. At times I'm not sure these perceptions are real; at times I very much am and I get chills."

A psychiatrist she had seen before felt she was on the verge of psychosis, yet she maintained her level of function quite adequately. "I felt scared yet liberated to admit these things," she said, adding that there was a certain "willed" quality in stoking up these disturbing emotions. After the breakup of her last love relationship, for example, she would " . . . play games with people in order to see what it would suggest to me, what I could stir up . . . I felt thrilled by the fears I would get." Though wary of men, her involvements each began with a *coup de foudre* suddenness and ferocity, and were highly erotic. If she could not have sex three times a day she assumed the man no longer loved her, and she would weep bitterly; it was all she could do on such a day to attend to her daughter and to her canvases.

This pattern of hypersexuality appeared as the continuation of incestuous overstimulation by both her parents. When she was 8, her father began to invite her into his bed, especially on Sunday mornings, and would stroke her genitals with either his hand or his penis. There was never intercourse. Her mother resented this practice but did nothing to stop it. Instead, she contributed in her own way to this premature erotization—by rubbing her daughter's vulva, as a means of "checking" to see if she had "done anything wrong." She masturbated her daughter, that is, to determine if her daughter had masturbated. Highly jealous, the mother accused her father of carrying on extramarital affairs with various black women who worked in his dress factory. She would then speak of these "affairs" to her daughter, embroidering the "horrific" details after the manner of someone composing a steamy novel. This so offended Susan, who vastly preferred her father to her mother, that when she was 11 she briefly ran away from home. As she grew older, it became more and more clear to what extent she was the "oedipal winner": her father lavished gifts, cars, trust funds, vacations, and jewelry on Susan, rarely giving much of anything to her mother. It never became clear whether the father was the philanderer her mother made him out to be; however, considering the disaffection between her parents and the strength of her father's own sexual needs, the stories her mother told her may well have been at least half true.

As in the preceding vignette, there were no schizophrenia-spectrum relatives in Susan's family, leaving one with the same question as to whether such genetic endowment was merely silent in them but reached clinical recognizability in Susan or whether her schizotypal traits arose from different factors. My impression was that the extreme and "bi-parental" erotization contributed so importantly as to have etiological significance in the evolution of her personality, a "phenocopy" of a schizotypal disorder.

A Schizotypal "Genophenocopy"?

Shelly was admitted for long-term hospitalization because of overwhelming fear of death, alongside profound social withdrawal and mystical beliefs. All these symptoms had been sparked by the sudden death of her father when she was 23, a year and a half before admission. The mystical thinking took the form of preoccupation with I Ching, palmistry, and "astral psychology." Her speech was vague and rambling. She would often smile cryptically and make gestures that seemed mannered and readable only by herself, as though she were locked inside her own solipsistic bubble. She had one close male friend, with whom she had lived for the year before coming to the hospital, but she had no female friends and was not on good terms with either of her two sisters.

Shortly before her admission Shelly had become pregnant by her boyfriend. She went to an abortionist who botched the procedure (this was in the '60s before abortions were legal), necessitating a hysterectomy. Since she had always been eager to have children when the time was right, this trauma was as severe as that of her father's death, the two events combining to precipitate her panic-state.

The relationship with her father was characterized by marked ambivalence, and though love outweighed hatred, both were intense and extreme. He himself was cyclothymic in temperament; however, his "highs" could be as notable for irritability as for euphoria. His rage outbursts were frequent and explosive: he would beat his wife and all the three children, and a moment later feel remorseful and apologetic. He might then hold the patient in his lap and sing to her and rock her. He taught her to read when she was 3, and tutored her in various subjects such that she was always ahead of her classmates even though she skipped two grades. She found school boring, got into trouble with the teachers for her inattention, and made no friends among her peers.

Her mother was chronically depressed, for which she received antide-pressant medication. She was also irascible—only a little less so than Shelly's father, such that the family atmosphere was violent almost continu-osly; the girls were as likely to be hit by their mother as by their father.

On Rorschach testing her responses showed considerable confabulation, contaminations, magical thinking, and autistic logic, suggesting a blurring of boundaries between reality and fantasy. Before entering the hospital, and for several months afterwards, she was subject to experiences where she would stare at the ceiling and "see" the skull of her dead father. Her speech was at first vague and at times rambling, but she never showed signs of "formal thought disorder."

Shelly's history, like Susan's and Paul's, is replete with the kind of trau-mata that can, in someone with certain vulnerabilities, engender a schizo-typal disorder—even in the absence (as far as one can tell) of significant genetic liability for schizophrenia. But in addition, Shelly's family history suggested genetic predisposition for *some* form of emotional illness, just not schizophrenia. In her case the predisposition seemed to be for affective illness; each parent appeared to suffer from a manic-depressive illness, ei-ther in a distinct form (her mother's recurrent depressive episodes) or an attentuated form (the father's cyclothymic temperament). All these fac-tors—traumatic background, miserable luck, probable genes for anxiety and hypohedonia (and perhaps for introversion)—seem to have conspired to produce a disarming imitation of schizotypal personality disorder, com-patible with Meehl's notion of a "*geno*phenocopy" of the schizotype. Her course over the next 20 years was one of recovery and much improved function, both socially and occupationally—also suggesting that her condi-tion was not related to a *true* schizophrenia-spectrum condition.

TREATMENT ISSUES

Elsewhere I have discussed guidelines for the treatment of schizoid and schizotypal patients in some detail (Stone, 1989e & f).

Schizoid Patients:
Educative and Cognitive Approaches

With respect to *schizoid* personality disorder, few clinicians have the oppor-tunity of treating in any great number patients who are *predominantly* schizoid, as the term is currently employed. The following remarks will have relevance mainly to patients who have noteworthy schizoid *traits*, but whose "main" personality features may be obsessive-compulsive, paranoid, borderline, or something else. When I refer to "schizoid patients," the phrase will usually be a shorthand for these latter kinds of patients.

As a rule schizoid patients are fearful of intimacy; this includes (as we saw with Samuel of the first vignette) opening up to a therapist. Intensive psychotherapy at two, three, or more times a week will seldom be comfortable and may even be quite contraindicated (cf. Markowitz, 1968; Rosenfeld, 1969). Paul's previous therapist met with him three times a week and tried to "get out the facts" concerning the sexual molestation by his father. This brought too many painful memories to the surface, far more quickly than the patient could deal with them, and led to panic. Perhaps as a rule of thumb, one might recommend that the more closely a patient approximates the prototypical (DSM) schizoid PD, especially if there are paranoid features, the more a therapist should aim for a once-a-week therapy rather than a "depth" therapy of an analytically oriented nature.

As a corollary to these comments, therapists should be advised to fashion a treatment that accords with the schizoid patient's prospects for becoming more at ease socially. These may be very meager (as in the case of Samuel). Many a schizoid patient needs to be helped to expand his repertoire of pleasurable hobbies and activities that do not involve other people, rather than pushed to "loosen up" in group settings (cf. Battegay, 1981). Paul, for example, at first avoided what he loved best, which was going to the opera or the ballet, having felt "unworthy" or such pleasures. Once this pathological feeling was overcome, he attended such performances frequently, and his life became much more bearable.

In less paranoid or less markedly schizoid patients, in whom intensive therapy may be feasible, the emphasis will often be directed to certain narcissistic dynamics having to do with the desire to be omnipotent or omniscient, as a compensatory mechanism defending against feelings of inadequacy (especially those derived from not fitting in with the group) (Grinberg & Rodriguea-Perez, 1982). One could discern such a mechanism in the dream of Samuel, where he saw himself as Superman. Since the isolation of affect in schizoid patients tends to be even more pronounced than what is seen in obsessive-compulsive patients, the therapist will need considerable skill in tuning in empathically to the feeling-state of the moment—in order, by translating this emotion back to the patient, to help the patient connect up various fragmentary and affectless comments with the emotion that would most likely have accompanied them (cf. Khan, 1960; Liberman, 1957).

Because it is a common characteristic of schizoid persons to have a less than adequate sense either of social customs, habits, manners, etc., or of what reactions would be most typical of people in various situations, a good deal of time in therapy sessions will be devoted to *educational measures* (Eidelberg, 1957) directed at teaching the patient what is expectable and what is appropriate. One does not cheer up a mourner at the funeral parlor, for example, with a risqué joke, no matter how funny the joke might have been in some other context. Schizoid patients are not always aware of social taboos of this sort, and will be spared many embarrassments if their treatment includes attention to such matters, as well as to more conventional topics like the identification and resolution of conflicts.

Akin to education of a patient is the cognitive/behavioral approach, such as that outlined by Beck and Freeman (1990, Chapter 7) in relation to schizoid and schizotypal patients. These authors point out how schizoid patients tend to complain that they get *no* pleasure from activities that do, on closer inspection, afford them some pleasure (viz. collecting phonograph records, in the authors' example). The therapist needs then to encourage them to engage more often, and with less pessimism in advance as to the outcome, in these kinds of activities.

A particularly gifted therapist, vis-à-vis behavioral techniques with schizoid patients, was Harry Albert (1983), one of the first to have his patients record their gestures on video, which could then be used to help them correct habits and gestures that were socially awkward or offensive. He used role-playing and "problem-solving" a great deal also. Once, when working with a schizoid patient who was facing a job interview and who had little idea of what to say or even what to wear, Dr. Albert spent the afternoon with the patient in Brooks Brothers, helping to get him properly outfitted in a suit that would make the best impression on the interviewer. In subsequent sessions he would then act the part of a typical interviewer, in order to get a better notion of what kinds of questions made the patient anxious, etc.

Another therapist willing to go to great lengths to help a schizoid patient come out of his shell was Norwegian psychiatrist Truls-Erik Mogstad (1979). Dr. Mogstad was working at that time with a talented sculptress who had suffered a psychotic break and was still in a state of prolonged muteness (whether she was catatonically or merely electively mute was unclear). Her premorbid personality was schizoid. She was enmeshed in a hostile symbiotic relationship with her mother—apparently a difficult, censorious woman. For nearly two years the sculptress would come faithfully twice a week for her sessions, during which she said not a word. Mogstad would from time to time utter a sympathetic comment or make a gentle interpretation. But the patient did bring in little sculptures she had made during the week—depicting most often the aridity, or the lethality, as she saw it, of the mother-daughter bond. At first Mogstad would place each piece on his desk, but when the sheer number of sculptures grew too great, he cleared the books from his library shelves to make room, eventually converting much of his office into a museum of her works. He might hazard a guess as to what emotions this or that piece was portraying. In this indirect manner he conveyed to her that he sympathized greatly with her suffering, respected her as a person, and admired her art enormously—since all of his other patients could not help but be aware that this one patient occupied a special place in his attention. She came to realize that he was willing to expose his admiration of her to his other patients, even at the risk of their being put out with him for doing so. This seemed to constitute a "corrective emotional experience" for her; at all events, at about the two-year mark, she began to speak, and from that point on she made a rapid and excellent recovery.

Schizotypal Patients:
The Therapist as Auxiliary Ego

A number of the suggestions proposed for the treatment of schizoid patients apply also to those with *schizotypal* PD or with prominent schizotypal traits. The need for educative measures will be relevant routinely, since by definition schizotypal patients tend to be eccentric and also to misinterpret many signals from their interpersonal world. Schizotypal patients are more apt to seek and to remain in treatment than are their mostly-schizoid counterparts. Therapists will often find themselves functioning, among other ways, as an *auxiliary ego* for their schizotypal patients—a function that may be necessary for prodigious lengths of time.

As mentioned above, concretistic thinking and the corresponding difficulty in analogizing a lesson learned in therapy to similar situations in the future create a seemingly endless need for the therapist to keep the patient on the track. Otherwise the patient may miss some social cue, make a dreadful gaffe unwittingly, or else make a perilous social decision and in very short order end up in some disadvantageous situation (alienating a boss, getting rejected by a friend or lover, etc.).

As an example, a schizotypal patient with whom I had worked for many years had great trouble sizing up potential "dates." She once told me about a man she had met at a company picnic who then called her the next day to ask her out. It became clear that he was calling from a pay-phone when the operator asked him to deposit more coins. He said he had no phone in his apartment and also said the pay-phone had no number on it so she couldn't call him back. She asked how come he had no phone, and he replied that he had only a four-month lease on his apartment, and there was no use asking the phone company to install one because his lease was just about up. All this sounded extremely fishy to me (no number on the pay-phone? a "four-month" lease?).

She asked, "Should I accept a date with him or not?" I went over the details with her one by one, and she did begin to see that something wasn't quite right about his responses. "But," she said, "I'm so lonely. I'd rather give him a second chance. . . . You think he'd hurt me?" I told her I couldn't give her a scientific answer to that, but that she herself must have some worries or why would she ask me. Then she recalled his having said something about "I want 100% honesty!" which seemed to come out of the blue. She now asked, "Do you think maybe he gives all this talk about 100% honesty because he's not on the level?" I asked her, "Well, if you were in the Maine woods and I wasn't around, what would your instincts *tell* you?" "I think he's shifty," she finally said, "I think he was conning me." So in this lumbering fashion, half getting her to listen better to her own impressions, half exposing my own impressions, I nudged her in the direction of declining a date with what sounded like a most unpromising person. As the months and years go on, however, similar situations arise, and I have again and again to serve as her "reality organ," i.e., as her auxiliary ego.

Another advantage to long-term psychotherapy for schizotypal patients, besides being able to serve as auxiliary ego, comes from the very continuity that such a lengthy relationship provides. Many schizotypal patients experience bewildering discontinuity regarding their own identity; time itself seems chopped up in pieces of unequal length, patched together in random sequences and with whole chunks missing. As one such patient put it, becoming tearful before a separation, "Now I'm seven and you're my mother"—this spoken as though at that moment she had indeed time-warped back to seven and I had transformed momentarily into her often and unpredictably abandoning mother. The continuity of our relationship, now spanning many years, allowed her to reflect each piece of her psyche, as it were, off me—enabling her to capture, from my sameness, a sense of her own sameness.

Perhaps better put: she exposed to me over time the whole mosaic of her past experience, feeling states, and the like, but randomly, as though dumping the contents of a jigsaw puzzle box onto a table. Because the "doer" of the puzzle was the same person—myself—when the picture was mostly completed there was a certain integrity and wholeness about the emerging picture, more than there might have been if, say, seven therapists spread over the years, each with his own perceptions and style, had put together various portions of the picture.

As with borderline patients, the mechanism of *projective identification* is often discernible in schizotypal patients: the patient who at times confused me with her mother would even more often accuse me of being angry at her or envious of her when, primarily, she was angry or envious or whatever at me. Schizotypal patients may try, unconsciously, to induce the feeling in us that they are struggling with (viz., making us really angry through some annoying gesture, such that their projection now seems accurate, etc.) It is useful at such moments to begin interpreting what is happening, with a comment like: "You seem to be seeing me as. . . . " This implies (a) that the therapist understands the nature of the projection, but (b) by virtue of being able to make a comment of this kind, must *not* actually be the same as the patient had imagined, or must *not* be enveloped in the feeling-state the patient assumed.

Over time, transference "dissections" of this sort help the schizotypal patient distinguish more accurately between self and other. This is the work of analytic therapy in general, to be sure, but the confusion between self and other is apt to be greater in schizotypal than in other personality-disordered patients, and of a qualitatively different sort: ego-boundary confusion is seldom a problem in the other disorders, but is a common feature of schizotypal personality. The work of Harold Searles is of special importance in getting to understand these processes more fully (cf. Searles, 1961).

Vanggaard (1979) has drawn attention to hypochondriasis as another common accompaniment of schizotypal disorders. There is often rich psychological symbolism behind the various hypochondriacal symptoms, but as Vanggaard mentions there may also be a curious reciprocal relationship between symptom and general level of comfort. If the patient's success in the interpersonal world can be enhanced, the bodily symptoms tend to diminish automatically. If that success remains elusive, hypochondriasis may continue to serve as the patient's refuge. In some instances the area of the body singled out for exaggerated attention in fact symbolizes some ambivalently regarded but much needed person—such that the important person, in reality perhaps estranged or living far away, or perhaps dead, is still very much "there" for the patient, embedded uncomfortably in this or that part of his flesh. One schizotypal patient used to walk bent over, complaining of back pain—likening her pain to having big weights sitting on her back. It became clear later on that, in her words, "my parents are always on my back," and that, in her case, this metaphor had become hardened into symptom.

Correct interpretation is an important first step in ameliorating a hypochondriacal symptom of this kind, but more solid improvement will require further movement into, and success with, the external world. It is here that the other modalities alluded to above—suggestion, education, behavioral modification—come into play in complementary fashion to the interpretive remarks.

A reduced pleasure sense is a less uniform feature of (predominantly) schizotypal than of schizoid patients. In the preceding vignettes hypohedonia was a major problem in Sandra ("phenotypic" schizotypal) but not in Susan (schizotypal "phenocopy"). Hypohedonia tends to manifest itself particularly in the interpersonal realm: people are more complicated than any objects; getting enjoyment out of closeness with others, though potentially the greatest pleasure, is attended by the most pitfalls and hazards. Whereas mood-disordered persons underreact or (more often) overreact to interpersonal stresses, even though their perceptions are more realistic, schizotypal persons are more at risk for *misinterpreting* what is going on between them and other people. This tendency, along with the hypohedonia which may also affect them, interferes with the establishment of intimate ties. The outcome depends on the balance of these two forces: prototypical schizoid persons have such a reduced pleasure sense as to make intimacy too threatening, irrespective of their ability to interpret correctly the intentions of others. Those schizotypal persons with a fairly well preserved pleasure sense (like Susan), will keep trying to achieve harmonious relations with others, even though handicapped by their tendency to misinterpret. Therapists working with schizotypal patients must take the measure of these two forces, and work toward the amelioration of either or both in whatever order seems most feasible. From a practical standpoint it will usually prove easier to expand the patient's pleasure sense than to clear up a lifelong tendency to misread the "signals" from other people.

In the treatment of schizoid or schizotypal patients who either are near, symptomatologically, to frank schizophrenia or experienced extreme early traumata (in cases of "phenocopy"), therapeutic goals may have to be pared down considerably. The development of friendships may be possible, but intimacy may not; work may be too stressful except in the most routine and interpersonally uncomplex settings. The therapy itself offers a human relationship that may take on special value to the patient just for this one reason.

One schizotypal patient I worked with some years ago had been unusually bright and promising as a boy: he became a radio "Whiz-Kid" answering tough science questions on a major network show. His parents pushed him to become a physicist or some other kind of scientist. But his schizotypal disorder became evident when he was an adolescent. He did manage to finish college and was able to make a few friends. Nervous and maladroit with girls, he fell hopelessly in love with a college classmate who had no interest in him; when she rejected him he became suicidal and had to be hospitalized. All he could do comfortably when I knew him was to play computer-baseball games (based on sophisticated game-statistics) with a few friends in his city or, via modem, in other cities around the country. He was also severely hypochondriacal, talking about bizarre pains that went from the "arteries" in his face down into his chest.

Though they hounded him mercilessly about his not working, his parents were quite wealthy and could support him easily. My treatment goals were (a) to educate his parents about the chronicity of his difficulties, in the hope that they would stop being so judgmental about his inability ("laziness" in their perception) to work, and (b) to serve as an accepting and nonthreatening person for him to relate to. Many of our sessions, once the outlines of his early life were clearly delineated, were taken up with baseball-talk: how he managed to beat So-n-So in Boston by staging a (computerized) double-steal in the ninth inning, etc., etc. In the process he became much more life-oriented and less suicidal; there was substantially more pleasure in his life. For the patient, and for me, this was a satisfying outcome, though his parents could only see his continuing inability to work as a failure.

Ancillary Treatments:
Group Therapy and Pharmacotherapy

Other modalities that have relevance to the treatment of schizotypal personality include group therapy and pharmacotherapy. We have already alluded to cognitive/behavioral therapy in some of the examples above; Beck and Freeman (1990) make more detailed recommendations about this approach. They emphasize the utility of keeping the sessions structured and of social-skills training. The latter, where role-playing and other educative techniques are used, helps reduce the extent to which the schizotypal patient may feel like a "misfit." The frequency with which paranoid trends are admixed with the schizotypal traits is acknowledged in the typical attitudes and assumptions outlined by Beck. Two such attitudes are: "People will get you if they can," and "There are reasons for everything; things don't happen by chance" (1990, p. 140).

Regarding *group therapy*, Leszcz (1989) mentions that the eccentricity of the schizotypal patient may present an ambulatory group with discomforts beyond what many of the other group members can tolerate—leading to dropout or exclusion from the group. If eccentricity is not a prominent feature, these patients may benefit, though from a *supportive*, rather than an (analytically oriented) exploratory, group approach. In this supportive approach there will be fewer demands for the kinds of self-revelation that the schizotypal patient would experience as threatening.

As for schizoid patients, Leszcz finds it useful to get the patient ensconced in a comfortable, supportive individual therapy first; then the patient can be introduced to a group setting—one that permits, and here Leszcz cites Yalom's words (1985), "slow, steady engagement, encouraging differentiation of affects and relationships, rather than a potentially overwhelming and cathartic breakthrough" (Leszcz, 1989, p. 2671).

Group therapy will often seem like a useful measure to help schizoid or schizotypal patients overcome shyness, since in the presumably more accepting environment of a psychotherapeutic group the exposure of embarrassing thoughts and behaviors might be much less traumatic than in the midst of strangers or casual acquaintances. There will be certain schizoid or schizotypal patients for whom this theory works out just as the therapist hopes. But if paranoid traits are prominent, even the protected setting of the group may be too uncomfortable, and, as Leszcz warns, dropout or extrusion may follow. Thus, an awareness that other people (viz., the other group members) also harbor disturbing thoughts and feelings can be fostered to great advantage, via group therapy, in not-so-paranoid schizotypal patients, but seldom has a chance to develop where paranoid fearfulness and mistrustfulness are entrenched.

Schizoid patients seldom show concomitant symptoms of the sort that could be "targeted" by neuroleptic or other medications. *Pharmacotherapy* has a very limited role, if any, in this patient group. In contrast, a goodly proportion of schizotypal patients do benefit from psychoactive medications, especially those patients who are prone to brief psychotic episodes. Early reports of favorable response include those of Serban and Siegel (1984) and Goldberg, Shulz et al. (1986). Goldberg et al. drew attention to certain clinical features that were most apt to be associated with positive response to low-dose neuroleptics—namely, illusions, ideas of reference, "psychoticism," phobic anxiety, and obsessive-compulsive symptoms. In their study low-dose thiothixene was utilized. In a subsequent study by Hymowitz, Frances et al. (1986), half of a group of 17 schizotypal outpatients responded favorably to haloperidol (2 to 12 mgm/day), especially on measures of ideas of reference, odd communication, and social isolation. Sedating side-effects were troublesome to a number of the patients and contributed to the 50% dropout rate from the study. This led the authors to speculate that " . . . only a selected subgroup of schizotypal patients is likely to tolerate and show clinically significant change with neuroleptic treatment" (p. 270). Many of their patients were able to tolerate only low dosages of haloperidol. (4 mgm/day or less), suggesting the need for low dosage with slow buildup in this patient population.

Clinicians need to keep in mind that single- and double-blind studies such as the above-cited are based on schizotypal patients who conform closely to the standard criteria of DSM, rely on medications for which placebos exist (viz., haloperidol), and therefore do not always approximate the kinds of patients that confront therapists in everyday practice. I have worked with one schizotypal patient who, merely on one or two meprobamate pills a day, became less irritable at work and less referential. The man mentioned above who liked computer-baseball became less hypochondriacal on trifluoperazine, 6 to 8 mgm/day. Paul, the case of schizoid "phenocopy," took it as a sign of weakness to have to rely on medication—especially a neuroleptic. Were I to recommend such drugs, he assumed I considered him "crazy" and flatly refused. When he at times became severely paranoid and referential, my hand was forced, and I would recommend small amounts of thioridizine, accompanying my suggestion with a comment to the effect: "Those uncomfortable experiences you tell me about [of people muttering 'faggot' under their breath when he passed by] do, after all, make you very anxious, so perhaps a few days of Mellaril might take the edge off the anxiety. . . . " In this way I could cajole him into accepting some medication whenever his referentiality became too disruptive. As for the better functioning schizotypal patients with whom I have worked—who showed signs of cognitive slippage, odd speech, and the like, but not the symptoms mentioned by Goldberg et al.—medications were not necessary at any phase of their treatment.

10

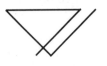

Paranoid Personality Disorder

Leontes: Is whispering nothing?
Is leaning cheek to cheek? Is meeting noses?
Kissing with inside lip? stopping the career
Of laughter with a sigh
. . . Is this nothing? . . .
Camillo: Good my lord, be cur'd
Of this diseas'd opinion, and betimes,
For 'tis most dangerous.

Shakespeare: *The Winter's Tale* I, ii, 284ff

THE TERM "PARANOID" has a long tradition in psychiatry, having been used by the ancient Greeks to denote a disorder characterized by abiding suspiciousness and irrational thought. Since "paranoid" was reserved mostly for disorders that included delusional thinking and other psychotic phenomena, there was little mention of *paranoid* as a modifier of a personality disorder until this century. The paranoia of Schreber in Freud's famous case (1911) was that of a psychosis—thought to be schizophrenic, but probably of manic-depressive origin. The mechanism of *projection*, in which unacceptable aspects of the self are externalized and situated (in the patient's mind) in other persons or agencies, is applicable nonetheless to paranoid personalities as well. Freud emphasized what seemed to him the essential nature of the projective dynamic; namely, that paranoid persons (particularly if male) are struggling with ego-alien, suppressed homosexual urges that are then turned around and projected onto the object of these urges. The paranoid person says, in effect, "It is not I that love him; rather, *he* loves *me*!"

Frosch (1983), while in basic agreement with Freud's assumptions, expands upon them in an important way, stating that " . . . unconscious homosexuality is denied, rejected and projected onto a replica of a significant childhood object" (p. 109). The paranoid patient experiences the "per-

194

secution" as an anal-sadomasochistic attack that is at once degrading and humiliating. But, in the case of sons who go on to become "paranoid," it so happens that there often *had* been actual persecution, in the form of unwarranted criticism, abusive treatment, and the like—from the *same-sexed parent*. Frosch offers a number of compelling clinical examples of this scenario.

I feel Frosch is quite correct in drawing attention to the frequency with which this dynamic is encountered in male paranoid patients. One also finds, however, that paranoid women often have in their background an abusive or incestuous father. The opposite-sexed parent, that is, can also play a prominent role in the pathogenesis of the paranoid condition.

Paranoid patients with an underlying functional psychosis (schizophrenia, manic-depression) will not so often be found to have suffered abusiveness or other traumata at the hands of either parent. In these instances the paranoid personality distortions appear to have a heredo-constitutional basis. Perinatal damage, idiopathic epilepsy, and certain other "organic" conditions can also predispose to paranoid personality formation. Unfortunate examples exist, of course, where a patient with one of these psychoses has also had a traumatic childhood, of a sort that conduces to this aberration. Traumata consisting of patterns and events that would lead to massive mistrust would be the relevant factors. Parental betrayal, gross parental infidelity, as well as parental vilification, would be more likely to promote paranoid "solutions" than traumata that people do not generally take in a personal way, such as illness, the death of a parent through an accident, etc.

In some (nonpsychotic) patients with paranoid personality, traumata of both sorts are found in the early background. Charles Rycroft (1960), for example, in an unusually poignant and beautifully written account of his four-year analysis of a "Bohemian" actress, mentions that, although she was her father's favorite, he eventually "betrayed" her, as she experienced it, by sending her to a reformatory when her behavior had become grossly unruly. Her mother died when the patient was two. This loss ushered in at first a profound depression. Later she appeared to deal with this depression, as best Rycroft could reconstruct, via paranoid defenses (and also grandiosity). Rycroft was at a loss to explain the "paranoid twist to her personality," though he also mentions her many manic qualities, including her extreme emotional intensity; these may have represented a biological push toward bipolarity (of which paranoid traits are a common accompaniment), inclining her to paranoid/grandiose personality rather than purely depressive traits. As an example of her intensity: a lover once said to her, "It's the glorious irrelevancy of you. You look at the sugar-bowl with intense hatred and talk of the weather with an expression of ecstasy" (p. 63).

The manner in which disappointment and depression can serve as stimuli to paranoid trends has been underlined by Searles (1979). A borderline, paranoid/blaming woman with whom Searles once worked, and who filled years of sessions with "ragefulness, resentment and dissatisfaction," said of her young son: "Billy—goddam' dirty trick that he was born a boy!" (p. 488), as though he had maliciously conspired against her in being born opposite in sex to what she would have preferred. Another intriguing mechanism that may exacerbate paranoid trends in already paranoid personalities is the too successful complementing of the patient by another person (including a therapist), such that the patient comes to experience the " . . . loss, beyond redemption, of [his] individuality as a part-person" (Searles, 1979, p. 137).

We can see from the authors just cited that the original notion of paranoid ideation as a defense against forbidden homosexual impulses is now considered too narrow, even though relevant to a fair proportion of cases. Modlin (1963) also sought to extricate us from the metapsychological straightjacket, vis-à-vis paranoia, in which the old formulation had placed us. Modlin studied a number of higher-functioning (i.e., nonschizophrenic) women with paranoid personality. He could discern no latent or disguised homosexuality in this group; instead, he found considerable underlying depression. The paranoid trends appeared to have been marshalled against this otherwise overwhelming emotion. In these women, removal of the stressful situations in their lives and therapy directed toward strengthening of their self-esteem succeeded in reducing the intensity of the paranoid trends.

In a like vein, Salzman (1960) felt that Freud's hypothesis needed revision. He cited first of all the work of Klein and Horwitz (1949), who found evidence of underlying homosexual concerns in only a fifth of their large series of hospitalized patients with paranoid conditions. Salzman went further and expressed his own view: that certain narcissistic patients develop a grandiosity early in life, leading to irritating personality traits (arrogance, presumptuousness) which then "antagonize the environment" (1960, p. 680). The grandiosity itself will usually have arisen as a compensatory mechanism for dealing with humiliation from the family. But the arrogance, Salzman felt, then elicits derogation or scoffing. These incursions into the grandiose person's inflated self-estimation lead to assumptions of malevolence and conspiracy, as though the world is in league to "burst his bubble." Paranoid developments thus seem *secondary*; the grandiosity *primary*, according to this schema.

While I think Salzman's point about the importance of grandiosity in paranoid persons is correct in the main (there are patients with mildly paranoid personalities who show little or no grandiosity), I don't think it is valid to assert that the paranoid cognition is necessarily, or even routinely, "secondary." Instead, I suspect there is, in certain persons, a *preparedness* to think in a paranoid manner, which may then be actuated by key life stresses (having to do with belittlement, rejection, etc.).

This preparedness, akin to the preparedness certain other persons show to dissociative phenomena, may stem, as indicated above, from heredo-constitutional factors or from specific and repetitive traumata in early life (or some combination of such factors). Even parental "brainwashing" in the absence of traumata may conduce to paranoid trends—as when a child is cautioned repeatedly to be wary of various social groups (this may then become a source of bigotry) or of people in general. Once the brain is "hard-wired" into a configuration predisposing to paranoid ideation, the latter will become manifest when triggered by the relevant interpersonal stresses.

One of the salient characteristics, in this regard, of "paranoid ideation" is *oversimplification* or, glimpsed from a different angle, the tendency to make hurried and unrealistic assumptions based on skimpy evidence.

OVERSIMPLIFICATION: PATHOLOGICAL AND NONPATHOLOGICAL

In *paranoid* assumptions, oversimplification is combined with suspicious-ness. Paranoia is an "early warning mechanism" alerting one to imminent danger. Since we reserve the term for pathological reactions, estimation of danger in paranoia is exaggerated or unrealistic; the "snap judgments" of the paranoid person are faulty (at least in part).

Nonpathological oversimplifications and instant reactions are a part of everyday life, and even more dramatically a part of the lives of those in military combat or other life-threatening situations. Men engaged in jungle warfare, such as in World War II, used passwords that were difficult to pronounce by soldiers of the opposing army. If a "wrong" sound was elic-ited from a stranger, survival was ensured by shooting first and then asking questions. In civilian life detectives investigating the suspicious death of a marital partner, knowing that 90% of spousal homicides are committed by the surviving spouse, fix their attention upon that spouse, no matter how good the alibi, etc. Such reactions are not "paranoid," though persons with a "touch" of paranoia excel in detective work. People living in large cities develop "street smarts"—which amount to a wariness that is realistic, even if not always accurate. A woman walking down a dark street in certain sections of town, noticing three or four tough-looking young men coming in her direction, is best off *assuming* the worst and running the other way. Perhaps the "real" risk (viz., of her being accosted) is "only" 5%, and the likelihood the men are merely exchanging anecdotes about the day's base-ball scores 95%. That is an uncomfortably high risk, so her street smarts serve her well.

The paranoid person's assumptions are distorted along the lines of emo-tional conflict, such that small and incomplete cues are misinterpreted as hostile threats touching on this or that important conflict. The following clinical example is illustrative.

Clinical Example

Paul, a paranoid man I treated for some years, though he was homosexual, vehemently denied his homosexuality, having been brought up in a family that strongly disparaged homosexuality. He often complained to me about the rudeness of New Yorkers, compared with the people in the small town where he grew up. If he stopped right there, one could not call him para-noid. But he insisted that strangers in large numbers, in movie lines or in the subway, were muttering "faggot!" under their breath as he passed by. This was an unfalsifiable hypothesis—at which paranoid persons excel—but it did not seem realistic, even if this were true occasionally, that it was happening as often as he indicated. I could picture how someone ahead of him in the movie line might suddenly discover he had left his wallet home. He might mutter (in the local accent), "Fuggit! I fuh-gaht it!" My patient might have been too far away to hear the words distinctly, perhaps picking up only: "F..g..t, f..g..t!" Someone not burdened with his specific conflicts, standing equally far away, would tend to fill in the blanks correctly. But my patient would insert just the vowels that would correspond to his feared assumption. *Any* sounds that could vaguely be interpreted as "faggot" would be heard/misheard in that fashion.

Here, suspicion, combined with a brain-wiring oversensitive to the possi-bility certain key words were being uttered, would conspire to "convince" the paranoid person that his worst fears were being actualized. As far as my patient was concerned, it was much too *dangerous* to assume the oppo-site, for what if he trusted and befriended the nine out of ten strangers who were truly beneficent, or at least harmless. That would still leave him with one out of ten who was an enemy. Since he experienced any hostility as just about lethal, a one-in-ten gamble, to him, seemed terrifyingly high.

This concern about the potential lethality of another person's hostility (imagined or real) constitutes a separate dynamic operative in many para-noid patients—a concern that need not be related in any way to conflicts about homosexuality. Paul had been abused severely by an older brother (who would throw lit matches at him, force his hand down on a hot radia-tor, etc.) until he reached the same size and weight as the older brother. When he was nine, his father sodomized him on a number of occasions.

The wonder is that he had never attacked anyone as an adult. He once did explode in a rage at me, in the very beginning of therapy, when he experienced me momentarily, and despite my being 20 years his senior, as a "powerful man who could hurt him." He himself "pumped iron" and had built himself into a quite powerful young man—though one who still carried with him the feelings of puniness and vulnerability from his latency days. Thanks to the delicate balance in his psyche, where self-restraint happened to exceed his anger, he lived—like Bartleby the Scrivener, in Melville's famous story—simply as a glowering and censorious hermit, alienating everyone but harming no one.

Paranoid patients in whom the balance is tilted the other way—where rage is greater than self-restraint—may readily become combative. This was the case with a "borderline" (but more prominently, paranoid) man I once interviewed at a conference. He had been severely abused also: fostered at age five because of his parents' poverty, he had lived with foster parents, among whose innumerable acts of cruelty was their practice of making him kneel on rice kernels for hours at a time, as a punishment for some trifling misbehavior. As he grew up in this hostile environment, he developed a hair-trigger sensitivity to slights or "negativity" of any kind. If another man offended him, he would instantly "deck" him—and just as quickly regret that he had lost his composure.

He had sought treatment, actually, because he was afraid that, in an unguarded moment, he might hurt his wife or his two small children. Here again, his paranoid personality had to do primarily with repeated threats to his survival, not to worries about homosexuality. He was also convinced of being "unlovable," constantly misinterpreting the kindness and compassion of his (female) therapist as insincere—"something she was taught in school," as he put it—so that, although he liked her friendliness, he did not trust it, whereas the hostility of others he of course didn't like but "trusted" implicitly as how the world "really was."

The tendency of paranoid persons to misread the intentions of others has been studied recently in a methodical way by Turkat et al. (1990). They compared the responses of paranoid vs. normal control subjects to a series of vignettes where two people were interacting: one was doing something to the other in ways that could be interpreted as hostile, unintentional, ambiguous, or helpful. Where the intentional direction was clear, the paranoids did as well as the controls. But where there was ambiguity, the paranoid subjects tended to identify the intention as hostile. As the authors concluded, the paranoid person's difficulties are not limited to misreading of ambiguous situations; there is also a problem of responding with anger where none is called for. This then " . . . suggests hypersensitivity and difficulty with emotional control" (p. 268).

VARIETIES OF PARANOID PERSONALITY

As we have seen, the dynamic underpinnings of paranoid personality are not unitary. Even where homosexual fears do play a role, struggle with actual homoerotic impulses may be a less commonly encountered aspect, clinically, than the struggle of a "pseudohomosexual" kind (as defined by Ovesey, 1965)—where a male patient, feeling inadequate sexually (cf. Cameron, 1963), equates this uncomfortable emotion with "not being a real man," and "therefore" (in the irrational logic of such persons) being homosexual. This state is not accompanied by sexual arousal to persons of the same sex.

Akhtar (1990) regards the main components of paranoid personality as *suspiciousness, grandiosity, and feelings of persecution.* But there are many clinical forms in which we find this triad. One may find a *generalized hostility* (Blum, 1981), especially where there is a history of intense family bickering (Jacobson, 1971a). Here the patient's early identifications are of hostile, complaining people, so that, besides the emotional hurt probably suffered at the hands of this or that family member, the patient becomes, in effect, programmed to behave this way also, absent early exposure to more humane and diplomatic ways of interaction. The *querulous,* reproachful patients Schmideberg (1946) described often came from families where chronic complaining and blaming-the-other were the order of the day. A related quality of *contentiousness* has been noted in many paranoid persons (Bleuler, 1908).

The *grandiosity,* which may be either secret or blatant, has already been mentioned (Salzman, 1960) and has been emphasized more recently by a number of other authors (Bursten, 1973; Kernberg, 1982; Searles, 1979), all of whom speak of the paranoid person's intense fear of dissolution of self (loss of identity) as a central dynamic. This dynamic takes on special significance when we discuss treatment.

The characteristic *hypervigilance* of paranoid persons has relevance both to their hostility and to their fear of boundary-loss. The need for a wide psychological and even geographical space between paranoid persons and those with whom they interact is a reflection of both (a) fear of hostile invasion by others (for which real distance has survival value) and (b) fear of being "unduly" influenced by others, to the point of losing a sense of separate self (for which extra psychological "space"—not getting intimate with others—is a solution).

Hypervigilance is often accompanied by oversensitivity to slights and to extremely subtle nuances of tone or gesture, even when no criticism or disapproval has been intended. A boss could be 99% satisfied with a work-er's performance, and could wear an expression that would be read as "approving" by 99% of workers—but the paranoid employee will detect the muffled and negligible disapproval, and will read the one tiny aspect of facial expression that might convey the negative feeling, or will altogether misread the boss's expression so as to "find" disapproval where there is not even a faint trace. Paranoid persons are thus often "*injustice collectors*"— registering all correctly interpreted negative reactions and all misperceived slights, dwelling on them, and holding eternal grudges against the (actual and imaginary) offending parties.

Finally, we may encounter either *pathological jealousy* or, less often, *erotomania*. The most severe forms of pathological jealousy do often contain a cryptic homosexual motif, again not so much the expression of true homoerotic interest as a "pseudohomosexual," erotized version of what was originally a preoedipal, nonsexual longing for closeness with the same-sexed parent. Men whose fathers were largely unavailable to them emotionally (or women whose mothers were distant, died early, etc.), and who are heterosexual in orientation, may yearn to be held or touched or soothed by the same-sexed parent—a yearning that becomes confused with "being homosexual."

The pathologically jealous male, for example, suspects his girlfriend or wife of being enamored of some other man. Consciously he resents the man for "taking away" his woman. Unconsciously, he resents the woman—that she might keep for herself the man he actually wants (but could never admit to wanting). A beautifully crafted dramatization of this triangle is to be found in Arthur Miller's "A View from the Bridge" (1957), in which a paranoid older man, outwardly fond of his niece, comes to resent her interest in a young man. Unable to accept his own wish to be close to this young man, he instead vilifies and mocks him.

The pathologically jealous woman, *mutatis mutandis*, has a secret yearning for the "other woman" she accuses her lover or husband of preferring. But in her conscious preoccupations with the other woman, she is aware only of envy and resentment. Underneath this is the resentment of the man for (supposedly) monopolizing the very woman she would like to be close to herself.

Erotomania, strictly speaking, is usually of a delusional nature, consisting in the "paranoid" misinterpretation that some other person (of exalted status, customarily) is secretly in love with you. As Segal (1989) points out, this condition may occur without concomitant schizophrenia, is noted more often in women than in men, and is probably set in motion by unmet narcissistic needs. A phenomenon of a related kind, which may also be the other side of the coin of pathological jealousy in certain patients in psychiatric treatment, is an obsessive love of the therapist. The usual scenario is a male therapist and a nonpsychotic but intensely deprived and lonely female patient, who becomes overwhelmingly preoccupied with and seemingly in love with her therapist, but who, as in the triangle of pathological jealousy, secretly envies the therapist his closeness with his wife, whom the patient would much prefer to have as a surrogate mother. Such patients are not usually paranoid to the extent of satisfying DSM criteria. They may instead show more dependent/hysteric/depressive traits, with only a few "paranoid" qualities (such as hypervigilance and suspiciousness) noticeable mostly just within the context of the "love triangle."

CORE FEATURES

These varieties aside, there are certain core features in patients with paranoid personality, some apparent to the casual observer, others that reveal themselves only after long acquaintance or after a fair amount of time in therapy. Akhtar (1990) summarizes these features well, dividing them into the *overt* and the *covert*, according to six frames of reference. As to *self-concept*, one finds overt arrogance, self-righteousness, and a readiness to anger, but covert feelings of inferiority and envy. In *interpersonal relations* mistrustfulness, humorlessness, and emotional coldness are on the surface; underneath, oversensitivity, fear of dependence and closeness, vengefulness, grudge-holding. In *social adaptation* there is industriousness, drivenness, but an inability to sustain friendships or become part of a "team" at work.

Overtly, in the area of *love and sexuality* one finds a lack of romantic interests and a priggish aversion to sexual humor; covertly, extreme anxiety about sexual prowess. In the domain of *superego* (values and ideals) there may be moralistic attitudes, overscrupulosity, and even religious fanaticism outwardly, but inwardly an idiosyncratic moral system or even a readiness to lie and distort. Overtly, the *cognitive style* is hypervigilant, nit-picking, searching for "evidence" to back up irrational assumptions; yet underneath there is an inability to "grasp the big picture" and a tendency to dismiss evidence that runs contrary to personal belief.

Akhtar's summary serves as a useful guide to orient therapists in their work with paranoid patients.

A FUN HOUSE MIRROR
THROUGH A WARPED LENS

In contrast to better integrated paranoid patients who are aware of their paranoid tendencies and in whom misperceptions are localized to narrow sectors of their life, more seriously disturbed patients with paranoid personality misperceive grossly. They are veritable geniuses at twisting the meanings of other people and at misconstruing the realities of everyday life, as might someone inspecting a fun house mirror through a warped lens. Since the subject matter under debate is emotional or speculative, rather than something easily verifiable, there is no "getting through" to the paranoid patient—certainly no *direct* access. Direct confrontation is if anything counterproductive, since it only elicits anger and vehement denial.

Thus a pathologically jealous newlywed, reacting to a not very tasty dinner prepared by the wife of one of her husband's old friends, screamed at him afterwards: "That bitch cooked slops to put me down!" Flabbergasted, the husband (my patient) asked, "How could you even think that? Cooking just isn't her forte. Anyhow, what woman would risk marring her reputation as a hostess by cooking poorly, just to deliver a hidden insult to another woman?" To which the wife retorted, "You're just covering up for her because you have the hots for her; I saw how you . . . ," etc., etc. Now the husband was faced with two impossible tasks: to prove that Mrs. _____ was really a mediocre chef, and to convince his wife that he didn't really find her attractive. This is a his-word-against-hers situation, with no appeal to external validation. Soon the atmosphere becomes electric with menace and accusation. To live with a paranoid person is to live perpetually in the defendant's box.

Kernberg (1982) gives another excellent example from his work with a narcissistic/paranoid man who accused him of billing him for a session that was never scheduled. The patient was in the wrong, but no matter: he kept up his vilification of Kernberg as a "liar" and a "cheat," until Kernberg finally suggested that there was a confrontation here between two separate "realities," where ultimately one of them must be "crazy." Unwilling to stigmatize either himself or Kernberg to quite that degree, the patient relented—not acknowledging that he was wrong, of course, merely adopting an attitude of noblesse oblige in which he was "willing to forgive and forget." For more outrageous examples of paranoid touchiness, where the accused can't win in the discussion, I can suggest the movies "Raging Bull" (about the pathologically jealous prizefighter, Jake LaMotta) and "Goodfellas" (depicting a paranoid Mafia underboss who distorts innocent comments by friends into life-and-death confrontations).

In psychotherapy, the seriously paranoid patient misreads the therapist's intentions, and then misreads the subsequent explanations meant to clarify the original misunderstanding, misreads the still further attempts to clarify the clarifications, and so on in an infinite series of distortions. This may create an insuperable hurdle for the therapist, who has neither the time for infinite explanations nor the ability to take the patient into his life—there to acquaint the patient with his honesty and trustworthiness.

In patients with mild paranoid trends, especially where these trends do not invade the therapeutic relationship to any great extent, this problem of the infinite distortions does not arise. But where the severity of the personality disorder is such as to approximate chronic delusion, this problem does arise and will tax the therapist's ingenuity to the utmost—in what will usually be an unsuccessful venture. Some of these points I hope to illustrate in the following vignettes.

CLINICAL ILLUSTRATIONS

Mild Paranoid Trends in a Well-Functioning Patient

Peter, an associate in a large law firm, sought therapy because of anxiety, at times of near-panic proportions, when having to converse with the senior partners or to give a public address. Though he kept his background as secret as possible, he felt that his Jewish origins would be found out and that the higher-ups of his very "Anglo-Saxon" firm would never promote him to partnership. They already seemed unfriendly to him, in his opinion, which he attributed to their "envy" of his expertise in a certain area of corporate law. Peter himself admitted he was "a bit paranoid" about the partners, and that his doubts and worries had made him more irritable with his wife. Though he did not question her fidelity, he did pick on her for all manner of trivial shortcomings; he was slow to forgive and quick to blow up in anger. He realized he was "a bit paranoid" with her also, in that the first time she broke a dish through carelessness, he was "merely" angry, but the second or third time he began to think she had done so on purpose, as if to annoy him.

Peter and his mother had come to this country from Russia when he was 11. His father, a minor official, had been held by the authorities for "political offenses" and was not permitted to rejoin his family until the patient was 15. The family had Americanized their name from Pozolotchik to Gilder (the name means "goldsmith"); his first name from Lev to Lou. As "Lou Gilder" he felt he could "pass," though at his firm he felt discovery and rejection were around the corner. This came through in a dream:

I am in prison. I needed to be in one of two sections if I were to be released. I believed I was in the wrong section, and would be discovered. I go to the head guard, who tells me I'm in the wrong section, so I run to the other. The scene changes, and I'm in a room where a mask is suspended in midair. An eye stares down at me. I stare back at the eye, like a contest of wills, and I awake in a sweat.

The *two sections* reminded him of the Nazi concentration camps where the guards divided the Jews into two groups: those (who couldn't work) for immediate extermination, and the "arbeitsfähige" (the work-capable) who were safe for a while. The *eye* was like "Big Brother," a political tyrant who spies on everyone. His law firm had become like a prison: a hostile environment, where he had no way of knowing where he stood.

Over the course of the next year and a half Peter was made partner, but he still did not feel at ease with his colleagues. He grew weary of the constant efforts required to hide his identity and of the anxiety of not knowing whether the partners would spurn him socially if they did find out. The longer he worked there the less the risk seemed to him—but how could he be sure? He finally rendered the problem "moot," as he put it, by taking the bold step of leaving the firm altogether and setting up a law office with himself and a few friends. His anxiety and paranoid fears lessened. His dreams still at times were cast in the paranoid mold, centering on themes of being under attack. Now, however, he was the victor instead of the vanquished; he was now the watcher rather than the watched:

I'm in a room with a shelf on all sides. There are lots of leopards on the shelves, and they jump down at me. I have a sword, and I dexterously dispatch them. I could even sense the ones behind me as if I had eyes in the back of my head.

His paranoid tendencies were by now much less in evidence.

A Paranoid Patient Functioning at the Borderline Level

Twenty-six when he began in therapy with me, Paul had been in treatment for two years in another city near his home in New England. Unemployed when he first moved to New York, he was supported by his parents. This was the man described briefly above (in the section on Oversimplification), who had been sodomized by his father and physically abused by his older brother. Depressed and discouraged initially, he was unable to articulate clear goals. He was unsure whether he wanted to return to graduate school or to work, whether to live a heterosexual or an asexual life. His family was contemptuous of homosexuality (despite the father's behavior). Identifying with their values, he could not accept the idea that the orientation he would be most comfortable with was homosexual.

He had been an outstanding student in graduate school, majoring in linguistics. At one point a male professor made a "pass" at him. This sent him into a panic and led to his dropping out of school and starting therapy back in his home town. Paul was so guarded, and remained so throughout the years I worked with him, that I could never form an accurate picture of the past. Had the professor made an unmistakable pass, for example, or had Paul misinterpreted an innocuous gesture? The previous therapist, at all events, pursued the topic of "unconscious homosexuality" too vigorously, or so Paul felt, and this too led to intense anxiety—so much so that patient and therapist grew uncomfortable with one another. This prompted Paul to seek help elsewhere and move to a different city.

His personality traits, especially at the beginning, were these: angry, bitter, censorious, cold, compulsive, overly controlled, cynical, dour, envious, fastidious, grudge-holding, guarded, humorless, hypercritical, insecure, intimidating, irritable, judgmental, mistrustful, moralistic, prissy, reproachful, seething with hatred, self-righteous, unapproachable, uncompassionate, and unsociable. His cynicism came through in his initial assumption that I would "prefer to treat a Rockefeller for nothing" than to treat him for a fee—as though treating a famous person would be a feather in my cap, whereas working with him gave me no social advantages.

He became less "paranoid" about our situation after I asked him whether he perhaps saw me that way as a reflection of his own self-disparagement: that no one would want to treat him because he was a "worthless" human being. This made sense to him, and he mentioned how he would buy a ticket to the opera—his favorite form of entertainment—only to then tear it up on the way to the concert hall because he felt he didn't "deserve" to experience anything pleasurable. Once, in a session that just preceded the opera, he told me he was again going to rip up his ticket. I hastily wrote out a prescription-form: "Go to the damn opera and enjoy it!" This was a turning point, at least with respect to concerts. He went, enjoyed the event, and continued afterwards to go attend the opera with some regularity.

Given what happened with the previous therapist, I opted for a treatment program that emphasized getting him to work, no matter at what, as a first step toward self-sufficiency. I doubted whether he could ever talk about the sexual molestation by his father so long as he still saw himself as a totally dependent and damaged person. To be able to support himself would mean that the events of the past had not altogether ruined him; therefore, he would not have to feel unbearable anguish at the mere recounting to me of the events he up until now equated with his "hopeless" condition. Since his means were limited, I reduced our sessions from two to one a week and encouraged him to meet once weekly with a vocational rehabilitation counselor. Within a short time he did find work, first as an assistant in an insurance company, later as a translator at a foreign bank. At both jobs, he came early, left late, impressed his superiors with his industriousness, and remained aloof from everyone. Openly disdainful of those who were less hardworking than he, or who "cut corners," he developed a reputation of being a gloomy crank. People who were cheerful, or who had a sense of humor, he considered frivolous. He often complained to me of the unfairness of his bosses or the "meanness" of his coworkers—who would "mutter things under their breath" about him. I suspect people at work did mutter things under their breath, not at first, but after being "put off" or "put down" by him enough times.

Though I worked with Paul eight years, and though he had finally reenrolled in graduate studies in his area of interest, he never softened with regard to coworkers or people his age. He made friends with his new professors, but with no one else. He did begin to make his peace with his family and even had some kind words for his father, with whom, after a lapse of many years, he effected a rapprochement. But in therapy, he still never spoke of the incest. He prided himself on his scrupulous honesty and excellence of character, yet to judge from his dreams—where mass annihilations of his many "enemies" formed the usual scenery—his good character was like the gift-wrapping over a terrorist's time bomb. If the mantle of power were suddenly draped around his shoulders, it would be easy to picture him a duplicate of Himmler. He was, and remained, without compassion. My efforts to broaden his understanding of people's motives, or to nudge him toward a more sympathetic attitude about the suffering of others, invariably fell flat.

The following incident, which stems from the sixth year of treatment, is illustrative. Paul was once returning home, he told me, on an almost empty subway, reading the newspaper and, as usual, minding his own business. A young woman sitting nearby, well dressed but "lonely looking" in his opinion, tried to engage him in conversation. He scowled at her "impertinence" and told her "Can't you see I'm reading?" A few stops later, she got off, muttering (or so he insisted) "faggot" or "fuck you," as she disembarked. "The nerve of some people!" he exclaimed to me, "You *see* what I'm up against out there?! Do you still wonder why I feel I'm not of the same species as all these people?"

My response was along these lines: "Well, let's assume you heard correctly and she said just what you told me she said. It's at least thinkable though, isn't it, that if you weren't always expecting the worst, and if you could feel a little sorry for her as a lonely person, etc., you might have been inclined to say something that put her down gently. You could still have gotten out of having to chat with her, without being abrupt, without hurting her feelings, and without prompting her to make a retaliatory remark. Like if you'd said, 'Gee, lady, I'd have been happy to talk with you, except I'm reading something for a report I have to make, and I'm under some pressure; I hope you can excuse me if I go back to my reading?' That would have gotten you off the hook, and I doubt she would have said anything insulting as she got off the train."

To this he replied, "The bitch didn't deserve all that diplomacy." The idea that she started out innocent and that he turned her into a "bitch" by his iciness was something he could not, or would not, see. My encouraging him to try diplomacy on the next such occasion—as a test of whether people would be friendlier in return—met only with puzzlement. The experiment seemed too risky.

TREATMENT ISSUES

There are a number of general points one can make about doing psychotherapy with patients who exhibit significant paranoid traits. Though candor and honesty are necessary ingredients of any therapist's character, with paranoid patients these qualities will be looked for with special keenness and tested to the maximum. The ease with which the therapist can deal with the mistrustfulness of paranoid patients—especially with those that make open demands for "100% honesty"—will depend in part on the source of this mistrustful attitude. Parents who had been abusive but not deceitful create distrust based on fear of hurt, yet without the added suspicion of being lied to. Paranoid persons from such backgrounds may actually be easier to deal with than those who had been lied to repeatedly, even if abuse was not in the picture. The tendency in the latter case would be to assume, in the transference, that the therapist would be a liar "like everybody else."

When (as alluded to above) the man in the last vignette became enraged with me in one of our first meetings, he pounded on the chair with his fists and in a menacing tone said: "I feel like kicking you in the balls!" I told him I felt intimidated, adding that if we were to accomplish anything together, we would have to talk things out to the point where he felt he could trust me and I felt I was safe in the room with him. I asked him to share with me if he could what raw nerve I had inadvertently touched that angered him, since this was not clear to me. He appreciated my being honest with him in this way and took some reassurance from the fact that if I were scared of a "puny" person like him, perhaps he was not such a pushover as he had always felt himself to be. He never exploded like that again in the remaining eight years of our work.

Paranoid patients who had been lied to during their formative years must often get to know a therapist over many months or even years before they can accumulate enough first-hand experience to overcome their initial doubts. Such patients often try, like a cross-examining attorney, to polarize subtle comments of a therapist into the language of "black-and-white." A therapist may, for example, speak of having been annoyed, momentarily and to a modest degree, with the patient. To the paranoid patient this may sound like proof that "you hate me." It becomes necessary to teach the patient about the shades of grey ordinary folk recognize and adapt to. This is not a matter of ten easy lessons; rather, of a thousand painful lessons.

Among authors who describe their approach to paranoid patients there is consensus on two main issues: direct attempts to confront and refute the paranoid assertion should be avoided (Colby et al., 1979), and the therapist should endeavor to introduce an element of *doubt* in the patient's mind concerning the validity of the assertion. The latter point has been made repeatedly since the first generation of psychoanalysts who sought to apply the analytic method to patients showing not only paranoid personality but frank persecutory delusions (Bjerre, 1912; Maeder, 1910).

Poul Bjerre, for example, recounts the case of a paranoid woman who became referential about men in the street who, she thought, were "sticking their tongues out at her in a mocking way." It developed that she had recently been rejected by a lover and had become disconsolate over the loss. Bjerre responded: Perhaps things happened just as you related them to me. But isn't there also a possibility that, under the impact of the severe loss that you suffered, your mind became impressionable, and that you might have misinterpreted the gestures of certain men who were perhaps wetting their lips, or making some other movement that was not intended for you? In this way Bjerre gradually got her to view the matter in a more realistic light. He kept in touch with her for a number of years, during which she gave evidence of a lasting recovery.

Ruth Mack Brunswick reported similar success with a paranoid woman she treated a generation later (1929), also relying on the technique of half agreeing with the patient while at the same time half wondering if there might also be alternative, more innocent interpretations. More recently, Salzman (1960) and Kernberg (1982) reiterate these points, stressing in addition the need to be aware of the paranoid patient's sensitivity to "invasion" of personal boundaries and to the related fear of losing a sense of self.

Searles (1965), in a paper first published in 1952, drew attention to a fear of dependency in certain highly paranoid patients, along with fear of strong emotions of any kind. One such patient answered a comment of Searles with the words: "One has to be cautious." "About what?" Searles inquired. "About people," he said, "Otherwise there is dissension and resentment. I keep out of things: that's the way *I* like to operate." When pressed to explain what was so intolerable about feeling resentment, the patient went on: "It leads to violence" (p. 84).

The need for interpersonal distance, typical of paranoid persons, is also apparent in the language of this patient: detached, impersonal, abstract (*one* has to be . . . , otherwise *there is* . . . , etc.). Therapists will often try to nudge such patients, unless they are particularly contentious and oversensitive, to accept ownership of their feelings—through adroitly pseudo-naïve comments like: "When you were saying "one" just then, I guess you had yourself in mind, also; would that be correct?" or "When you said, 'It leads to violence,' were you saying in effect that you're afraid *you'd* be tempted to get violent? Or that someone might get violent toward you?"

Obsessive-compulsive patients also tend to use impersonal phrases of this sort (as part of an overall tendency to "isolation of affect"), which need to be countered with similar techniques. Millon (1981) has pointed out that paranoid patients are in fact often compulsive as well, and that certain other trait-combinations are common in the domain of paranoid personality—namely, narcissistic, passive-aggressive, and antisocial. The passive-aggressive/paranoid patient, like the more purely paranoid "litigious" patient, is particularly challenging in therapy, because of his massive distrust of authority and general negativism. The negativism is such that the patient takes greater satisfaction in proving the therapist wrong and in defeating treatment than in "getting better" or acknowledging some benefit from the therapist—since this would be tantamount to a humiliating "submission."

Other points about which there is good agreement among therapists from different schools of thought concern the need to enhance the paranoid patient's self-sufficiency. Beck and Freeman (1990), writing from the perspective of cognitive therapy, underline this approach as a way of helping such patients overcome their feelings of inferiority—especially in the area of sex. Paranoid persons tend to disparage "weakness" in others, which, as the authors mention, probably represents a projection of their own sense of not measuring up. In general, paranoid mechanisms are mobilized in the interest of warding off shame and humiliation. Paranoid patients are inordinately preoccupied with "losing face." But if self-esteem can be bolstered in one area (viz., work or artistic pursuits), this better feeling about oneself can, it is hoped, spill over into the even more sensitive areas of sex and intimate involvement.

It is of interest that, despite the differences in vocabulary and despite the rarity with which proponents of one technique cite the works of the other school, cognitive and analytically oriented therapists have evolved similar techniques with paranoid patients and emphasize the same hierarchy of tactics. Meissner (1976), writing from the analytic perspective, speaks of the need to convert paranoid/projective mechanisms to "depressive/introjective" mechanisms. The latter more easily admit of being worked through in the course of psychotherapy.

Paranoid mechanisms (viz., projection, projective identification, externalization) are, as Meissner mentions, not limited to patients with fully developed paranoid personality. They may be found in patients of most any personality type. Wherever they are noted, the therapist will have the same tasks: "calling into question the projective assumptions" (i.e., introducing an element of *doubt*, as mentioned earlier) (p. 97), and "tactfully pointing out where the patient's knowledge of the world may be insufficient" (p. 98).

Toward the end of the therapeutic experience, the paranoid patient may, as Meissner notes, "retreat into pseudoautonomy" (p. 110). This, I believe, is conceptually the equivalent of what Salzman and Kernberg were drawing attention to in describing the difficulty paranoid patients have in either acknowledging dependency or retaining a comfortable sense of self when in a "dependent" relationship. In the rare situation where dependency is excessive in a paranoid patient; namely, where there is concomitant erotomania, one tries to foster in the patient the ability to be less dependent: Segal (1989) capsulized this neatly in recommending "neuroleptics and distance."

Apropos this need for "space" in paranoid patients there is usually a need for more space between appointments than would usually be scheduled for other types of patients in the same kind of therapy. Patients with distinctly paranoid personalities tend to become ill at ease if treated in a "classic" psychoanalytic mode, with four or five visits a week. This frequency fosters a depth of self-revelation and a level of transference involvement that may easily become threatening. It does not matter that the "dynamics" are clear to the therapist and that the patient "ought" to be able to work through the various conflicts. Paranoid patients will sooner break off treatment than suffer the anxiety that, for them, is attendant upon such closeness with the therapist. It will often be wiser for the therapist, faced with this situation, to accede to the patient's wish for a less intense schedule.

It is true that for some patients—in whom the paranoid traits are milder, or where there is a liberal admixture of depressive/intropunitive traits—analytically oriented or even full-scale analytic therapy may be comfortable and may succeed. Perhaps it is patients of this latter type that formed the basis for the above-mentioned articles by Kernberg and Meissner. But within the whole domain of paranoid personality disorder, at least as defined by DSM, I suspect that these patients are in the minority.

It is for similar reasons that one must ordinarily set less ambitious goals for paranoid patients and be guided often by their goals (rather than impose loftier but unrealistic goals upon the patient), especially as concerns the sphere of intimate relationships. If we were to divide the personality types into two fractions—those that cling vs. those that shun dependency, wishing to go their own way—the latter form more tenuous attachment to a therapist and are correspondingly more challenging to treat. This distinction, by the way, is the same as Balint (1969) designated by the terms "ocnophilic" and "philobatic" (as explained in Chapter 6). Paranoid, schizoid, passive-aggressive, antisocial, and certain narcissistic patients belong generally to the "philobatic" group; hysteric, dependent, masochistic, depressive, and many borderline patients to the "ocnophilic" group. Treatment strategies and prognosis are determined in large measure by the prominence of one or the other attribute.

Cluster B

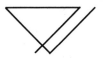

Dramatic Disorders

11

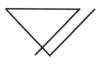

Borderline Personality Disorder

> I sit on the ledge
> looking down at the city.
> My view of the sidewalk
> is really quite pretty.
> I turn and I jump,
> it's over and done—
> the windows are washed
> and lunchtime's begun.
>
> Jane D. (1963)

IN THE PAST GENERATION, more space in the psychiatric literature has been devoted to *borderline* than to any other personality disorder. Earlier, the psychoanalytic literature concentrated upon the so-called character disorders: hysteric, obsessive, phobic, depressive, and to a lesser extent, narcissistic and paranoid. As we currently use the term, "character" refers predominantly to one's inner self and to one's value system, as these are formed and solidified through parental rearing. Nonpsychoanalytic psychiatry focused on matters of temperament, on forensic issues relating to antisocial personality (or, if you will, persons of "bad" character), and on personality types associated with schizophrenia or manic-depression (cf. Kraepelin, 1921).

Why so many articles, books, symposia, meetings, etc., on borderline patients? Since persons with hysteric (histrionic), obsessive-compulsive, or depressive traits vastly out number borderline patients, I can only assume it is the *difficulty* in treating the latter that has brought about their popularity in our field. They are not the only difficult patients: passive-aggressive, schizoid, and paranoid patients are also very challenging to a therapist's skills. Antisocial persons are mostly *beyond* our skills. But borderline patients are more commonly encountered than, say, schizoid patients: perhaps 1½–2½% of the population would meet DSM criteria for "BPD," whereas schizoid persons are either fewer in number or, almost certainly, less disposed to use the services of the mental health profession. The symptomatology of borderline patients clamors for our attention: manipulative suicide gestures, angry outbursts, midnight calls, sudden and inexplicable mood swings, moments of delusional thinking, "acting out," etc.

Recent Books on Borderline Personality Disorder

The reader may find it useful to view the literature on borderline patients, the books in particular, in chronological fashion, much as one might walk past their shelf in a psychiatric library. The list in Table 16 is not complete, but it does give an accurate picture of how crowded this shelf had become during the 1980s. Most, but not all, the books used the term "borderline" in the title; their contents centered around cases we would now call "borderline" by one or another of the more popular definitions. I have listed multi-authored and edited books by their first author or by the editor, using an asterisk. Those whose orientation is primarily or exclusively psychoanalytic I have designated with the abbreviation "(Psa)."

This table, of course, does not do justice to the many important chapters on various aspects of borderline conditions in books not primarily centered on this topic, nor to the thousands of articles in psychiatry and other mental health journals that have appeared, especially over the past 25 years. In beginning our discussion of this vast and complex subject, it may be helpful to provide a brief history of how the "borderline" concept evolved. More detailed accounts are to be found in several earlier contributions (Stone, 1980a; 1985a; 1990b).

Evolution of the Borderline Concept

Alienists of the nineteenth century, having begun to utilize the terms "neurotic" (first used by William Cullen, 1807), to designate less serious mental conditions and "psychotic" for more serious conditions, noticed that some persons exhibited conditions intermediate between these two extremes. Some were nondelusional patients who were nevertheless so handicapped with either depressive or cognitive symptoms as to warrant assignment to a place in the "borderland" between neurosis and psychosis (Rosse, 1890). Others were recidivist criminals, also nondelusional, but hardly "healthy"— so they too were relegated to this in-between zone (Lombroso, 1878).

As psychoanalysis began to make its impact, shortly after the turn of the century, the analytic pioneers began to notice that some of their analysands, though, again, not "psychotic" (or only briefly so), seemed never to improve much with even a lengthy course of analytic therapy. They were thus sicker than the ordinary "neurotic" patients who proved amenable to Freud's

TABLE 16

Books on the Borderline

YEAR	AUTHOR	MAIN CONTENTS
1954	Knight*	(Psa) Two articles by Knight on definition and therapy of borderline states
1967	Bryce-Boyer*	(Psa) Treatment of schizophrenic, borderline, and characterological disorders
1968	Grinker*	Study of 52 hospitalized borderline patients; description of 4 main sub-types
1968	Balint	(Psa) The "basic fault" described; the limitations of classic technic
1971	Kohut	(Psa) Self psychology as applied to narcissistic and borderline patients
1973	Wolberg	(Psa) Origins of borderline seen as identification with parents' unfulfilled needs
1974	Blanck*	(Psa) Pathological narcissism and borderline states; use of dream analysis
1975	Bergeret	(Psa) Three levels of mental function; psychoanalytic approach to borderline and depressive states
1975	Mack*	Definition, drug therapy, inpatient psychotherapy of borderline patients
1975	Kernberg	(Psa) Description and psychoanalytic therapy of borderline patients; object relations theory
1977	Grinker*	Case studies, follow-up studies, family of the borderline patient, "stable instability"
1977	Chessick	(Psa) Intensive psychotherapy of the borderline patient; discussion of narcissism
1977	Hartocollis*	(Psa) Concept explained; empirical studies; individual group, and family therapy
1979	LeBoit*	(Psa) Metapsychology; transference and countertransference issues; jealousy
1979	Vanggaard	(Psa) Schizophrenic borderline states; severe neuroses; borderline affective conditions
1980	Kernberg	(Psa) Discussion of Klein, Fairbairn, Jacobson; narcissism; transference in borderlines
1980a	Stone	Overview of concept; multidimensional diagnostic approach; clinical examples
1980	Kwawer*	The Rorschach test in borderline patients, including children and adolescents; treatment implications
1981	Aarkrog	(Psa) Study of borderline adolescents (diagnostic criteria resemble our schizotypal patients)
1981	Klebanow*	(Psa) Chapters dealing with treatment issues
1981	Little	(Psa) Transference and countertransference from British object relations standpoint
1981	Masterson	(Psa) Therapy of borderline and narcissistic patients; focus on separation/individuation
1981	Stone*	Definition, genetics, abuse factor, family factors, structural interviewing
1981	Millon	Description of all the DSM-III personality disorders, including borderline
1981	Battegay	(Psa) General discussion of borderline patients
1982	Rinsley	(Psa) Therapy of borderline patients, focusing on Mahlerian concepts, part-objects
1982	Slipp*	(Psa) Chapters on definition, therapy, turning points in treatment
1983	Abend et al.*	(Psa) Therapy from object relations orientation, with 4 case reports
1983	Akhtar*	Chapters on new psychiatric syndromes, including borderline and narcissistic states

(continued)

217

TABLE 16

Continued

YEAR	AUTHOR	MAIN CONTENTS
1983	Frosch	(Psa) Psychotic defenses, unconscious homosexuality in paranoia; borderline states
1983	Rohde-Dachser	(Psa) Definitions; theories of Kernberg, Searles, Wolberg, Mahler; psychotherapy
1983	Steingart	(Psa) Splitting, ambivalence, pathological play in borderline and narcissistic personalities
1983	Robson*	Etiology, diagnosis, treatment of borderline child; attention-deficit disorders
1984	Kernberg	(Psa) Therapy of severe personality disorders (borderline and narcissistic); hospital treatment
1984	Meissner	(Psa) Levels of psychopathology; etiology; criteria of analyzability
1984	Gunderson	Diagnosis, dynamics, ego-psychological therapy, multimodal treatment
1985	McGlashan*	Empirical research: follow-up, self-report instrument, defenses, transitional object
1985a	Stone*	Historical review and commentary on 24 reprinted articles from 1884 to 1984
1985	Adler	(Psa) A deficiency model of borderline pathology; focus on psychotherapy
1986	Searles	(Psa) Focus on transference/countertransference work with borderline and schizophrenic patients
1986	Wallerstein	(Psa) Follow-up report on Menninger project: 42 borderline, mostly ambulatory patients
1987	Dahl	Symptom patterns, family backgrounds, ego function in hospitalized borderline patients
1987	Grotstein*	Dynamic and genetic aspects of etiology; analytic and other forms of therapy
1987	Volkan	(Psa) A six-step approach to therapy of borderline patients, with detailed case report
1987	Waldinger*	Diagnostic and prognostic patterns; dynamic therapy; five case reports
1988	Kroll	Core features; "affective" vs. BPD; therapy, including drugs; countertransference
1988	Meissner	(Psa) Limit-setting, confrontation, interpretation; group and family therapy
1988	Slavinska-Holy	Use of self psychology; expressive group therapy; auxiliary modalities
1989	Kernberg*	Articles on narcissistic disorders, including some with BPD comorbidity
1989	Kernberg, Selzer et al.*	(Psa) Principles and phases in dynamic therapy of borderline patients; acting out
1990	Stone	10–25-year follow-up study of 300 borderline patients (206 meeting DSM-III criteria)
1990	Links*	Family environment in BPD; role of childhood abuse, especially sexual abuse
1991	Cohen & Sherwood	(Psa) Focus on helping borderline patients achieve object-constancy
1992	Clarkin*	Etiology, diagnosis, treatment: dynamic, dialectical, group, multimodal
1992	Silver*	Diagnosis, follow-up, biologic factors; dynamic, behavior, and group therapies
1992	Cauwels	Overview of all aspects of borderline personality disorder
1993	Paris*	Focus on etiological (especially, traumatogenic) factors and on therapy

*First author of multi-authored work.

method. These patients were now regarded as "borderline"—neither neurotic nor psychotic, but somewhere in between. This usage reflected their *level of function*—mirrored later in Kernberg's definition of borderline as the intermediate of three levels: neurotic, borderline, and psychotic.

Whereas the original descriptions by such analysts as Stern (1938) and Helene Deutsch (1942) were imprecise, Kernberg (1967) sought to give "borderline" clearer definitional boundaries, limned within the framework of object relational theory. It should be added that during mid-century most analysts felt that their "borderline" cases were not only "in between" with respect to analyzability, but probably also at the border of a particular psychosis, namely, schizophrenia (H. Deutsch, 1942). Presumably, one could be "borderline" in relation to manic-depressive psychosis as well, but this possibility received little support, except from the work of Edith Jacobson (1971; 1971a).

Knight (1953), though he felt borderline states were probably affiliated with schizophrenia, tended to use "borderline" as a name for a separate clinical entity, thus de-coupling the concept from that of schizophrenia. The reader should remember that in the U.S.A. at mid-century (and well before the advent of lithium for manic patients) the major definition of schizophrenia was Bleulerian: very broad by contemporary standards, such that "psychosis" and schizophrenia were nearly indistinguishable.

Kernberg extended Knight's tendency further, defining borderline in a manner quite distinct from schizophrenia. In his definition (Kernberg, 1967), the views of Erikson (on identity diffusion: 1956) and Frosch (on reality-testing capacity: 1964) are synthesized: *borderline personality organization* is that characteristic level of functioning where the sense of identity is weak (unlike the situation in neurosis), yet the capacity to test reality is preserved (unlike the situation in psychosis). Still, the Kernberg definition is quite broad and may be applicable to some 10 or 11% of the population—mapping onto that segment of the bell-curve of mental health situated between one and two standard deviations from the norm, on the "ill" side, just next to the extreme 5% who are psychotic (Stone, 1988).

In an effort to define *borderline* along less inferential, more directly observable lines, Gunderson and Singer (1975) developed a six-item criterion set: impulsivity, brief psychotic episodes, manipulative suicide gestures, poor work history, adequate socialization, and depressed mood in the face of rejection or loss of an intimate relationship. This was another definition separate from schizophrenia: in the latter, socialization was usually impaired. Neurotic persons usually had a better work history. Gunderson's criteria constitute a *syndrome*, relying partly on personality traits but mostly on symptoms. The same is true of the DSM definition—an outgrowth of some features of Kernberg, others of Gunderson—though borderline in DSM is classified solely as a *personality disorder* (Spitzer et al., 1979).

Three other ways of understanding "borderline" remain in current use, though they have less acceptance and popularity than they once enjoyed: borderline as a special *dynamic constellation* (involving separation/individuation problems), as emphasized by Masterson (1981) and Rinsley (1982); as a *prognostic statement* (a *post facto* label applied to unsuccessful attempts at resolving narcissistic disturbances via self-psychological psychoanalysis: Kohut, 1971); finally, as a *forme fruste* of schizophrenia—one of the original uses of the term, as carried forward in the work of psychogeneticists like Kety, Rosenthal et al. (1968).

DEMOGRAPHIC AND CULTURAL FACTORS

The currently more popular and objectifiable definitions of borderline—those of DSM or Gunderson—besides being narrower than the Kernberg definition, also emphasize serious symptoms to a greater degree, and thus single out a more psychiatrically ill population than the broader Kernberg criteria. As mentioned in Chapter 7, in the P.I.-500 study (Stone et al., 1987), the suicide rate was 9% among DSM-III borderlines, but only 2½% in Kernberg borderlines who met criteria for neither dysthymia nor BPD, and zero in the dysthymic (but non-BPD) group.

No matter which definition one uses, however, a preponderance of female patients is customary, at least in the U.S. The excess may be in the range of 2:1, 3:1, or even higher. This is not the case in Norway, Sweden, or Denmark, where more reserved, "schizotypal" traits are common in the patients labeled "borderline" (cf. Aarkrog, 1981; Dahl, 1987). Schizotypal traits seem in general more evenly distributed between the sexes. In the U.S. the marked female preponderance may have to do with a different base-rate for schizoidal traits in the general population, as compared with Scandinavia. It is possible, however, that this imbalance is a reflection of the differential incest rates in the two regions. Though epidemiological incest studies of comparable elegance to that of Russell (1986) are not available from European countries, the incest rate may be higher here. Because of the close connection between a history of *transgenerational* incest (especially father-daughter) and the development of BPD in females, a female preponderance would be expected. This type of incest is about six times as common among girls as among boys (Finkelhor, 1984; see also Chapter 17).

In Japan, where the incest rate is thought to be considerably lower than in the U.S. (Kuninao Minakawa, M.D., personal communication), there is a female preponderance in BPD—but the typical patient is a young woman who has made a suicide gesture after a broken romance, but who shows little anger, etc.

DIFFERENTIAL DIAGNOSIS

The general topic of borderline personality and its diagnostic near neighbors has been elaborated by Kernberg (1967), Gunderson (1984), and Stone (1992).

The currently important definitions of borderline are much more closely allied, phenomenologically, to the affective than to the schizophrenic disorders. BPD needs to be distinguished from more serious affective conditions such as bipolar II manic-depression (similar to "hysteroid dysphoria" as outlined by Liebowitz and Klein, 1981) and recurrent depression, when the latter is accompanied by high irritability. Less dramatic forms of affective illness, such as cyclothymia, dysthymia, and "irritable temperament" (cf. Kraepelin, 1921) may also resemble BPD, especially in young persons suffering from the first of what will turn out to be a long sequence of irritable/depressive episodes.

There is a rough correspondence between the patients whom diagnosticians are currently calling "borderline" and those whom psychoanalytically-oriented therapists had spoken of as their most difficult or challenging patients. It is of interest that several clinicians at Menninger's write about a special group of hospitalized patients as "difficult" (Allen, Colson et al., 1986; Colson, Allen, et al., 1986)—where the word *difficult* becomes something of a specific diagnostic term. There is considerable overlap, for example, between the characteristics of their "difficult" patients and those of DSM borderline patients. The four main attributes Colson and Allen mention are: (a) character pathology (verbal hostility, inappropriate demands, manipulativeness), (b) withdrawn psychoticism (regressed, not involved in treatment), (c) violence or agitation (viz., poor impulse control), and (d) suicidal/depressed behavior (self-damage, depression).

Women subject to the more severe forms of premenstrual tension ("late luteal dysphoria") often exhibit depression and irritability shortly before or during the early part of their menses. Some are prone to self-damaging acts in order to relieve the tension; a few others even experience suicidal feelings. They thus resemble BPD patients. To complicate matters, a high proportion of women with established BPD experience an aggravation of their symptoms during this part of their cycle (Stone, 1982).

The physical or sexual abuse suffered by many BPD patients will often have been extreme enough to set in motion the syndrome of "PTSD" (post-traumatic stress disorder), with its flashbacks, nightmares, etc. But some patients with PTSD do not show enough of BPD "items" to qualify for a comorbid diagnosis (i.e., they might not show inordinate anger, self-damaging acts, etc.).

Certain conditions with a primarily "organic" underpinning (as best one can determine) may resemble BPD. This is true of temporal lobe epilepsy ("partial complex seizures") or of "episodic dyscontrol" (especially in adolescent males prone to explosive rage outbursts: cf. Andrulonis et al., 1981).

BPD may be confused with other personality disorders, particularly with those of the "dramatic cluster." More importantly, almost all the other category-based personality disorders can be "fellow travelers" with BPD, as pointed out by Oldham et al. (1992). BPD will often be found in conjunction with several other—even four or five—"PDs," if one relies on DSM criteria, such that a whole "profile" is established: BPD with narcissistic, antisocial, and histrionic traits, for example, or BPD with depressive, avoidant, and passive-aggressive traits, and so on. It is always important to determine whether and which of the other PDs are present, since treatment and prognosis depend heavily upon the combination encountered. Schizoid PD is the one disorder seldom found in conjunction with BPD, at least in the U.S.

A complicated reciprocal relationship exists between BPD and illicit drugs, inasmuch as abuse of alcohol and certain drugs (viz., amphetamines) can intensify the symptomatology of BPD, by making the impulsivity even worse. Substance abuse is common among BPD patients. But it may also happen, especially among adolescents or young adults, that abuse of amphetamines, marijuana, or psychedelics occurs first, setting in motion a deterioration of habits and self-control and leading to a clinical picture resembling BPD (cf. Chapter 2, section on chimerical personality).

There are several species of *impulse control disorders* that also resemble, overlap with, or could be confused with BPD. Repetitive "acting out" of the transference in psychoanalytic patients may be seen as a form of impulse disorder; many articles by analysts were devoted to this topic a generation ago (Frosch, 1977; Rangell, 1955). We now recognize that certain syndromes such as trichotillomania (Winchell, 1992), intermittent explosive disorder (Lion, 1992), and repetitive self-mutilation (Favazza, 1992; Grunebaum & Klerman, 1967; Pao, 1969; Pattison & Kahan, 1983; Rosenthal et al., 1972) are often noted in patients with BPD, yet may also exist as separate impulse disorders in persons who do not manifest enough other BPD traits to justify a dual diagnosis.

Over long periods of time one can discern patterns in impulse dyscontrol in BPD: bulimia is more common in recent years and is often accompanied by kleptomania and self-cutting. Kleptomania by itself was more common a generation ago. These manifestations are more common in women, especially during times of stress, including that of the premenstrual phase.

PERSONALITY TRAITS COMMONLY
ENCOUNTERED IN BPD

In the preceding section we enumerated some of the symptoms one may see in persons whose impulsivity goes beyond the level of "spontaneity" or mild recklessness. Since impulsivity is the one trait all definitions of "borderline" agree on (Perry & Klerman, 1978), it is not surprising that BPD patients are often "comorbid" for one or another of these Axis I conditions. They are, after all, two sides of the same coin.

If, for reasons of purism, we were to redefine "borderline" solely within the language of personality *traits*, a list would emerge of two dozen or more adjectives, such as I outlined in earlier papers (Stone, 1989, 1992). There I mentioned the following: alternatingly adoring and contemptuous, chaotic, childish, clingy, cranky, demanding, desultory, going to extremes, fickle, flighty, fragile, hostile, importunate, inconstant, irritable, manipulative, mercurial, moody, possessive, reckless, restless, seductive, shallow, unpredictable, unreasonable, vehement, and volatile. Oldham and Morris (1990) have emphasized the trait, "mercurial," in their description of BPD.

At present there is no way of rationalizing the trait-component of BPD with the symptom-component: though all patients of BPD show one or another combination of the above traits, many persons exhibit some of these traits without in addition fulfilling the other criteria for BPD as it is currently understood.

Certain other traits also occur with especial frequency in patients with BPD, though they are less closely related to the "central" borderline qualities of irritability (cf. Stone, 1988), mercurial mood (lability, volatility, etc.), and unreasonableness. *Jealousy*, for example, is a common, and intense, problem in many borderline patients (cf. Mullen & Maack, 1985; Stone, 1985), but the pathological forms of jealousy also occur in other personality disorders, especially paranoid and narcissistic PDs (cf. White & Mullen, 1989). Perhaps very "rigid" personalities of any type are, by virtue of inflexibility, prone to severe jealousy; likewise, very dependent persons may be vulnerable—to the extent that the love-object at hand seems utterly irreplaceable. The trait of *intensity* is itself also very common in borderline patients: they tend to have "all-or-none" responses (Kernberg, 1967) and to hug the extremes of any opinion, emotion, or behavioral tendency.

NATURAL HISTORY

The criteria for BPD, as set forth by DSM or Gunderson, rely upon a number of items—stormy relationships, manipulative suicide gestures—

that do not manifest themselves with great clarity until late adolescence. This means, in effect, that BPD has little relevance as a diagnosis before this time of life. There are children and early adolescents who are "in between" what might be considered neurotic or else clearly psychotic for this age group. Some attempts have been made to establish norms for a diagnosis of "borderline" in persons 16 or under (Vela et al., 1983), but these schemata have yet to win wide acceptance. Furthermore, there has not yet been time enough to perform long-term follow-up studies on "borderline" children, by way of determining what correlation exists, if any, between "borderline" in this younger age group and BPD in adults. Tove Aarkrog in Copenhagen is in the process of carrying out such a study on the former borderline patients of her residential unit, but these adolescents were more "schizotypal," on average, than the adolescent patients of most hospital units in the U.S.

This controversy aside, the usual debut of BPD is in the latter part of the second decade of life to the early part of the third. In my experience, there are two main sets of underlying factors. One has to do with an *innate predisposition to affective illness*, especially of the depressive/irritable sort, surfacing in late adolescence as rebelliousness, extreme moodiness, demandingness, and self-damaging acts. The other has to do with *parental abusiveness* (which is more apt to be sexual in the case of daughters, physical in the case of sons). Physical abuse is apparently the more common than incest in many locales (including Western Europe and Australia: cf. Stone, Unwin et al., 1988), particularly in this generation. Abuse-engendered BPD shows the same array of rebellious, impulsive, hostile behavior, moodiness, suicidal feelings, etc., as BPD that is more genetically determined. Promiscuity and substance abuse are common accompaniments of late-adolescent BPD, irrespective of the mix of underlying factors. (Of course, the future borderlines in some families *both* have inherited "risk genes" for bipolar II or other affective conditions *and* have been mistreated by various family members.) The separation/individuation problems emphasized by Masterson (1981) and Rinsley (1982) are noted in some borderline patients, but not to the extent that would be suggested by the samples upon which their contributions were based; also, the tighter and more symptom-oriented definitions now in use may create patient samples where abuse figures more importantly; separation problems, less so.

Borderline patients often come to the attention of the mental health profession via suicide gestures during high school or college (or during the often painful transition between high school and moving away to college). Or drug abuse may lead to dangerous, reckless behavior that, even in the absence of anything so alarming as suicidal acts, serves to alert family or others in authority. In other patients, severe eating disorders may mark the debut of illness. In the decade between the mid-60s and the mid-70s there appeared to be not only an increase in the incidence of anorexia nervosa (Willi & Grossman, 1983), but also, in young women with BPD, an increase in bulimia with self-induced vomiting. An abuse history is common in the latter group (Root & Fallon, 1988).

As to the typical clinical pictures BPD patients eventually present, Hurt et al. (1990), analyzing data from 465 BPD cases (gathered from four sources), developed a statistical strategy for compartmentalizing the cases into three major groups: an *identity* cluster (where the prominent features were identity disturbance, intolerance of being alone, and boredom/emptiness), an *affective* cluster (marked by anger, affect instability, and unstable relationships), and an *impulse* cluster (characterized by impulsivity and self-damaging acts). The latter two types were more common than the identity-cluster variant.

This differentiation has important prognostic implications, inasmuch as suicide risk is greatest in those manifesting the "impulse" cluster; less, though still substantial, in the "affective" group (especially in males); and least (almost negligible) in those showing mostly just the "identity" features. The borderline patients whom the earlier generation of psychoanalysts wrote about, and whom they treated with primarily exploratory or (in Kernberg's term) expressive (i.e., modified analytic) therapy, probably belonged mostly to this identity-disturbed (and less impulsive) group.

The long-term fate of borderline patients is discussed at greater length in Chapter 7. Here, we simply point out that patients with BPD regularly have a stormy course during their twenties. Many will require residential or brief hospital care at some point, though it is unclear what percentage of all persons who would fit this diagnostic category ultimately will have spent time in institutional care. Those who make serious and repetitive suicidal acts are perhaps best treated in long-term facilities, where stays of several months or a year or more are possible. The indications for this admittedly expensive and no longer so easily available form of treatment have been well delineated by Fenton and McGlashan (1990).

There is a general tendency for BPD patients to do rather poorly during their twenties, struggling with the difficulties of leaving home and of achieving emotional and occupational security. In their attempts to form intimate relationships, they run into the "need-fear" dilemma highlighted by Burnham et al. (1969). They crave closeness but fear being hurt or disappointed. This paradox can come about either because of innate nervous system irritability in those from relatively nurturing homes or because of deep (and quite understandable) distrust of others engendered by abusive caretakers during the formative years (Stone, 1988a).

Borderline patients, as they enter their thirties, often show a mellowing:

less self-destructive behavior, improved ability to form close and supportive relationships (or, in some, a better ability to get along without intimacy), a giving up of alcohol or other dangerous substances (often through the help of AA).

The fifth decade constitutes another critical period, when either the gains in emotional stability and gratification garnered during the preceding decade solidify or, as McGlashan discovered in his long-term follow-up study (1986), the clinical picture deteriorates under the impact of rejection or divorce and the ensuing loss of emotional support. It appears that the decisive variable here, determining whether a borderline patient continues to do well in midlife and beyond or suffers an exacerbation of illness, is *hostility* (Stone, 1990d). Those whose anger and querulousness continue to smoulder on into middle life eventually wear out the patience of spouses or other intimates upon whom they depend. Serious depression, resumption of drug abuse, suicide: these may be the results of having destroyed important relationships through anger. Meantime, many former BPD patients, by virtue of parting with self-destructive or rageful behavior and by virtue of solidifying their once enfeebled sense of identity, reach a higher plateau in their forties and fifties, such that the "borderline" label is no longer applicable. Factors conducing to good outcomes of this sort, versus those that militate against recovery, are discussed in detail in Chapter 7.

BIOLOGICAL, NEUROPHYSIOLOGICAL, AND PSYCHOLOGICAL-TEST MARKERS

The clinical signs of BPD are usually flamboyant enough to permit diagnosis without the aid of special tests. In an effort to validate the diagnosis, or to better elucidate the nature of this disorder, some markers have been suggested.

With respect to *psychological tests*, Gunderson and Singer (1975) drew attention to the tendency of BPD patients to perform poorly on the unstructured portions of the standard test battery (viz., on the TAT, the Rorschach), whereas performance is adequate on the structured portions. Rorschach responses are often overinclusive, confabulated, or flamboyant. Schizophrenic patients, in contrast, tend to show difficulties even on the structured portions. Carsky and Bloomgarden (1981) found significant distinctions in the responses of borderline patients (diagnosed by the broader Kernberg criteria) with predominantly affective features, in comparison to those with predominantly schizotypal features. Rorschach responses considered highly "affective" were overrepresented in the former; those considered mostly "schizoid" were noted more frequently in the "schizotypal" patients. Others addressing this topic in detail include Kwawer et al. (1980) and Collins et al. (1992).

Since the diagnosis of BPD rests upon anamnestic and interview data, psychological tests should be regarded as having some corroborative value, rather than as providing a definitive "marker." They may have considerable value in highlighting the psychodynamics, which often otherwise remain hidden during the opening phases of therapy (especially with BPD patients who are evasive or coy, and who do not volunteer the important data about their past).

Though dreams are not ordinarily regarded as neurophysiological markers, there will be dreams that borderline patients report from time to time that carry some diagnostic value. In contrast to Freud's comment (1900, p. 431) that the ego (of the dreamer) cannot conceive of its own death (and therefore one does not have dreams of being dead), certain borderline and psychotic patients *do* have dreams either of being dead or of being severely mutilated (Stone, 1979).

An example: a male patient with BPD, hospitalized because of a suicide gesture, had a dream just after he signed mortgage papers for a house his wife had been pressuring him to buy. In the dream he saw a gaping hole in his groin where his penis should have been; blood was pouring out; his severed penis was lying in the puddle of blood at his feet. Neurotic patients almost never have grotesque dreams of body dismemberment of this sort (though they may have dreams where they lose some hair or teeth).

Another patient with BPD reported this dream the session before I was to leave for a vacation: "I'm strapped to an electric chair. The man turns on the voltage switch, and I'm dead. I awakened with a start, surprised to realize I was still alive." Still another patient, whom I had thought at first was not so fragile, made me aware of her being "borderline" (as later became clear through her self-destructive behavior) via a dream in which she saw herself lying on a bed in a recovery room, eviscerated, with all her abdominal organs arrayed around her in a semicircle (à la Jack the Ripper's victims), while her inebriated surgeon waved to her on his way out of the room, saying, "Don't worry, you'll be fine!" (The transference implications—that, in beginning to work with me, she did not feel herself to be in the best of hands—are obvious just from the manifest content!)

A number of *biological* or *neurophysiological* markers have been proposed as relevant to BPD. The subject is discussed in review articles by Cowdry (1992) and Stone (1992c). The high proportion of BPD patients, especially females, comorbid for major depression has led to research into abnormalities known to be associated with affective illness. Persons given a dexamethasone challenge will, for example, normally show suppression of endogenous cortisol levels in their plasma for a certain period of time. Early "escape" from this normal suppression is seen in patients with depression— but also in a high proportion of BPD patients (13 of 21 in the study reported by Carroll et al., 1981). But Baxter et al. (1984) see the abnormal dexamethasone test as relating to the depressive component in BPD patients who are simultaneously depressed; those without concomitant depression mostly have negative tests. Because of this nonspecificity, the test is not much relied on at present.

Persons with primary affective disorders often exhibit shortened REM latency during somnographic testing. Akiskal, Yerevanian et al. (1985) found shortened latencies in BPD subjects not only when concomitantly depressed but also in between times of depression, suggesting that the finding is a trait, not merely state-dependent. It remains as yet unclear how solid a correlation exists, particularly where BPD seems to have derived from non-affective sources (viz., early abuse, attention-deficit disorder).

BPD patients who symptomatically resemble bipolar II (hypomania/severe depressions) disorder tend to show "augmentation" on tests of evoked potentials. This "positive feedback" correlates with the typical *over*reactions of these patients to all manner of interpersonal stimuli (Klein, 1988)—spoken of as "all-or-none" responses by Kernberg. I have referred to this phenomenon under the heading of excessive irritability, predisposing borderline patients to oscillate between attitudes of total adoration and total hatred (Stone, 1988a). Either heritable/constitutional factors (viz., for bipolar II or ADD) or a nervous system "kindled" during the early development years via physical/sexual abuse can foster this response augmentation. In other studies of CNS-evoked potentials, certain BPD patients have shown increased latency and diminished amplitude in the P300 component, such as is noted also in schizophrenia—suggesting that these borderline patients have "schizotypal" features, electrophysiologically and perhaps clinically (Kutcher et al., 1987).

In recent years great advances have been made in brain imaging, through the use of positron emission tomography (PET scan), magnetic resonance imaging (MRI), etc. These techniques have furthered our understanding of cognitive dysfunction, especially in schizophrenia. Despite strong hints that patients with BPD may, at least when stressed, manifest limbic system dysfunction (diminished access to long-term memory, rage outbursts, etc.), as yet structural abnormalities have not been demonstrated, as Cowdry points out (1992), that might correlate with the clinical abnormalities (cf. Lucas et al., 1989).

The chain of interacting factors—genetic, constitutional, and developmental—that conspire in the formation of BPD is illustrated in Figure 22. According to this etiological model, the various contributory factors lead to abnormally heightened irritability, and this in turn to a diminished capacity to modulate responses (viz., to interpersonal stresses). The personality becomes distorted along lines we later recognize as the key "items" of BPD: impulsivity, lability, ragefulness, storminess, self-damaging acts.

Figure 22: *Etiological Factors in Borderline Personality Disorder**

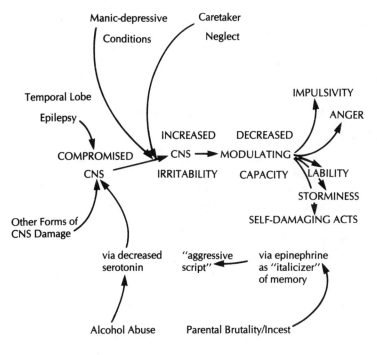

*From Stone, 1992c

TREATMENT OF
BORDERLINE PERSONALITY DISORDER

Though we think of borderline patients as being therapeutically challenging, there is really a kind of circularity in any such statement. For, as we
can see from Colson, Allen et al.'s description of the "difficult" (hospitalized) patient, there are certain attributes which by their very nature lie at
the edge, or uncomfortably beyond, our abilities as mental health professionals to contain and ameliorate: violent outbursts, psychotic episodes,
suicidality, demandingness, etc. It is these same attributes that got swept
together at some point in the evolution of our field, and placed under a
new label: "borderline."

As clinicians, we usually come to recognize who our "borderline" patients are, not because they have this or that item from the latest version of
DSM, but because they refuse to leave the session when the time is up, or

they come in with a wrist bandaged up from a self-mutilative gesture after rejection by a lover, or they call us at two in the morning in some (to our way of thinking) quite preventable crisis.

The list is a long one, but each of these acts announces to us that the patient is thinking/acting/feeling in an *unreasonable* manner; the patient is "going to extremes." In a word, the patient is being "difficult." And it often turns out that the patient is (by one criterion set or another; perhaps by all of them) *borderline*. I mention this perhaps trivial-seeming point by way of emphasizing that "borderline" is a label of convenience. I wish to take the mystery out of it. The sequence (in the mental processes of the therapist) is, I believe, important: we first experience certain patients as "difficult," and a bit later we categorize those who are not clearly psychotic as "borderline."

Currently, there are several therapeutic techniques, some competing, some overlapping, that are commonly employed in the treatment of border-line patients. In an earlier article I defined the *pragmatic* approach vis-à-vis borderline patients as a matter of "A,B,C,D": Analytically-informed therapy, Behavioral therapy, Cognitive therapy, and Drug therapy (Stone, 1990c). The "complete" therapist would not only be comfortable with all these modalities, but would also be at home with group therapy techniques (cf. Leszcz, 1992), Kohut's approach, and the kind of teamwork necessary to the treatment of hospitalized borderline patients. Since no one can master all the requisite techniques, each therapist must be quick to invite another colleague into the treatment when a joint venture would be optimal (viz., psychotherapist and pharmacotherapist), or willing to refer a patient to another colleague or resource when such a change would be in the best interests of the patient. Therapists must be comfortable with limit-setting, since this is a crucial element in the treatment of almost all borderline patients. In addition, they must be familiar with the many special anony-mous groups upon which ambulatory patients often rely to firm up the limit-setting interventions an individual therapist can suggest but not imple-ment alone: besides Alcoholics Anonymous, Overeaters Anonymous may be helpful in working with bulimic patients; incest survivor groups for BPD patients in this category, etc.

In the sections that follow, I discuss a number of these techniques, and touch on the role of supportive interventions that, for most borderline patients (especially during the early phases of the work), serve as the foun-dation upon which the more specialized modalities are built.

Psychoanalytic Approaches

In the early years of psychoanalysis, analysts would begin to notice that certain patients seemed not to improve within the usual (two-to-four-year) time frame. They seemed "clingy" (and were perhaps examples of what Grinker et al. [1968] were later to call the "anaclitic/depressed" type of borderline patient). Others acted out the transference over and over again: picked up sexual partners in unsavory bars, rather than dealing in words with their erotic feelings toward the analyst, etc. Still others showed self-destructive tendencies. Some could not tolerate the relative "sensory deprivation" of not being able to see the analyst while lying on the couch. To deal with all these difficulties, analysts began, rather apologetically at first, resorting to "parameters"—interventions considered inappropriate to the carrying out of a proper analysis. These included having the patient sit up and face the analyst, giving the patient strongly worded advice not to go through with some dangerous plan of action, permitting the patient to call at late hours under certain circumstances or to have an "extra" session during some crisis. Many such practical interventions are mentioned in an unusually (for the era) straight-from-the-shoulder article by Melitta Schmideberg (1947).

Because of the broad, and not well-defined criteria for "borderline" during this earlier time, and because the term was hardly employed outside the psychoanalytic community, the patients treated by Schmideberg or by Helene Deutsch or by Stern, Bychowski, Zilboorg, Zetzel, Jacobson, and others—the "borderline" patients from roughly 1930 until 1970—were often from fairly well-to-do families, were disinhibited (but not *so* disinhibited as those we now identify as cases of BPD), and may well have shown more identity confusion and depression than violence or life-threatening impulsivity.

So long as "borderline" remained primarily within the purview of psychoanalysis, the major controversies regarding optimal treatment centered on such topics as: Should one continue to use the couch or not? What was the optimal number of sessions per week? How many and which parameters were legitimate? How much limit-setting was necessary, and how did one go about implementing it? When was it appropriate to bring in family members either for conjoint sessions or for gathering certain pieces of critical information? These topics were addressed in several symposia in the analytic journals of the day (cf. Rangell, 1955, 1968). Others addressed the important topic: in the therapy of borderline patients, how much value was to be placed upon the *words*—the interpretations themselves—and how much upon the hidden, nonverbal, largely unconscious aspects of the transference—the person of the analyst, the mise-en-scène of the analytic office, etc. (Greenson & Wexler, 1969; Nacht, 1963)?

As "borderline" became a more popular term during the '60s and '70s, due in part to the influential papers of Kernberg, its use was still largely confined to the domain of psychoanalysis. Controversies concerning treatment centered around the issue of whether therapists should first address the "negative transference" that typically pervaded the atmosphere during the early phases (Kernberg) or whether the proper stance was that of sympathy, empathic resonance, and the withholding of confrontative remarks until a trusting relationship had been built up (Kohut) (cf. Stevenson & Meares, 1992). Debates of this sort tend to be casuistical: assigned the very same patient, proponents of both schools usually behave in a similar fashion, guided by the needs and personality traits of the patient. Kernberg's experience was accumulated in equal measure from hospitalized and office patients; Kohut's just from office patients. The more "difficult" patients Kernberg encountered in all likelihood would elicit—from most any therapist—strong limit-setting and confrontative interventions around their impulsivity and suicidality. With the typical patient of Kohut, one could afford to bide one's time, hear out the patient's narcissistic complaints without making too quick interpretations about the patient's demandingness, etc. Furthermore, the personality and cognitive style of the therapist shape to a certain extent the nature of the preferred interventions, their timing, etc. So therapist factors also account for some of the "variance" in recommendations about optimal therapy (cf. below: Chapter 18).

The Kernberg-Kohut debate is not the only controversial area relevant to the therapy of borderline patients. Controversy also surrounds the issue of when and how to confront borderline patients about their distorted perceptions concerning themselves and persons important to them. Kernberg promulgates a theory emphasizing an excess of aggression, either "innate" or secondary to adverse parental interaction early in life. This is primarily a *conflict* model. Kernberg advocates first a limit-setting approach to rein in the patient's tendency to act out the transference; then, the use of a special kind of confrontation, where contrary, inconsistent assertions are challenged. The challenge might come in this form: "You just got through claiming your mother was a faultless woman, yet a few minutes ago you told me how she beat you with a cord if you misbehaved, and used to lock herself in her room after supper, so you never heard her read you a bedtime story. Is that the picture of a perfect mother?" The purpose of such a confrontation would be to help the patient see his parent in a more realistic light. Borderline patients are usually able (sooner or later) to resonate with confrontative interpretations of this sort. In line with an emphasis on the borderline patient's innate (or early-determined) aggression is Kernberg's contention that, should the patient relate initially in an idealizing mode toward the therapist, this idealization may well be a cover-up for suppressed, hostile feelings, which need to be unearthed and dealt with.

Adler (1985) has put forth a contrasting view: one that sees as primary the borderline patient's need, oftentimes, to maintain an idealizing posture, the too early interpretation of which might be taken as a painful criticism, thus destabilizing the treatment. In a like vein, Adler mentions that: "Often the [hospitalized] patient is seen as manipulative when he is most suicidal and desperate" (p. 206). Here Adler, like Maltsberger and Buie (1974), puts the sympathetic foot forward, ahead of the confrontative/critical foot. Adler cautions that to lose sight of the patient's pain and distress is to foster the splitting and projective identifications, such that they come to constitute the therapist's or hospital staff's only view of the patient. Elsewhere, Adler and Myerson (1973) advise against the kind of confrontation Kernberg advocates, urging instead a more openly sympathetic stance (not unlike that of Kohut). Adler believes that borderline psychopathology is better understood as a *deficit* phenomenon, stemming from an inability to internalize good, soothing images of the parents—because the parents were actually insufficiently nurturing and soothing. The rage of the borderline patient is seen as an outgrowth of the patient's desperation over this critical deficit.

Whereas just about all commentators on borderline personality speak of the need for therapists to create a "holding environment" or to act as a "container" (in Winnicott's language) for the patient's tempestuous emotions, some give primacy to interventions and attitudes (of sympathy, for example) of this sort, while others give primacy to dealing with the patient's open and hidden aggression. In the former position we might place, as well as Adler and Buie, also Giovacchini, Chessick, and Volkan. Kernberg has been a staunch advocate of the second position. Similarly, Kernberg might be more accepting of the position that certain borderline patients had reasonably "good enough" parents, yet (because of excess innate aggression) distorted their image of those parents, seeing them instead as dreadful, sadistic, etc. Adler, Buie, and also Masterson would tend to see the parents as truly bad (Masterson's belief [1981] was that the mothers of borderlines were themselves borderline), implying that the patient had not been distorting after all.

It seems to me that the best way to resolve this apparent dilemma is to acknowledge two facts. I call them "facts" because I believe my assertions here are near enough to the truth to warrant so bold an assertion. First, the borderline domain, even by the narrower definitions, is quite vast and contains patients with such a variety of primary and secondary causative factors that some exist who do justice to the hypotheses of Adler, Giovacchini, Masterson, Kohut, etc., while others are best understood according to the hypotheses set forth by Kernberg. The clinical situation is thus not "either/or."*

Second, there are distinct personality differences among the theoreticians mentioned, which exert a more profound impact upon their theories than any of them would comfortably acknowledge. Each "magnetizes" to himself (in his private patient work, for example) mostly those borderline patients who "click" with his personality and therapeutic style. Patients who do not "click" will be more prone to drop out early and to journey on to another therapist with whom they are more at ease. There is thus a certain self-serving (and solipsistic) quality to the theories, alongside a certain measure of "universality." Not true universality, that is, but at best, wide applicability.

Good therapists all have a range of emotion and attitude, allowing them to work well with a variety of borderline patients—but not with *all*. None of us sees himself as accurately as he sees others (as Robert Burns would remind us: "To see ourselves as ithers sae us/'Twoud fra' mony a blunder free us . . . "). In my own work over the years I can see that I have, with various borderline patients, been avuncular, giving, withholding, stern, accepting, judgmental, sympathetic, crotchety, and so on. It may be that Adler or Chessick remain avuncular in circumstances where Kernberg, Searles, and I become stern. Any one of us must surely at times enjoy working with a patient whom most of the others would find exasperating. Yet we seem to do creditable work with a reasonable percentage of the borderline patients who are referred to us.

As Waldinger and Gunderson have shown (1984), we all have a "dropout" rate of similar proportions (this side or the other of 40%), suggesting (because such a high percentage of borderline patients ultimately do well) that those who fail with one therapist may succeed with another. Each of us has had the experience of succeeding where other colleagues have failed, and of having failed where subsequent therapists have succeeded. I am no longer bothered by this state of affairs.

The *totality* of theoretical works in this field could be set side by side so as to constitute a sourcebook or dictionary, containing (on one page or another) much that is useful and pertinent to any given patient. The whole

---

*Horwitz, Gabbard et al. (1993) make a similar point, arguing that BPD is not a discrete, homogeneous clinical entity. They endorse Meissner's notion of a continuum from the near-psychotic to the near-neurotic cases: analytically oriented therapy would be indicated more often in the healthier group (Zetzel's more conservative approach would be more appropriate to the former group). They agree with Gunderson's contention that confrontations made too early account for some of the high dropout rate among BPD patients.

set of therapists who devote themselves to this clinical area may be seen as a large army of potential helpers, with certain basic skills and ethical values serviceable for all borderline patients. But each of us also has special skills, interests, temperaments, and personalities, which will make us adept at working with particular kinds of patients and rather handicapped in relation to other borderline patients, with whom we do not "click" or who push us beyond our comfort zone.

Many of the theoretical debates about the "ideal" method of treating borderline patients could be clarified greatly, if not resolved altogether, were the participants to carry out methodical long-term follow-up of their patients. Such an exercise yields precious data concerning which patients, treated by method X, really made dramatic improvement, and which failed to improve. Meticulous follow-up also provides clues about the therapist's own range of preference and adequacy.

For example, I have recently written about persistent hostility as a markedly negative factor in borderline patients (Stone, 1990d), mentioning my many failures with those at the extremes of the anger spectrum. Some of the vignettes in this book derive from these experiences. Have I hit upon a factor that has wide reverberations within the whole realm of therapists who work with borderline patients? Or have I merely zeroed in on a variety of psychopathology in persons (loudly hostile, violence-prone) whom I dislike and with whom, partly for that reason, my therapeutic efforts do not flourish? To what extent is my theory (that chronically hostile borderlines don't get better) widely applicable "out there," and to what extent have I merely revealed something peculiar to my own personality? Would Adler do better with these patients? Kernberg? A Kohutian like Ernest Wolf? None of the above? The answer to important questions of this sort lies in follow-up, truthfully and unflinchingly reported.

My impressions on this point have been seconded recently in the excellent review article by Higgitt and Fonagy (1992). There the reader will find thoughtful discussions not only about the need for long-term follow-up but also about the above-mentioned controversies concerning genetic vs. developmental factors in borderline patients, and concerning the differing views among psychoanalytically oriented therapists on optimal treatment strategies. The typical defenses utilized by borderline patients—splitting, projective identification, overvaluation and devaluation, and clinging/hostile dependency—are all defined in detail.

Higgitt and Fonagy, in their descriptions of analytic/interpretive vs. supportive approaches and their advocates, argue in favor of adopting one or the other, but not both, techniques, adding that "there is no indication for the judicious combination of the two" (p. 34). As is clear from my own remarks above, I would take issue with them on this one point, because in my experience I rarely encounter borderline patients, unless they have stabilized after years of therapy with other colleagues, who do not experience periodic crises necessitating supportive interventions. Support and reeducation are usually indicated for the many borderline patients one currently encounters who have been seriously abused during their formative years—even if they are, in other respects, amenable to analytically oriented therapy.

Higgitt and Fonagy make a poignant, and altogether apropos, comment at the end of their article: "Unfortunately, suitability (or otherwise) for treatment will most commonly become self-evident only after several months of heartache, of struggling with negative therapeutic reaction, of massive distress during breaks, of insistent demands for special treatment . . . of suicidal gestures, and sometimes physical violence." They add, with respect to prognosis, "Sadly, none [of these phenomena] appears to guarantee either therapeutic success or failure" (p. 39).

As a useful bridge to the discussion of supportive and other techniques, Aronson's review (1989) deserves mention. Commenting on the "recent . . . retrenchment from the intensive psychoanalytic model" (p. 526), Aronson speaks of the utility of combining individual with family or group therapy in many cases. Within the psychoanalytic community, as Aronson underlines, there has always been a spectrum of opinion, even before the 1980s and the new follow-up studies, concerning exploratory vs. supportive interventions. Aronson provides a scale, similar to the one I constructed (Stone, 1990c), showing the advocates of a predominantly supportive approach at one end (exemplified by Grinker, Knight, Zetzel), and the advocates of a predominantly exploratory approach at the other (Boyer, Giovacchini, Bion, Searles, Kernberg). In between he places Schmideberg, Adler, Gunderson, and myself. I believe this is a reasonable characterization, especially in view of the pragmatic comments made by Gunderson some years ago: "From a technical point of view, a therapist [of borderline patients] ranges from the early phases of treatment, where repeated limits and behavioral monitoring are required, to the later stages of treatment, in which a more passive stance . . . accompanied by a demand for borderline patients to explore their internal life responsibly are required." He sums up by saying: "Allegiance to any isolated technical approach simply restricts the ability to work with such patients altogether or restricts one's usefulness to [merely] a limited aspect of the total problem" (1984, p. 180).

Supportive and Cognitive/Behavioral Techniques

With the appearance of DSM-III in 1980, "borderline" expanded into all domains of psychiatry, not just the psychoanalytic. And because the condition was defined along narrower and more dysfunctional lines, the old arguments about two vs. four sessions per week and about how best to handle the negative transference became less relevant, even supererogatory. Patients from all walks of life were being diagnosed "BPD," and psychoanalytically oriented ("expressive," "exploratory") psychotherapy could no longer rationally be regarded as the treatment of choice for all those who now fit under this diagnostic umbrella. Clinicians became more aware that the "remainder" of a borderline patient's personality traits carried important prognostic implications: those with strong antisocial traits, for example, as a rule made a mockery of treatment; those with compulsive traits tended to get much better (Stone, 1990).

Meanwhile, the *supportive* aspects of therapy, long regarded by psychoanalysts as the country cousins among the various therapeutic interventions, were reevaluated in a more positive light. Supportive therapy includes expressions of sympathy, reassurance, exhortation, education about the interpersonal world, limit-setting, advice, the ventilation of long-withheld secrets on the part of the patient, etc. For the majority of BPD patients, supportive therapy—on a once- or at best twice-a-week basis—was all that was affordable. Moreover, as Wallerstein declared in his resumé of the Menninger study (1986), evidence was quite compelling that patients whose therapy had been conducted mostly along supportive lines did as well as those whose treatment had been mostly "expressive."

My long-term follow-up study of borderline patients showed similar results (Stone, 1990). Numerically, those who worked well within the framework of expressive therapy and who appeared to benefit greatly constituted a small group: perhaps one patient in six. Many other borderline patients in my study did equally well with a predominantly supportive therapy or with some mixture of the two styles, the ratio of expressive to supportive interventions varying from one phase of treatment to the next, even from one day to the next, depending on whether the patient was in some life crisis or not.

Similar conclusions about the efficacy of supportive therapy were reached by Mary Lee Smith and her colleagues (1980) in their elegant study of different types of psychotherapy. Their research suggested that therapists trained in a particular school of thought—so long as it provided them with a workable model of psychopathology and with workable guidelines for ethical therapy—did well, and that psychotherapy proved useful, *independent* of the particular school in which they were trained.

That having been said, one can still argue, as I did in a recent article (Stone, 1990c) that for certain borderline patients a particular treatment method is more congenial and therefore more useful, if for no other reason than that it conforms better with the culture and cognitive style of the patient.

In recent years *cognitive* and *behavioral* therapies have become more widely used in the treatment of borderline patients. Aaron Beck and his colleagues in Philadelphia have been instrumental in popularizing cognitive techniques (Beck, 1976; Beck & Freeman, 1990), and have shown how these may be applicable to all the different personality disorders of DSM. For each disorder, for example, there is a corresponding thought pattern (cognitive style), consisting of a *view of self*, a *view of others*, a set of *main beliefs and attitudes*, and a set of *main strategies*. Persons with each disorder can also be seen as showing a neglect of certain other strategies, adaptive for most people, but deemed not useful by those with a particular personality disorder. By way of illustration, the *obsessive-compulsive* person, in Beck's schema, views himself as "responsible and fastidious," views others as "incompetent and irresponsible," entertains the main beliefs, "errors are bad, I know what's best, and details are important," and pursues as main strategies "perfectionism, adherence to rules, quest for control." The obsessive's undeveloped strategy would be spontaneity.

Beck refers to the set of beliefs that inform one's behavior as the "schema" of that individual. This is similar to the analyst's reference to "psychodynamics" or to my phrase for the whole collective of one's dynamics and the life plan that arises from this source: one's "inner script" (Stone, 1988). There is an important difference in the two schools of thought—a difference that Beck misconstrues. Beck states (Beck & Freeman, 1990, p. 4) that psychoanalysts see the core structures as unconscious and not easily available to the patients, whereas cognitive therapy holds that the *products* of this process are largely in the realm of awareness. Exactly so. The products (Beck's main beliefs, etc.) *are* what is in awareness. No analyst would deny this, because it is self-evident. What gives rise to the main beliefs, however, are memories of interpersonal events with parents and other early figures that are no longer conscious (that is, the *underlying* dynamics).

Beck's school simply relies on the capacity of certain patients to override, with the help of the cognitive therapist, the main beliefs, gradually supplanting these with newer, more adaptive beliefs—all via an appeal to reason and without a preliminary discovery of the hitherto unconscious dynamics (such as an analyst would foster via dream analysis). The technique advocated by Beck relies upon the cataloging of these main beliefs and the subsequent dialogue with the therapist, who attempts to demonstrate to the patient the superiority of strategies until now overlooked or underutilized by the patient.

What is truly different from traditional analysis is Beck's advocacy of "homework" by the patient, who might, for example, make a list of his beliefs or of various advantages and drawbacks to a certain plan of action, all of which can then be reviewed and discussed in the next session. The ensuing dialogue between cognitive therapist and patient tends, however, to resemble remarkably the type of dialogue one would overhear between a psychoanalyst and a patient who does not remember dreams. The latter, in effect, forces his therapist (no matter how that therapist was trained) into becoming a "cognitive" therapist.

What gives cognitive/behavioral therapy credibility is that, like analytic/supportive therapy, it often works. Of a hundred borderline patients, I would imagine that, say, seventy would improve with either method. But there would be some nonoverlap: a few of the patients would respond just to the one method; a few others to the second.

Beck's Recommendations vis-à-vis Borderline Patients

Patients with BPD may show any of a number of "maladaptive schemata." These include the *anticipation of abandonment, conviction of unlovability, subjugation of one's own will to the will of other(s), mistrust,* and *guilt.* Beck also mentions "lack of self-discipline" (Beck & Freeman, 1990, p. 183), but this is perhaps better regarded as a deficiency, probably stemming from lack of parental encouragement and control, rather than as a "life plan." In dealing with the borderline patient's maladaptive schemata, the cognitive therapist would first point out the characteristic distortions in the patient's beliefs. The therapist would then focus on the penchant for "dichotomous" thinking, also characteristic of borderlines. This is the same quality analysts refer to as "all-or-none" thinking and is understood as a persistence of childhood-type "splitting" of the internal representations of self and others into polar opposite pairs: "I'm (alternatingly) all bad/all good," "Mother" (or whoever) is (alternatingly) all bad/all good."

Beck gives a clinical vignette of a dialogue between cognitive therapist and borderline patient (Beck & Freeman, 1990, p. 199ff). In this example, the patient was dividing the world into "trustworthy" people, whom you can completely trust, and "treacherous" people, whom you can't trust at all. The therapist then asked about his sister-in-law; the patient said, "Oh, I can trust her." But the therapist reminded him: "Don't I remember that last week you were mad because she didn't call when she said she would?" This led to a discussion of how trust is not a black-or-white affair; rather, one can be "mostly" trustworthy, etc.

I mention this interchange at some length because if differs in no way from the "confrontations" Kernberg would make about the patient's unrealistic all-or-none position, with the goal of getting the patient to see that there are shades of gray. Kernberg's style relies heavily on "cognitive" interventions of this sort (in contrast to Searles' more intuitive style), even though Kernberg is solidly allied with the psychoanalytic, not with the cognitive, school of thought.

As I have indicated, as a therapeutic approach, this method is quite often effective. What Beck is offering *conceptually* is merely a retranslation into cognitive language of what the analytic community has done (and described in its own language), when working with borderline patients, for a long time. Here Beck has succeeded, if I may reverse the adage, merely in pouring old wine into new bottles.

The outline of techniques used by the cognitive therapist for converting the borderline patient's impulsivity into a more reasoned and modulated kind of behavior is similarly sensible—but not innovative. One gets the patient to (a) identify the impulse before it is acted on; (b) inhibit what would have been the automatic ("knee-jerk") response; (c) think of various alternatives; and then (d) select the one that is the most adaptive. This sequence has of course been advocated as a program of interventions by skilled therapists who work with borderline patients, whatever their training (Stone, 1990c).

The "schema" of mistrust is important in understanding the inner mechanisms of borderline patients, especially incest victims, who have suffered overwhelming betrayal in their early years. What one often sees clinically is a cycle of behavior along the following lines: (a) adoration ("limerance") of the loved one, (b) growing dependence upon the loved one, which (c) reawakens old fears of betrayal, such that the patient "sees" the lover as about to stage a betrayal. This prompts the patient to (d) become provocative and rageful, thus alienating the lover, who indeed breaks off the relationship. But this (e) causes intense despair and loneliness, which become as intolerable as the fear of betrayal had once been, prompting (f) a desperate craving for reconciliation. If the lover returns, the cycle begins anew (Stone, 1988)—unless the therapist has in the meantime succeeded in helping the patient to recognize these steps and to adopt a more trusting attitude (if the lover realistically merits trust), allowing the relationship to continue without storminess and interruptions.

As for the list of schemata relevant to borderline personality, one would want to add a theme of great importance in many such patients, namely, *vengefulness*. Borderline patients who have been abused—and this seems now to be the majority—develop strong wishes early on to "get even." This inclines such persons in the direction of making sexual partnerships with unworthy or abusive mates, in relation to whom "getting even" seems all too justified. This "spares" the patient the awkwardness of having to examine the past, to reacquaint himself with those who had been the original authors (an incestuous father, an abusive mother) of the patient's wish to seek vengeance. In the event a vengeful borderline patient makes a healthier choice—of a mate who is faithful, tender, understanding, etc.—what often happens is that the patient becomes provocative, goading the otherwise nonabusive partner to become angrier, more uncontrolled, i.e., to become *like* the abusive parent. This effectively trashes the relationship, since the healither partner soon tires of the provocations.

This oscillating schema of mistrust/reconcilation (Melges & Swartz, 1989; Stone, 1988) is most often mobilized in borderline patients with a history of incest by a caretaker, since in this situation love and hatred are both fueled to the maximum. Without successful treatment, there is usually no possiblity of integration; "splitting" remains intense; the victim wants both to cling and to kill.

Linehan's Dialectic Behavior Therapy; Treatment Goals

Allied conceptually with cognitive therapy is a technique developed by Marsha Linehan (1987, 1992) during the early '80s: dialectic behavior therapy. "Dialectic" here refers to the dialogue between therapist and patient, acknowledging their conflicting views of the world, which the therapist, while respecting the patient's original picture of reality, attempts to resolve via persuasive dialogue—in such a way as to promote in the patient more adaptive patterns of thought, feeling, and behavior. This approach is reminiscent of Sullivanian "interpersonal" psychotherapy, and also partakes of what Spillane (1987) called "noble rhetoric." The latter relates to "an ethcial hierarchy of language and values, based on the principle of responsible autonomy" (p. 217). It is this "responsible autonomy" that the therapist hopes to foster—not only in borderlines, but in all patients.

Linehan outlines a number of relationship strategies that may be used by the dialectic-behavioral therapist working with a borderline patient. Besides acceptance of the patient and problem-solving, Linehan also advocates therapist self-disclosure, by way of providing feedback and fostering appropriate modeling (i.e., promoting opportunties for the patient to identify with the more reality-adapted *modus vivendi* and life philosophy of the therapist).

I believe judicious use of self-disclosure can be valuable in the treatment of borderline patients, so long as one does not descend into maudlin and embarrassing self-revelation. Usually the self-disclosure will be in the form of an anecdote or perhaps the acknowledgment of a transitory emotion. If, for example, a borderline patient threw an ashtray at the therapist, it would be quite natural to admit that one felt angry and frightened. *Not* to do so would probably duplicate the parent's mendacious avoidance of telling simple truths of that sort; the patient may at such moments be "testing" to see whether the therapist can be more honest and forthright than the parent. Psychoanalytically trained therapists who work with borderline patients will make self-disclosures when the occasion seems appropriate (cf. Searles,

1986), though in writing about recommendations for therapy they tend to downplay, or even interdict, this type of intervention.

Linehan offers a useful hierarchically-arranged list of treatment goals. These are commonsensical and are utilized instinctively by therapists of all persuasions; yet it is remarkable how seldom we see such a schema in print. The goal that takes precedence over all others is: to deal with and prevent suicidal or self-injurious behavior. Next, one addresses behaviors that would jeopardize the therapeutic relationship (threats to quit treatment precipitously, for example). Thirdly, one treats any serious and potentially disruptive symptoms—such as substance abuse. If all the above are adequately dealt with (or are not present), one turns one's attention to less disruptive symptoms and to problems in day-to-day life at work or at home. A step further down in the hierarchy would be the more subtle aspects of the patient's personality and character, which may contain elements negatively affecting the quality of the patient's life. Finally, one focuses upon the patient's life goals and ambitions: the nature of her dreams and hopes, how realizable (or not) they are, etc. It should be clear from the nature of borderline personality disorder, especially within the context of hospital treatment, that the therapist will be preoccupied for a long time with the first three levels in Linehan's hierarchical schema, more so than would be the case with other personality disorders.

Psychopharmacological Approaches

Because BPD usually declares itself via symptoms (viz., rage outbursts, self-mutilation, suicide gestures), rather than via personality traits alone, psychopharmacological agents often play an important role in treatment, especially during the early phases. A number of investigators figure prominently in this area (Cowdry, 1992; Cowdry & Gardner, 1988; Liebowitz & Klein, 1981; Soloff et al., 1986). The whole subject of pharmacotherapy in borderline personality has been extensively reviewed by G. Stein (1992). Elsewhere I have discussed the topic from the vantage point of a psychotherapist/psychoanalyst in clinical practice (Stone, 1989d; 1990c).

The target symptoms clinicians will encounter in their borderline patients include depression, anxiety, ragefulness, hypomania, and premenstrual intensification of mood and irritability. In some patients with schizotypal comorbidity, one may see cognitive distortions of sufficient magnitude to warrant psychopharmacological intervention.

Whereas an earlier generation of psychiatrists relied upon tricyclic antidepressants, such as imipramine, for the depressive component in their borderline patients, Liebowitz and Klein argued for the greater efficacy of monoamine oxidase inhibitors (MAOIs), such as phenelzine or tranylcypromine. Some controversy persisted as to the relative merits of these two classes of antidepressant. Soloff et al. (1986) showed a way out of the controversy through their research suggesting that BPD patients who exhibited simple depression without concomitant hostility/irritability might very well improve with tricyclics. Those who did show considerable anger, etc., did better with the MAOIs. But Soloff also found that a neuroleptic (haloperidol) in low doses (up to 6 mgm/day) would do equally well, and was not, in this low dose range, associated with tardive dyskinesia.

In BPD patients with hypomanic traits lithium may have a stabilizing effect. In those who do not respond to lithium an antiepileptic medication such as carbamazepine may be helpful. Where attention-deficit disorder (ADD) is a complicating factor, tricyclic antidepressants may be helpful (Satel et al., 1988). Pimozide has been recommended for patients with pathological jealousy (Byrne & Yatham, 1989), though this has not been widely used in BPD patients.

Many borderline patients have frequent bouts of mild to moderate anxiety; some are prone to panic attacks. Benzodiazepine anxiolytics may be of benefit in these situations, though one should be aware that some BPD patients become more irritable on benzodiazepines (cf. Cowdry & Gardner, 1988). There is a risk of habit-formation, especially with alprazolam, necessitating caution—especially in a condition like BPD, where symptoms may persist for long periods.

Therapists carrying out psychoanalytically oriented psychotherapy with borderline patients often prefer to eschew the use of medications altogether, on the grounds that alleviation of what might otherwise have been tolerable levels of anxiety would detract from the motivation necessary to explore relevant dynamic areas. Past a certain level of anxiety, one could no longer justify, in contemporary psychiatry, withholding medication. Where the boundary line is to be drawn is a matter of clinical judgment.

Ambulatory borderline patients with intense suicidal feelings, especially those who have made serious attempts in the past, represent serious risks with respect to the use of certain medications. If clinical indications for an MAOI exist, these must be weighed against the possibility that the patient may make a suicide gesture via a deliberate overdose. This is a "catch-22" situation, since the drug was supposed to diminish the risk of such suicidal feelings to begin with. But these medications do not work immediately. The clinician, faced with a two- or four- or six-week wait until the desired effect is achieved (assuming the patient is going to respond ultimately), must choose between the MAOI and some other medication, abuse of which carries less ominous consequences. The more reliable the patient, the more an MAOI becomes a reasonable choice; the less cooperative or trustworthy the patient, the more risky a choice.

Female patients with concomitant BPD and premenstrual syndrome will usually require medication at least during the phase of symptom aggravation. This may be anywhere from a week or so before the expected period till a few days after the menses begins. There is no set regimen that will alleviate symptoms for all women with this pattern; the correct regimen must be discovered empirically. For some women a mild anxiolytic will suffice; for those with severe symptoms small doses of a neuroleptic may be useful during the days of maximal discomfort. A trial of an antidepressant will be useful for some patients; a few may even require lithium or carbamazepine. Some women undergo a radical change of personality in the paramenstrual phase, becoming extremely irritable, self-destructive, and depressed. They are, in effect, "borderline" for four or five days out of the month, and buoyant, cheerful, quite normal, the other three-fourths of the cycle. If untreated, this tendency could lead to serious disruption of family or occupational life. Psychotherapy plus the appropriate medications will usually restore equanimity; occasionally, the medication alone will be sufficient (Stone, 1982).

The Need for Pragmatism

Though each person—and each personality—is unique, the disorders of personality we currently recognize do not all cover equal shares of the human population, nor do they all describe circles of equal diameter, with regard to the variety of "subtypes," from some central concept. BPD seems to describe a very wide circle; the patients who fall within the circle seem more diverse than is the case, say, with schizoid PD. As we saw, even the range of etiological factors is broad in BP, whereas it is narrow in schizotypal PD (perhaps, in the latter, just moderate genetic liability for schizophrenia).

Because the "borderline" population is so diverse, it seems only natural that optimal treatment for so large and diverse a group could not be unitary in its description. We would not expect that someone whose BPD arose mostly out of an abusive childhood would emerge into adult life so similar to another patient whose BPD had more to do with genetic predisposition for affective illness (and who came from a nonabusive home) that their treatment plans would be identical. Quite to the contrary, clinical experience suggests that, in the domain of BPD, what is needed on the part of the therapist is a high degree of *pragmatism*. With this goes diversity of treatment approach, according to the shifting demands of the situation, i.e., eclecticism; also, flexibility, patience, optimism—and humility (every therapist will fail with some borderline patients, who then go on to succeed with a colleague!); in addition, respect for the patient and a flair for persuasive dialogue, as Linehan has emphasized.

CLINICAL VIGNETTES

The following clinical vignettes show some of the variety in personality characteristics and symptom display in the domain of borderline personality disorder. All the patients met the criteria for DSM-III BPD, the number of items ranging from five to all eight. The long-term outcome of these patients also covers a broad range—from "recovered" to suicide. The reader will find additional examples, filling in some of the gaps in this necessarily incomplete sample, in an earlier publication (Stone, 1990). Figure 23 shows the life course of the patients in the next four vignettes.

A Borderline Patient with an Excellent Outcome

Betty, a single woman of 26, had been referred to me for psychotherapy after her release from residential treatment. She had entered a hospital unit specializing in the therapy of borderline conditions some two years before, because of a series of suicide attempts.

She had grown up in an affluent New England family with her three older brothers. Her upbringing had been free of any physical or sexual abuse. She experienced her father as easygoing and affectionate, whereas she saw her mother as perfectionist and controlling. If she did something or embarked upon a course of action her mother disapproved of, her mother would characteristically rebuke her with the comment: "You're killing your father!" Her father had had a mild heart attack when the patient was eight, but, contrary to the impression her mother wished to convey, had been in good health ever since. When the patient was 15, she began to stay out until all hours, frequenting bars in the seedier parts of town, where she would pick up men from backgrounds her parents would have regarded as totally unacceptable. Shortly before she was to go to college (the choice of which had led to screaming arguments with her mother), she cut her wrists and took an overdose of hypnotics, necessitating a brief hospitalization.

During her college years, Betty kept up her pattern of casual sexual affairs and began to abuse alcohol. Ultimately she completed her journalism course, but not before two more suicide gestures and brief hospital stays, each occasioned by a romantic disappointment.

While working as an editorial assistant after graduation, she began to feel lonely and depressed, made another suicide gesture after the breakup of a brief love affair, and this time entered a long-term facility. Exploratory psychotherapy was the mainstay of her treatment, although she was given tricyclic antidepressants in the beginning.

When I began working with her, she had gotten a job in a publishing company, lived with a roommate, and was fairly stable, except for episodic

Figure 23: *Life Trajectories of Four Borderline Patients*

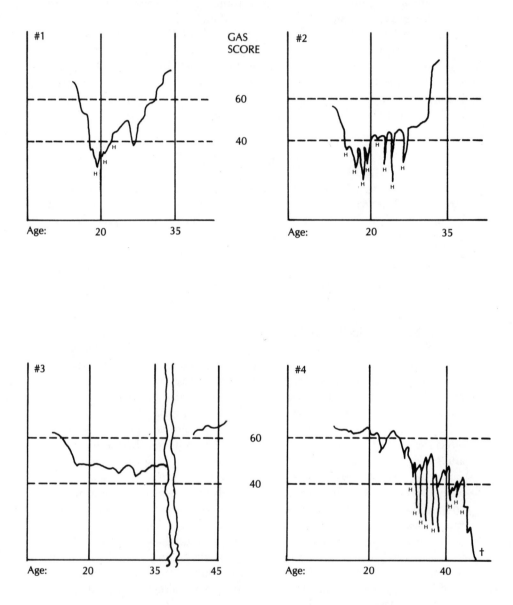

"H" indicates a period of hospitalization

abuse of alcohol. If her roommate was away, she would become anxious and would compulsively "bar-hop," engaging in "one-night stands" with men she met earlier in the evening.

Shortly after our work began, Betty reported the following dream:

> I was in the lobby of some hotel; there was a patio with a lot of people milling around; on one side there was a thin partition, and there was a gathering of people on the other side of this partition. I had a gun and shot it in the direction of the partition. It turned out the manager of the hotel was on the other side, and the bullet killed him. I felt guilty, and went up to some room on the second floor, where I put the gun to my head and killed myself.

The "translation" of the dream, via her associations, concerned the "killing" of her father, who would have "died" if he knew about all her partying and casual affairs. The price she had to pay for this unintentional patricide was her own life, via suicide. This led to a reexamination of her mother's "curse" and to the realization that use of alcohol and sex to fight loneliness were maladaptive activities that needed to be changed — but were not mortal sins that would literally kill her father if he ever found out.

Other key problems were low self-esteem and her conviction of being ugly, even though she was actually attractive. Our work, which spanned two and a half years of twice weekly sessions, shifted gradually from mostly exploratory to a mixture of exploratory and supportive. Except for rare lapses, she conquered her drinking problem with only minimal help from AA (she attended for only a few months). Therapy focused on her anxiety when spending an evening alone. Over time, she developed some interests and hobbies that were able to sustain her during such periods. She was able to take an apartment by herself, in the meantime widening her circle of friends, so that her life was less solitary than it had been. Her supervisor at work considered her an outstanding employee: she came early and stayed late, did "two people's work," and was friendly and uncomplaining.

After a year in therapy, one of her friends introduced her to a man in his early forties. Well-established and far more suitable than the men she had been with before, he was nevertheless very skittish about a committed relationship, owing to a bitter marriage and divorce some years before. Their involvement became "serious" five or six months later. Therapy now centered on this relationship; many sessions were taken up with discussion of the "optimal strategy" — how to get her friend comfortable enough to overcome his nervousness about marriage. Fortunately, my opinion and recommendation — that patience and applying no pressure would be the best attitude — coincided with her own instincts.

Perhaps because her self-esteem had been low for so long a time, she asked little of life and was of an uncomplaining disposition. Inordinate anger was one of the BPD items she did *not* show. I met with her friend a few times alone; a few times with both together. Apparently these sessions helped alleviate his anxieties, for shortly afterwards he proposed. The termination of her therapy coincided with their marriage and their move to a different city. We correspond once or twice a year, from which I learned that she has been happy in her marriage, has a child, and pursues her journalism from home on a free-lance basis. She has also become more compassionate toward her mother.

A Borderline Patient with an Unexpectedly Good Outcome

Barbara, a single woman of 24, sought treatment with me shortly after discharge from a hospital, where she had spent three weeks because of depression, panic attacks, and a suicide gesture. This had been her seventh hospitalization—all of them brief, and all for similar symptoms—since age 17. Cheerful and cooperative as a young girl, she underwent a radical change of personality at the time of her menarche. Thereafter she became irascible, rebellious, moody, and demanding.

Compulsive behavior developed, taking the form of refusal to eat meals unless the foods were arranged in a particular color coordination and sequence on the plate. For a time she was anorexic; later on, bulimic (maintaining her normal weight by vomiting). Schoolwork deteriorated, and she took up with a wild crowd, abusing marijuana and other drugs and engaging in promiscuous sex. At one point she ran away from home with a boyfriend, and didn't return for three months.

She quit high school with one year to go. Her life became even more chaotic; she scratched her wrists on a number of occasions, and consorted with abusive men who would use her sexually and then beat her up. Her work history was nil, apart from a sinecure at the factory which her father owned. A number of close relatives had serious affective disorders, including agoraphobia, bipolar illness, and recurrent depression.

By the time I began working with Barbara, she had been abusing alcohol for about a year, and had also become addicted to benzodiazepines. Her proneness to panic-level anxiety now took the from of agoraphobia, necessitating her being accompanied by a parent to her thrice weekly sessions. Premenstrually, her irritability rose to fever pitch: she would strike her parents with her fists, sometimes necessitating help from the police. She would then threaten to kill herself.

I would get frantic calls at all hours. Her tone with me varied from one minute to the next, from pleading to sassy (her parents saw only her sassy self). She had no talent for insight therapy and was too frantic for support- ive therapy, taking up most of the session time with an unending litany of complaints about her family. It seemed hazardous to give her antidepressant medications because she abused almost anything given her; it proved impos- sible to taper her from the benzodiazepines, since the less she took of those, the more alcohol she would consume that day.

She was frightened of hospitals, and refused my recommendation to enter one — until I managed to convince the family that her alcoholism could not be controlled on the outside (she refused AA, as well as any day pro- grams in her area). She spent a month in an alcohol treatment center and actually conquered that habit — only to become all the more addicted to benzodiazepines. Lacking any hobbies or interests, apart from dancing, she was bored to distraction at home, yet afraid to venture out. Nothing gave her any pleasure except glitzy clothes (which her agoraphobia rendered irrelevant) and her puppy.

For a few weeks Barbara dated a man from her neighborhood, and although she was able to leave the house if she were with him, she used the opportunity in a self-destructive way, going to wild nightclubs and pro- voking him with demands to the point where he drove her only halfway home, pushing her out of the car, so that she had to hitchhike home at 2 a.m. This precipitated a suicide attempt with a variety of medications, which gave me the leverage to force her into a long-term treatment unit.

Despite the panoply of symptoms and personality traits (which filled up half the pages of DSM), there was something likeable about this patient: her sassiness, her clinginess, and querulousness seemed like an overlay, as though a consequence of her "bipolar II" affective disorder, underneath which was a potentially friendly and generous person.

When she was hospitalized, the first order of business was to taper her off the benzodiazepines. She was extraordinarily sensitive, like the Princess and the Pea, to the least decrement in daily dose. The task required three months, during which she made herself unpopular with the nursing staff because of her complaining. A pastmistress at "splitting," she would call her parents, playing on their sympathies, urging them to take her out of "this prison" and let her return home. Thanks to many meetings with the staff about this manipulativeness, they stood their ground.

When the drugs were finally out of her system, her personality under- went a profound change. Her "likeable" self, which had gone into hiding the past 14 years, reemerged. She joined in various patient activities, which she had studiously avoided beforehand; as her hospital "privileges" in- creased, she volunteered to do favors for other patients; she became cheer- ful, optimistic and calmer. Having shown no self-discipline at any earlier point in her life, she was now able to apply herself to various assignments in recreational and occupational therapy, as a preparation to resuming extramural life on a more solid footing.

The residential phase of Barbara's treatment lasted two years. She was then able to maintain herself in an apartment with a roommate and to sustain herself at a job with only minimal help from her family. At the time of this writing, five years later, she is still doing well socially and at work, is drug-free, and is getting along comfortably with her family. Her eating disorder, finickiness, and agoraphobia have not returned. Though much of the credit for her recovery belongs with herself and the dedicated hospital staff (and she bit many a hand that fed her, in the beginning), much credit also goes to her parents—who, despite having been "enmeshed" with her for many years, were never abusive and always supportive.

A Borderline Patient with a Marginal Course for Many Years, but with Eventual Recovery

A single woman of 35 had worked with four analysts over a period of 11 years, before the last of these referred her to me. Since Beatrice had graduated from college at age 22, she had seemed to circulate in a holding pattern. She saw herself as an executive-to-be in the corporate world, but in actuality had held just a few entry-level jobs, and those only briefly. Once or twice she quit in a huff because the job was "not interesting enough" or because "they weren't promoting me fast enough." She had no distinct career goals, nor had she taken any special courses to prepare herself for some particular path. The work problem did not pose a threat to her well-being, since she lived off a large trust fund that her family had set up for her.

On the relational side her situation was not much better. Beatrice had never been "serious" with anyone and had little interest in men apart from their ability to pay compliments to her appearance. Her self-image was contradictory: she alternated between seeing herself as "model pretty" or else ugly. While buying an ice cream, she would feel devastated if the counterman did not make eyes at her; if he did, she would feel "insulted."

Bulimarexic since her teens, she maintained a weight ten pounds below the ideal by means of brief binges and long periods of starvation. She had no hobbies or sustaining interests and found evenings with nothing to do intolerable. On such evenings she would usually engage her mother in long phone conversations (her parents lived in a different city), demanding that her mother come and visit. If this were not possible, she would slam the phone down, only to then call her mother back half an hour later to apologize.

During the time I worked with Beatrice, her most noticeable personality traits were those of *anger*, *argumentativeness*, *scornfulness*, *irritability*, and *vanity*. Her intensity and demandingness made her troublesome in her family; her parents and siblings were mostly good-natured and got on well when she was not in their midst. She satisfied six criteria for BPD: all but impulsivity and self-damaging acts.

She spoke with considerable pressure and was very circumstantial. Being "in analysis" meant a great deal to her, since she associated this with high intellectual status. Yet she had little aptitude for working with symbolism. Just how rich a mine was left unexplored in this regard may be gleaned from one of the dreams she did mention—but to which she did not have any associations:

> You're gay, though you have a crush on me. I tell you I'm quitting therapy for good, and you make a pass at me. You pull a gold chain off my neck. Also, you kept my mail. In one envelope there was a picture of me, which you jealously hold onto, in order to masturbate with.

Premenstrually, Beatrice became markedly more depressed, tearful and irascible. At such times she had suicidal thoughts, though she never acted on them. I saw her more and more as temperamentally cyclothymic, perhaps as a bipolar II manic-depressive in attenuated form, with accompanying borderline personality disorder. I recommended antidepressants; later, a trial of lithium. The very idea of needing a medication meant "craziness" to her.

It was after 11 months of three-times weekly therapy that I suggested the lithium. At that moment she walked out of the office and did not return to therapy. I became the fifth analyst she quit seeing. She did call me a year later and told me that she was now working with a female analyst. Her life was no less constricted than before. She was not employed and still had only her narrow circle of friends. But she liked this analyst and was more comfortable with her than with any of the five men she had seen over the years before.

*   *   *   *   *

In connection with a recent effort to follow up the patients with whom I have worked in private practice since 1966, I recently called the woman of this vignette. I did so with some trepidation, since she had been angry with me and disappointed. I had not spoken to her in ten years, and was concerned that, now in her mid-forties, she might have become more discouraged and embittered than she had been a decade earlier. Quite to my surprise, she was most pleased that I had phoned, saying, "Why, Dr. Stone, how sweet of you to call!" She went on to tell me how she had continued in treatment with the female therapist for many years, and had, over the past two or three years, begun to socialize in a much more effective way. She now not only made friends easily but also retained them, whereas before she used to alienate friends by becoming overly critical. She no longer had an eating disorder. Though she still lived alone, she was more at peace with herself even on evenings when she was not with friends. She could relax and devote time to hobbies and interests. For the first time in many years, she was working, and was preparing to assume a more advanced position in a media-related corporation. Furthermore, she had been willing to stay at one place of employ and progress slowly through the ranks, whereas in her twenties and thirties she had entertained magical hopes of swift success that would come automatically.

It is not clear to me what were the ingredients of this woman's remarkable improvement. Surely, some of it must have to do with the last therapist—with whom she "clicked" in a way that had not happened with her former therapists, including myself. The maturation and emotional calming that are supposed to occur with the advancing years (as Cicero once spoke of in his *De Senectute* oration) seem to have had their good effects. Fortunately, she did not experience a downturn in her mid-forties, as do some borderline patients (McGlashan, 1986) who abruptly lose a sustaining relationship in that decade. In the PI-500 study counterintuitive results of this sort occurred with about one in 10 or 12 patients at long-term follow-up (Stone, 1990). Thus far, I am finding a similar ratio among my former private patients.

A Case of Borderline Personality Disorder
Ending in Suicide

Some years ago I was consulted about a legal dispute over the validity of a will. The "decedent" had been the wife of a wealthy manufacturer, from whom she had been separated for about a year. Embroiled in an acrimonious custody battle over their three children, which she was clearly about to lose, she hastily wrote out a will that bequeathed her half of the estate to some distant relatives. The motivating factor behind her choice of legatees was apparently spite—a way of getting even with her husband—since these relatives lived abroad and she had never seen them. Two days after penning the will she killed herself with an overdose of secobarbital. The main issue to be adjudicated, aside from whether the husband's factory was legally separate or really half hers, concerned the wife's soundness of mind at the time she drew up the document.

My task was to perform a "psychological autopsy," reconstructing as best one could her mental state and her personality merely from records, rather than from interviews with the living patient. Paradoxically, in the case of a highly "negative" personality, the appraisal emerges with greater clarity from contact with acquaintances than with the person in question (who is likely to evade and dissimulate), and may often be made more easily with a dead subject than with a live one, since people (especially those in subordinate or dependent positions) may garner the courage to say about someone who can no longer hurt them what they would have feared to say if the person were still alive. As it was, I had available to me 11,000 pages of depositional material, derived from 35 relatives, friends, employees, physicians, etc., some of whom had taped their conversations with her. How often does a psychiatrist get to know a patient's personality "in depth" to this degree?

Forty-three years old at the time of her death, Mrs. B., as I shall call her, had been married for 18 years. Her immediate family was of modest means and was substantially free of adverse factors: no divorce, no deaths, no alcoholism, no abuse. Several aunts and uncles on the mother's side had affective disorders. After finishing high school, she supported herself as a department-store clerk, in which capacity she caught the eye of her future husband: a considerably older man who was attracted to her good looks and her "bubbly personality."

Her early married life was like a fairy tale come true, as she suddenly found herself in a situation of great wealth and high social position. For a year or two all went well, until after the birth of her first child. She found the obligations of motherhood a severe strain, despite having servants and nannies at her beck and call. Ascribed initially to "postpartum depression," her moodiness persisted long beyond the expected time. Having once been the life of the party, she now became reclusive. She seemed content only when alone with her husband on a trip; the presence of the baby made her morose and irritable.

Persuaded to seek treatment, she went to a prominent analyst, chauffered five days a week from her suburban home to his downtown Atlanta office. After some months, her behavior became more irascible and eccentric. She began to abuse alcohol. One day she appeared for her session in a negligée. A man of considerable probity, the analyst told her that he could no longer regard her as serious about getting help, and that he could no longer work with her. He modified his original diagnosis from "hysteric character" to "borderline personality disorder."

Her course from that moment was steadily downhill—in a slide that spanned 13 years before the final dénouement. The care of the next two children was entrusted almost entirely to their nannies. She seldom left her bedroom. What had been moodiness earlier was now frank depression; periodically she would become suicidal and make a gesture or a more serious attempt (cutting her wrists, taking overdoses; once she tried to hang herself). Her care was now entrusted to a psychiatrist who saw her only a few times; otherwise he went along with her insistence on having just "telephone sessions," consisting of two- or three-hour tirades in which she complained nonstop about her husband, the children, and the "help."

Whenever she did make a suicide gesture, she would spend a few days (never more than four) in a psychiatric hospital, then return to her bedroom and the endless "sessions." During the last 12 years of her life there were 11 such incidents. Fascinatingly, all but one occurred within a three-day span around the "central" day of December 12th. Since this was not the anniversary of anything, I would assume that this eerie predictability must have reflected a "seasonal" affective disorder (running alongside, or perhaps underlying, her BPD) that might have been alleviated by proper treatment. However this may be, her behavior deteriorated to the point where she grew abusive, hurling scatological insults at her family and household help, at times smashing objects around the house.

Her life became morbid theater. Toward the end, her abusiveness took on grotesque overtones, as when, while in the family car on the way to her middle daughter's confirmation, she cut her wrist with a penknife and smeared blood on her daughter's white dress, turning a joyful ceremony into a nightmare. This was the next to the last straw. The last straw came a few months later, when the children returned home a half-hour later than expected from some event. She flew into a rage, threw a bookend at one of her daughters and chased the other two around the house with a cane. Her husband purchased another house within days, moved the girls into it, and served papers for legal separation, as prelude to divorce.

Apparently because of her ambivalence and her unwillingness to admit how much easier life would be for her without the children, she sued for custody. Experts were brought in for both sides, but the evidence was overwhelming that the children belonged with their father. A hearing had been scheduled before a judge, who would decide the matter after the reports were completed (a process that took up several months). The day before the judge's decision, her body was found in her bedroom by her servants.

Comments

Although the patients described in these vignettes met DSM criteria for BPD (Mrs. B. showed all eight items), this fact alone has little explanatory value in relation to their eventual outcome. Hospitalized borderline patients with all eight items tended, in my follow-up study, to do poorly (Stone,

1990), but many of the patients who committed suicide had not been "pan-symptomatic" in this way, as had Mrs. B. What figures more importantly in determining prognosis, I believe, are certain other factors: some subtle and hard to measure, such as *likeableness* and *character*; others more observable and measurable, such as the level of *anger* or *hostility*. Whether one is *self-disciplined* or *chaotic* constitutes another more objectifiable variable.

Elsewhere, I offered a list of some dozen prognostic measures (Stone, 1985b) that might be of help in distinguishing easily treatable borderline patients from those who seemed at the "border of treatability" (or even untreatable). These included: friendliness, likeability, intelligence, motivation, psychological-mindedness, moral sense (i.e., good vs. bad character), self-discipline, intro- vs. extrapunitive defensive style, and empathy. Parental and social supports, or their lack, were another set of factors, external to the patient.

Most of these are "soft" measures, in the sense that they are subjective and require that the therapist know a patient over a long period of time. Some are interrelated: chances are a consistently likeable patient is someone who is not consumed with hostility (especially with hostility that spills over into the therapeutic relationship). Likeableness and hostility (or "unfriendliness") could therefore be seen as one measure, not two: polar opposites along an axis concerning "attitude toward others."

The patients of the vignettes, in any event, differed considerably in relation to this dimension. The first patient, Betty, not only was likeable, but showed no "inordinate anger" toward anyone (though she did, years earlier, toward her mother). The second, Barbara, was friendly toward me (albeit drainingly demanding), but had been harboring resentments against her whole family for many years. When she was in residential treatment, the nursing staff found her unfriendly, imperious, and manipulative—all of which she was until the drugs she had been abusing were out of her system. It was as though she started out in life with a friendly personality makeup, then became irritable (at menarche) in response to genetic predisposition (to manic-depression), made herself more irritable through the side-effects of the drugs she took via "self-medication," and only reverted to her former likeability when tapered from those drugs and rehabilitated. In her case, hostility was a patina (though one that had covered her for a long time), not her "true" self. Her friendliness now interacts synergistically with other positive steps in cementing in place her improved status: by virtue of getting along better with family and friends, for example, she now has a solid support system, whereas before she was scarcely endurable even to her parents.

The patient in the third vignette, Beatrice, though tantrumy and hot-tempered all her life, preserved a tolerable balance between the pleasing and the irritating qualities of her personality up through her late twenties. The balance swung toward the irritating side during her thirties, but then toward the pleasing side later on.

Mrs. B. blamed others entirely and during the last decade of her life became uninterruptedly malicious. Her wealth, which would have facili- tated therapeutic success, had she been motivated (and had she been re- spectful of other people's feelings), only made her situation worse. Wealth can fan a spark of nastiness into a conflagration of wickedness. Her millions having lifted her outside the circle of social control, she could, like Elena Ceaucescu, do just as she pleased. What therapist ever humbled an abusive tyrant?

Actually, Mrs. B.'s case is all the more intriguing in that a manic- depressive "diathesis," not so apparent during the first half of her life, became manifest during the latter half. Some patients in this situation re- spond to lithium or carbamazepine, etc., so well as to become transformed into the calm and friendly selves they may once have been. This was the pleasant outcome of the trichotillomania patient—combative and verbally abusive when in the hospital; on phenelzine, a sweet and tractable person— I described in my long-term study (Stone, 1990, p. 331). But no one in- volved in the care of Mrs. B. prescribed the medications that might have both melted away the (admittedly very thick) façade of irritability and reexposed the friendly person who had once dwelt underneath.

Borderline patients, more than patients with most other types of person- ality disorder, exhibit what Gleick (1987) called "sensitive dependence upon initial conditions." As in the meteorological conditions Gleick was describing, tiny differences at the outset (the butterfly flapping its wings in South America) can, in certain "chaos" prone systems, multiply into huge differences further down the line (a tornado in Oklahoma). In many human situations, small differences can multiply in this fashion, as suggested in the adage "the rich get richer." In the realm of personality disorder and its treatment, we observe something similar: the nice get nicer (and often, the mean get meaner). Patients who are even a little above some threshold of likeableness, for example, tend to respond well to therapy, and end up much better adapted. Those just a bit below this threshold (to say nothing of those way below this line) tend to spiral the other way.

This phenomenon is not limited to borderline personality; we have had ample opportunity to witness something similar among the entrepreneurs who made the headlines of the '80s. To judge from their biographers (cf. Rothchild, 1991), a good many of these men seemed narcissistic (power-hungry, egotistical, ruthless, etc.) and hypomanic (grandiose, over- exuberant, extraverted, etc.). Those who had self-restraint and good business sense were able, after owing a billion dollars a year, to take in $1,050,000,000. These men flourished. They were even able to put something aside for a rainy day. Those who, facing a similar debt structure but with poorer business sense and incurable grandiosity, took in $950,000,000 suddenly found themselves with a major creditor they could not pay. This was the butterfly flapping its wings. Other creditors got wind of trouble and stormed the doors, banks would no longer extend loans, "junk bond" sales suddenly found no buyers—and after a time the grandiose plans ended in disgrace and ruin. This was the tornado.

None of the patients in the vignettes had been abused physically or sexually (though Mrs. B. had grown up in a "high expressed-emotion" household: Vaughn & Leff, 1976). In the many instances where these factors have been present in the background of a borderline patient, a special countertransference problem will often arise. Such patients routinely show the kind of inordinate anger and vindictiveness Mrs. B. exhibited. An abuse history makes these negative qualities more "understandable" and will tend to evoke great sympathy on the part of the therapist. This is a very human response and up to a point causes no difficulty.

But the day will come when such patients must take responsibility for their hostility toward others, their jealousy, their vengefulness—or whatever form their pent-up anger may assume. Therapists who suppress the impulse to confront in this situation, no matter how long they have been working with the patient, make a serious mistake. To pussyfoot around the hostility endlessly, because one "feels sorry" for what the patient had endured years earlier, does nothing to check the patient's habit of abusing others in the here and now. Therapists must have the integrity to speak openly about a patient's destructiveness, even if the patient leaves treatment in a huff. The alternative is a kind of dishonest nontherapy, where one listens to stories of abusiveness and, for fear of "offending" the patient, does nothing about it.

12

Narcissistic Traits and Personality Disorder

THOUGH *NARCISSISTIC* IS A WORD in everyday language, when it is used technically as a modifier of certain personality traits and disorders, we encounter formidable problems in definition—no less so than the problems besetting our use of the term "borderline." Since Freud's time *narcissistic* has had a place in both normal and abnormal psychology. As Cooper (1984) mentions, Freud (1905) spoke of a sequence in early development progressing from the infant's "primary autoerotism" (total self-absorption or "narcissism") to eventual normal object-relatedness. Psychoanalysts found it meaningful to postulate various "lines of development" (A. Freud, 1963), including the *narcissistic* path, relating to one's evolving attitude toward one's own self, in contrast to the object-relational path that concerned attitudes, inner representations, etc., about other people. Citing Pulver (1970), Cooper (1984, p. 42) lists four meanings Freud gave to *narcissism*: a sexual perversion, a developmental stage, a type of object choice (where one loves someone because of that person's resemblance to oneself), and an ego-state relating to self-esteem.

In contemporary psychiatric parlance *narcissistic* refers to an exaggeration of various attributes of what would otherwise be normal self-regard: in the place of "enlightened self-interest," one might find an all-consuming self-centeredness, or a cavalier indifference to the legitimate needs of family members, coworkers, etc., or a grandiose and inflated sense of self-worth. DSM-III-R outlines nine traits (briefly: pathological reaction to criticism, exploitativeness, grandiosity, sense of uniqueness, preoccupation with power/success/beauty, entitlement, admiration-seeking, lack of empathy, and envy). Requiring only five of these nine, DSM permits 256 combinations in its polythetic definition, a reflection of the many varieties of *narcissistic personality disorder* (NPD) encountered in actual practice.

As with borderline personality disorder (BPD), NPD may coexist with any of the other "official" disorders. These "fellow travelers," depending on their nature, may exert strong influence on prognosis (Stone, 1989b). In addition, there is a multitude of narcissistic *traits*: those alluded to in DSM, and many others. In my trait-profile, I include: affected, "arriviste," arrogant, boastful, conceited, contemptuous, dandyish, haughty, hypercritical, know-it-all, mannered, name-dropping, patronizing, pompous, pretentious, "prima donna," sanctimonious, self-righteous, smug, snobbish, stilted, and vain—over and above the narcissistic traits in DSM. And this list relates only to the attitude of thinking oneself better than others. Greediness, stinginess, indifference, demandingness, spitefulness, and crankiness also bespeak a "me-first-ness" that we associate with the concept of (pathological) narcissism.

The number of persons exhibiting significant narcissistic traits, even short of "NPD," but enough to cause difficulty in interpersonal life, is clearly very great. Lasch (1978) and Restak (1982) concur in considering narcissistic disorders symptomatic of our era. Absent comparable epidemiological data from the nineteenth century vis-à-vis personality disorders, it is not easy to validate this impression. But these authors are probably correct. We do seem to be living in a time when inhibited personality types are not as frequent as they seemed to be in Freud's day; disinhibited self-centeredness does seem a strong feature of our nosologic landscape; and NPD is certainly a prominent feature of any therapist's patient-roster.

THE ORIGINS OF PATHOLOGICAL NARCISSISM

Contributory factors must belong to one of three compartments: hereditary, constitutional, or environmental. Hereditary factors would include genetic liability for either schizophrenia or the bipolar form manic-depression. Some schizophrenic persons display prominent narcissistic traits that stem seemingly from their inability to form close ties with others: they remain, in effect, with the self-absorption and self-centeredness of the young child. Grandiosity may be present, though not as regularly as would be noted in bipolar manics. In the latter, grandiosity is often flamboyant or messianic: an "end-stage" of the spectrum of euphoria and self-confidence.

Physical beauty might be seen as a constitutional factor, though hereditary influences are important also. Men and women of unusual beauty elicit favoritism, good opinions, sexual attraction, etc., from others, which, if not handled sensitively by parents, can predispose to certain narcissistic traits: disdainfulness, haughtiness, arrogance, and the like.

In contrast to schizoid or schizotypal disorders, however, narcissistic traits probably derive more from early environment than from "innate" sources. Under ordinary circumstances, one's parents and one's culture accept with good humor and a loving attitude a child's grandiose dreams and sense of specialness. As children grow and mature, they are "let down gently," learning little by little to pare down their dreams to the size of their talents and possibilities. The desire to "have it all" is sacrificed, in tolerable stages, to the more reasonable wish for "fairness." Of three sibs, none gets the whole pie; each learns to be satisfied with a third.

Narcissistic traits can develop, curiously, when there are deviations from ideal rearing on either side: pampering or neglecting; expecting too much or too little. Excessive praise of a child (whether the child is unusually talented or not) can give rise to what Tartakoff (1966) called the "Nobel Prize complex." Feelings of superiority, of being destined for greatness, may arise in this situation. But compensatory feelings of a similar kind can arise where there has been parental indifference and neglect, for in this situation a child may develop an exaggerated desire for "greatness" by way of shoring up a sense of self-worth in the absence of the ordinary parental praise. Whereas the overly praised child may regard himself as better than he really is, the neglected child may present a dual picture: an outward sense of (compensatory) specialness covering an inward sense of worthlessness. Neglected children of the very wealthy often show these paradoxical features (Stone, 1972). Parental cruelty can have this same dual effect, teaching the child not only to undervalue himself, but also to conclude that "it's every man for himself" — a narcissistic assumption.

CONTEMPORARY PSYCHOANALYTIC VIEWS

Discussion about narcissistic disorders has centered in recent years around the contrasting metapsychologies of Kohut and Kernberg. Freud argued at the turn of the century that patients with "narcissistic neuroses" did not form a transference. His impression stemmed from their characteristic aloofness. Freud was referring to what we now call schizophrenia, not to nonpsychotic persons with (DSM-type) narcissistic traits.

Kohut (1971, 1977), speaking actually of the latter, nonschizophrenic "narcissists," asserted that their seeming inability to form a transference was better understood as a " . . . specific primitive form of object tie which appeared in patients who had suffered significant damage to the nuclear self during early psychological development" (Cooper, 1984, p. 43). Kohut's views are further explicated in a recent article by A. Goldberg (1989).

It is important to remember that Kohut and Freud did not have the same kinds of patients in mind when they formulated their ideas about transference potential. Kohut also stretches language a bit beyond its flexibility in claiming that aloofness or tenuousness — in patients whose parents were neglectful, rejecting, etc. — represents their brand of "transference." While it may be that they transferentially assume the analyst will also be indifferent to them, as were their parents, in many, especially severely narcissistic patients, there is no longer a hidden self waiting for the chance to form a bond with someone. The capacity for any kind of meaningful connectedness has simply been lost (as with vision, in a child whose otherwise good eyes were blindfolded the first five years of life and whose brain no longer processes "visual" stimuli).

In contrast to Kohut, for whom a *developmental arrest* was the prime factor in narcissistic disorder (brought about by inadequate parenting), Kernberg places the emphasis on the pathological effects of rage, including a superabundance of "innate" (heredo-constitutional) rage, as causing distortions in the representations of self and other that the clinician sees in "narcissistic" patients. Kohut's and Kernberg's positions seem irresolvably opposed, though the difference may be in part a reflection of Kernberg's greater familiarity with hospitalized borderline patients — many of whom have a manic-depressive component or attention-deficit component, either of which would lend weight to his more biologically-based theory. Rageful-ness even from postnatal sources (parental abusiveness, incest) acquires a "hard-wired" quality in adult life; the anger of hospitalized borderline patients with concomitant NPD will also appear "innate."

Cooper has offered an integrative view of "narcissism," incorporating the most cogent aspects of Kohut, Kernberg, and other psychoanalysts specializing in this area. A unified sense of selfhood is essential in normal development, as Cooper mentions (p. 45). *Infantile grandiosity* is a normal stage in early childhood; residues of this state may reemerge under stress or during either sexual enthrallment or periods of intense creativity. Normal development also requires the achievement of an *integrated, internalized self-image*. Given empathic parenting, the child's failures and victories are not blown out of proportion. The reassurances and realistic expectations of a "good enough" parent (to use Winnicott's term: 1965) help modulate the child's responses and evolving self-image so that both humiliation and pathological grandiosity are avoided. Again, under normal circumstances, a realistic and healthy *self-esteem* develops, allowing one to withstand constructive criticism and to recognize destructive criticism as stemming from a flaw in the critic, not from a flaw in the recipient. Failures in the development of self-esteem may take the form of paranoid, persecutory ideation, or of depression (as though one deserved the bad notices), or may predispose to the obsessive's perfectionism.

Acknowledging the contributions of Searles and Ornstein, Cooper mentions that during the *oedipal* phase the father's acceptance of the child's normal narcissistic strivings and the mother's acceptance of the child's emerging sexuality and exhibitionism contribute to healthy sexual and personality development; the father's competitive anger or the mother's ridicule leads to fearfulness and humiliation. On the topic of narcissism and the *body*, Cooper reminds us that persons whose self-esteem is vulnerable react with intense dismay to signs of aging and are apt to mobilize various "narcissistic" defenses: resorting to unnecessary plastic surgery, courting sexual partners a generation younger than oneself, etc.

Finally, the need for age-appropriate *idealizations* is underlined: it is these that provide a template for one's own ego-ideal and healthy ambitions. Idealizations also may serve as the source of grandiose, inflated notions of one's worth at times of disappointment, loss, group-criticism, etc. (As to the latter point, imagine the fate of an opera singer, actor, or other performer who could not draw on some reserves of "unrealistic" grandiosity when faced with a tough audition, a huge audience, or an unkind review.) For most people, this unrealistic but vital inner sense of specialness comes from having been loved by one's parents and from being loved by one's sexual partner in the here and now. One might say it is the overestimation of our worth and goodness by those who love us that permits us to endure the awareness, which grows ever more keen throughout life, that we are not quite that valuable, not quite that good. Those not fortunate to have this storehouse of love must face life "on their own." Unless they are, in Cooper's word, extraordinarily self-sufficient, such persons will be prone to feelings of unworthiness, given any reversal, especially a rejection or even the temporary absence of a lover.

Clinical Examples

Narcissistic personality disorder and prominent narcissistic traits can coexist with any of the other personality disorders. In my experience this is less apt to occur in the case of avoidant and schizoid disorders, whereas narcissistic traits, if not the full-blown disorder, routinely accompany antisocial PD and are quite common in BPD. The following vignettes show something of the range and variations of narcissistic pathology.

Narcissistic Personality Disorder with
Schizotypal Personality Disorder

Nancy, who has been in therapy for many years, came from a family where both her mother and maternal grandfather were schizophrenic. Apart from a brief marriage, she has lived alone, although she has had a number of long relationships with men. Short-tempered and markedly self-centered, she has told me that the nuances of social interaction baffle her; she has no ability to make "small talk"; she feels superior to and different from her coworkers. But when either I am away on vacation or her male companion is away, she suddenly complains of feeling "worthless" or "ugly." If someone is a bit inattentive because of feeling "under the weather," she takes offense, never imagining the person might be ill, to say nothing of inquiring how that person is feeling. Her ability to empathize correctly with others is, and has remained over the years, very low.

Narcissistic Personality Disorder with
Paranoid Personality Disorder

Ned, a man in his mid-twenties, sought therapy following a brief hospital-ization for a psychotic depression. There was a strong family history of affective illness, plus soft signs of "organicity," probably stemming from birth complications. Though raised in an affluent family with all the "advantages," he also suffered verbal and (to a lesser extent) physical abuse from both parents. The home atmosphere was one of high expectations, hypercriticalness, and humiliation.

Beginning in adolescence, Ned became preoccupied with proving his worth to the world; he elaborated grandiose fantasies of becoming super-friendly, super-good, super-moral, etc. He immersed himself in martial arts, in an effort to shore up feelings of sexual inadequacy.

Conversations, whether with therapist, relative, or acquaintance, began and ended with pleas for reassurance that he was bright, talented, and likeable. Any suggestion that he might have handled a certain situation slightly differently from how he did was experienced as a withering criticism and as an intolerable intrusion into his efforts to "be his own person." Though empathic in nonthreatening encounters, when dealing with not-so-friendly people Ned became blunt, at times hostile, preferring to "remain honest" and lose an opportunity, rather than use diplomacy and achieve his goal. Warm and helpful with his close friends, he reacted with exaggerated mistrust and resentment to the merest whisper of a difference of opinion, voiced by a girl he was courting or by an authority figure. His impatience to win fame, fortune, and the love of beautiful women was so great as to hinder his steps along the path of even pared-down versions of these ambitions. The grudge he held against his parents for their harshness two decades ago led to a feeling of entitlement about what they now "owed" him in "reparations."

Narcissistic Personality Disorder with Borderline Personality Disorder

Naomi, age 21, had dropped out of college in her final year because of mounting depression, alienation, and several suicide gestures. There was no family history of mental illness. Her mother was an imperious "grande dame" from a wealthy family and was herself highly narcissistic. Her father was from an even more prominent family. Of a much more gentle disposition, he found the marriage intolerable and divorced when the patient was four. She rarely saw her father afterwards.

During her teens, Naomi took art courses, hoping to become a great painter whose works her father would read about and rush to see; he would then beg to be reunited with her. Her talent was meager in this area (though considerable in other pursuits she deemed as less likely to appeal to her father), and her dreams were not realized. Her suicide gestures led to her spending a year and a half in a residential treatment unit. Highly attractive, she was equally haughty and made no friends in the residence. Intensely lonely and longing for maternal nurturing, she hesitated nonetheless to bare her soul to anyone, including her therapists—all of whom she treated like so many hired servants of inferior status.

Ironically, young men of her "class" found her insufferably cold, so she consorted, *faute de mieux*, with macho barroom types, who would use her sexually, beat her up, and then leave her. (These encounters were also the acting out of her oedipal longings: forbidden sex and the punishment for it were rolled into one experience.) Her sense of entitlement was so extreme that she would at times come unannounced and knock on the door of mere acquaintances at one or two in the morning, fully expecting to be welcomed with open arms. Despite her beauty, wealth, and aristocratic status (things *other* narcissists merely hope for!), she was eaten up with envy toward the many "lesser" persons in her life—including her therapists—who were brought up in, and who created in their adult lives, warm and loving families.

Narcissistic Personality Disorder with Antisocial Personality

Nicholas, age 27, was referred for therapy in hopes (by his family) that he would "find himself and settle down." Single and unemployed, he was the scion of a wealthy family, almost all of whose members led dissolute lives, amply supported by trust funds. Alcoholism was rampant in his immediate family and in his uncles, aunts, and cousins on both sides. He himself had been severely alcoholic since age 16 and had spent many months at various treatment centers "drying out." When he was 20, he maimed a man in a barroom brawl, but was exonerated for "lack of evidence," partly through the manipulations of his powerful family.

Nicholas played many destructive and costly pranks during his adolescence, but was always bailed out by the family. Sometimes the "joke" was on them, as when he was given a $20,000 Piaget watch for high-school graduation: driving while drunk, he got into an accident two days later and smashed the watch to smithereens. The same afternoon he marched into Cartier's and charged an identical watch to his trust account. His father never noticed anything amiss.

I noticed, as I began my work with him, that Nicholas' affect was bland, his speech evasive and full of clichés. He "settled down" to the point of getting a sinecure job with a relative. Fancying himself a young tycoon-to-be on the "fast track," he would regale me with stories of giant "deals" he and the firm were consummating. The executors of his trust assured me all these Bunyanesque tales were figments of his imagination. Pathological lying pervaded other areas of inquiry as well, such that no reliable account of his past could be pieced together, except from the few scraps of information known to the executors. As he became more comfortable in his sheltered life, he would skip more and more sessions until, as in a prolonged taffy-pull, treatment finally thinned out to nothing.

Narcissistic Personality Disorder with Histrionic Personality Disorder

Nora, a married woman of 40 with two children by a previous marriage, sought therapy for episodes of irritability and depression. These occurred a few days before her period and often led to cat-fights with her husband of such severity as to threaten the new marriage. A woman of great beauty, she had married into European nobility and now maintained six homes: four in America and two abroad. Her narcissistic traits were the prognostically least ominous: she was not exploitative, envious, or unempathic. Apart from the conflicts with her husband, she was generous, cheerful, dramatic, rather shallow, and highly impressionistic. She had a sense of humor about her entitlement: enamored of all her new finery, she once quipped, "Why, Dr. Stone, I'd rather eat thumbtacks on my Sevres china than caviar on dime-store dishes!" Sometimes her husband would whisk her away for a few days to one of their other homes. In order to reschedule our next session, she would leave word for me to call her—invariably omitting to mention in which home I might find her. I had a 20% chance of guessing right the first time. Usually, of course, I failed.

"Pure" Narcissistic Personality

Norman was an unmarried surgeon in his early thirties when he was referred for psychoanalysis because of feelings of unfulfillment and problems making satisfactory relationships. Envious of colleagues who were getting academic posts, he complained that the "system" favored certain men who "sucked up" to the chief. It did not occur to him that success had eluded him because he developed no special techniques, did no research, and published no papers. He had always felt special, partly because he came from a highly respected family and was quite handsome and athletic. Among the four children in the family, he was also the unquestioned favorite of both parents. His "moment of greatness" came during his senior year of high school, when, having scored the winning touchdown against the school's big football rival, he was carried aloft on the shoulders of his teammates. Life had been downhill ever since.

Idolized by the most sought-after women, Norman "went through" one after the other, never falling in love with any particular one, always convinced he could easily find another superior to the last. He treated women shabbily, but with men (except for a few friends) he was worse: intensely competitive and irascible, he was openly critical of his colleagues; when he played basketball or tennis, he was "out to kill." Outspokenly bigoted, he was contemptuous of people from all groups except the favored one from which he came.

In two years of analysis, Norman moved from "A" to "B," reporting but one dream, and that a banal one to which he had no associations. During a two-week vacation at the close of the second year, he took a trip to Florida, fell in love with a four-times divorcée he met on the beach, married her at the end of his vacation, phoned to let me know his plans, and has remained there ever since.

Narcissistic Personality Disorder with
Passive-Aggressive Personality Disorder

Nathaniel, a single man in his early twenties, came for psychotherapy because of uncertainty about work goals. His parents wanted him to enter the family business. Meanwhile, he was going through the motions of working as a journalist, but his secret ambition was to be a boxing champion. He was highly ambitious, but his grandiosity far outstripped his ambition. He had gotten fired from a number of writing jobs because of surliness and uncooperativeness. Living at home with his parents, he alternated between compliance and sassiness. A younger brother was a college football player of local renown, about whom the patient felt great pride and even greater envy.

A weight-lifting buff, Nathaniel took to coming to his sessions clad only in his gym shorts and sneakers, looking like the men in muscle-magazine covers. This created quite a scene in my waiting room. Gentle interpretations on my part to the effect that this was a rather inappropriate way to show up at the office of one's analyst, and perhaps there was some hidden motive, elicited all manner of rationalizations about "no time to change," etc.

I found him a little contentious, but mostly good-natured and friendly. He was much more argumentative at home or at work. There was a curious sense of entitlement that bespoke not so much arrogance as an insensitivity to social convention. Once, for example, when my office was being repaired, we had to meet at my apartment. Waiting there in the living room, he noticed the housekeeper and asked her for a turkey sandwich, adding his specifications (salt, pepper, lettuce, light on the mayo). By coincidence these ingredients were available, so, nonplussed but gracious, she made him his sandwich.

Toward the end of Nathaniel's therapy, he moved into an apartment of his own. He became serious about a woman he had been dating. When both were on the bed one evening, his mother called, as she did almost every night, and held him on the phone for an hour. He felt like killing her. (His girlfriend felt like killing him.) In relating this incident, he told me: How could I have hung up on her? It'd hurt her feelings. I hate when she does that, but she's my mother. I pointed out to him that if he were diplomatic, her feelings would probably not be hurt. But if she did react badly, that was a reflection on her, not on him: he had every right to privacy with his girlfriend. This led to a salutary change in him: he no longer stored up resentment until he finally exploded in anger, but came to rely more on a gentle remark at the first sign of trouble.

Narcissistic Traits with
Obsessive-Compulsive Personality Disorder

Nelson, a married man in his thirties, underwent psychoanalysis because of a gnawing sense of failure—in his more openly acknowledged goal of achieving great academic success, and in his more hidden goal of receiving top accolades for his research. A perfectionistic "workaholic" since his university days, he had recently been promoted to associate professorship for his outstanding work and was given assurances that full professorship would be "automatic" when a few more pages had fallen off the calendar. Yet he was impatient for that day to come and was consumed with anxiety lest some adversary in the department "screw things up" for his advancement.

Though he had capable lab assistants, Nelson hovered over them in relation to every detail, never quite trusting that they could carry out his instructions to the letter as he insisted. Each year when the Nobel prizes were awarded, he would read the announcements tense-jawed and with bitterness, as though the medals had been stolen out of his pocket and given to others. His wife was on the brink of asking for divorce: the fun-loving qualities and raucous sense of humor that had attracted her originally had gradually disappeared, and in their place was just a dour "research robot."

Narcissistic Personality Disorder with Hypomanic Personality

Neil, a man of 40, was referred for therapy at the suggestion of the courts, while he was awaiting trial on charges of securities fraud. Years earlier he had started out as a broker in the commodities market, and he had then worked his way up into becoming a major player in precious metals. Athletic in build and expansive in demeanor, he exuded charm, optimism, and energy. Fast-talking, self-confident, and utterly convinced of his "genius" at predicting how the market would go, he was like the supersalesman in Mamet's *Glengary Glen Ross*. His self-confidence was not even shaken by the staggering losses his trading-positions had created for certain banks, which had suddenly found themselves hundred of millions in the hole. This was after a period of equally impressive gains, during which he bought diamond brooches for his wife, two Jaguars (a pink one for her, a blue one for himself), and a condo in Monaco.

Having grown up poor, Neil's ambition had always been to "make a killing" on Wall Street. As it turned out, he had done nothing illegal; he had merely succeeded, helped along by his manic exuberance, in cornering such a large share of the market and in winning the confidence of so many large investors, that when circumstances beyond his control flip-flopped, huge gains became huge losses. In his heyday, however, he was so much a genuine hero—idolized by the financial community, invited to give lectures about his "surefire" method—that his pathologic fantasies of greatness were camouflaged by the appearance, albeit temporary, of real greatness. During that time, he would have been impervious to treatment for his NPD. Afterwards he was more amenable to the idea there might be something the matter with him, but his situation was much less salvageable.

Narcissistic Personality Disorder with
Masochistic Personality

At age 36, Nina entered therapy because of her inability to break loose from her original family. Her father was a manufacturer, living comfortably; her mother had never worked. Two older brothers had married and lived in other parts of the country. In her twenties she had been married briefly to a man from a similar background, only it "just so happened" he was a heroin addict, who died of an overdose a few months after their honeymoon. Following this she had a series of affairs with men who resembled each other only in their disinclination to marry her: one was already married, one was a gangster, one was 12 years younger and poor, etc.

Nina's parents supported her, since the kind of work she aspired to she refused to train for and the kind of work she could do was "beneath her." Her mother was infantilizing and critical to the point of abusiveness. But interspersed with each act of cruelty was an act of generosity: a trip to the Caribbean or a new coat or dinner in a posh restaurant. Her father fostered dependence in similar, though less dramatic, ways.

Nina herself, spoiled, without interests or hobbies, envious of her friends who had husbands and children, seemed curiously content to remain locked in this relationship of "sweet torture" with her parents. I felt that one underlying motif was this: her mother received her only real gratification from being an (active) mother; if her daughter grew up and away from the family, mother would feel useless and forlorn. By undermining the daughter's self-confidence, etc., mother would always remain "necessary," have a role to fill, etc. Interpretations of this sort led nowhere; the patient seemed determined (unconsciously) to play her part in her parent's malignant drama — remaining their girl-child until they died, choosing unsuitable suitors along the way, so as to play at striving for independence, all the while staying attached to her parents.

Comments

Each of the vignettes highlights a particular area within the wide domain of narcissistic disturbances. The *schizotypal* patient (Nancy) had an abusive father and a rejecting, neglectful mother, each of whom contributed to the distortion in the "narcissistic" path of her early development. But her poor empathic capacity probably stemmed more from genetic liability for schizophrenia.

The *paranoid* man (Ned) was exquisitely sensitive to feelings of shame: saw himself as inadequate and unattractive, worried about organ-inferiority and about others regarding him as weird or a "loser," etc. These feelings of narcissistic injury underline the importance of *shame* as a theme relevant to narcissistic personalities (Morrison, 1986).

The *borderline* woman (Naomi), though born with all the advantages, by virtue of her lonely upbringing and her self-centered mother became pathologically narcissistic, dreaming of even more success and power than she already had. These "compensatory" mechanisms failed her, and she did not become a real success until she let go of these unrealistic ambitions. (In her thirties she became a highly successful businesswoman.) While in therapy she reported a number of poignant dreams that pictorialized various aspects of her narcissism: in one, she was chased and overtaken by horrid green monsters (her envy!). In another, she saw herself as an infant in a baby carriage; her mother stood nearby, with an immensely long penis issuing from her groin—that curved around, and bypassed, the baby, inserting itself into the mother's own mouth. Her mannish/domineering mother, instead of feeding the baby, that is, fed herself, while the infant looked on and cried. (This dream provides a new twist, by the way, to the shopworn concept of "penis envy.")

The *"pure" narcissistic PD* patient (Norman) is reminiscent of Joyce McDougall's paper (1989) on the "anti-analysand in analysis." There she spoke of certain ostensibly "analyzable" patients, who talk—and talk, and talk—of people and things, but rarely of the relations between people or between things (p. 364). The analysis becomes stagnant, or rather, it never really begins. Yet some of these patients cling to their "til-death-do-us-part" analysis like a frightened child to its parent. In my experience, a number of such patients (not this particular man, so much) had suffered "narcissistic injuries" consisting of an unavailable mother or an unapproachable father—so that the stalemated, endless non-analysis *becomes* the parent-child relationship they never had. Allowing something positive to happen would, in their minds, "destroy" the blissful togetherness they enjoy—and guarantee for themselves by making sure the treatment never goes anywhere.

The *antisocial* man (Nicholas) came by his narcissistic disturbances mainly from his parents' outrageous neglect and unfair criticisms. The latter were examples of the "idle rich": frivolous, inattentive, self-centered, who at times inflict as severe narcissistic wounds upon their children as do the desperately poor (Stone, 1972). His psychopathy rendered therapy a mostly losing venture. He was unmotivated, and so caught up in his private world of grandiose fantasies and prevarications as scarcely to inhabit our world.

The *passive-aggressive* man (Nathaniel) was similar to the "phallic-narcissistic" character disorder described by Wilhelm Reich (1929) and later by Ben Bursten (1986). These patients, most of whom are men, typically parade their masculinity, and are exhibitionistic and reckless. They often have a "dual attitude toward women . . . talking about them in contemptuous locker-room language . . . [but] they are the defenders of motherhood and the sanctity of women" (Bursten, p. 385).

The dynamics of the *obsessive-compulsive* researcher (Nelson) were like a page out of Tartakoff's article on the Nobel Prize complex (1966). His demeanor during his analysis also resembled the obsessive/narcissistic man described by Kernberg (1970), who was quite derogatory toward the analyst, reveling in his own interpretations while viewing the analyst as a background figure whose role was merely to endorse enthusiastically the patient's insightful remarks.

The *hypomanic* commodities broker (Neil) illustrates the difference between the narcissistic pathology to which schizophrenia predisposes and that engendered by manic-depressive heredity. Whereas the schizotypal woman was, in a manner of speaking, driven back onto self-preoccupation by her inability to connect up empathically, to "resonate" with others, the hypomanic broker, with his infectious good humor and his (truly) incurable optimism, connected up all too readily with others and thought of himself, even after the financial debacle, as "God's gift" to Wall Street. Kernberg (1970) has pointed out the difficulties in getting through, therapeutically, to a narcissistic patient whose outward success has come to equal his inner fantasies. In addition, hypomanic patients often show poor psychological-mindedness and are not well tuned in to the nuances of feeling in other people, such that their narcissistic defenses are not easily dealt with even when outward success is not a complicating factor.

The problems posed by the *masochistic* patient (Nina) have been addressed from a theoretical vantage-point by Cooper (1989), who sees a "structural unity" of the two characterological modes: narcissism and masochism. "Interpreting masochistic behavior produces narcissistic mortification," Cooper mentions, "and interpreting narcissistic defenses produces feelings of masochistic victimization, self-pity and humiliation" (p. 308).

Some Notes on Therapy
with Narcissistic Patients

Much of the by now extensive literature on the treatment of narcissistic conditions (whether strong traits short of DSM criteria or of "full-fledged" NPD) has been generated by the psychoanalytic community. Kernberg has recently written an excellent summary of his approach (1989a); Kohut and Wolf (1978), of Kohut's recommendations; Steiner (1989), of the methods advocated by Melanie Klein and her adherents. Mardi Horowitz and his colleagues (1984) have shown how analytic principles can be applied to the short-term treatment of narcissistic patients. Many of the comments concerning the analytically oriented therapy of "severely disturbed patients," put forth by Giovacchini (1982) were intended for, and apply to, those with severe narcissistic disturbances. Beck and Freeman (1990) show how the cognitive approach can be utilized to advantage in working with narcissistic patients.

The differing theoretical positions of Kernberg and Kohut have therapeutic implications as well. Because Kernberg sees narcissistic grandiosity as an outgrowth of rage elicited by maternal indifference or rejection, he assigns an important place, in the armamentarium of the therapist, to confrontation/interpretation concerning the patient's anger, contemptuousness, envy, devaluation, etc. In this way the underlying conflicts, including the conflictual view of the therapist (as hated depriver, as envied possessor of the "answers," as idealized, magical provider), can ultimately be resolved.

Kohut envisions narcissistic disturbances as a manifestation of developmental arrest, brought about by a mother who fails in her role of "mirror" (fails in effect, to validate the child's burgeoning sense of self-worth), or who fails to instill in the child a realistic sense of limitations, both hers and the child's. Using empathic understanding and sympathetic acceptance and relatedness, the (Kohutian) therapist aims at helping the patient give up some of the child-like grandiosity, and at helping the patient accept the limitations of hitherto overidealized parents and parental figures.

Because of the extreme sensitivity to criticism shown by narcissistic patients, Horowitz et al. (1984) emphasize the need for "tact and timing." Certain narcissistic patients—perhaps this is true more of men than of women—find themselves in an almost unworkable situation when beginning therapy: a patient must be able to acknowledge some degree of "mature dependence" upon the therapist if the latter is to be of any help; yet, paradoxically, such acknowledgment is anathema to the patient, who experiences even this "normal" dependency as being put down, as a humiliation. As for the therapy, sometimes the ship sinks before it is launched. If the therapist can deal in a gentle but effective way with this sensitive situation, treatment may then proceed much more favorably. The special tact and timing are needed in order to select most judiciously the moment when an interpretation about the patient's dependency can be tolerated. If made too soon, as Horowitz et al. point out, the patient may become defensively rageful, disavowing any such "inferiority" to the therapist. Strong countertransference problems often arise in one's work with narcissistic patients, who may evoke reactions of self-protectiveness, anger, sarcasm, or boredom (p. 210).

The "negative therapeutic reaction"—of hostility to the therapist's efforts to be helpful—is not restricted to narcissistic patients (those with masochistic or other types of personality disturbances may also show this reaction).

But when present in narcissistic patients, the reaction can be treacherously difficult to counteract. The man with the paranoid traits (of the second vignette above), for example, having worked with me for several years in what had come to be a comfortable therapeutic alliance, entered a phase where he insisted I serve only as a sounding board, better still as only an endorser, giving my seal of approval to the various occupational and social plans he made for himself from week to week. The encouraging remarks he used to appreciate hearing from me he now experienced as intrusions, as though I were busy trying to "insert" my thought-habits, my way of doing things, into his brain. Or, worse yet, that I was trying to somehow "ingratiate" myself with him, in order to "foster a codependent relationship."

Had I dared, at this juncture, to interpret this man's instructions to me as a projective identification of his no longer comfortable dependency on me, I suspect his rage would have become volcanic. Prudence dictated that I (1) shift gears into a "Kohutian" mode, just quietly resonating with his quite exaggerated need to "be his own man" by denying my utility altogether, and (2) maintain this posture until such time as he achieved certain goals. Having once achieved these goals (so I theorized to myself), he would no longer feel "unmanned" by suggestions and comments coming from me—and real therapeutic dialogue could resume.

The situation with this man illustrates, I believe, another paradoxical aspect of the Kernberg-Kohut controversy—namely, that sometimes theory and therapy pass one another by. The man in the vignette, for example, came by his narcissistic pathology chiefly as an end product of the hostile and abusive atmosphere in which he grew up. He suffered not so much a want of maternal mirroring etc. (though there was some of that), as outright humiliation from unwarranted criticism. Kernberg's etiological model had the most explanatory value here. Yet Kohut's therapeutic style was the more appropriate during the phase of treatment just alluded to.

There is probably an analogy between this being-sympathetically-*there* for the patient and the kind of *soothing* presence Giovacchini (1982) speaks of as an essential element of the analytic *mise-en-scène* or "background"; "Unless the relationship can provide some degree of soothing, there cannot be sufficient self-observing ego to permit analysis" (p. 47). For "analysis" here, one could substitute therapy of any sort for narcissistic patients who cannot—or cannot as yet—tolerate the fuller "confrontation with the truth," as Horowitz (1989) counsels, that dynamic therapy requires. It may be that narcissistic patients who are particularly overwhelmed with shame and belittlement need to feel accepted by their therapists before they can speak more candidly about the sources of their embarrassment. Until this atmosphere of safety is created, such patients may continue to evade, or tell falsehoods, by way of presenting themselves in a better light.

A man I once worked with had been humiliated repeatedly throughout his early years by a spiteful mother. Impotent with women (including his wife during their brief marriage), he would make up stories about his sexual "conquests" to his buddies at the office. He would then feel ashamed at having lied. Only when he began to feel comfortable with me—that I would not judge him as a "wimp"—could he begin to explore the underpinnings of his sexual difficulty (inaugurated by a dream in which he was hanging onto the edge of a cliff, where his mother then came and stepped on his fingers) and to stop the empty boastfulness with his friends.

The opposite paradox—a narcissism brought about by factors Kohut saw as primary but best treated by interventions Kernberg recommends—also exists. I had once worked with a young surgeon, for example, who sought help for mild depression. Equally narcissistic, but more compulsive, than the surgeon of the earlier vignette, he was dissatisfied with his lack of advancement and even more dismayed that he was not beating as many opponents at tennis as he had hoped he would. For many narcissistic persons, tennis, as a "one-on-one" sport, serves as an excellent yardstick for success, since who you beat is who you're better than. Both his parents were themselves highly narcissistic, his mother in particular tending to intrude and to "live through" her son, hoping he would attain the heights that had eluded her. When he was growing up, she was too preoccupied with her own agenda to listen with any patience to his concerns or needs of reassurance.

He was highly motivated for treatment, had a much wider zone of "tolerable anxiety" (Horowitz et al., 1984) than the man of the preceding vignette, and had much more ability to accept the transitory dependency of the therapeutic situation. In the beginning he was openly contemptuous of his chief (a "bumbling" surgeon) and of me. He would get after me about my ears sticking out too far (which he offered to correct surgically) or my having the wrong number of buttons on my jacket (he could recommend a superior men's shop). Here, confrontation about his devaluation of others, coupled with an invitation to explore the sources of this captiousness, proved beneficial. He could see how he had unwittingly become a Xerox-copy of his hypercritical mother; he could also admit, eventually, that he really hadn't done anything to distinguish himself at the operating table—so why should his chief rush to give him promotions?

In the second year of therapy he worked feverishly hard to develop an improved technique for a type of hand-surgery, wrote eight papers, and gave ten addresses at conventions. He was now quickly advanced to assistant professorship and given the number-two spot at another teaching hospital. He became in the process a mellower and much less envious person. This experience led me to add a footnote to the remark of one of my teachers in analytic school, Alberta Szalita. She had once remarked to our class: the cure for envy is gratitude. A wise remark. But when gratitude is long in coming, *hard work* also works wonders: with hard work envious narcissistic patients can begin accumulating the same tokens of success enjoyed by those whom they were busy envying before. This does not exactly "cure" this pathological trait by exploring and pulling out its roots, but it may render it inoperative.

Group Therapy and Cognitive Approaches

As for *group therapy* with narcissistic patients, a number of valuable recommendations have been made by Norman Wong (1988) and L. Hearst (1988). Wong points to the increased opportunities for identification and internalization when group therapy is added to individual therapy, and to the greater potential for the narcissistic patient to engage in reconstructive therapy (p. 43). Group therapy is best added to the regimen, Wong feels, only after a period of time in individual treatment. Since the other patients in a group can, collectively, offer strong support to the fragile self-esteem of the narcissistic patient, this supportiveness may allow certain confrontations (about unwelcome traits and habits, for example) to be made that the patient might not otherwise tolerate.

There is much controversy as to the choice of (diagnostically) homogeneous vs. heterogeneous groups for narcissistic patients. Hearst favors homogeneous groups (p. 124) as " . . . more likely to fulfill the required functions of these patients than the classical heterogeneous analytic group." Particularly for the "narcissistically most disturbed, a small homogeneous group may be the only social setting in which they can function with safety to themselves and their fellow patients" (p. 141). As in the classical group, it is the special group itself which, in Hearst's view, is the therapeutic agent.

Therapists who opt for a *cognitive* approach will find in Beck and Freeman (1990) useful guidelines for dealing with what these authors regard as the three major components of NPD: namely, grandiosity, hypersensitivity, and lack of empathy. All therapy of personality disorders aims at the eventual *discontinuing* (deprogramming) of maladaptive attitudes and behavioral tendencies and at *reconditioning* along more adaptive lines. The cognitive approach with NPD seeks specifically to replace the grandiose ambitions and need for specialness with more adaptive paradigms, by reinforcing healthier notions, such as, "One can be human, like everyone else, and still be unique," or "There can be rewards to being a team player," or "Colleagues can be resources, not just competition." Beck and Freeman offer some dozen and a half such "alternative beliefs" which the cognitive therapist tries to inculcate in the narcissistic patient (p. 249).

The Need for Flexibility

As with therapists of borderline patients, those who work with narcissistic patients will tend either to ally themselves with the teachings of one recognized authority, adhering as closely as possible to the interventions recommended by that authority, or else to pursue an eclectic course, creating an amalgam of all the relevant schools of thought, molded to the particularities of the therapist's own personality. One cannot prescribe *ex cathedra* which path will be the more suitable for any given therapist. Those who follow one authority closely will have the advantage of depth, but at the sacrifice of breadth in terms of the range of narcissistic subtypes with which the therapist can work efficiently. The eclecticist will enjoy greater breadth, but at the sacrifice of some depth and perhaps of some measure of conviction about the correctness of his theoretical stance.

Given the complexity of people and the multiplicity of clinical variations, I find it hard to speak in absolutes; I find eclecticism and flexibility more congenial. With respect to treating narcissistic patients in particular, I believe it is also important to feel genuinely, and from the depths of one's being, nondefensive and noncompetitive. Much of the sarcasm, devaluation, etc., "inflicted" on one by one's narcissistic patients has been learned the hard way from their sarcastic or devaluing parents. Dealing in similar ways with the therapist may thus be understood in part as a kind of "testing"—to see whether the therapist is "just like the parents" (and thus not much to be trusted) or is indeed a different kind of person—who will not put them down, not show them who's boss, etc.—and to that extent might prove a reasonably safe repository of the patient's trust.

13

Antisocial Personality Disorder and Psychopathy

IN AMERICAN PSYCHIATRIC LITERATURE the space devoted to antisocial personality disorder (ASP) is, in its bulk, second only to that on borderline personality disorder (BPD). In countries such as England, where BPD is less popular as a personality descriptor, ASP enjoys pride of place. Unlike the other personality disorders, books and articles about which concern mostly diagnosis and treatment, written material about ASP focuses primarily on epidemiological, social, forensic, and political issues. Questions about etiology also occupy a fair amount of space, as to a lesser extent do ethical problems. Little is said about treatment.

DIAGNOSIS AND CONTRIBUTORY FACTORS

In addressing the matter of diagnosis, we need to take into account historical trends over the past century and a half in the terminology psychiatry has used to designate socially deviant—especially criminally deviant—persons. "Antisocial personality" is only the latest in a sequence of labels for such persons; the criteria in DSM-III or III-R (cf. Chapter 2) differ in important ways from those in their nosologic predecessors.

277

Nineteenth-Century Terms

Prichard, the English alienist writing in the 1830s, used the term "moral insanity," defining it in the following way:

> Under the head of *moral insanity* I have adverted to a form of a disease of which the principal or sole manifestation is a propensity to break or destroy whatever comes within reach of the individual; in short, an irresistible impulse to commit injury or do mischief of all kinds.* (1835, p. 404)

Later in the century, the popular books of Cesare Lombroso on criminality combined the then current psychiatric theories with impressions stemming from the now discredited beliefs concerning physiognomy. Criminals, the majority of whom were not delusional, were relegated to a "borderland" between normality and insanity. The physiognomists comforted the popular imagination by suggesting that criminals somehow *looked* different from normal people. Lombroso's books are filled with portraits of admittedly quite mean-looking cut-purses, forgers and assassins (1878, 1887). We are now well aware that many of the most violent criminals look bland and unthreatening; they even capitalize on their ordinariness into deceiving their victims (cf. Herman Mudgett, Chapter 21).

Kraepelin, in his comprehensive text of mental disorders (1909–1915), outlined the various abnormal personalities. He did so under the generic heading, *psychopathische Persönlichkeiten*, or "psychopathic personalities." Here the word *psychopathic* meant only "mentally abnormal," and carried none of the overtones of antisociality it does for us. Kraepelin listed many abnormal types, including the "haltlosen" (uninhibited), the "Verschrobenen" (eccentric), those exhibiting "Zechprellerei" (leaving restaurants without paying), "Streitsücht" (quarrelsomeness), "Genussucht" (he-

---

*As Berrios reminds us (1993, p. 19), Prichard's term *moral insanity* cannot really be understood as the precursor of our term *psychopathy*. This is because Prichard spoke of "moral" not only in the manner we might now use this word (to connote the measure of one's adherence to social rules) but in the broader way, borrowed from the French, to refer to the spiritual life in general. *Moral insanity* was close to Pinel's concept (1799) of *manie sans délire*. The latter phrase signified persistent hyperexcitability or furor ("manie"), yet without a disorder of intellect or thought (i.e., "sans délire"). Thus, a manic patient showing frantic movement and irritability, yet without grandiose or other delusions would be diagnosed *manie sans délire* by Pinel and *moral insanity* by Prichard. The above example, where furor takes the shape of an irresistible impulse to harm others, is therefore a special case of "moral insanity" closer to our current concept of psychopathy, but lacking any mention of the personality traits (viz. callousness) we would now insist on before calling someone "psychopathic."

donism), and "Reuelosigkeit" (unrepentance). The latter comes closest to the contemporary notion of the "psychopath"—as characterized by callousness and lack of remorse for acts hurtful to others.

Words denoting antisociality inevitably acquire a pejorative connotation; in time "psychopath" smacked of making a moral judgment (which of course it does) and was replaced by "sociopath." The newer term seemed more acceptable, because it says merely that something is wrong with one's actions in society, whereas the older term implied there was something seriously wrong with one's mind.* The distinction is casuistical, really, since many of the people to whom these ever-changing phrases refer appear to indeed have something the matter with their minds—something that affects how they behave among their fellow human beings. That "something" is only occasionally a recognizable organic lesion of the sort Kraepelin, and his neuroanatomist colleague, Alzheimer, had hoped to find as neurological underpinnings of the various mental disorders.

An example where an organic lesion probably served as a predisposing factor would be the case of the "Mr. Goodbar" killer, Joe Willie Simpson (Fosburgh, 1975). Following severe head injuries during adolescence, Simpson showed impulse dyscontrol, irritability and impairment in thinking. These abnormalities apparently predisposed to irresponsibility, inability to work (because of thought impairment, etc.), vagrancy, and violence. Brain damage in this situation would play an important role in the pathway analysis of the eventual psychopathic disorder. More commonly, however, our search for causative influences would lead back to parental abuse and neglect, probably in combination with a defect affecting the (postulated) neurophysiological substrates of empathy.

As Millon (1981) cautions us, there are many persons who show a few traits customarily associated with the psychopath, but who never engage in criminal activities, never even break the law, and may even serve society in special ways as a result of these noticeable but less pathological traits. We will return to this point momentarily, after reviewing the diagnostic schema adumbrated by Cleckley. In the meantime, we may take note of the efforts made by the psychiatric community in this century to remove the stigma of moral opprobrium that attached to nineteenth-century designations, of which "moral insanity" would be the most striking example. Millon (1981, p. 197) urges us to " . . . progress beyond the perspective of moral and social judgments as a basis for clinical concepts. . . . " This admonition,

---

*The transition from *psychopath* as a general term for someone with a disturbed mind to the contemporary, and more specific usage (connoting extreme callousness and proneness to socially offensive behavior) is to be found in the writing of Kahn (1931).

very much in the spirit of a nonjudgmental psychoanalytic psychology, causes us little trouble when dealing, say, with persons whose "antisociality" consists of vehement disagreement with an oppressive political regime. In the heyday of Communism, a Russian citizen who spoke out against the KGB might find himself labeled "antisocial," or even "schizophrenic." We experience only a little more trouble when confronted with an unscrupulous used-car salesman or with a truant adolescent who shoplifts but does nothing worse. The term "psychopath," at least in contemporary parlance, signifies tendencies which are much more serious.

The severity of this personality disorder, both from a social and a psychological standpoint, may be more readily grasped from a review of the contemporary diagnostic criteria.

Current Definitions of Psychopathic Personality

The term *psychopath* is now in a kind of competition with *antisocial personality disorder*. The latter is championed by the widely used DSM, but does not convey the essence of the *inner state* of certain socially deviant persons the way *psychopathy* does. Persons who are habitually mendacious, glib, egotistical, predatory, exploitative, and deceitful are notorious for their ability to fool others. This includes not only neighbors, coworkers, mates and strangers, but also mental health professionals.*

The most serious problem the psychopath (as I am using the term here) presents to the diagnostician concerns the difficulty in piercing through the cloud of disinformation, behind which the psychopath's mendacity lies concealed. This is true even of the merely disruptive, as well as of the more dangerous subtypes. Precisely because the psychopath would answer the question, "Do you habitually tell falsehoods?" with a "No," the straightforward approach may not be very revealing diagnostically. Truly to know the personality of such persons, one will often have to rely upon the impressions of employers, coworkers or intimates—those whose initial trust was eventually betrayed. Diagnosticians will not routinely have access to the first two, sometimes not even to friends or relatives, and must instead make do with inference, "street smarts," and a certain flair for detecting glibness and insincerity.

The great diagnostician, Hervey Cleckley, seems to have had the most highly developed "sixth sense" about the psychopath of any psychiatrist of

---

*Something comparable came to light in the experiment of Rosenhan (1973), where actors posing as patients fooled psychiatrists into hospitalizing them as "schizophrenics." As Maher (1991) points out, this was the correct thing for psychiatrists to do, given the high base-rate of *real* patients who come to emergency rooms, as against the negligible rate of pseudo-patients.

his era. This comes through in his famous monograph, *The Mask of Sanity* (1972), where he outlined some 16 attributes that might alert us to the presence of this abnormality of personality. They include superficial charm, unreliability, insincerity, egocentricity, lack of remorse, etc. Cleckley's list was later reworked by Robert Hare, who has done much excellent research in this area over the past 25 years. Reid, Dorr et al. (1986) reproduced this 20-item checklist in their book, *Unmasking the Psychopath*. The Hare checklist (Hare, Harpur et al., 1990; Schroeder, Schroeder, & Hare, 1983) consists of the items listed in Table 17. (Two additional items are mentioned in the 1983 list: "many types of offense"; "drug/alcohol abuse not direct cause of antisocial behavior.") The scoring system allows for a "0," "1" or "2" for each item, yielding a maximum score of 44. A score above 30 is considered diagnostic for "psychopathy."

These 20 attributes differ in their prognostic seriousness. Some reflect merely the narcissism that is an invariable accompaniment of the psychopath (viz., grandiose sense of self-worth, shallow affect), but an accompaniment also of many law-abiding and socially integrated narcissistic persons. Promiscuity and irresponsibility, even glibness and lying, need have no implications vis-à-vis criminality. Lack of remorse and callousness are more ominous, in that their presence makes the slide toward criminality easier and more likely.

TABLE 17

Items in the Revised (20-Item) Psychopathy Checklist*

---

1. *Glibness/superficial charm*
2. *Grandiose sense of self-worth*
3. *Need for stimulation/proneness to boredom*
4. *Pathological lying*
5. *Conning/manipulative*
6. *Lack of remorse or guilt*
7. *Shallow affect*
8. *Callous/lack of empathy*
9. *Parasitic lifestyle*
10. *Poor behavioral controls*
11. *Promiscuous sexual behavior*
12. Early behavior problems
13. Lack of realistic long-term goals
14. *Impulsivity*
15. *Irresponsibility*
16. *Failure to accept responsibility for own actions*
17. Many short-term marital relationships
18. Juvenile delinquency
19. Revocation of conditional release [e.g., from prison]
20. Criminal versatility

---

*Reproduced with permission of Multi-Health Systems, Inc., 908 Niagara Falls Blvd., North Tonawanda, NY 14120-2060 (800-456-3003).

I feel Hare's modification of Cleckley's checklist should add "egocentricity" to item #2 (i.e., egocentricity and a grandiose sense of self-worth) and should also add a 21st item: imperviousness to shame. This goes further than his item #6, in that shamelessness represents the absence of *any* deterrence to offensive (including violent) behavior: not even the presence of others serves as an inhibiting influence. It goes without saying the psychopath lacks any *internal* inhibitions against such behavior; i.e., there is no *guilt*. In speaking of certain habitual criminals, in fact, Hampson (1988) makes the important point, stressed by Yochelson and Samenow (1976), that " . . . the criminal does not see himself as a criminal but as an exceptionally superior and good person . . . lacking in any kind of insight into the immorality of [his] way of life" (p. 273).*

From the standpoint of linguistic purity, Hare's list is not an ideal catalog of descriptors of psychopathy as a personality disorder. For this purpose, we would want to prune the list of items that are not traits. This would leave us with items #1–8, 10 (= "recklessness"), 11, 14, 15 and 16 (= the "disresponsibility" of White and Walters, 1989); i.e., the italicized items of Table 17.

One could view about half the psychopathic traits as extreme points on personality continua at whose other ends normal, or at least socially useful, traits are encountered. Table 18 illustrates the kinds of persons or their occupations we might find at the "normal" end of these continua.

A Note on Statistics

Statistical surveys of personality disorders rely on the more readily diagnosable criteria of DSM rather than on such criteria as Cleckley's. The latter are more inferential and usually require considerable acquaintance with the person being evaluated. As mentioned, the DSM definition of "antisocial personality" (ASP is built more around acts than traits). Even so, the extensive epidemiological survey of Robins et al. (1991) established that most antisocial persons are noncriminal (53%), and only 37% of persons arrested met criteria for ASP. Most persons with ASP have job troubles (94%) or show violence (83%).

Robins and her group (1991), when they used questionnaires that tapped

---

*The annals of crime are replete with examples (cf. Chapter 21). To cite but one: Nineteen-year-old Pattie Columbo became annoyed with the objections of her tradition-oriented parents to her flimsy attire and promiscuity. Her parents were a bother. So she conspired with one of her boyfriends—whom she conned into thinking her father was a "mafioso" who was out to kill him—to join hands with her in killing her parents and her brother (Remsberg, 1992). To her, these three murders seemed sensible and justified.

TABLE 18

Psychopathic Traits: Mild Variants
Associated with Social Advantages

Trait	Persons/Occupations Associated with Mild Degree of Trait
glibness	talk-show host, negotiator, televangelist
grandiosity	stage performer, entrepreneur
need for stimulation	circus performer, entrepreneur
pathological lying	spy, diplomat
conning/manipulative	used-car salesman, circus barker
lack of remorse	infantryman
shallow affect	undertaker
callousness	general in wartime
poor behavior controls	daredevil
promiscuous sex	reproductive advantage; go-go dancer
impulsivity	people with great spontaneity

activities not permissible within government survey guidelines, estimated a lifetime incidence of 4% for ASP in the U.S. as a whole. Without the proscribed questions (about fencing, prostitution, drug-dealing, etc.), the overall lifetime rate was about 2½%. In all age groups there is a marked male excess of those with diagnosed ASP—in the range of 4 : 1 to 7 : 1 or higher. Among those with felony convictions, half of white felons and a third of black felons met criteria for ASP.* Lifetime ASP rates were low for persons with a college degree (1.2%); high for those with multiple failed marriages (e.g., 15 + % for white males). ASP " . . . typically begins about age eight with a variety of behavioral problems . . . and is fully expressed by the late twenties or early thirties" (p. 289). Few persons with ASP seek treatment; available treatments were rarely efficacious in any event. But in the fourth decade of life, and beyond, the symptoms by which ASP would be diagnosed tended to abate.

Because the Cleckley/Hare criteria are not the current standard for measuring antisociality, and are difficult to assess, we have no ready estimate of the incidence of psychopathy or of the degree of overlap with ASP. Just as with ASP, there are many who meet Cleckley's criteria who do not have criminal records and have never murdered.

Though psychopathy (as exemplified by Ted Bundy, for example) may arise "spontaneously"—in the absence of child abuse or neglect, the latter

---

*According to a recent national survey, there are 1.15 million persons now in prison in the U.S.; the incarceration rate is about 300/100,000 population (US News, Sept. 16, 1991)

factors do predispose to this aberration of personality in many instances. Examples would be Charles Manson or Henry Lucas or Joseph Kallinger (cf. Chapter 21). Unfortunately, there are no epidemiological data that would reveal how many children are maltreated to the extent Manson or Kallinger were — and who then go on to become law-abiding, productive members of their communities. This is a key issue for the next generation of epidemiologists to address.

The following vignettes may, in the meantime, give the reader some appreciation of how difficult it is to predict, in the presence of a "sordid background," which young person will emerge as an innocuous, productive citizen — and which will become a violent criminal:

Vignette A   A man of 27 from a middle-class family in Cuyahoga county in Ohio was the younger of two sons. He had always been shy and introverted; he rarely dated, and had never been intimate with a woman. His father was generally aloof, rejecting, and unsympathetic. When the older brother, for example, would hold the younger brother's hand against a steaming radiator, the father would later turn a deaf ear to his younger son's complaints, saying: "You're lying! Your brother wouldn't do any such thing!" Actually, the man endured a whole variety of tortures from the older brother until, at 14, he was as tall and husky as the brother. On several occasions when the man was in grade school as a boy of nine, his father would shove himself on top of his son and sodomize him anally.

Vignette B   A man of 30 from a middle-class family in Cuyahoga county in Ohio had grown up shy and introverted. He had never dated. His parents were never abusive toward him or his younger brother, but they constantly argued, often acrimoniously and loudly, finally divorcing when the man was in high school. His parents openly preferred the younger son. His mother suffered a "nervous breakdown" of some type shortly after the divorce. When he was a boy of eight, some older boys in the neighborhood molested him sexually. As a teenager, he kept a pet cemetery, was cruel to cats, dogs, and frogs, and was mocked by his schoolmates as being a "weirdo." After the parents' divorce, each parent went his/her separate way, leaving the young man at home alone much of the time.

These men grew up within a few miles of each other, almost in the same grade at school. Both were brighter than average. The first was a patient of mine, a man of a decidedly paranoid caste, who had dropped out of graduate school temporarily because of intense anxiety in connection with a certain professor. After several years of supporting himself with unstimulating jobs, he eventually was able to resume his studies. The second is Jeffrey Dahmer, who confessed, in July and August of 1991, to the sexual assault, murder, necrophilia, and dismemberment of 17 young men, some in Ohio, some in his current residence, some in Europe when he was in the Army. He was sentenced to life imprisonment in February 1992. The point of these stories is that, if either one had been identified in advance as a serial killer of young men, most people would have said, "Well, with a background like *that*!"

The Interplay of Psychopathy and Antisociality

For the foreseeable future both the terms *psychopathy* and *antisociality* will be with us. Both the DSM definition of ASP and the Cleckley/Hare definition of the psychopath have their utility. Rather than politicizing the issue by arguing for scrapping one or the other term, it is probably better to live with both, taking advantage of their respective utilities, only in a more integrated way. One way to do this is to create a 2 × 2 table of the diagnostic possibilities in the combined domain, as suggested by Figure 24.

Region I of this domain is occupied by persons who not only manifest clear-cut psychopathic traits, but habitually commit antisocial acts. Many of the serial killers and perpetrators of premeditated homicide that we will confront in Chapter 21 exemplify the overlap of these two concepts. The same is true of many less savagely antisocial persons, such as men who, having abandoned their wives and children, change their names and flee to remote places to weasel out of paying $50 a month in child support.

Figure 24: *Diagnostic Possibilities in the Combined Domain of Psychopathy and Antisociality*

CRITERIA FULFILLED:	I	II	III	IV
DSM—ASP	+	−	+	−
Psychopathy*	+	+	−	−

*As defined by *traits only*: items #1–8, 10, 11, 14, 15 and 16 of Table 17

Key to Regions I–IV:
I: Persons who manifest psychopathic traits and habitually commit antisocial acts.
II: Persons who manifest psychopathic traits but have not (yet) committed antisocial acts.
III: Those in outcast social groups who behave antisocially toward those outside their group.
IV: People who are neither psychopathic nor antisocial.

Region II consists of persons who exhibit psychopathic *traits* (viz., egocentricity, glibness, manipulativeness, imperviousness to shame) but do not—or have not as yet—committed distinctly antisocial acts. Certain college students who can lie with impunity about an "illness" that prevented them from taking an exam they hadn't prepared for, who will "stand up" one girl for a date having subsequently met another girl they like better, who pass off as their own a research paper culled from the files of their fraternity, etc., but who have never assaulted anyone or broken into a house to commit theft would occupy this diagnostic region. In some the transition from psychopathic personality to antisocial activity never occurs; in others, the transition is rapid—as in the case of Pattie Columbo mentioned earlier. At ten Pattie already showed signs of "malignant narcissism" (Kernberg, 1992): callousness toward her brother, contempt toward her parents, selfishness, hostility. But by 11 she had already assaulted another girl at a party; at 15 she was vampish, seductive, and rebellious, and was arrested for credit-card theft.

Region III would include large numbers of persons from fringe or outcast social groups, who behave respectfully and honestly toward others within their own group but steal and cheat outsiders without any sense of wrongdoing. In times of war or social ferment, many formerly respectable, or at least "contained," non-aggressive persons (young men, especially) turn to thuggery—as sketched so well by Doris Lessing (1987)—their morality extending only so far as expediency and conformity to the mob or gangster-group of which they have become a part. Some will remain antisocial even after the crisis/riot/war passes; the majority revert to outward respectability. In the recent firebombings of Turkish residents in Germany, the ringleaders are probably psychopaths, but some of their accomplices appear to have been respectable but morally weak adolescents—converts to antisociality under group pressure. They exemplify the "banality of evil" of which Hannah Arendt (1977) spoke. Not surprisingly, one such youth, horrified at the evil he had participated in, committed suicide in prison, whereas the psychopathic ringleader "could care less" (*New York Times*, Dec. 12, 1992).

Region IV, included for the sake of completeness, simply refers to the large majority of people who are neither antisocial nor psychopathic.

* * * * *

As matters stand, the DSM definition of ASP is not likely to disappear overnight, despite its overreliance on actions (truancy, stealing, drunk-driving, etc.) rather than on traits. There may be some value in retaining both terms—antisocial and psychopathic—because of the special legal implications of the former and prognostic implications of the latter. Many persons reared in adverse circumstances (viz., inner-city males) get labeled "antisocial" because of their actions, even though a good proportion of these same persons are not psychopaths (cf. A. A. Stone, 1985). This distinction is important, since, as we shall see, one can envision treating, or resocializing, a nonpsychopathic person with ASP whereas our ability to treat (or "reform") a psychopath meeting Cleckley's or Hare's criteria is negligible. The hero of Hugo's *Les Misérables*, Jean Valjean, stole bread when he was poor (an "antisocial" act), but was clearly not "psychopathic."

Underlying Motives and Scripts

Silvan Tomkins (1987, 1991) has written extensively on the "scripts," elaborated early in life, that give shape to our personalities and that direct our attitudes and behavior. Most scripts evolve from a combination of innate and learned factors (1987, p. 148). Scripts are sets of ordering rules that govern how we interpret, predict, and behave in any of the many typical and repetitive situations in which we are likely to find ourselves. They are generally self-validating and usually contain "corollaries," allowing for deviations from the script under certain circumstances (1987, p. 155ff). A compulsive person's script might run: "I must work diligently at all times," though with the corollary, " . . . except when I'm laid up with illness." Someone with psychopathic tendencies, who has not ascended very far in the moral stages outlined by Kohlberg (1976; Kohlberg, Levine, & Hewer, 1983), may live according to a script dictating: "I mustn't steal," but with the corollary " . . . unless, of course, there's a riot, and everybody's smashing store windows and looting what's inside." This kind of "expedient" morality answers to the middle level of Kohlberg's six stages, in which one recognizes being part of a social order requiring rules and regulations, but where strong temptations to break rules are not reliably resisted (cf. Hampson, 1988, p. 258).

In the lives of psychopathic and antisocial persons, there are a number of common motifs. These could each serve as the title for a particular inner script (cf. Stone, 1988). Some may be understood as the dark side of *love* and *work* (Liebe und Arbeit), which Freud saw as the two major themes of life. In the pathological scripts we find, instead, *jealousy* and *greed*. Other pathological scripts of special relevance to psychopathy are wounded pride, envy, hunger after control and power, and self-hatred. These in turn may spawn *hostility*, *vengefulness*, *contempt*, and *sadism*.

The boundless egocentricity of the psychopath and the fear of discovery constitute *nonspecific* motifs, and answer to the low stage of moral evolution, where (a) one wants anything and everything one desires, and (b) one wishes simply to avoid the inconvenience of being thwarted. The majority of people, who respond not only with shame (having to do with public exposure) but also with guilt (requiring the recognition that one has betrayed one's own values), find it difficult to grasp the essential nature of the psychopath. Many *cannot believe* that someone caught in a criminal act can continue eternally to deny responsibility (cf. Chapter 21).

These script-words and motif-words are also personality *trait*-words. In the lives of persons animated by these concerns, the "script" will refer to *specific* situations and ambitions. Someone with the trait of vengefulness, for example, may be driven by a script specific to that person: a desire to "get even" for having been jilted or divorced in favor of another partner. The serial killer, Ted Bundy, was markedly envious and hostile toward women. In him, these traits were the manifestations of a specific script, having to do with contempt for his blue-collar origins and hatred of the woman to whom he was briefly engaged, who came from a wealthy family he could never fit into.

Further Comments on Diagnosis and Contributory Factors

It is necessary to preserve the semantic distinctions both between psychopathy and antisociality and also between the latter and certain other concepts often conflated with it — namely, aggressivity, violence-proneness, and dangerousness. To many of the murderers discussed in Chapter 21, *all* of these concepts are applicable. But many con artists (such as the men hawking fake Rolex watches along Fifth Avenue), while they may be psychopathic, are neither aggressive nor dangerous.*

Specific factors pertinent to genetics and constitution in antisociality or psychopathy I have touched on in Chapter 3. To summarize the pertinent neurophysiological findings in "primary" psychopaths, the list drawn up by Lilienfeld (1989) is useful: (a) poor passive-avoidance learning, (b) diminished spontaneous skin-conductance fluctuations, (c) a slow recovery rate of the electrodermal response, (d) slow electrodermal classic conditioning to aversive stimuli, (e) diminished electrodermal and augmented cardiovascular activity to impending aversive stimuli, and (f) excess theta waves during resting EEG (p. 568). All these innate neurophysiological differences point to a diminished behavioral inhibition (and to high novelty-seeking),

---

*Not all dangerous persons are psychopathic. On rare occasions both dangerousness and a transitory psychopathy can be brought about by prolonged abuse of anabolic steroids, as in the case of Nathan Jones of Brisbane, Australia. He became a 6' 8" giant, and committed a series of armed robberies, until jailed and taken off the steroids — after which his personality reverted to its former mildness (F. Robson, 1989; Stone, 1992a).

and play a role in heightening the risk for psychopathy as an eventual phenotype.

Differing points of view on the topic of dangerousness are to be found in a book edited by Webster, Ben-Aron, and Hucker (1985); the interplay of aggression and violence in a monograph by Valzelli (1981); and discussion of biological aspects of criminality in Mednick, Moffitt, and Stack (1987). Cultural, familial, and constitutional factors predisposing to criminality are addressed extensively in Wilson and Herrnstein (1985). The findings of Brennan et al. (1991) are useful in pointing up the independence of socioeconomic status and genetic factors in their impact on criminality: they found an increase in criminality in adoptees of biological parents with a criminal record, over and above the level of variance that could be explained by SES.

Two Subtypes of Psychopathy

While Hare and his coworkers have sought to improve the reliability of "psychopathy" as a clinical entity (Hare, Harpur et al., 1990; Schroeder et al., 1983), Collins Lewis (1991) has found it useful, both for heuristic and prognostic purposes, to divide this diagnostic realm into two subgroups: a "primary" group, with pathological *lack* of emotion (the callous, guiltless, unemphatic psychopaths), and a "secondary" group, exhibiting a pathological *excess* of emotion. Low CNS serotonin activity may be present in both types, and may help account for the inability of the psychopath to respond to punishment (p. 725). Psychopaths are, in any event, slower to learn through aversive conditioning than are most people (p. 720). As for those with excess emotionality, Lewis notes that one ordinarily finds, in studying groups of hypomanic/manic persons, a higher than expected proportion of delinquency and socially unacceptable behavior (cf. also: Metzner, 1991).

These observations are in line with those of Smith and Newman (1990), who found no link between abuse of alcohol or other substances in the callous group, but did find such a correlation in the emotional-excess group. In the latter, instability, boredom, and short-temperedness were the rule—their disinhibited nature becoming even more disinhibited under the influence of alcohol (Finlay-Jones, 1991). The sensation-seeking style of psychopaths, especially of the emotionally excitable group, may be an expression of underlying cerebral response tendencies, as suggested by evoked-potential studies (Raine, 1989; Raine & Venables, 1988). Psychopathic subjects tend to show cortical *augmenting* (which would correlate with overreaction to stimuli); they also show a superiority, compared with other groups, in the ability to attend to events of particular interest (Raine, 1989, p. 7).

While neurophysiological and neurochemical research has shed considerable light in recent years upon psychopathy and upon the tendency to violence, early family environment, as Coid (1989) points out, probably still plays a crucial role in most instances. Psychopaths, especially those who later commit antisocial acts, usually have in their background some combination of domestic violence, sexual misuse, parental alcoholism, and abandonment by the father or other early losses. Fortunately, the majority of children raised in these circumstances does not become antisocial, thanks either to "intervening protective factors . . . or the absence of constitutional predisposing factors" (Coid, 1989, p. 754).

In view of the wide range of contributory factors and of the various clinical subtypes encountered by the clinician, Coid finds it more sensible to speak in the plural: of the "psychopathic disorders," rather than of a single entity. Certainly there is wisdom in this approach from a clinical standpoint. For example, the serial killers discussed in Chapter 21, almost all of whom were psychopathic, can be separated into several groups: the callous but outwardly sociable (e.g., Bundy); the callous but schizoid/unsociable (e.g., Joubert); and the hyperexcitable/sensation-seeking (e.g., Gallego, Buono). The four murderers among the 196 traced borderline patients in my follow-up study (Stone, 1990) were antisocial persons of the disinhibited, hyperexcitable type.

A Note on Criminality

In their study of offenders, both violent and nonviolent, Mednick, Brennan, and Kandel (1988) noted that violent offenders were more apt to come from unstable/broken homes than from stable homes. These authors noted a previous study comparing the conviction rates in biological and adopted fathers of convicted male adoptees, which indicated a significantly greater likelihood that the biological fathers would have a conviction record. Mednick et al. could confirm such a connection in relation to property crimes, however, such a genetic link was not noted for violent crimes. Their study was carried out on a Danish population, whose base rate for violent crime is substantially lower than in the U.S., making it harder to discern a genetic effect if one existed.

Embedded in Mednick's extensive study of the Danish offenders is, nevertheless, a suggestion that the tendency to violence is, to a certain extent, transmissible. Defining violent offenses as assaults, murders, robbery, domestic violence, illegal possession of weapons, and threats of violence, Mednick observed that the percentage of sons born to non-mentally-ill parents (N = 8981) who went on to become violent was 4%. Among the 144 children of schizophrenic or psychopathic parents, the proportion of violent sons was about the same: 16½%. If the mother was mentally ill (viz., schizophrenic) and the father had been convicted of a crime, 27% of their sons eventually became violent. This proportion rose slightly to 30% if, besides the mother being mentally ill, the father was a *recidivist* criminal (Mednick, 1992). About half the violent offenses came from sons with the combination: mother with at least some emotional disorder plus father with a criminal record. Since there is no real evidence for "criminal genes *per se*," just *what* these sons inherited remains unclear—perhaps (cf. Chapter 2) a tendency to sensation-seeking or to low empathy or to high drive-levels.

ASP is one of the two most common DSM diagnoses in a prison population: the lifetime prevalence rate was 62% in a recent study of 495 Canadian inmates (Côté & Hodgins, 1990). Alcohol abuse was even more common: 67%. But schizophrenic disorders, bipolar disorders, and major depression were found at rates six or more times as common as in the general population; comorbidity (ASP plus one or more of these other conditions) was the rule rather than the exception.

What proportion of these inmates would meet Hare's criteria for psychopathy is unclear. In their study of violence and aggression Hare and McPherson (1984), using their psychopathy checklist as the yardstick, found that psychopaths committed a greater percentage of crimes than nonpsychopaths, and that their crimes tended to be more violent and aggressive.*

Hare's group was also able to use the checklist *dimensionally*, in studying post-release recidivism: men with low, medium, and high psychopathy checklist scores showed 27%, 49%, and 65% rates of reconviction, respectively. Likewise, the chances of not being convicted within the first year of release were related to these scores: 80% of the "most" psychopathic men were convicted within the first year after release, as against 23% of the men with the lowest scores (Hart, Kropp, & Hare, 1988).

The Criminal Mind and the
Ubiquitousness of Narcissism

Several authors who have focused on criminals, in contrast to psychopaths (only a portion of whom become criminals), have enumerated qualities they feel characterize the "criminal mind." Scott (1989) mentions, among these characteristics, sensation-seeking, "expensive habits," egocentricity, poor conscience development, the use of projection (blaming others) and rationalization as defenses, and a hunger for power. White and Walters (1989) invoke the theme of what they call *disresponsibility*: a contemptuousness of social convention, accompanied by the attributes of irresponsibility, intru-

*It was of interest, nonetheless, that the nonpsychopaths in their study typically persisted in criminal activities over the years, whereas the psychopaths often "burned out" after age 40, no longer committing crimes (Hare, McPherson, & Forth, 1988; cf. Robins et al., 1991).

siveness, self-indulgence and rule-breaking. All commentators on psychopathy, as the reader will note, allude to the attribute of (pathological) narcissism — whether under the rubric of egocentricity, self-indulgence, or some similar term. In effect, all psychopathic persons are at the same time narcissistic persons. The likelihood of psychopathy given a diagnosis of NPD is, of course, much smaller. The overlap of ASP (as defined by DSM) and NPD is also not as great as that of psychopathy and NPD, since, as mentioned above, *some* antisocial persons are antisocial by virtue of membership in organized crime families and other "pariah" groups.

In relation to homicide, there is a tendency for non- (or only mildly) psychopathic murderers to kill those known to them, often in the midst of domestic disputes, whereas psychopath offenders frequently kill strangers (Williamson et al., 1987; Yarvis, 1990).

Apropos psychopathy and the topic of *criminal personality*, Hampson (1988) makes the point that our assessment of deviance from social norms is hampered by cultural relativism (p. 250), given that different societies (or the same society at different stages of its evolution) place different values on the same behavior. She cites infanticide as an example of a practice that was at one time felt to be an acceptable means of population control (and still is in some societies), but is now considered a crime in most countries. A daughter who consorts with an "infidel" may be legitimately killed by her father in some cultures, but in others such an act is plain homicide. Hampson feels we can never arrive at a universally acceptable definition of ("antisocial") deviance, but remain at the mercy of what a particular society evaluates as "deviant" at a particular stage of its history. As she argues: "The definition of deviance does not depend upon some quality inherent in a person or a behavior, but on the rules . . . which determine the boundary between deviance and conformity" (p. 251). Hampson at the same time reminds us that there are no thriving cultures which look the other way at murder, rape, and theft.

Hampson notes that some theoreticians of personality emphasize supposed internal characteristics which cause certain persons to behave in a deviant manner. She finds it more relevant to ask why, and under what circumstances, certain behaviors and persons come to be labeled as deviant by the majority of others. The personality theorist looks, that is, for *within-person* variables that predispose to criminality. This approach Hampson regards as embodying a bias, in not acknowledging the great importance others place upon *situational* variables. Given that autocratic societies have dubbed persons with nonconformist political views as either crazy or criminal, her argument is not without its cogency. Few would deny that many seemingly ordinary people behave monstrously (or, for our purposes, *antisocially*) under the impact of group pressure, in times of social upheaval.

Despite my own obvious bias in favor of internal variables — or at least in favor of *searching* for such variables — I will certainly grant Hampson the point about the impact of the environment. Certain bigots, to take but one example, who could readily be drawn into a lynch-mob, there to become identifiably antisocial personalities (and criminals as well), might otherwise have lived out their lives innocuously (though not without a measure of obnoxiousness) had they been raised in a community where the targets of their bigotry happened not to exist. But what predisposed these persons to active hatred in the first place? It is here that I believe Hampson fails to give intrapersonal and preexisting (including innate) factors their due. What makes some people raised in unfavorable circumstances (abusive parenting, morally lax parents, neglectful parents) antisocials, others antisocials-manqué, and still others incorruptible? There are no easy answers to these questions, but I believe the most promising approach is one that is *interactive*, combining the best available information with data concerning both innate and environmental factors. For heuristic purposes, Figure 25 offers a way of integrating these disparate factors.

Track 1 of the diagram relates to persons burdened with the worst of both sets of factors, who are easily nudged in the direction of habitual criminality. They are both psychopathic in personality and antisocial in behavior.

Track 2 concerns those with somewhat less serious innate factors and fairly good familial/social factors, leading to milder, non-antisocial forms of psychopathic personality: exploitative, amoral but nonviolent and prone to getting away only with those acts that will still not land one in trouble with the law.

In *Track 3* mildly adverse innate factors are modulated by a nurturing home environment, leading to someone who, though in general neither antisocial nor psychopathic, may show moral weakness and corruptibility under situations of strong temptation or social disorder. This person is guided by expediency and outward conformity rather than by a set of well-internalized and unwavering moral principles.

In *Track 4* the genetic/constitutional factors are only mildly unfavorable, but early home life was abusive and social factors were adverse, conducing to antisociality (violent or otherwise) in the absence of full-blown psychopathy. *

---

*An example: the life of William Mothershed (Rivele, 1992), a brilliant, socially awkward college student who had been severely abused and humiliated by his father. Formerly well-behaved, he took up with a gang of amoral, sensation-seeking students, embarked on a spree of armed robberies, and, when accosted as a suspect by a policeman, shot the policeman to death.

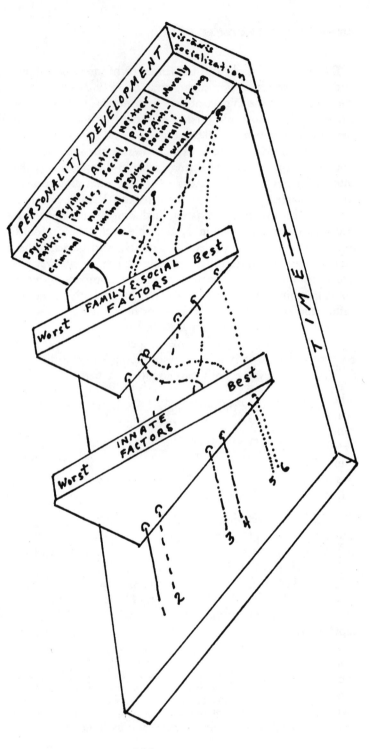

Figure 25: The Interaction of Innate (Genetic/Constitutional) and Environmental (Intrafamilial/Social) Factors in the Formation of the Moral Aspects of Personality

Track 5 pays homage to persons exposed to just about the worst family and social factors, yet with apparent freedom from predisposition to psychopathy, who manage to take, and remain on, the moral high road in situations where many become vengeful, violent, and dissolute. I give a detailed example of such a person in Chapter 17.

Track 6 shows the path taken by most persons who are fortunate in both innate and environmental factors: the path of strong—and for all intents and purposes incorruptible—morality. The highest stage of development, corresponding to Kohlberg's "Stage VI," is exemplified by those who stand by high principles even when exposed to intense group or community pressure to engage in devious or reprehensible acts.

These tracks constitute only a few of the myriad possible paths we might have chosen as illustrations. The "Bad Seed" path, for example, presupposes the *worst* innate factors, capable of determining a psychopathic outcome even in the face of the most nurturing home and noncorrupting social influences.

Merikangas' Schema Concerning Violence

Complementing the division of psychopathy into callous vs. hyperexcitable types (C. E. Lewis, 1991) is the model proposed by J. Merikangas (1981), who uses a tripartite schema for categorizing violent persons. His three parameters are (a) *drive level*, (b) *stimulus threshold*, and (c) *response inhibition*. Since any of the three can vary from high to low, this generates 2^3 or eight subtypes. In his study of 128 assaultive patients there were 16 murderers, five of whom were considered "psychopathic." Six of the eight possible groups contained at least one murderer, all except groups II and VI, which were characterized by high response inhibition (p. 182). These observations would have important treatment implications: while it is difficult to change one's innate drive level, clinicians could aim at heightening response inhibition, through such means as lithium, alcohol treatment programs, beta-blocking drugs like atenolol, behavior modification programs, etc.

Walker's Typology of Sexual Offenders

Apropos sexual violence, Nigel Walker (1991) offers a typology of dangerousness with four compartments: (a) persons responding to "chance" situations that are provocative or sexually tempting, (b) those who "follow inclinations" (viz., child molesters who then look for jobs in day-care centers), (c) "opportunity seekers," and (d) "opportunity makers." The latter two types are, in Walker's words, "unconditionally dangerous" (p. 755), and typically show the traits of psychopathy. Walker (1991) makes a compelling argument for the extended segregation of repeat sexual and other violent offenders.* His studies show that offenders with four or more convictions for violence have a 50% or greater likelihood of committing similar offense(s) in the future (p. 753).

Sexual attacks that seem spontaneous are often the end result of conscious planning "slowly formulated in the flawed sexual imagination of the assailant" (Wyre, 1986). Because even mental health professionals can predict dangerousness only to a limited extent, and because society has the right to protect itself against those most likely to commit serious harm to others, there is the need for prolonged segregation of such offenders, but also, as Walker emphasizes, the need for this segregation to take place in a reasonably pleasant, let alone humane, surrounding: "If [an offender] has reached a stage at which treatment no longer offers hope of rendering him harmless . . . then he deserves something by way of compensation for being sacrificed to the interests of others" (p. 757). Society's privilege, that is, for retaining repeat offenders indefinitely is purchased at the cost of some "false-positives" (offenders whom we feel would commit further crimes if released, but who actually might not); this carries with it the obligation to improve the quality of life on the inside for such retainees. The humanity and wisdom of Walker's article commend it to all who are interested in criminology and in the study of "intractable" personality disorders.

Psychotherapy in the Realm of Antisociality

Severe Forms of Antisociality

In the brief, but accurate, comment of Dulit et al. (1993), "Unfortunately, most clinicians agree that the prognosis for treatment of antisocial personality disorder is extremely bleak." They, and most other authors, agree that the goals of correcting the maladaptive behavior patterns of antisocial patients and of enhancing their sense of responsibility are best accomplished in specialized inpatient units. In such units strict limit-setting can be instituted, and the staffs are trained to provide consistent responses to the patients' behaviors, along with a "strictly enforced hierarchical structure" (p. 409) for granting privileges. As Kernberg underlines (1992, p. 80),

---

*Readers interested in the complex forensic issues presented by violent offenders with *multiple personality* will find the article by D. Lewis and Bard (1991) useful. As for violent sexual offenses, such as rape, Kutchinsky's study (1991) has shown that the easy availability of pornographic material, in the four countries examined, has had no detrimental effect in the form of increased sexual violence.

closed units are necessary, as are extended time-periods of institutionaliza-tion in an incorruptible environment, if remediation is to occur. Even so, as Gabbard and Coyne (1987) point out, the success rate is generally poor.

The clinical subtype is an important consideration: certain explosive or violence-prone antisocial patients become better controlled when treated with lithium, β-adrenergic antagonists or with serotonergic drugs such as fluoxetine.

In general, the more pronounced the *psychopathic* traits in antisocial patients (callousness, lack of remorse, imperviousness to shame, mendacity, etc.) the poorer the chance of any success that can be attributed to the therapeutic interventions. As we shall note in discussing follow-up, remedi-ation sometimes occur through factors not directly related to therapeutic efforts: certain life events, the adoption of a new religion, advancing age.

Kernberg (1992), in his discussion of psychotherapy in relation to se-verely antisocial persons, recommends diagnostically the broad division, utilized by Henderson and Gillespie (1969), into a *passive-parasitic* type (where such behaviors as swindling, forgery, prostitution, and lying are common) and an *aggressive* type (where violent acts such as armed robbery, assaults, and murder are characteristic). Kernberg also emphasizes the co-existence of pronounced narcissistic traits in antisocial persons: envy, deval-uation of others, entitlement, exploitativeness and an incapacity for empa-thy. Attitudinally, antisocial persons (and psychopaths) routinely show a stimulus-hunger and a "diffuse sense of the meaninglessness of life" (p. 80).

There is a paradox inherent in discussing treatment of antisociality — namely, that there is *some* hope for remediation in antisocial persons who have been remanded by the courts to a special treatment unit, because of the total control such units (in prisons or elsewhere) can exert. As Yochel-son and Samenow (1976) remind us, hard-core criminals are dominated by criminal thinking patterns (scripts). Rehabilitation can only be effected by totally eradicating such thinking patterns. This requires tremendous persua-sive powers on the part of the prison or hospital staff, if the antisocial tendencies are to be permanently suppressed. Only rarely can this be achieved, and in the case of serial killers and other maximally dangerous criminals, it is not really worth the effort, considering (a) the risks to society should the treatment fail and (b) the high likelihood of failure. Still, some less dangerously antisocial persons leave their criminal ways behind under the impact of such treatment programs. But with antisocial persons who elude prison or do not commit grossly illegal acts, the likelihood of ending up in a controlled treatment environment is minuscule and the chances of remediation via outpatient therapy negligible. It is easier to cure pneumonia than a cold.

The psychotherapeutic treatment methods brought to bear upon severely antisocial patients are usually those stemming from cognitive-behavioral theory—as promulgated by Beck and Freeman (1990) and as outlined by Barley (1986). Barley described various interventions one might employ, including keeping a diary (in which all one's thoughts throughout the day are recorded and discussed), cognitive-behavior programs designed to curb sensation-seeking, the use of token economies for rewarding prosocial behavior, social-skills training, behavioral psychodrama (where immature, dyssocial responses to problem situations can be exposed, critiqued by one's fellow inmates, and modified in prosocial directions), and community-level programs for those who have progressed toward acceptable levels of social function. Some of these techniques were advocated and used by some of the pioneers in working with delinquent youths (Schmideberg, 1959, 1961). Despite the short-term gains therapists can often achieve with these techniques, Barley warns that " . . . there is much less evidence that they produce long-term alteration of behavior" (p. 183).

Insight-Oriented Psychotherapy

The utility of classical psychoanalysis with antisocial (and especially with distinctly psychopathic) patients is nil. Occasional modest gains may be achieved using intensive, long-term insight-oriented (psychoanalytically-oriented) psychotherapy with certain nonviolent and less ruthlessly antisocial persons—as in the case of patients manifesting "malignant narcissism." Kernberg characterizes this latter group as showing narcissistic personality disorder, ego-syntonic sadism, a paranoid orientation, some antisocial behavior, yet still retaining the capacity for loyalty to at least some persons in their milieu. They may also have the capacity to experience guilt (1992, p. 77).

Dyadic forms of therapy, by themselves, are severely handicapped when confronted with antisocial persons. Simply being incorruptible and above all temptation, though essential to the therapist's task, is hardly sufficient. Patients who "con" their therapists, who are habitually dishonest, deceitful, exploitative, etc., if they enter one-to-one therapy at all (and few do unless "cornered" by failures and rejections in their daily life), do so with hopes of gaining an "ally" against those who are closing in on them. They do not seek help for their bad character. I have never heard a patient announce as his "chief complaint": "Doc, you have to help me get control of myself. I treat people shabbily, I cheat on my fiancée, I pad my expense account . . . you gotta help me stop!" What I have heard instead are complaints like: "I'm turning 40 now and I worry that my hairline is receding. I go to the beach to see if I can still attract girls of 18 or 19. My wife pissed me off the other day when she came home unexpectedly and caught me talking to one of them on the phone. What do you think, Doc? Do I look 40?"

The therapeutic task here is to listen sympathetically to the display of narcissism, to learn what one can of its sources, and eventually to confront the patient about the destructiveness or self-defeating nature of this sort of dishonest behavior. The hope is that enough of a positive relationship can be created with the therapist that the therapist develops some "leverage," where the confrontation can be accepted, metabolized, and integrated in such a way as to lead to new and more socially acceptable behavior patterns. This having been said, favorable outcomes that exemplify this scenario are *rare* with antisocial/psychopathic patients, even of the passive-parasitic, nonviolent type.

Psychoanalysts will occasionally have experience in treating a particular variety of narcissistic patient with rather pronounced psychopathic features—namely, the entrepreneur. Not all entrepreneurs are of this mold, but among their ranks are unquestionably a number of super-charmer or else super-aggressive (martinet-type) wheeler-dealers who often enough become major figures in the business and political world. Person (1986) has written about the special problems in doing analytic (or more often, analytically-oriented) therapy with such patients. They are usually men, brimming with self-confidence and "sure-fire" ideas for success, manipulators of people rather than of ideas, and often supercharged in their stream of mental activity, energy level, and ability to get by on little sleep. Many of these men like to live fast, gamble, philander, make splashy purchases at auctions, and indulge in various other forms of thrill-seeking behavior. Person cites a colleague who mentioned that these entrepreneurs "need to be distinguished from manic-depressives" (p. 263), but this does not do justice to the situation: these men often *are* bipolar manic-depressives,* with all the expansiveness, overambition, extraversion and grandiosity characteristic of bipolar persons.

In elaborating on the unfolding of the transference during analytically-oriented therapy with the narcissistic/psychopathic entrepreneur, Person (p. 271) describes an opening phase of overidealization and "brutal" honesty. The latter turns out to be pseudo-candor, in which the patient assuages his conscience by confession. Later on, the denigration of the analyst, which was hiding underneath the rosier images, surfaces and threatens to scuttle the treatment. On the countertransference side, in cases where the entrepreneur is genuinely successful, powerful, or famous, the analyst must not succumb to feelings of awe or false pride (at having such a mover and shaker as a patient), and must resist any temptation to profit from the encounter (buying certain stocks, getting invited to gatherings of celebrities, etc.).

---

*Among the more seriously psychopathic entrepreneurs of this type are several who have murdered their mates in fits of jealous rage: Einhorn (Levy, 1988), Minns (Finstad, 1991), Masters (Gibson et al., 1991).

Cognitive-Behavioral Therapy

In their recent book on the cognitive therapy of personality disorders, Beck and Freeman (1990) devote a chapter to the treatment of antisocial personality disorder. They speak of the delay in the development of moral maturity noted in antisocial persons: "arrested" at intermediate stages of Kohlberg's hierarchy, they cannot entertain another person's point of view at the same time as their own. This, of course, maps onto our understanding of narcissism, since what the antisocial person is saying in effect is: "I don't care what *you* think or what *you* feel; all that matters is what *I* think and feel." Since conventional supportive and analytically-oriented therapy presupposes a capacity for shame and guilt, they must perforce be of limited efficacy, as the authors contend, in the treatment of persons lacking these capacities. The logic of their point is compelling.

Beck and Freeman suggest that one might improve the moral and social behavior of antisocial persons via enhanced cognitive functioning (p. 152). This approach progresses, under optimal circumstances, through several stages. An antisocial man in one of the authors's examples wanted sex with his girlfriend but was unwilling to spend anything on her. The cognitive therapist suggested he consider the alternative of taking her to dinner or a movie, as a *quid pro quo* step that might make her more willing to offer him what he wanted. To begin behaving in this way is to advance to a more *utilitarian*, rather than purely *selfish*, level. This is still some distance from the higher plane of interpersonal conduct where one gratifies another person's wishes out of love and respect. But it is an improvement, and one that may result from convincing the antisocial person to reconsider the risk/benefit equations for the various moves he anticipates making.

In the cognitive-behavioral approach, the thrust of therapy is toward making constructive, longer-range decisions, in place of destructive, good-only-for-the-moment decisions. Here Beck and Freeman offer the example of a man who has just been demoted at work for poor performance. The man's first impulse is to tell the boss to "shove it" (the active-aggressive solution). The "advantage" is revenge. The disadvantage: getting fired and having to search for a new job. The therapist encourages the patient to think of alternatives. Some of these will still be pretty maladaptive, albeit not as rash as the first "plan." To do the next assignments as slowly as possible (the passive-aggressive solution) is a step up from cursing the boss to his face. The most mature strategy—to work extra-diligently at the next series of assignments in order to please the boss and get reinstated at the higher position—is the next higher goal (the utilitarian solution). Only a few antisocial/psychopathic patients will scale this height. And even then, it would be a long and arduous journey to see the patient embrace this strategy not simply because it "pays" in the long run, but because it is the sensible, mature way to go about one's work, and because the patient's egocentricity has been replaced by genuine compassion for the boss as a person with his own problems and worries (the brotherly solution).

The best one can hope for, except in the rarest of instances, through cognitive-behavioral or any other type of therapy with antisocial patients (especially those with pronounced psychopathic traits), is an ascent to the *utilitarian* level. At this level, the patient is simply substituting a totally selfish con game ("I promise her if I get laid I'll take her to the movies, only then I don't take her") with a socially less repugnant con game ("OK, so I *do* take her . . . "). What is still missing is any *sincere* regard for the other person. The improvement consists merely in *pretending* to be like an ordinary person and in *play-acting* the part in a more tolerable fashion. The *inner* control mechanisms of shame and guilt (most especially, guilt) will still be lacking or present only in an inchoate, rudimentary form. Conversion of the "primary" psychopath to a guilt-sensitive person who would recoil at the thought of hurting or conning someone does not occur. Certain "secondary" psychopaths, in whom these control mechanisms exist to some extent, may achieve more genuine states of prosociality. This will occur more often under the impact of some overwhelming life event that shakes such persons to their very foundation, and which impels them to join a religious organization capable of serving, in perpetuity, as a kind of external superego. With enough years and the maturation that may develop as one rounds the turn of 30 or 40, prosocial attitudes may even get *internalized*.

Psychoanalytic Therapy with Less Severe
Forms of Deviant Behavior

A number of psychoanalysts of the pioneer generation sought to treat socially deviant adolescents and adults with modified forms of psychoanalysis. They did so under several headings: "wayward youths" (the "verwahrloste Jugend" of Aichhorn, 1925), pathological liars (Deutsch, 1921), psychopaths (Schmideberg, 1947), imposters (Deutsch, 1955), even, on occasion, murderers (Williams, 1960). The "psychopaths" Schmideberg treated were of the passive-parasitic type: irresponsible, extractive, but not violent or callous. The more common label at mid-century for this whole group of socially deviant persons was *sociopath*.* A psychoanalytic theory

---

*This term now connotes, in the U.S., a less serious, less criminally-inclined form of deviance than is currently implied by "psychopath." In England "sociopathic" is still often used to designate the whole antisocial group. Tyrer and Alexander (1979), for instance, describe two categories under the rubric of sociopathy: an *explosive* type and a *sensitive-* (or paranoid-) *aggressive* type. The former is characterized by marked impulsivity and irresponsibility; the latter by suspiciousness, aloofness, and aggressivity.

of psychopathy was elaborated by Wittels (1938). This was followed several years later by Adelaide Johnson's influential hypothesis (1949) of a "SuperEgo lacuna," wherein a defect in a particular compartment of *conscience* was, in a way, transmitted from parent to child; i.e., a moral value missing in a parent, by virtue of that value not being inculcated into the child, ended up as an "absence" (or *lacuna*) in the child.* Although this mechanism seems to operate in many cases, some children of amoral parents develop an excellent set of moral values by some other, often mysterious, means. Likewise, as I discuss earlier, some young persons (the sort we subsequently label "Bad Seed") become psychopathic even when reared by parents of high moral character. Many of the patients treated by the above-cited analysts were of reasonably good character although given to imposture or pathological lying. They were motivated for therapy and wanted to overcome their symptoms. They were *not* the callous or ruthless or totally self-centered "psychopaths" as defined more rigorously (and negatively) by Cleckley or Hare.

In the more recent psychoanalytic literature one also finds case reports concerning the treatment of persons who habitually engage in socially unacceptable acts. As in the older literature, these patients usually also have a well-developed sense of shame and even of guilt, a corresponding tendency to depression after the commitment of such acts, and enough motivation to seek help in order to correct their behavior. Such patients fall far short of the criteria for ASP, let alone the contemporary criteria for psychopathy.

One such report (Myers, 1991) concerned a married man who practiced a form of paraphilia: *frotteurism*. He did this when riding the subways. He also made obscene telephone calls. Both acts were accompanied by masturbation to orgasm. In the course of the analysis, the patient, who also when under the influence of alcohol was physically abusive to his wife, came to recognize his hostility toward women: a carryover, in his case, from the time, until age four, when he shared the bedroom with his parents, overheard their lovemaking, endured their anger when he interrupted them, etc. This patient, a corporate executive, was highly motivated for treatment, became symptom-free during the latter part of his analysis, and had remained so at follow-up a year and a half later.†

The interesting question "Can a liar be psychoanalyzed?" formed the basis for a recent article by O'Shaughnessy (1990). She does not provide

---

*Cf. the recent novel, *Before and After* (Brown, 1992), in which the father of a teenager who murders a girlfriend disposes of the lethal weapons and stonewalls the police.

†It is likely that, had his therapist been schooled in cognitive-behavioral therapy, the outcome would have been equally favorable.

enough data to permit judgment on this issue, simply expressing the view that if the liar can admit he lies, and if the analyst can accept sympathetically the (hopefully, only temporary) "need" for this defense, then "a genuine analytic process can be set in train" (p. 194). One of the two patients she mentioned had certain psychopathic traits: glibness, superficial charm covering over the underlying hostility, and *habitual and pervasive* lying. I can see no room for optimism for therapy, certainly not for psychoanalytic therapy, here.

Obviously, the habitual liar creates a false persona — such that the therapist is, in effect, treating *someone else*. Pervasive lying is an impenetrable shield, deflecting all the therapist's "bullets" (attempts to pierce through to the real self) to one side or the other. This is a very different situation from dealing with patients who are basically truthful with the therapist, but who speak candidly of their need to prevaricate "out there" about certain embarrassing facets of their life. The man I once treated who bragged of sexual exploits to the other executives of his corporation, when actually he had no experience at all, is an example. This was a "treatable" patient. There is an important point to be made here: namely, that the combination of *good character and bad habits* usually makes for a workable situation, whereas *bad character and bad habits* predict treatment failure. "Good" character, in this context, would imply the presence of appropriate moral values and social conscience; the ability to admit fault; a susceptibility to shame, guilt, and depression; and an active striving to improve.

Since mental health professionals tend to trust the statements of patients who come willingly for help, even the most astute clinician can be "conned" by a talented psychopath. Not long ago, as an example, a colleague — one with forensic training — undertook to treat a young man who was known to have engaged in some minor delinquent acts. The patient seemed motivated, and in other ways unremarkable. Unbeknownst to the psychiatrist, the patient was a serial killer who had been raping and murdering women even during the time he was in "therapy" — until he was apprehended by the authorities.

On Making Moral Judgments in Psychiatry

My comments about "good character" and "moral values" raise a thorny issue concerning a therapist's own proper stance vis-à-vis the antisociality or offensiveness of certain patients. Must we be *always* neutral and nonjudgmental? With respect to psychoanalysis, which was not devised in the first place as a technique for treating psychopathic persons, Freud recommended years ago that " . . . patients who do not possess . . . a fairly reliable character should be refused" (1904, p. 263). While this rule is still pertinent for psychoanalysis, one might argue that the rule is too rigid and would destroy at the outset any hopes of amelioration, via other modes of therapy, of patients who offend others, including their therapists, let alone of actual "offenders" in the legal sense.

A number of writers have gone so far as to recommend scrapping "psychopath" as a diagnosis altogether, because of its pejorative connotation (Blackburn, 1988), or even "personality disorder" (Lewis & Appleby, 1988)—lest the negative overtones of this appellation lead to an unsympathetic attitude by the therapist. Maier (1990), who works on a forensic unit, asks: Could it be after all these Freudian years, that psychiatrists have denied the hatred they feel for psychopaths and criminals, and thus have been unable to treat psychopaths adequately because their conceptual base for treatment has been distorted by unconscious, denied feelings from the start?" (p. 766).

One catches the aroma, in these communications, of sanctimoniousness. Worse, it seems never to have occurred to these authors that there are persons who are "too far gone"—in whom malice is too deeply entrenched—to be treatable by any method whatsoever, by any therapist no matter how skilled. As for therapists' "unconscious, denied feelings" (of animosity, fearfulness, etc., toward violent or psychopathic patients), one need only read Searles (1979a) on *Violence in Schizophrenia* to be reminded that therapists are customarily quite in touch with this stratum of "countertransferential" feeling.

The key issue, again, as with patients who lie, is the balance between pervasiveness vs. limitedness of the destructive symptom. The husband in Myer's report, who made obscene calls and who was at times abusive toward his wife, was violent only occasionally and to a moderate degree; he sought to contain his violent impulses, and was eventually able to do so. This is a very different picture from the limitless vengefulness of the young man in Searles' interview, to say nothing of the venomous remarks about women made by the serial killer, Jerry Brudos, cited in Chapter 21.

If the balance pertaining to destructiveness tips toward the positive—where good character outweighs destructiveness—treatment may succeed. If tipped in the other direction, treatment will usually fail. To imagine otherwise, and to castigate a therapist's despair and hostility given a thoroughly destructive patient, as a countertransference impediment that, if removed, would permit therapy to flourish strikes me as naïve.

If we are really to treat persons who do hurtful things to others, we must be able to confront them about their actions. We must do so with honesty and, to the extent this is possible, with compassion. The alternative is to tiptoe around the destructiveness, letting the patient merely "ventilate"—in hopes that the patient will eventually be inspired to behave in a more socially acceptable way. The inability to recognize evil (by which I mean unremitting malice, scheming to hurt others) and the refusal to label it as such when confronted with it do not lead to a program for therapeutic success with extremely and unrelievedly destructive patients. But then, when dealing with psychopaths at this extreme end of the spectrum, remediation through therapy is not a reasonable expectation.

With *less* destructive antisocial persons, who show lesser degrees of the prognostically most ominous psychopathic traits (viz., callousness, lack of empathy, lack of remorse), the outlook for treatment is not as bleak. Even so, most therapists have little contact during their professional lifetimes with incarcerated offenders; only rarely does a patient referred for psychotherapy or analysis turn out to have prominent psychopathic traits. Those whose professional life involves psychiatric hospitals or residential treatment centers do encounter patients with ASP and/or strong psychopathic traits—including the violence-prone.

Gabbard and Coyne (1987) offer a number of useful suggestions for the management of such institutionalized patients. These include strict hierarchical structure, along with firm and promptly enforced rules—where the consequences of breaking those rules are made abundantly clear and enforced with unanimity by an "unsplittable" staff. A variety of countertransference problems may arise, such as the assumption by some staff members that what the antisocial patient really needs is the "love he didn't receive as a child" (this leads to a lack of firmness about rules, etc.) and staff's denial about the likelihood that the patient may fail to improve. This may occur because staff members " . . . have a deep-seated need to see themselves as capable of treating the untreatable patient" (Gabbard & Coyne, 1987, p. 1184).

A similar note is sounded by Strasburger (1986) in his well-reasoned recommendations for working with antisocial patients (in this less-than-hopeless region of the spectrum). Focusing on the therapist's feelings, Strasberger points out that there will be times when it is prudent for the therapist to speak candidly about his own fearfulness to an antisocial patient who inspires such fear. This teaches the patient something about the reactions he elicits in others, and it teaches the therapist something about his own vulnerability. Countertransference feelings are, in any case, a useful index to emotions relevant to the patient, which the latter is unable to recognize or articulate (Searles, 1986, p. 190). The therapist must be comfortable with his own anger, including his own sense of "righteous indignation," when some action or statement evokes these feelings. The patient's hatred and mistrust of others stir up similar emotions in the therapist, who must learn to "contain" these feelings and deal with them nondefensively, all in an effort to reorient the patient about the trustworthiness and friendliness of at least *one* other human being.

With the more "treatable" antisocial patients this effort may be re-
warded, in which case a bridge will have been built to the outside world.
The patient may then be more able to view the world, formerly seen in
black-and-white terms, in a more realistic, less hostile way. At times we do
succeed in rehabilitating antisocial patients—a doubly gratifying result,
since both the patient and the community at large benefit. But along the
way, as Strasburger underlines, the therapist must acknowledge his negative
feelings, which are an " . . . integral part of an intimate relationship with
people who commit antisocial acts. Not to be adversely affected would be
a denial of one's humanity."

Minor Forms of Psychopathy

Like a spoonful of India ink in a quart-jar of water, even a "little" psychopathy goes a long way in coloring the personality and in determining the
direction of the life-course. In ordinary, everyday society one encounters
with frequency: crooked salesmen, company embezzlers, scam-artists, philanderers, schemers who blackmail their lovers, "rip-off" cheats of every
description, dishonest politicoes, etc. The complete list would be very long.
Most have never spent a day in jail nor ever raised a hand against another
person.

My first major encounter with a psychopath of the nonviolent, not so
readily noticeable sort was during my internship in medicine, at Memorial
Hospital in New York. As one of three interns on the medical service, I
shared my duties with a former classmate from medical school and another
man whom neither of us knew. We were responsible for some 60 patients
spread over ten floors. Toward the end of our rotation, my friend and I felt
overworked even beyond the usual burdens interns carry. Comparing notes,
we discovered that he and I were taking care of 52 patients—26 apiece—
meaning that our colleague was carrying only eight. We then recalled how
he would phone us on his day "on call," claiming that so many new patients
had been admitted that he couldn't manage them all: could we help out?
Going over the records in the admissions office, we learned that on those
days, on average, only three were admitted: he "worked up" one and saddled us with the remainder. He left work at 2 p.m., we then ascertained,
while we both worked till late into the evening. We had someone "tail"
him, and it turned out he spent the afternoons "shacking up" with another
woman, while his wife was in her ninth month of pregnancy.

When we finally spoke of these matters with the head of medicine, the
chief scolded us for tattling and "making up stories." He did not believe us,
until some weeks later we caught our colleague "sink-testing" urine speci-
mens of his patients (meaning he tossed the urine in the sink and proceeded
to write fake numbers in the chart, as though he'd done the lab work). The

chief suspended the man, but only briefly; he is still in the profession, I'm sure, cheating family and public in whatever way he can.

As to "treatment," how can one even speculate about the most "effective" therapy for someone who, unless he were caught good and proper, would never present himself to a therapist in the first place? Indeed, one could even say that public humiliation is "Step 1" in the remediation of the psychopath — but this is something that lies far outside the sphere of legitimate intervention, just as one cannot "prescribe" religious conversion, despite the singular power of such conversion to remediate many an antisocial or psychopathic person.

There is an ironic point to be made here, in connection with the nonviolent, less flamboyant forms of antisociality and psychopathy. It is often easier to do beneficial therapeutic work with institutionalized antisocial patients who show a depressive component (cf. above: Woody et al., 1985), than it is to treat their nondepressed counterparts in office practice. The institution, or hospital, makes of the patient, for a while at least, a captive audience. Interpretations that might lead an ambulatory psychopath to take umbrage — and take off — have to be listened to, perhaps in time absorbed, by the inpatient who cannot run out the door.

IMPACT ON THE LIFE-COURSE: FOLLOW-UP DATA

Nigel Walker (1991) has stressed the importance of follow-up, preferably long-term, as the crucial step in improving our ability to predict the life trajectory in persons with antisocial/psychopathic personalities. He points to the woeful lack of such studies, and how this lack impairs the prediction of dangerousness in the case of violent offenders.

Of the studies that have been carried out, that of Lee Robins and her colleagues (1991), based on the DSM-III criteria for ASP, is particularly impressive. Among their conclusions:

(a) The disorder typically begins around age eight (with behavior problems at home and at school) and peaks in the twenties and thirties.

(b) Job and marital problems and violence are the most common symptoms; only a minority have (serious) difficulties with the law, and only about half of prison inmates meet these criteria.

(c) ASP is predominantly a male disorder.

(d) Remission is high, especially after age 40.

(e) A strong association was noted between ASP and substance abuse;

a lesser but still impressive association between ASP and schizophrenia and manic-depression.

(f) Persons with ASP tended not to seek treatment; effective means
of treatment were seldom available for those who did.

The study of Woody et al. (1985) compared outcomes of nonpsychotic
opiate addicts from various diagnostic groups, including those with ASP
with and *without* concomitant depression. They found that, while ASP
alone was a negative predictor of response to psychotherapy, those with
ASP *and* depression did respond favorably.

As interesting as these studies are, we would be even more eager to know
about the impact on the life-course of *psychopathic personality traits*, since
these are contained *within* the envelope of *personality*. It would be important from an epidemiological standpoint to know how many persons with
ASP score high on a psychopathy checklist and how many psychopaths
commit antisocial acts. These questions for the most part await future
research. In the meantime, Rice et al. (1990) have reported on their study
of recidivism in rapists — and they did use Hare's psychopathy checklist as
one of their indices. The presence of psychopathy proved one of the strong-
est predictors of recidivism in this group.

In my long-term study of hospitalized borderline patients (1990), comorbid antisociality, (by DSM-III criteria) was common among the males (12
of 57, or 21%). Sixteen other males were borderline by Kernberg criteria
only, but also showed ASP. These 28 patients were difficult to trace, since
many were hiding out from the law when I sought to learn of their outcome
10 to 25 years later. I found only 19 (68%), whereas I could trace 95% of
the 145 BPD females. The distribution of outcome Global Assessment
Scores for the 19 traced males with ASP is shown in Table 19. As can be
seen, only six (32%) are now doing well (as defined by being in either the
"good" or "recovered" groups). This is a much poorer average than for the
borderline group as a whole, 64% of whom are now well.

Initially, I did not evaluate the patients with a psychopathy checklist.
Reexamining the ASP males now, using Cleckley's list (with such variables
as charm, lack of nervousness, unreliability, untruthfulness, lack of remorse, pathological egocentricity, etc.), I can assign 11 to a group where
ASP is combined with psychopathy. Only one of these patients is in the
"good" outcome group; none, in the "recovered" group. In fact the five
"recovered" males were all adolescents, what Dilalla and Gottesman (1989)
call *transitory delinquents*, as opposed to *continuous antisocials* (who continue on to become criminals as adults). Four came from broken homes
and had taken to the streets, turned to drugs or alcoholism, engaged in
petty thefts, and had poor work records. They exemplified my comment

TABLE 19

Global Assessment Scores at Follow-up
of Nineteen Males with ASP

GAS RANGE	CLINICAL STATE	N
>70	"Recovered"	5
61 to 70	"Good"	1
51 to 60	"Fair"	4
31 to 50	"Marginal"	4
01 to 30	"Incapacitated"	3
zero	"Suicided"	2

above about "good character with bad habits." All are now continuously employed and are married (four with children). As for those with psychopathy, three have been in prison (one died in prison; one suicided after, as the police were about to rearrest him for arson; one is still in prison for murder); another killed three persons via arson when he was 14 and escaped punishment; another died in a motorcycle accident; and one has been missing for 23 years and is presumed dead.

Not one of the recovered antisocial males could be considered to have improved as a direct result of the treatment received at the hospital. Alcoholics Anonymous was instrumental in the recovery of two; Narcanon, of another. One of the alcoholic patients solidified his determination to stay well by joining a Buddhist religious group in addition to AA. Many of the borderline patients in the study chose this route, joining a number of different religious groups, whose "group-pressure" had the salutary effect of strengthening their ability to curb impulsivity. Of the three parameters of violence suggested above by Merikangas, response inhibition is the easiest to modify; it is not surprising that the group-pressure of a religious group succeeded in many of the more impulsive borderline patients, where one-to-one psychotherapy failed.

The impact of psychopathy has also been assessed in relation to risk factors in erotomanics. Meloy (1989), commenting on "unrequited love and the wish to kill," noted that in erotomanic persons, the presence of psychopathic traits predicted a greater likelihood of unexpected assault against the "erotomanic object." Usually the latter is a woman, as in the celebrated case of the psychopath Hinckley and his "love" of the actress, Jodie Foster, though sometimes, as in the case of Diane Schaefer (Brenner, 1991)—who followed a famous surgeon all around the world, intruding into his life—the woman is the huntress and a man the prey. In Meloy's experience, the addition of paranoid traits and alcohol abuse raises the risk of violence still higher.

In the design of future follow-up studies concerning antisociality and psychopathy, it will be desirable where feasible to use a prospective approach, beginning with detailed evaluations of school-age children, who could then be followed at various intervals on into their thirties and forties. It is clear already that physical abuse is a predictor of future aggressivity (Dodge et al., 1990; Huesmann et al., 1984). One should also take temperament factors into account, and as the personality begins to solidify in late adolescence, one should evaluate psychopathy as well as antisociality, using appropriate, reliable checklists. Perhaps assessment of chronic hostility would also be relevant, if for no other reason than that persistent anger is apparently associated with diminished life-span, over and above the impaired relations with others engendered by the pattern of angry or bitter reactivity (Angier, 1990).

In summary, the prognosis in ASP, while not altogether gloomy, is guarded: better for those who are not violence-prone and who show little in the way of psychopathic traits (as enumerated by Cleckley or Hare); worse for those with marked psychopathy, especially if accompanied by paranoid traits and repeated acts of violence. There is a tendency for the former group to ameliorate as they approach midlife—often through the help of various support and limit-setting groups, less often through the agency of psychotherapeutic intervention.

Where therapy is of help, the approach will usually have been cognitive-behavioral, emphasizing skills training, improved social skills, etc.; dynamic therapy in the one-to-one has little to offer. There is continuing debate as to the legitimacy of moral judgments on the part of the therapeutic community: Blackburn (1988) and Appleby and Joseph (1991) arguing against such judgments; others, including Strasburger (1986) and myself, taking the view that, at least when confronted with the most callous and malicious of psychopaths, such judgments are inescapable.

CLINICAL VIGNETTES

In the following vignette, I myself ended a treatment relationship—the only time I have felt moved to do so in 26 years of practice—because the patient's unremitting hostility and destructiveness toward those close to her were, in the absence of institutional controls, beyond my powers to ameliorate.

A Patient with Many Psychopathic, But Only a Few (DSM-) Antisocial, Traits

A single woman of 34 sought help because of difficulties with her family and her boyfriend. Anna, as I shall call her, had been unemployed for the past year and a half, subsisting on an allowance sent her by her parents.

She had been fired from her last job, as from several previous jobs, because of her abrasiveness (this I later learned from her father). In her mind, she had been doing "outstanding work," and was now suing her employer for "breach of oral contract."

She came from a large middle-class family with a strong history of affective disorder. Two siblings were currently taking lithium for bipolar manic-depression, as was an aunt on the maternal side. Neither parent was affected. She portrayed her parents as hateful, uncaring ogres bent on placing roadblocks in the path of her development, rejecting her suitors, etc. Her parents, with whom I met on several occasions, seemed quite different: soft-spoken, intimidated, earnestly concerned about their daughter's welfare, but bewildered about how to relate to her. For a number of years she had behaved abusively toward them, arguing over nothing, insulting them in front of her siblings at family meals, defending her own behavior with contemptuous remarks to the effect that: "You gave me bad genes; it's all your fault!" Her parents, mentioning "She hates us with a passion," feared that she would become violent.

Each session was a Niagara of vituperation—mostly at her parents, partly at her boyfriend—which I could no more easily interrupt than I could a real waterfall. During our fourth meeting, she flung a photo of her parents at me, so I could "see the monsters" who had made her life miserable. She announced to me: "I'm going to cut out their eyes with a razor and send it to them!" as if to dispel any lingering doubts as to how she regarded them. I managed to pose the question: "Do you think that would be a wise move on your part, since they are sure to take offense—considering the fact that they support you financially, and by the way also pay for your therapy? If you really hope I can help you, wouldn't you be jeopardizing that chance if you did something politically unwise, like sending a mutilated photo?" At which point she yelled, "Fuck them! I don't care how they feel!" Raising my own voice, I told her: "Listen—I think sending that photo would be so destructive that I'm going to plain *ask* you not to do it. Instead, you tell *me* why you felt such a need to carve up their picture. Give me the words that go with the action—and forget the action." Reluctantly, she promised that she wouldn't send the photo. Three days later, as the reader will already have surmised, I received a phone call from Anna's parents, expressing shock and horror over the photograph. Their equilibrium was restored when I recounted to them my efforts to intervene.

The year-end holidays were approaching, and her attention shifted to her boyfriend, an engineer seven years her junior. She pictured him as bumbling, ineffectual, unable to commit himself to their relationship, and ungratifying as a lover. Accusing him of having given her herpes, she said that was half the reason she was insistent that he marry her, despite his shortcomings. The other half: she wasn't getting any younger. Since I didn't trust her description of him any more than I did that of her parents, I suggested that I meet with the two of them. There was a meekness about him, but he was a very decent fellow, naïve, inexperienced, totally dominated by her. Though he had spoken of marriage at one point, he was clearly anxious about such a step, given her constant criticisms and the storminess of their relationship in the recent months. Nothing emerged during our first two meetings, but in the third "joint" session he felt emboldened to set matters straight about the herpes. He was actually a virgin when he and Anna met. The infection couldn't have come from him; he must have gotten it from her. This led to a screaming denial from her.

We met a week later, after the Thanksgiving holiday, which she had spent with her "future in-laws." Her boyfriend told me that in front of them, and the assembled guests, she exclaimed: "Bryan's going to have to marry me, you know . . . he's given me herpes, so nobody else'll have me. Bryan *owes* me!" Just to underline her point, she added: "And that's what Dr. Stone said!" Her boyfriend knew she was simply backing up one lie with another, but this hardly made the occasion any more bearable. Shocked by her outrageousness, he finally broke off the relationship. For similar reasons, I told her I would no longer work with her.

Anna was not looking to me as a therapist, she was seeking an accomplice. This not only makes a travesty of the treatment contract, but also subjects the therapist to the same intolerable emotion she evoked in others: betrayal. It occurred to me at the beginning that her irritability and her volubility were "soft signs" of the manic-depressive condition more readily diagnosed in several of her family members. Perhaps lithium, carbamazepine, or another medication might have reduced these tendencies. But she refused to try them. I suspect medication would not have made a major difference. This was no charmer psychopath of the snake-oil salesman type. This was someone animated by revenge, domination, and malice: the "malignant narcissist" of which Kernberg speaks (1989a, 1992). She dealt with insecurity about her inability to retain a man's affection by "brainwashing," undermining his self-confidence through her criticism, destroying his defenses through humiliation, until he was her helpless puppet. Husbands who batter their wives are attempting to exert dominion for the same reasons, though with the use of physical rather than psychological force. Some battering husbands at least love their wives. Anna wanted Bryan solely for her own ends.

Anna furthered her aim (of psychological enslavement) by alienating all of Bryan's friends (all of whom refused to see him anymore, unless he promised to come without her), then making him choose between her or them. One might claim: there are many people in the world who are cruel, intolerant, misanthropic, manipulative; by no means are all such persons "psychopathic." What is different about Anna? Consider for a moment the great Australian author, Patrick White, the subject of a recent biography by David Marr (1992). White is described as: "a despicable human being, consumed by self-hatred," "a truly unpleasant character: moody, arrogant, spiteful, incapable of forgiveness, [who would] yell at dinner-party guests, explode in rage at friends, etc."—earning him what Sullivan (1992) called, the "Nobel Prize in misanthropy." The difference lies in self-awareness, remorse, and the nature of one's hurtfulness. White had self-awareness, remorse, and a ruthless honesty about his own crustiness. Reading over Marr's biography shortly before his death, White cried—but did not change a word. He hurt others through bluntness or irascibility; he did not lie and scheme to gain advantage. But in Anna there was malice; remorse and self-awareness were lacking.

A Patient with Many Antisocial Traits But Only a Few Psychopathic Features

Alfred was 25 when admitted to a long-term psychiatric center because of ragefulness, feelings of inferiority, and suicidal impulses. He had come from a family that had been well-off when he was young but whose fortunes had seriously declined because of business reverses. Feisty and ill-tempered even before these reverses, Alfred felt inferior to his friends, who were still able to go to summer camp, etc., while such pleasures were no longer possible for him. He became frankly belligerent at this point and earned a reputation throughout adolescence as a bully.

At college Alfred was anxious about maintaining a high average, so that he could realize his dream of going to law school. To this end, he at times cheated on exams, in order to convert a "B" into an "A." He drove his car recklessly, got many speeding tickets, compounding the problem by "giving the finger" to the arresting officers, who occasionally hauled him down to the station for disorderly behavior.

Finally he did get accepted at a prestigious law school, but this was not without its drawbacks: he did not win entrée into the more "aristocratic" set, as he had hoped. He did become engaged to a girl from that set, but the relationship ran aground because he was not accepted by her family. Disconsolate over that loss, he was inattentive to his studies and flunked out of law school. This led to a prolonged tantrum in which he trashed his room and went around scratching Cadillacs and Jaguars with a hunting knife "to get back at the wealthy." He threatened to kill himself and one of his professors. It was at this point that he was persuaded to enter the hospital.

During the first eight months of his yearlong stay, Alfred's behavior was much as it had been on the outside. Powerfully built and menacing, he spoke and acted abusively toward the staff and intimidated the other patients, to whom he would show his contempt by doing repugnant things in front of them, like masturbating into a cup and drinking his semen out of it. Yet he seemed "reachable" to his therapist; he could express sadness at times over the crazy drama he was enacting—in which he would repel potential friends and then bemoan his loneliness. In the last few months of his stay, he got much more in touch with the underlying depression, apologized to the many people he offended, worked through some of the grief over his losses, and became a "human being." At follow-up 13 years later, he was running a successful business and had married. Still intense and somewhat short-tempered, he was much less hostile, and no longer engaged in antisocial acts.

Both Anna and Alfred illustrate what Gabbard (1989) was referring to in his article on "patients who hate." Though they are filled with hatred, they also elicit hatred from those upon whom their lives impinge, including therapists and hospital personnel. Certain symptoms are common in these patients: self-mutilation, suicide gestures, substance abuse, rage outbursts, and assaultiveness. Borderline, antisocial, narcissistic, and paranoid traits are present in one combination or another. Underlying dynamics may include a desire to offend first, before others have a chance to initiate "rejection," in patients convinced of their own unloveability. Gabbard also mentions the need, in some patients, to "get under the skin" of others, lest they be "forgotten." This might be the case with patients raised by openly rejecting parents, where the alternative to rageful attachment was an even less tolerable no-attachment-at-all.

In the hospital treatment for such patients, Gabbard underlined the need for the staff to form a "good-enough" holding environment, while the therapist sought to help the patient explore and resolve the crucial dynamic issues. One needed to resist, insofar as humanly possible, the countertransference temptation to "rise to the bait"; i.e., to engage in sarcasm or other displays of contempt. It will be easier to carry out Gabbard's recommendations when one can find some small spark of humanity, some sign, however exiguous, of vulnerability, in the patient, onto which the therapist's hope can fasten and toward which his efforts can meaningfully be directed. This fosters the possibility that the patient will one day sense this (genuine) hope and respond to the genuinely positive feelings reflected in these efforts. This can set in motion a "positive feedback," where the patient becomes more likeable, because he can see that the therapist (unlike most others in his early life) can like *him*, making it safer still for the patient to become more likeable, and so on. Probably it is easier to get this therapeutic machinery going in the institutional setting, because, as mentioned above, it is more difficult for the patient to run away before the curative processes can begin. At all events, Anna remained hating and hateful; Alfred largely gave up hating and became likeable, and therefore treatable.

14

$$\bigtriangledown$$

Histrionic Personality Disorder

HISTRIONIC PERSONALITY DISORDER is the DSM term replacing the older designation, *hysterical* character neurosis, that enjoyed wide currency in the psychoanalytic literature. The latter derived from the ancient term, *hysteria*, used by the early Greek physicians to describe a pattern of behavioral excess and wild emotionality exhibited by certain women, especially around the time of their menses. "Hystéra" was the Greek word for "womb" (a cognate both of "gaster," [stomach, hollow organ], and of Sanskrit. "udára" [womb]). The idea was that the womb, in this overexcited state, somehow traveled throughout the body, settling at times in the brain, where it led to the aberrant behavior we call *hysterical*.

Since overemotionality is not limited to women, nor, in women, to their premenstrual phase, "hysterical" acquired a pejorative connotation offensive to women. This prompted the change to "histrionic." Despite the similarity of sound, the two words are not related, *histrionic* stemming from a Latin word "histrio," borrowed from the Etruscan, a *stage player*. "Histrionic" thus signifies *theatrical, overemotional, stagey*, etc. With this revision, it would seem the architects of DSM have merely gone from the linguistic frying-pan into the fire. But there you have it.

A HISTORICAL NOTE

DSM's laudable (though not very successful) aim to replace *hysterical* with a gender-neutral term less prejudicial to women may be seen as a step toward undoing some of the wrongs men have inflicted upon women for many centuries. In Europe during medieval times in particular, the normal sexual desires of women were harshly suppressed by the Church, engendering (among other things) periodic outbreaks of unruly behavior, often sexually tinged, among nuns. Aldous Huxley's *The Devils at Loudun* (1953) recounts such an episode. Women were seen as dangerously lustful, inconstant, and as somehow responsible for sexual failures on the part of men — as though impotence was brought about by women's "sorcery."

We could afford to regard these notions as absurd, were they not also the wellspring from which unconventional or overemotional women came to be persecuted as "witches" from the late fifteenth to the mid-nineteenth centuries. The authors whose work gave sanction to this persecution were two German monks, Krämer and Sprenger; their *Malleus Maleficarum* (1496) [The Witches' Hammer] serving as a handbook for judges presiding over the Inquisition.

In the sixteenth century, though the clergy continued to endorse the belief in witches (Bodin, 1589), a few dared to debunk such belief as superstitious; most notable was the father of modern psychiatry, Johann Weyer (1564). The first English book on hysteria was published in the seventeenth century by Jorden (1603), who claimed that the so-called witches were not "possessed" by Satan, but were mere unfortunate women with mental disturbances. Some still held fast to the belief in witchery (DelRio, 1679), but anatomists like Willis (1668) now considered hysteria to be an affliction of the brain, unrelated to any "traveling womb."

Physicians of the eighteenth century understood fainting spells, "convulsions," and other "hysteric" phenomena as disorders of the "spirit" brought about by improper diet or by poisonous wastes not properly eliminated. According to Purcell (1707) the hysteric "Vapours" occur more often in women:

> . . . Because their menses is an excrement more apt to cause obstructions than any . . . excrement in Man's body, and being retained produces more various and dismal accidents. . . . Secondly Because from the weaker texture of their Brains and Nerves they are more subject to violent passions . . . than men are. Thirdly Because their Diet is more irregular. (p. 38)

These formulations are to be found in other eighteenth century commentators on hysteria (Beauchêne, 1781; Mandeville, 1730; Pinel, 1799; Whytt,

1765). Pinel, noting that some women were prone to violent alterations in mood around the time of their period, recommended early marriage and frequent pregnancies — as a way of diminishing the number of periods such women need endure. Aubin (1716) meanwhile described the outbreak of hysteria in the nuns of Loudun, upon which Huxley based his monograph.

In the early nineteenth century the cause of hysteria continued to be ascribed to purely biological factors. Tate (1831), for example, felt that dyspeptic symptoms preceded the nervous ones, and that if mental shocks (deaths in the family, disappointments in love) played any role in hysteria, they did so "by putting a sudden check to the catamenia during their flow" (p. 132). French alienists of this era wrote in a similarly biological and rather unsympathetic vein (Louyer-Villermay, 1816; Esquirol, 1838). Voisin (1826) saw nymphomania as the product of some cerebral affliction, curable, if at all, by early marriage to a vigorous male.

We begin to see a more complex, and more modern, view emerge after mid-century. Briquet (1859), originator of the eponymous syndrome of hysterical paralyses, headaches, swallowing difficulties, etc., first of all refuted Louyer-Villermay's assertion that, lacking a uterus, men could not develop hysteria. LePois (1618) long ago realized men could become hysteric, as Briquet mentions (p. 12), but the fact was then forgotten. Though Briquet used *hysteria* as solely a symptomatological, not a characterological, term, he was keenly aware of the impact psychological influences made upon the clinical picture of hysteria. Of the emotions that could trigger hysteria, all were of the painful type: sadness, jealousy, disappointment, fear, and boredom. One of the first to underline "dynamic" factors, reflecting untoward early experience, Briquet mentions: "First, the bad treatment children may receive on the part of their parents, or that women suffer at the hands of their spouses; second, the worries and troubles in intimate life, whether in the family or in illicit affairs; third, business failures or unfavorable changes of employment. . . . " (p. 116, my transl.). Since not all persons subjected to these negative influences developed hysteria, Briquet invoked the idea of *predisposition* (viz., hereditary, constitutional), hysteria resulting from the precipitating factors affecting predisposed persons.

In the latter half of the nineteenth century there was a growing awareness that, over and above menstrual "causes," women with hysterical conditions often suffered from disturbances in their sexual life. The utility of hypnosis in alleviating hysterical symptoms was recognized and legitimized, through the work of Charcot (1875) and LeGrand du Saulle (1891). The photographs of Richer (1885) reveal the ways in which sexual conflicts could be kept hidden from consciousness but acted out in body posture. Hysteria remained primarily a condition of women, and was sometimes accompanied by erotomania and even "double personality." LeGrand du Saulle (p. 266ff) gives a lengthy case-history of the latter: a virginal young woman who alternated between a dour, sad self and a cheerful self, convinced (in the cheerful state) she was pregnant.

In 1893 Breuer and Freud published their first paper on the psychical mechanisms in hysteric phenomena — a landmark work that gave etiological pride of place to unconscious sexual frustrations and conflicts, and that pointed to the efficacy of bringing these conflicts to the surface, via psychoanalysis, as the best means of relieving the hysterical conditions. Freud had made clear, in a letter to Fliess a year before (1892), that among the causative factors in hysteria was "sexual traumas before the age of understanding" (Masson, 1985, p. 38). These traumas, Freud was aware, could include incest, a subject about which Freud knew more than he was comfortable to say, owing to the political climate of the times (Stone, 1992b).

Other prominent psychiatrists at the turn of the century continued to focus on descriptive issues (Janet, 1911; Kraepelin, 1909; Krafft-Ebing, 1902), whereas Freud began to use *hysteric* not only as a designation for the symptoms outlined by his predecessors, but also as a label for a *characterological* style and, in 1905, for a stage of normal development. The *hysteric character* (whose features we may take as the precursor of DSM's description of *histrionic personality disorder*) was sketched in greater detail by Wilhelm Reich in the 1929 portion of his *Character Analysis*. Here Reich mentions: "obvious sexual behavior, with coquetry in females, overpoliteness and feminine gestures in males; an agile, nervous, lively disposition; an extraordinary capacity for sexual attachment of an infantile character; fixation at the genital phase of development, with incestuous attachment; and a diminished tendency to sublimation" (p. 189ff).

AREAS OF CONFUSION IN
MODERN USAGE OF "HYSTERIC"

In speaking of "hysteric" patients or "hysteric" character neurosis, Freud and the early generation of analysts tended to focus on symptoms, on underlying defense mechanisms, and on "causative" psychodynamics. Less attention was paid to clinical description or to distinctions between typical symptoms and typical personality patterns. The same was true, as Baudry (1989) points out, for obsessive conditions: "Freud's use of the term obsessional neurosis suggests that what he had in mind was the total personality organization . . . [rather] than just the symptoms" (p. 36). Many of Freud's early case histories concerned women who had "hysteric conversion symptoms" (such as globus hystericus), plus what we would now consider hysteric/histrionic personality traits (exaggerated emotionality, seductiveness, impressionistic speech, need to be the center of attention, overconcern with attractiveness).

The conversion symptoms—to which the nineteenth century nosologists paid so much attention—can occur, however, in patients with few or no histrionic traits. This was actually my first lesson in psychiatry. The first patient I examined as a medical student on the psychiatry rotation was an overburdened mother of four children, hospitalized because of hysterical paralysis of her right arm. Having grown terrified that she might take a kitchen knife and stab her children, she then developed paralysis of the arm with which she might have carried out this unacceptable wish. But her personality was compulsive and paranoid, without a trace of histrionic traits.

Using "hysteric" as a double-duty term for both symptom and trait is not the only difficulty one encounters in psychoanalytic theory on this topic. There was been a tendency to ascribe causative significance to certain dynamics which may have little, or only symbolic, relevance to the development of "hysterical character" or histrionic traits. Thus the notion of "penis envy" was invoked as a way of explaining the hysteric woman's sexual conflict—specifically, the paradoxical combination of seductiveness and dissatisfaction with being female. But it is reductionistic to imagine that penis envy is the keystone to the whole edifice of hysteric/histrionic personality. What matters is the whole pattern of interaction with the parents, the degree of satisfaction of the mother with her lot as a woman, the emotional availability or seductiveness or aloofness of the father, one's culture (does it foster or inhibit a woman's ambitions to a career?), etc.

Parallel to the oversimplified statements about cause are the unrealistic efforts to match up a particular condition with a particular defense and a particular locale on the linear path of early development. There is more to hysteria than repression, just as there is more to obsessiveness than isolation of affect and intellectualization. Statements cast in this mold lack the explanatory power they aspire to, as when Sandler (1985) comments: " . . . in hysteria a problem such as that arising from hatred of the mother due to penis envy is solved by repression" (p. 108). How to explain histrionic personality in males? And in a culture where women had equal access to life's riches, would a grown woman still prefer male appendages?

Similarly, the effort to situate each separate condition at a specific locus on the developmental track proved reductionistic and confusing. The three neurotic characters—depressive, obsessive, and hysterical—"belonged," according to this schema, to the oral, anal, and genital stages of development. This made hysteria seem more "healthy" than obsessionality, since it represented trouble at a more advanced level. Easser and Lesser (1965) noted, however, that certain "hysterics" were more dysfunctional than typical obsessives. This is paradoxical only within the confines of a rigid, linear model of psychopathology (Stone, 1980b).

A model with greater explanatory power would posit that subtle differences in biologically-based cognitive style and in right/left brain differences between the sexes account, in part, for the tendency of men to excel at certain (e.g., visuospatial) tasks; women, at others (e.g., linguistical, identification of emotion). Differences of this sort, in turn, load the dice in favor of the "histrionic" style for women, and (to a lesser extent) the obsessive style in men. From an ethological standpoint there is survival value attached to these differences, having to do with child-rearing vs. hunting tasks in our remote ancestors. In a sense, then, what we are calling *histrionic* and *obsessive* disorders may be understood as exaggerations of subtle, normal gender differences in cognitive/behavioral predisposition.

Considerations of this sort underlie my discomfort with either "hysteric" or "histrionic" as a label for a personality disorder which happens to be more common in women. The terms, though meant to be designations for a relatively uncommon disorder in either women or men, seem, at the same time, reflective of a tendency to disparage women in general as childlike or irresponsible.

Histrionic personality is seen in certain family studies as occurring with greater than expected frequency in the female relatives of antisocial males. The hypothesis is: the two conditions may be the phenotypic expressions of a similar genetic liability to sensation-seeking, etc. (Cloninger et al., 1975). This model is probably correct in relation to the pedigrees analyzed in these studies. But because so many women exhibit one or two traits listed as the items of histrionic PD, one must be careful that they not be tarred with the same brush we use in depicting the (usually much more disturbed) female relatives of antisocial men, as though "histrionic" were the reverse side of the coin of antisociality.

It would be good if a term with less negative overtones could be found when referring to those with only a few minor traits (in place of "somewhat hysteric" or "a little histrionic"). In the meantime it will be useful to think *dimensionally* about a *continuum* of a trait-cluster we might call "over-expressive," reserving terms like *histrionic* or *hysteroid* only for men and women who are truly at the dysfunctional extreme.

A Continuum of Emotional Overexpressiveness

We might picture such a continuum as part of a gaussian curve of variation relative to the whole population, as shown in Figure 26. Persons in regions I and II belong to the normal population and would seldom seek psychiatric help. Persons in Region III, exhibiting only a few HPD traits, are encoun-

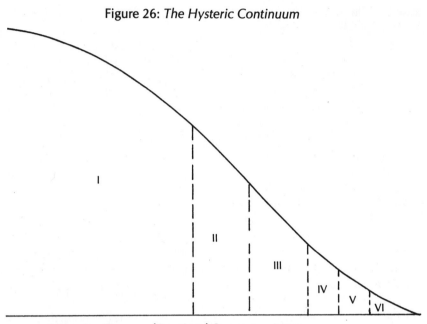

Figure 26: *The Hysteric Continuum*

Increasing Degrees of Emotional Overexpressiveness

Key to Regions I to VI:
 I: Normal expressivity   IV: Meets criteria for HPD
 II: Mild overexpressivity   V: "Hysteroid" (HPD × BPD)
 III: Some troublesome HPD traits   VI: "Hysterical Psychosis"

tered often by psychotherapists; most function well and are well-integrated; some have more serious conditions, as well as a number of traits "belonging" to other personality disorders. As for the traits ordinarily associated with HPD, they may show exaggerated need for reassurance (as might many dependent persons) or overconcern about appearance (as would be typical of narcissistic persons). Region IV represents HPD as described in DSM.

Region V contains the kinds of patients Easser and Lesser (1965) characterized as "hysteroid"; Kernberg (1967), as "infantile." These are patients with "histrionic" disorders, but who show inordinate hostility or ragefulness, and who function at a borderline level; the "hysteroid dysphorics" of D. Klein (1977) and Liebowitz and Klein (1981)—basically, patients with BPD, HPD, and dysthymia—also belong to this diagnostic region.

Finally, in region VI are found the rare patients with what has been called "hysterical psychosis"—a term used by Breuer and Freud and revivi-fied by Hollender and Hirsch (1964). Modestin and Bachmann (1992) re-cently studied 22 such cases (21 were female), and noted that this group could be distinguished from schizophrenia (they had fewer delusions or hallucinations, recuperated quickly, had good rapport), but were quite sim-ilar to patients with reactive (psychogenic) psychosis. The only real differ-ence was that the former had underlying histrionic personalities. For this reason Modestin recommended the diagnosis of "hysterical psychosis" be dropped in favor of "reactive psychosis with comorbid HPD." In general, the overrepresentation of females grows greater as one nears the extreme end of the curve in Figure 26.

MODERN CONCEPTIONS OF
PSYCHODYNAMICS IN HPD

Millon (1990) has succinctly captured the essence of the histrionic/hysteric style, analyzed into various domains of discourse. Thus he desribed patients in this category as behaviorally *affected*, interpersonally *flirtatious*, cogni-tively *flighty*, relying on mechanisms of *dissociation*, in mood *fickle*, in self-image *sociable*, in their internalizations *shallow*, and in morphological organization *disjoined*. By "affected" Millon meant sensation-seeking, rather impulsive, hedonistic, not very reflective. One could add "unmethodical," since persons with this disorder tend to be unpunctual and easily daunted by certain "adult" obligations, such as balancing a checkbook; they are the opposite, that is, of the "compulsive" person.

The dissociative defenses include the use of socially "charming," attrac-tive façade to disarm criticism, the use of self-distracting activities to avoid reflecting on unpleasant emotions, the use of repression to block awareness of unacceptable wishes, etc. By "disjoined" Millon refers to a psychic organ-ization in which the processes of internal regulation and control are scat-tered and poorly integrated (p. 364).

The remarks by Easser and Lesser (1989) about the typical dynamics of persons with "hysterical character neurosis" and about the strategies used in dealing with their major conflicts are particularly apt, the more so as the authors offer excellent recommendations for treatment (plus suggestions about how to avoid the "tender trap" these patients tend to create within the therapeutic setting).

Easser and Lesser allude to Freud's comment about the hysteric's com-bined coquetry and apprehensiveness: there is preoccupation with sexual wishes, yet fearfulness about actually engaging in sex. Fenichel (1945) spoke of this as "pseudo-hypersexuality" (p. 528), where sexual strivings are suppressed, only to reemerge in (thinly) disguised form—as coquettishness and fleeting but intense enthusiasms of all kinds. A turning away from reality and toward fantasy is a related characteristic—sometimes leading to the creation of a rich and elaborate "inner world," where the patient "really" lives (i.e., where one's emotions are primarily invested).

The "hysteric" typically maintains a child-like self-image, employing the child's charm and insouciance to win his way into acceptance by important others. Many hysterics come from environments that have sent a double message about sex: one or both parents *talk* as though it were dirty and unacceptable, but *behave* as though it is highly excitable and desirable. This contributes to a "hysteric" mechanism where sex can only be indulged in if one pretends one didn't really want it but was "forced" into it by a partner who "wouldn't take 'no' for an answer." That is, sex is permissible as long as one can disavow responsibility for it.

In speaking of the hysteric's "emotional way of life" Easser and Lesser point out how intensification of emotion and exaggerated display of feeling can be used as a defense against the cognitive recognition of the underlying conflicts. One may see a dismissiveness about the connections a therapist might try to make concerning these conflicts: not merely an overvaluation of emotion, in other words, but a depreciation of reason. In juxtaposition to these mechanisms, one sees an action-orientedness or, in the case of someone in treatment, a proneness to dramatize in behavior "out there" what the patient is reluctant to face and to talk about in the therapist's office. Especially because the hysteric may do so in an entertaining or amusing way, this defense constitutes a formidable "character armor" (as Wilhelm Reich spoke of it). This evocation of emotion may be used not only to "enliven" the sessions, in becoming the therapist's "favorite" patient, but also to deflect criticism or trivialize an interpretation. In less well-integrated hysterics (especially those with borderline features), one may see a particular type of unreasonableness, in which emotionality and counterattack (externalization) are used to "demolish" someone else's point. An example: Spouse A says, "Gee, the expenses are really piling up; do you think you could get along with the clothes you have for a while?" Spouse B retorts: "Well, you didn't get me what I wanted for Christmas anyway; and besides I don't think you love me anymore!" (which totally derails any further discussion about fiscal prudence).

In many instances the hysteric's emotionality and seductiveness had been encouraged by parental seductiveness. This will more often have been the case with the father-daughter than with the mother-son relationship. Partly this reflects cultural reinforcements, where girls are permitted emotional display but boys are encouraged to suppress such display. The efforts hysteric patients make to be "appealing" serve to recreate the pleasurable aspects of the early environment; however, in psychotherapy the danger is that the patient will try to make of treatment a mere reenactment of the past (viz. of the forbidden oedipal attachment), and will show little interest in exploring with the therapist the relevant connections between past and present. There is less interest in ascending to the higher ground of mature sexuality than in remaining in a "holding pattern" of inhibited, ersatz sexuality via flirtatious attachments to unavailable partners.

Because of powerful resistances of this sort, a psychotherapy or psychoanalysis may appear to be going well—with all manner of "fabulous" material, "fascinating" dreams, etc.—but, as Easser and Lesser caution, may actually be going nowhere: no depth of exploration, no working-through of conflicts, no ameliorative changes in external life. Still, the combination of a motivated hysteric patient with an adroit therapist who knows how to navigate around these obstacles is a very favorable one for a successful treatment outcome.

As with any personality disorder, there is of course an inverse relationship between "sickness level" and outcome: HPD in borderline patients is a less certain situation for successful treatment than HPD in better integrated patients; the latter may not do as well as still better integrated patients showing only a few, less intense histrionic traits. The reader should consult Chapters 7 and 11 for detailed indices of positive and negative predictors. In general, highly traumatized, incestuously victimized, chronically angry patients will do worse; those without these factors, better.

ATYPICAL AND MIXED FORMS; POORLY INTEGRATED PERSONALITIES

Within the broad domain of patients with pronounced "hysteric" traits (some conforming to DSM's HPD, some not) there are a number of mixed or atypical disorders. We already alluded to "hysteroid dysphoria," which can be seen as the confluence of HPD, BPD, and "depressive" PD (the latter not an official term but corresponding closely to dysthymia).

Most of the patients Helene Deutsch (1942) described under the heading of "as-if" personality are also predominantly hysteric, though with marked narcissistic features as well. These patients were usually raised in wealthy families where the children were decidedly *not* the center of the parents' attention, and where enormous emphasis was placed on "good form" and very little on self-discipline and on solid moral values. Left to their own devices and hungering for connectedness, "as-if" persons form quick and tenacious attachments to one lover after another, playing up to the tastes and attitudes of each in turn—in hopes of earning a spot in the lover's affections. This accounts for the "as-if" quality: it is *as if* their personality were in harmony with that of the desperately needed other.

The men and women Deutsch sketched in her vignettes had the shallowness, the fleeting identifications, and the "hyped" (insincere and exaggerated) emotions we associate with the "hysteric character." The as-if person can thus be a right-wing fanatic one month (if the lover broadcasts those attitudes) and next month, with equal fervor, champion the downtrodden (if that would be in accord with the new lover or new group-affiliation). Because there is no solid inner core, as-if persons can oscillate between good and evil, as Deutsch mentioned, with hardly any awareness of the inconsistency. Though they long for meaningful attachment, they are so "wired" for non-attachment, that they usually remain aloof, shallow, hard to reach, and harder still to treat. The therapist is often left as one trying to grab hold of a cloud.

Hysteric traits (whether these meet or fall short of HPD criteria) can be found in conjunction with most of the other "categorical" personality disorders. The same is true of most of the other disorders, so one might envision a matrix of 11 × 11, or 121, combinations; if one included sadistic and self-defeating (masochistic) PD's, the table would enlarge to 13 × 13 or 169 combinations. Some of these would, of course, be rare or nonexistent. It is hard to imagine a schizoid hysteric. Mixed compulsive/hysteric disorders do exist, especially in subcultures where women are brought up in a harshly repressive atmosphere (conducing to unemotionality and "up-tight" compulsiveness), yet are taught to act "gushy" and little-girl-like. Some have called such persons pseudo-hysterics, since their excessive emotional display is studied and eerily hollow.

Dependent and masochistic traits are much more common accompaniments of hysteric disorders, since both are in the direction of playing the child, or courting suffering (the price for forbidden sexual pleasure), by way of making themselves more appealing to a strong "rescuer." Though hysteric patients are usually sensation-seeking and extraverted, some are even avoidant and outwardly timid. One sees this combination more often among borderline-level hysterics than among those who are better integrated. In all my years of practice I have seen one schizotypal hysteric: a woman who had been incestuously misused by both her father and her mother, and who, in adult life, presented a curious mixture of seductiveness, hypersexuality, eccentricity, suspiciousness, odd—but impressionistic—speech, and magical thinking.

Though in general women are less often sadistic, and much less often antisocial, than men, the combination of hysteric PD and sadistic PD is, alas, not a null set. This mixture is seen in both men and women, perhaps in equal numbers (there are no data on the subject). Despite the saying "De mortuis nihil nisi bonum" (Of the dead we must say nothing except what is good), I would venture to say, having read his biography (Clarke, 1989), that Truman Capote showed these combined traits. He was well-known both for his overemotionality and his witty insults to the hosts and hostesses who lionized him.

At the clinical level, sadistic hysterics may show such extremes of either set of traits—and do so with such lightning-like shifts from one state to the other—as to call to mind Dr. Jekyll and Mr. Hyde (Stevenson, 1886/ 1990). The character in the novel was not hysteric, to be sure: Dr. Jekyll was dour, saturnine, obsessional. But this same kind of *unintegrated* personality may be seen in patients with borderline PD, and in outwardly better functioning persons who alternate rapidly between a hysteric-like, overdramatic pretense of warm emotion and a sudden cold cruelty.

The character of Mildred in Maugham's *Of Human Bondage* (1915), modeled after a lover of Maugham's, was fundamentally cruel: scheming, grasping, tyrannical, etc. The hysteric traits were as an overlay. But I have seen patients in whom these contrasting trends, and the coexisting sweetness and cruelty (or vengefulness), were so neatly balanced that one could not say that the one trend was any more the "real" self than the other. Not only that, but the sweetness and the enjoyment in taking care of others were genuine, when these emotions and attitudes were center-stage. When some disappointment or annoyance suddenly triggered the opposite traits, the cruelty was also genuine. Here the personality is truly unintegrated (to the point where it is not easy to give it a diagnostic label). Perhaps Maugham's "Mildred" was only "pseudo-unintegrated," since her sweetness was only a veneer, a thin icing on a rancid cake.

As for the truly unintegrated hysteric/sadistic patient, there has usually been a highly traumatic past—incest is a common feature—and the situation from a therapeutic standpoint is not hopeless. The genuine warm feelings for others, though capable of being suddenly swept away for a time, constitute an oasis, one that with proper treatment can be expanded. If an offending parent had some human qualities, forgiveness and compassion are possible; one should help the patient achieve these more mature attitudes. If an offending parent had been thoroughly cruel, unremittingly evil (as one will from time to time encounter if one works, as I do, with borderline patients in large numbers), it may be quixotic to expect that the patient can "forgive and forget." Here the task is more difficult: one must help the patient grasp fully the difference between the cruel parent and the majority of humankind "out there" who might deserve the patient's trust and friendship.

Besides undoing the transference distortions of this kind, there is also the task of compartmentalizing the painful emotions that surround the memories of the parent; the patient may have to build a thick wall, henceforth excluding the parent (or other damaging intimate), while at the same time building up the ability to trust others and to make a better life with them. The therapist will often be the first person to establish trustworthiness in the life of the patient, and thus becomes the first hurdle on the path toward a trusting, gratifying relationship with a friend or lover. Here the therapist's integrity, steadfastness, acceptingness, ability to "contain" stormy emotion, and genuine conviction about the patient's humanity (despite the occasional flare-ups of rage and sadism) would be essential curative factors—as much, or more so, as the correctness of interpretive remarks.

Epochal Changes in Personality: Implications for "Hysteria"

It should not be surprising that certain personality differences between men and women would arise owing to the difference in their average bulk and strength. Since women typically weigh only two-thirds as much as men, confrontations would be one-sided were brute strength the only deciding factor. But a woman can humiliate a man with words—a technique that works quite well except with a man intent upon murder. This realization might foster—in women more so than in men—the development of a certain giftedness for putting an opponent down with words.

If we shift attention from negative to positive interactions, we note that women can attract, elicit help from, or at least neutralize a man via charm and the promise of sexual favor. Even in our own culture up through recent times, the "game" women were compelled to play, in the interests of survival and security, favored "feminine charms," whetting male rescue fantasies by acting helpless, being deferential and accommodating—in hopes of lifetime support by a loving husband. Divorce was frowned on and rare, so this strategy was adaptive. The hysterical personality, as it was depicted at the turn of the century, represented merely an exaggeration (sometimes to the point of caricature) of these "feminine" traits.

This intermingling of concepts is reflected in much of the writing by psychiatrists until very recently (cf. Chodoff & Lyons, 1958). Attitudes have begun to change in the last 25 years, as reflected in Wolowitz' comment (1972):

> Given the cultural ideal . . . of socialization it is not surprising to find that hysterical character more frequently characterizes women than men. . . . The psychodynamics of the hysteric are uncomfortably close to the dynamics of the idealized normal feminine personality. (p. 313)

Harriet Lerner sounded a similar note (1974):

> . . . if we examine societal notions of masculinity and femininity we
> find that the pressures on women to adopt a hysterical style are intense
> and continue throughout a lifetime. (p. 159)

Thanks to the efforts of those who have championed the causes of
women, cultural changes are taking place, slowly but surely. The effects
are already discernible, in that the old feminine ideals, and the personality
style that supported these ideals, are giving way to a different set of norms,
more in keeping with the social verities of our time and place. For most
women in our culture to bat eyelashes, wear frills, etc., under the assumption this will win eternal support from a man whose one income will suffice
for the needs of the family, is no longer an adaptive strategy; it is in fact
suicidal for all except the wealthiest and the luckiest. Because of economic
changes, work is now a necessity, not a luxury, for most women; the high
divorce rate renders this necessity all the more compelling. Self-sufficiency
is also an effective remedy against a battering husband: one can leave him
and still survive.

As these changes continue, the old *hysterical personality* will resemble
less and less the new optima for women's personality. In step with these
changes, the optima for men's personality will resemble less and less the
old "Me Tarzan, you Jane" stereotypes of male swagger. In male-female
relationships, as the balance between dominance/submission behavior and
cooperative behavior shifts toward the latter side, the catalog of ideal personality traits optimal for the two sexes will be rewritten. Women will
continue to be different from men, but "hysterical/histrionic" personality
may end up of interest more to historians than to psychiatrists.

CLINICAL ILLUSTRATIONS

In line with the remarks from the preceding section, it is perhaps of some
significance that examples of "classical" hysteric character (or "histrionic
personality") are no longer so common among patients in private practice,
whether male or female, as was apparently the case in Freud's day. There
may still be some women like Freud's "Anna O."; in my own practice I
have seen only one. I have not treated many patients who would meet DSM
criteria for HPD: two males and approximately a dozen females. Perhaps
the majority of women treated by the analytic "pioneers" had hysteric
"character neuroses." What I see much more often now are women with a
mixture of traits—self-defeating (masochistic), dependent, histrionic, com-

pulsive—whose early experience seemingly programmed them to fall in love with men who are afraid of commitment. Often, the array of traits do not add up to a personality "disorder" of any sort; instead, I am confronted with a rather normal personality "driven" down blind alleys (in the area of intimate relationships) by the maladaptive "program." Sometimes, the patient has strong fears of commitment: choosing a commitment-shy partner serves as a camouflage for the patient's own reluctance. I see this pattern as often in men as in women, leaving me with the impression that this form of "masochism" does not have much of a gender tag attached to it.

The following vignettes concern patients who do meet criteria for HPD and who functioned at different levels: one neurotic, one borderline, and one psychotic, as these levels are defined by Kernberg (1967).

Histrionic Personality Disorder at a Neurotic Level in a Woman with Jealousy

Helen sought therapy because of uncontrollable jealous rages during the course of a romantic relationship. She was 29, a ballet dancer with a considerable reputation and an excellent income. Her boyfriend was a photographer of 43 with a spotty work record. He got by mostly by his good looks and bon vivant air, mooching off well-to-do women. Like the charming sociopath in Brian Friel's "Dancing at Lughnasa" (1991), he was always promising to marry his "true love" when his ship came in . . . only his ship never came in.

Helen had grown up in a small town in Illinois. Her father worked as a middle executive in the phone company. Her mother was a woman with great affection and "sparkle." When Helen was in high school, she was elected "beauty queen" in her hometown contest.

Family life had been harmonious for her and her younger brother until the year before she entered high school, when her father began to drink to excess and stay out late. He had begun an affair, which he maintained clandestinely for many years, until the death of her mother when Helen was 24—at which time he married the other woman.

Helen first became jealous when dating in high school, which even at the time seemed paradoxical to her, in view of her popularity. Having taken ballet lessons since age five, she succeeded to the point of winning a scholarship to a prestigious New York ballet school. In the parent company, she rose from chorus to soloist to "prima" by age 25. Once, at age 23, during a visit to her home, she was attacked at gunpoint and raped. The man was caught and imprisoned. Following this incident, her relationships with men (most of whom were much older and much less successful than she) were punctuated by outbursts of jealous rage, which could be triggered by the man's glancing at a waitress, discussing an old girlfriend, or being inattentive. Her current boyfriend, Charles, was a truly masochistic choice, since he really did leer at other women and try at times to arrange covert meetings when Helen would be away on a tour. Charles also seemed to go out of his way to frustrate her craving for compliments about her looks, telling her she "should be above that sort of thing."

In personality Helen was usually cheerful, but could break into tears easily if recounting some unpleasantness with Charles. She was intense, remarkably candid, spoke with great vividness, and launched immediately into the heart of things, showing as much instant trust of me as she characteristically showed mistrust of the men she had been with. Her first dream:

> Charles and I try to have sex, but we couldn't because it seemed we weren't alone. I ask him to at least rub me, but instead he stuffs mashed potato up me.

Her associations centered around the "intruders," who were perhaps her parents; the rapist also came to mind, since he "stuffed something up there that didn't belong there." As for the mashed potatoes: that was her mother's favorite dish—something very "fattening." That led her to thoughts about wanting a child, being pregnant, which would nevertheless interfere greatly with her career and also force her to confront a hidden fear: if she had a child, her husband would desert her emotionally, as happened in her own family.

Helen's jealousy seemed always alien and out of character to her. There were several layers one could detect. She was fond of her father, yet he was an untrustworthy man who betrayed her mother. Her distrust of men's steadfastness was thus easily understandable. The rape added a traumatic dimension to the problem, causing nightmares and flashbacks from time to time. She could begin to see that she contributed to her difficulty by picking a man like Charles, whose ogling would incite jealousy in any woman. At first she claimed she didn't mind supporting him, but after a while this eroded her respect for him. I suggested that her lack of self-confidence led her to select men whose dependence on her she could purchase, since they were poor and she was well-off. This gave her "assurances" she wouldn't be abandoned (as her mother had been, psychologically), though the arrangement created more problems than it solved. Her ambivalence toward Charles emerged in a "slip" she made in responding to my asking her what attracted her to a man who treated her so shabbily: "Well, but he's a gorgeous skunk . . . I mean, hunk of a man."

Later, another facet of her jealousy became apparent: a deep attachment to her mother, intensified after the latter's death, had become "erotized."

She found it disturbing to acknowledge that she wanted to be sexually close with a woman; this wish could remain hidden within her jealousy. She hated Charles because he paid attention to other women. On the surface this meant to her only that she wanted Charles, and therefore resented his interest in another woman. Underneath this, however, *she* wanted that other woman (= mother), and hated Charles for getting that woman away from her. There was a dream to this effect:

> I cheated on Charles with a certain guy. He was in love with me. Charles finds out about it. The guy turned into a woman.

And a few days after, another:

> A big burly teddy-bear of a guy falls in love with me and hugs me. I tell Charles about it backstage. The man shows up—only now he's changed into a fat ugly woman with big breasts. Then another woman appears, who's also my lover: she's very pretty, and Charles says, "she's adorable." I get jealous at him for that.

As these conflictual feelings toward mother were beginning to surface, Helen got an offer with a European company, and within several weeks moved abroad, ending her therapy after eight months. She had grown more self-confident about the prospect of giving up Charles and looking for a more suitable partner—someone who would not openly stoke her jealous tendencies. This would leave still unresolved her hidden, and unacceptable, longings for closeness with a (maternal) woman, which constituted a deeper source of her jealous feelings. She agreed to continue in treatment with a colleague I recommended to her, in the country where she was to resettle. As for her "hysteric" traits, she was less in need of reassurance about her skills or her appearance; her emotionality and vivid speech served her well in her professional life—they were "ego-syntonic"—and did not change.

Histrionic Personality Disorder at a Borderline Level

Harriet was 22 when she began therapy. She came not of her own accord so much as at the prompting of her mother, who became distraught upon learning that her daughter was living with a man of 60. Harriet was the product of her mother's first marriage at age 17; her current husband—her fifth—was a physician. Though she liked her latest stepfather better than the other three, Harriet quit college and ran away to the east coast a few months before I first saw her. She detested her mother, considering her a "whore" for running through so many men in such a short time. The mother considered Harriet a "whore" for having affairs with older men. Though Harriet did not contact her home after running away, her mother hired private detectives, from whom she learned not only the address but also of the affair with the "retired millionaire from England" (if indeed that is what he was).

When her mother finally tracked her down, Harriet made a suicide gesture with an overdose of aspirin and Valium, necessitating a brief stay in an emergency room.

At the initial consultation, Harriet came seductively attired in a cocktail dress and in what seemed like several kilograms of gold bracelets, pins, rings and chains—presents from her English "beau." She exhibited all eight of the HPD criteria, but little in the way of symptoms—except a dread that her mother would somehow interfere with her plans to work as a model and to marry her newest (oldest?) beau. The subject of her mother made her enraged and tearful, especially as she dwelt on her lifelong feelings of having been emotionally abandoned: "It's just like her to barge in on my life when I don't want her; when I did want her, she was never there for me." Her biological father she had never known: he had made no attempt to see her (Harriet was one when this divorce took place), and she was as angry at him as at her mother. Curiously, the only person who did show genuine concern about her was her aging beau—who was actually a retired millionaire, divorced with children older than Harriet, and eager to be of help in any way he could.

Harriet had little motivation for treatment. She felt she was "fine" as long as her mother left her alone, but if she did have to see a psychiatrist, she preferred to work with a woman. I learned from her English friend that she was extremely unpredictable in her moods, tempestuous, changing her mind from one moment to the next about where to go, what to do, and given to crying spells over things she refused to discuss. After a few months, she became erratic about her appointments. When she missed two in a row, I tried to get in touch with her. I spoke with her friend, who told me that she had run away from him a few days before and was apparently living with a girlfriend. They had not argued; she had simply packed (the jewelry included) and disappeared.

Histrionic Personality Disorder at the
Psychotic Level: "Hysterical Psychosis"

Hilary was 31 when she was referred to me for continuing treatment of her eating disorder. She had been in residential care for a year at age 24, following a suicide attempt. She was anorectic on admission, but regained and retained normal weight until a second bout of anorexia a year before I began working with her.

This, as it turned out, was only one of a whole variety of crippling symptoms. At the time of her menarche, for example, she developed a severe "germ phobia." Her obsessive-compulsive disorder had by now reached such proportions that she washed her hands 50 or more times a day, took four showers a day, changed clothes and bedsheets three or four times a day, pretreated all fruit with alcohol, then eating the fruit only with rubber gloves. Though fond of dancing and of men's attentions, she dated rarely and engaged in no sexual activity.

Hilary met all eight criteria for HPD, carrying many of these to "psychotic" extremes. Ordinarily compliant and sweet, she could become tantrumy and enraged, as though inhabited suddenly by a different person, if someone thwarted her will. Oversentimental to the extreme, she showed a maudlin oversensitivity to scenes in movies, pictures in magazines, or footage on the TV that "touched some nerve." Once, on a date, she was at a movie about a Nazi higher-up from her original home-city of Lyons, France. In response to the horror scenes, she began hallucinating and had to be escorted home.

Morbidly fearful of "fatness," Hilary felt that, if she breathed the same air as that of a fat woman walking past her in the street, she too would "weigh 200 lbs. the next day." From her dreams it was clear that she made a chain of associations: fatness, pregnancy, sex, defilement, sinfulness. Anything freighted with such symbolism became similarly "defiled." If a magazine article touched on death, AIDS, blood, murder, etc., she had to throw it away. If there was a book visible in my office that had a black cover, she implored me to remove it from view, since it carried the "color of death." Noticing a book on depression or suicide would move her to tears, as would any newspaper article she might come across dealing with some tragedy or injustice. Since the bulk of newspapers consists of such accounts, she seldom permitted herself to read them. Though friendly and generous by nature, she eschewed the company of others, to the point of leading a cloistered existence—partly to reduce exposure to the many occurrences in daily life that would have elicited in her uncontrollable crying or other overwhelming emotions.

THERAPEUTIC APPROACHES

As with maladaptive personality-traits of all types, hysteric traits are generally dealt with by a therapeutic approach that stresses the *opposite* of the patient's natural tendency. Hysteric patients start out with the assumption of not being up to various tasks of life. In this they resemble depressive patients. But, as Beck and Freeman (1990) mention, hysterics have some confidence that by playing up to others via appealingness, attractiveness, etc., they can get them to come to the rescue, to make up for the hysteric's deficits. The depressive elicits help through tears, while the hysteric relies on charm.

While in therapy, the hysteric will attempt to win favors from the therapist, in order to end up feeling "special" or "loved." If the therapist yields to these blandishments, the patients will feel (temporarily at least) content—but will make no progress. If the therapist resists, the patient may feel sad, rejected and angry. Optimally, therapists need to navigate around both dangers—by helping hysteric patients to recognize these mechanisms and to explore their origins. These would be the initial steps in ultimately selecting and developing more adaptive, specifically more self-reliant, coping techniques (cf. Horowitz et al., 1984).

The cognitive style of hysteric patients, as alluded to in the DSM definition, is impressionistic, relying on colorful language and hyperbole. There is a tendency to exaggerate, so that events that are a bit good or a bit bad are experienced, and described, as "super" or "horrible." Minor illnesses are fatal tragedies (till proven otherwise); finding a dime in the street makes for a "lucky day." Therapists confronted with exaggerations of this sort will instinctively make comments that steer the patient in the opposite direction: "How is it every pimple and sore becomes 'cancer' in your mind?" or "But there's really not much magic in a dime," etc.

In a similar way, one tries to foster "compulsive" behavior, as a replacement for the hysteric's lack of methodicalness. This may even take the form of educative suggestions—about buying a phone-number book rather than relying upon bits of paper strewn all over the house, about getting a pocket calculator to aid in balancing the checkbook, about carrying a watch to enhance punctuality, etc.

The patients in the vignettes differed in their habits: Helen was methodical and organized in her dancing, but poorly organized in the social sphere and quite haphazard about appointment times. She handled leisure time poorly, lacking hobbies or interests in any other activities besides dancing. During weekends off she tended to abuse alcohol, which then fueled the jealous outbursts (these never occurred except under the influence of alcohol: the major curative intervention was to get her to reduce or abolish drinking). In contrast to truly paranoid patients, Helen's jealousy was an isolated and ego-alien phenomenon, in an otherwise very trusting personality. Harriet was not organized in any sphere. Because she was not motivated for treatment, there was no opportunity to encourage her to overcome her chaotic patterns. Hilary had adequate self-discipline in completing coursework at school, unless she was in "crisis." Apart from that, she behaved like a caricature of the hysteric, in relying almost totally on the emotional resources of others.

Readers interested in guidelines for short-term, analytically informed psychotherapy of hysteric/histrionic patients will find much that is useful in the book by Horowitz, Marmar et al. (1984). Their method combines elements of expressive and supportive techniques. Guidelines for the cognitive therapy of this personality type are provided in Beck and Freeman (1990).

Cluster C

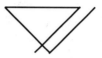

Anxious Disorders

15

Dependent, Obsessive-Compulsive, Avoidant, and Passive-Aggressive Personality Disorders

THE LAST GROUPING WITHIN DSM, cluster C, includes four personality types, whose common property is the tendency to experience anxiety and to show outward signs of fear. The four types—dependent, obsessive-compulsive, avoidant and passive-aggressive—share in another feature: inhibition in the assertion of socially acceptable impulses. Customarily, these include inhibitions in the sexual sphere, but also a fearful reluctance to express irritation or anger, even when the interpersonal circumstances (an unfair coworker, an unreasonably demanding family member) would justify such emotion. This inhibitedness is encountered commonly in histrionic personality disorder (currently classified within the "dramatic" cluster), the as yet unofficial "self-defeating" personality disorder, and in dysthymic persons, who, though presently classified in Axis I, could usually be said to show a "depressive" personality disorder (Phillips, Gunderson et al., 1990). I discuss the self-defeating personality under the heading of pain-dependent personality disorders, in the next chapter.

These inhibited personality types are precisely the ones which Freud and the psychoanalytic pioneers first encountered and sought to treat. Psychoanalysis and the related psychotherapies have their greatest efficacy in this domain: in the alleviation of inappropriate inhibition (Stone, 1990c). Whereas we are taught to regard *personality* attributes as ego-*syntonic*, inhibition

339

inevitably carries with it a measure of suffering—therefore, of ego-*dystoni-city*. It is this suffering that motivates the patient to seek help and, having done so, to endure the discomforts that accompany the steps toward recovery: self-revelation and the gradual entry into the territory of fear.

With the exception of the passive-aggressive types, inhibited patients typically *internalize* blame for the frustrations in their life, even in situations where observers (including the therapist) would hold the patient blameless. This quality, too, facilitates treatment, in the sense that the patient shows a willingness to accept some responsibility for contributing to the unhappiness in his personal life. This puts therapist and patient on the same "wavelength" and fosters the cooperative dialogue we now refer to as the "therapeutic alliance." As mentioned earlier, those who blame others (externalizers; viz., antisocial, paranoid and sadistic patients) pose far greater challenges to the therapeutic process; their prognosis is correspondingly more guarded.

In the sections that follow the nature and treatment of the four cluster C disorders are discussed in detail.

Dependent Personality

Diagnosis and Etiology

The traits that most readily call to clinicians' attention the likelihood of their dealing with a *dependent* personality are submissiveness, passivity, timidity, and clinginess. The psychodynamic wellspring from which these traits develop in early life is fear of being abandoned. This fear does not always originate from the same source: in some persons death of a parent during one's childhood seems the most important causative agent, but in others repeated experiences of neglect or outright rejection by caretakers is the primary noxious influence. The psychoanalytic pioneers were drawn to the notion of dependency as reflecting "oral" traits, owing to the close connection between the infant's need for sustenance from its mother and our concept of "dependency" (cf. Fenichel, 1954/1989). Further comments on the nature of dependency and the innate repertoire of the human infant's attachment behavior are to be found in Bowlby (1969).

At least three of the defining items in DSM-III-R may be viewed as reparative tactics designed to maintain a hold on the important other(s) in one's life: pressuring others for reassurance, mindlessly agreeing with others lest disagreement lead to rejection, and doing favors and tasks one would rather not do simply to ingratiate oneself with these "vital" others. These are true "dependency" attributes (Livesley, Schroeder, & Jackson, 1990).

The remaining six items may be seen more as characterological symptoms of the failure of these defensive maneuvers. Being inordinately hurt by criticism or mild disapproval, for example, represents an adaptive failure. The dependent person may try, at the same time, to turn such failure into a victory, as when breaking into tears at some slight criticism elicits volumes of reassurance and perhaps a hug from a lover or spouse one was afraid of "losing." Letting others make all the decisions is both a failure and a defense: here the defensive aspect takes the form of overcompliance (submissiveness). Submission reduces the probability of offending the other person, hence of "insuring" loyalty or steadfastness. Clinginess—never letting the other out of one's sight—is one of the most common manifestations of the dependent personality, and is a sign of "pathological attachment." This tendency often backfires, in the sense that it alienates most people and drives away the very person(s) to whom one clings the most tightly. In less disablingly dependent persons, one can see the good effects of likeableness: the various traits of the supertrait agreeableness ("+A") are often found in abundance in dependent persons—as a way of ensuring the enduring affection and support of the vitally-needed other person(s) (cf. Chapter 6).

Dependent personality will often be found in conjunction with the features of avoidant personality (Trull et al., 1987) or with the characterological attributes of depressive persons (viz., low self-esteem, pessimism, constant worrying). In the older classification of borderline conditions (Grinker, Werble, & Drye, 1968), the "healthiest" type of borderline was the "anaclitic depressed type": the patient who was simultaneously depressed and clingy. Many patients with borderline personality disorder are also markedly dependent. At the extremes of dependent personality one may encounter erotomania (including erotomanic preoccupation with the therapist).

Though patients with dependent personality disorder have a higher than expected proportion of first-degree relatives with dependent and other anxious cluster personality disorders (J. Reich, 1989), especially avoidant personality disorder, much of the psychopathology stems from "cultural transmission" via a similarly dependent parent—who inculcates in the future patient a propensity to fearfulness and clinging.

Treatment

The *treatment* of dependent personality, unless the disorder is found in conjunction with distinctive symptoms (belonging, e.g., to Axis I disorders) amenable to various pharmacological or other biological measures, relies upon verbal therapies. Currently, these might include any of the following: (a) psychoanalysis, (b) psychoanalytically oriented psychotherapy, (c) supportive therapy, (d) cognitive therapy, (e) behavioral therapy, or (f) group therapy. Apart from "classical" psychoanalysis, the other forms of psycho-therapy will often need to be combined flexibly and in different ways during the course of treatment. How many modalities are used depends on the breadth of training of the therapist, as well as on the nature and severity of the problems presented by the patient. The best approach is pragmatic, not parochial.

The *length of therapy* likewise cannot be determined on theoretic or doctrinal grounds, but only on the basis of the patient's motivation, the intensity and urgency of the problems, and the realistic goals of the patient. A dependent patient who, for example, is young, single, highly motivated, and possessed of some inner resources (hobbies, skills, etc.) may wish to overcome the pathological dependency in a thorough way, with the goals of living autonomously, relying less on parents, becoming self-reliant at work, and forming a sexual partnership. These goals might be realized in an intensive therapy (two or more visits per week) spanning two to five years, or even longer. With a more seriously handicapped patient, one might use the same forms of psychotherapy, but with the more modest goals of substituting dependency upon the original family with a less severe dependency upon a marital partner — bypassing what might be the unrealiz-able ambition of "complete" autonomy.

Dependent patients are usually exquisitely sensitive to being alone; worse yet, to being jilted. Many will have devoted years to "perfecting" the tech-niques of clinging to others — to the neglect of outside interests, casual read-ing, the cultivation of friends, or any other potentially sustaining activities. To be alone on an evening or a weekend, for such a patient, may lead to intense anxiety or even to panic. In this situation, supportive interventions are of critical importance.

Therapists must encourage dependent patients of this sort to expand upon whatever activities (if any) they may have found enjoyable and divert-ing in the past or (and what is substantially more difficult) to develop such interests for the first time. Joining church groups, political organizations, lecture series, and the like, may go a long way toward conquering the fear of being alone, while also helping to expand the patient's social network. In the meantime, psychotherapy (of whichever mode is most congenial with the therapist) can assist in helping the patient overcome fears connect-ed with meeting new people at social gatherings, expressing opinions in public, etc.

Group therapy may be useful in helping such patients see that other people can continue to like and accept them even if they should give vent to an opinion discordant with views of the others (a maturational step depen-dent persons experience as extremely risky). Patients who are particularly clingy will need to be taught (via a supportive or cognitive intervention) about the terrible "catch-22" inherent in this tendency, namely, that excessive demands upon the attentions of others will (almost invariably) drive away—and provoke abandonment by—the very persons to whom they have so tenaciously clung. The lesson (that if someone loves you, he will stay if you give him breathing space, but flee if you confine him), though absolutely crucial to the amelioration of dependent personality disorder, goes contrary to a lifetime of thought on the part of the patient.

The therapist's task here will be no brief skirmish. Inevitably, the therapist will be caught up in the clinginess (demands for extra time, nighttime calls, symptom outbreaks before vacations, etc.). As Freeman and Gunderson (1989) mention, a certain measure of dependence upon the therapist is to be expected at the outset, and can be a useful quality: a good working alliance will tend to develop, which the therapist can eventually utilize in moving the patient toward greater autonomy. Excessive dependence, of course, will elicit countertransference annoyance, riddance-wishes, and the like, all of which must be controlled and dealt with reflectively and compassionately—so that the resulting emotional material can be used rewardingly for the patient's benefit. Otherwise, such feelings may lead to a redramatization of the patient's original plight (of getting rejected), intensifying the dependency and clinginess.

When under the stress of personal loss or rejection, patients with dependent personality disorder often become anxious in a way that will warrant the employment of the milder anxiolytic drugs, such as the benzodiazepines. These medications reduce the "crisis" atmosphere and help restore the patient's equilibrium, permitting the strengthening effects of therapy to solidify. A proportion of patients with dependent personality disorder also show marked depressive traits or the picture of dysthymia; they may respond favorably to tricyclic antidepressants (Kocsis et al., 1988).

Clinical Examples

Darlene, a 19-year-old college sophomore, was the only child of a suburban family in comfortable circumstances. She had grown increasingly anxious just before final exams of the fall semester. She felt overwhelmingly lonesome, tearful, and frightened, and without quite knowing *what* she was afraid of, decided she had best take "incompletes" and return home. Her parents arranged for me to see her in consultation. The college she had chosen was several hundred miles from where she grew up, and represented her first time away from her parents.

In personality Darlene was compliant, amiable, unselfconfident about her scholastic abilities despite being an "A" student, and though relaxed during her sessions, quite anxious at the prospect of resuming her studies. She was convinced she couldn't master the various courses. Apart from the ease with which she could visit friends or travel the few miles to my office, she behaved like an agoraphobic patient. She had always been markedly dependent on her mother, whom she still used as her confidante.

In speaking about her parents she related incidents in which the dependency seemed a two-way street. As a young girl, she had been reluctant to go to camp, and her parents let her remain home during the summers. The few times her parents had taken vacation trips Darlene had always accompanied them. I had the impression they were no more inclined to part with her than she was to absent herself from them.

After three months of twice-weekly therapy, I decided to meet with all three for one of the sessions, reserving the other for individual work. It developed that her parents' marriage had grown cooler, and this had become much more apparent when Darlene left for college. Each parent could talk freely to Darlene, but not to the other. As long as Darlene was home, her mother and father found enough satisfaction in their relationship with her so as not to mind the communicational barriers that had arisen between them. When Darlene was away, her parents either quarreled or didn't talk at all.

Darlene's dependency and anxiety attack at school seemed like manifestations of some "ESP" that told her she was needed at home. Having a breakdown at college gave her an acceptable excuse to return home, without her parents' having to admit they desperately wanted her back home. When these issues were brought to the surface, the parents were able to acknowledge that they had been overly dependent on their daughter.

Fortunately, they were mature enough to realize that she had a right to get on with her life and that she could not be expected to serve as the "solution" to their problem. The parents worked toward the improvement of their own situation, and Darlene now aware that they were not going to "collapse" if she left them, was able to return to college, no longer so dependent upon either parent. By the time she graduated, she had become engaged and was now quite self-sufficient.

＊ ＊ ＊ ＊ ＊

Deborah was 26 when she began twice-weekly therapy for dysthymic symptoms that followed the breakup of a romantic relationship. Both her brother and her father had bipolar illness. Her father was a highly successful businessman, but her brother had a violent temper, which was poorly controlled by medication, and had never worked.

When Deborah was four, her father had the one breakdown necessitating hospitalization, and she was sent for eight months to live with an aunt. Since that time she had been clingingly dependent upon her mother and was always anxious when starting something new: elementary school, camp, college, her first job, etc. Her brother tyrannized the family and diverted much of her parents' attention away from her, since she was the better-functioning one.

Her most noticeable quality during her sessions was her tendency to break out into tears almost constantly, easily going through a whole Kleenex box in the course of an hour. Curiously, she was lachrymose without being maudlin. That is, there was no hysteric oversentimentality; rather, one sensed a deep and inexpressible sadness—over her lonely childhood, her loneliness after her boyfriend left her, and her lonely job: she was a book editor, and rarely came into contact with the other employees at her company.

Always deferential and considerate, she almost never called me after hours—yet she spoke to me of calling her former boyfriend numerous times throughout the day. She did so ostensibly to "make sure he was all right" or "to see if he arrived on time at work," but really to allay her own dependency worries: she needed to hear his voice, to reassure herself he still loved her, etc. He found her neediness intolerable, wounded her with epithets like "crybaby" or "whine-o" to the point where, though she "couldn't live without him," she couldn't bear his insults any longer either.

Immediately after they broke up, she became so depressed that she could barely work. I started her on a course of imipramine, 125 mgm/day, and for a few weeks met with her more frequently until the crisis had passed. Altogether her treatment lasted two and a half years, by the end of which time Deborah had become more self-reliant, less tearful, and no longer clinically depressed. She met another man, toward whom she was able to behave in a much less clingy manner. They married shortly after she left treatment. We keep in touch through Christmas cards, which nowadays contain snapshots of their two children.

OBSESSIVE-COMPULSIVE PERSONALITY DISORDER

History, Etiology, Diagnosis

Of the characterological abnormalities that preoccupied the "pioneer" generation of psychoanalysts, obsessive-compulsive traits received attention second only to the hysteric—as judged by the volume of literature devoted to these topics. Hysteric and obsessive-compulsive traits are both very common, partly because they represent extremes of mental-processing modes linked biologically to gender (Stone, 1980b). Subtle structural differences in male vs. female brains predispose to advantages in verbal, sequential, digital tasks in men; analogic, synthetic, intuitive tasks (including the grasp of emotional nuances) in women (Robinson et al., 1983). These differences correlate with our descriptions of obsessive vs. hysteric traits. These traits may be seen as exaggerations of normal gender-linked variations in CNS function, exaggerated still further, in all likelihood, by cultural influences and rearing patterns. A possible link between obsessive-compulsive ideation and panic attack, as a reflection of left frontotemporal lobe dysfunction, has been suggested by Yeudall et al. (1983).

The traits of obsessive-compulsive personality disorder (OCPD), as enumerated in DSM-III-R, reflect abnormalities in all three "compartments" of mental life: behavior, thought, and mood. "Compulsive" refers to the behavioral aspects: preoccupation with lists, rules, schedules, etc.; indecisiveness; hoarding; overemphasis on work to the exclusion of pleasurable activities; stinginess with money or time (unless there is "something in it" for oneself). The cognitive component usually takes the form of overconscientiousness, moral rigidity, or else of repetitive worries and self-reproaches that one cannot obliterate from one's mind. The abnormality of mood associated with OCPD is in the characteristic restriction in the expression of emotion (the situation opposite, in effect, to that of the histrionic person).

The obsessive worries are often dystonic, just as the preoccupation with "doing the right thing" can pass over into truly symptomatic ritualistic compulsive behavior (making sure the door is locked, the stove turned off, etc.). Some patients with OCPD, in other words, also show the Axis I "obsessive-compulsive disorder" (OCD). Though each disorder figures in the differential diagnosis of the other, one must keep in mind that OCD patients may show any of a number of personality disorders (viz., avoidant, histrionic, dependent) besides OCPD (Mavissakalian, Hamann, & Jones, 1990). When both OCPD and OCD are present, the clinical picture usually consists of (a) rumination and indecisiveness, (b) urges to carry out unacceptable acts, with concomitant guilt and anxiety, and (c) superstition- and magic-tinged rituals (Guidano & Liotti, 1983).

Regarding the sex ratio in OCPD, it is usual to find a male excess in the range of 6 : 4. Men and women tend to have similar dynamics and personality traits, but gender gives rise to different caricature-types within the culture: women with OCPD often appearing as fussbudget housewives for whom every ashtray and curio must be in exactly the same place, and who beg off from sex because the laundry isn't yet finished; men appearing as "uptight" professionals who check their watch every five minutes to make sure they're "on schedule," and who feel unnerved by the unstructured time of holidays and weekends, to which they bring no spontaneity. The latter situation was aptly called the "Sunday neurosis" by Ferenczi (1919).

As can be seen, many of the traits upon which the contemporary diagnosis of OCPD rests reflect the original notions of Freud (1908), who felt obsessionality derived from abnormalities in the "anal" stage of development and showed itself via the triad of "orderliness, obstinacy, and parsimony." From a dynamic standpoint, OCPD patients are overwhelmed with concern about loss of control (being too messy, or sexy, or naughty, etc.). Hence, their overcontrollingness, their urge to dominate others rather than submit, and their striving for "machine-like" *perfection* and for the stifling of the "messiness" of emotional life. Loss of control also of *angry* feelings looms as a major issue in most patients with OCPD. Their fear of retaliation is often accompanied by "magical thinking," where they fear that if they were to reveal (say, to a therapist) an angry thought about a parent, the parent, though living miles away, would somehow "know" what they had said, and would exact punishment.

As for the perfectionistic tendency, Guidano and Liotti (1983) point to the compulsive person's need to present an *ideal* self to the world (beginning with his parents), as contrasted with his *actual* self*. This leads to an obsession about foreseeing all dangers and possible slip-ups. The compulsive person thus lives in the *future*, whereas the "dramatic cluster" persons live mostly in the *present*. The compulsive person is concerned with *details* rather than the whole picture, thinks "digitally," makes black-and-white distinctions, and is often weighed down with overscrupulosity (exaggerated ethical concerns), his general approach to life being reminiscent of the lawyer as opposed to the artist. The ritualistic behavior may also be understood as having a propitiatory quality—as though the anger of the parent (or other authority figure) over one's "badness" can be warded off by double-checking that one's tie is straight, that one hasn't stepped on any cracks in the sidewalk, etc.

Other important *defensive* maneuvers encountered in OCPD are intellectualization, rationalization, and reaction-formation (A. Freud, 1936). All these represent attempts to deal with fears and other disturbing emotions via *logic*. As a result, in OCPD speech becomes arid, peppered with irrelevant detail, such that one never quite gets to what should have been the emotional "point" of any discussion. Obsessive-compulsive patients talk *around* the central issues, not directly about them (Horowitz, Marmar et al., 1984).

---

*This new footnote is a reflection of a similar view expressed earlier by Karen Horney (1939).

Since reason and logic are part of the normal mechanisms of survival, it is a matter of clinical judgment as to when these mechanisms have "spun out of control" enough to warrant a diagnosis of OCPD. Reliance on these mechanisms will differ from one culture to another, so one must also take into consideration the patient's cultural background. In general, it may be said that, whereas the histrionic "style" represents exaggerations having to do with the ability to *love*, the *compulsive* style concerns the domain of *work*, and emphasizes the issue of *respect*.

From the standpoint of etiology, data suggest a significant measure of heritability in OCPD. The genetic contribution to the emergence of the personality traits of "neuroticism" (roughly similar to the set of anxious-cluster disorders) has been assessed at the level of 50% (Andrews, Stewart et al., 1990), but what "breeds true" is not so much the whole disorder as certain specific traits. The concordance rate for compulsive personality in MZ twins is greater than that of DZ twins (Pauls et al., 1991), yet in a family study of OCPD, despite the higher incidence of mental illness in the close relatives of the patients (as compared with those of the controls), the illnesses were more apt to be either depressive or other types of cluster C disorders, rather than OCPD itself (McKeon & Murray, 1987).

OCPD may thus get its impetus from a genetic factor (predisposing, perhaps, to a predilection for structure, viz., lining objects up in neat rows), but is licked into final shape by rearing patterns that overemphasize conformity, neatness, automatic obedience to authority, and punitiveness. At the extremes, obsessive-compulsive persons may show themselves as *tormented* souls, struggling between what they know they must do and what they feel like doing: the "ideal" vs. the "actual" self. Parental punitiveness or abusiveness can easily lead to retaliatory hatred and revenge-seeking— which the compulsive person must then strenuously suppress, becoming, in effect, a Jekyll & Hyde manqué.

Though psychological test findings show characteristic abnormalities in OCPD (spikes in the "2-7-8" scales of the MMPI [Greene, 1980]; overattention to fine details on the Rorschach test), the diagnosis can usually be made readily enough simply on the basis of the clinical presentation.

Treatment

The treatment of OCPD tends at best to be time-consuming and tedious, owing to the patient's adroitness at evading the significant emotional issues. The therapist is apt to hear endless monologues of self-justification, of lofty goals and ambitions, of "reasons" why the patient's family members and intimates need to be rigidly controlled ("the wife'd buy out the dress shop if I let her have a credit card"), browbeaten ("my daughter'd go to bed with any guy that'd look at her, unless I got a private investigator to check out his family"), or neglected ("work comes first: I don't have time for all this romantic stuff when there's a job to be done"). The loneliness that underlies possessiveness or the fear (of love's "chaoticness") that pushes the compulsive person to frenzies of unnecessary work or trivial pursuits remains buried underneath the patient's verbiage and diversionary concerns.

OCPD is often found in conjunction with passive-aggressive PD, paranoid or avoidant PDs, or at least with some of their traits. The prognosis, as well as the optimal therapeutic strategy, will depend on these factors. When OCPD is characterized mainly by inhibition of enjoyment—with little in the way of meanness, pettiness, hostility, or controllingness—the response to treatment will be better (though not necessarily briefer) than when those qualities dominate the clinical picture.

Different treatment approaches for dealing with obsessive-compulsive patients have been outlined by a number of authors: the psychoanalytic, by Salzman (1973); the cognitive-behavioral, by Beck and Freeman (1990) and Guidano and Liotti (1983). Whichever form of psychotherapy is used, therapists working with compulsive patients must develop ways to parry the thrust of the patient's indecisiveness, ruminative thinking, and suppression of emotion.

When doing short-term therapy (Davanloo, 1986) or cognitive therapy, the therapist will have to establish priorities as to which problems deserve the most urgent attention (lest the patient set up endless "decoy" problems to throw the therapist off the scent). Problem-solving methods will be useful. As an antidote to perfectionism, it is useful to point out that (1) the fastest way to conquer certain problems is to acquire skills gradually and to be willing to make mistakes without undue embarrassment, whereas (2) the patient's hope to succeed even quicker by being "perfect" the first time around is illusory.

When time is not a pressing consideration, a psychoanalytically oriented approach may be especially useful: the use of dreams and free association are helpful in piercing the compulsive patient's intellectual armor and in getting through to the painful feelings underneath. I recall in this connection a lonely, unemotional man with obsessive-compulsive personality I once treated: shortly before I was to take a month's vacation, he denied having any reaction to the separation and indeed wished me a pleasant holiday. But he reported a dream in which he found himself all alone on an old-fashioned ship that had become unmoored from the pier and was floating aimlessly out at sea. From his associations to the dream he could grasp that behind his blasé and self-confident façade were feelings of a very different kind. As with many compulsive patients, he often brought lists of topics to discuss, which he had written out beforehand. It is appropriate to discourage, in a compassionate way, this kind of overcontrol, since it robs the sessions of the very spontaneity that the compulsive patient—more than other types—needs to develop.

OCPD patients, particularly those with the passive-aggressive trait of procrastination, often evoke countertransference irritation, boredom, and fatigue. These problems, and the stalemated treatment that might result, can usually be circumvented by forthrightness and honesty—in letting the patient know that, "Yes, you have gotten me a bit tired or cranky with all this talk about unimportant things: so perhaps you're doing this to avoid something uncomfortable. Let's see if we can't discover what that may be."

Despite the obstacles that confront the therapist who works with OCPD patients, their dogged persistence and task-orientedness are positive traits, which often help create a good therapeutic alliance and lead eventually to a favorable outcome. In the long-term follow-up of borderline patients, for example, those whose next most prominent personality traits were obsessive-compulsive outperformed those with all other accompanying personality features (Stone, 1990).

Clinical Examples

Otto, a college student of 19, urgently sought help because of panicky states, accompanied by what he called "the dream feeling," whenever he was away from home. The dream feeling was largely one of depersonalization. These anxiety symptoms could be alleviated by returning home. Treatment lasted only a few months, owing to his having to resume classes in a different city. He experienced some relief with benzodiazepines.

Several years later, Otto took up his treatment where it had left off. By now he had undergone a divorce after a ruinous marriage: his wife was frigid, but also paranoid and hypercritical, and he had primary impotence.

The only child of war-refugees, Otto was raised by a sympathetic but seldom available father, and a mother whose meanness could scarcely be matched except by the witches of fairy tales. There is something about a parent's repudiation of a child's gift that hugs the very edge of cruelty. Once, when he was 11, he had saved up money from his newspaper route to buy a comb and brush set for his mother's birthday present. Upon opening it, she shouted at him: "What kind of a shit-present is this?!" and tossed it in the basket.

One might wonder how he developed agoraphobic symptoms in a home that offered so little soothing, but this he did. Even more remarkable, he was always good-natured and cheerful. His compulsivity was extreme, but only in the area of orderliness and "isolation of affect." He was generous to a fault, and not at all stubborn.

He had risen by now (at 27) to a middle executive position in a large company, and had many friends among his coworkers. But he was terrified of sexuality and took to lying to his buddies about sexual conquests that never took place. He was quite remorseful about the white lies, which offended his high sense of ethics, but he could not bring himself to alter the pattern. It was difficult to get behind the armor of his intellectualization and impossible altogether to get him in touch with the long-buried anger at his mother's humiliating remarks. He seemed afraid she could hear through the walls if he said anything negative about her.

His dreams told a different story. In one, for example, he was climbing up a cliff, and just got his hands over the edge, when his mother crushed his fingers with her shoe, and he fell off. He could see the castration theme, apparent even in the manifest content, yet spoke of it with no emotion: "Gee, Doc, I guess I must feel my mother'd step on my efforts to succeed at anything, or to have sex . . . but it all seems so unreal to me."

By the time Otto left treatment—to take a post in a different city—he was in his mid-thirties. The closest he came to having sex was with the wife of a friend: the couple was about to divorce, and the wife "came on to him" at a party. He ejaculated before entering her. Despite her entreaties that they meet again, he became very righteous about the whole matter, covering up his fear of failing again with moral scruples about sex with a married woman (though she was no longer even living with her husband).

It has been ten years since I have seen him, and I don't know whether he has remained an ascetic bachelor (as I would guess) or whether he has finally overcome his inhibitions. There was much evidence that his failure at sex and his (by now outgrown) need to be at home "to feel safe" were, in a way, acts of loyalty to his lonely, if witch-like, mother. Emotionally, he never left her.

Many patients with predominantly obsessive-compulsive personality structure not only show traits of one or more of the other cluster C disorders, but may, under certain stressful situations, develop various anxiety reactions (or "anxiety neuroses" as they were called in the analytic literature). The patient in this vignette had mild agoraphobia and depersonalization. There are a number of detailed accounts of psychotherapy with compulsive patients who experienced such reactions. Mann and Goldman, for example, discuss the treatment of a man with an acute phobic reaction, successfully treated by short-term psychotherapy (1982); Vanggaard (1989) has offered the complete records of a compulsive professional man whom he treated psychoanalytically, and with an excellent outcome, for a panic state that occurred within the context of a difficult employment and marital situation. The latter case is of especial interest because of a 17-year follow-up in which the former patient reported being well since the cessation of treatment. Fear of expressing angry feelings at cherished love ones or at authority figures lay behind the panic (a dynamic typical of persons with this personality configuration).

* * * * *

Oscar was referred to me because of compulsive handwashing and severe "separation anxiety." The latter consisted of a fearfulness about being alone, either at home, because his parents were insisting that he get an apartment by himself, or at college, when his roommate would leave for the evening. His parents had made it plain that, when he turned 21, they would no longer support him or tolerate his living at home. This birthday was little over a year off when I first began working with him.

Oscar was the youngest of seven children in a wealthy family proud of its "Mayflower" lineage. Having to be "on your own at 21" was an inflexible family rule, relaxed only in the case of one of his sisters, who had been in and out of mental institutions. In Oscar obsessive-compulsive personality and obsessive-compulsive disorder were combined. His most noticeable traits were orderliness and scrupulosity—in addition to which he dressed, at all times, and contrary to contemporary fashion among young people, in immaculate and somber suits. Because he was unusually handsome, he resembled a model for a conservative men's fashion magazine.

Oscar was also rigidly conformist and overly polite, obsequious really, and presented an idealized picture of perfection as to the nature and behavior of his parents, recited nevertheless in a stilted monotone, suggesting that this is what he *had* to say about them—as though an invisible gun were pointed at his forehead, poised to go off if he said anything even mildly critical of either parent. He washed his hands 50 times a day, and would shake my hand, gingerly, at the end of our sessions, only because his sense of good manners was even more powerful than his fear of contamination.

I worked with Oscar until he was 25, though for a year and a half we spoke only occasionally by phone when he was away at college. The first phase of the work lasted a year, during which time he revealed nothing of emotional relevance. No dreams, no painful memories from the past, apart from his having been intensely lonesome when his parents sent him to a military-run summer camp when he was eight. He spoke of having had a girlfriend, but apparently he had little sexual experience. Given the much-written-about connection (in the early psychoanalytic literature) between compulsive handwashing and childhood masturbation, I thought masturbatory guilt lay behind this symptom. But the topic remained taboo during this first year.

The parents, whom I had met with several times, seemed affable and understanding. There must have been at least a small flame of family conflict to account for the dense smoke of his psychopathology, but I could not find it.

During the second phase of our work, Oscar was initially in great torment. His 21st birthday was just a few weeks away, and he felt not at all ready to move away from home. He begged his parents to let him stay a while longer, but they were adamant. At one point he was on his knees, crying and grasping his father's legs. His father brushed him aside, berating him for being a "sissy." Oscar moved into quarters he shared with two friends, and within a few weeks no longer found the separation from home so intolerable. I stepped up our sessions to four times a week (from two), partly to help cushion the change. By now, there was enough of an alliance between us, and enough consternation about the unsympathetic stance of his parents, that he felt emboldened to expose his long-buried resentments.

Home life had been far from idyllic. The first intimation of this was heralded by his first dream:

> He and three of his high-school friends were being driven by his mother down a steep embankment; she was going too fast and swerved over the edge, crashing the car; mother was all right, but he and his friends were grievously injured and bleeding.

Little by little he revealed the "Hyde" aspects of his mother's Jekyll & Hyde personality. As sweet as was her public persona, she could be equally harsh and destructive within the four walls of the house. Her moods were unpredictable, and she could "turn on a dime" from graciousness to cruelty. Before his therapy he never dared oppose her in anything. But shortly before his "exile," as he now told me, he had protested against some unfair rules she was imposing on him—and she picked up the hi-fi set she had given him for the holidays and smashed it on his bedroom floor. His father he experienced as a cold and rigid martinet, though less capriciously destructive than his mother.

This still did not explain the handwashing. I raised the issue of masturbation at this point (the third year of our work). He could talk fairly comfortably about this now and did not seem unduly troubled either by his experiences or accompanying fantasies. There *was* a sexual secret, but he was not yet ready to share it with me. We even met with his parents once, and in that meeting his father told him, in a tone of scarcely concealed contempt, "You know, we could accept you, Oscar, even if you were ho-mo-sek-syu-ell."

Six months later, Oscar was finally able to reveal the secret. Toward the end of high school he had gotten his girlfriend pregnant and had helped her with the expenses of an abortion. It was then that the compulsive symptom began. Had his parents discovered the truth, he would have gotten off lightly had they merely disowned him. He was shocked, though relieved, at the ordinariness with which I regarded this bit of his history—something that in his culture was apparently a sin even God would not have forgiven. After this revelation, Oscar grew more self-assured and at ease with himself; his handwashing was less frequent (this was in an era before serotonergic drugs) and his anxiety attacks disappeared.

*   *   *   *   *

Oliver began psychotherapy when he was 21, close to the time he was to graduate from college. He came because he was lonely, depressed, and tormented by suicidal and homicidal urges. He was the eldest of five children. His father was the owner of a steel factory. Oliver considered the family's lavish home a "well-appointed prison."

There seemed to be considerable tension between his parents. His father was authoritarian, a harsh disciplinarian, and unaffectionate. His mother, in contrast, "gushed with emotion," spilled out all her complaints to Oliver about the shortcomings in her marriage, and behaved seductively toward her eldest son—her clear favorite among the children. She would often walk into his bedroom naked after bathing, as though searching for a towel, and excusing herself with feigned naïveté: "Oh, Ollie, I didn't realize you were here!"

The better to "make a man of him," the father insisted that Oliver work his way through the last two years of college, despite the ample resources of the family, plus Oliver's own trust fund. Unable to find work locally, and eager to get away from home in any case, Oliver joined the Merchant Marine between his sophomore and junior years. He had all kinds of "rough" experiences, including getting drunk and getting into fights while on board, and getting gonorrhea after being with a prostitute in a Cape Town brothel.

My work with him began shortly after his return from sailing around the world. Oliver was fastidious, stiff in his movements, and older-appearing—mostly because he dressed, like his father, in pinstripe suits and conservative ties. He had only one or two friends, kept mostly to himself, and was very touchy about classmates who made noise when he was trying to study or who bothered him in other ways. There was one particularly annoying student toward whom Oliver harbored overpowering fantasies of wanting to set fire to his room. Oliver never carried out any such fantasies, but often tensed his muscles and clenched his fists while talking about these wishes, as though it cost him all his self-control to refrain from becoming violent.

Though strongly attracted to several girls on campus, he consorted with prostitutes instead. Considering his mother a "manipulative whore" anyway, he felt he was better off with an acknowledged whore, whom he could pay and forget about, rather than let himself get ensnared, and exploited, by some Circe from his own social milieu. If I suggested that there were many young women who were affectionate, genuinely caring, and *not* just out to "suck men dry," he reacted as though I were an extraterrestrial creature with no knowledge about earthlings. He did have some notion that not all men were carbon copies of his ungiving and competitive father, but there were few he trusted enough to sustain friendships.

His dreams were filled with murder, fire, and mayhem — scenes in which he got even with his tormentors. He often awoke with nightmares of this sort.

Oliver strove to live according to the high moral code his parents preached but did not practice; his life had become a constant struggle not to let Mr. Hyde take over. He left treatment after he graduated college, and I do not know whether he succeeded in this struggle, or succumbed. I do strongly suspect that the "anal sadism" of which the early analysts spoke has rather less to do with obsessive personality per se than with parental mistreatment. There are many obsessive persons who were not mistreated during their youth, who very much like to make lists of things and stack objects in neat rows, but who do not become Jekyll & Hyde's or struggle with sadistic fantasies.

AVOIDANT PERSONALITY DISORDER

Diagnosis and Etiology

The description in DSM-III-R of avoidant personality disorder (AvPD) is composed of several key traits (reticence in social situations, avoidance of activities that demand interpersonal contact) and mild symptoms (easily hurt by criticism, fear of showing visible signs of anxiety in public). The latter are at the crossroads between trait and symptom proper: a pronounced *fear* of blushing or crying is still one step removed from the actual outbreak of these symptomatic behaviors. There appears to be a dynamic equilibrium between avoidant personality and certain symptom disorders of Axis I (Tyrer, Casey, & Gall, 1983), most notably social phobia, but also agoraphobia and obsessive-compulsive disorder. Patients with these conditions often show an underlying AvPD. Some patients with social phobia create for themselves an environmental niche, where social contacts are reduced to a bare minimum of superficial encounters, such that they are "left with" only the AvPD. If unanticipated circumstances suddenly pushed them into the social arena, signs of severe anxiety (viz., crying in public, marked blushing or sweating) will quickly reappear. There are many similarities between *avoidant* and *dysthymic* persons, though the latter tend to be more conscientious, self-denigrating, and suspicious; the avoidant persons, more shy and vulnerable (Tyrer & Alexander, 1988, p. 55).

It is common for persons with AvPD to manifest comorbidity within the confines of cluster C, with enough traits of dependent or obsessive-compulsive personality to justify either or both of these disorders by DSM-III-R criteria.

Patients with AvPD often have close relatives with cluster C conditions, including AvPD itself (J. Reich, 1989). In a twin study, however, concordance was noted in MZ pairs where the proband was agoraphobic, but not where the proband had social phobia (Torgersen, 1983). It may be that mild genetic loading for the depressive forms of manic-depressive illness predisposes to AvPD (and to social phobia), since patients with major (including recurrent) depression or with dysthymia often have concomitant avoidant traits, along with a family history of affective illness and cluster C disorders (Akiskal, Bitar et al., 1978).

Environmental influences are important, and in many instances probably sufficient, in the etiological background of AvPD. Children "programmed" to fear and avoid many kinds of persons and situations most people consider harmless will tend to develop AvPD; they often have a parent who is as fearful and avoidant as the future patient. This tendency may carry down the generations, as in the family of an agoraphobic patient in my care: the maternal grandmother was agoraphobic and depressed; the mother, depressed and overly dependent upon the patient; the sister, avoidant and depressed; and the patient herself, avoidant, anorectic, depressed, in addition to her agoraphobia and obsessive-compulsive disorder. All were pathologically ("symbiotically") attached one to the other and afraid of encounters with persons other than members of the immediate family.

Certain traumatic patterns in early development seem sufficient by themselves as causative of AvPD. Parental brutalization, incest, and sexual molestation in childhood have been implicated not only in post-traumatic stress disorder, but also in a lasting pattern of social avoidance and fearfulness toward those who even remotely resemble the victimizers of the past (Stone, 1989a). Early sexual exploitation often leads to pain-dependent, self-defeating (i.e., "masochistic") personality traits, alongside those of avoidance (van der Kolk, 1989); in this setting, AvPD may be accompanied by gaze-avoidance and intense shame.

Treatment

Fashioning a suitable program of *treatment* for the patient with AvPD will depend in part upon whether the personality traits themselves are admixed with symptomatic phobia or with such anxiety symptoms as palpitations, blushing, or trembling. The psychodynamic underpinnings of each case also enter into the equation: patients who have been "taught" the language of fearfulness and withdrawal by a similarly avoidant parent will require a different therapeutic strategy than would be appropriate for an avoidant patient who had been an incest victim. Fortunately, there is a wider array of potentially useful modalities to choose from than is so for most of the other disorders.

As for *psychopharmacological* measures, the social anxiety that often accompanies AvPD may respond to an MAO inhibitor such as phenelzine. For patients with blushing, "stage fright," etc., beta-blockers such as atenolol may interrupt the autonomically mediated anxiety symptoms (Liebowitz et al., 1986). Benzodiazepine anxiolytics may curtail the brief panic episodes to which AvPD patients are prone. Favorable response to medication often converts a highly symptomatic, hence highly fearful, avoidant person into someone far less afraid of the once anxiety-engendering life situations. This, in turn, helps the psychotherapist make a more convincing case that these stressors (meeting people, going on a "date") need not be so frightening. The patient can then respond more enthusiastically to whatever form of psychotherapy seems most useful.

Because of the conjunction of AvPD, in so many instances, with social phobia, various forms of treatment that focus on the latter will often prove useful. These include social skills training, desensitization (cf. Marks & Marks, 1990), cognitive therapy, and other methods within the umbrella of behavioral treatment. One technique involves the selection of social tasks graded hierarchically as to their difficulty: once a level of comfort is achieved in talking with salesclerks in a store, a harder task can be tried, such as making small talk with strangers in a "singles" bar. As for social phobia, *in vivo* exposure techniques of this sort are considered more effective than desensitization. Cognitive and dyadic therapies seem equally if not more effective than exposure techniques. Even though forced exposure to strangers in an atmosphere of *acceptance* would seem particularly advantageous, group therapy (which usually provides this acceptance) has not thus far proven more effective than one-to-one supportive or exploratory psychotherapies (Emmelkamp & Scholing, 1990). Where AvPD has been a sequel to incest or other interpersonal traumata, however, *problem-specific* groups, as developed over the past decade, and composed of patients with similar backgrounds, are considered especially helpful.

Clinical Examples

Andrew had emigrated to America after graduating from college. He worked in the administrative section of a small hospital, having become the number-two man after ten years at this post. What led him to begin psychotherapy was his dissatisfaction with the meagerness of his life. He lived alone, seldom dated, and had only one close friend. Despite a strong desire to expand his social horizons, perhaps one day to marry, he could not bring himself to attend parties or other social functions, out of fear others might think he "looked funny." Though a man of pleasing appearance, he studied himself in the mirror as one might a laboratory specimen, inspecting minutely every square centimeter for peculiarities or flaws: Was one nostril bigger than the other? Did his left ear stick out too far? etc.

Andrew came from a large farming family in Scotland. "Pleasure" and "humor" were not part of his parents' vocabulary. In addition, his father was given to mocking and criticizing his sons — Andrew most of all, since he was the "rebel son" who, partly out of protest against his father's harshness, detested farming. Andrew's damaged self-image traveled with him, however, even as he put family and country behind him.

Compulsive traits were about as marked as his avoidant ones. He was overmeticulous, rigid, perfectionistic, and judgmental about his more fun-loving and less punctual coworkers. This could be seen as identification with his father, but also served the purpose of providing him with excuses not to mix with these "ordinary people" who were much more at ease, in socializing and in sexual encounters, than Andrew was.

I worked with him on a twice-weekly basis for three years, using an eclectic approach that incorporated psychodynamic, cognitive, desensitizing, and behavioral interventions. There was an approximate sequence in the choice of these therapeutic styles. In the beginning I focused on dynamic issues, particularly his fear of sexual failure and subsequent embarrassment — an outgrowth of his having being humiliated so consistently by his father.

We next attacked his unrealistic assumptions about being "ugly" through a more cognitive approach (cf. Beck, Rush, & Shaw, 1979). I could not effect a desensitization to his social phobias in a direct manner, but with strong encouragement to confront the feared situations he was (during the second year of treatment) willing to take his chances in office parties and the like. Alprazolam, 0.5 mgm t.i.d., was useful in quelling his anxiety during the beginning phase of this enhanced socialization (cf. Marks, 1982).

The social-skills training that forms a part of behavioral therapy (cf. Curran, 1977) was, likewise, something I could recommend rather than carry out directly. I suggested he enroll in ballroom-dance lessons and join a concert-and-lecture series, to broaden his range of interests and possible topics of conversation. All these steps led to a "positive feedback": compliments on his appearance, made by several girls whom he met at various social gatherings, eventually undermined his long-held conviction of ugliness.

Andrew began to have a few successful sexual experiences, usually within the context of brief two- or three-week affairs. At first he had retarded ejaculation—a symptom related, apparently, to his continuing fear of any prolonged involvement with women. This did not resolve until the final year of treatment. He left therapy at this point, content with having become more confident socially and more relaxed at work. His hopes for an intimate relationship of a more lasting nature were not yet realized, but no longer seemed so remote a possibility.

* * * * *

Anita was 23 when admitted for the first time to a psychiatric hospital. She had become depressed and dysfunctional—no longer able to work or even maintain her few social contacts. Two years earlier she had graduated from college in Ohio, where her family lived, and had come east primarily to get away from her family. She had been supporting herself in meager fashion as a file clerk.

Her early history had been extremely traumatic. Her father was a manic-depressive, hospitalized on three occasions for violent behavior. He was once arrested for vehicular manslaughter while inebriated. Anita was the eldest of three daughters, her father's "favorite." This did not work to her advantage. Beginning when she was eight, he would take her into the family basement and, under the guise of teaching her some Satanic "religion," have sex with her. This occurred on a frequent basis (orally, at first; when she was older, vaginally). At times he would get into an alcoholic debauch and beat everyone in the house. During these rage outbursts he did not spare Anita.

The incest did not stop until the mother divorced him when Anita was 14. Meanwhile, she developed various somatic complaints, skin rashes, etc., and became withdrawn and timorous. Shame-ridden and seething with anger at her father, she felt like a pariah and was, with one or two exceptions, unable to make friends at school, or later, at college.

During the 18 months she spent in the hospital, Anita kept her gaze averted whenever talking with anyone; despite a hunger for acceptance and closeness, she would blush if anyone approached her, and immediately look down at the floor. She made only one friend among the other patients and was comfortable only with one nurse. Anita also showed "dysmorphophobia," inasmuch as she harbored near-delusional conviction of being ugly, even though she was reasonably attractive.

She was diagnosed as having borderline personality with strong avoidant comorbidity. None of these outward signs changed appreciably by the time she left the hospital. She afterwards went to Tennessee, where she joined a religious cult that practiced "speaking in tongues." Some of the higher-ups were unscrupulous and did her out of her savings.

Disillusioned and even more "avoidant," Anita returned home to Ohio, where an aunt took care of her until she could get back on her feet. She found work as a secretary, found some solace in a more standard religious organization, where she also made a few friends with some of the older women. Anita entertained distant hopes of marriage and family, but, when followed up 20 years later, had still not overcome the effects of her father's exploitation, had dated men only on three or four occasions, and continued to harbor the conviction she was ugly and unacceptable.

This case illustrates some of the shattering effects that physical and sexual violation of a child often bring about. Besides a whole host of somatic conditions, symptomatic acts such as running away from home, promiscuity, substance abuse, suicidal and self-mutilative gestures, etc. (cf. Chapter 17), *avoidant* personality is a common sequela. Elsewhere in this text I have mentioned that innate factors alone can predispose heavily, in certain persons, to dysthymic/depressive, obsessive, or irritable personalities, even in the absence of parental maltreatment. I suspect persons with avoidant, passive-aggressive, and perhaps also dependent personalities can usually point to some significantly unfavorable interactions at the hands of their parents or caretakers. In Anita's case, her depressive tendency may have had a genetic component: not only her father but also seven of his eleven siblings had also been hospitalized with affective psychoses! Yet the extreme and treatment-resistant nature of her avoidant traits seemed attributable primarily to the early abuse.

Passive-Aggressive Personality

Characteristics

The passive-aggressive personality style, characterized by a mixture of passive resistance and grumbling compliance, has probably been an aspect of human nature for millennia. The term itself was coined only quite recently (in the mid-1940s) by wartime psychiatrists who found themselves confronted from time to time with reluctant and uncooperative soldiers (Whitman et al., 1954). The smoldering resentment and chronic, but veiled, hostility of passive-aggressive persons is not strictly limited to this personality type. In actual practice, many persons with paranoid trends show passive-aggressive features. So do many obsessive-compulsive persons, even though anger, irritability, and hostility are not part of the definition of OCPD.

Passive-aggressive personality disorder (PAgPD) implies at least some measure of hostility; three of the nine item criteria ("becomes irritable or argumentative," "resents useful suggestions . . . ," "scorns people in authority . . . ") speak of hostility directly. The remaining items center around obstructionism, curmudgeonliness, and procrastination. Some passive-aggressive individuals are anxious, some are not.

PAgPD shares some common ground with (the admittedly much more severe, and openly aggressive) sadistic PD in that persons of either sort typically *externalize* and cannot accept blame for any of their shortcomings. Even those who do accept some responsibility for their plight (for alienating superiors, for example, or for causing unhappiness to their intimates) will set up counter arguments to nullify any positive suggestion, such that no beneficial change occurs. This tendency asserts itself just as strongly, of course, in the therapeutic milieu, constituting a major impediment to treatment.

The captiousness, verbal nitpicking, contrariness, and sulkiness that characterize PAgPD are not known to be the latter-day phenotype of any genetic influence; rather, the condition would seem to have its origin in a pattern of unending power struggles with one's parents. The comparative helplessness of youth made it impossible to "win" these battles at the time, certainly not in any directly confrontative way. Instead, the future PAgPD patient developed face-saving techniques of passive resistance. One such technique has been brilliantly pictorialized in the cartoon where the mother asks her youngster, "Where did you go?" (Answer: "Out!"); "What did you do?" ("Nothing!"). The effects of parental nagging tend to grow more severe over the years: constant nagging may interfere with a child's steps toward self-fulfillment; lowered achievement may then make the child (or adolescent) more vulnerable to criticism and more impaired in self-esteem; this renders the child more sensitive to, and resentful of, further parental criticism and nagging; allusions to his failures cut deeper with the advancing years, as the possibilities of living up to the parents' (often unrealistic) expectations grow ever dimmer.

Parental overcontrol is arguably the most common and most important psychodynamic factor in PAgPD, but it is not the only underlying mechanism. In some cases parental neglect or else blatant favoring of another sibling can alienate a child and conduce to the formation of the silent protest and grudging obedience we associate with this condition.

Within the realm of PAgPD, several subtypes have been described: (a) those with anxiety or depression (about one patient in three), (b) a self-defeating type, locked in a frustrating relationship with a "punishing partner," (c) those who are primarily vindictive, and (d) those who voluntarily but begrudgingly keep their lives on hold by caring for aging parents (Perry, 1989; Perry & Flannery, 1982). Those with a "punishing partner" will occasionally erupt into outbursts of not so passive aggression (striking a hypercritical parent, for example), if their "button is pushed." One such patient in my follow-up study, in a fit of anger at his girlfriend, knocked out her cat's front teeth (Stone, 1990).

Treatment

Problems in *treatment* usually center on extreme indecisiveness and on the undermining of one's own ambitions, alienating others via uncooperative or argumentative interactions. There are many paradoxical situations therapists will encounter again and again in dealing with passive-aggressive patients. By the time they enter treatment (late teens or early adult life), they are often in the midst of a "sit-down strike," as an indirect protest against parental pressure or insensitive authority in general. They may refuse to work, stage impasses, refuse stubbornly to progress in any direction, etc. — all of which ultimately defeats *their own* cherished hopes and ambitions, let alone the unrealistic dreams of their parents.

This leaves the therapist in the position, after therapy has gone on for a certain length of time, of urging the patient to take up where he left off years ago, to get a job, to enroll in a course, to do *something*! But this immediately reawakens feelings of parental pressure. The patient may retort: "You're just twisting my arm like *they* twisted my arm!" To such thrusts I have found myself parrying with comments like, "Yes, indeed, I'm suggesting you do something, *anything* . . . but unlike your parents I don't really care if you go to Harvard Law School or if you stack cans in the grocery down the street. Just so you do *something* that would gratify *you*. I'm not comfortable with the spectacle of collecting my fee till you're 47 and I'm dead, just so you can 'win' the battle with your parents by disappointing them totally." Sometimes I mention the wonderful Steinberg cartoon depicting a man at the far end of a seesaw perched at the edge of a cliff. At the other end of the seesaw is another man, his "enemy." He shoots the man — and of course drops into the abyss.

A common form of passive aggression, where one defeats one's goals just to get back at the parents, is the refusal to go through some course of study or training — which happens to be the very thing one always wanted to do — simply because the parents urged the same course of action in a humiliating and intrusive way: "You want me to go to Harvard Law!?

Good! I'll take up astronomy (even though I don't like astronomy)." Excessive parental pressure robs a child of spontaneity and any feeling of independence, of *being one's own person*. The passive-aggressive solution is to be nothing, to be an idle dreamer, to be something else entirely — and thus "independent" — since to gratify the parent would mean losing one's identity.

Medications have not been found beneficial in passive-aggressive patients, except in those who are prone to episodes of depression or anxiety. Because of their externalization and argumentativeness, they do not do well in group therapy, often quitting or getting extruded by the other members. Cognitive therapy may be helpful, if one can get the patient to understand, and to modify, the entrenched pattern of expecting the worst from others — and then creating a "self-fulfilling prophecy" by bringing out the worst in others. Supportive and analytically oriented psychotherapy may also succeed in selected patients, though the task is long and arduous (Liebowitz et al., 1986).

The analysis of dreams is potentially helpful in getting to the heart of the central conflicts, especially since passive-aggressive patients are so adroit at trivializing the therapist's interpretive remarks. Dreams may provide the "smoking gun," demonstrating the patient's anger, fear, etc., in an undeniable fashion. But first the therapist must make a convincing case that this therapeutic approach is not (as the patient will artfully contend) so much hocus-pocus. This may consume many months of "resistance analysis." If successful, one will arrive at the underlying feelings of littleness, of unworthiness, of having received only "conditional" love (i.e., "if you get straight A's . . . "). Optimally, the therapist will also enable the patient to see that an authority figure can actually be benign and genuinely concerned about his welfare, whereas in the patient's view the therapist's only motives were to emerge "superior" and to "keep the patient down." Perry and Flannery (1982) have commented on the potential benefits of a technique based on *assertiveness* training, an aspect of *behavioral* therapy.

The recommendations offered here should not be construed as an indication that treatment can succeed with any regularity in PAgPD. The battle is not even. On the therapist's side (it is to be hoped): wisdom, skill, compassion, and nearly infinite patience. But these may be no match for the passive-aggressive patient's skipping appointments, paying late, coming in a few minutes before the session was to end, saving the emotionally crucial material till two minutes before the session is over, and then announcing a few weeks later that "not much is happening here, so I'm quitting." In the absence of adequate follow-up data on this disorder, it is unclear what the proportion is between favorable and unfavorable outcome. But in the opinion of most seasoned clinicians, good outcomes are the exception.

Clinical Examples

Patrick was the younger of two sons in a middle-class, Midwestern family. He came to New York after graduating college and took a post as a teacher in a private school. There were a number of dissatisfactions in his life that led him to seek therapy—primarily, problems in getting along with girlfriends. He was ill at ease with the idea of "getting serious" because of his reluctance to take on the responsibilities at this time in his life (he was in his late twenties) of marriage and children.

Patrick was an active member of a political group dedicated to protesting against the corruption and certain unfair practices of the major political parties. Most of his social contacts came from his group. There was a parallel between the unfairness he sought to change in the social system and that which prevailed in his original family. His older brother got the lion's share of parental love and attention.

This emerged early in the therapy, which consisted of thrice-weekly psychoanalytic sessions. The first dream, for example, involved an expensive sports jacket that he spotted in a department store window. The feeling tone was one of frustration, since he felt he could not afford such a jacket. The scene made him recall a similar-looking jacket that his parents had once given his brother, and which came to him only as a hand-me-down.

The overarching theme during his analysis was resentment at having to give to others, when he himself had been so shortchanged by the people in his family. This expressed itself through procrastination and being late with many obligations. On one occasion, having paid the phone bill at the last moment, he found that his service was temporarily disconnected. His school had a standing offer to give its teachers a substantial annual bonus if they completed their master's degree. He did so shortly after the beginning of treatment, yet delayed sending in the requisite form for two years. I recall having a "countertransference dream" toward the end of that time, where I sneaked into his apartment, found the envelope, and mailed it myself.

His father disapproved of Patrick's political views; before Patrick moved east there had been frequent, and bitter, arguments. The transference counterpart of that relationship showed itself in his tendency to doubt my good intentions toward him. He would test me in various ways regarding my political beliefs, as though these might be a yardstick of my attitude toward him in general. He was wary of authority figures of whatever stripe and was also uncomfortable with all of life's "musts." As a relationship with a woman would deepen, for example, there would come a time when the woman expected him to be with her on Saturday night, expected him to treat her to dinner now and then, expected him to listen to how her day had gone—all of which made him feel put upon and cornered.

Patrick decided to end treatment at a time when he was in the midst of a relationship with a woman that seemed to go fairly smoothly, and when his work situation was also more stable. He was more at ease with his brother, though between him and his parents there was as much distance as ever.

At follow-up 22 years later, Patrick was teaching at a more advanced level than before and had achieved job security. He had mellowed considerably with respect to his passive-aggressive traits. It is not clear what had brought about this change. Perhaps it was the maturation that comes with age. In any event, he was no longer involved in "protest" groups, but rather, groups made up of people with various life-problems who were devoted to "being there" for one another: being available for help at a moment's notice, for example, or taking turns advising one another from within their sphere of expertise. He had had a number of relationships with women lasting a year or two during the follow-up interval, but now was involved with a woman toward whom he felt more at ease and more committed than he had with previous women-friends. Ironically, he was now eager to "tie things up," whereas his friend, owing to some unfortunate experiences in her own past, was apprehensive — just the reverse of his situation during his twenties and thirties. He had become a more sympathetic and understanding person than he had been years before and was more confident about the future.

* * * * *

Phillip was 25 when I first saw him in consultation. He had been in therapy two years earlier for difficulties in finding a direction in life. There had been no visible progress in that treatment, so Phillip changed therapists. He was the youngest of four sons. His father, who had started out poor, had become prosperous as the owner of a furniture store; he had sold the store and now lived in retirement off the proceeds.

Phillip's memory for his early years was spotty, but it seemed that the family atmosphere was one of continual bickering and contentiousness. The eldest brother had become a Jesuit priest and professor of philosophy, creating a virtue, as it were, out of the cross currents of hair-splitting and argument that took the place of dinner-table conversation. Their father was a man of solid moral values, but in temperament was scrappy and domineering. He did not so much talk as pontificate. He was also very "territorial" about business matters, sharing nothing of his work-life with his wife.

Phillip's parents had never been compatible in general, and the marriage was held together more by habit than by love. When he was little, Phillip had been extremely dependent upon his mother and had a measure of "school phobia" during kindergarten and first grade. At some point in his life, disillusionment set in, and Phillip became markedly ambivalent: still dependent on his mother, but contemptuous of her superficiality and nagging.

Between the verbal bullying of his father (who had a long list of things his son "must" do with his life) and his mother's nagging, Phillip felt at once robbed of self-esteem and burdened with impossibly high expectations. A kind of paralysis set in, where, by doing nothing, he could preserve the illusion of being still capable of doing anything—whereas if he tried his hand at something, he would surely fall short of his parents' ambitions. As a further complication, an unspoken conspiracy had arisen—a Faustian bargain in reverse—in which Phillip was to keep his parents company in their old age, giving up accomplishments and the beautiful girl, in return for the comfort and securities of home.

As for his therapy, he mounted a nearly insuperable defense against anyone (such as a therapist) trying to break up the "conspiracy" and to help Phillip get on with his life. He fended off any remark or interpretation with casuistical arguments about the unproven nature of psychotherapy, or about the irrelevancy and the inherent subjectivity of my comments, since they were the emanations of my brain, not his brain. Yet there was a certain attachment. I felt a psychoanalytic approach was indicated, in hopes that his dreams would make clear what he was so reluctant to acknowledge about the negative attitudes toward his parents. When I would ask him what kept him coming, four times a week, given that he viewed analysis as a life-raft made of cotton candy, he replied: "True, but what other hope do I have?"

Diagnostically, Phillip showed prominent traits of all four of the cluster C disorders: passive-aggressive, avoidant, compulsive, and dependent, in that order. Though fear of male authority, stemming from interactions with his father's blustery temper, was a dominant dynamic issue, the fear of assertion took on a life of its own and became magnified through a negative feedback. The more that assertive steps into the outside world (toward work and sexuality) were avoided, the more daunting such steps seemed, as time went by. This for two reasons: the longer one delays taking a "scary" step (skating, dating, driving, etc.), the more one remains at the mercy of one's childhood assumptions about how difficult they are (and the less experience one has by which to measure a therapist's claim that the assertive step need not be so anxiety-provoking). Secondarily, the older one gets, still not having mastered certain ordinary life-tasks, the more embarrassed one feels (i.e., the greater the narcissistic injury) about finally attempting them, since one's beginner-awkwardness will stand out in bolder relief. At 17, for example, one's sexual partner is usually very forgiving about fumbling with straps, difficulty getting aroused, and so on. At 27, one's partner expects more finesse, such that the fumbling, etc., is more embarrassing. And at 37. . . .

In Phillip's situation, after two years, the "passive-aggressive" defenses — the verbal sparring about the efficacy of analysis, etc. — were mostly resolved. A certain amount of work was done vis-à-vis the oedipal dynamics. But this was all "armchair" work. Phillip's anxiety (about dating, leaving home, etc.) did not diminish enough to make these tasks easily negotiable. At this phase of the treatment, exhortation (to move gradually into the phobic areas) took its place side by side with interpretation. This "behavioral" intervention must occur eventually in one's work with avoidant patients, irrespective of whether one is trained as (or identifies primarily as) a behavioral therapist or not. As work with patients like Phillip demonstrates, the treatment of passive-aggressive patients makes lawyers of us all; therapy of avoidant patients makes behaviorists of us all.

SUMMARY

In this chapter, in the preceding chapters dealing with the other disorders recognized by DSM, and in the next chapter on pain-dependent personalities, I comment on the general level of treatability and on some of the techniques currently employed. I have touched in passing on the abnormal temperaments associated with manic-depressive illness: depressive, (hypo-)manic, irritable, and cyclothymic. In these four, personality traits and symptoms are combined (Stone, 1978) — much as they are in borderline, schizotypal, and antisocial disorders. The term "dysthymic" has begun to replace "depressive temperament" or "depressive neurosis."

Since this book is subtitled "Within and Beyond the Realm of Treatment," this might be a useful place to capsulize impressions about amenability to treatment. I will ask the reader's indulgence in my making, for didactic purposes, a broad generalization about amenability. I believe it is justifiable to submit the whole set of DSM disorders, including the provisional ones, plus the abnormal temperaments, to a kind of triage. We can divide them into three groups: the typically amenable; those of intermediate treatability; and the typically non-amenable or scarcely amenable. The emerging schema would look like this:

1. *Typically amenable to therapy:* dependent, histrionic, obsessive-compulsive, avoidant, self-defeating (pain-dependent), and depressive temperament.

2. *Personality disorders of intermediate treatability:* narcissistic, bor-

derline, schizotypal, hypomanic temperament, cyclothymic temperament.

3. *Scarcely amenable or non-amenable to therapy:* paranoid, passive-aggressive, schizoid, irritable/explosive, sadistic, antisocial/psychopathic.

It is not easy to well-order the list further because there is such diversity within the confines of any one personality type. Obsessive-compulsive persons who are conscientious, highly motivated, and not authoritarian will clearly be more amenable to psychotherapy than will obsessive-compulsive patients who are rigid, authoritarian, and woodenly insensitive to emotions and psychological symbolism. Patients of the latter kind might be less amenable to treatment than someone who, though he had passive-aggressive PD, had only a "touch" of it.

Since most patients are unlike the prototypical descriptions, but instead show mixtures of traits from several of the above-mentioned disorders, we could take the triage-list a step further and say that prognosis is dependent in good measure on the degree to which the traits of the disorders in the third group are present. The corresponding traits constitute the rate-limiting ingredients of the personality mix, from the standpoint of treatment. *Any* disorder, that is, if admixed with prominent antisocial, sadistic, or paranoid features, becomes correspondingly more difficult to treat, especially in one-to-one psychotherapy.

Prognosis in patients with a temperament abnormality depends in part on their responsiveness to medication. Mood-regulating drugs like lithium, carbamazepine, or valproate may restore euthymia, sometimes without much further therapy. Often, medication helps define the boundary-line between the trait and symptom aspects of the overall condition. Some hypomanic patients improve, for example, with lithium alone. In others it becomes apparent that, even after lithium restores normalcy of mood, there is a good deal of personality pathology "left over." This then becomes the work of our psychotherapeutic efforts. The same is true with many borderline patients.

Psychoanalysts and psychiatrists in private practice concentrate their attention on patients in the first group, for the most part, and to a lesser extent on (mildly) narcissistic patients. Self-defeating qualities are characteristic of almost all patients who come voluntarily for help. Many improve considerably when their maladaptive patterns (in choosing mates, for example) are worked out and worked through. Here again, the *most* self-defeating patient will remain beyond the reach of treatment. I once heard of a young man who compulsively gave all his money to strangers. A friend urged him to get help. But with no money left for therapy, he could not get the treatment he needed to get over his problem of giving all his money away. So even though in other respects he may have been a very suitable patient, there was no easy way to interrupt the "vicious circle" his problem created.

As for the prospective patients in the second group, therapists with special training, a special interest in working with personality disorders, and/or many years of clinical experience may be able to do effective treatment. This extends also to the more mildly paranoid and passive-aggressive patients of the third group. The remainder of this group make up the "hard core" of scarcely treatable or non-amenable persons, sketched in greater detail in the chapter on antisocial personality and in the last two chapters of the book.

Part Three

SPECIAL ISSUES IN TREATMENT AND BEYOND

16

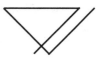

Pain-Dependent
Personality Types

A neurotic is not happy; on the contrary, he suffers terribly, yet no
one can relieve his suffering without his consent and this he so often
withholds. He insists on suffering because his ego cannot bear the
pain of facing reality and the diminution of self-importance which a
cure would involve.

   If there are any souls in Hell, it is not because they have been
sent there, but because Hell is where they insist upon being.

W. H. Auden (1962)

THE PSYCHOANALYTIC LITERATURE is rich in descriptions of a personality
type characterized by paradoxical courting of painful situations. The term
"masochistic" was affixed to this abnormality, because of the similarities,
on the psychological plane, to the even more extreme courting of actual
physical pain in the sexual perversion described by Count Leopold Sacher-
Masoch (1901), for whom the disorder is named. Sacher-Masoch had described his own abnormal tendencies, craving humiliation from the woman
he loved, in his most widely known novel, *Venus in Furs*. Actually we
owe both terms *masochism* and *sadism*, to Krafft-Ebing (1886), who, as
Ellenberger (1970) reminds us, coined the pain-dependent perversion in
honor of Sacher-Masoch and the cruelty-dependent perversion in honor of
the Marquis de Sade.

   Freud and the pioneer generation of psychoanalysts depicted the masochistic character as one in which the person is unusually submissive and seems
to seek out situations in which he or she can experience humiliation or
defeat. Masochism was seen as something of an extension of "normal"
femininity, as though representing the far end of a spectrum of compliance
and submissiveness. Helene Deutsch wrote, for example, in a 1930 paper
on hysteria: "Coitus is after all the best reservoir for the man's aggression

373

and the woman's masochism . . . " (1965, p. 70). Perhaps in fin-de-siècle Vienna this was so.

Currently, we no longer understand masochistic personality as an exaggerated form of femininity, recognizing that the typical personality traits occur about as frequently in men as in women. J. Reich (1987) made this point in his study of personality types detectable in an outpatient sample. About 18% of his 82 patients met the criteria for "self-defeating personality disorder"—the term that replaces *masochistic* in DSM-III-R. Of these, 58% were women; 42% men: a ratio no different from the gender distribution typical of Reich's clinic.

I used the term *pain-dependent* in the chapter heading to avoid both the narrowness of "masochistic" and the excessive breadth of "self-defeating." As Cooper rightly underlines, all neurotic persons suffer, and they also undermine their own ambitions (Cooper & Sacks, 1991). Not many people seek the help of a psychotherapist who are not in some sense "self-defeating." To be sure, DSM attempts to give the label meaning by defining it as, in effect, *very* self-defeating, i.e., chooses people and situations that lead to hurt or disappointment, rejects help, elicits angry responses, is unattracted to persons who would be genuinely caring, engages in unnecessary self-sacrifice, etc. But the new definition conflates items from concepts which, for clinical reasons, have generally been distinguished within the psychoanalytic community—namely, masochistic and *sadomasochistic*.

Kernberg (1988) argues for the preservation of these distinctions, and provides an excellent taxonomy of personality disorders and character types where either seeking pain or inflicting pain constitute the salient diagnostic features. At the least pathological end of the (emotional-) pain spectrum one confronts compulsive persons whose ordinarily realistic self-criticism becomes exaggerated under certain circumstances, leading to a kind of dysphoric mood. The "moral masochist," in contrast, seeks, out of unconscious guilt, the position of "victim," without sexual pleasure being involved. The figure of the Professor in *The Blue Angel* is an oft-cited example: the older man who becomes hopelessly enamored of the young siren, before whom he humiliates himself, enduring all manner of suffering and rejection.

The "depressive-masochist" is a common clinical type, along with the hysteric and compulsive types, of relatively high-functioning "neurotic" persons. Kernberg draws attention to the excessive harshness of conscience in the depressive masochist, who presents with excessive seriousness, humorlessness, perfectionism and overconscientiousness at work, impossibly high standards, a tendency to feel "righteous indignation" and to maneuver himself into situations where he can be taken advantage of. Such persons often cycle between overcompliance and expressions of (hitherto suppressed) anger. They are unduly sensitive to small slights, and may also make excess demands, make others feel guilty, and get themselves criticized or rejected. Some masochistic persons of this type may have masturbatory fantasies of being beaten, though without ever actually seeking to include such activities in their sexual life.

Further toward the pathological end of the pain spectrum, Kernberg places the "sadomasochist." Here one sees alternation, in love relationships, between self-debasing behavior and sadistic attack. Sadomasochists are apt to function at the borderline level of psychic organization (Kernberg, 1967) and see themselves as the victims of other people's aggression. They are prone, through their hypercriticalness, to elicit anger from those they depend on. They experience this anger as mistreatment, not realizing the extent to which they may have brought it upon themselves. (In a more subtle form: the sadomasochist *chooses* an abusive partner who is quite capable of being mean without provocation, thus permitting the sadomasochist to feel all the more "justified" in being indignant and bitter.) Still, there is a greater capacity to get close to others than is displayed by persons who are primarily narcissistic.

The sadomasochist often reports that the parents, especially the mother, were sadistic and controlling. In Cooper's view (1985), which matches my own clinical experience, the background in patients with "moral masochism" and depressive-masochistic personality is fraught with parental indifference, failure to appreciate the child's uniqueness, etc., but is not usually abusive. This engenders low self-esteem, a craving for affirmation of one's worth, vulnerability to narcissistic injury and to occasional outbursts of anger if such injuries occur. The sadomasochist, on the other hand, probably *did* experience verbal, physical, or even sexual abusiveness from one or both parents. Home was a more unpredictable, violent atmosphere, and the "survivor" of this atmosphere may indeed grow up to become aggressive (in this case: more evenly divided in masochistic and in sadistic behavior).

Adding to the description of the "sadomasochistic" character, Malenson (Cooper & Sacks, 1991) mentions that such patients, having been truly victimized by "deeply needed but disparaging others," develop attitudes of martyrdom, become "injustice collectors" or "grudge holders," and control those close to them via "emotional blackmail." The sadomasochist, drawing on heavy reserves of righteousness indignation stemming from adverse childhood experience, finds it easy to misconstrue the good intentions of others, reacting with intense anger at those whose responses seem uncaring or unsympathetic. Hyperalertness to even minimal cues of such "negativity" prompts the sadomasochist to bring out the heavy artillery when none is called for, creating in the recipient a negativity that is no longer imaginary or minimal. The other person has now become, willy-nilly, an actor in the drama, replayed from childhood, taking the part of the offending parent, while the sadomasochist shifts into the role of the injured innocent.

Cooper and Sacks have argued that pathological narcissism is a common accompaniment of masochism: the tendency to indignation, wounded pride, and narcissistic rage at having been treated unfairly is never far from the surface. The desire for revenge is also near the surface, even in the more outwardly submissive "depressive-masochists." The latter often induce a sense of shock and betrayal in others (including their therapists), as Malenson points out, when their anger ultimately shows itself. This in turn leads to counterattack, which the masochist takes as proof that even the most trusted persons are "against" them, thus reinforcing the masochist's conviction of being the eternal victim.

There is disagreement about whether narcissism always hovers below the surface of masochism (Cooper's position, but not Kernberg's) or whether injurious childhood experiences underlie sadomasochism. Since pain-dependent personalities are common and varied in their presentation, it may be that disagreements of this sort relate to the inevitable differences in the "sample" of patients with which various experts becomes familiar, over the course of their professional life.

A PARADOX OF THE "PLEASURE-PAIN" PRINCIPLE

One of the most puzzling aspects of masochism from the standpoint of psychoanalytic theory was its apparent violation of Freud's pleasure-pain principle. As he enunciated in 1924:

> If mental processes are governed by the pleasure principle in such a way that their first aim is the avoidance of unpleasure and the obtaining of pleasure, masochism is incomprehensible. (p. 159)

Wilhelm Reich argued that masochism was not so paradoxical after all, since masochists also strove for what was pleasurable, but anxiety and the fear of punishment, which came to be associated with otherwise pleasurable acts, caused the original goal to be obliterated or else reevaluated as unpleasurable. Reich gave as an example (1929, p. 221) a patient who, having soiled his pants as a three-year-old, was beaten severely by his violent father; he had feared his father would literally castrate him, so it was with some relief that he found he was merely to be beaten on the buttocks. He developed fantasies of being whipped or beaten, afterwards, which of course looked on the surface as though they violated the "pleasure principle," but which represented, ironically, a pleasurable reprieve from the far worse punishment he had anticipated.

There would appear to be other forces impelling patients with pain-dependent personalities to repeat, and to recreate, seemingly undesirable experiences. Some of these forces can be understood as reflections of a "repetition compulsion." The latter concept is applicable to behavior across a wide spectrum, not just in the domain of masochism. And there is more to the story than can be explained by the tendency of the sadomasochist to convert the passive suffering of childhood into the victimization of others during adulthood (via the defense of "identification with the aggressor"). One must also acknowledge what Modell has explained as the compulsion to seek perceptual identity between past and present objects (cited by Edelman, 1992, p. 182).

The psychological language of the early years, in those who are reared by indifferent or even cruel caretakers, *is the only language such persons know*. They are strangers in the world of ordinary tender and considerate people. Their whole psychological machinery is geared to avoid hurt or, if it seems safe enough, to dish out a little as revenge. As adults, such persons are faced with the choice of speaking the language of normality "with an accent," or else of remaining comfortably fluent in the language of indifference and hurt. The second alternative—the one taken by pain-dependent persons—is obviously both easier and grossly maladaptive.

Learning the language of kinder and gentler folk, which becomes the primary task of therapy, is extremely difficult and is fought by the masochist every inch of the way. The world of indifference and hurt constitute "home" to such patients; despite the suffering, it is not something they walk away from easily. Familiarity breeds content. Considerations of this sort may help explain why such patients seem perpetually to see the worst in other people. There is an intense loyalty to one's family, no matter how disastrous a family it was. To see others as uncaring, selfish, and mean is to see one's parents as "not so bad, after all," as though one is not really worse off compared to others, etc.

In some masochistic patients one sees a self-defeating object choice repeating itself over and over in their search for a mate. This can occur even in the absence of any abusive or guilt-tinged relationship with a parental figure. I have worked with several depressive-masochistic patients who had been abandoned by their fathers during infancy. They have no recollection of their fathers, only a brief catalog of anecdotes about what kind of men they had been (a "charming stinker," according to one of their mothers). But once these women began dating, they sought out, with the unerring sense of direction for which the unconscious is famous, just such charming stinkers as had once made their mothers' lives transitorily pleasant and then enduringly miserable. It was as though the patients sought to splice in some important piece of life that had been missing from their childhood—a task more important to them and, despite the suffering attached to it, more gratifying than finding a devoted and caring man who, by his very virtues, could not supply that missing link.

Stolorow et al. (1988) recently provided a poignant example of paradoxical pain-seeking in a psychotic young woman who was also intensely masochistic and self-mutilative. She would plead with her therapist again and again: "Hit me!" If the therapist asked, "Why do you want me to hit you?" or said, "I don't want to hit you," her response was only, "Hit me!" Finally, the therapist said, "I don't want to cause you pain." To this she said her first sentence other than "Hit me!": "Physical pain is better than spiritual death." During her childhood she had experienced her mother as grossly indifferent to her and as shattering her sense of selfhood by insisting on absolute conformity to mother's rules and beliefs. The patient's masochism was not so much a form of self-destruction as a pathetic attempt to restore a sense of existing (I hurt, therefore I am).

GENDER DIFFERENCES AT THE CLINICAL LEVEL

Challenging the older assumptions about a link between masochism and femaleness, Baumeister (1988) conducted an intriguing study comparing men's and women's anonymous letters written to sex-oriented magazines. To begin with there were more letters written by men, than by women, that had a distinctly masochistic caste (in a ratio of 55:45).

Baumeister noticed a number of differences in the typical scripts embodied in the men's vs. the women's letters. The male correspondents, for example, sought painful experiences that were more intense than those sought by the women, though the women wished to submit to pain on a more frequent basis. The men's scripts bespoke more intense humiliation and more use of third persons (ménage à trois) and transvestism. The women masochists saw their painful submissions as punishment for having been "bad." The women were more eager to have their sexual acts observed by spectators.

Baumeister felt that the differences in the scripts of male vs. female masochists (and here the term is used to describe persons with both masochistic sexual inclinations and personality traits) related primarily to cultural stereotypes of masculine/feminine behavior. Our culture emphasizes individual ambition, autonomy, and self-reliance for males. Men who find these cultural demands uncongenial may rebel along "masochistic" lines, showing such traits as self-sacrifice and suffering for the sake of others: traits that are more incompatible with maleness than with femaleness in our culture.

Masochism, as Baumeister sees it, represents among other things a denial of stereotypical masculine aspects of identity in both men and women.

We see submissive men as "less masculine," therefore, in a way, more "feminine." Women who are particularly submissive we may see as "ultra-feminine," after the manner of Cio-Cio-san in Madame Butterfly, who, had she ever gotten to marry Pinkerton (no masochist he!), would surely have walked ten paces behind him. Sadomasochistic women, especially those where the balance between suffering and counterattack is tilted clearly toward the latter, are often viewed as "masculine." Men of this stripe (such as Pinkerton) are seen not so much as hypermasculine, but rather (and correctly) as cads.

Pain-dependent personalities, masochistic more so than sadomasochistic, are apt to be found in conjunction with the "inhibited" group of (cluster C) disorders, the compulsive and passive-aggressive in particular. Because of the indirect expression of anger peculiar to both masochistic and passive-aggressive persons, Widiger and Frances (1988) have expressed the concern that perhaps the concept of masochism overlaps, clinically at least, with that of passive-aggressivity — enough to render the label of masochism less useful or distinctive. Overlap with "depressive personality" (akin to the dysthymic person) is also common, as noted both by these authors and by Kernberg (1988).

The concepts underlying these various disorders, as well as the constellations of traits by which they are characterized, seem, nevertheless, sufficiently distinct to warrant retention of "masochistic" as a separate personality label. If "self-defeating" or "pain-dependent" seems more appropriate, I have no quarrel with such a change, though "masochistic" enjoys the longest usage. "Pain-dependent" covers the conceptual territory the most accurately. As for the "negative therapeutic reaction," this phenomenon seems to correlate quite strongly with pain-dependent personalities of all types (masochistic, sadomasochistic, etc.), whereas there are many passive-aggressive and depressive patients who do not show this reaction.

OBSESSIVE LOVE AND JEALOUSY AS
SPECIAL FORMS OF SADOMASOCHISM

There are many forms of pathological love relationships that are pain-dependent in the extreme and for which "self-defeating" is a limp euphemism. "Masochistic" or "sadomasochistic" seem better linguistic containers for such morbid love, since both underline the intense suffering that follows inevitably in the train of unrequited love, hopeless passion, cycles of rejection and reconciliation, and other such patterns of desire gone awry. These terms also imply that the psychic pain, though not consciously sought, is brought about through the sufferer's own actions or choice of partner, and is thus in a sense "willed." What is at work here is not unkind fate but (to steal a phrase from a bad movie) "fatal attraction." Many an opera is based on masochistic, obsessive, and ultimately doomed love, as in *Carmen* (where Don José deserts his regiment for Carmen, and then kills her when she flippantly deserts him for the Toreador) or La Traviata (where the high-born Alfredo falls desperately in love with the courtesan, Violetta).

Enslavement to an unattainable love-object, whether or not the love is returned, often goes by the name "pathological infatuation" (cf. Cooper, 1985), and usually has its source in an unresolved incest- (Oedipus) complex. This would seem to be true, whether on the lofty plane of Don Quixote's longing for Dulcinea or on the grotesque level of Hinckley's preoccupation with Jodie Foster. Masochism in these situations crosses beyond the borders of personality trait into frank symptomatology. One may see erotomania (where someone imagines being "loved" by a person, usually of high social status, who is not even aware of the existence of lover); obsessive love (where someone may even "stalk" the love-object, even though aware that the love is not returned); or the various forms of pathological jealousy.

In the case of Diane Schaefer, imprisoned for aggravated harassment of her "quarry," there were features of both erotomania and obsessive love: she shadowed and hounded for years a man who had no interest in her at all, yet whom she delusionally believed was "very much in love with" her (Brenner, 1991). As with many sadomasochistic persons, Schaefer had been abused during childhood (her mother was verbally and physically abusive). Her self-defeating tendency came through in a comment she made after her trial: "There were so many times in my life where I could have made the right turn. Something always went wrong" (p. 265).

Pathological jealousy, which may be found in association with almost any of the defined personality disorders, contains strong sadomasochistic elements. Pathological jealousy is, in effect, a compartmentalized delusion: the conviction that one's lover or spouse is being sexually unfaithful. The false belief is itself a source of intense humiliation and suffering, but also leads to what White and Mullen (1989) have called "inquisitional cross-questioning" (p. 183). Jealous persons often become "snoops" as well, checking their partners' clothing, wallet, checkbook, wastepaper basket, address book, etc., for "evidence" of the "other" man or woman.

Paranoid ideation is also a strong element in pathological jealousy: no amount of evidence, no "sworn statements" from the partner (no matter how sincere and believable), are ever sufficient proof, in the eyes of the jealous person, that the partner was "innocent." The inquisition is, of course, a technique of sadistic control and revenge—the jealous person's antidote to the masochistic suffering from the imagined betrayal. Carried far enough, such inquisitorial treatment makes real the fantasy being played out in the mind of the jealous person: eventually the partner may react to the harassment with either actual infidelity or with severing the relationship — "proving" that the jealous person was "right all along."

Pathologically jealous people often have an unerring eye for the potential masochists in the crowd — for partners, that is, who will endure their jealous taunts and minute inspections longer than most others would. As White and Mullen mention, jealousy " . . . places the partner in the subservient role, for he or she must either confess or otherwise respond to the accusations" (p. 242). In many instances, the jealous person will even choose someone with a known "track record" of philandering or infidelity: this just about ensures ultimate betrayal (and this is the downside of the bargain), but also ensures that the jealous person's view of the world (you can't trust anyone) is confirmed (this is the great "advantage"). In this situation the jealous person is spared having to realize the gross distortions in his or her picture of reality, can feel justified in not seeking therapy, and can bask perpetually in the glow of righteous indignation. Within this solipsistic world the jealous person is indeed "right," behavior and attitudes become increasingly ego-syntonic, and the possibility for amelioration by psychotherapy ever more remote. It is because of this sealed-in quality (plus the delusional nature of pathological jealousy) that serious forms of jealousy are inordinately difficult to threat.

CLINICAL VIGNETTES

Depressive-Masochistic Patients

A single woman of 35 sought help because of intermittent depression. She had never completed college and had never worked. Supported by a modest trust fund, she had "bummed around Europe" during her twenties, and had had a few brief affairs, none of which gave any promise of fulfilling her hopes of marrying and raising a family. She had grown up on a huge estate owned by her wealthy parents, who had divorced when she was ten. Her mother was schizophrenic, and had spent months at a time in institutions. These absences were spoken of as "vacations abroad" by the nannies who raised her and her three siblings.

She lived in straitened circumstances, owing to the helpless attitude with which she confronted her financial situation. With one call to her trust-executor she could have converted stocks that paid almost no interest into bonds that paid high yields. Her income would have trebled, allowing her to complete college and to live in reasonable comfort. It took four years of factual discussion, exhortation, and resistance-analysis to convince her to make that call. Once it was made, her life did change for the better: she did enroll in courses, and eventually got her degree.

Still, she complained bitterly that she was a "nobody," whereas she had always yearned for a career as a musician. Yet she had never taken lessons on any instrument. Now that she had money to spare, I suggested that she set up a scholarship-award for a promising young soloist — an award that would bear her name and thus give her a measure of the recognition she desired, including the chance to meet notables in the musical world, have her name in the papers, etc. She would have none of it. To be a patroness was "second-rate." She would be either a virtuoso or nothing.

Whereas this narcissistic trend got in the way of her vocational ambitions, her self-defeat in the romantic sphere stemmed from other sources. Never having enjoyed any closeness with her mother (who was as crotchety outside the hospital as she had been unavailable while in it), she sought "mothering" from sources guaranteed not to supply any. During the first six years of our work, and for three years before, she had been enveloped in a hopeless, one-sided love affair with a homosexual neighbor who had been living with the same partner for 20 years. Despite his paying her no attention greater than a perfunctory "good morning" on his way out to work, she left mash-notes under his door several times a week and baked cookies for him, which she left in tins outside his apartment.

Dynamically, it seemed clear that she was deeply conflicted about sex and motherhood, such that an attachment of this sort was eminently "safe": she could preserve to herself the illusion that she "really" wanted a husband and children, but failed in these goals simply out of the "bad luck" of falling in love with a man who was gay. Given the barrenness of her life, I felt it necessary to challenge her illusions only in the most gentle and slow-paced way. It was only after she won her degree, and had begun to feel there was *some* hope for a gratifying life, that her obsessive love of her neighbor grew less intense. Her masochism did not disappear, though it had now become less disabling.

A divorced woman of 39 requested treatment because of depression and a sense of purposelessness about her life. The latter had grown more keen since her divorce, and was mitigated only slightly by the attentions she had to devote to her two small children. The eldest daughter of an irascible and abusive engineer, she had had to endure many a beating and tongue-lashing for the most trivial "infractions" of her father's tyrannical rules (for example, that the three children were never to speak at the dinner table). She chose for a husband a man who, though less physically abusive than her father, was equally hypercritical. He "bad-mouthed" her to the children during his visiting days after the divorce, undermining her ability to gain their respect.

An artist of no mean accomplishment, she had painted in the Chinese style for a number of years, under the tutelage of an acknowledged master. During the few months she remained in therapy, she began to learn Chinese calligraphy in order to make more credible titles and signatures on her canvases.

The focus of therapy was on her loneliness. She felt a hunger for companionship and for a sexual relationship with a man. Customarily shy and ill at ease with men, most of whom she experienced as predatory and ultimately rejecting, she approached the dating game with a mixture of desperation and defeatism. She would go to "pick-up" bars, usually in the company of women friends more lively and attractive than herself. This would lead to a "one-night stand" with someone who would never call her again, leaving her feeling desolate and worthless. These were pretty much the feelings her father left her with on countless occasions during her growing up.

Comments on my part to the effect that looking for "Mr. Goodbar" in this fashion was her way of guaranteeing failure and hurt led to angry protests that I was being critical of her, that I was just like her father and all the others. Feeling particularly lonely on Thanksgiving, she impulsively invited into her apartment an elevator boy 20 years her junior. After their "quickie," she felt humiliated and deeply embarrassed over the stories she assumed he would spread to the other workmen of her posh building. Here, too, my attempts to get her to see how she set up painful encounters of this sort backfired: "First you encourage me to put some pleasure into my life, and then when I try to, you tell me I did it all wrong!" Not long after, she grew discouraged about learning Chinese calligraphy and, in a fit of pique, ripped up her canvases and quit treatment.

Sadomasochistic Patients

Lydia, a widowed woman of 36, began therapy in hopes of becoming independent from her parents and of learning what was "wrong" with her that kept her from finding a mate and starting a family. She had grown up in an affluent home, where her father was a manufacturer of stationery products. Her brother was a physician, and had had little contact with her parents since entering college. She married at 23 only to be widowed three years later, when her husband died in a car accident. Since that time she worked only sporadically, eschewing "entry-level" jobs as "beneath" her, but resisting all efforts to train for positions she could be more proud of. Besides, she "could only be her own boss," since she could not get along with authority figures.

The reason was not far to seek. Both her parents, but especially her mother, carried verbal abusiveness to the level of caricature, like Waxford Squires and his wife in *Nicholas Nickleby*, but all the more malignant for their being real and not mere characters in a Dickens' novel. Remaining totally dependent upon them financially, she had no escape from nightmarish scenes in restaurants, where her father would upbraid her at the top of his lungs ("You don't know what the fuck you're talking about!"), and her mother, in a similar decibel range, would savage her with comments like: "You look like shit! No wonder you haven't met anybody!" or "Don't worry about not giving us grandchildren: you'd ruin them!" After wiping away her tears, she would assail them with similar epithets: "Some way to talk to your own child! I hope you both get leukemia and bleed out in front of me!" The next day, her father would give her a big check for a week in Europe, and her mother would treat her to an expensive outfit in the swankiest shop.

Her self-esteem in tatters from this unending rhythm of hostility and reconciliation, she by now felt that she was not good enough for any man she could admire and that she would be "stuck" with her parents until they died. I began to feel (especially after meeting her parents) that, secretly, she was very precious to them (their "baby," the consolation of their declining years) and that they had gone about (unconsciously) ensuring that she could never leave them, by annihilating her self-confidence vis-à-vis any other milieu except home. I could not pry her loose from this destructive pattern: too many years had gone by, too many skills not acquired, too many chances thrown away.

* * * * *

A married couple with three children came for "couple therapy" because of tensions in their relationship. The husband was a physicist in a research center. He had met his wife while stationed in Germany during his Army tour in the '60s. He came from a Jewish family in New England; she from a Lutheran family in Hamburg. Their marriage had been characterized by a fair amount of bickering from the beginning, but this had grown worse since he became embittered over a failure on the part of his higher-ups to give him credit for a certain invention. His criticisms of his wife became more intense and frequent, as though she had become his "whipping-boy" for anything he was disgruntled about.

Her reactions were more along "passive-aggressive" lines: she would find excuses to do the laundry till 2 a.m., thus denying him sex. Though if she did come to bed "on time," he would get after her the next morning: "How am I supposed to go to work without even a clean shirt?!" Nothing she could do was "right." She had mostly a long-suffering attitude about his criticisms—as part of a depressive-masochistic character structure—whereas he was chiefly the one to go on the attack.

The Jewish/German issue played a prominent, though seldom openly stated, role in their quarreling: at first he professed to have "no feelings" about marrying a German girl (despite his family's vehement protests); he now began to condemn her, as though she was personally responsible for the Holocaust. Actually, she had been only two when the war ended; her father (whom she had never known) was a foot-soldier killed at Stalingrad. At first his being Jewish added to his attraction, helping her to assuage her guilt about the crimes of her countrymen. He in turn fancied himself "magnanimous" in choosing her, as if this meant he had risen above parochial prejudice and was willing to let bygones be bygones.

All this altruism proved to be a very thin patina indeed once their quarreling became heated. Once he had even struck her when she was pregnant with their last child: ostensibly over some minor expense she had incurred (ordinarily she was quite frugal); covertly, over his embarrassment at not being able to take care of the family expenses adequately, owing to his not getting the promotion he felt he deserved.

The sexual side of their marriage had "classical" sadomasochistic overtones: arguments would reach a fever pitch, with nasty language, occasional blows, threats of leaving . . . and these scenes would suddenly usher in, like a storm lifting, a mood of reconciliation, accompanied by tears of remorse and protestations of affection. War-making gave way to lovemaking. After a few peaceful, even idyllic days, the alternate pattern—of his fault-finding and her staying up till all hours "taking care of the house"—would reassert itself.

The outcome in this couple was favorable. Their love for one another was still readily apparent; their motivation was high; neither had come from a malignant or abusive family. The husband was able to recognize how shabbily he had been treating his wife; she could grasp how lonely he was for her affection, underneath his judgmental façade. He became less critical; she became less compulsive about her housework. They found a solution to their once irresolvable arguments about the religion in which their children were to be raised: in place of "either/or" (Jewish or Protestant), they began to celebrate both sets of holidays. This meant, in effect, the children would be "neither and both," i.e., neither exclusively one nor the other, but a blend of the two, the 50:50 fairness of which appealed to the couple and did not seem to bother the children. When I made a follow-up call 15 years later, the husband told me they were getting along much better, the children had turned out nicely, and when they went away to college, his wife completed a master's degree and started teaching. Not every couple spins out of the turbulence of a sadomasochistic relationship as this couple had, but it is encouraging to know that some respond well to therapy and make significant gains.

A "Sadomasochistic" Relationship
(Where One Member Was
Depressive-Masochistic; the Other, Sadistic)

Whereas the term "sadomasochistic" is usually applied to persons who are capable of warm feelings toward a sexual partner (though these are periodically vitiated by the sadistic component), we reserve the term "sadistic personality" for those in whom the capacity for warm intimacy is barely developed, if at all. When we speak of a whole relationship as being "sadomasochistic," at least one partner will usually be found to have that personality configuration—as in the foregoing examples. But a similar kind of tormented, pain-ridden pattern can unfold where one member is the willing victim and the other is outright sadistic. Unrelievedly sadistic people are often psychopathic as well, though exceptions exist on both sides: psychopaths who are not sadistic (e.g., charming con-artists who never say cruel things), and (mildly) sadistic persons who are not psychopathic (e.g., extremely stingy, mean-spirited, and abusive spouses who are scrupulously honest, "pillars of the church"). The following vignette concerns a couple, one of whose members was sadistic, the other, a "long-suffering" person with depressive and masochistic qualities.

The couple (to condense a very long story) consisted of a university professor and his wife. The relationship had many of the features of Maugham's *Of Human Bondage*—the man from an upper-class family, the woman from a background that was uncultured and sordid. The glue that held it together for so long was not sexual attraction, as in the novel, but instead the husband's fear of being alone. The marriage began to come apart after ten years, owing to the cruelty and lack of compassion on the part of the wife. The process of divorce took even longer, because of the innumerable roadblocks she placed in the path of any settlement (unreasonable demands, frequent changes of attorneys, "no-shows" at court, etc.). One may glimpse the nature of the wife's personality from a sampling of the incidents recorded by the husband (my patient) over a five-year period somewhere in the middle of the lengthy divorce proceedings, when the husband was already living apart:

item: "W. [the wife] bursts into my office at the college, when I was on my lunch-hour: my desk was overturned, and the drawers searched, their contents scattered in every direction. She accosts me when I return, screaming "I found the number of the other woman!"—even though we have already been apart three years."

item: "She tells our two daughters I am 'crazy,' a 'sadist' . . . and that I give her no money. When the girls tell me this story, I show them a canceled check for $5,000 I'd sent their mother two weeks before."

item: "W. bursts into my office again, and begins yelling at me and hitting me, saying that I should never have sued for divorce. After she hits me in the face, I try to call the campus police, but she rips the phone out of the socket."

item: "As the girls were about to visit me on Fathers Day, W. got in their way, forbade them to see me, and screamed so loud at the elder girl that she ran into her room. W. yanked the door open with such force as to break it off its hinges, and then proceeded to rip the posters off my daughter's wall, and hurl her books off the shelf."

item: "W. screamed at our younger daughter for half an hour, demanding that she tell her mother where I was living, whom I was seeing, etc."

item: "W. eventually found out where my apartment was. One afternoon, when I was teaching, she came round to the apartment and boarded up the entrance-door with planks and nails. A sign, in her handwriting, was affixed to one of the planks: 'Go to Hell, You Bastard.'"

These are but a few of the many dozens of such incidents, both before and after the decision to divorce. Clearly, if my patient had been abusive to his wife, her actions, though still extreme, would have to be viewed in a different light. But (and here the reader must take my assertion on faith) this was not the case. The husband's neurosis consisted not in provocative behavior such as might elicit counterattack, but (as with so many masochistic patients) in an unfortunate attraction to cruel partners. Truly sadistic persons scarcely ever change under the impact of treatment, and it will come as no surprise to learn that for a period of time before the divorce was initiated the couple went for marital counseling, which was unavailing, and that the wife went for psychotherapy, which was also without benefit.

SOME THOUGHTS ON THERAPY

The damned-if-you-do-damned-if-you-don't choices portrayed so cleverly in Heller's *Catch-22* come to mind again and again in one's work with pain-dependent patients. A psychiatric resident whom I supervise was telling me recently of a depressive-masochistic woman in her mid-sixties, agoraphobic for 40 years, fearful of life, fearful of death, extremely inhibited in sex, who denied her husband's requests for the past 20 years. At one point, when she was about 60, he had a brief affair. She found this out two years later. Apart from that her husband has been devoted to her throughout the 37 years of their marriage. Still, as she said, "I can never forgive him." Would she have preferred that he had divorced her and *then* taken up with the other woman? Certainly not, she indicated: that would have been the death of her; she cannot exist apart from her husband. Can she understand, then, how her refusal of sex — for a whole decade — could have nudged him in the direction of a discreet dalliance with another woman? Certainly not: "We took a vow before the priest at the altar to be faithful forever and ever. . . . " In other words, every solution is wrong, the fault always lay with the other person. Catch-22.

The wife in this example was not outwardly angry or strident and could be persuaded by her therapist, eventually, to forgive her husband — on the grounds that "to forget was human; to forgive, divine." This appealed to her self-image: she was a "better person" in being able to forgive. One might have liked to see her forgive on the more earthly grounds that, having been almost perfectly faithful for almost 40 years under trying conditions, her husband actually merited forgiveness. But at least she mellowed, and life with her husband became more satisfying.

Many depressive-masochistic patients are compliant and easy to get along with, do very little that contributes to the downfall of their intimate relationships, and do not set their therapists on edge via the evocation of hostile countertransference feelings. They manage to make their lives unhappy all the same through the unconscious selection of ungratifying partners: viz., pleasant persons who happen not to love them, unpleasant persons who do profess to love them, or (perhaps most commonly) persons incapable of commitment to a long-term relationship. Popular books about "women who love men who don't love women" are replete with examples of this phenomenon. The corresponding situation of men who love obsessively women who do not return their feelings is also by no means rare.

Confronted with patients of this sort, the therapist's first task is to help the patient recognize the pattern. Next comes the far more difficult task of helping the patient readjust his erotic wiring sufficiently so as to be able to fall, if not "madly," at least sufficiently, in love with someone who *returns* the love and who *is* motivated for a committed relationship. Since the "inner script" that dictates which sexual partners are "ideal" is etched early and deeply, this task usually requires the relinquishment of the so-called ideal partner and a gradual shift toward compromise. That is, they have to find satisfaction with a "good-enough" partner who has *some* of the qualities of the "ideal" (usually, the unobtainable oedipal/incestuous dream-man or dream-woman) — enough to support a stable love relationship — but who lacks the once-so-eagerly-sought-after qualities that routinely spelled the doom of all previous object-choices.

One patient of mine who struggled with this problem—an attractive and gifted woman whose irresponsible and probably alcoholic father abandoned the family shortly after she was born—fell in love with one after another self-centered and commitment-shy, but exciting and unconventional man. Each seemed to replicate certain aspects of what she had gleaned about her father's personality. As for the suitable men—less exciting, but more caring—who constantly asked her out, she waved them aside as so many "boring bankers in three-piece suits." Perhaps she will one day find the satisfactory compromise (a dashing entrepreneur in a two-piece suit?)—in what I have called "Tatyana's Choice." In Pushkin's masterpiece, the heroine first is swept off her feet by Yevgen'y Onegin, the suave and handsome egotist from the big city. Gradually, she realizes a marriage to him would be a disaster (Pushkin has this realization come through a dream, though he was writing 60 years before Freud's *Traumdeutung*). She reluctantly breaks the engagement and (later on) marries the less urbane, less handsome prince who truly cherishes her. She chucks hopeless love, in other words, for enduring affection; she makes a mature choice in place of a masochistic choice.

Pain-dependent patients with more pronounced sadomasochistic tendencies usually present greater challenges to therapy than do those with predominantly masochistic tendencies. This becomes all the more true if the typical defenses of externalization and counterattack are directed with some regularity at the therapist. Sadomasochistic patients frequently come across as aggressive; their responses may range from hypercriticalness to outright sarcasm or other expressions of contempt. A steady barrage of this will tend to unnerve most recipients, whether these be family members, spouses, friends, coworkers—or therapists.

Among therapists, various countertransference feelings will be elicited: impatience, annoyance, hatred, riddance-wishes, and the like. This is apt to bring out the worst in us—which the sadomasochist seizes upon as proof of our inadequacy. The charged, unpleasant atmosphere thus generated will usually turn out to be a duplication of the patient's early home-life. Therapist swept up in this atmosphere must steel themselves to not take personally the specifics of the verbal attacks or, at the very least, to admit candidly as to when and where they have misunderstood or otherwise been in error. This will usually restore calm, creating an environment more congenial to the patient's acceptance of partial responsibility for the strained atmosphere.

In time patients may be able to understand how the attack-mode brings out defensiveness and counterattack in others (including the therapists), and how not *all* these "others" can be correctly construed as hostile and uncaring, the way the parents may (or may not!) truly have been. Ultimately, this means sadomasochistic patients must dismantle the attack machinery with which they have hitherto defended themselves. Perhaps in the home of origin this machinery was necessary to survival. Now, as they must learn, it is prejudicial to survival, or at least to the harmony of their most important relationships.

At all events, the therapist who is able to "contain" (in Winnicott's excellent image) the patient's accusations has the best chance of helping that patient distinguish those criticisms that are fair from those that are unfair, and of helping the patient grasp how an accusatory tone, by bringing out the worst in others, simply courts alienation, perpetuating the illusion that there is only "injustice" in the world. This helps one get to the sadomasochist's more hidden layers—of mistrust, of wounded pride, and, deeper still, of forlornness over being cut off from the simple pleasures that come so easily to other people.

Unhappy love relationships, including unhappy marriages, often consist of a victimizer-victim pairing: sadomasochist with masochist. For therapists who grew up unexposed to the indignities which such couples visit upon each other, the stories they will hear constitute a kind of *terra incognita*, carrying them deep into an unfamiliar realm. It becomes difficult to understand the dynamics of such egregious behavior, difficult at times to sympathize with the more openly abusive partner (even though the latter had probably been tormented by caretakers years before). The lives of sadomasochistic persons, in particular, seem orchestrated by a misplaced genius for making life uncomfortable where it needn't have been. Unlike the lives of persons who are primarily sadistic (as in some of the vignettes in Chapters 13 and 21), sadomasochistic persons often have amicable relations with non-intimates. It will be helpful to keep well in mind the genuine suffering they once endured, since this awareness will make it easier for the therapist, even when under attack, to maintain an appropriate attitude of compassion and sympathy.

Since many patients with pain-dependent personalities are animated by the hope of "getting even" with an abusive or disappointing parent (or with persons in their current life who serve as transferential "equivalents" of the offending parent), it will become a major goal at some point in the treatment that this unrealizable hope be given up. Impressing upon such patients the old lesson that "living well is the best revenge" is not easy, and requires the kind of encouragement and persuasive argument that Spillane (1987) had in mind in analogizing the art of psychotherapy to a "noble rhetoric": an "ethical hierarchy of language and values based on the principle of responsible autonomy" (p. 217).

The demandingness and accusatoriness of certain sadomasochistic patients may represent attempts to "get even" with the abusive figures from the past, through a transference operation in which the therapist is misconstrued as this or that hurtful caretaker. If, of course, such patients succeed in evoking hatred or rejecting responses from the therapist, they will have actually managed, not so much as to misconstrue, but to *convert* the therapist into a "bad" person. Revenge motifs can now be enacted directly against the therapist-qua-bad-parent, which permits the patient to proceed along his preferred path of getting even rather than getting better. Needless to say, this is no kind of therapy—merely, a kind of wasteful psychodrama. The way around this pitfall is to contain, rather than to react (in effect, to "keep cool" rather than retaliate) and to treat angry outbursts as one would a dream: as communications that beg to be "translated," understood, and interpreted. I don't think any therapist can respond so adroitly on every such occasion. To err is human, and it is very easy to err when under attack. But if one can preserve goodwill, and utilize even one's lapses as vignettes to be understood and metabolized, then in time the patient may be able to grasp the essential humanity and benevolence of the therapist. In time, this may overpower the internal images of authorities, parents, or whatever, as being only malevolent or dishonest.

17

The Impact of Abuse
on Personality

WE HAVE KNOWN FOR A LONG TIME that parental abusiveness regularly has a deleterious impact upon the developing personality. This is in contrast to parental *sternness*, even when occasional slaps are included to interrupt a child's truly outrageous or dangerous behavior. Mild, occasional corporal punishment—"for cause" and administered without meanness by a loving parent—is common in many cultures throughout the world. While one might hope that even that degree of physicality could be avoided in an "ideal" world, it would be folly to assume that occasional cuffs of this sort need necessarily lead to a serious deformation of the child's personality. But severe, senseless, unprovoked, or cruel physical punishment or verbal humiliation, inflicted by an enraged or rejecting parent, is extremely difficult for even the most emotionally strong and the most forgiving child to overlook. The impact upon personality will often be damaging—and sometimes shattering.

In the last 15 years we have become aware of how many relatives commit incest—daughters will be victimized about six times as often as sons—and here again, the impact will often be damaging and, in the case of parent-child incest, *often* shattering.

The burgeoning literature on these subjects includes books by Courtois (1988), Finkelhor (1984), Forward and Buck (1978), Herman (1981),

392

Goodwin (1982), Justice and Justice (1979), and the fine epidemiological study by Russell (1986). I myself first became aware of the frequency of incest histories in women admitted to psychiatric hospitals with borderline personality disorder (Stone, 1981a); the literature on that subject is now voluminous (cf., e.g., van der Kolk, 1989, Zanarini & Gunderson, 1990).

In the mental health profession we try to avoid cause-effect statements, since the paths between past events and an outcome of such complexity as a "personality" are usually tortuous, crisscrossing, and, as the years between those past events and *now* increase, ever more blurred. But I defy anyone to read the biographies of the author/composer Paul Bowles (whose father left him exposed to the cold, to die), Beethoven (whose alcoholic father beat him on the back with a stick while he practiced his scales: Stone, 1976), Turgenev (whose despotic and insanely cruel mother beat him to within an inch of his life), the Schreber of Freud's famous monograph (the elder Schreber roped his children to metal rods, to "improve" their posture), or Hitler (toward whom we feel no sympathy, but whose father whipped him daily, and much harder than he whipped Hitler's half-brother, who ran away from home)—I defy anyone to read the accounts of parental cruelty in these biographies and still to assert: yes, but we can't say there is cause and effect. And to the hold-outs who are still unimpressed, I say, read the biographies of some of the notorious murderers of our own day and place. With the exception of Turgenev's mother (cf. Pritchett, 1977), none of the parents alluded to above comes close in viciousness to the father of John Gacy (the serial killer of 38 men in Chicago: Cahill, 1986), or of Albert DeSalvo (the "Boston Strangler": Frank, 1966), or of the stepfather of James Armstrong (who went on to strangle cats as a child; women, as an adult: E. Keyes, 1976), or the mother of Jerry Brudos (the Oregon serial killer: A. Rule, 1983), or of the brutalizing fathers of the Texas tower shooter, Charles Whitman (Nash, 1982), the "Yorkshire Ripper," Peter Sutcliffe (Burn, 1985), or the Philadelphia torturer/killer, Gary Heidnick, whose alcoholic father used to hold him outside the window, threatening to drop him if he didn't behave (Englade, 1988).

From this wealth of biographical material we come away with the impression that with parental cruelty—and luck—one may emerge as a cranky musical genius (Beethoven) or as a pathologically shy novelist (Turgenev); with the same or worse cruelty—and no luck—one may come out as the incarnation of evil. These are the extremes. In between is the far greater number of our patients, especially those with borderline or antisocial personality disorders, famous neither for good nor for evil, but whose histories of abuse are just as seering, often more sickening, than anything in biographies I have alluded to. Every so often I have heard a story—from a patient of my own, or from a colleague—that at the time I thought surely must represent the nadir of parental abusiveness. I have long since come to realize that below each such "absolute zero" of depravity lies a more gruesome story, underneath which is a story more horrifying still. I offer the following by way of example, knowing full well that you the reader have gathered in your clinical practice stories that make mine pale by comparison.

While visiting an Australian hospital unit specializing in borderline patients, I encountered a suicidal young woman whose religious-fanatic mother, by way of "purifying" her daughter before church, would lock her in a closet for a day, then scrub the girl's vulva with steel wool. Upon my return to the States, I did a case-conference on another borderline inpatient whose breakdown occurred after her mother, enraged at the type of boyfriend she brought home, went ahead and served her daughter a sandwich made of (the mother's) feces. A college student with a severe compulsive personality disorder came from a family where the father was so violent as to have thrown this young man and his mother *through* one of the walls in their house; when the student chanced to vomit some of his food during supper, his father then forced him to eat the vomitus. When lecturing at a hospital in Boston, I made the acquaintance of a psychologist who listened indulgently to these tales of "supreme" child abuse, then told me of an adolescent patient of his whose father, after raping the boy anally, proceeded to pour boiling water over his penis and then to blow apart his puppy with a firecracker.

But these are the stories of young people who, after all, lived to become our patients. What do we really know of the systematic torture inflicted upon the six-year-old Lisa by her "adoptive" father, Joel Steinberg (Ehrlich, 1989)? And how do any of these vignettes compare with the worst of the tragic stories amassed over the past 25 years by a pioneer in the field of child abuse like Dr. Arthur Green (1978)?

Given the epidemic proportions of family violence in the United States (van Hasselt et al., 1988), we can be grateful that only a small percentage of the victims grow into hardened criminals. Few escape without abnormalities of personality. These abnormalities are diverse and include social avoidance and shyness, extreme rigidity and compulsiveness, a crippling envy (toward the majority of persons, who have not been exposed to comparable cruelty), defiance, abusiveness and combativeness, bitterness, mistrustfulness, cynicism, bigotry, amorality, tyranny, sadism, vengefulness— to mention only some of the more important. I do not mean to imply that persons exhibiting these traits have invariably been the victims, during childhood, of cruelty or humiliation, but rather, that in the histories of persons with these traits there would be an overrepresentation of such histories, compared with the general population. As for incest victims, because of their conflicting loyalties, exposure to parental possessiveness and betrayal, they often develop intense and intractable jealousy and sometimes a crass seductiveness and manipulativeness, among a multitude of other symptoms (Stone, 1985, 1990).

THE INCIDENCE OF PHYSICAL ABUSE AND INCEST

The precise incidence of *physical abuse* of children in our country is unknown, for reasons that, as Starr (1988) mentions, go beyond mere problems in finding an acceptable definition as to what constitutes "abuse." Abuse occurs in the privacy of the home; there is also underreporting by neighbors, teachers, and mental health professionals who chance to become aware of battered children. In 1983 some 280,000 children were reported to have been physically abused in the U.S.A., along with 190,000 who were abused and neglected, and another 460,000 who were neglected. According to a random sample of American households, 3½% of parents admitted committing acts of violence against a child (Gelles, 1978), which extrapolates, as Starr points out, to approximately one and a half to two million children subjected to forms of violence that might cause physical injury. Since the American Humane Association began compiling data in 1976, there has been an increase of about 150% in reported cases, but it remains unclear how much this reflects an actual increase in the base-rate vs. a heightened tendency to report such cases.

Though for a time it had been argued that child abuse was equally represented in all social classes, merely underreported in middle and upper classes, more convincing evidence points up that the preponderance of maltreating families are from lower-middle to lower class in status (Straus, Gelles, & Steinmetz, 1980). Methods for coping with intrafamilial stress may differ along class lines, such that "dominance/submission" strategies may predominate in less well-off families, while "negotiation" strategies may be more the norm in better-off families.

In line with this socioeconomic factor is my own observation, based on analysis of famous murder cases (cf. Chapter 21), that histories of parental brutality were grossly overrepresented among the lower two SES classes: of 39 instances, the distribution was: SES I—0%, II—2½%, III (middle class)—26%, IV—51%, and V—20%. Murderers without a history of parental brutality showed a reversed pattern (N = 111): SES I—11%, II—31%, III—27%, IV—22%, and V—10%. Excluding the middle class cases, it turns out that 28 of 63 murderers from the lower two classes had been brutalized (44%), but only one of 47 from the upper two classes

(2%). Cultural factors may also play a role, as suggested by the absence of a parental physical abuse history in the 11 Jewish murderers (most of whom had strong *hypomanic* features, which were seldom noted in those from other religious groups).

Incest had once been considered extremely rare, as though occurring only in Greek plays and Egyptian kings. Quite to the contrary, recent epidemiological studies show that 5% of a sample of female college students report an incest history (Finkelhor, 1984); Russell's careful study (1986) of San Francisco women from all cultural and socioeconomic groups showed a 16% history, where incest was broadly defined (forced intercourse at the one extreme, sexual kissing or hugging at the other). Thirty-one percent of the 930 women interviewed by Russell and her colleagues reported at least once incident of sexual abuse by a non-family member before age 18. With respect to the impact upon personality in the victim, transgenerational (e.g., father-daughter, uncle-niece, father-son) incest is more damaging than same-generational (Farrell, 1990), involving, as it does, betrayal of the protective responsibilities on the part of the older person toward his or her relative.

There is an interrelationship between incest and the pathological emphasis on male "superiority" mentioned above in connection with physical abuse in lower SES families. Father-daughter (and other forms of older male-younger female) incest has the effect of subjugation of the victimized woman. There is also a curious interrelationship between incest and prostitution, at least in America, in that (a) the incidence of an incest history among prostitutes is extraordinarily high (viz., 90% among those working in massage parlors; K. Harter, 1992, personal communication), and (b) some men will consort with prostitutes by way of avoiding incest, while still others resort to incest to avoid the (for them) excessive complications of adultery or going to prostitutes. But the "sparing" effect prostitution has on incest (and this is more visible in certain cultures, where prostitution is more condoned and incest more vehemently prohibited than in the U.S.) means that some incest victims who turn to prostitution save some of their younger "sisters" from the predatoriness of their fathers, which might otherwise be visited on the daughters. This is reminiscent of the coy vs. fast strategies discussed in Chapter 4.

One of the more lurid examples of this "equilibrium" — from the annals of criminology concerns the case of Gene Simmons, the Air Force sergeant who sired a child by his favorite daughter. Even though he, for years, terrorized his family into absolute submission, the news did eventually leak out, at which point he murdered all his dozen family members, including his daughter and his son (grandson?) by her (Marshall & Williams, 1991).

PARENTAL CRUELTY AS A FACTOR
PREDISPOSING TO ANTISOCIALITY

The shibboleth "violence begets violence" is fortunately not always true. Starr (1988) estimates that about 80% of abused children do *not* go on to abuse their own children. Some (the women more than the men) make a special pact with themselves not to mistreat their children as they themselves were once mistreated. Still, there is an overrepresentation of formerly abused children among the ranks of adults who, as they became parents, continued the same pattern. Furthermore, as Dietz (1985) suggests in his catalog of predictors of future criminal behavior, a history of having been abused as a child—coupled with an arrest later on for any violent offense— is associated with repeat criminal offenses in the range of 10 to 50% (p. 94). The same is true for (a) morbid jealousy or (b) alcoholism, when either is associated with a history of a violent offense.

In my study of murderers who became the subjects of a biography, 31% had had a clear-cut history of severe parental abuse. Most of the murderers showed strong antisocial/psychopathic and narcissistic traits. Though other factors contributed, such as a pronounced family history of felony, alcoholism, or incarceration, this 31% incidence is higher than the baserate of parental abuse in the U.S., enough to suggest that the parental cruelty predisposed in some instances to the development of antisocial personality.

Other personality attributes that may figure as predictors (though not strong predictors) of criminality are, as Dietz suggests: (a) incapacity to feel sympathy, (b) inability to learn from experience, (c) impulsivity, (d) narcissistic traits, (e) paranoid traits, (f) borderline traits, (g) inner rage, (h) overcontrolled aggression, (i) an external locus of control (cf. Foon, 1987), and (j) a hypertrophied sense of justice (p. 94). Parental cruelty could foster the development of factors a, c, e, g, h, and i from this set; incest, of factors c, e, f, g, h, and i.

Here is an illustration of how incest can predispose to the formation of paranoid traits: a woman in her late thirties had sued her husband for divorce. She was convinced he was going to molest their 13-year-old daughter. I was asked by their attorneys to evaluate the family. The woman, it developed, had been "gang-raped" by her four older brothers when she was 13. When she complained to her (alcoholic) father, he yelled at her: "They did no such thing!" Shortly before her daughter's thirteenth birthday, she and her daughter drove to a motel in another town, registering under an assumed name. The mother did this to "protect" her daughter from incest, even though there was not the slightest indication that her husband had any such designs on his daughter. Reconciliation proved impossible. The mother could admit that she knew she was "acting crazy," yet she was too mistrustful to remain in the marriage.

Other clinical features associated with an incest history are to be found in an earlier article (Stone, 1989a); other vignettes concerning the impact of physical and sexual abuse in a paper focusing on borderline patients (Stone, 1990a). The heightened vulnerability of female incest victims not only to borderline and multiple personality disorders, but also to become rape victims in adult life or to choosing battering husbands has been underlined by Coons, Bowman et al. (1989).

A Note on Obsessive-Compulsive Disorder

There has been a resurgence of interest over the past decade in obsessive-compulsive disorder, and a burgeoning literature devoted to this condition. In part the development of several serotonergic medications that offer symptom relief in a good proportion of cases has prompted this interest. Meanwhile, improved techniques in brain imaging have yielded promising clues as to the neurophysiological correlates of OCD (Rapoport et al., 1981). Baxter, Schwartz et al. (1991) argue for the heads of the caudate nuclei and the left orbital gyri as the sites of relevant neuroanatomical disturbances. Kellner and his colleagues (1991), using a magnetic resonance imaging technique, could not confirm the presence of gross brain structural abnormalities in OCD as compared with a healthy control group. Despite the appellation, patients with OCD are by no means concomitantly "obsessive-compulsive" in their personality (Mavissakalian et al., 1990; Sciuto et al., 1991), but may show a wide range of personality types.

What I have been struck with, in connection with OCD, is the frequency with which a history of severe physical or sexual abuse is present. Examining the records of the 180 patients I have treated in private practice since 1966 (and who remained in treatment at least three months), I noted there were 14 who showed the DSM-III-R picture of OCD (Stone & Pine, 1993). Four had compulsive handwashing. One had to turn the key to her apartment 20 times before she could leave; another had to touch everything four times. Thirteen of these patients had been abused either verbally, physically or sexually (in 13, 12, and 4 cases, respectively). Only one had no abuse history. Among the 166 patients who did not have OCD, an abuse history was significantly less common: 25/166 or 15%. Both groups of abused patients came from similar socioeconomic backgrounds (avg. SES 1.9 in the OCD group; 2.3 in the non-OCD group). All but one of the OCD patients were comorbid for a personality disorder: BPD (5), OCPD (3), schizotypal, avoidant, paranoid, explosive and passive-aggressive (1 each).

These data derive from a relatively small sample. The correlation cannot be as robust as a similar finding based on independent evaluations of a larger sample rated by persons blind to the diagnosis. Still, it merits closer attention, since it points to the intriguing possibility that, as in borderline personality disorder (which five of the OCD patients also had) and post-traumatic stress disorder, a history of abuse may be an important contributory factor in OCD. In the case of OCD, some underlying neurophysiological abnormality of the basal ganglia may be a necessary, but not always sufficient, cause. In persons with the (perhaps) serotonin pathway abnormality, severe abuse may set in motion the clinical picture we identify under this heading.

Though four of the OCD patients in my series had suffered physical abuse severe enough to cause bodily injury, none of the four (nor any of the other six) had gone the route of antisocial behavior. Seven, in fact, were unusually guilt-ridden people who blamed themselves for family problems, illnesses (in themselves or their intimates), etc., which had nothing to do with them. They were persons of unusually good character, but with low self-esteem, having identified with the abusive remarks and treatment of the offending parent(s), as though they "deserved" their misery.

HEROIC PERSONALITY INTEGRITY IN THE FACE OF EXTREME ABUSE

Psychiatry does well at offering plausible explanations for how emotional disorders (of whatever sort) may have come about when the childhood antecedents, in the way of abuse, neglect, etc., were flagrant. When the personality is severely disordered in the absence of such childhood antecedents, we tend to evoke "birth trauma," "risk genes for schizophrenia," etc., wherever we can find some scraps of evidence for constitutional or genetic liability. Where the "nature" factors are unfavorable *and* the nurture factors were clearly horrendous—and *still* the personality emerges whole, or even unusually courageous—the explanatory powers of psychiatry fall to just about zero. Normality eludes us. Instances of this latter sort are a great challenge to psychiatry. But until we can explain why some people become whole who, according to theory, should have been "basket cases," our work is only half done. I offer the following vignette as an example of what psychiatry *cannot* explain about personality.

The "Case" of Eileen Franklin

In January of 1989 Eileen Lipsker, née Franklin, while holding her five-year-old daughter, Jessica, in her lap, had a sudden return of memory from an incident she had witnessed some 20 years before when she was a girl of eight. The incident in question was that of an "outing" in which her father had driven Eileen and her best friend, Susan Nason (also eight), in his van to some secluded spot, where he then proceeded to rape her friend, and then kill her by smashing her in the face with a rock. Eileen had kept this memory locked away from awareness (with generous encouragement from her father, who threatened to kill her if she ever told anyone) until the image of Jessica, a near look-alike to her old friend, flashed this "state-dependent" memory back onto the screen of consciousness.

After this realization, and with full emotional support from her husband, she proceeded to tell the authorities. The hitherto unsolved murder case was eventually opened—but not before reassurances from the district attorneys that there was an excellent chance that her father, George Franklin, would be not only convicted but also incarcerated for life, so that she and her family need not worry about the father's threats, were he let off or released. Despite the 20-year gap and the virtual absence of evidence from the crime scene, the case went forward. The rest, as they say, is history. The father was convicted and put away for life (Franklin & Wright, 1991).

Had this been the sole "unpleasantness" in Eileen's early life—a temporary aberration of her father's, in the midst of an otherwise nurturing home-life—the experience would still have been shattering, I believe, for most children; the chances of most children in such a circumstance escaping without personality abnormality I would judge to be vanishingly small. Eileen's childhood, however, was a horror story of which the murder was merely the worst chapter. Her father had committed incest with Eileen repeatedly from the time she was three until her parents finally divorced, when she was 14. Her father committed incest with her three sisters as well, and Eileen knew about this. He was explosively violent and abusive toward all five of the children. He also began battering his wife after the birth of the youngest child. His temper was particularly vicious when he had been drinking.

At times their mother also drank and joined in the beatings of the children. Otherwise she was so neglectful as to be "nonexistent" as a mother, and often had nervous breakdowns (of a depressive type) necessitating hospitalization. When Eileen was 18 her mother kicked her out of the house, leaving Eileen to fend for herself. She went through a period of drug abuse and chaotic living, until, at the age of 20, she met her future husband. Thereafter, the many positive forces in her personality were able to co-alesce, creating the poised, resolute, courageous, emotionally warm, and morally unshakable woman she now is.

I had the good fortune to meet Eileen and her husband when she spoke about her experiences before the American College of Psychiatrists at the

February 1992 meeting, which was devoted to the topic of memory. She came across in person, as in her book, as engaging, lively, not exhibitionistic or overdramatic, integrated, and perhaps most remarkable of all, lacking in bitterness. I asked her (rhetorically—I did not expect a convincing answer) what enabled her to fly in the face of expectation, emerging whole from the wreckage of her disastrous childhood. She shrugged her shoulders and said something about a nice aunt, and about her husband's support. Really, she had no idea. She was her father's "favorite"—but that is not a big advantage, given the history of her father's sexual violation. He did stop beating her after the murder of her friend (as though he didn't quite trust her to keep quiet about it), but that, too, can hardly explain her strength of personality.

Eileen is attractive and intelligent—but so are her three sisters, none of whom had the same ability to put what is morally right before matters of family "loyalty." Besides, though attractiveness and intelligence are "pluses," they are no guarantors of emotional wholeness, as witness the story of Barbara Hoffman—born into a socially more advantaged family than Eileen's—whose attractiveness and IQ of 145 did not offset whatever happened during her childhood (there is suspicion of incest): she became a serial killer, using her knowledge of chemistry to poison unsuspecting men whom she would lure with sexual favors into making her the beneficiary of insurance policies, etc. (Harter, 1990).

Why Barbara Hoffman opted for a life of vengeance, and Eileen Franklin for a life dedicated to social betterment, is not answerable from what we know at present. For the moment, I must assume that Eileen Franklin got dealt all the genetic high-cards, arranged in such a way as to allow her to have more compassion for the suffering of others than bitterness over what she had suffered, more empathic ability, more capacity to distinguish good from evil, once she was finally exposed, as she grew older, to people who were not evil (certain neighbors, her "nice" aunt, for example), and, most surprising of all, a trustingness, wholly out of keeping with the series of betrayals she experienced as a child, in the goodness of those she was later to meet who actually merited such trust. I wish we knew the "wiring-diagram" for this supra-normal personality and for the development of good character in the absence of positive influences, but we do not. Perhaps "absence" is too strong a word here: ironically, Eileen's father, despite his own mendacity, had always admonished her to "tell the truth." Somehow, she was able to pay more attention to his good words than to his bad deeds, so that, even though she loved him as well as hated him, when she was finally in a stronger and safer situation, she could do the right thing— and turn him in.

Heroic Integrity in the Child of a
High-Ranking Nazi

After the defeat of Germany in 1945, many of the Nazi leaders met their death either on the gallows at Nuremberg or, in a last-minute effort to dodge that fate, through suicide. The majority left wives and children behind; the children would now be men and women in their fifties and sixties. Gerald Posner (1991) attempted to interview a number of these descendants recently, and found that, to no one's surprise: (a) several declined to be interviewed altogether; (b) many had only positive things to say about their fathers (as Edda Göring said, "I love him very much and cannot be expected to judge him any other way"); and (c) others had ambivalent attitudes, with loyalty taking precedence over the negative feelings (Mengele said, "I was ashamed of him, but he was my father. . . . I couldn't turn him in"). Blood is thicker than water.

Except in the case of Niklas Frank. The younger son of the Nazi Governor-General of Poland, Hans Frank, Niklas grew up in a huge castle in Cracow, witness to his parent's systematic plundering of the Poles and Polish Jews, and growing ever more aware of the extermination of the Jews, over which his father presided. From the windows of Frank's castle one could actually watch the smoke billowing from the nearby crematoria. As for the plundering, sometimes Niklas' mother would take him along in the limousine as she would swoop into the ghetto, buying up mink coats for a few zlotys from Jewish women about to be transported, unknowingly, to Auschwitz (who could refuse the wife of the Governor-General?).

Far from suffering the outrages *within* the family that Eileen Franklin's parents subjected her to, Niklas was not abused by his parents and grew up in the lap of luxury—until, when Niklas was seven, his father was hanged at Nuremberg. Somehow, Niklas was able in the years that followed to get a clear fix on his parents, recognizing them for exactly what they were. No one in his entourage, least of all his predatory mother, enlightened him about the real nature of his father or the Nazis in general. Niklas devoted years of his life to amassing material and uncovering the truth about his father's life.

The book-jacket of Niklas' biography speaks of his "impassioned condemnation of his father's life and deeds." These are pallid words next to what is inside the book. In describing his father's apprehension that Hitler and Himmler were scandalized by his looting art works from museums and were about to reprimand him, Niklas writes:

The fear inside you must have been dripping with cancerous lesions by now. . . . You are stinking from your putrefying snot, and my heart rejoices. . . . I'm filled with an unspeakable joy that your regime is finally coming to an end, an insane satisfaction that you are going to feel with your own body at least a taste of that nameless horror we caused millions of others to feel. (p. 294)

Elsewhere, in response to the many letters of sympathy and admiration for his father that his mother received over the years, Niklas comments:

I look at us Germans and I am frightened. . . . There are two people inside each German: One of them is well behaved, hardworking, a solid citizen. That is the official version of the respectable German. But beneath it . . . there are the authentic Germans, a people of murderers. (p. 350)

After reading this overwhelming book, I wrote Niklas Frank, asking him, as I had asked Eileen Franklin, if he had any clues as to what enabled him to escape the moral squalor of his family. What allowed him to rise above the usual knee-jerk love and loyalty to a parent no matter how evil, and to speak so eloquently *against* the evil within his family? Whence this integrity of personality, coming from such a background? In the touching letter he sent me in reply, Niklas Frank had no more idea where his nobility of spirit came from than did Eileen Franklin; like her, he was embarrassed at being praised in this way. He even added in his letter:

For even from my own text, it became clear to me how much danger we ourselves are in — who knows whether, if I had lived in his time, I might have become like my father? (my transl.)

Most mental health professionals would agree that (a) there is a strong connection between child abuse and subsequent deformations of personality, yet at the same time (b) many victims of child abuse go on to lead either very productive lives, without crippling disorders of personality, or (c) some become both productive and "normal" without any discernible ill effects from the earlier abuse. The latter group are analogous to the "invulnerable children" psychogeneticists speak of, in connection with infants at "high risk" for schizophrenia who seem impervious to all "insults" (i.e., adverse factors), whether prenatal, perinatal, or postnatal (Anthony, 1974; Marcus, Auerbach et al., 1984). Niklas Frank and Eileen Franklin belong to this group, where *personality* is concerned (the painful flashbacks of memory Eileen Franklin experiences are ill effects, but ones involving symptoms, not personality).

18

The Personality of the Therapist as a Factor in Treatment

THE COMPLEXITIES OF TREATING PATIENTS with personality disorders or with troublesome traits — which means virtually every patient seeking help through psychotherapy — impel many a clinician to seek assistance from a book about how to do psychotherapy. The utility of any such volume depends upon a number of assumptions: most importantly, that the cases being highlighted in the book resemble closely the cases with which the reader is struggling. No less importantly: that the reader-clinician has a personality, a training, and a basis of experience that do not differ too markedly from those of the clinician-author.

The latter assumption, it need hardly be said, figures much less in the equation when the subject is, instead of personality disorders, more biologically-caused conditions like acute mania. Even in the realm of the psychopharmacology, as opposed to the psychotherapy, of borderline personality, the peculiarities of the clinician weigh much less in the balance. Paul Soloff, Rex Cowdry, and Michael Liebowitz, for example, have all made important contributions to the psychopharmacology of borderline conditions. But the impact of their personalities upon the patients who were the subjects of their studies, while not altogether negligible, must be very small when compared with the impact of psychotherapists' personalities upon the patients with whom they are working in intensive treatment. There is, after all, near universality of agreement about the advisability of prescribing lithium to a borderline patient "comorbid" for bipolar II affective disorder (a common occurrence) or of trying an MAOI antidepressant with a borderline patient who is simultaneously depressed and hostile. The medications will tend to work in these situations irrespective of the particularities of doctor or patient. The situation with psychotherapy is not nearly so neat.

If one thinks about all the interventions one might recommend in relation to the psychotherapy of borderline patients, there are certain dos and don'ts that would appear on everyone's list, no matter what the personality or background of the clinician. One should take a careful history; one should not become overfamiliar or overindulgent with the patient's demands, etc., etc. These comments are reminiscent of what chess books advise concerning opening moves: some are almost always useful; certain others are disastrous. Beyond the opening moves, however, lies a vast region of "chaos": a quintillion octillion octillion possible moves—the optimal of which cannot be predicted with certainty beyond the next two or three. In large part this unpredictability stems from the unpredictable responses of the other participant—the same situation that obtains in the doctor-patient dyad.

The clinicians of renown in the domain of borderline conditions have, collectively, elaborated many theories and suggested many formulae and guidelines for "ideal" or optimally effective psychotherapy. One can find various features in common, such as the need for limit-setting. This becomes important when dealing with the tendency of borderline patients to act impulsively or to make unreasonable demands either upon the therapist or upon other persons of importance to the process of treatment. In Chapter 11 I sketched in detail the six hierarchical steps outlined by Linehan (1987). These help orient the therapist as to what needs to be accomplished, and in what sequence, during the course of treatment. Linehan's first two steps concern suicidality and substance abuse: rescuing the patient from self-destructiveness. Step three consists of resolving conflicts about the therapist that, if neglected, might threaten the continuity of the therapeutic relationship. In treating milder personality-disordered patients, where issues of life and death, self-destructiveness, and "negative transference" are not present, therapists will instinctively "skip" to steps four and five: dealing with symptoms and disturbing personality traits.

In any event, once one advances beyond the "opening moves" (about which there is usually considerable agreement), one is in the vast and deep ocean of details. The details concern particular moments in the therapy of any given patient by the one and unique therapist with whom that patient is currently working. It is in this region of the deep that, in the case of borderline patients, the recommendations of Kernberg, or Gunderson, or McGlashan, or Perry, or Masterson, or Meissner, or Adler, or Searles, or

Kroll, or Kohut, or Grotstein, or Balint, or Schmideberg, or Beck, etc., etc., not only begin to differ in no longer trivial ways but also begin to reveal something about the individuality of each theoretician.

To take as one example, the theoretical stance embodied in the writings of Searles places great weight upon the ability to grasp intuitively the hidden dynamics that so often figure in the lives of borderline patients, especially those dynamics that are foreign to the experience of the average therapist: the wish to become a dog (that being the only creature that ever received any love within the family); envy of a certain brocaded chair (upon which one's former lover was fond of sitting), etc. This is not merely the empathy whose importance the Kohutians underline, but rather an uncanny ability to tune in to the uncanny.

There are many therapists but only a few who possess Searles' ability, just as there are many musicians but only a few with perfect pitch. Those without "perfect pitch" clearly must make do with what they have. It comes naturally to Searles to rely upon extrasensory-like intuition, even to the point of making it the cornerstone of his psychotherapeutic edifice. Those who try to emulate him yet who lack this gift will have no better success than will the violinist, lacking perfect pitch, when he plays high up on the "E" string. To the average therapist, then, Searles' reliance on intuition will seem overemphasized or somehow off the mark: it doesn't work (as indeed for them it does not).

To the non-perfect-pitch majority it might seem prudent at this point to toss Searles' books aside and reach for another author: Kernberg, perhaps. Kernberg's style, as well as tenor of the theoretical stance adumbrated in his books, is more methodical, more systematic. One analyzes the negative transference that commonly pervades the atmosphere early in the intensive therapy of a borderline patient. One confronts the patient about the paradoxical positions maintained in descriptions of important persons: mother was neglectful/mother was a saint; father was a pillar of the church/father was grossly seductive; you (the therapist) are corrupt and mercenary/you are the only one who can save me, etc. Gradually, the various split-images of these persons are knitted together into more integrated pictures.

Kernberg's theory about treatment, and the specific recommendations that flow from it seem appealing and convincing to a wide readership, just as did the theories and the clinical examples to be found in Searles' writings. But even if Kernberg's system is *mostly* attuned to external reality and is of therapeutic use over a wide array of cases (the same as could be said of Searles, though focusing on different aspects of the patients' reality), it is still in part a reflection of Kernberg's "cognitive style"—the way his brain is "wired," in contrast to the different wiring of Searles. Kernberg's cognitive style emphasizes precision, hard edges, sharp distinctions, categorical more than dimensional thinking. But what if the therapist who immerses himself in Kernberg's writings has a cognitive style characterized by dimensional more than categorical thinking, confluence of impressions at the expense of precision, etc.? Such a therapist will not feel himself to be in harmony with Kernberg's system. The recommendations seem sound yet they do not quite work for him, and he may search for a still different expert with whom to identify and whose works seem more congenial to the therapist's intrinsic style.

Because no theoretician has woven a fabric so complete as to cover all situations, therapists, as they mature, absorb and assimilate the wisdom contained in dozens of books and in dozens of supervisors. For each therapist, a new theory evolves (not often written down explicitly) that derives from one or two "main" mentors and from many subsidiary influences. Except in the case where the therapist "swears" by just one expert (becoming, in the process, something of a religious acolyte), his new, personal theory will be an amalgam—a heterodoxy. Not a monochrome fabric but a quilt.

THE THERAPIST'S TRAITS

The subjectivity of therapists, including psychoanalysts (who are never the "blank screens" Freud and the pioneers assumed they could be), inevitably influences ("intrudes," if you are a purist) the therapeutic mise-en-scène. This will occur with all patients. Perhaps compliant patients will experience this subjectivity less than "difficult" patients, since the latter, by virtue of being overemotional, threatening, irritating, seductive, demanding, or whatever, elicit stronger counter-reactions in us. Patients whose personalities incline toward the paranoid, aggressive, or narcissistic may place great strain on our efforts to be gracious and benevolent. One might claim that the object-relational, self-psychological, and Sullivanian/interpersonal schools, which have risen to such prominence in the analytic world after mid-century, were themselves reactions to the unrealistic "blank-screen" (read: one-sided) view of the therapist-patient dyad (Gedo, 1979; Kernberg, 1982a; Kohut & Wolf, 1978; Sternbach, 1983; Sutherland, 1980).

Therapists trained at the same center and of the same generation will certainly show noticeable differences with respect to many personality traits. We can think of a number of relevant personality "axes": silent vs. chatty, permissive vs. strict (viz. in limit-setting, scheduling, and fee arrangements), phlegmatic vs. reactive, detached vs. interactive, serious vs. humorous, decisive vs. tentative, authoritarian vs. egalitarian, formal vs. casual. One could extend the list to quite some length. Since therapists have their own personality profile, to say nothing of their own families of ori-

gin—each with its own cast of characters, its own unique experiences—
there will be a range, within the whole spectrum of patients, where each
therapist does his or her best work. Outside that range, the work becomes
unfamiliar and difficult. Having had a depressed parent, for example, may
make a therapist more sympathetic to, more understanding of, more able
to help similarly depressed patients. If that parent were at the same time
rejecting or abrasive, depressed patients might be "off limits" for that therapist.

Certain therapists have an expansive humanity and an ability to sympathize with persons whom most others find intensely disagreeable or threatening. Harry Albert (1983a) was such a therapist, and could do amazing
work with paranoid patients most other therapists would back away
from—including the paranoid man who wielded a gun. The man was about
to "blow away" his wife in the delivery room, believing the baby was from
another father. Dr. Albert, finding a way to sympathize with this man's
plight, and to communicate this sympathy to him, was able to restore the
man's equilibrium.

One time a patient said she would kill me first, if I went ahead and
warned her husband she was about to buy a gun and kill him. In this
situation I found I could not sustain sympathy (especially after, in a family
session, she berated her daughter who had just rescued her from a suicide
attempt). I even recall thinking at the time: "This is a case for Harry."
Or perhaps "for Frieda." Frieda Fromm-Reichmann, as is clear from the
impressions of those who knew her during her days at Chestnut Lodge,
was remarkable for her compassionate acceptance of patients who seemed
"impossible" to others, including those who seemed unreachably "regressed" and out of contact.

For many patients, especially for those who are better-functioning, the
stylistic differences and particularities of personality among various therapists make little impact upon the outcome of treatment. The therapists'
peculiarities are so much "grist for the mill," perhaps altering the sequence
with which important topics emerge, but making little difference in the
long run. The situation is more precarious with patients who have been
severely traumatized: they may be too uncomfortable for therapy even to
get started if the therapist is, say, of the same gender as the offending
parent. For this reason, borderline female patients who have been incest
victims often prefer to work with female therapists, at least at the beginning, if not for the duration of treatment. An obsessive-compulsive analy-
sand raised by laconic and uncaring parents may find a too-silent analyst
intolerable, and will switch to a more talkative colleague.

Baudry (1989a) offers an interesting vignette highlighting the need for
flexibility and creativity—*dramatic flair* might be nearer the mark—if cer-

tain therapeutic stalemates are to be overcome. The vignette concerns an analyst who was treating a wealthy Parisian woman to whom "money meant nothing." After a time, the analysis failed to move forward. As Baudry tells it: "All the interpretations of the patient's resistance, aggression, and contempt failed to resolve the impasse." The analyst then announced to her one day that " . . . until further notice, he had decided not to charge her a fee." This *beau geste* took her by surprise, and allowed the analysis to go forward (p. 403). What, in the complex chemistry of his own personality and in the unfolding of his own life-history, led him to this *coup de théâtre* the analyst himself could probably not fathom. Yet, as Baudry emphasizes, the personality traits of the therapist form an integral part of the therapeutic equation—one that is customarily left as so many x's and y's, unrevealed and unavailable, when we later try to explain our technique to others. One can add: The most gifted supervisors are those who take stock of their trainees' individuality. Harold Searles, for example, rather than explain what *he* might do in a given clinical situation, helped his supervisees to create useful interventions based on the particularities of *their* personalities and experiences (Stone, 1982a).

Ultimately, patients with pathological personality traits will tend to ferret out the real (as opposed to transference-fantasied) qualities of their therapists—partly in an effort, as Baudry suggests, to make more personal contact, to counteract the one-sidedness of who gets to know whom in the therapeutic encounter. There may be other reasons. I can think of certain sadomasochistic patients who have had an inordinate need to find my flaws, to bring me down to size, to see me as "no better" than their abusive parents (this, out of loyalty to the hated, but also loved, parents), and also to see me as no better a master of my life than they are of theirs—thus to win a kind of Pyrrhic victory, one in which they can lament their own failure to get better, but enjoy the spectacle of the vaunted therapist flailing about in equal helplessness. In a curious way, exposure of my imperfections may have helped, rather than hindered, the bond between us, with some of these patients, to whom in my quirkiness I no longer seemed so distant or so different. Baudry makes the valuable comment, though, that: "If the patient engages the character of the analyst at a point in which the latter is [too] vulnerable or sensitive, the treatment may not make progress at this point" (p. 408).

EQUAL OR OPPOSITE REACTIONS

In physics one speaks of a force impinging upon an object as producing an "equal and opposite" reaction. Human reactions do not always follow so neatly along such Newtonian lines. Often they do, as I indicated (Liebowitz, Stone, & Turkat, 1986) when commenting that therapists, in dealing with particular personality traits, usually summon an *opposite* trait: we become emotional when confronted with the arid obsessive; super-logical and low-keyed in working with histrionic patients, etc. Actually, mothers do this as a matter of course with their small children: they ooh and ahh when the child has underreacted; they soothe and speak calmly when the child is crying. Mothers augment or diminish their responses, that is, in order to bring their children's reactions more into line with what is normal or average. Therapists try to do something similar, also without dwelling on the process consciously.

This process has been called "complementarity" in the psychoanalytic literature (Deutsch, 1926; Servadio, 1956). But, as Baudry cautions (p. 407), " . . . a character attitude in one person has its effect to stimulate . . . a mirror reaction . . . in the other person who is the target of it, *depending on the latter's character style*" (emphasis added). Contentiousness on the part of a patient may elicit an aggressive rather than a calming response in certain therapists. There are even occasions when the (usually effective) New Testament advice about a soft answer turning away wrath does not work. Certain patients who go over the edge in expressing anger may need a sharply worded response before calm can be restored (in which case a therapist with too little anger in him to make such a response might be at a disadvantage). Of late I have found myself handicapped in dealing with vituperative patients—ones who push me beyond my ability to remain gracious—owing (as far as I can tell) to my contact with certain extraordinarily gracious analysts like Dr. Jean Bergeret of Lyon and Dr. Keigo Okonogi of Tokyo. Patients whose anger keeps me from being "wa-o-tootobu" (harmony-respecting), I wind up for the moment resenting twice over: once for unnerving me, and once again for making me aware of failing to emulate these men.

Most human behavior patterns and responses to specific situations—our patients' as well as our own—however maladaptive some may seem during the unfolding of therapy, were surely adaptive in various important contexts at earlier phases of life. Even the woman who threatened her husband (and me) with a gun grew up, after all, in a house where, if you didn't scream, you didn't eat.

19

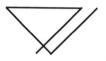

Some Special Traits and Types Amenable to Psychotherapy

IN THIS CHAPTER and the next I offer a number of vignettes built more around individual traits than around specific personality disorders. Some patients have fairly serious conditions, including near-disabling symptoms, yet ultimately do well because of special positive traits that allow them to overcome tall hurdles. Strong self-discipline and conscientiousness may make the difference, or else an unusual degree of compassion or friendliness, of the sort that inspires people to overlook a host of faults. If these positive traits seem clearly to outweigh certain bothersome traits (bossiness, procrastination, impulsivity), the latter may also cease to be so annoying.

The situation changes where offensive traits dominate the clinical picture. With persons who are *very* offensive, there often is no "clinical picture," since such persons generally pooh-pooh the idea of "getting help" and derogate psychiatry in all its branches. Whereas the most aggressive and antisocial persons come to the attention of forensic psychiatrists, there is an intermediate group that represents the dark side of the moon, almost never actually seen by therapists—except in their private lives or in their exposure to the news of the day. As mentioned in Chapter 7, these people inhabit what is underneath the tip of the iceberg containing the relatively few persons who both (a) have easily treatable personality disturbances and

411

(b) come voluntarily for help. Some persons, and some patients, strike us because of markedly pathological traits that do not fit very neatly into the standard nomenclature. I have alluded to a number of these throughout the text: rude, cheap, abrasive, indiscreet. Several of the vignettes in the next chapter depict patients who displayed such traits — traits that overshadowed whatever DSM disorder they may also have exhibited.

As a prelude to presenting the clinical material, it may be useful to enumerate in condensed fashion the positive and negative traits that occupy the two sides of the personality balance. Instead of looking at all 600+ traits outlined in Chapter 5, here it will suffice for the most part to focus just on the five dozen resulting factors.

The *positive* factors included: affiliative (with such traits as empathic, grateful, friendly), assertive, attentive, conscientious, docile, honest, jovial, kind, open, respectful, self-assured, and serene. It is not to be expected that the "ideal" person would display all these qualities. We do not look for docility in a drill sergeant, though he ought at least to be conscientious and respectful. A music student need not be self-assured or jovial, though docility and openness would be valuable traits.

The *negative* factors I had divided into two broad groups: those troublesome to others and those troublesome mostly to the self. Fifty factors (cf. Chapter 5) seemed sufficient to capture the main synonym-clusters, even allowing for the arbitrariness of allocation. "Jealousy," for example, belongs under *mistrustful*, but in its more extreme forms also fits under *offensive*. For the purposes of this chapter, it will be useful to break down the offensive factor into a number of further subdivisions. We might do this as in Table 20.

If we apply this factor-based schema to the patients in this chapter—

TABLE 20

Varieties of Offensiveness

Abrasive (insolent, cheeky, brazen . . .)
Backbiting (bitchy . . .)
Disreputable (sleazy . . .)
Exploitative (manipulative . . .)
Humiliating (indiscreet, teasing . . .)
Ill-mannered (rude, uncouth, vulgar . . .)
Inconsiderate (thoughtless, interrupting . . .)
Intrusive (snoopy, nagging, importunate . . .)
Stingy (cheap . . .)
Unruly (disorderly, messy . . .)
Vindictive (scheming, treacherous . . .)

patients who were highly amenable to treatment—I note that all three initially displayed the same eight factors and lacked the same four. None was assertive, jovial, self-assured, or serene. The first patient became much more assertive, jovial (outgoing), and self-assured toward the end of her therapy three years later. Judging from our exchange of Christmas letters over the past 26 years, I would say she has also achieved a measure of serenity. The third patient has undergone a similar evolution. (The second patient I have been unable to trace, though she was more self-assured and assertive at the end of six years of therapy.)

TREATABLE TRAITS

Personality traits most amenable to psychotherapy are apt to be those associated with *internalization* of conflict, as distinct from *externalization*. There is a correlation between internalization and anxiety, inasmuch as internalizing patients, by definition, are those who blame themselves for what is wrong in their lives, and who worry a great deal whether their behavior, or what they say, will hurt or offend others. Their conscience is, if anything, overactive, and they experience anxiety more often and more keenly than others do. In the earlier psychoanalytic literature, one spoke of "autoplastic" vs. "alloplastic" defenses—concepts that addressed the same issues. Some persons cope, that is, via making changes within themselves (auto-), while others attempt to make other (allo-) people change, so as to be more in conformity with what the alloplastic person wants.

Those who blame others for their troubles (many of whom show a surplus of paranoid, antisocial, passive-aggressive, or narcissistic traits) are correspondingly more challenging to work with. The terms "active" and "passive" have sometimes been used to convey similar polarities. This was the case, at least, when I was in training at the Columbia Psychoanalytic Institute. "Passive" referred to those who internalized, who were introspective, who were often anxious and slow to make decisions or to act on them. "Active" was applied to persons similar to the hard-driving businessman, who is ambitious, not very sensitive to emotions, a "doer" rather than an introspective type, etc. In the roster of patients undergoing analysis at the Institute there were, as might be imagined, very few "active" persons. I don't think it is prudent to use "active" and "passive" in this way, however, particularly because this definition of *active* is really a gloss for persons who ride roughshod over others (who are, that is, hardboiled, abrasive, driving, and thick-skinned). There are, after all, many busy, energetic, assertive (read: "active") people—some of whom seek our help in psychotherapy—who are also sensitive to feelings and who are introspective.

THE BALANCE BETWEEN POSITIVE
AND NEGATIVE TRAITS

As a patient's personality unfolds in the course of treatment, a therapist will become aware of the balance between likeable and unlikeable characteristics, between pleasing and offensive traits. Some traits are maladaptive yet not offensive, and do not come into the reckoning. For instance, shyness or self-criticalness may be distressing and socially limiting, but does not intrude in an unpleasant way within the therapeutic setting.

When I speak of "balance" here, I am aware that the arena is one of personality, where precise quantification is not possible. But I believe that people in general, therapists included, develop impressions of those whom they get to know well—that the latter are "more likeable than not," or "more good than bad," etc. Where the personality is predominantly pleasant and socially adapted, the few unpleasant or annoying traits that are, so to say, left over will be much easier to address, and to remedy, than would be the case if almost every action and utterance were offensive.

This much is self-evident. But from the standpoint of therapy there is one point worth elaborating. A patient who is mostly annoying, like a child who is mostly naughty, will come in for criticism continuously, say, from those in the workplace or in the family. Therapists, who usually try very hard not to be critical, will at first do a slow burn, until they too feel driven to say something, however diplomatically couched, about this or that annoying trait. The (realistically) mostly unlikeable patient will feel (realistically) mostly unliked, and will also feel a growing awareness that the part of him that needs no modification is quite small, whereas the part of him that needs to change is quite large. Even for a highly motivated patient this is a discouraging revelation. It is a matter of clinical experience that offensive patients are seldom much motivated for constructive change anyway. Patients who are, for example, contemptuous, predatory, smug, who constantly interrupt, etc., tend to be "externalizers" with little psychological-mindedness and little interest in changing themselves. The patient who is, at all events, not very likeable—and senses this—and whose need for change is massive and sweeping is more apt to quit treatment than to stay for the duration.

In pointing out to the mostly likeable patient some minor shortcoming in the interpersonal sphere, therapists have an easy time of it: they can count on the patient's *awareness of being liked and respected* as a strong buffer against the potential hurt of any criticism. Similarly, children who are mostly loved and mostly pleasant take a parent's occasional criticism ("You really should have told Aunt Jane you liked her new dress, even though you thought it looked silly, because she's sensitive . . . ") in stride:

these children know such comments are meant to help them adapt even better to those around them, etc.

Patients who have few, or no, offensive traits enjoy another advantage over those whose personalities are difficult: people are not always cognizant of offending others, but even when they are, they tend to be reticent about sharing the actual circumstances with a therapist. If we get to learn about such traits or about the situations in which they show themselves, the source will often be those external to the patient: a spouse, a parent, a friend. (We are rarely privileged to hear from coworkers or employers.) But in the least offensive patients, the information that we are missing is negligible. With patients at the other end of the spectrum, the information we would need to know, which is being withheld by the patient, is vast— and the therapist is seriously handicapped. Worse, if the therapist did come to learn of the offensive traits, in their numerous manifestations, not much good could come of it: as mentioned above, the patient would almost surely take umbrage, would not hear the criticism in the manner in which it was intended, and would break off treatment.

For all these reasons, those who need to change very little—in the way they affect others—can usually make these changes within the context of treatment, and thus get "better." Probably treatment will have ameliorated their symptoms also, such that the whole therapeutic venture is a success. Those who treat others abominably, if they come to therapy at all, have a poor foundation upon which to build. Ideally, from the standpoint of society, we would want to help those who are offensive become socially acceptable. To make the socially acceptable even more acceptable would, in a way, be gilding the lily, but if the resources were available, this would be a reasonable secondary goal. But psychotherapy concentrates on the individual, and with the tools presently at hand, it seems, lamentably, that we can make the good better, but not the bad, good.

The reader may wonder whether, in speaking moralistically here—a taboo in psychiatry—I have not been the fool who rushes in where angels fear to tread. I worry about this, too. Yet I do not know how to avoid mention of these concepts—good, bad, offensive, etc.—since the topic of personality, taken in its breadth, reaches out at its boundaries to some persons who are very bad indeed.

The first generation of psychoanalysts encountered in their daily work mostly people of good character (cf. Ruitenbeek, 1973). Those who did not possess good character were rejected for treatment, and thus glimpsed only with peripheral vision. As Freud mentioned (1904):

One should look beyond the patient's illness and form an estimate of his whole personality; those patients who do not possess . . . a fairly reliable character should be refused. It must not be forgotten that there are healthy people as well as unhealthy ones who are good for nothing in life, and that there is a temptation to ascribe to their illness everything that incapacitates them. . . . (p. 263)

Elsewhere, Freud acknowledged (1919):

Against the vast amount of neurotic misery which is in the world . . . the quantity we can do away with is almost negligible. Besides this, the necessities of our own existence limit our work to the well-to-do classes, accustomed to choose their own physicians. . . . (p. 401)

Today, of course, psychotherapists from all the disciplines reach out to persons from every social class; nor does psychiatry limit its perspective to those with "reliable character." The forensic psychiatrist, in particular, has a familiarity with bands of the characterological spectrum normally exposed only to the police. While some have contended that moral judgments have no place in psychiatry,* to me it seems inescapable that at times we will find ourselves forced to make such judgments in relation to our patients and their intimates. It is enough that we be slow in making these judgments and that our attitude, besides being compassionate, is one of practicality and realism.

In the clinical examples of this section I limit myself, in any case, to those whose positive traits greatly outweighed the negative, and whose negative traits troublesome to the self greatly outweighed those negative traits troublesome to others. These were patients whose personalities needed only modest revamping, and who were able to make the desired changes during the course of psychotherapy. Usually the changes were in the direction of becoming less inhibited.

In the light of retrospect, it seems reasonable to state that psychoanalysis, as a form of therapy, is especially well adapted to the task of *dissolving excessive inhibition*. The typical patient of Freud and of the pioneer generation of analysts was someone overly inhibited in one or more of the following areas: expression of emotion, sexuality, socialization, assertion, or independence. Such inhibitions would give rise to what were called the "character neuroses": obsessive-compulsive, hysteric, phobic, depressive, or passive-dependent, respectively.

Today we speak of these conditions by somewhat different terms, but when we encounter them clinically they still enjoy the favorable prognosis

---

*Cf. Chapter 21. There is more to "psychopathy," in my view than a "moral judgment masquerading as a clinical diagnosis," as Blackburn contends (1988, p. 511).

they did in Freud's day and are still amenable to dyadic forms of therapy, including, but no longer limited to, the psychoanalytic. Some inhibited patients know what is socially permissible but hesitate to take advantage of this degree of freedom, out of guilt or out of various fears. Others scarcely know what are the permissible limits and have kept themselves constrained within much narrower borders, out of even greater fear or as an outgrowth of parental rearing so strict that they never learned about the customary freedoms ordinary people enjoy.

Clinical Examples

The patient, a married woman in her twenties with two small children, had been raised in a stifling, repressive atmosphere at home and educated under the harsh codes of a convent school. Her mother, a dour, straight-laced woman, had been treated for depression and hospitalized on one occasion. The one spot of warmth in the family was her father, who would wink at the patient when her mother was on the warpath and would see to it that unreasonable punishments were not carried out. He was much less rigid than the mother about religious matters, though he shared her abstemiousness where alcohol was concerned. During the patient's adolescence, he had an affair, which his daughter somehow discovered. She kept the secret, not even telling her confessor. What brought the patient to treatment was her irritability with her children. She would occasionally fly off the handle and spank one of her daughters for misbehavior she herself realized was trivial.

As the various facets of her personality became apparent, it became clear that irritability and disproportionate anger were her only traits "troublesome to others." Of the positive traits I have listed, she had nearly all—except that she was not unflappable or serene, not even-tempered or independent, and as yet deficient in self-control. In the beginning of her treatment optimism and joie de vivre were not much in evidence, though they were to become so later on.

Highly intropunitive, this woman blamed herself not only for her own failures, but also for sins not committed. If one of her daughters caught a virus, she felt this was a reflection of a weakened constitution "caused" by her having had sex once with her husband before they were married. This same peccadillo she held responsible for her being anorgasmic with her husband. Her maladaptive traits centered around anxiety and compulsiveness: she was highstrung, moody, fastidious, perfectionistic, overly self-conscious, and scrupulous.

She was also unselfconfident and self-effacing. An example of the latter: having read something about Australia in a magazine, she told her husband, "Did you know that koalas don't eat anything but eucalyptus leaves?" Her husband, an engineer and a man of military bearing, "chauvinistic" long before the term became popular, told her she didn't know what she was talking about. Three days later, apparently having picked up the same magazine, he told his wife, "Hey, did you know that koala bears. . . !?" She smiled sweetly (so she told me) and walked away, muttering curses under her breath.

This incident came during a turning-point phase of her therapy. She not only had begun to reexamine her attitude toward her husband (she no longer saw him as "all right" and herself as "all wrong"), but also saw her mother in a new light. In the past she regarded her sexual desires as shameful and felt hopeless about her situation because, in her view, the Church decreed them so. I told her these views were a gross distortion of Church teachings, but she pooh-poohed my reassuring remarks on the grounds that I was not raised in the same religion. The dispute was settled after she reported a dream where she saw herself in Hell, being lashed on her back by her mother, who was using her rosary as a whip. She began to realize that the severity of her own mores concerning sex had very little to do with any agents of the Church and had a great deal to do with her mother.

The patient's life course was all uphill from this point. After three years of thrice weekly expressive psychotherapy, she had become more assertive, sexually responsive, and much less irritable with her children. She moved with her family to a different city, but has kept me abreast, through letters, of the changes in her life over the past 25 years. She eventually left her husband, married someone more compatible with the person she had now become, completed graduate school, and achieved a high administrative position in her chosen profession. Since both her daughters turned out well, I am left with the impression that her irritability toward them years ago had no lasting ill effects.

*   *   *   *   *

The patient of this vignette was a nursing supervisor at a small hospital: a single woman of 29 when she first sought help. An only child, she had been raised in a rural area in Maine. Memories of her early years were pleasant. She was cared for by her mother and maternal grandmother— both mild-mannered and affectionate. Her grandmother died when the patient was four; her mother, when she was seven. Her father then put her in the hands of his parents in a nearby village. This was disastrous for the patient, since these grandparents were harsh and exploitative. She was treated like Cinderella, having to do all the household chores—an unpleasant but not intolerable fate, had it not been for the fact that she was also sexually abused by her grandfather, her father's brother, and her cousin.

Her father did not seem well enough off to care for her himself; in any event, she chose not to reveal anything to him about the incest.

Among her many positive traits were: affectionate, calm, compassionate, compliant, cooperative, deferential, docile, eager to please, empathic, even-tempered, humorous, possessing moral integrity, modest, neat, orderly, polite, reasonable, self-disciplined, tactful, trusting, and trustworthy. Her few maladaptive traits consisted of her being shy, somewhat aloof with her coworkers, insecure, socially unselfconfident.

The precipitant leading to her seeking therapy was her increasing discomfort with a longstanding love relationship in which she was essentially the "girl Friday" of a prominent, married executive. He spent one day a week with her, but it was clear he had no intention of leaving his wife. Though women in her situation are often made into confidantes, he did not even complain to her about his wife. The patient's self-esteem was so low that she barely protested against the awkwardness, let alone the hopelessness, of this relationship.

The thrust of her treatment was to make her realize that her degraded situation, during the ten years she lived at her grandparents, was not at all of her doing. Though she was made to feel that she was a "bad girl" who had to do the menial tasks and "service" the menfolk (in order to "work off" the points against her), this system arose out of their viciousness, not out of any wrongness on her part. Even as she developed more realistic views about the past, however, she still felt unworthy, as though a "good" man would surely find her inadequate — as a homemaker, as a cook, as a companion, etc. She thought of herself as "boring," having noticed that she seldom had much to say at social gatherings. People considered her "aloof," even stuck-up, because of her taciturnity. It gradually became clear that it was her feeling of shame about the incest that rendered her silent when among people. As she worked through this facet of the past, she grew less inhibited socially. She gathered the courage to leave the married man, and embarked upon a series of love relationships with progressively less "hopeless" choices: a single, but self-centered man who treated her shabbily; a kinder man with whom she had not much in common; finally, a more suitable man, whom she eventually married. This process took some seven years, after which she left treatment — more self-confident, less self-effacing, more at ease and interactive socially.

This patient's history is in some ways similar to that of the man with paranoid personality described in Chapter 10. Both were incest victims (though he had been molested by his father; she by non-parent relatives). Economic circumstances were worse in her family than in his. Still, she had the advantages of spending her formative years with a loving mother and with a father whom she remembered fondly. Neither parent had been punitive or abusive. In the case of the man, incest involved his own father, whereas in her case the offending relatives were not those of her immediate family. Physical cruelty by parents or siblings appears to have worse effects on long-range prognosis than does non-parent incest. At least this was the case in my follow-up study of hospitalized borderline patients (Stone, 1990).

GUILT IN PERSONS WITH
PROVOCATIVE FAMILY MEMBERS

In recent years I have become aware of a number of patients whose personalities are distinctly "guilt-ridden"—in whom the guilt was evoked largely by siblings or by other family members whose behavior toward these future patients had been unusually provocative. A typical family setting is one in which there is a set of well-meaning, rather placid parents, and several siblings, all but one of whom are also placid, even-tempered, and reasonable. The "exceptional" sibling will have emerged, almost from moment of birth, as cranky, irritable, touchy, demanding, and *un*reasonable.

The parents, to the extent that they are placid and nonconfrontational, pursue the path of appeasement—not from the beginning perhaps, but after an exhausting and largely unsuccessful attempt to control the demanding child through exhortation, withholding favors, and outright punishment. The parents shift tactics, in the hopes of preserving some modicum of tranquility in the home, in the direction of urging the even-tempered children to acquiesce a bit to the admittedly unreasonable demands of the tantrumy sibling.

In this situation, the parents purchase peace—but at the price of engendering *entitlement* in the irritable child (who falsely concludes that it got what it wanted because it "deserved" it, rather than that the other family members decided to give in so as to minimize the level of tension). Another price: the more normal children have to endure the unfairness, and also have to endure knowing that they must do so specifically because they *are* more normal, hence better able to live under tyranny, than the tyrannical child would be able to accept the customary limits. Worse yet, the tyrannical child will, on numerous occasions, goad the normal siblings into defending themselves and into becoming momentarily "hostile," by way of protecting themselves against the provocativeness of the irritable sibling.

An unreasonable family member can, in this way, reduce the healthier members to a similar kind of "craziness"—inducing in the others a temporary and out-of-character "bitchiness" or irascibility that much resembles the, if you will, innate irascibility of the provocateur. Ironically, the provocative child, incapable of appraising the world by the usual standards, feels genuinely shortchanged, sees his demandingness not as demandingness at all but as righteous indignation, and therefore experiences no guilt. Meanwhile, the healthier children, having become regulated by guilt (rather than simply by the less mature mechanism of shame), and capable of greater empathy and compassion, will feel guilt over their own annoyance at the unreasonable actions of their demanding sibling. This tendency to feel guilt for one's own negative feelings would be maximized in a family where the parents bent over backwards to protect the *amour propre* of the fragile child, encouraging the healthier children to "be sympathetic," to "understand," etc., and who never permitted these other children, even behind closed doors, to voice a justified complaint about the unfairness of the provocative child.

The problem I have sketched here can be magnified a hundredfold where the family members are almost all highly unreasonable people—except for one child, lucky enough to have been born without constitutional predisposition to abnormal personality, but unlucky enough to have entered an Alice in Wonderland world where everyone else is very strange and often cruel. Since it takes years for a child to expand its world outside the confines of the family, the child will tend at first to assume the parents, etc., are "all right." Even after the child grows up, it is difficult to shake off a distorted picture of the world—a picture laid down early, after all, and the only picture available till much later. The patient in the following illustration, though she was exquisitely sensitive to the feelings and needs of others, and led an essentially faultless life, experienced inordinate guilt, and was often keenly depressed, largely in response to having been "put down" her whole life by the other members of her family.

Clinical Example

A woman of 34, having moved with her husband from a different city, was referred to me for continuing therapy. She was one of two sisters, the other of whom was vacuous and manipulative. The patient's nephew was a paranoid schizophrenic; her niece was an impulsive, "borderline" adolescent. The mother was schizophrenic, many times hospitalized. She was hypercritical and impossible to satisfy. The father was a moody and depressed alcoholic, though he did not impose unreasonable demands upon her as did her mother. The maternal grandmother, fault-finding, irascible and imperious, was the "grande dame" of the town where the patient grew up—the wife of the man who owned the town factory. The grandmother made a habit of driving up to one of the local grocery stores, then "testing" the fruit, while her chauffer and her granddaughter (the future patient) waited in the car. If the oranges, or whatever, failed to please the old lady, she would push them all into the street with her cane, while the horrified grocer (and mortified granddaughter) looked on.

The patient, when I began to work with her, led a constricted life, socializing with a few close friends, spending much of her day practicing the piano in preparation for her volunteer post as a church organist on Sundays. Her parents, who lived in a nearby city, would call every day. Her mother would place various demands on her—that she choose upholstery fabrics for her parent's new settee, that she get such-and-such from the department store, that she come out to visit them on the weekend, etc. To refuse her mother seemed impossible: though furious at the unreasonable requests, she felt guilty and near-panicky at the thought of saying no.

Treatment was largely supportive: as someone external to her and her situation, I could validate her impressions of her mother's unreasonableness and could embolden her to put her own realistic needs first. In her view, for example, because her church work was voluntary, it was not "real" work and therefore did not exonerate her from running out to do her mother's errands. It took many months for her to feel appropriately entitled to refuse one of her mother's inconvenient demands. Until then I helped her get around the problem by installing a second, unlisted phone—to be used only by friends. The "mother" phone she could now leave disconnected until she had finished her day's music practice.

20

$$\nabla$$

Traits Less Amenable or
Not Amenable to Therapy

THE LIST OF TRAITS TROUBLESOME to others is, as we have seen (Chapter 5), long and not easily rearranged into nonoverlapping categories. In the context of the five-factor model, most of these traits belong to the "−A" branch: the opposite of agreeableness, i.e., antagonism. Besides the generally "offensive" traits alluded to at the beginning of the last chapter (see Table 20), disagreeable traits fall into such categories as angry/irritable, argumentative, mistrustful, deceitful, aggressive, etc. Those whose leading characteristics are violent, malicious, ruthless, depraved, or cruel seldom seek help spontaneously. Those who are particularly aggressive, sadistic or antisocial are, as mentioned, apt to be persons we read about, not patients we treat.

The spectrum of aggressiveness does contain, at its milder end, some traits we will occasionally encounter: tantruminess, gruffness, contentiousness, and vehemence. I have seen "domineering" persons among the parents of some of my patients, only rarely in the patients themselves. In 25 years of practice (consultees and treated patients together numbering some 350), I have encountered only eight patients in whom vengefulness was a pronounced trait. Of these, five were borderline; the rest, paranoid personalities. Some of these patients are included in the clinical vignettes in the chapters on borderline and antisocial personality disorders. One of the

423

vignettes in this chapter concerns a notorious figure from the annals of crime.

In this chapter I will give examples of personality configurations that generally pose serious obstacles to change by any methods of treatment currently available. Some of the examples in the beginning sections of the chapter are derived from my clinical experience. These concern patients with prominent personality traits of a sort that rendered therapeutic work unusually difficult (though not necessarily impossible). In some instances the trait in question overlaps several DSM categories, and seemed better discussed under its own heading—as a separate condition, in effect—rather than as a subtype of a DSM category. *Cheapness*, for example, partakes of the obsessive-compulsive (where parsimony is a defining item), the passive-aggressive, the depressive (fear of poverty), and the sadistic (meanness). But extreme cheapness has a life of its own: it is the prime irritant that those close to the person with this trait must endure. Cheapness then becomes the chief focus of the therapist who works with the person, were he or she to enter treatment.

Certain other traits, though of critical importance to the treatment situation (by virtue of being that patient's most noticeable characteristic), lie outside conventional nosology altogether. Examples are *plasticity* or the habitual inappropriateness and dreamy disconnectedness that we allude to by the colloquialism, *"flaky."*

Further on, in the concluding sections, I have tried to provide a catalog, admittedly condensed and incomplete, of personality configurations that in all likelihood render their possessors quite beyond the realm of treatment. Some of these are highly egocentric and hostile persons in positions of power. So long as they remain in power they do not think of themselves as having "personality problems." They would never present themselves at a therapist's door. If one day "brought low" by circumstance, they may then become treatable, though this will not be true in all cases. There will always be a residue of totally untreatable persons, even among those who have never raised a hand against others. In the next chapter, the focus is on those in whom violence (usually in the form of murder) and untreatability are combined: irremediably dangerous persons.

My point in presenting this material is to demonstrate that there are limits to what we can accomplish in the realm of treating abnormalities of personality. In trying to define where these limits are, I am sure other specialist might draw the lines a little to one side or the other of where I have drawn mine. But it is important to recognize our limitations. Even in treating mild disturbances of personality, the process is usually lengthy and costly. It would be prejudicial to the welfare of the many who *can* benefit from our efforts if the therapeutic community allocated too much of its resources to those who are not at all likely to benefit.*

PATIENTS IRRITATING TO THERAPISTS

Not all the various unpleasant traits impinge with equal discomfiture upon a therapist. Even vengefulness, if it is directed at someone else, may not bother a therapist in any direct way, though it may inspire countertransferential feelings of dislike, apprehension, and indignation. Here I am using "countertransference" in the broadest sense, by the way: it need not be "neurotic" to dislike a patient who schemes to do hurtful things to a family member or lover—or to his therapist. Harold Searles once worked with a schizophrenic patient who left fecal matter on the chair he was using in Searles' office (1965). The repugnance Searles felt might belong to the most general category of countertransference, but it is obviously an average human reaction to such an occurrence, not anything unique to his or to any other therapist's psychic makeup. I would like to think that my own disdainful feelings toward a schizophrenic patient of mine—who after each month's bill was presented, stole the same amount in dollar value from Bloomingdale's department store (sweaters, mostly)—were more averagely human than neurotic.

But calling therapists at all hours, prying into their personal affairs, showing open hostility and contempt: these qualities are quite different, because they tend to throw therapy off its track (by throwing therapists off their track), destroying what Bion (1961) rightly called the *work* atmosphere of the therapeutic hour and threatening to nullify the possible benefits of treatment. It is a surplus of just such traits that makes us single out certain patients as "borderline" or "paranoid" or (with less diagnostic precision) "difficult" (cf. Colson, Allen et al., 1986) or outrageous—something, that is, that places such persons in our minds as *different* from the "ideal" neurotic (neurotic, in Kernberg's sense of a *level of function* [1967]) or "analyzable" patient. DSM diagnoses aside, one might say, we tend to characterize our patients as comfortable to work with or else as difficult. Demandingness, intrusiveness, and hostility are the kinds of traits that "carve nature at the joints" with respect to treatability.

---

*The efforts of Göransson and her colleagues in Sweden (1992) to treat (and ultimately, release) recidivist rapists represents an approach opposite to what I am recommending. Time and follow-up study will show whether their optimism or my pessimism was the more justified stance. One must hope that not many women will be endangered in the experiment.

In this chapter, for considerations of space, I can do no more than give a sampling of persons who grip our attention because of a dramatically pathological trait, independent of whether other aspects of the personality would warrant a DSM diagnosis. Probably there is a vivid example for each of the 500 negative traits somewhere in the memory of the reader, based on an acquaintance, a patient, or a figure from public life.

The patients I have found the most difficult to work with (limiting the discussion, for the moment, to those in my practice), have been those with one or more of the three attributes alluded to above: making frequent calls at times outside the working day, intrusiveness (prying into personal life), and open hostility or contemptuousness toward me. Of these attributes, the most vexatious is frequent calling, since it invades the boundary between professional and personal life. The working day, in effect, never comes to an end.

The other attributes add only to work-strain during the session itself, since more active and creative interventions are needed if the therapist is to preserve the work atmosphere. Prying questions, for example, usually reflect intense anxiety patients have in their own lives about the aspects of the therapist's life touched on in the questions. This much is obvious on the face of it, but to lead such patients back to the relevant area in their own lives can at times be inordinately difficult. Some would much rather the therapist do the sweating than get down to work themselves. If this tendency cannot be reversed, it may be a sign that the patient's motivation for therapy is not all that great, and that treatment is not going to flourish.

As for hostility or contemptuousness toward the therapist, when these qualities are shown only infrequently or to a mild degree, they need not impose intolerable burdens on the process of treatment. The problem comes when the hostility is pervasive and present from the beginning, such that a therapeutic alliance never really forms, or if it appears to have formed, in a fragile and tentative way, never really solidifies. Patients who show hostility or contempt toward the important people in their lives, *except* the therapist, may be easier to work with at first—but the "honeymoon" may be brief, and the day will usually come when these attitudes suffuse the transference as well.

When any of these attributes persists over a long time, treatment failure is the usual result. There are, of course, other reasons why treatment may fail. Patients who lack motivation, who give strong evidence of antisociality, who show extreme degrees of suspiciousness, jealousy and the like, may also fail to get better, even if the bothersome traits mentioned above are not present.

In Table 21 I have outlined those treatment failures that I attribute mainly to intrusiveness, hostility, or frequent calling (especially if the latter

TABLE 21

Difficult Patients Who Became Treatment Failures

#	Sex	Diagnoses	C	H	I	E	V	Left Rx	Outcome
1	F	BPD, MAD, PMS, AB, OCD, AG, ALC, N	+			+		Hosp	G
2	M	SZ, DrAb	+					Quit	P
3	F	BPD, ExPD		+		+	+	Quit	P
4	F	BPD, ADD, OCD, P	+	+				Left	F
5	F	BPD, Factit. Il.		+		+	+	Quit	R
6	F	BPD, AG		+		+	+	Hosp	F
7	F	BPD, N		+		+	+	Quit	F
8	F	BPD, MDP, PMS	+	+	+			Quit	F
9	M	P, N, SZ (prob.)		+		+	+	Quit	?
10	F	BPD, OCD, AB, PMS, MAD			+			Quit	F
11	M	MDP, P	+		+	+		Term	F
12	F	BPD, MAD, PMS, AN, N	+	+		+	+	Quit	F
13	F	BPD, MAD, PMS, N, P	+	+		+	+	Term	F
14	M	P, MAD		+				Term	?
15	F	BPD, MPD, OCD, PMS, MAD, DepPD	+			+		Quit	M
16	F	BPD, MAD, DepPD	+					Hosp	G

Key: AB—anorexia/bulimia, ADD—attention deficit disorder, AG—agoraphobia, ALC—alcoholism, AN—anorexia nervosa, BPD—borderline personality disorder, DepPD—dependent personality disorder, DrAb—drug abuse, ExPD—explosive personality disorder, Factit. Il.—factitious illness, MAD—major affective disorder, MDP—manic depressive illness, MPD—multiple personality disorder, N—narcissistic personality disorder, OCD—obsessive-compulsive disorder, P—paranoid personality disorder, PMS—premenstrual syndrome, SZ—schizophrenia

C—calling frequently, H—hostility/contemptuousness, I—intrusiveness, E—entitlement, V—vengefulness

Manner of leaving treatment: Hosp—had to be hospitalized; Left—left to go to a different city; Quit—abruptly quit treatment; Term—treatment had to be terminated because of inability to pay, or for other reasons

Outcome: R—recovered (current Global Assessment Score > 70); G—good (GAS 61–70; F—fair (GAS 51–60); M—marginal (GAS 31–50); P—poor (GAS < 30)

is accompanied by a tone of demandingness or entitlement). These are the cases where my limitless patience and boundless tolerance came to an end. Because treatment usually ended on a sour note, follow-up has not been easy. I know at least the short-term fate of many; two I have lost track of completely.

Making Frequent Calls

Patients who make frequent calls to a therapist are for the most part lonely, dependent, and depressed. These are the patients who exemplify most strikingly the DSM-III item (subsequently modified in the DSM-III-R version) in its definition of BPD: "problems tolerating being alone." Seven of the nine in Table 21 who made frequent calls were BPD patients.

The emotional forces impelling these patients to call at odd hours were not always the same. The first patient who had this tendency was a young woman I had worked with during my residency training, and whom I continued to treat when I began my practice. Noticeably shy since childhood, she had become markedly "avoidant," as well as depressed and lonely, since the death of a parent during her adolescence. While at college, she entered treatment with a psychiatrist. When her therapist went on his summer vacation, she made a suicide gesture and was hospitalized.

A similar pattern unfolded after I took over her care at that hospital: she made suicide gestures before the first two vacations I took during the year and a half I worked with her. For many months the traits most apparent in her personality were mournfulness, tearfulness, and taciturnity. She spoke barely above a whisper, inviting others, so it seemed, to draw very close to her so that they could hear her. She also tended to remain in her chair when a session would be at an end. The net effects of all this were to make me feel cruel and uncaring, since I obviously gave her so little of what she hoped for in the way of attention and affection. No matter how tactfully I would remind her that the time was up, her look of bitterness and suffering made me feel like a Nazi commandant who had ordered her "nach links!"— i.e., to the side of the tracks for those destined for the gas chambers.

Interestingly, in her dreams, she often sent *me* to the gas chambers. It took almost the whole year and a half in the hospital before she could acknowledge any anger toward me—for going away at times, for sharing so "little" of my time with her (an ironic accusation, considering that our four weekly sessions amounted to more time I spent actually listening to any one person, including my wife . . .), or for what was surely my greatest sin: in the midst of all her suffering, I seemed to be enjoying life.

Thus far I have stressed the burdensome aspects of our work. There was another side to it. I felt great compassion for her. She was, in some respects, including her appearance, like a magnified version of my mother; I'm sure this accounted in large part for the intensity of the "rescue fantasy" she inspired in me. The latter must have played a role in my own suppression of anger toward her, in relation to her guilt-provoking and demanding qualities. I only began to acknowledge this anger when she became a private patient after leaving the hospital.

For a few months all went smoothly. She found a roommate with whom to share an apartment. At first she was seldom alone, since she and her roommate took their meals together, went to the movies together, and so on. But the roommate was more comfortable socially, began to step out with boyfriends—or, worse yet, bring them home—making my patient intensely aware of how great were her social deficits. On the evenings she would be alone, she began to call me—sometimes during the dinner hour, eventually during the later (including the "wee," hours). Her talk had no focus, and would, had I permitted it, have lasted the whole night.

By now I was well aware of my irritation, and I tried to make her understand that her making me angry must surely be her (as yet unconscious) method of showing me her anger. I had learned of this mechanism—of instilling into the therapist the unacceptable emotions with which the patient is himself struggling—from Harold Searles: not only from Searles' writings, but from his personal supervision of this case. I would fly down from New York to Washington on a Saturday morning for this supervision, encouraging myself earlier in the week to "keep her alive for Searles"—meaning, to help her get through another week without her killing herself, so Searles could help me to help her get through another week without. . . .

All this came to a crashing climax when, one evening, after her roommate had left the apartment, my patient called me frantically, telling me, "Dr. Stone, I don't know what to do. I can't stay alive. I can't keep myself going. *I can't even make tea!* I DON'T KNOW HOW TO MAKE TEA!" I knew, and suspect she knew as well, that this was not literally true. She was telling me she was at the end of her rope. I insisted on rehospitalizing her, and the next day she entered a long-term facility.

Happily, the story ends better than it began. In the course of my follow-up work, I contacted her 10, and again, 20 years later. By the tenth year she had completed not only college, but graduate school. By the twentieth, she had become self-supporting at a prestigious job, and had been living for some years with a man in the same profession as hers. She had become much more self-confident and was more at ease socially than she used to be, though she still tended to worry excessively about the future. She retained a measure of bitterness about the tormented life she had led during her twenties and about the seeming impotence of the mental health profession vis-à-vis her condition at that time.

What determines a therapist's reactions to a patient who makes frequent calls is, I believe, the balance between the patient's positive and negative traits. This balance will affect the "ratio," in the therapist, between sympathy and annoyance. The length of time with which one has worked with a patient enters these equations. Even the most difficult patient will elicit mainly sympathy in the beginning, especially because, with very difficult patients, there will usually have been a history of parental neglect or abusiveness. After some months (four or five months, in my experience), the therapist begins to hold the patient more responsible for his/her own actions. Clingy, overly dependent behavior (of which frequent calling may be a manifestation), which one may tolerate at the outset, becomes burdensome later on, the more so if the therapist feels the patient is now secure enough to do without the extra measure of attention. One will attempt to place limits at this stage—partly to encourage self-sufficiency in the patient, partly to safeguard the necessary degree of comfort in one's professional life. This comfort, by the way, is a precondition to doing good therapeutic work: if an annoying trait goes unchecked, the therapist's irritation will soon mount to the point where further work with that patient becomes intolerable. What might have been a salvageable situation leads instead to dissolution of the treatment relationship.

Termination of treatment is what occurred, for example, with two borderline patients, each of whom was depressed and prone to suicide gestures. Each had been an incest victim. Both had suffered physical abuse from a parent. Each came across an unstable, pitiable, unable to handle reverses or rejections; at the same time, demanding and entitled. One was quick to anger, often storming out of a session early, slamming the door upon her exit. The other was given to begging and pleading, or to crying, in order to persuade me to let her go on for another minute or two on the phone. Each, having elicited sympathy in the beginning, became an albatross around my neck later on.

Their dependency on me, as on their previous therapists, was heightened to the extent that neither had more than one or two friends. The narrowness of their social circle was in part due to their shyness; in part, to their tendency to exhaust the patience of people they had once been close to. With each I attempted to fix a limit to the calls: in duration (no more than five minutes), as to time of day (no later than 10:30 p.m.), and as to frequency (no more than once a day). For a while this arrangement worked well. But then a "crisis" would arise that (in their eyes at least) justified an exception.

The nighttime calls, in particular, served as a kind of transitional object (the need for which, in borderline patients, has been noted by Arkema, 1981), much as does a mother's lullaby. But pointing out such a "dynamic" to these patients—though they heartily agreed with the interpretation—did not lead to any salutary decrease in their need for soothing responses of this kind.

When I found myself unable to accommodate comfortably to these demands, I let them know that I could no longer be of help to them—unless they could find ways to curb their anxiety through other means. Each eventually broke off treatment. Interestingly, both then "made do," partly for reasons of economy, with psychopharmacologists, whom they saw much less frequently, and who relied much more on soothing via medication rather than by conversation. For certain borderline patients (it is not always easy to tell who they are in advance) intensive psychotherapy ends up more of a temptation (to get the parenting they felt they lacked, for example) than an opportunity for growth. They do not all "fall apart" (contrary to what they and, often, their therapists at first assume) when forced by circumstances to settle for the comparative sparseness of once-a-week psychopharmacological or group or supportive treatment.

SENSATION-SEEKING

Those who crave strong sensation do not necessarily run into major difficulties in life if (a) this tendency is not at the outermost edge of the bell-curve, and (b) their friends, intimates, and life pattern all conspire to gratify the desire for novelty. A woman who is happiest when she can go to a different theater or nightclub every other night, dance at her favorite discothèque the nights in between, and take frequent trips to exotic countries, and who in addition has a well-to-do husband with similar tastes, a nanny to take care of the children, etc., can go to her grave never knowing she had a problem (let alone a "personality disorder"). Absent these favorable conditions, the same woman might find herself alone more often than she can tolerate, "crawling the walls" for want of excitement and companionship. She may then consult a therapist, and enter treatment for her (as it might now be identified) histrionic personality disorder. Since it is most unlikely that the exploration of her psychodynamics will make any measureable change in her novelty-seeking pattern, some other approach will be necessary.

According to the general rule that whatever "sticks out" from the hypothetical norm must be pushed back toward this ideal-line, the therapist will be well advised to help the patient acquire some modicum of self-discipline. Order (in the form of disciplined activities) is the natural antidote to chaos (here, the directionless sensation-seeking). All this can of course be said in one sentence. To effect such a change is something else. What the therapist must bring about is a modification in the "profile" of traits, such that "histrionic-ness" grows less and compulsiveness grows stronger.

Much of this task, in the treatment of hospitalized patients, falls to the lot of the occupational and recreational therapists. Theirs is not always considered a glamorous role, and their efforts—absolutely critical to the recovery of sensation-seeking, poorly disciplined patients—are seldom sufficiently appreciated.

In 25 years of private practice I believe I have helped two patients of this type learn the "compulsive" habits necessary to the better toleration of nights and weekends alone; another two eventually mastered these skills, more or less on their own, after they had interrupted their treatment with me. I learned of their successes only when I contacted them in a follow-up study 20 years later.

Of the two who improved while still in therapy, one was alcoholic, besides suffering from a mood disorder and severe premenstrual tension. I was finally able to persuade her to enroll in AA (which excels in the fostering of discipline); following this, she resumed the piano lessons she started when she was little. Between the meetings and the frequent lessons, her evening time was now structured. She rarely experienced the kind of anxiety that, literally, used to drive her to drink. Currently (14 years later), she is married, working, and raising two children. One might argue that she was already half-disciplined to begin with (she had always loved the piano, she had fairly good work skills), and that the influence of therapy was, in a manner of speaking, just to nudge her back off the shoulder onto the main road. I would accept this appraisal.

Far more difficult, in my experience at least, is to foster a sense of self-discipline, a devotion to this or that hobby, an ability to enjoy activities that do not involve thrills and spills, where no such patterns have ever existed in the first two or three decades of life. My failures in this regard outnumber my successes by an embarrassingly wide margin. The following vignette is instructive as to the perils of thrill addiction, though it is not informative as to cure.

Clinical Examples

A "middle-level" executive in a large banking firm sought treatment after he had become embroiled in a tempestuous, and seemingly hopeless, love affair. Now in his early forties, he had been married briefly 15 years before. His fiancée was 24. Emotionally volatile, she would provoke "scenes," sparked by her intense jealously. The usual steps in their sadomasochistic dance were these: passionate lovemaking would be followed by an equally passionate argument. They would break off the engagement. Two days later he would pick up a "bimbo" in a bar, take her home, and have a rapturous night. Two days after that, the fiancée would reappear, rummage through his trash basket, find a champagne cork, and fly into jealous rage — as though they hadn't really broken up and should therefore have been faithful to one another.

In one such scene he broke her wrist and she took him to court, only later to drop the charges. She trashed his car in another such scene, and he tried to sue her, but also dropped the charges later on. He knew she was "no good" for him, but could not give her up. He had the candor to admit that he was no good for a conventional woman who might want a man with some stability.

Both he and his fiancée hired private investigators to spy on the other. Each threatened to kill the other. Alcoholism intensified all these problems.

He had no hobbies, no sustaining interests, no patience to watch TV or read a book if he were by himself. Hypomanic and gregarious, he had a million acquaintances and zero friends. Having long grown past the age when he and his buddies could go bar-hopping every night, he was now alone while they were with their new families—alone, that is, unless the on-and-off engagement was in an "on" phase.

I tried hard to get him into AA. He went to one meeting. In our next session he told me, "It's not going to work. AA's not my cup of tea." "Indeed," I said, "Tea itself is not your cup of tea. Alcohol is your cup of tea. It will also be your undoing." He continued to pursue his rudderless path, coming to some sessions, skipping others, getting fired for padding his expense account in order to buy jewelry to placate his fiancée, getting evicted when there was no more expense account to "absorb" the rent, punching a cop during a melee, then using his "connections" to get the case thrown out—his life a concatenation of crises.

Treatment ended in a characteristic way: after apparently dropping out for several months, he reappeared at my office one evening unannounced and quite drunk, just as I was about to leave. I told him I could see him for just five minutes, to get the flavor of what the latest crisis was all about, and we would have to schedule a session of regular length the next day. He stormed out, cursing me for "not caring" about him. Later I learned from the doorman that the patient, on his way out, urinated into a flowerpot in the lobby. Several months after, he called again, urgently requesting an appointment, but then never showed up.

This man is an example of someone with "cyclothymic" temperament. He was a curious blend of a competent, impeccably attired, most of the time high-functioning executive, and a restless, episodically violent thrill-seeker. Appreciative of my help (except during the impromptu visit), he seemed to work well in treatment: he understood the nature of his problem, knew he needed a mate less chaotic than his fiancée, knew he needed to conquer his alcoholism, itself an unsuccessful antidote to a worse problem: intolerance of being alone after work-hours. But his restlessness swept away his good intentions. Lithium and anxiolytics did not stem the tide either.

Since I could never get him to settle down with a good book, I hoped I could at least get him to settle down with a good woman. What kind of woman, however, could put up with so unstable a man? Only an equally sensation-seeking woman like his fiancée. Such people are "augmenters," overreacting to all perceived threats, neither able to calm the other. They are "meant for each other" only in the sense that no one else can put up with their storminess.

Sometimes age leads to mellowing, by "turning the heat down" on the intensity of the drives. But if adaptive, sublimatory activities do not take up the space once occupied by the thrill-seeking, one is left either with a hollow, "burnt-out" person, or else with an ever more restless, lonely person, spinning ever more out of control, veering ever closer to premature death or suicide.

Patients of this sort evoke strong countertransference emotions: rescue fantasies, disappointment, irritation—because the cures seems so obvious. One knows exactly what needs to be done. The implementation of the "cure"—getting the patient to develop internal controls, simpler and less dangerous pleasures—remains in all too many cases next to impossible.

* * * * *

A stewardess in her mid-twenties asked if she might begin psychotherapy with me because of indecision about which of two men she should marry. She was the elder of two daughters born in the Midwest to a prosperous engineer and his wife. A pert and attractive woman, she had been popular in school and had had many brief affairs since she was 18.

She became a stewardess shortly after graduation from college. Working for a major carrier, she was able to travel all over the world. When by herself, she became restless, anxious to the point of desperation, and unable to sleep. Television might hold her interest on such evenings, but only for a half-hour or so. She would then feel driven to go to a bar, where she could be assured that, because of her looks, some man would offer her free drinks and would be more than happy to take her home with him for the rest of the night. If she were in luck, she might find a man who would, in between the drinks and the sex, also take her to a nightclub with a show or to a play. Though she usually felt forlorn and "used" the next day, her escapades had a calming effect while they lasted. Her pattern reminded one of the Spanish saying: "El raton que no sabe mas de un agujero, el gato lo coge presto" (the mouse that only knows one hole, the cat catches quickly).

During the few months before her consultation, she managed to meet not one, but two men that took a more lasting interest in her. She seemed equally fond of both. The details of her predicament were such as could happen only to a stewardess: the one man was an older, wealthy hotel owner from Madrid; the other was a man her age—a soldier stationed in Los Angeles. Since these were stops on her regular route, she could see each beau every other week.

Her chopped-up schedule made any attempt at regular sessions impossible. If she were in New York for a week, she would come for three or four sessions and appear to make some solid progress. But then she would be out of the country for several weeks, and it would be as though we were starting from the beginning.

She had a number of revealing dreams along the way. In one, for instance, she saw herself rolling on the front lawn of the house where she grew up, in a fast embrace with a tiger. Her mother was staring at them disapprovingly. This seemed to point pretty clearly to some lusty, oedipal feelings for her father. She herself had no associations to the dream. In another, she was in a subway, standing up with the other straphangers—only the straps were the penises of all the men she had had sex with. She could make no sense of this dream either, though I found myself wondering: was she referring to her need to hang onto a man, via sexuality? to her anger at men, who were all castrated in this fashion? to her lack of interest in any other aspect of men except this one part of them? to her sense of triumph at having so many sexual trophies?

All this was taking place in the 1960s. As I think about her situation now, I wonder whether her sensation-seeking pattern had gotten initiated by gross seductiveness on the part of her father? Had there been incest? Could she sustain enthusiasm for any man besides her tiger-father? When I made some interpretation, in any event, to the effect that her "quandary" over the Los Angeles man vs. the Madrid man was her way of not committing herself to any man, she "acted out" her response, flying off to Rio de Janeiro, where she got pregnant during a brief dalliance with a pilot. She terminated the pregnancy, and not long thereafter terminated the therapy.

Though she lacked what Kernberg has aptly called "sublimatory channels," just as did the man in the preceding vignette, she ultimately was able to settle down. Twenty-two years later I learned from her that she had at first moved around the country a lot, married neither of the men she had been discussing with me, but did marry a few years after. That marriage ended unhappily, but over the past 13 years she has been in a good marriage, and has a son of 12. She still gets bored easily if there's no excitement in her life, but her family serves a "stabilizing rudder."

"Primitive" Personalities

Under the heading "primitive personalities," M. Robbins (1989) and Miller (1992) have grouped a number of the common personality types which share the features of destructiveness and poor integration. Robbins placed *borderline, narcissistic, paranoid, and schizoid* types under this heading; others would add the *hysterical* and the *"impulsive."* I would be reluctant to include the schizoid, since many schizoid persons, though marginal in function and aloof, are not at all infantile or destructive. I have given examples in various chapters of higher functioning paranoid and narcissistic, to say nothing of hysterical, patients: they too cannot be subsumed neatly (certainly not exclusively) under the "primitive" rubric.

The concept of "primitive" is most nearly coextensive with that of borderline—especially of the "infantile" type, as enunciated by Kernberg (1967). Some of the personality traits common to the infantile patient are: demandingness, irritability, tantruminess, unreasonableness, and a childlike poutiness or petulance. One also sees marked projective mechanisms (viz., blaming others), along with a tendency to be wantonly hurtful toward others, unfair, entitled, bitter and envious.

Primitive persons live in the immediate present and have strikingly poor memories, under stress, for the totality of the interpersonal history pertinent to key relationships. This gives the personality its unintegrated quality: a minor act of forgetfulness on the part of a spouse, for example, may lead to an explosion of anger—as though the spouse were "always" forgetful. The thousand kindnesses, large and small, that preceded the oversight are temporarily blanked out, as the "primitive" partner swings swiftly into action. As Miller speaks of this action: "The inability to form and sustain affect representations leads [primitive persons] to emote with little restraint or control" (p. 95). Instead of experiencing what Rado (1956) called the "welfare" emotions, the primitive person feels mostly "emergency" emotions (rage most typically, but fear or, at times, guilt), as though they are constantly in a survival mode.

The utility of an otherwise vague, and perhaps depreciatory, concept of the "primitive" personality lies in its applicability to a wide spectrum of patients whose typology cuts across traditional nosological lines. From the standpoint of the therapist, certainly, the challenge is in the primitivity *per se*, not in the hysteric or obsessive or whatever other form the personality may take.

I have given many examples of primitive patients in the chapters on borderline, antisocial and paranoid disorders, and also in this chapter. There is a clinical variety I believe deserves further discussion, nevertheless, because it is a rare family that can boast of being untouched by this phenomenon somewhere within its ranks. This variant is the bitter/envious person, which we as therapists see now and then in our practices, but more often hear about: as the spouse or sibling or parent of one of our patients (for instance, Lois' mother in the next example). Bitterly envious persons are notorious for creating a "living hell" for those close to them, whether through petty acts of meanness, spiteful remarks, dyspeptic looks, or some other "dig" chosen from the thick catalog of hostile expression.

As to the matter of treatment, I agree in principle with the recommendation put forward by Miller:

Rather than uncovering conflict, the emphasis of psychotherapy with primitive personalities should be educative. For these individuals, analysis of cognition and affect must occupy the central position that analysis of conflict and defense occupies in the treatment of more classically neurotic patients. (1992, p. 102)

The practicalities of the problem are much more challenging in many instances. Not all persons with marked degrees of envy, spitefulness, or other "primitive" traits even *feel* the need for help (because in their eyes the rest of the world is at fault, not themselves). If they do seek treatment, chances are it will be for some problem *other* than the traits that so much alienate them from even their own families. By the time they reach adulthood, family members can no longer give a "word to the wise," because they will appear to have been merely self-serving (as if trying to get the offensive relative off their backs).

The oversensitivity of "primitive" persons makes them react—ragefully— with what to them seems like complete justification—to minor annoyances, unintended slights, etc., that ordinary people would scarcely notice. A therapist's task in educating such a patient to the cultural norms of what people do and don't take offense at is monumental. One often feels it would require two lifetimes to complete the work. Group therapy is theoretically useful, since the other group members could "level" with someone who was hostile and bitter, in hopes the comments of peers might be easier to assimilate than those of an authority figure. Sometimes this turns out to be a successful strategy, though all too often embittered and blaming persons quit under fire and leave the group. Dyadic therapy, in the meantime, is at a disadvantage, because those who know the other side of the story are not invited into the therapeutic process.

BITTERNESS

As with many of the special traits in this section, *bitterness* cuts across the lines of our standard characterology: the trait can be found in persons with almost any personality disorder. Bitterness is particularly common in persons with paranoid, irritable, and depressive qualities. These qualities are discernible in many pain-dependent personality types, such as I sketched in Chapter 16.

Clinical Example

Lois began treatment with me after leaving her previous therapist. She was 41 at the time, supporting herself in a comfortable style through her post as chief technician of a chemistry lab. Her marriage ended in divorce after four years, when she was 30. There were no children. Lois had a half-brother by her mother's earlier marriage; her mother made little effort to conceal her preference for her son. Her father seemed to favor her, but he was not very communicative; nor was he at home much since he often had to work two jobs to make ends meet. Both parents came from large families, the other members of which were demonstrably more successful than Lois' father. Her mother was bitter about this, and derogated her husband because of his "blue-collar" jobs. She was also hypercritical toward her daughter, whom she turned into a "Cinderella," making her do much of the cooking and cleaning. Lois was as a result "housebound" throughout much of her adolescence, and had little time for friends.

Her father died suddenly when she was 15. She became severely depressed, and two months later made the first of many suicide gestures. Her first hospitalization occurred when she was 18, shortly before graduating high school. This had followed an ugly scene in which her mother, insisting that Lois go to college near home so she could continue to "help out," threatened not to support her in any way if she went to the college of her choice in a different state. Lois had to give in, and this became a source of a bitterness toward her mother that did not diminish in 20 years.

This bitterness only increased when her marriage failed. Her husband wanted children and she did not, convinced that she had "nothing to give to a child, since I got nothing from my mother." She saw the defective mother-daughter relationship as the root cause of the failure in her own marriage. During the intervening years she had a few brief affairs, but otherwise lived alone. She became increasingly crotchety, impatient and critical of her friends and lovers, alienating them to the point where she had little in life besides her work, and that none too gratifying. A vicious circle of bitterness began to spiral: the fewer the friends, the more she was alone, the more irritable she became, the more abrasive she was with the few friends she had left . . . until they too deserted her, leaving her still more alone, more bitter, more petulant. . . .

During her thirties, she had several brief hospitalizations for suicide gestures with overdoses of sedatives and antidepressants. Throughout this period she was in treatment with a succession of therapists, including psychopharmacologists. With each, "things were all right" in the beginning, but after a time her captiousness took over—to the point where sessions were no longer focused on her situation and what she could do to improve it, but on her catalog of complaints. Her coworkers didn't appreciate her; her boss gave her the minimum raise; she couldn't stand friends who were married "because they have each other"; she couldn't stand single friends "because they're in the same boat I'm in," etc. If a therapist took notes: "All you seem to care about is those notes, not me." If another therapist didn't take notes: "You're not taking any of this down: does this mean I don't matter to you?"

Her bitterness and suicidality would heighten each year before her mother's birthday: that seemed the ideal time to "teach the bitch what she did to me." During my work with her, I tried to pry her away from her preoccupation with her mother; I tried to get her to end her self-enforced isolation; I encouraged her to resume playing the violin that she seemed to enjoy as a child. Success was brief and episodic. She could hardly look at her violin, since it reminded her of how her mother made her practice it in the closet, so as not to disturb the rest of the family. I even addressed the issue of her bitterness directly, telling her it was like a creeping poison spoiling her life—a poison that she now administered to herself, over and beyond *whatever* had happened to her.

For a time she began to speculate whether her father had molested her sexually, and whether that "explained" why she couldn't get along with men. There seemed to be no evidence for this; rather, it seemed that she was fishing for something else to be bitter about—something that would justify her giving up on life. Certainly her childhood had been less than ideal. But it was much less traumatic than were the formative years of many other patients.

I assumed it was her predisposition to recurrent depression that led her to experience the negative things of her life as more intensely negative than others might.

She had reached a time in her life when her own efforts to enrich her life were an essential ingredient to her recovery; endless sympathy from a therapist would not add to her circle of friends, give her a hobby, secure her a mate. Lois was rarely willing to make such efforts, preferring instead to brood, under the covers, about her deprived childhood. The one dream she reported in the year and a half I worked with her addressed this feeling: she sees herself in the gourmet section of a department store, where she eyes a fruit basket. She swipes it, warning herself on her way out of the store: you shouldn't have done this, you'll get caught. The security people did catch her.

During the course of our work, her attitude toward me shifted. At first, she was comfortable with me, as someone with whom she could confide, even though the therapy, as she often reminded me, was "getting nowhere." Later, as I began urging her to take some positive steps in her life, I was no longer a "transitional object," just a pest. She made a serious suicide attempt the day before I returned from a brief absence. She was still groggy during the next session, and no less suicidal. I brought her to the hospital. This enraged her: "Who told you to save my fucking life?!" She broke off treatment with me after her release, remaining with the doctor who had treated her while at the hospital.

This vignette makes plain how *bitterness* as an enduring trait may act synergistically with a constitutional predisposition to depression, enhancing the tendency to suicide and keeping this tendency at a worrisomely high level decade after decade.* As Angst et al. (1990) have shown in their survival-analysis study, the "constant group risk for committing suicide [in the affectively ill patients] is remarkable from a clinical point of view. . . . the patients never escape their risk. In an individual case the risk may vary . . . and be dependent on the presence or absence of episodes and symptoms. . . . the risk of suicide comes up again and again" (p. 183).

In Lois' case, premenstrual symptom aggravation, episodic abuse of alcohol, and poor responsiveness to conventional medications fed into the suicide risk, but personality factors — her chronically embittered attitude, especially — also figured importantly in making her prognosis guarded. As I noted in my follow-up work, the combination of depression, borderline personality, and alcohol abuse was associated with a poor five-year survival. If the accompanying personality was such as to wear out the patience of one's relatives and to state before the world "The hell with all of you!" the risk was higher still. Those who were more life-oriented and less bitter had a better chance of working cooperatively with a therapist and of overcoming their infatuation with suicide.

PLASTICITY

Related to the "as-if" personality described by Helene Deutsch, with its emphasis on blandness and chameleon-like adoption of attitudes espoused by the important people in one's life, is the trait of "plasticity." Usually one uses only the adjectival form: "plastic." We confront the "plastic" person most commonly among the younger or middle-level workers in large corporations. They are opportunistic, conformist in the extreme, and readily disposed to agree with the opinions and proposals of higher-ups.

Unlike the hypocrite, who thinks one thing and says something else, the plastic person feels utterly sincere in his agreement with the boss, even though he may have been on record as having a different view before the boss made his ideas explicit. More often, the plastic person entertains as

*From the standpoint of outcome, depressive inpatients studied by Duggan et al. (1990) had poorer outcomes to the extent that they scored high on "neuroticism" (as judged by the Eysenck inventory) or on obsessionality (during the recovery phase in the hospital, as measured by the Leyton scale).

few views as possible, until they have become endorsed by higher authority—except for the very safest of opinions that already bear the stamp of approval of the whole country. Thus, "Plastic man" is "for" God, America, Mom, baseball, gun ownership, and apple pie, in approximately that order.

Getting to know such a person is no easy task, because he will have shorn himself of as many identificatory "hooks" as possible, by way of being pleasing, or at least acceptable, to the greatest number of people. "Plastic man" may come across as upright and moral, but the morality will prove, under trying circumstances, to be easily bent—in whatever direction the prevailing political winds are blowing at the moment.

This phenomenon is similar to what Hannah Arendt (1977) wrote about, concerning the Nazi rulers and their henchmen, under the heading of the "banality of evil." The biographies of many such "ordinary men," who became willing instruments of the Holocaust, are depicted in Browning's recent book (1992). Hitler's foreign minister, Joachim von Ribbentrop, was a man of this sort—an Anglophile and fluent speaker of English in his younger days, a man with Jewish as well as Christian friends, who, once he became mesmerized by Hitler, instantly turned anti-Semitic, and anti-English. As John Weitz (1992) tells us in his excellent biography, von Ribbentrop even affected no longer to understand the English language, when meeting with British diplomats.

Example

The man who in my experience most exemplified this trait was the husband of a patient who had begun treatment in the hopes of patching up a deteriorating marriage. Both actually were executives in large corporations, except the wife functioned well at her job and received frequent commendations, while he was constantly getting fired from one high post after the other. His behavior exasperated her because he took no steps to better his situation: he felt he was "doing fine," was "well-liked," and had no problems.

At her request I saw him alone and with her on a number of occasions. He wore the navy blue suit and "rep" tie that was apparently standard at his company. Coupled with his equally "standard" good looks (like the picture under "MAN" in a child's dictionary), the attire gave him the appearance of the businessman with the bowler hat—and no face—in Magritte's famous painting. I could not "get through" to him regarding any area of his life, past or present. He described everything using corny phrases, referring to his childhood as "peachy keen," to his children as "super," and to his marriage as "hunky-dory." His mind was a dictionary of platitudes.

Apart from a measure of anger at his wife for suggesting that anything was wrong with him in the first place, he had expunged strong emotion from his behavioral repertoire—like the Scientology zombies who keep smiling sweetly even when you insult them to their face. At work he apparently did display that peculiar translucency of personality Helene Deutsch wrote about: he spoke the party line with seeming conviction—once his two superiors at the company announced what the "party line" was.

If he made himself so agreeable, how was it that he kept getting fired? It turned out that his studied agreeableness was not enough to earn him a permanent spot. Some originality was required, and of that he had none. To make matters worse, he was so convinced he was (in his words) the "cat's meow" at his firm that he took liberties with vacations (overstaying without notification), padded the bill too noticeably, and made himself expendable.

Shortly after I saw him, his wife's prediction (that he would lose the current job too) proved correct. Even that did not shock him into becoming more "real." This pushed her beyond her limit, and she filed for divorce. During the acrimonious legal tussle that ensued, it developed that he had been cheating on her for over a year, pretending to have no assets, yet siphoning off large sums from an account he was supposedly managing. Besides being "plastic," he proved to be passive-aggressive (at home) and sociopathic. This is not a treatable combination.

INDISCRETION

For the recipients of indiscretion, it is a vexatious trait, even when the indiscreet one is blithely unaware of the social gaffes he or she is committing. There is a more malignant variety where the indiscreet person is well aware that his remark or act will have an immediately hurtful effect. An example of the latter might be that of a husband quipping to the assembled dinner guests: "Don't mind how Martha overcooked the beef: if it's too tough, you can always use it to make wallets." Here, indiscretion passes over into vengefulness, and should probably be discussed under that heading.

Where this conscious intention to wound is not present, indiscretion may take the form of tactlessness or carelessness, or it may be the byproduct of the behavior of those whom we call scatterbrained—or, in the colloquial language, "flaky." Those who are "flaky" sometimes offend others with an apparent genius for doing everything wrong, while at the same time being friendly, well-meaning, and seemingly guileless. Culture enters into the equation: foreigners will inadvertently violate cultural norms, yet not be deemed indiscreet. A common form of indiscretion is blurting out a secret, but even this tendency will vary in valence from innocent to hurtful, depending on whether the secret involved a job promotion or a malicious rumor.

Example

The person I will be describing in this vignette was not a patient, but rather, the nanny for the three children of my neighbors some 15 years back. (All the names here have been change.) The Harrises had hired Marie a few months before the family was to spend an August in France. Marie, a sophomore in college and of French descent, seemed at first an excellent choice, since she was vivacious, cheerful, and seemingly eager to work with children.

The Harris' daughter and two sons warmed to her quickly. Trouble started almost as quickly. The Harrises began to regale me with "Marie stories"—the first of which were not too disturbing but so amusing that I took to writing them down at the time. One of Marie's indiscretions was to flop down on the bed next to Mrs. H. around 11 in the evening, to watch whatever program Mrs. H. was watching on the television. This, despite Marie's having a TV in her own room. Not wishing to hurt Marie's feelings, Mrs. H. let this go on for a time; however, Marie gave no indication that she was about to depart for her own quarters even when Mr. H. came in, obviously wanting to turn in for the night. Mrs. H. had to tell Marie that positioning herself on the bed next to the lady of the house wasn't something one did—though making this explicit made Mrs. H. feel awkward and snobbish.

Mr. H. then noticed that the monthly grocery bill had suddenly escalated skyward—a mystery that did not resolve until it became clear that Marie was charging to the family's account five or six bottles (a gallon) of Perrier water every day. Was she selling some on the side? Did she bathe in it? At all events, Mr. H. felt he had to lay the law down—gently, so as not to bruise Marie's feelings—pointing out that it was not quite proper to charge $160 worth of water in a month without asking permission.

Though her behavior was outrageous, he couldn't sustain his own indignation, since at the same time he felt cheap at having to expose his finances to the nanny, imagining as he did that a really rich man wouldn't notice such a "trifle." But then a new wave of indignation would sweep over him—at Marie's having forced him to feel like a piker. Still, the children liked her, and nothing Marie did was exactly *dangerous*.

Once abroad, this was to change. While touring toward the south of France, for example, the Harrises came to a mountainous terrain where the road was a succession of hairpin turns. As Mr. H. was nervously negotiating these turns, Marie was busy in the back seat telling the children about her relatives. Her brother, she gleefully told them (they were 12, 10, and 7 at the time), was currently in jail after being arrested for "homosexual activities." When asked what those were, she went ahead and explained that he'd been "sucking penises" in the subway bathrooms.

After regaining his composure, Mr. H., afraid to criticize Marie too sharply for fear of undermining her authority with the children, requested quietly that she change the subject to a topic more within the children's range of experience. As indeed she did: she got them to participate in a word game, elevating her voice for some reason to piercing soprano level, such that Mr. H. was sure he would become unnerved and pitch the car over a ravine, where the six corpses would be discovered the next day. He now simply told "everybody" to please be quiet, again so as not to embarrass Marie in front of the children.

The next day the family stopped at a rather posh hotel near Puy. At lunch the Harrises ordered modestly: crôque-monsieurs for the children, a local fish for Mr. and Mrs. When the waiter turned to Marie, she piped up: "I'll have the caviar." Again Mr. H. had to smother his fury—more at the gall in Gaul than at the sixty dollars—but there was nothing he could say, until later when the children were not around.

Two days later, arrived in Cannes, the family went to the beach in the morning. Just before lunchtime, Mrs. H. called over to Marie, who was in the water with the children, to bring them in for their food. The older boy was pokey about coming out of the water. Marie punished him by shoving his head under the water. That so infuriated Mrs. H. that she "lost her cool" and screamed at Marie to release him instantly.

The boy was still shaken, and shivering, after the meal, so Marie, now contrite, sought to make amends—by taking him to her bed and holding him next to her naked body, while the two younger children romped about the room. When Mrs. H. came upon this scene she was aghast, but powerless to say much until she could get Marie aside and explain why, despite the centuries-long tradition of nannies seducing their young wards, it was not *comme il faut*, especially in plain view of their siblings.

Next stop, Arles—where Marie proceeded to walk with the children atop the colisseum, a hundred feet above the plaza, and with no guard rail. The Harrises spotted them from down below, and of course could do nothing but pray that at least some of the children would be able to get down without falling to their death. All survived, whereupon Mrs. H. immediately fired Marie—but only in her mind at this point, since to tell her she was fired, while letting her stay until the end of the trip, would invite even more trouble. And to send her home on the next plane would allow Marie, if she so chose, to rob them blind. Saddled with Marie's endless indiscretion and poor judgment, the Harrises had still to preserve civility until their return to the States. Once home, they had her pack her belongings and leave the premises, while summoning the locksmith to change the locks.

I have culled these details from a much lengthier notebook by way of stimulating the reader's curiosity as to what a therapist might do, if faced with the task of treating even a good-natured person like Marie, where everything that person did seemed socially jarring and indiscreet? Where would one begin? If Marie had become a patient in one-to-one therapy, she would not have been likely to reveal the details pertinent to her "personality disorder," since whatever she said or did seemed justifiable and normal to her. Her employers, whom she would have seen as fussy and straight-laced, would not have come to her sessions to expose the other side of the story.

Possibly, the scope and breadth of her peculiarities might have come out in group therapy. Even so, there seemed to be no solid place in her personality, no zone of commonality with ordinary people (including the hypothetical therapist) to serve as a foundation upon which the needed changes could be constructed. She gave no sign of "lateral spread," where a lesson learned in one context is at once applied to all similar contexts. Her innnovativeness in creating social mistakes was therefore infinite. One would have had to *start all over*, and this requires more magic than even the most gifted therapists have at their disposal. As a consequence, therapists, while they may not always escape personality aberrations of this sort in their personal life, rarely confront anything similar in their professional life.

VENGEFULNESS

Few people go through their lives without having been betrayed, jilted, cheated, misused, unfairly treated, unreasonably punished, denied opportunities, etc., etc., at least on a small number of occasions, by someone. The wish to get even is very powerful. I am not even speaking here of tragic situations that turn one's life upside down in an instant, such as having one's child mowed down by a drunken driver. It would be presumptuous for anyone who has not suffered a catastrophe of that magnitude to preach about the "adaptive" way of handling the vengeful feelings such an event would awaken in one (though, miraculously, some people surmount even this kind of loss).

I am referring instead to the more common situations: of learning that one's spouse has been unfaithful, that one's boss has promoted a less deserving employee, that a confidante turns out to have a disreputable character. It is in these circumstances that the old adage rings especially true: *living well is the best revenge.* Yet many people are slow to learn that, if you discover someone you were involved with, in romance or in business, was untrustworthy, was a "pychopath" even, the best remedy is to absorb the harsh lesson, to walk away, and to rebuild one's life with people of a better sort.

A good example of someone who pursued this mature strategy is Agatha Christie. Her first husband, a dashing military man, proved unfaithful. Devastated for a time, she emerged as the great mystery writer, penning a hundred-and-something thrillers in which, often enough, bounders like her "ex" end up shot, or stabbed, or poisoned. Instead of "sublime" revenge, *sublimated* revenge — far the better course. She had, by all accounts, a wonderful life with her second husband, which, along with her fame, must have expunged pretty completely all remnants of hurt, and of the attendant anger, over the original betrayal.

Fortunately, one does not have to have talent of the magnitude of Agatha Christie's to recover, via living well, from the usual vengeance-inspiring events in one's life. Finding a better mate, a better job, a fancier dress, a spiffier car, a consuming hobby — there are many alternatives. In the chapters on borderline and antisocial personality disorders I offered some clinical vignettes of remarkably vengeful patients who most emphatically did *not* take the high road, but who instead mired themselves in vindictiveness, attempting to bring others into the muck with them. They ended up in the muck all by themselves, though they did teach me, to the extent my treatment efforts were a total failure, just how difficult it is to extricate someone from this characterological quicksand.

To find the ultimate in vengefulness I had to search the annals of crime. The biographies of notorious violent criminals, which I used in my reexamination of psychopathy (Chapter 21) are replete with examples of murderers and terrorizers motivated by vengeance. Many had wretched childhoods, having been brutalized themselves, which makes their crimes, if no less unspeakable, somewhat more "understandable." In this respect, the vengefulness of Betty Broderick is much less understandable, so far as any childhood predisposing factors are concerned, and therefore in a way more instructive. To grasp just how far beyond the scope of psychiatric treatment she stood, one would have to read the whole of Taubman's biography (1992). Here I can give the reader only a flavor.

Betty Broderick was born in a wealthy home in the suburbs of New York City. She was one of six children in an intact family, with nurturing parents and none of the "abuse" factors that permeate the histories of most prominent murderers. Highly attractive and intelligent, she married a domineering, egocentric, "workaholic" and equally good-looking man, very fashion-conscious, who completed first medical school, and then law school, as stepping-stones to a career in malpractice law. Settling in San Diego, the Brodericks had four children. Within a few years Dan Broderick became partner in a prestigious law firm and was earning over a million dollars a year.

The marriage, never very solid, deteriorated. Dan began an affair, clandestine at first, with Linda Kolkena, a former stewardess who became his receptionist, then his mistress. Taking "life begins at 40" literally, Dan walked out on Betty three months after his fortieth birthday with a red Corvette and a 21-year-old (Taubman, p. 63). He sued for custody of the four children, and in the no-holds-barred battle that followed, Betty burned his clothes with gasoline in front of the children; she rammed her car into the new house Dan purchased; she smashed his windows, broke his mirrors, sprayed paint on his walls.

No paragon of compassion himself, Dan reacted to the news that their younger daughter was developing a drug problem and had dropped out of high school by formally disowning her and writing her out of his will. In 1988, Dan married Linda (who, at 21, looked just like Betty at 21), by which time Betty's behavior had descended to that of a foul-mouthed and abusive virago. Compared to her mild-mannered and soft-spoken comportment of the pre-Linda years, this was a 180° turnabout. She was consumed with rage, obsessed with fantasies of killing Dan, and no longer capable of speaking a sentence that was not peppered with four-letter words. No one would have said she had any kind of "personality disorder" beforehand (unless one counts naïveté about a blatantly philandering husband); now she emerges as an explosive, antisocial, even somewhat psychopathic person hell-bent on murder. All this occurred without any "push" from alcohol or other disinhibiting drugs.

Betty made no secret of having purchased a .38 revolver, with which she planned to repeat Medea's revenge, and kill her ex-husband for good measure. Before she carried out her plan (she sneaked into their house and shot both to death in November of '89), several friends urged her to get psychiatric help, but she refused adamantly on the grounds that Dan would use this as proof she were "crazy"—one more reason to justify his getting custody.

In the meantime Dan was ordered by the Court to pay her $16,000 a month in alimony. Even so she ended up broke much of the time, because she squandered large sums on dresses she hardly wore, and because Dan tried to curb her use of foul language by subtracting a certain amount each time she uttered any on the phone. She would not delete the expletives even for her own advantage, however, as was documented on many tape-recorded phone conversations with her children. Taubman excerpted a poignant interchange, the original lasting over a half-hour, in which her then ten-year old son, Dan Junior, with a wisdom beyond his years, begs his mother to stop the bad words, so that a settlement can be reached, and so that life can return to normal. Here are some of the relevant passages:

> Danny: How come you won't stop saying bad words?
> Betty: Because I'm mad.
> Danny: Yeah, well how can you be mad for two years? And you're just going to get worse and worse and worse until you get your stupid share of money, and you're never going to get your stupid share of money until you stop saying bad words! . . .
> Betty: Where's the cunt? [her sole term in referring to Linda]
> Danny: Nowhere, Mom. I don't know.
> Betty: It's not time to come over and screw him yet, huh?
> Danny: She's with her family.
> Betty: Oh, with her family . . . I wonder what her family thinks of her fucking her boss who's married with four kids?
> Danny: . . . You better stop saying bad words or else . . .
> Betty: No matter what bad words I say, I still own half.
> Danny: Fine. After you stop saying bad words, you'll get your stupid half.
> Betty: You're a little monster. . . .
> Danny: (crying) Why do you do it? . . . Because you're being selfish, you want everything, you want all the kids, you want to get all the money, you want to get him away from Linda, and you want to still say bad words. . . . It's not going to work, Mom. (Taubman, pp. 103, 107)

Danny may not speak the language of DSM, but he was "on" to his mother's narcissism, paranoid grudge-holding, explosiveness, antisociality, and obsessiveness, and he was fully aware of the inappropriateness of it all. At ten. Are we to imagine psychiatry could neutralize vitriol that was impervious to the tears of one's ten-year-old son?

As for rebuilding her life, this was no woman from the culture of poverty, with but one joy in her life—her mate—and that now taken away from her; this was an attractive woman of 40 with a beautiful home, four children, a circle of friends and $16,000 a month. She had options. But apparently all the options—going back to school, getting a job, traveling, joining organizations that might, among other things, add to her chances of finding another mate—must have seemed like pale stuff, compared to the winner-take-all/loser-kill-all game to which Betty Broderick devoted her energies. She became a monster of entitlement. How did this happen to someone who did not even seem to have grown up "spoiled" by her parents?

Her biographer, Taubman, called her book *Hell Hath No Fury*, as if a woman scorned might react that way. Yet Danny, at ten, knew that the hatred and vengefulness of a rejected woman are supposed to melt away in a few months, surely before two years. Therapists help many "scorned" partners through the process of recovery—but only those who wish to be helped. Persistent vengefulness erases our sympathy. With those who put revenge above recovery we are powerless.

CALLOUSNESS

A resident I was supervising told me of a patient he was working with on the drug-rehabilitation unit. The patient—a man in his late twenties—had, in the course of a robbery, shot a policeman, rendering him paraplegic. During the trial the policeman was wheeled into the courtroom by his wife and small child. In recounting the story to the resident, the patient expressed fury over the courtroom scene: "How the hell was I going to get a fair trial with the jury looking at the wife crying her eyes out over this cop in the wheelchair?!"

Here, as I mentioned to the resident, was callousness in the extreme. Had the mechanism of shame (never mind guilt) been present in this man, presumably he would not have committed armed robbery in the first place, let alone squawked about the wheelchair. What could the resident hope to accomplish now in someone with a record of armed robberies and incarcerations stretching back to his teens? If therapy succeeded *now* in planting within this man the seeds of remorse, what might be the result? The heartfelt acknowledgment of such crimes—particularly the last one (the policeman died a month after the trial)—might lead a man capable of remorse to kill himself. Perhaps, as I suggested, the only alternative would be to go on the lecture circuit, speaking to young audiences about the horrors of violent crime and about the ruin and waste that characterizes the life of the violent offender.

The resident organized a group of men, including this patient, all of whom had committed crimes of violence. Vincent (as I shall call him) eventually was able to admit, "If I thought too much about that cop's kid, I couldn't live with myself." This comes close to acknowledging the paradox I had alluded to: if treatment of a murderer is maximally effective, suicide may beckon strongly as a therapeutic "outcome." In this situation the cured murderer does not live to enjoy his regained humanity, while the remorseless (read: persistently psychopathic) murderer lives on free of the pangs of conscience. Later, Vincent admitted: "If I think about what I did even to the cop, I can't stand myself—so then I go and drink, only once I get drunk I know I'm going to go out there and do another crime."

Here is another vicious circle that can be interrupted only by committing oneself to a prosocial course of action. Actually, Vincent did give a lecture at a local high school—one that was emotionally very moving for himself as well as for the students. He has not as yet felt emboldened to "go on the circuit" in a more committed way. But I am convinced that if recovery is possible in cases like his, this is the way the process must begin. Here the therapist's compassion must be combined with a still-preserved capacity for moral outrage (so often this is benumbed in our culture). Ideally, it is this compassion that fosters identification, on the part of a callous and anti-social patient, with the moral values of society (of which the therapist is a representative).

By itself, the "talking cure" is not enough. Evil acts can be redeemed only by good acts—acts of genuine contrition and self-sacrifice. The cure for antisociality is "prosociality"—the development, if and when this is possible, of a heartfelt social conscience. The callousness in Vincent was one step short of the maximum, and to that extent perhaps remediable. One is reminded of the cures sometimes effected by religious adepts, such as the Zen master, Ryohkan (Stevens, 1993) whose forgiveness led the town troublemaker to mend his ways. Where the rudiments of conscience are still present, amelioration is a possibility. Beyond this point, we are in moral vacuum and most likely beyond the realm of treatment. This like-lihood becomes certainty once grievous acts (murder, torture) have been committed—as is true with many of the persons we will encounter in the final chapter.

HIGHLY DESTRUCTIVE PERSONS (SOME WITH PSYCHOPATHIC TRAITS) WHO CAUSE GREAT HARM TO OTHERS, DRIVE OTHERS TO SUICIDE, BUT WHO HAVE NEVER COMMITTED ACTUAL MURDER

As a closing to this chapter, and a prelude to the final chapter, I can mention a number of destructive personality configurations not commonly encountered by therapists. Occasionally, the patients with whom we work will have among their relatives or acquaintances persons embodying one or another of these character types. To those in forensic psychiatry, or in the field of child or spousal abuse, many of these character types will be part of their routine work.

Most readers will be familiar with these character types from their pe-rusal of various biographies and newspaper accounts. For considerations of space, I will give only one example in detail, alluding to the rest only briefly and with a few pertinent references.

One such character type is often spoken of as the "Hollywood Mother." These are typically narcissistic and intrusive women who live "through" their children's accomplishments, and who push their children to the outer edges of their capacities (and beyond) in hopes of earning a kind of vicarious fame. An example is that of Brenda William-Taylor Frazier, whose ambitions for her daughter ("Little" Brenda—a famous debutante in the 1930s: DiLiberto, 1987) ultimately ruined her daughter's life. Similar in personality, but more indifferent than domineering toward her children, was Rebecca Semple Harness (Unger, 1988).

Tyrannizing fathers constitute another destructive type. The kind of bullying and egocentricity they display is well documented in Niederland's biography (1984) of the jurist Daniel Schreber (of Freud's "Schreber case"). Schreber's autocratic and domineering father drove one son to suicide, and crippled the lives of his whole family. Archibald Douglas was another such man. His personality is set forth in the eloquent biography of his son, Geoffrey (1992), who managed, after many difficult years, to extricate himself from the effects of his father's vanity and contemptuousness.

Still more destructive was the father of the actress, Edie Sedgwick (Stein & Plimpton, 1982). Two of his sons committed suicide after years of humiliating taunts from their father, whose incestuous involvement with Edie contributed later on to her suicide at the age of 28. The damage inflicted by fathers of this sort has been characterized as "soul murder" (Shengold, 1989; Stone, 1991a).

Despotic bosses whose abrasiveness and insensitivity make torture-chambers of the workplace are known all too well. Some examples are to be found in Stewart's documentary (1991) about the Wall Street scandals of the 1980s.

Certain explosive-tempered, violent persons stop short of murder, but come to our attention (or to the attention of the authorities) because of pathological jealousy and wife-battering (as in the case of Jake LaMotta, the prizefighter whose life was dramatized in the film, *Raging Bull*). Diagnostically, they fall into the category now called "impulsive-aggressive" (Hollander, 1992; Lidberg, 1992).

Power-mad narcissistic leaders constitute a truly untreatable group. Pacepa (1987) has documented the lives of the Ceasescus, whose son, Niku, was in a fair way to becoming as ruthless and predatory as his parents— until they were executed by the new government in Romania.

Mendacious psychopaths who cheat and betray, relying on their charm and acting skill to "con" and exploit others, may be said, as is true of power-made leaders, to inhabit the realm of evil. Their imperviousness to treatment has been commented on by Bursten (1989).

Still less debatable as occupants of the realm of evil are sadistic tortur-

ers—especially those who victimize children. Though there is, as I speculated in Chapter 17, no worst case of sadism, the following example may
serve to convince the skeptic that the realm of evil and the realm of treatability do not overlap. I learned of this case in the course of a seminar on
child abuse that is now a requirement for renewal of medical licensure in
New York State. The seminar leader told of a girl of seven who had been
molested sexually by her uncle on an ongoing basis. One day he took the
child down to the basement of her house where there was a basket for the
family cat and her kittens. Opening the furnace door, the uncle pitched
first the mother cat, then the kittens, one by one, into the flames, warning
his niece: if you ever tell anyone about what we do, I'll throw your mother
in here—and then you!

The realm of evil is defined by the presence of *malice*: the active desire
to harm others. In the preceding example, malice took the form of sexual
violation and terror—enough to bring about, possibly, the psychological
death of the victim (the "soul murder" of which Shengold spoke). In the
final chapter we look at malice in its ultimate form: murder, especially
premeditated murder and serial homicide.

21

Beyond Psychotherapy: The Psychopath Reexamined

> Only then did [Inspector] Kostoev see who Chikatilo really was. At
> the core. Beneath the mask of grandfather, the mask of communist,
> the mask of the insulted and injured. . . . And what Kostoev saw
> was . . . the vengeance of which weakness dreams. Abdications of
> everything human as impediment. Surrender to the might of evil,
> mysterious as God and death, real as the wounds in a child's flesh.
>
> Richard Lourie (1993), *commenting on the*
> *pedophile/serial killer, Andrei Chikatilo, captured after*
> *the sexual murders of 53 boys, girls, and young women*

TO UNDERSTAND BETTER THE LIMITS of psychotherapy in ameliorating
personality disorders, it is useful to examine the issue from "the other
side"; i.e., from the study of persons who stand clearly on the far side of
treatability. A convenient starting-place in this exercise is the domain of
habitual offenders, such as would occupy the attention of the criminologist
and the forensic psychiatrist. Almost by definition, habitual criminals, and
even felons who have committed only one or two serious crimes, will exhibit one or another disorder of personality.

While untreatable personality disorders are hardly confined to the realm
of the violent (many an embezzler, forger, or bank-robber also lie beyond
the pale of treatment), violent acts more readily attract attention. As I have
mentioned elsewhere (Stone, 1989c), spectacular cases of murder or of
killing in self-defense are apt to become the subjects of biography, thus
contributing to the annals of "True Crime."*

---

*I have purposely focused in this chapter on civilians and on those who are *not*
members of organized crimes. As Lessing (1987) reminds us, many men who had
led unexceptional lives during peacetime suddenly succumb to baser instincts
during war, becoming violent psychopaths-of-the-moment—raping and murdering
noncombatants.

There are many biographies rich enough in personal details to permit the reasonably accurate assessment of personality pathology. These details may include impressions by persons who knew the perpetrators at various stages of their lives. Such material is potentially of greater value to the diagnostician than what is "revealed" by the killer, since the latter is usually at pains to mislead and misinform.

Details amassed from the study of large numbers of violent offenders contribute to the establishment of *profiles*, such as those created from the extensive research by the FBI (Ressler et al., 1988; Ressler & Shachtman, 1992). Governmental authorities concentrate on details pertinent to detection and prosecution; here we will turn the spotlight on the issues of personality assessment and treatability.

Forensic specialists mention several attributes, personality traits among them, noted with unusual frequency in persons who murder. Rebelliousness and aggressivity are common, as are mendacity, entitlement, and social isolation. Murderers are typically beset by surpluses of hatred and impulsivity. These attributes, especially when fueled by alcohol, conduce to *ragefulness*, characterized by episodic outbursts of violent behavior directed against others. These factors help account for the strength of the murderous impulse, but do not address specifically the "releaser mechanisms" that presumably underlie the transition from murderous fantasy to murderous act.

An important element in this releaser mechanism is *callousness* (implying a lack of empathy and compassion), the cardinal feature of the psychopath (cf. Chapter 13). Possible innate factors predisposing to callousness have been discussed by Hare (Goleman, 1987), and are probably present more often in men than in women (Zenhausern et al., 1981).*

Compassion may require that an adequate empathic mechanism be fortified by warm and positive interactions with caretakers during the first few years of life — interactions whose net effect we speak of as "humanizing." The capacity for compassion can be crushed in some persons by unremittingly cruel parents, yet in others parental cruelty seems only to fortify compassion — along with a determination never to become like those parents when they later become parents.

Although the correlation between abusive childhood and murder is impressive, correspondingly good epidemiological data are simply not available concerning the (immensely greater) proportion of persons with abys-

---

*This may help account, along with the lesser aggressivity of women, for the much better record women have (by a factor of ten or more) in relation to murder. Until recently, for example, there were no female serial killers at all in the United States.

mal childhoods who never come close to murdering. Abusive parenting *heightens the risk* for future murderous acts, but is not in and of itself a sufficient cause. I cannot as yet demonstrate scientifically that what one might call the "compassion-quotient" is the essential variable distinguishing those capable of murder from the majority who are not. The assessment of such a quotient would depend on "soft" data, having to do with the quality of parenting, the manner in which the parents (or any important caretakers) actively taught respect for the rights and feelings of others, etc. Such data are hard to extract and measure. Much easier to computerize are data relevant to early fire-setting, cruelty to animals, delinquency, and the like. The best one can do at present is to glean what one can about the presence or absence of humanizing influences from the more detailed biographical accounts of murderers. As of this writing, I have perused some 164 biographies, many of which were inspired by "counterintuitive" examples: murderers who came from seemingly good families, from middle-to-upper class circumstances, etc., which we would not customarily regard as the breeding ground for heinous crimes.

One might take as the zero-point on the scale of compassion the remark of the serial killer and schizoid psychopath (cf. Gallwey, 1985), Jerry Brudos (Rule, 1983). After Brudos' 1969 arrest, a detective was trying to get to know how the mind of such a person works. He asked him: "Do you feel some remorse, Jerry? Do you feel sorry for your victims—for the girls who died?" As Ann Rule quotes his response: There was a half piece of white paper on the table between [the detective and the prisoner]. Jerry " . . . picked it up, crumpled it, and threw the ball of paper on the floor. 'That much,' he said. 'I care about those girls as much as I care about that piece of wadded up paper . . . '" (p. 238).*

GRADATIONS OF EVIL

Quelques crimes toujours précèdent les grands crimes.
Quiconque a pu franchir les bornes legitimes
Peut violer enfin les droits les plus sacrés;
Ainsi que la vertu, le crime a ses degrés;

---

*Brudos appears to have had a predisposition to a schizophrenia-spectrum condition. He came from a family that was neither very nurturing nor abusive. An older brother developed along normal lines. In 1974, the prison psychologists assessed Brudos as paranoid (though not psychotic) and dangerous, and recommended against release. The biographer underlined, in her 1988 addendum, that "There is no psychiatric treatment today that cures a sadistic sociopath" (p. 226).

Et jamais on n'a vu la timide innocence
Passer subitement à l'extrème licence.*

Phaedre, iv, 2
(Jean Racine, from Hippolyte's reply to Thésée)

It has become commonplace in our culture, and in the current generation, to express the belief that, if certain persons who have committed
felonies had only received psychiatric help—when they were adolescents,
say—they would not have carried out the violent, including murderous,
acts by which they eventually became identified. Or, more optimistically
still, people will assert that if a convicted felon were to receive therapy
during his prison stay, he could change his antisocial ways and live peaceably, upon his release, in the community.

The distinctions drawn in Chapter 13 between *antisociality* and *psychopathy* are important here. The famous case of Leopold and Loeb is instructive. Caught and imprisoned shortly after their murder of a young acquaintance, Loeb, a psychopathic "charmer" in personality, was killed in a prison
brawl in 1936. The gullible and transitorily antisocial Leopold, a more
scholarly type, spent 34 years in prison; since his release in 1958, he has
led an exemplary life and is considered a totally changed person (Glyn
Jones, 1989).

Examples of the other sort—where an imprisoned felon, once released,
quickly resumes his criminal path—are legion (Rule, 1983, 1983a). Sometimes this resumption becomes a dramatic proof of the ineffectiveness of
one or another treatment program.†

The psychiatrist who reported to the prison officials about Jerry Brudos,

---

*Crimes of lesser degree always preceed great crimes.
  Whoever disregards the boundaries of the law
  Is capable ultimately of violating the most sacred rights.
  Just as with virtue, crime has its degrees,
  And one never sees shy innocence
  Pass over on a sudden into the extremes of licence.

(My translation)

†I once interviewed a man on a forensic-psychiatric unit who had been remanded
there originally for killing his mother, grandmother and aunt. Twenty at the time,
he had been reacting to his mother's verbal abuse. He was without remorse, stating
glibly that her abuse made it right for him to "put her away." A prison psychologist
had earlier taken an interest in this man, and treated him in psychotherapy twice
weekly for seven years when the man was in his forties. Concluding that his patient
was a "cured man," was no longer sociopathic, etc., he recommended release. Ten
days after regaining his freedom (after a lapse of 31 years), the man was invited to
dinner at the home of his girlfriend's mother. He became enraged at something she
said, whereupon he struck the woman and raped her, in full view of her daughter.

for example, though he saw him " . . . as a potentially very dangerous individual were he to be released into the community," felt compelled to add: "The situation will continue *unless he has intensive and prolonged psychotherapy* . . . " (emphasis mine). In relation to Jerry Brudos, comments of this sort, though expressive of a laudable humanistic spirit, seem nevertheless naïve. How much better it would be if we were able to distinguish in a more reliable way between the curable and the incurable, not only so that we can allocate therapeutic resources more appropriately, but also for the (to my way of thinking) *more* humanistic goal of sparing innocent persons. What is at stake here is the balance between the rights of the individual, which our country properly prizes very highly, and the rights of the community, to whose welfare, by virtue of its greater numbers, we might well accord an even higher status.

To sharpen our intuition concerning which persons who appear at first glance to be unreachable by any psychotherapeutic means would actually turn out to be socially irremediable, I thought it might be useful to create a *scale* relevant to this issue. The scale reflects my impressions about the degree of inhumanity—or, viewed another way, the measure of "compassionlessness"—demonstrated by those who have taken the life of another person, and who, in the process, managed to rouse the attention of a biographer.

Since the scale focuses on the extremes of inhumanity, where social rehabilitation is unlikely, I refer to it as the *Gradations of Evil* (Table 22). A moral allusion of this kind may seem disturbing coming from a psychoanalyst. Certainly, psychoanalysis discourages one from making value judgments about one's patients. But most persons who voluntarily seek the help of psychiatrists or of psychoanalysts do not inhabit the moral vacuum of, say, the serial killer, and thus do not place their therapists in a state of conflict relative to moral judgment. More to the point, the miserable childhoods many (but by no means all) murderers endured help make their crimes *understandable* to the mental health professional (whose orientation is, in any case, the *individual*), but hardly *excusable* when viewed, as inevitably they must be viewed, within a social context. Once one has shown an ungovernable propensity to harm others, he has, irrespective of the tragic circumstances of his early life, propelled himself outside the realm of psychotherapy (though he will still be an object of study to the forensic psychiatrist), and into the lap of the moralist or the court-judge. The purpose of the Gradations of Evil Scale was to help solve two related questions: How far do the actions of a person distance him from amenability to psychiatric treatment? Is there a gray zone between amenability and obvious unreachability, where psychotherapy might in some instances, and despite pessimistic indicators, still prove beneficial? (See Figure 27.)

TABLE 22

Gradations of Evil, with Examples of Persons
Who Have Killed and Have Been
the Subjects of Detailed Biography

CATEGORY	NAME	BIOGRAPHY
1. Those who have killed in self-defense, and who do not show psychopathic personality	Pierson	Kleinman, 1988
2. Jealous lovers, who, though egocentric or immature, were not psychopathic	Harris	Harris, 1986 (autobiography)
3. Willing companions of killers; aberrant personality—probably impulse-ridden, with some antisocial traits	Campbell	Olsen, 1987
4. Killed in self-defense, but had been extremely provocative toward the victim	Patri	Englund, 1983
5. Traumatized, desperate persons who have killed abusing relatives, and also others (viz., to support a drug habit), but who lack significant psychopathic traits and are genuinely remorseful	Barfield	Barfield, 1985 (autobiography)
6. Impetuous, hot-headed murders, yet without marked psychopathic features	Muller "Curly" "Billy the Kid"	Goodman, 1990 Partridge, 1955 Utley, 1989
7. Highly narcissistic, but not distinctly psychopathic persons, with a psychotic core, who kill "loved ones" (jealousy, an underlying motive)	Poddar	Blum, 1986
8. Nonpsychopathic persons with smoldering rage, who kill when rage is ignited	Whitman	Nash, 1987, vol. 3
9. Jealous lovers with psychopathic features	Minns Snider	Finstad, 1991 Bogdanovich, 1984
10. Killers of people "in the way," or of witnesses—egocentric, but not distinctly psychopathic	List	Sharkey, 1990
11. Psychopathic killers of people "in the way"	Chambers Crafts MacDonald Stuart	Taubman, 1988 Herzog, 1989 McGinnis, 1983 Sharkey, 1991
12. Power-hungry psychopaths who killed when they were "cornered"	Jim Jones	Reston, 1981
13. Inadequate, rageful personalities	Simpson	Fosburgh, 1975
14. Ruthlessly self-centered psychopathic schemers	Benson Marshall	Anderson, 1987 McGinnis, 1989
15. Psychopathic, "cold-blooded" spree or multiple murders	Cavaness G. Jones	O'Brien, 1989 Moore & Reed, 1988
16. Psychopaths committing multiple vicious acts	Coe	Olsen, 1972
17. Sexually perverse serial murderers (among the males, rape usually a primary motive, with killing done to hide evidence; systematic torture not a primary factor)	Bundy Nilsen	Michaud & Aynesworth, 1987 Masters, 1985
18. Torture-murderers, with murder the primary motive	Brudos Gallego	Rule, 1983 Biondi & Hecox, 1987

TABLE 22

Continued

CATEGORY	NAME	BIOGRAPHY
19. Psychopaths driven to terrorism, subjugation, intimidation, and rape—short of murder	McElroy	MacLean, 1988
20. Torture-murderers, with torture as the primary motive, but in psychotic personalities	Kallinger	Schrieber, 1984
21. Psychopaths preoccupied with torture in the extreme, but not known to have committed murder	Hooker	McGuire & Norton, 1988
22. Psychopathic torture-murderers, with torture their primary motive	Brady	Williams, 1968
	Cottingham	Leith, 1983
	Eyler	Schwartz, 1992
	Gacy	Cahill, 1986
	Mudgett	Franke, 1975; Nash, 1982, vol. 2

Figure 27: *Amenability to Therapy in Relation to the Gradations Spectrum*

Amenability		Category	Example
probably		1.	Pierson (justifiable homicide)
amenable		2.	Harris (crime passionel)
to		3.	Campbell
therapy		4.	Patri
grey zone		5.	Barfield
		6.	"Curly"
		7.	Poddar
persons		8.	Whitman
		9.	Snider
		10.	List
not	P	11.	Stuart
	S	12.	Jim Jones
	Y	13.	Simpson
	C	14.	Marshall
amenable	H	15.	Cavaness
	O	16.	Coe
		17.	Bundy
to	P	18.	Brudos
	A	19.	McElroy
	T	20.	Kallinger
therapy	H	21.	Hooker
	S	22.	Brady

THE TWENTY-TWO GRADATIONS,
WITH EXAMPLES FROM THE BIOGRAPHIES

Category 1

For the purposes of creating an *anchored* scale spanning the whole spectrum of homicide, the first category concerns persons not facing mortal threat at the moment of their attack, who killed a relative in what therefore seemed at first to be murder, but which was later shown to equate with self-defense.* The typical protagonists in these family dramas are either battered wives (Sandiford & Burgess, 1984; cf. Yglesias, 1981), abused sons (Mewshaw, 1980), or incest victims (Kleiman, 1988).

For example, Cheryl Pierson's father committed incest with her, besides humiliating her physically and verbally to an extreme degree. Because she was an adolescent, much less powerful physically than her father, she could not count on being able to subdue him the next time he became abusive.

Regrettably, she chose to hire a friend to kill her father, such that self-defense (from the threat not of death but of continuing sexual abuse) was admixed with premeditation and the use of a third party. Because of this, she spent a brief time in a minimum-security facility. Currently she is married and, as reported by her biographer Kleiman (1988), living quietly with her husband and working in an office. Her personality does not appear to be abnormal.

Category 2

Category 2 relates to *crime passionel* of the sort committed by Jean Harris (Harris, 1986). When she found out that her lover, Dr. Tarnower, was two-timing her (she discovered another woman's lingerie in a dresser-drawer in his bedroom), she killed him. She appeared to have been driven by depression, jealousy, and the rageful feelings that accompany betrayal. The psychological abnormalities predisposing to a murder of this type relate not to psychopathy, but to impulsivity and a certain lack of maturity. Those with greater self-restraint, faced with a similar betrayal, would walk away from the situation, grieve, entertain all manner of revenge-fantasies for a while, and then get on with their lives.

Category 3

Category 3 concerns those with clearly aberrant personalities, who have goaded a companion into committing murder. The personality shows some

---

*Murder implies the unlawful killing of person(s) with malice, and also includes the inhumane or barbarous killing of other persons.

antisocial traits, but is predominantly impulse-ridden, rather than psychopathic. Cindy Campbell, for example, (Olsen, 1987) conspired with her friend, David West, to kill her parents. Her history points to the possibility of her having been sexually molested by her father. Her behavior was generally chaotic (rages, seductiveness, drug abuse, etc.); she may have had BPD.

Category 4

In Category 4 I placed those who killed in apparent self-defense (viz., from battering husbands), but whose own behavior was so provocative as to make it unclear whether the assault upon their person that seemed to justify lethal counterattack would have taken place apart from their provocativeness. Example: Jennifer Patri (Englund, 1983).

Category 5

The moving autobiography of Velma Barfield (1985) prompted me to create a separate Category 5 for genuinely remorseful persons who have killed abusing relatives (and also a few innocents), yet who lack significant psychopathic traits. A North Carolinian woman raised in poverty by a terrifyingly abusive father (and not much gentler mother), Barfield saw her father mellow toward her only after he had sexual relations with her when she was 12. She did well for a while when she married, only to have her husband die shortly thereafter. She abused drugs, poisoned her dying mother to get insurance money to support her habit, and eventually poisoned three other persons. One of the few women sentenced to death in recent years, she became ardently religious while in prison, where she also wrote her autobiography. A potentially good person, rendered "wicked" through crushingly harsh experience, she seems an inappropriate choice for condign punishment, when compared with many of the persons in categories to be described below.*

Category 6

There are few biographies devoted to persons in Category 6—impetuous, hot-headed murderers without marked psychopathic features—because their acts seem more "understandable," and their lives more mundane, than would conduce to an instructive moral tale of much interest to general readers. Yet there are many murderers who share these characteristics. One

---

*Karla Faye Tucker, one of the few women currently on Death Row (for a Texas pickaxe murder), underwent a similar transition from unrepentant to remorseful, ruthless to empathic, once she was imprisoned and forced to become drug-free (Lowry, 1992).

such is Franz Müller, the first recorded railway murderer (Goodman, 1990). A German immigrant living a penniless life in London, Müller, whom his neighbors remembered as "a quiet, well-behaved, inoffensive young man of a humane and affectionate disposition" (p. 19), killed an elderly gentleman on the train, in order to steal his watch. He pawned the watch for a few pounds to pay steerage to New York, where he hoped to start a new life. Apprehended in New York, he was returned to England, where he was hanged for his crime in November of 1864, three months after the murder.

A more flamboyant example might be the volatile Henry McCarty, better known to us as "Billy the Kid," the New Mexico desperado who flourished briefly in the 1870s till he was gunned down at the age of 21 in 1881 (Utley, 1989). Some of Billy's personality traits, as mentioned by those who knew him: daring, courageous, reckless, ambitious, resourceful, with a hair-trigger temper, abstemious, always in a good humor and ready to do a kind act for someone. The turning point in his life was the death of his mother when he was 14, following which he was "on his own." He took up with "bad company": members of a rival group warring for control of a small New Mexico town.

As for "Curly" (Partridge, 1955), he was the youthful, handsome farm-hand who had come to work for an wealthy skinflint (Mr. Ainsley) in upstate New York. Ainsley had just married a beautiful woman of 20 (Zelda) whom he proceeded to keep secluded on their farm, lest she become enamored of some younger man. She and Curly (he never revealed any other name) predictably fell in love, and made plans to run away. She left a note to that effect for her husband. Unbeknownst to her, Curly killed and robbed Ainsley just before the two ran off. They lived happily for a short while, but then he began to drink and become irascible. Zelda escaped back to the farm; Curly disappeared for a time in South America, but then in 1885 returned to the States where he was caught and hanged.

Category 7

In Category 7 are to be found jealous murderers whose impulse-dysregu-lation is an expression more of psychosis than of psychopathy. The most well-known example to psychiatrists is that of Prosenjit Poddar, a Hindu exchange-student in California, who became despondent when a woman he delusionally thought was his fiancée made it clear she had no interest in him. Increasingly paranoid and depressed, he sought psychiatric help at the urging of a friend. He told the psychiatrist he was going to kill the woman (a Miss Tarassow), and ultimately did so. The family brought suit for not having been forewarned, and won their case: the famous *Tarassow decision* directing psychiatrists henceforth to break confidentiality and to warn the parties at risk, when a patient reveals serious intention to kill or injure someone.

Category 8

This category includes such persons as Charles Whitman, the ex-marine who, after killing his mother, his wife, and a receptionist, shot 16 more people from his perch in the University of Texas tower. Not a Cleckleyan psychopath, Whitman had been an outwardly friendly and caring person, a former Eagle scout, and better-than-average student at the university (Levin & Fox, 1985). But he was also, as Levin and Fox (1985) mention, "oozing with hostility" (p. 16). This stemmed in large part from the abusiveness of his father toward himself and his mother.

What places him further along the spectrum than those who kill the object of their hatred is the indifference to the lives of strangers.

Category 9

This is a relatively crowded compartment, containing jealous lovers with psychopathic features. One such example became the subject of a movie, depicting the life of the actress/model and former Playboy "centerfold," Dorothy Stratten. She had been discovered by Paul Snider, a Vancouver man who dealt in drugs and prostitutes. Stratten, having come from a respectable family, would not ordinarily have crossed paths with him. But their paths did cross, and Snider persuaded her to marry him; he became her "agent." Their paths began to diverge: her charm and grace allowed her to ascend high in the social scale; his crudity left him many rungs below. Inevitably, she tired of him and formed a relationship with a more suitable man. During the ensuing estrangement, Snider, possessive, jealous and enraged, lured her back to his place, tortured and killed Dorothy, and then shot himself (Bogdanovich, 1984).

Several of the killers in this category have distinct hypomanic features, and were also men in "mid-life crisis" who fell in love with beautiful women 20 years younger. One of the more dramatic instances: Richard Minns, millionaire owner of exercise spas, though remaining married, diverted his attentions to a striking young woman, Barbra Piotrowski (Finstad, 1991). He became obsessively in love with her, in a way more reminiscent of addiction than of affection. These were the traits that characterized Minns: extraverted, charismatic, intensely narcissistic, entrepreneurial, litigious, a habitual liar, grandiose, braggart, alternatingly stingy and generous, pathologically jealous, volatile, intense, unethical, manipulative, vindictive, paranoid, arrogant, daring, sensation-seeking, vain, and abusive. A man devoid of scruples, he would stop at nothing to get his way or, failing that, to get back at whoever thwarted him. For a time, Barbra was as madly in love with Minns as he with her. But as his negative (especially, abusive) qualities became more apparent, she lost her infatuation. He became even more assaultive toward her, and finally she left him. Minns then hired hit-men to kill her. They shot her and left her for dead, but she recovered (though still partially paralyzed). Minns escaped the country and has thus far eluded justice.

Category 10

This level deals with persons who, though capable for the most part of "fitting in" both socially and in the workplace, have shown themselves disposed, under special circumstances, to eliminate even family members whom they have come to regard as "in the way." The most notorious recent example is that of John List, the joyless and compulsively religious accountant who, having been fired from his job not long after he'd taken out a big mortgage on an enormous house in New Jersey, saw fit to, as it were, decrease his overhead, by killing his mother, ailing wife, and three children. Escaping to Colorado, he eluded the authorities for 18 years until his face (reconstructed as it might appear after so long a lapse) was shown on a TV program devoted to killers still at large. In the meantime, he had changed his name and remarried. An extremely obsessional, cold, expediency-oriented, but not distinctly psychopathic man, List offered the thin rationalization for his act that (in the case of his perky 16-year-old daughter who was beginning to date boys) he had "spared" them from eternal damnation (Sharkey, 1990).

Category 11

Reserved for distinctly psychopathic killers of people (usually spouses) deemed "in the way," this category contains many dramatic examples that have caught the public's attention. The usual scenario is that of a man considered respectable in his community who does away with his wife when he has become involved with another woman. Glib, egocentric, and skillful at lying, these men often try to make it appear as though the crime were an accident or as though someone else was responsible. They bank on their good reputation and appearance to gull the authorities. Almost never do they admit their guilt, even in the face of overwhelming evidence.* Many naïve people are taken in, unable to believe that "such a nice looking man could have. . . . "

---

*As of this writing, I have come across 17 biographies of wife-killers (uxoricide). Sixteen of the men denied guilt even after conviction, as did seven of eight women who killed their husbands.

Examples include Robert Chambers, whose date for the night caught him stealing from her purse (Taubman, 1988) and Jeff Macdonald, the army doctor who killed his pregnant wife and two daughters (McGinnis, 1983).

Not all these men have charisma. In one of the uglier recent examples, the dour pilot, Richard Crafts, had been carrying on an affair for years; when his wife finally sued for divorce, he killed her, and disposed of her body by passing it through a woodchipper, near a river. It took the skills of a forensic odontologist to establish his guilt.

The cynical con artist, Charles Stuart, counted on racial tensions in Boston to make the public believe a Black man tried to kill him and his pregnant wife, when actually Stuart killed her in their car, parked in a Black neighborhood, and then gave himself a non-fatal wound, to make it look as though he, too, had been a victim. Stuart had shifted his affections to a young woman with whom he hoped to "build a new life." As with many cornered psychopaths, Stuart committed suicide when caught (Sharkey, 1991). His reason for not simply divorcing his wife was purely monetary: he did not wish to be burdened with the extra expense.

Category 12

The psychopaths referred to in Category 12 I have limited to those whose scope encompassed only peacetime activities. The tyrants whose names are writ large in the annals of the twentieth century—Hitler, Stalin, Ceaucescu, Pol Pot, Saddam Hussein (to mention only the more prominent)—are larger-than-life figures whose complex personalities are not easily categorized within the confines of diagnostic manuals. Suffice it to say, they all seem grandiose, ruthless, charismatic, egomaniacal and (with the exception of the meek-appearing Pol Pot) nakedly aggressive. For what it is worth, brutalization by a father was a part of the backgrounds of Hitler, Stalin, and Saddam. Readers who wish to familiarize themselves more fully with the histories of these men would do well to consult such biographies as those of Flood, 1989 [Hitler], Antonov-Ovseyenko, 1980 [Stalin], Pacepa, 1987 [Ceaucescu], al Khalil, 1989 [Saddam], and Ngor, 1987 [Pol Pot].

The "civilians" in Category 12, though highly destructive, operated perforce on a much smaller scale than their political counterparts. The most stunning example within recent memory is that of the Reverend Jim Jones (Reston, 1981), the arrogant, manipulative, paranoid, and grandiose (he thought he was the second coming of Lenin) psychopath, who set up in the middle of the Guyanese jungle his ill-fated community of the gullible. A combination of evangelist, con artist, and communist of the what's-yours-is-mine-and-what's-mine-is-mine school, Jones called his church the "People's Temple"; himself, the "Father." He came to exert total dominion, in all matters of sex, money, and life itself, over his pathetic flock. When investigators, including a U.S. congressman, began to close in on Jones, he had them killed. That spelled his doom; but rather than surrender to the authorities, he persuaded his entire congregation—some 913 persons—to drink cyanide, following which he added his own suicide to theirs.

Category 13

The inadequate-rageful type represented in Category 13 accounts for a large proportion of murderers, but only a small proportion of the biographies. These are the impulsive killers who make the headlines for a day or two because of the senselessness of their crime, or because of the special appealingness of their victims. They are usually persons of no promise; their backgrounds, wretched; their current lives, sordid. Such was the case with Joe Willie Simpson, the 24-year-old drifter, thief, and homosexual prostitute who charmed his way into the good graces of the schoolteacher, Kathy Cleary, in a New York City bar on New Year's day in 1973. Joe was actually bisexual and had a 17-year-old wife in Florida at the time, who was five months pregnant. The lonely teacher invited the stranger (who gave her the name "Charlie Smith") to her flat. They attempted sex, but he could not perform. He grew enraged, stabbed her to death, and then grew aroused enough to complete the sex act. This murder formed the basis of the movie, "Waiting for Mr. Goodbar."

Category 14

Although the psychopathic persons of Category 14 are for the most part preoccupied with the urge to get rid of someone—a spouse, a creditor—"in the way," they differ from those of Category 11 in that they show unusual degrees of premeditation and cunning. Among those I studied, half had hired hit-men or had enlisted the aid of an acquaintance to do the dirty work. Whereas Jeff Macdonald's act was impromptu—the final scene, a rampage—Rob Marshall's murder of his wife, Maria, whom he wanted out of the way so he could luxuriate in a new life with his mistress, was planned long in advance, carefully orchestrated with hit-men to make it look as though robbers had tried to kill both his wife and himself (recall Charles Stuart, who copied this scenario). A social-climbing insurance salesman (he saw to it that Maria's life was heavily insured, with himself as beneficiary), Marshall passed for an upstanding citizen of Tom's River, New Jersey. But he was insincere, amoral, cowardly and philandering (McGinniss, 1989). Like Minns, Marshall was experiencing "mid-life crisis." His early years did not contain many hints of what was to unfold years later. Marshall's father was alcoholic, but his childhood was not particularly traumatic. He is perhaps an example of what happens when mediocrity, overweening ambition, and amorality come together.

Category 14 concerns for the most part those who plotted against one other person and whose murderous intent was directed toward one person. Sometimes a few other "inadvertent" fatalities might occur, if someone happened to be in the wrong place at the wrong time. Steven Benson, for example, though from a wealthy family, was improvident with money and found himself in financial straits. He planted a car-bomb rigged so as to kill his mother, thus accelerating the process of inheritance. His cousin and sister were in the car also: the cousin was killed; the sister badly wounded.

Category 15

Those who make up the ranks of Category 15 (psychopathic and unusually callous multiple or "spree" murderers) usually come from traumatizing or neglectful families. Sometimes, for reasons probably related to constitution, persons from unremarkable families can develop a similar ruthlessness. This seems to have been the case with Dr. John Cavaness, the southern Illinois surgeon who verbally abused and physically brutalized his wife and four sons, and who was sadistic toward his employees, his many mistresses, even toward his patients (O'Brien, 1989). He became increasingly alcoholic and violent; his Jekyll and Hyde personality began to tilt toward Mr. Hyde. When faced with money troubles, he killed his first son, Mark, in 1977, cashing an insurance policy of which he was the beneficiary. He did the same thing in 1984, killing another son, Sean. Sentenced to death when apprehended, he also committed suicide in prison. In my reading of the literature, Cavaness is the only parent to have killed his children for insurance proceeds.

The women whose crimes would place them in this category have usually been the victims of sexual molestation, either by a relative or by a stranger. Genene Jones, the nurse who killed a number of babies in an intensive care unit with succinyl choline (a curare-like muscle relaxant), was an adoptee and had probably been abused as a child. There was a grotesquely grandiose motive to her crimes: she hoped to stage a dramatic rescue of the babies whose lives she put in mortal danger—so as to emerge as a "heroine." When she was not quick enough, the infants died. Despite the overwhelming evidence by which she was convicted, Jones continues to deny her guilt.

Category 16

Category 16 may be seen as an extension of Category 15 rather than as marking out a whole new territory. Here there is an extra measure of viciousness in the direction of torture (as compared with the "quick" deaths by shooting, cyanide, etc., inflicted by those in the preceding section).

Since rape is in itself a form of torture and has caused the psychological death of many women who have survived physically, multiple rapists, even if they have not murdered, belong in this category. One of the most chilling examples is that of Fred Coe, an outwardly charming but breezily contemptuous man from a "good" family in Spokane. His father was on the editorial staff of the Spokane *Chronicle*. The whole family was intensely narcissistic, preoccupied with looks (the mother had been a model), and gilded the lily by undergoing cosmetic surgery (Fred included). A psychopath embodying every characteristic mentioned by Cleckley, Coe forged report cards, plagiarized papers, did shoplifting, well before he embarked upon a career of rape. Eventually caught, he was sentenced, because of the enormity of his crimes and the callousness of his attitude, to life plus 75 years. At that point, his mother, whose behavior toward him had always been seductive, pampering and pathologically jealous (of his ex-wife, for example), conspired with potential hit-men to murder the prosecutor and judge who had put her son away. She, too, was caught and sentenced (albeit lightly) for criminal solicitation to commit first-degree murder. The sister still adamantly refuses to accept the fact of her brother's guilt. In the absence of an abusive background, Coe's psychopathy is probably attributable to a combination of genetic factors plus the extreme seductiveness and grandiose ambitions of his mother.

Category 17

This category and those following it concern mostly sexually perverse serial killers. Those in Category 17 had rape as their primary motive (apart from the one female example); murder was done usually to hide the evidence. Systematic torture was not a primary factor.

In almost all instances, the early background was traumatic, and included various combinations of neglect, death of a parent, humiliation and abuse. The family tree was often an unmappable tangle of liaisons, multiple marriages, fosterages and incest, yielding a picture of instability, parental irresponsibility, and chaos.

The serial murders by Dennis Nilsen of young men who either were, or whom he thought were, homosexual, may be the culmination of interacting genetic and environmental factors (Masters, 1985). Nilsen never knew his father, a Norwegian soldier in World War II, who disappeared after marrying his Scottish mother. Nilsen was very attached to his maternal grandfather, and was shattered by his death (when Nilsen was six), much as Berkowitz was when his adoptive mother died. A great-aunt died in a mental asylum. Nielsen's personality evolved along schizoid lines. Quiet, withdrawn, unobtrusive, he blended in among coworkers, whether in the Army catering corps or in his "white-collar" job in London, without much notice.

He would invite men to his flat, strangle them, and keep the bodies under the floorboards as long as practicable, for necrophiliac purposes.

Arguably the most notorious occupant of Category 17 is Ted Bundy. His story has been recounted in detail by a number of authors (Leyton, 1986; Michaud & Aynesworth, 1987; Ressler & Shachtman, 1992; Wilson & Seaman, 1992); Bundy grew to despise the fact of his illegitimate birth and the working-class environment in which he was raised. Obsessed with status, he stole luxury cars and other expensive items during his adolescence. By this time in his life, he was already introverted, sadistic, hypersexual and overwhelmed with fantasies of rape and necrophilia. He aspired to the *haute bourgeois* life, but could never fit in. This became clear to him when his attempt to marry a girl from that stratum failed. His attacks against women of his ideal-type—who were young, beautiful, long-haired and "classy," began just after this failure, in 1972. The attacks became murderous in 1974. Taking advantage of his high intelligence, good looks and superficial charm, Bundy would lure unsuspecting women into his car by feigning helplessness (a splint over a pretend-broken-arm). He would then immobilize them or knock them unconscious (or dead), and abuse them sexually, making sure they were dead when he was "finished" with them. Some of his comments after his eventual capture (which did not come until after he had killed three dozen or more women) create a veritable textbook of psychopathy: "I don't feel guilty for anything; I feel sorry for people who feel guilt" or "What's one less person on the face of the earth, anyway?" (Leyton, p. 73). Even before his execution in 1989, he admitted to only a few of his murders, and then blamed them on the "effects of reading pornography."

Ressler, who interviewed Bundy shortly before his execution, mentions Bundy's last "ploy," promising to inform the police about *all* of his murders—but saying that the telling would take another eight months or so! Unlike Scheherezade, he was not granted endless reprieves to tell these stories. He *was* allowed, during the decade he awaited execution, conjugal visits—managing in this interval to marry and sire a child. (I leave it to the reader to conclude what it signifies for American justice that Bundy, who destroyed the lives of 38 or more young women, was himself permitted the luxury of parenthood.)

Wilson and Seaman (1992), drawing attention to the need of serial killers to subjugate and exert total dominion over their victims, coined the apt phrase, "Roman Emperor syndrome" (p. 260). Because no one could deny an emperor his wish, no matter how depraved, Caligula and Nero were cruel out of what seemed a total and uncheckable *self-centeredness*. Bundy, as well as most of the murderers in Categories 17–22, exemplify this quality to as great a degree as one is likely to see in peacetime.

Category 18

The murderers in Category 18, some sexually perverse serial killers, others not, are distinguished by the more significant role of torture in their crimes (as compared with persons in the foregoing categories), although murder still took precedence from the standpoint of motive. In some instances I have included perpetrators of unusually heinous crimes, where the macabre nature of the murder, even in the absence of bodily torture, lifted it to this level.

The example of Brudos, who flayed his victims while they were still alive, was mentioned earlier in this chapter.

Another who typifies this category is Gerald Gallego. Born in Sacramento in 1946, he showed serious delinquency at age 12, getting arrested five times for burglary, vandalism, and "lewd acts" with a six year-old girl. After a year in a reformatory, he committed armed robbery upon his release in 1961. His first wife, whom he married when he was 17, divorced him after he struck her with a hammer. Later he was to engage in incestuous relations with their daughter. Alcohol abuse contributed to his violence. The serial killings, which took the lives of nine women, a man, and a child, began after his sixth marriage—to Charlene—when he was 32. They would pick up young women, using Charlene to disarm their suspicions and to lure them into a van. Once captive, the women would be led into a secluded area, to be struck with a hammer and then shot by Gerald. Basically a pedophile, if he got fired from a job, he would become impotent with Charlene, unless she then dressed up like a prepubescent girl. At his trial, Gallego proved himself totally without remorse. In this he seems to have followed a family tradition. His father, whom Gerald never knew, had been executed (when Gerald was about eight) for killing a policeman in Mississippi. Even the technique was the same: driving someone to a secluded spot off the side of the road and executing him. The remarks of Gallego, Sr. concerning his crime give as good a view into the mind of the psychopath as one is likely to get, and are worth quoting at some length:

> When I killed the cop, it made me feel real good inside. The sensation was something that made me feel elated to the point of happiness, for I achieved in putting to death one of my tormentors. . . . For what I've done, I feel no regret or sorrow whatsoever, and if I die I'll know I was perfectly right in killing that cop. I honestly believe I've committed no wrong. (from the Death Row statement of Gerald Albert Gallego, Mississippi State Prison, 1954; cited by Biondi & Hecox, 1988, p. 154)

Category 19

Thus far in my review of the literature Category 19—psychopaths who terrorize, subjugate, rape, but stop just short of murder—has but two occupants. One of these was Ken McElroy, who terrorized the whole town of Skidmore, Missouri. He was the fifteenth of 16 children born to a southern Missouri tenant farmer and his wife. Tony, the father, was alcoholic, hot-tempered, violent, and a womanizer. Ken took after him in all these qualities. On their first day in a school bus Ken and one of his brothers pulled knives on two other boys, to "settle" an argument. When still quite young, Ken stole from a grocer, who then called Tony and told him what his son had done. As Maclean (1988, p. 28) tells it, later that day, "Tony burst into the store with a long hunting knife . . . , slammed the owner up against the wall and held the knife up to his throat. 'If you ever touch my boy again,' Tony snarled, 'I'll cut your heart out.'" The lessons of his father's knife-point morality stayed with Ken all his days. Ken bullied the townspeople, never worked, stole at will from the local farmers, maintained a stable of women whom he terrorized and by whom he had a warren of children, mostly illegitimate.

For the last 30 years of his life, McElroy robbed, raped, assaulted, and maimed various townspeople, along with his mistresses, was charged with over 20 felonies including rape at gunpoint and placing rattlesnakes in mailboxes. He eluded conviction on every occasion but one, thanks to lawyers who knew the loopholes and to the intimidation of witnesses. One day in 1981, when Ken was parked in a truck outside a Skidmore tavern, some of the local citizens put the town out of its misery with their rifles. Unfortunately, it required vigilantism to accomplish what ought to have been carried out by the Law.

* * * * *

The last three categories are set aside for those who betray the utmost contempt for human feeling, as manifested by their committing murderous acts that not only subject the victims to prolonged agony, but that strip them of the last vestiges of human dignity. We speak here, in other words, of crimes we prefer to call "inhuman"—even though we remain aware, as Lorenz (1963) reminds us, that we are the only species that behaves this way towards its own kind. Applying some latinate term like "sadistic personality disorder"* to such persons, as diagnosticians feel compelled to do,

*Or terms of Greek derivation, like "erotophonophilia," by which John Money (1990) designates lust murder and serial killing.

is already to distance ourselves from their acts, to stifle nausea through euphemism. These final bands on the spectrum of inhumanity are thus close together. Torture was the primary motive in all three. The distinctions I have made here will be seen by some as arbitrary and subjective. I have placed, for example, sexual sadists who were psychotic a little further in from the extremity of the spectrum, even though their victims suffered as horribly as did the victims of sadistic murderers who were sane. My thought was: the psychotic killers probably had less awareness of the wickedness of their acts. The penultimate band I reserved for nonpsychotic sadists who stopped short of murder, or whose intent to kill was thwarted. The last band: nonpsychotic killers whose sadistic acts were particularly repugnant.

Category 20

Category 20, where psychosis, murder and torture are combined, is numerically small.* The case of Joseph Kallinger is of special interest, since his story elicits great sympathy for the victims, yet no small measure of sympathy for the killer as well, considering the torture to which he was himself subjected during his early years.

An adoptee, Kallinger's biological mother was from a Canadian Jewish family: the Renners. Judith Renner married for the first time to a James Scurti, by whom she had a daughter. The marriage lasted just over a year. She later remarried, but carried on a relationship with a married man, Tony Patelli, by whom she had Joseph in 1936. After a few weeks of caring for him herself, Judith placed her son in an orphanage. He was adopted at age two by a German-Catholic couple in Philadelphia: Stephen and Anna Kallinger. This joyless pair took the position that Joseph "owed" them a life of hard work; consequently, all play was interdicted. On one occasion Anna hit Joe on the head with a hammer because he'd asked to go to the zoo. When he was seven, he underwent a herniorraphy. Anna used this opportunity to instruct Joseph about the "evils" of sex, telling him that the

---

*Sheila Hodgins (1992), studying the entire 1953 birth cohort of Sweden up through the age of 30, found that males admitted for a psychosis were four times as likely to have committed criminal, including violent, offenses as were normals. It is not clear how great the excess of murder was in the psychotic (largely schizophrenic and manic-depressive) group, compared with the normal group. Glancy and Regehr (1992), reviewing the world's literature on the subject, point out that most studies show an increased rate of homicide in schizophrenics—when the rate is assessed for the time they are *not* in the hospital and therefore free to carry out homicidal urges to which those with high anger level and low impulse control may be predisposed.

surgeon "drove out the demon: he fixed your *bird* so it will never grow big
. . . it ain't ever gonna get hard!" (Schreiber, 1984, p. 25).

Psychotic signs were already apparent when Joseph was 15: he heard
God's voice commanding him, telling him he was a special person. He
married at 17 and had two children; this might have reassured him about
his "bird," but after three years his wife ran off with another man. Just
before she left, she taunted him about his small penis. He quickly remarried, at 22, and had five more children. As Kallinger entered his thirties, his
mental stability deteriorated. He experienced "command" hallucinations,
consisting of God's voice bidding him kill all three billion people on earth.
Later, he heard God making the more modest request that he kill merely
his son, Joey, Jr. Kallinger lured Joey, in July of 1974, to a construction
site where there was a deep waterhole. He made another son, Michael,
accompany him. He then tied Joey to a plank overlying the hole, and
commanded Michael to shove his brother into it. Michael declined, whereupon Kallinger threatened to push Michael in the hole. But he then returned
to his original objective, and took it upon himself to shove Joey to his
death. Half a year later, Kallinger, again accompanied by his son Michael,
broke into a home in Leonia, New Jersey. They bound the occupants,
threatening them at gunpoint. In the midst of this activity, a visitor dropped
by—a nurse by the name of Maria Fasching. Kallinger bound her along
with the others, and then, pointing to one of the male occupants, commanded her to chew his penis off—or he would kill her. She of course
refused, and Kallinger then stabbed her to death—himself under the "command" of his hallucinated double, whom he called "Charlie." Kallinger was
eventually apprehended, brought to trial, and sentenced to life imprisonment. Diagnosed "paranoid schizophrenic" at the time of his trial, he has
apparently been less delusional while in prison.

Category 21

Category 21—torturers who do not also kill—is sparsely represented in the
literature. I would like to think this is a reflection of their rarity in the
general population. I suspect, however, that there are many who subject
other persons to bodily pain, in a habitual if not in a systematic manner.
Child abusers, wife-batterers, "S&M" enthusiasts, etc., are too commonplace in our country to merit biography; they would have to be unusually
wicked just to win attention in the local newspaper.

The man who serves here as the prototype for this category, Cameron
Hooker, brings a certain diabolical originality, not to say perseverance, to
his craft, which elevates him above the crowd. Hooker is the man who in
1977 kidnapped Colleen Stan, as she was hitchhiking out West, and for

seven years made her a slave of his sadistic sexual impulses. Skilled in the carpenter's trade, Hooker built a coffin-like box, in which he imprisoned Colleen—under his and his wife's bed. Janice, his wife, had already gotten a taste of Hooker's perversion, when, before their marriage, he would tie her up to a tree and beat her. A taste *for* Hooker's sadistic perversion might be more accurate, because on one occasion Hooker tied Janice up and dunked her in a creek, almost to the point of drowning—yet she still went ahead and married him. As for Colleen, early in her captivity, she too was "dunked"—in the bathtub of the Hooker home. Bound, gagged and blindfolded, she was led from her coffin-box to the tub, where Hooker held her head under the water till she lost her breath and started sucking in water. He then "rescued" her and repeated the process about two dozen times. She became, as a result, Hooker's brainwashed "love-slave."

Curiously, there is really nothing in Hooker's background to make comprehensible why he evolved into the compulsive sadist he became. He had grown up in a blue-collar family in Arkansas. His parents were not abusive to him or to each other. They were an intact family presenting him and his sister with no unusual stresses other than moving every few years because of work circumstances. There is no indication that his parents humiliated him or mocked his burgeoning manhood, as had Kallinger's adoptive parents. Hooker was a loner during his adolescence, with no close friends, no team-sport activities, no "passions" except for pornographic magazines. These gave shape and substance to his sadistic inclinations. This story ends better than it began: Hooker was eventually arrested and brought to trial, where he was convicted and sentenced to 104 years in prison. The presiding judge said: "I consider this defendant the most dangerous psychopath I have ever dealt with" (McGuire & Norton, 1988, p. 376). Colleen has recovered slowly from the prolonged traumatization, though she is still, understandably, fearful of crowds and of going out alone.

Category 22

Category 22, the final band on the spectrum, concerns psychopathic murderers who subjected their victims to intense pain and terror before killing them. Numerically, they form a large group—not only when compared to the other categories outlined here, but when examined in the light of other source material, such as news articles and brief vignettes in crime-anthologies.*

---

*This would not have been the case if one were writing at the turn of the century or even before World War II. Having pored over microfilms of the *New York Times* for the 1890s and the period before World War I, I can report that, apart from a handful of persons like Herman Mudgett, the most "dastardly" murders of that

If we confine ourselves to this past century, the first figure we encounter worthy of inclusion in this category is a man, Herman Webster Mudgett, who, for the nineteenth century, was as spectacular as he was rare. Serial killers were almost unknown in his day (they began to appear in small numbers only in the 1860s), yet he did not break new ground in a modest way: he may have killed as many as 200 women.* Mudgett was born in New Hampshire ca. 1860, one of four sons of a prosperous and non-abusive Methodist farm family. Throughout his career, his primary goal was self-enrichment via insurance fraud. Harming others was not part of his *modus operandi* during the initial stages. As a medical student at the University of Michigan, Mudgett would steal cadavers from the dissecting room, deface them with acid, bury them in various places, meantime having taken out insurance policies on the corpses under different names. This relatively innocuous phase of his career was interrupted by a campus police-man who intercepted Mudgett dragging the corpse of a young woman from the lab. For this he was expelled from medical school.

Mudgett, alias Holmes, resurfaced in Chicago as a pharmacist, in the meantime acquiring several wives in several different cities, via separate aliases for each. It was in Chicago, though, that Mudgett realized his dream: the creation of an assembly-line for murder. To this end he had constructed, firing and hiring successive sets of laborers, such that none of them knew *what* they were actually building, a three-story office—replete with hidden stairways, false walls, rooms without doors and a chute that led down to the basement.

Mudgett then enlisted the aid of local employment agencies in supplying him with young secretaries. Relying on his good looks and easy charm, he would then seduce them, one by one, making promises of marriage, but

---

era were generally motivated by jealousy, greed (as in the case of armed robbery), or conspiracy to do away with a spouse so that the surviving spouse could be free to marry a hitherto secret lover. In comparison to the murders in Category 22, or to pre-adolescents in the big cities who throw a boy off a roof or who set fire to a schoolmate, or to the juvenile rapists of the "Central Park Jogger", these *fin-de-siècle* crimes strike us as quaint, almost genteel. The increase in *gruesome* murder since World War II is real, and although still an uncommon event, must surely be a symptom of some, more widespread, less dramatic disintegration within the body social. Here we are concerned not so much with the sociological issue, important though it is, as with the increasingly more common disintegration of personality, for there must be some kind of dynamic equilibrium between tendencies on the social plane and tendencies on the plane of the individual in society.

*Mudgett is known for certain to have killed 27 persons, mostly women, but he may have killed many more (Franke, 1975).

making sure they met their end of the "bargain" by signing over to him insurance policies and their savings, as well as by making out a will in his favor. Then, after favoring each with a night of "prenuptial" intercourse, Mudgett would awaken early, overpower the woman with chloroform, and thrust her down an elevator shaft, secured thereafter with a sliding glass sheet. Upon awakening, the women would realize they were trapped. Mudgett would savor their terror for a while, and then pump in poison gas. Once death occurred, Mudgett's next task was to haul the bodies over to the chute leading to the basement. There, on a large dissecting table, Mudgett would, with surgical precision, remove portions of special interest to him—for ghoulish experiments in his "laboratory" on another floor. Conducting these anatomical remnants thither up a secret stairway, Mudgett would hum a particular melody, overheard at times by his janitor. The remainder of the bodies he would saw into more manageable sections for cremation. Parts that did not burn well he would relegate to vats of lime and acid. Occasionally, Mudgett did away with all formality and merely butchered the girls alive and screaming in a soundproof room. Apparently Mudgett revealed some of these details, after having denied all guilt when he was first apprehended, just before he was sent to the gallows in 1896. But just before the trapdoor was sprung—on Mudgett himself, this time— he again protested his innocence.*

Most of the contemporary figures in this category have either come from a background of parental cruelty or else were homosexual men who acted out their inability to accept homosexuality by raping and killing other men. Eyler is an example of the latter phenomenon. In Gacy both these factors were present. A few others were raised in nonviolent homes, but for reasons that are not clear were consumed with rage against women. Concealed for varying lengths of time behind a surface amiability, the rage would erupt periodically in the torture and murder of women. This was the case with Richard Cottingham, a married insurance representative, father of three, who, after the birth of his last child, lost interest in his wife and began to kill women he thought were prostitutes. In his youth he was heavily involved with bondage, sadomasochism and pornography. Cottingham removed the heads and hands of his victims, hoping to elude detection by rendering the women unidentifiable.

Near as we are to the outermost edge of evil in these cases, the torture of children is a greater evil still. The closest one comes to this ultimate derangement of personality is the story of Ian Brady and Myra Hindley—

---

*The consummate con artist, Mudgett had several wives and sets of children, in cities other than Chicago, with whom he spent as much time as his other activities permitted, and who found him charming and devoted.

the "Moors Murderers"—who in the mid 1960s kidnapped and killed five children. Brady, the more responsible party to these acts, was the son of a Scotswoman, Maggie Stewart, by an unknown man. He was given into the care of a Mrs. Sloan, who was regarded as nurturing and nonabusive. His natural mother reclaimed him when he was 16. She was now married to a Mr. Brady, from whom Ian took the new last name. Delinquent from adolescence on, Ian Brady once tied a boy up and set him afire. He was a devotee both of Nazi hate-literature and of pornography. He would bury cats and rabbits partway in the ground, then sever their heads with a lawn-mower. Irritable and aloof, Brady had no friends—until he somehow mes-merized Myra Hindley, when both were in their mid-twenties. It was the fatal synergism created by their meeting (recall Gerald and Charlene Gal-lego) that led to their luring children (more easily accomplished by the woman), bringing them to their cottage (in the British moors country), where the children would be bound, tortured, killed, and eventually buried in the moors. The detail that makes their crime the more appalling is the tape-recording of the children's screams—which Brady and Hindley would then replay as a stimulus to sex. Certainly this is an example of *recreational* torture; it falls short of being a child-version of Mudgett only in that Brady, though probably a "genetic" psychopath like Mudgett, was suffused with hatred throughout his life, and was not as "cool" as his American counter-part. Perhaps Brady inspires in us more revulsion only because a century separates us from Mudgett. Still, his torture of children as an *aphrodisiac* strikes me as the ultimate in evil.

THE ROLE OF PSYCHIATRY IN PSYCHOPATHY

Justice, when she peeks out from under her blindfolds, keeps one eye on the individual, one eye on society. Psychiatry also takes both into consider-ation, but focuses on the individual or on small groups.

In some respects psychiatry is more vulnerable than the law to the blan-dishments of psychopathic persons, since the mental set of psychiatrists, psychologists, etc., inclines us to believe what our patients tell us. Persons of a psychopathic bent have little difficulty manipulating mental health professionals to, for example, gain admission to a psychiatric hospital when prison might have been the more logical residence, or in getting released from hospital when retention would have been the wiser decision. Some-times a tragic result occurs because we, or someone in a position to in-fluence both legal and psychiatric authorities, pay more attention to the admittedly heartbreaking—and valid—stories of childhood abuse certain criminals have suffered, than to the now intractable nature of their violent tendencies, as these have become manifest in adult life.

The most notorious example is that of the murderer, Jack Henry Abbott, whose writings from prison drew the attention, and the hopelessly misplaced sympathy, of the much more famous author, Norman Mailer. Mailer, who had already penned a lengthy romanticization of the life (and execution) of Gary Gilmore, championed the cause of Abbott. Mailer ultimately persuaded those in charge to give Abbott another chance — as though his murderous impulses and general hatred of humanity were now safely "sublimated" through his writing. It was not long after Abbott was freed that while dining in a New York restaurant with two women, he got into a senseless argument with a waiter — whom he proceeded to stab to death.

I think the argument can be made that psychiatry bears some of the responsibility for episodes of this kind. Psychoanalysis made substantial contributions to our understanding of the psychological factors that underlay not only the "psychoneuroses" that were treatable by psychoanalysis, but also the more serious and less reachable conditions, including schizophrenia and psychopathic personality. In the heyday of enthusiasm about psychoanalysis as a treatment method, psychoanalysts — and through their writing, the public — began to hold out more hope than was hitherto customary that even violent felons could be resocialized. The idea was that classical analysis might not be able to accomplish this task, but that an analytically-informed therapy of a different sort would prove effective. Furthermore, the closer examination of childhood history, spurred by the psychoanalyst's emphasis on early development, unearthed the stories of abuse, often outrageous abuse, that many murderers and other felons had once suffered.

A paradoxical outcome of this humanistic trend in psychiatry has been that, in our violence-drunk culture especially, mental health professionals and the public alike will at times bestow more sympathy upon the killer than upon his victim. Such was the case with Richard Herrin, the killer of Bonnie Garland (Gaylin, 1983). Many also make the grievous error of assuming that if such-and-such serial killer, or recidivist rapist, "had gotten therapy" or gets it now, he could have been or could still be converted from his psychopathic ways.* As it turns out, whether one is dealing with

---

*This leads to the odd stories we read in the tabloids, such as the case of a recidivist rapist in New Jersey whom the court had to release because he had "done his time," but whom the judge considered so dangerous as to have him under "house arrest" with round-the-clock police supervision. The judge also stipulated the man "must get therapy" (even though the man cannot go anywhere to get it), as though one can command a person to benefit from a form of treatment (psychotherapy) for which the *spontaneous seeking of help* is an absolute requirement (*Daily News*, Jan. 6, 1993).

early-onset psychopathy, *late-onset*, or *schizoid*, therapy has little to offer; less, once the taste for blood has been actualized (cf. Gallwey, 1985; Coid, 1989, p. 753, concerning this tripartite division).

One of the clearer windows into the mind of a psychopathic murderer, regarding treatability before vs. after taking the life of another person, is provided by the confessional remarks of the Anchorage, Alaska serial killer, Robert Hansen. Apprehended in 1983 for a dozen (out of perhaps 30 or more) rape/murders committed over the past 12 years, Hansen told his interrogating officers how at various times he toyed with the idea of telling someone of his crimes: "But who do I go to for help?" he asked: "I sure in hell can't go in to somebody and tell them I killed somebody. I don't want to spend the rest of my life in jail any more than anybody else." He thought of telling a minister: "I walked around the block [of the church] till I damn near wore out the sidewalk." But he stopped short of going inside the church: "No, no, Bob, you can't do this now. Goddam, now, you can't talk to him." And he added: "You can't go talk to a doctor. Boy, a psychiatrist was about the first 'no-no'. . . . " As for his wife, he ruled her out as a confidante also: " . . . how in hell do you tell your wife that you're going out, having sex fantasies and having sex with another woman, and worse than anything else, you killed one of them?"

When he first got into trouble (for arson, during high school), a judge recommended Hansen get psychiatric help. "Boy, you know, I would have; I knew I had a problem way back then" (Gilmour & Hale, 1991, p. 279). But the facts speak for themselves: *before* the killings he had no motivation for change, let alone for psychiatric help. Here his attitude is characteristic of psychopaths in general. And *afterwards* is too late: too many unpleasant consequences, too little hope for acceptance and forgiveness by the community, etc.

The judge at Hansen's trial, after sentencing him to "461 years + life" for his crimes, apologized to the community for the previous laxness of the authorities (both legal and psychiatric) who had let Hansen go on many occasions over the years, before his final arrest: "Society had better take another look when you've got people like this. And there should be laws which allow you to supervise and keep some kind of control over people like this, the rest of their lives if it's necessary" (Gilmour & Hale, 1991, p. 318).

Judge Moody's comments touch on a related issue at the interface of psychiatry and the law, namely, the use of an "insanity" defense. Current law derives from the celebrated case of the Englishman, Daniel M'Naghten, who, in 1843, killed a certain Edward Drummond in the belief he was the Prime Minister, Sir Robert Peel. M'Naghten was engulfed in the delusional belief that Peel was in conspiracy against him. The Crown acquitted

M'Naghten, judging him to have been unaware that the nature of his act was wrong.

This inability to recognize the wrongfulness of a felonious act is at the heart of the definition of *insanity*, which is actually a legal, not psychiatric, term. As the forensic psychiatrist, Daniel Lunde, mentions in his biography of the schizophrenic mass murderer, Herbert Mullin, most paranoid schizophrenics are legally sane because they can distinguish right from wrong. Lunde thinks of Mullin, and most other mass murderers, as "insane" (Lunde & Morgan, 1980, p. 205). He weakens his own point, however, by providing evidence that, in the case of Mullin anyway, the murderer made efforts to conceal his deeds, which would suggest that he knew they were wrong.

To be correctly regarded as insane, one would have to be so out of touch with social convention as to, for example, shoot someone in a public square (acting in response to a command-hallucination), and then stand triumphantly over the body, as though one had a perfect right to have done so: therefore, no need to hide what one had done. None of the biographees I have alluded to above would meet the criteria for insanity—not even Mullin or Kallinger. As for the man who attempted the life of President Reagan, and who won an insanity plea as though schizophrenic, Clarke (1990) makes a much more convincing argument that Hinckley was a psychopathic drifter (who knew his act was considered wrong), not a schizophrenic, much less an "insane" one.

In the adversarial situation of the law-court, in fact, it is quite possible for a psychopath, eager to save his skin, to affect "craziness," whether in the form of delusions, hallucinations, or, if it would be more advantageous, *insouciance* about the nature of his previous act (i.e., "insanity"). David Berkowitz, for example, told Robert Ressler during a personal interview that he fabricated the story about the *Son of Sam* and about the dog to make the police think he was insane, so he could avoid prosecution via the usual channels. He killed only when the chances were optimal he could escape detection; hence his acts were premeditated and not those of someone insane (Ressler & Shachtman, 1992, pp. 66–68).

Since society has the right to protect itself from those who show an inveterate propensity to commit violent acts, once such persons are apprehended for acts already carried out, it seems merely academic whether the perpetrators were psychotic and insane, clearly sane and nonpsychotic, or psychotic but sane. Persons in *any* of the three categories need to be sequestered somewhere—prevented from visiting further harm upon the innocent. Whether the incarceration were best effected in a conventional prison or in a forensic unit (as in the case of a truly bizarre felon who might need psychotropic medications, etc.) might best be determined *after* a jury decided about guilt. In this, to my way of thinking, more rational schema each group of experts—those connected with the law, and those connected with psychiatry—would be free to do their work in the most efficient manner, and in the proper sequence. Where rape, murder, aggravated assault, kidnapping, and other violent felonies are concerned, psychiatry would usually serve the community better *after*, than *in*, the courtroom.

As to Judge Moody's opinion about the need for lifetime supervision in case of serial murder and other forms of repetitive violent crime (rape without murder, for example), one can only say Amen.

Afterword

WE MAY VIEW ABNORMALITIES of personality in the whole population as ranging from mild (and blending into the general population) to the most severe. Creating a circle to represent the whole population, we can illustrate the issue of amenability vs. non-amenability to psychotherapy by means of a diagram containing circles within circles, demarcating zones of either greater or lesser amenability. Figure 28 shows such a diagram; its corresponding zones are explained in the Key.

In the broad domain of personality disturbances the likelihood of beneficial change depends on a number of variables. Does the prospective patient have the *motivation* for change? Does the patient have an *internal locus of control*? Is the patient well-socialized, in the sense of having *good moral character*, especially of the sort that would militate against harming someone else? Does the patient have a cognitive style characterized by *openness*, by *psychological mindedness*: the ability to make connections between present and past, the ability to work with symbolism, the ability to understand the "inner script" that directs one's life, and the ability to accept responsibility for one's thoughts and actions? Is there a measure of *flexibility*? Is there the *capacity to accept compromise solutions*?

Patients who show all the above-mentioned personality qualities are very likely to benefit from psychotherapy. Their corresponding region in the

Figure 28: *Personality Disturbances in the
General Population Amenable and Non-amenable
to Psychotherapy*

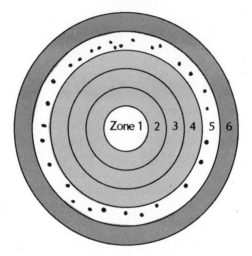

Key to Zones 1 to 6:
1: The large majority of the population with socially harmonious personalities that
require no amelioration through therapy.

ZONES 2, 3, & 4: THE REALM OF TREATABILITY

2: Persons with a few bothersome personality traits, or a mild disorder, readily
amenable to therapy.
3: Persons with some offensive traits and/or a personality disorder, but with good
character features distinctly outweighing the bad, and still amenable to therapy.
4: Persons with prominent and socially offensive traits and/or a severe personality
disorder (including antisocial), not easily modifiable with therapy, but who may
improve eventually with therapy or with other interventions, including religion
or 12-step programs.

ZONES 5 & 6: BEYOND TREATABILITY

5: Persons with personality traits or disorders not amenable to therapy by conventional means, who may occasionally improve with the passage of time (as may
occur with nonviolent antisocial persons in mid-life) or with the intervention of
some unusual set of circumstances, or through the intervention of an unusually
skilled therapist or special group. (The dots represent the occasional successful
outcomes in a zone where therapeutic failure is the norm.)
6: The realm of evil. Malice is a characteristic feature of the persons in this zone,
which contains violent criminal psychopaths who murder, terrorize, and torture,
especially those who experience "thrill" in the pain and subjugation of others.

diagram is Zone 2. Generally, persons in this zone have been reared in relatively nontraumatic homes, and are thus less burdened with the distrust and demoralization that is so often the outgrowth of a highly traumatic early environment. Commonly they will also show more in the way of anxiety, self-blame, and inhibition than of hostility and externalization; they will display a fairly good ability for give-and-take in close relationships, and relatively little aloofness or egocentricity. Such patients may be excellent candidates for an insight-oriented modality, ranging from psychoanalysis (with three to five sessions weekly) to an exploratory/expressive therapy with a less rigorous schedule. But, depending on the cognitive style of the patient and the training and preferences of the therapist, good work can be accomplished with supportive or cognitive-behavioral techniques.

Those with good character and many of the other qualities of persons in Zone 2, but who are more impulsive, and whose locus of control is predominantly external, will customarily require limit-setting interventions, along with whatever supportive or exploratory techniques seem applicable. Many borderline patients (for whom "impulsivity" is a defining trait) show these characteristics. Zone 3 of the diagram is the region relevant to their condition. This zone also contains persons with little impulsivity, but who show a number of irritating traits that place a strain on social relationships. The amelioration of such traits often depends upon cognitive-behavioral techniques, particularly because habits of long duration seldom automatically evaporate just because one has come to grasp the psychodynamic factors that may underlie or contribute to the maladaptive habits. If some of the maladaptive habit patterns are intimately bound up with certain symptoms (as in the case of obsessive-compulsive disorder), medications targeted to these symptoms will often be indicated.

Traumatic experiences often play a role in the early life of many persons in Zones 3 and beyond. Some persons, subjected to these experiences, develop tempestuous personalities: they may be highly irritable; once irritated, they cannot always readily calm down, etc. Here, too, medications (including the newer serotonergic drugs) may be useful.

Special groups (viz., for incest victims, compulsive gamblers, bulimics, etc.) may be helpful in restoring self-esteem and in diminishing intropunitiveness or accompanying depression. For others, nurturing and non-exploitative religious groups may be more appropriate. Beneficial changes in personality often result. The symptom-oriented and religious groups will sometimes be effective where dyadic or conventional group approaches fail.

Zone 5 is the "grey zone" where therapeutic failure is the rule, no matter what interventions are employed. Persons in this region may be antisocial and may exhibit many psychopathic traits, though their behavior inclines more to conning, desertion, irresponsibility, or petty crimes rather than to violent felonies. Possibly, certain "least violent" felons—such as the rapist reported by M. Kafka (1991), who did not use "greater than necessary force" and who responded temporarily to serotonergic medication—may be treatable, not by conventional psychotherapy, but by medications or other means.

This zone also contains many power-hungry narcissists who, unless they fall from grace, do not think of themselves as having any abnormality of personality.

Zone 6, the realm of evil, contains persons whose destructive or violent acts stem from aberrations of personality that are irremediable. It no longer matters that, at some earlier stage of the person's existence, remediation may have been possible. Such speculation becomes casuistical from the standpoint of the here-and-now: a propensity toward destructive acts that has long since become a fixed and deeply entrenched habit. In the face of incurable destructiveness, it would be better if psychiatry gave up the illusion of cure, and recognized that in this situation the welfare of society weighs more in the balance than the liberties of the offender.

References

Aarkrog, T. (1981). The borderline concept in childhood, adolescence and adulthood. *Acta Scand. Psychiat.*, suppl. 293, vol. 64. Copenhagen: Munksgaard.

Abend, S.M., Porder, M.S., & Willick, M.S. (1983). *Borderline patients: Psychoanalytic perspectives*. New York: International Universities Press.

Abraham, K. (1921). Ergänzung zur Lehre vom Analcharakter (Contributions to the theory of the anal character). *Int. Z. für Psychanalyse*, 9:27–47.

Adams, R.M. (Ed.) (1977). *Niccolò Machiavelli*. New York: W.W. Norton.

Adler, G. (1985). *Borderline psychopathology and its treatment*. Northvale, NJ: Aronson.

Adler, G., & Myerson, P.G. (1973). *Confrontation in psychotherapy*. New York: Science House.

Aichhorn, A. (1925). *Die verwahrloste Jugend*. Vienna: Internationaler Psychoanalytische Verlag.

Akhtar, S. (Ed.) (1983). *New psychiatric syndromes: DSM-III and beyond*. New York: Aronson.

Akhtar, S. (1990). Paranoid personality disorder: A synthesis of developmental, dynamic and descriptive features. *Amer. J. Psychother.*, 44:5–25.

Akiskal, H.S. (1981). Subaffective disorders: Dysthymic, cyclothymic and bipolar-II disorders in the borderline realm. *Psychiat. Clin. N. Amer.*, 4:25–46.

Akiskal, H.S., & Akiskal, K. (1992). Cyclothymic, hyperthymic and depressive temperaments as subaffective variants of mood disorders. In A. Tasman & M.B. Riba (Eds.), *Annual review of psychiatry*, vol. 11 (pp. 43–62). Washington, DC: American Psychiatric Press, Inc.

Akiskal, H.S., Bitar, A.H., Puzantian, V.R., Rosenthal, T.L., & Walker, P.W.

(1978). The nosological status of neurotic depression. *Arch. Gen. Psychiat.*, 35: 756–766.

Akiskal, H.S., Hirschfeld, R.M.A., & Yerevanian, B.I. (1983). The relationship of personality to affective disorders. *Arch. Gen. Psychiat.*, 40:801–810.

Akiskal, H.S., Yerevanian, B.I., King, G.C., & Lemmi, H. (1985). The nosologic status of borderline personality: Clinical and polysomnographic study. *Amer. J. Psychiat.*, 142:192–198.

Albert, H. (1983). Special aids to therapy with schizophrenics. In M.H. Stone (Ed.), *Treating schizophrenic patients* (pp. 246–273). New York: McGraw-Hill.

Albert, H. (1983a). Special technics with dangerous or armed patients. In M.H. Stone (Ed.), *Treating schizophrenic patients* (pp. 275–288). New York: McGraw-Hill.

Alkon, D.L. (1989). Memory storage and neural systems. *Scientif. Amer.*, 261(6): 42–51.

Allebeck, P., Allgulander, G., & Fisher, L.D. (1988). Predictors of completed suicide in a cohort of 50,465 young men: Role of personality and deviant behavior. *Brit. Med. J.*, 297, July 16th, 176–178.

Allen, J.G., Colson, D.B., Coyne, L., Dexter, N., Jehl, N., Mayer, C.A., & Spohn, H. (1986). Problems to anticipate in treating difficult patients in long-term psychiatric hospital. *Psychiatry*, 49:350–358.

Allport, G.W., & Odbert, H.S. (1936). Trait names: A psycholexical study. *Psycholog. Monographs, 47* (whole issue).

Alnaes, R., & Torgersen, S. (1990). Basic character inventory personality traits among patients with major depression, anxiety disorders and mixed conditions. *Europ. Arch. Psychiat. & Neurol. Sci.*, 239:303–308.

Andersen, C.P. (1987). *The serpent's tooth*. New York: Harper & Row.

Andreasen, N.C., & Olsen, S. (1982). Negative vs. positive schizophrenia. Definition and validation. *Arch. Gen. Psychiat.*, 39:789–794.

Andreoli, A., Gressot, G., Aapro, N., Tricot, L., & Gognalons, M.Y. (1989). Personality disorders as a predictor of outcome. *J. Personal. Dis.*, 3:307–340.

Andrews, G., Stewart, G., Allen, R., & Henderson, A.S. (1990). The genetics of six neurotic disorders: A twin study. *J. Affective Dis.*, 19:23–29.

Andrulonis, P.A., Glueck, B.C., Stroebel, C.F., Vogel, N.G., Shapiro, A.L., & Aldridge, D.M. (1981). Organic brain dysfunction and the borderline syndrome. *Psych. Clin. N. Amer.*, 4(1):47–66.

Angier, N. (1990, December 13). If anger ruins your day, it can shrink your life. *New York Times*, B-23.

Angst, J., Stassen, H.H., Gross, G., Huber, H., & Stone, M.H. (1990). Suicide in affective and schizoaffective disorders. In A. Marneros & M.T. Tsuang (Eds.), *Affective and schizoaffective disorders* (pp. 168–185). Berlin: Springer Verlag.

Anthony, E.J. (1974). The syndrome of the psychologically invulnerable child. In E.J. Anthony & C. Kupernik (Eds.), *The child in his family: Children at risk. International Yearbook, vol. 1*. New York: Wiley.

Antonov-Ovseyenko, A. (1980). *The time of Stalin: Portrait of tyranny*. New York: Harper & Row.

Appleby, L., & Joseph, P. (1991). Management of personality disorder. *Internat. Rev. of Psychiat.*, 3:59–70.

Arendt, H. (1977). *Eichmann in Jerusalem: The banality of evil*. New York: Viking.

Arkema, P. (1981). The borderline personality and transitional relatedness. *Amer. J. Psychiat.*, 138:172–177.

Aronson, T.A. (1989). A critical review of psychotherapeutic treatments of the borderline personality disorder. *J. Nerv. & Ment. Dis.*, 177:511–528.

Åsberg, M., Nordström, P., & Träksman-Bendz, L. (1986). Cerebrospinal fluid studies in suicide. In J.J. Mann & M. Stanley (Eds.), *Psychobiology of suicidal behavior* (pp. 243–253). New York: N.Y. Acad. Sciences.

Aubin, N. (1716). *Histoire des diables de Loudon, de la possession des Réligieuses Ursulines*. Amsterdam: D'Etienne Roger.

Auden, W.H. (1962). Anger. In I. Fleming (Ed.), *The seven deadly sins* (pp. 78–87). New York: Morrow.

Bachrach, H.M., Weber, J.J., & Solomon, M. (1985). Factors associated with the outcome of psychoanalysis (clinical and methodological considerations): Report of the Columbia Psychoanalytic Center Research Project. IV. *Internat. Rev. Psychoanal.*, 12:379–389.

Bailey, J.M., Pillard, R.C., Neale, M.C., & Agyei, Y. (1993). Heritable factors influence sexual orientation in women. *Arch. Gen. Psychiat.*, 50:217–223.

Baldessarini, R.J. (1985). *Chemotherapy in psychiatry: Principles and practice* (2nd ed.). Cambridge, MA: Harvard University Press.

Balint, M. (1979). The basic fault: Therapeutic aspects of regression. New York: Brunner/Mazel. (Originally published in 1968)

Barasch, A., Frances, A., Hurt, S., Clarkin, J., & Cohen, S. (1985). Stability and distinctness of borderline personality disorder. *Amer. J. Psychiat.*, 142:1484–1486.

Barfield, Velma (1985). *Woman on death row*. Minneapolis: World Wide Publications.

Barley, W.D. (1986). Behavioral and cognitive treatment of criminal and delinquent behavior. In W.H. Reid, D. Dorr, J.I. Walker, & J.W. Bonner III (Eds.), *Unmasking the psychopath: Antisocial personality and related syndromes* (pp. 159–190). New York: W.W. Norton.

Baron, M., Gruen, R., Asnis, L., & Lord, S. (1985). Familial transmission of schizotypal and borderline personality disorders. *Amer. J. Psychiat.*, 142:927–934.

Bataille, G. (1991). *Gilles de Rais* (R. Robinson, Trans.). Los Angeles: Amok Press.

Battegay, R. (1981). *Grenzsituationen*. Berlin: Hans Huber.

Baudry, F.D. (1989). The evolution of the concept of character in Freud's writings. In R.F. Lax (Ed.), *Essential papers on character neurosis and treatment* (pp. 23–45). New York: New York University Press.

Baudry, F.D. (1989a). A silent partner in our practice: The analyst's character and attitude. In R. Lax (Ed.), *Essential papers on character neuroses and treatment* (pp. 397–408). New York: New York University Press.

Baumeister, R.F. (1988). Gender differences in masochistic scripts. *J. Sex Research*, 25:478–499.

Baxter, L.R., Edell, W., Gerner, R., Fairbanks, L., & Gwirtsman, H. (1984). Dexamethasone suppression test and Axis I diagnosis of inpatients with DSM-III borderline personality disorder. *J. Clin. Psychiat.*, 45:150–153.

Baxter, L.R., Schwartz, J.M., & Guze, B.H. (1991). Brain imaging: Toward a neuroanatomy of OCD. In J. Zohar, T. Insel, & S. Rasmussen (Eds.), *The psychobiology of obsessive compulsive disorder* (pp. 101–125). New York: Springer.

Beauchêne, M.de (1781). *De l'influence des affections de l'âme dans des maladies nerveuses des femmes*. Montpellier: Méquignon.

Beck, A.T. (1976). *Cognitive therapy and the emotional disorders.* New York: International Universities Press.

Beck, A.T., & Freeman, A. (1990). *Cognitive therapy of personality disorders.* New York: Guilford.

Beck, A., Rush, A., & Shaw, B. (1979). *Cognitive therapy of depression.* New York: Guilford.

Belfer, M.L., & d'Autremont, C.C. (1971). Catatonia-like symptomatology. *Arch. Gen. Psychiat.*, 24:119–120.

Bellak, L., & Loeb, L. (1969). *The schizophrenic syndrome.* New York: Grune & Stratton.

Benjaminsen, S., Krarup, G., & Lauritsen, R. (1990). Personality, parental rearing behavior and parental loss in attempted suicide. *Acta Psychiatrica Scand.*, 82: 389–397.

Benton, A.L. (1991). The prefrontal region: Its early history. In H.S. Levin, H.M. Eisenberg, & A.L. Benton (Eds.), *Frontal lobe function and dysfunction* (pp. 3–32). New York: Oxford University Press.

Bergeret, J. (1975). *La dépression et les états-limites.* Paris: Payot.

Berrios, G.E. (1993). European views on personality disorders: A conceptual history. *Comprehen. Psychiat.*, 34:14–30.

Bion, W. (1961). *Experiences in groups.* New York: Basic Books.

Biondi, R., & Hecox, W. (1987). *All his father's sins: Inside the Gerald Gallego sex-slave murders.* Rocklin, CA: Prima.

Bjerre, P. (1912). Zur Radikalbehandlung der chronsichen Paranoia. *Jahrbuch für psychoanalytische und psychologische Forschungen.* 3:795–847.

Blackburn, R. (1988). On moral judgments and personality disorders: The myth of psychopathic personality revisited. *Brit. J. Psychiat.*, 153:502–512.

Blanck, G., & Blanck, R. (1974). *Borderline: Teori och Behandling: Jagpsykologins uppkomst, utveckling och tillämping.* Stockholm: Wahlström & Widstrand.

Blashfield, R.K. (1990). An American view of the ICD-10 personality disorders. *Acta Psychiatrica Scand.*, 82:250–256.

Blashfield, R., Sprock, J., Pinkston, K., & Hodgin, J. (1985). Exemplar prototypes of personality disorder diagnoses. *Compr. Psychiat.*, 26:11–21.

Bleuler, E. (1908). *Textbook of psychiatry.* (A.A. Brill, Trans.). New York: Macmillan, 1924.

Bliss, E.L. (1986). *Multiple personality, allied disorders and hypnosis.* New York: Oxford University Press.

Blum, D. (1986). *Bad karma: A true story of obsession and murder.* New York: Atheneum.

Blum, H. (1981). Object inconstancy and paranoid conspiracy. *J. Amer. Psychoan. Assoc.*, 29:789–813.

Blumenthal, R. (1989, December 18). Path from hate. *New York Times*, A-1, B-8.

Bodin, J. (1589). *Daemonomania degli Stregoni.* Venice: Aldus.

Bogdanovich, P. (1984). *The killing of the unicorn: Dorothy Stratten, 1960–1980.* New York: Morrow.

Bowlby, J. (1969). *Attachment and loss. Vol. I. Attachment* (pp. 228–232). New York: Basic Books.

Boyle, T. (1989). *Black swine in the sewers of Hampstead.* New York: Viking.

Brennan, P.A., Mednick, S.A., & Gabrielli, W.F. (1991). Genetic influences and criminal behavior. In M. Tsuang, K.S. Kendler, & M.J. Lyons (Eds.), *Genetic issues in psychosocial epidemiology* (pp. 231–246). New Brunswick, NJ: Rutgers University Press.

Brenner, M. (1991, September). Erotomania. *Vanity Fair,* 189ff.

Breuer, J. (1893/5). Studies on hysteria. In S. Freud, *SE,* vol. 2, New York: W.W. Norton.

Breuer, J., & Freud, S. (1893). Über den psychischen Mechanismus hysterischer Phänomene. *Neurolog. Centralblatt,* 4–10; 43–47.

Briggs, I.V. (1921). *The manner of man that kills.* Boston: Richard G. Badger.

Briquet, P. (1859). *Traité clinique et thérapeutique de l'hystérie.* Paris: J.-B. Baillière et Fils.

Brown, R. (1992). *Before and after.* New York: Farrar, Strauss & Giroux.

Browning, C.R. (1992). *Ordinary men: Reserve police battalion #101 and the final solution in Poland.* New York: HarperCollins.

Brunswick, R.-M. (1929). The analysis of a case of paranoia. *J. Nerv. & Ment. Dis.,* 70:1–22; 155–178.

Bryce-Boyer, L., & Giovacchini, P.L. (1967). *Psychoanalytic treatment of schizophrenic, borderline and characterological disorders.* New York: Aronson.

Burn, G. (1985). *Somebody's husband, somebody's son: The story of the Yorkshire Ripper.* New York: Viking.

Burnham, D.G., Gladstone, A.I., & Gibson, R.W. (1969). *Schizophrenia and the need-fear dilemma.* New York: International Universities Press.

Bursten, B. (1973). Some narcissistic personality types. *Internat. J. Psychoanal.,* 54:287–300.

Bursten, B. (1986). Some narcissistic personality types. In A.P. Morrison (Ed.), *Essential papers on narcissism* (pp. 377–402). New York: New York University Press.

Bursten, B. (1989). The relationship between narcissistic and antisocial personalities. *Psych. Clin. N. Amer.,* 12:571–584.

Buss, A., & Finn, S.E. (1987). Classification of personality traits. *J. Personal. & Social Psychol.,* 52:432–444.

Buss, D.M. (1991). Evolutionary personality psychology. *Ann. Rev. Psychol.,* 42: 459–491.

Byrne, R., & Whiten, A. (Eds.) (1988). *Machiavellian intelligence: Social expertise and the evolution of intellect in monkeys, apes, and humans* (pp. 1–11). New York: Oxford University Press.

Byrne, A., & Yatham, L.N. (1989). Pimozide in pathological jealousy. *Brit. J. Psychiat.,* 155:249–251.

Cadoret, R.J., Cunningham, L., Loftus, R., & Edwards, J. (1975). Studies of adoptees from psychiatrically disturbed biologic parents. *J. Pediatrics,* 87:301–306.

Cadoret, R.J., Troughton, E., Bagford, J., & Woodworth, G. (1990). Genetic and environmental factors in adoptee antisocial personality. *Eur. Arch. Psychiat. Neurol. Sci.,* 239:231–240.

Cahill, T. (1986). *Buried dreams: Inside the mind of a serial killer.* New York: Bantam.

Cameron, N. (1963). *Personality development and psychopathology.* Boston: Houghton Mifflin.

Carroll, B.J., Greden, J.F., Feinberg, M., Lohr, N., James, N.M., Steiner, M., Haskett, R.F., Albala, A.A., DeVigne, J.-P., & Tarika, J. (1981). Neuroendocrine evaluation of depression in borderline patients. *Psych. Clin. N. Amer.,* 4(1): 89–99.

Carsky, M., & Bloomgarden, J.W. (1981). Subtyping in the borderline realm by means of Rorschach analysis. *Psych. Clin. N. Amer.*, 4(1):101–116.

Casey, P. (1988). The epidemiology of personality disorder. In P. Tyrer (Ed.), *Personality disorders: Diagnosis, management and course* (pp. 74–81). London: Wright.

Cattell, R.B. (1945). The description of personality: Principles and findings in a factor analysis. *Amer. J. Psychology*, 58:68–90.

Cattell, R.B. (1957). *Personality and motivation: Structure and measurement.* Yonkers, NY: World.

Cattell, R.B. (1965). *The scientific analysis of personality.* Chicago: Aldine.

Cauwels, J.M. (1992). *Imbroglio: Rising to the challenge of borderline personality disorder.* New York: W.W. Norton.

Chance, M.R.A., & Mead, A.P. (1988). Social behavior and primate evolution. In R. Byrne & A. Whiten (Eds.), *Machiavellian intelligence* (pp. 34–49). New York: Oxford University Press.

Changeux, J.-P. (1985). *Neuronal man: The biology of the mind.* New York: Oxford University Press.

Charcot, J. (1875). *Leçons sur les maladies du système nerveux* (2nd ed.). Paris: Delahaye.

Cheney, D.L., & Seyfarth, R.M. (1988). Social and non-social knowledge in vervet monkeys. In R. Byrne & A. Whiten (Eds.), *Machiavellian intelligence* (pp. 255–270). New York: Oxford University Press.

Chessick, R. (1977). *Intensive psychotherapy of the borderline patient.* New York: Aronson.

Chodoff, P. & Lyons, H. (1958). Hysteria, the hysterical personality and "hysterical" conversion. *Amer. J. Psychiat.*, 114:734–740.

Chomsky, N. (1965). *Aspects of the theory of syntax.* Cambridge, MA: MIT Press.

Clarke, G. (1989). *Capote: A biography.* New York: Ballantine.

Clarke, J.W. (1990). *On being mad or merely angry: John W. Hinckley Jr. and other dangerous people.* Princeton, NJ: Princeton University Press.

Clarkin, J.F., Marziali, E., & Munroe-Blum, H. (Eds.) (1992). *Borderline personality disorder: Clinical and empirical perspectives.* New York: Guilford.

Cleckley, H. (1972). *The mask of sanity* (5th ed.). St. Louis: C.V. Mosby.

Cloninger, C.R. (1978). The link between hysteria and sociopathy: An integrative model of pathogenesis based on clinical, genetic and neurophysiological observations. In H.S. Akiskal & W.L. Webb (Eds.), *Psychiatric diagnosis* (pp. 189–218). New York: Spectrum.

Cloninger, C.R. (1986). A unified biosocial theory of personality and its role in the development of anxiety states. *Psychiatric Developments*, 3:167–226.

Cloninger, C.R., Reich, T., & Guze, S.B. (1975). The multifactorial model of disease transmission II. Sex differences in the familial transmission of sociopathy (antisocial personality). *Brit. J. Psychiat.*, 127:11–22.

Cloninger, C.R. (1993, March 4). *A general biosocial model of personality and psychopathology.* Presidential address presented at the 83rd annual meeting of the American Psychological Association, New York.

Coccaro, E.F. (1989). Central serotonin and impulsive aggression. *Brit. J. Psychiat.*, 155 (Suppl. 8) 52–62.

Cohen, C.P., & Sherwood, V.R. (1991). *Becoming a constant object in psychotherapy with the borderline patient.* Northvale, NJ: Aronson.

Coid, J.W. (1989). Psychopathic disorders. *Current Opinion in Psychiatry*, 2:750–756.

Colby, K.M., Faught, W.S., & Parkinson, R.C. (1979). Cognitive therapy of paranoid conditions. Heuristic suggestions based on a computer simulation model. *Cognitive Ther. & Research*, 3:5–60.

Collins, R., & Glassman, E.J. (1992). The psychological assessment of borderline personality disorder. In D. Silver & M. Rosenbluth (Eds.), *Handbook of borderline disorders* (pp. 229–249). Madison, CT: International Universities Press.

Colodny, L., & Gettlin, S. (1992). *Silent coup: The removal of a president*. New York: St. Martin's.

Colson, D.B., Allen, J.G., Coyne, L., Deering, D., Jehl, N., Kearns, W., & Spohn, H. (1986). Profiles of difficult psychiatric hospital patients. *Hosp. & Commun. Psychiat.*, 37:720–724.

Coons, P.M., Bowman, E.S., Pellow, T.A., & Schneider, P. (1989). Post-traumatic aspects of the treatment of victims of sexual abuse and incest. *Psych. Clin. N. Amer.*, 12(2):325–336.

Cooper, A.M. (1984). Narcissism in normal development. In M.R. Zales (Ed.), *Character pathology: Theory and treatment* (pp. 39–56). New York: Brunner/Mazel.

Cooper, A.M. (1985). The masochistic-narcissistic character. In R.A. Glick & D.I. Meyers (Eds.), *Masochism: Current psychoanalytic and psychotherapeutic perspectives*. Hillsdale, NJ: Analytic Press.

Cooper, A.M. (1989). The narcissistic-masochistic character. In R.F. Lax (Ed.), *Essential papers on character neurosis and treatment* (pp. 288–309). New York: New York University Press.

Cooper, A.M., & Sacks, M. (1991). Sadism and masochism in character disorder and resistance: Panel report. *J. Amer. Psychoanal. Assoc.*, 39:215–226.

Cooper, T. (1819). *Tracts on medical jurisprudence*. Philadelphia: James Webster.

Cordeschi, R. (1991). Brain, mind and computers. In P. Corsi (Ed.), *The enchanted loom* (pp. 315–320). New York: Oxford University Press.

Coryell, W.H., & Zimmerman, M. (1989). Personality disorder in the families of depressed, schizophrenic and never-ill probands. *Amer. J. Psychiat.*, 146:496–502.

Costa, P.T., Jr., & McCrae, R.R. (1985). *The NEO Personality Inventory manual*. Odessa, FL: Psychological Assessment Resources.

Costa, P.T., Jr., & McCrae, R.R. (1986). Personality stability and its implications for clinical psychology. *Clin. Psychol. Rev.*, 6:407–423.

Côté, G., & Hodgins, S. (1990). Co-occurring mental disorders among criminal offenders. *Bull. Amer. Acad. Psychiat. Law*, 18:271–281.

Courtois, C. (1988). *Healing the incest wound: Adult survivors in therapy*. New York: W.W. Norton.

Cowdry, R. (1992). Psychobiology and psychopharmacology of borderline personality disorder. In D. Silver & M. Rosenbluth (Eds.), *Handbook of borderline conditions* (pp. 495–508). Madison, CT: International Universities Press.

Cowdry, R., & Gardner, D.L. (1988). Pharmacotherapy of borderline personality disorder. *Arch. Gen. Psychiat.*, 45:111–119.

Crawford, C. (1988). *Survivor*. New York: Jove Books.

Crook, J.H. (1988). The experiential context of intellect. In R. Byrne & A. Whiten (Eds.), *Machiavellian intelligence* (pp. 347–362). New York: Oxford University Press.

Cullen, W. (1807). *First lines on the practice of physic.* Brookfield, England: E. Merriam.

Curran, J. (1977). Skills training as an approach to the treatment of heterosexual anxiety. *Psychol. Bulletin,* 84:140–157.

Dahl, A.A. (1985). Borderline disorders: The validity of the diagnostic concepts. *Psychiat. Devel.,* 3:109–152.

Dahl, A.A. (1986). Prognosis of borderline disorders. *Psychopathol.,* 19:68–79.

Dahl, A.A. (1987). Borderline disorders: A comparative study of hospitalized patients. (Thesis) Oslo: Gaustad Hospitalet.

Dahl, H. (1978). A new psychoanalytic model of motivation. *Psychoanal. & Contemp. Thought,* 1:373–408.

Davanloo, H. (1986). Intensive short-term psychotherapy with highly resistant patients. I. Handling resistance. *Internat. J. Short-Term Psychother.,* 1:107–133.

Dawkins, R. (1976). *The selfish gene.* New York: Oxford University Press.

DeLillo, D. (1991). *Mao II.* New York: Penguin/Viking.

DelRio, M. (1679). *Disquisitionum magicarum.* Colonia Agrippina: Herman Demen.

Dennett, D.C. (1988). The intentional stance in theory and practice. In R. Byrne & A. Whiten (Eds.), *Machiavellian intelligence* (pp. 181–202). New York: Oxford University Press.

Dennett, D.C. (1991). *Consciousness explained.* Boston: Little, Brown.

de Rivera, J. (1977). A structural theory of emotions. *Psychol. Issues: Monograph #40.* New York: International Universities Press.

Deutsch, H. (1921). On the pathological lie (pseudologia phantastica). (Unpublished manuscript)

Deutsch, H. (1926). Okkulte Vorgänge während der Psychoanalyse. *Imago,* 12: 418–433.

Deutsch, H. (1942). Some forms of emotional disturbance and their relationship to schizophrenia. *Psychoan. Quart.,* 11:301–321.

Deutsch, H. (1955). The imposter: Contribution to ego psychology of a type of psychopath. *Psychoan. Q.,* 24:483–505.

Deutsch, H. (1965). *Neuroses and character types.* New York: International Universities Press.

Diagnostic and statistical manual (3rd ed.) (DSM-III). (1980). Washington, DC: American Psychiatric Association.

Diagnostic and statistical manual (3rd ed., rev.) (DSM-III-R). (1987). Washington, DC: American Psychiatric Association.

Diekstra, R.F.W., & Moritz, B.J.M. (1987). Suicidal behavior among adolescents: An overview. In R.F.W. Diekstra & K. Hawton (Eds.), *Suicide in adolescents* (pp. 7–24). Dordrecht, The Netherlands: Martinus Nijhoff.

Dietz, P.E. (1985). Hypothetical criteria for the prediction of individual criminality. In C.D. Webster, M.H. Ben-Aron, & S.J. Hucker (Eds.), *Dangerousness: Probability and prediction, psychiatry and public policy* (pp. 87–102). Cambridge, England: Cambridge University Press.

Dilalla, L.F., & Gottesman, I.I. (1989). Heterogeneity of causes for delinquency and criminality: Lifespan perspectives. *Development and Psychopathology,* 1: 339–349.

DiLiberto, G. (1987). *Debutante: The story of Brenda Frazier.* New York: Knopf.

Dodge, K.A., Bates, J.E., & Pettit, G.S. (1990). Mechanisms in the cycle of violence. *Science,* 250:1678–1683.

Douglas, G. (1992). *Class: The wreckage of an American family*. New York: Henry Holt.

Duggan, C.F., Lee, A.S., & Murray, R.M. (1990). Does personality predict long-term outcome in depression? *Brit. J. Psychiat.*, 157:19–24.

Dulit, R.A., Marin, D.B., & Frances, A.J. (1993). Cluster B personality disorders. In D. Dunner (Ed.), *Current psychiatric therapy* (pp. 405–411). Philadelphia: W.B. Saunders.

Duruy, V. (1917). *A short history of France* (2 vols). London: E. P. Dutton.

Easser, R.-R., & Lesser, S. (1965). Hysterical personality: A reevaluation. *Psychoan. Q.*, 34:390–405.

Easser, R.-R., & Lesser, S. (1989). Transference resistance in hysterical character neurosis: Technical considerations. In R.F. Lax (Ed.), *Essential papers on character neurosis and treatment* (pp. 250–260). New York: New York University Press.

Edelman, G.M. (1987). *Neural darwinism*. New York: Basic Books.

Edelman, G.M. (1989). *The remembered present*. New York: Basic Books.

Edelman, G.M. (1992). *Bright air, brilliant fire: On the matter of the mind*. New York: Basic Books.

Eibl-Eibesfeldt, I. (1989). *Human ethology*. New York: Aldine De Gruyter.

Eidelberg, L. (1957). A schizoid patient. *J. Amer. Psychoanal. Assoc.*, 26:298–300.

Ellenberger, H. (1970). *The discovery of the unconscious*. New York: Basic Books.

Emmelkamp, P.M.G., & Scholing, A. (1990). Behavior treatment for simple and social phobics. In R. Noyes, Jr., M. Roth, & G.D. Burrows (Eds.), *Handbook of anxiety* (vol. IV) (pp. 327–361). Amsterdam: Elsevier.

Endicott, J., Spitzer, R.L., Fleiss, J.L., & Cohen, J. (1976). The Global Assessment Scale. *Arch. Gen. Psychiat.*, 33:766–771.

Englade, K. (1988). *Cellar of horrors*. New York: St. Martin's Press.

Englund, S. (1983). *Man slaughter*. New York: Doubleday.

Erikson, E.H. (1956). The problem of ego identity. *J. Amer. Psychoan. Assoc.*, 4: 66–81.

Erlich, S. (1989). *Lisa, Hedda and Joel*. New York: St. Martin's Press.

Esquirol, E. (1838). *Des maladies mentales*. Paris: J.-B. Baillière.

Essen-Möller, E. (1980). Intrafamilial correlations in Sjöbring's dimensions of personality. *Acta Psychiat. Scand.*, 62:89–98.

Eysenck, H.J. (1947). *The dimensions of personality*. London: Kegan Paul, Trench & Trubner.

Eysenck, H.J. (1967). *Biological basis of personality*. Springfield, IL: Charles C Thomas.

Fairbairn, W.R.D. (1952). *An objects relations theory of personality*. New York: Basic Books.

Falconer, D.S. (1967). The inheritance of liability to disease with variable age of onset, with particular reference to diabetes mellitus. *Ann. Hum. Genet.*, 31:1–20.

Farber, S.L. (1981). *Identical twins reared apart*. New York: Basic Books.

Farrell, W. (1990). The last taboo? The complexities of incest and female sexuality. In M. Perry, J. Money, & H. Musaph (Eds.), *Handbook of sexology Vol. 7: Childhood and adolescent sexology* (pp. 335–359). New York: Elsevier.

Favazza, A.R. (1992). Repetitive self-mutilation. *Psychiat. Annals*, 22(2):60–63.

Fenichel, O. (1945). *The psychoanalytic theory of neurosis*. New York: W.W. Norton.

Fenichel, O. (1954). Psychoanalysis of character. In *The collected papers of Otto Fenichel* (2nd series) (pp. 198–214). New York: W.W. Norton.

Fenton, W.S., & McGlashan, T.H. (1989). Risk of schizophrenia in character disordered patients. *Amer. J. Psychiat.*, 146:1280–1284.

Fenton, W.S., & McGlashan, T.H. (1990). Long-term residential care: Treatment of choice for refractory character disorder? *Psychiat. Annals*, 20(1):44–49.

Ferenczi, S. (1919). Sonntagsneurosen. *Internat. Z. für Psychoanalyse*, 5:46–48.

Ferrill, A. (1991). *Caligula: Emperor of Rome*. London: Thames & Hudson.

Feuchtwanger, E. (1923). *Die Funktionen des Stirnhirns*. Berlin: Springer Verlag.

Fiester, S.J., & Gay, M. (1991). Sadistic personality disorder: A review of data and recommendations for DSM-IV. *J. Personal. Dis.*, 5:376–385.

Finkelhor, D. (1984). *Child sexual abuse: New theory and research*. New York: Free Press.

Finlay-Jones, R. (1991). Psychopathic disorder. *Curr. Opinion in Psychiat.*, 4:850–855.

Finstad, S. (1991). *Sleeping with the Devil*. New York: Morrow.

Fisher-Dilalla, L., & Gottesman, I.I. (1989). Heterogeneity of causes for delinquency and criminality: Lifespan perspectives. *Development and Psychopathology*, 1:339–349.

Fiske, D.W. (1949). Consistency of the factorial structures of personality ratings from different sources. *J. Abnl. & Soc. Psychol.*, 44:329–344.

Flood, C.B. (1989). *Hitler: The path to power*. Boston: Houghton Mifflin.

Foon, A.F. (1987). Locus of control as a predictor of outcome in psychotherapy. *Brit. J. Med. Psychol.*, 60:99–107.

Forward, S., & Buck, C. (1978). *Betrayal of innocence: Incest and its devastation*. Harmondsworth, Middlesex, England: Penguin.

Fosburgh, L. (1975). *Closing time: The true story of the "Goodbar" murder*. New York: Dell.

Frances, A. (1985). Validating schizotypal personality disorder: Problems with the schizophrenia connection. *Schiz. Bulletin*, 11:595–597.

Frances, A.J., & Widiger, T. (1986). The classification of personality disorders: An overview of problems and solutions. *Annual Review*, V (pp. 240–257). Washington, DC: American Psychiatric Press, Inc.

Frank, N. (1991). *In the shadow of the Reich (Vater: Eine Abrechnung)* (A.S. Wensinger & C. Clew-Hoey, Trans.). New York: Knopf.

Franke, D. (1975). *The torture doctor: The only true account of the greatest criminal the police have ever handled*. New York: Hawthorne Books.

Franklin, E., & Wright, W. (1991). *The sins of the father*. New York: Crown.

Freeman, P.S., & Gunderson, J.G. (1989). Treatment of personality disorders. *Psychiat. Annals*, 19:147–153.

Freud, A. (1936). *Das Ich und die Abwehrmechanismen (The ego and mechanisms of defense)*. Vienna: Internationaler Psychoanalytische Verlag.

Freud, A. (1963). The concept of developmental lines. *Psa. Study of the Child*, 18:246–265.

Freud, S. (1895). Project for a scientific psychology. In J. Strachey (Ed. & Trans.), *The standard edition of the complete psychological works of Sigmund Freud* (hereafter *SE*), 1:295–397.

Freud, S. (1900). The interpretation of dreams. *SE*, 4 & 5. New York: W.W. Norton.

Freud, S. (1904). On psychotherapy. *SE*, 7:257–268. New York: W.W. Norton.

Freud, S. (1905). Three essays on the theory of sexuality. *SE*, 7:125–243. New York: W.W. Norton.

Freud, S. (1908). Character and anal erotism. *SE*, 9:169–175. New York: W.W. Norton.

Freud, S. (1911). Psychoanalytic notes on an autobiographical account of a case of paranoia. *SE*, 12:3–82. New York: W.W. Norton.

Freud, S. (1919). Turnings in the ways of psychoanalytic therapy. In J. Rivière (Ed.), *Collected papers*, vol. 2 (pp. 392–402). New York: Basic Books, 1959.

Freud, S. (1920). Beyond the pleasure principle. *SE*, 18:7–64. New York: W.W. Norton.

Freud, S. (1923). The ego and the id. *SE*, 21:3–66. New York: W.W. Norton.

Freud, S. (1924). The economic problem of masochism. *SE*, 19:159–170. New York: W.W. Norton.

Freud, S. (1933). Introductory lectures. *SE*, 22. New York: W.W. Norton.

Friel, B. (1991). *Dancing at Lughnasa*. New York: Faber & Faber.

Frosch, J. (1964). The psychotic character: Clinical psychiatric considerations. *Psychiatric Quart.*, 38:1–16.

Frosch, J. (1977). The relation between acting out and disorders of impulse control. *Psychiatry*, 40:295–314.

Frosch, J. (1983). *The psychotic process*. New York: International Universities Press.

Gabbard, G.O. (1989). Patients who hate. *Psychiatry*, 52:96–106.

Gabbard, G.O., & Coyne, L. (1987). Predictors of response of antisocial patients to hospital treatment. *Hosp. & Commun. Psychiat.*, 38:1181–1185.

Gallwey, P.L.G. (1985). The psychodynamics of borderline personality. In D.P. Farrington & J. Gunn (Eds.), *Aggression and dangerousness* (pp. 127–152). New York: Wiley.

Gaylin, W. (1983). *The killing of Bonnie Garland: A question of justice*. New York: Penguin.

Gedo, J.E. (1979). Theories of object-relations: A meta-psychological assessment. *J. Amer. Psychoan. Assoc.*, 27:361–373.

Gelles, R.J. (1978). Violence toward children in the United States. *Amer. J. Orthopsychiat.*, 48:580–592.

Ghiglieri, M.P. (1985). The social ecology of chimpanzees. *Scientif. Amer.*, 252(6): 102–113.

Gibson, E., Gibson, R., & Turner, R. (1991). *Blind justice: A murder, a scandal, and a brother's search to avenge his sister's death*. New York: St. Martin's.

Gilmore, M. (1991). Family album. *Granta*, vol. 37 (autumn). New York: Penguin.

Gilmour, W., & Hale, L.E. (1991). *Butcher, baker: A true account of a serial murderer*. New York: Penguin/Onyx.

Giovacchini, P.L. (1982). Structural progression and vicissitudes in the treatment of severely disturbed patients. In P. Giovacchini & L. Bryce-Boyer (Eds.), *Technical factors in the treatment of the severely disturbed patient* (pp. 3–64). New York: Aronson.

Glancy, G.D., & Regehr, C. (1992). The forensic psychiatric aspects of schizophrenia. *Psych. Clin. N. Amer.*, 15:575–589.

Gleick, J. (1987). *Chaos: Making a new science*. New York: Viking.

Glyn Jones, R. (1989). *Murder*. New York: Carroll & Graf.

Goldberg, A. (1989). Self-psychology and the narcissistic personality disorders. *Psych. Clin. N. Amer.*, 12(3):731–739.

Goldberg, L.R. (1982). From ace to zombie: Some explorations in the language of personality. In C. Spielberger & J. Butcher (Eds.), *Advances in personality assessment* (pp. 203–234). Hillsdale, NJ: Erlbaum.

Goldberg, S., Shulz, S., & Shulz, P. (1986). Borderline and schizotypal personality disorders treated with low-dose thiothixene versus placebo. *Arch. Gen. Psychiat.*, 43:680–690.

Goldsmith, H.H., Buss, A.H., Plomin, R., Rothbart, M.K., Thomas, A., Chess, S., Hinde, R.A., & McCall, R.R. (1987). Roundtable: What is temperament? Four approaches. *Child Develop.*, 58:505–529.

Goleman, D. (1987, February 27). Brain defect tied to utter amorality of the psychopath. *New York Times*, C-1.

Goodman, J. (1990). *The railway murders*. New York: Carol Publishing Group.

Goodwin, J. (1982). *Sexual abuse: Incest victims and their families*. Littleton, MA: PSG Publishing.

Gough, H.G., & Heilbrun, A.B., Jr. (1983). *Adjective checklist manual*. Palo Alto, CA: Consulting Psychologists Press.

Göransson, B., Järvholm, J., & Kwarnmark, E. (in press). Male offenders and their female victims: Treatment inside the penal system.

Gray, J.A. (1982). *The neuropsychology of anxiety: An inquiry into the function of the septo-hippocampal system*. Oxford: Oxford University Press.

Green, A. (1978). Psychiatric treatment of abused children. *J. Amer. Acad. Child Psychiat.*, 17:356–371.

Greene, R.L. (1980). *The MMPI: An interpretative manual*. New York: Grune & Stratton.

Greenland, C. (1985). Dangerousness, mental disorder and politics. In C.D. Webster, M.H. Ben-Aron, & S.J. Hucker (Eds.), *Dangerousness: Probability and prediction, psychiatry and public policy* (pp. 25–40). Cambridge, England: Cambridge University Press.

Greenson, R.R. (1967). *The technique and practice of psychoanalysis* (vol. I). New York: International Universities Press.

Greenson, R.R., & Wexler, N. (1969). The non-transference relationship in the psychoanalytic situation. *Internat. J. Psychoan.*, 50:27–39.

Gregory, R.L. (Ed.) (1987). *The Oxford companion to the mind*. Oxford: Oxford University Press.

Grinberg, L., & Rodriguez-Perez, J.F. (1982). The borderline patient and acting out. In P. Giovacchini & L. Bryce-Boyer (Eds.), *Technical factors in the treatment of the severely disturbed patient* (pp. 467–485). New York: Aronson.

Grinker, R.R., Sr., Werble, B., & Drye, R.C. (1968). *The borderline syndrome: A behavioral study of ego-functions*. New York: Basic Books.

Grinker, R.R., Sr., & Werble, B. (1977). *The borderline patient*. New York: Aronson.

Grotstein, J.S., Solomon, M.F., & Lang, J.A. (1987). *The borderline patient: Emerging concepts in diagnosis, psychodynamics and treatment* (2 vols.). Hillsdale, NJ: The Analytic Press.

Grunebaum, H., & Klerman, G. (1967). Wrist slashing. *Amer. J. Psychiat.*, 124:113–120.

Guidano, V.F., & Liotti, G. (1983). *Cognitive processes and emotional disorders*. New York: Guilford.

Gunderson, J.G. (1980, May 3). *Psychodynamic validation of borderline diagnosis*. Presented at the 133rd annual meeting of the American Psychiatric Association, San Francisco.

Gunderson, J.G. (1984). *Borderline personality disorder*. Washington, DC: American Psychiatric Press, Inc.

Gunderson, J.G. (1987). Interfaces between psychoanalytic and empirical studies of borderline personality. In J. Grotstein, M. Solomon, & J. Lang (Eds.), *The borderline patient* (pp. 37–59). Hillsdale, NJ: The Analytic Press.

Gunderson, J.G., Kolb, J., & Austin, V. (1981). The diagnostic interview for borderline patients. *Amer. J. Psychiat.*, 138:896–903.

Gunderson, J.G., Siever, L.J., & Spaulding, E. (1983). The search for a schizotype. Crossing the border again. *Arch. Gen. Psychiat.*, 40:15–22.

Gunderson, J.G., & Singer, M.T. (1975). Defining borderline patients. *Amer. J. Psychiat.*, 132:1–10.

Gunn, J. (1991). Human violence: A biological perspective. *Criminal Behav. & Ment. Health*, 1:34–54.

Gurrera, R.J. (1990). Some biological and behavioral features associated with clinical personality types. *J. Nerv. & Ment. Dis.*, 178:556–566.

Hampson, S.E. (1988). *The construction of personality: An introduction* (2nd ed.). London: Routledge.

Harcourt, A.H. (1988). Alliances in contests and social intelligence. In R. Byrne & A. Whiten (Eds.), *Machiavellian intelligence* (pp. 132–152). New York: Oxford University Press.

Hare, R.D., Harpur, T.J., Hakstian, A.R., Forth, A.E., Hart, S.D., & Newman, J.P. (1990). The revised Psychopathy Checklist: Reliability and factor structure. *Psychol. Assessment*, 2:338–341.

Hare, R.D., & McPherson, L.M. (1984). Violent and aggressive behavior by criminal psychopaths. *Internat. J. Law & Psychiat.*, 7:35–50.

Hare, R.D., McPherson, L.M., & Forth, A.E. (1988). Male psychopaths and their criminal careers. *J. Consult. & Clin. Psychol.*, 56:710–714.

Harris, Jean (1986). *Stranger in two worlds*. New York: Zebra Press.

Hart, N. (1832). *Documents relative to the House of Refuge, instituted by the Society for the Reformation of Juvenile Delinquents in the City of New York*. New York: Mahlon Day.

Hart, S.D., Kropp, P.R., & Hare, R.D. (1988). Performance of male psychopaths following conditional release from prison. *J. Consult. & Clin. Psychol.*, 56:227–232.

Hartocollis, P. (1977). *Borderline personality disorders: The concept, the syndrome, the patient*. New York: International Universities Press.

Haslam, J. (1809). *Observations on madness and melancholy*. London: J. Callow.

Hathaway, S.R., & McKinley, J.C. (1940). A multiphasic personality schedule (Minnesota): 1. Construction of the schedule. *J. Psychol.*, 10:249–254.

Hearst, L.E. (1988). The restoration of the impaired self in group psychoanalytic treatment. In N. Slavinska-Holy (Ed.), *Borderline and narcissistic patients in therapy* (pp. 123–142). Madison, CT: International Universities Press.

Heller, S. (1987). Personal communication.

Henderson, D.K., & Gillespie, R.D. (1969). *Textbook of psychiatry* (10th ed.). London: Oxford University Press.

Herman, J.L. (1981). *Father-daughter incest*. Cambridge, MA: Harvard University Press.

Herzog, A. (1989). *The Woodchipper Murder*. New York: Henry Holt.

Higgitt, A., & Fonagy, P. (1992). Psychotherapy in borderline and narcissistic personality disorder. *Brit. J. Psychiat.*, 161:23–43.

Hodgins, S. (1992, September 9). Aggression and violence among the mentally ill. First European Symposium on Aggression in Clinical Psychiatric Practice. Stockholm.

Hoffman, R.E. (1987). Computer simulations of neural information processing and the schizophrenia/mania dichotomy. *Arch. Gen. Psychiat.*, 44:178–187.

Hollander, E. (1992). Personal communication.

Hollender, M.H., & Hirsch, S.J. (1964). Hysterical psychosis. *Amer. J. Psychiat.*, 120:1066–1074.

Hollingshead, A.B., & Redlich, F.C. (1958). *Social class and mental illness.* New York: Wiley.

Holzman, P.S., Proctor, L.R., & Levy, D.L. (1974). Eye-tracking dysfunctions in schizophrenic patients and their relatives. *Arch. Gen. Psychiat.*, 31:143–151.

Holzman, P.S., Solomon, C.M., & Levin, S. (1984). Pursuit eye movement dysfunctions in schizophrenia. *Arch. Gen. Psychiat.*, 41:136–140.

Horney, K. (1939). *New ways in psychoanalysis.* New York: W.W. Norton.

Horowitz, M. (1989). Narcissistic pathology. *Psych. Clin. N. Amer.*, 12:531–539.

Horowitz, N., Marmar, C., Krupnick, J., Wilner, J., Kaltreider, N., & Wallerstein, R. (1984). *Personality styles and brief psychotherapy.* New York: Basic Books.

Horwitz, L., Gabbard, G., Allen, J., Frieswick, S., Colson, D., Newsom, G., & Coyne, L. (1993). *Borderline personality disorder: Tailoring the therapy to the patient.* Washington, DC: American Psychiatric Press, Inc.

Huber, G. (1966). Reine Defektsyndrome und Basisstadien endogener Psychosen. *Fortschritte der Neur. Psychiatrie und ihrer Grenzgebiete*, 34:409–425.

Huesmann, L.R., Eron, L.D., Lefkowitz, M.M., & Walder, L.O. (1984). Stability of aggression over time and generations. *Developmental Psychology*, 20:1120–1134.

Hughes, R. (1987). *The fatal shore.* New York: Knopf.

Humphrey, N.K. (1988). The social function of intellect. In R. Byrne & A. Whiten (Eds.), *Machiavellian intelligence* (pp. 13–26). New York: Oxford University Press.

Hurt, S.W., Clarkin, J.F., Widiger, T.A., Fyer, M.R., Sullivan, T., Stone, M.H., & Frances, A. (1990). Evaluation of DSM-III decision rules for case detection using joint conditional probability structures. *J. Pers. Dis.*, 4:122–130.

Huxley, A. (1953). *The devils of Loudun.* New York: Harper.

Hymowitz, P., Frances, A., Jacobsberg, L.B., Sickles, M., & Hoyt, R. (1986). Neuroleptic treatment of schizotypal personality disorders. *Compr. Psychiat.*, 27:267–271.

International classification of diseases (9th ed., ICD-9) (1977). Geneva: World Health Organization.

Isenberg, S. (1991). *Women who love men who kill.* New York: Simon & Schuster.

Itard, J.-M.-G. (1932). *The wild boy of Aveyron* (G. & M. Humphrey, Trans.). New York: The Century Co.

Jacobson, E. (1971). *Depression.* New York: International Universities Press.

Jacobson, E. (1971a). On the psychoanalytic theory of cyclothymic depression. In E. Jacobson, *Depression* (pp. 228–241). New York: International Universities Press.

Janet, P. (1911). *L'état mental des hystériques* (2nd ed.). Paris: Alcan.

Jenike, M.A., Minichiello, W.E., Schwartz, C.E., & Carey, R.J., Jr. (1986). Concomitant obsessive-compulsive disorder and schizotypal disorder. *Amer. J. Psychiat.*, 143:530–532.

John, O.P. (1990). The "Big Five" factor taxonomy: Dimensions of personality in the natural language and in questionnaires. In L.A. Pervin (Ed.), *Handbook of personality theory and research* (pp. 66–100). New York: Guilford.

Johnson, A.N. (1949). Sanctions for super-ego lacunae in adolescents. In K. Eissler (Ed.), *Searchlights on delinquency* (pp. 225–244). New York: International Universities Press.

Jolly, A. (1988). The evolution of purpose. In R. Byrne & A. Whiten (Eds.), *Machiavellian intelligence* (pp. 363–378). New York: Oxford University Press.

Jorden, E. (1603). *A brief discourse of a disease called suffocation of the mother.* London: John Windet.

Juel-Nielsen, N. (1965). *Individual and environment: Monozygotic twins reared apart.* New York: International Universities Press.

Jung, K. (1921). *Psychologische Typen.* Zürich: Rascher.

Justice, B., & Justice, R. (1979). *The broken taboo: Sex in the family.* New York: Human Sciences Press.

Kafka, M. (1991). Successful treatment of paraphiliac coercive disorder (a rapist) with fluoxetine hydrochloride. *Brit. J. Psychiat.*, 158:844–847.

Kahn, E. (1931). *Psychopathic personalities.* New Haven: Yale University Press.

Kantrowitz, J.L., Katz, A.L., & Paolitto, F. (1990). Follow-up of psychoanalysis five to ten years after termination. II: Development of the self-analytic function. *J. Amer. Psychoanal. Assoc.*, 38:637–654.

Kellner, C.H., Jolley, R.R., Holgate, R.C., Austin, L., Lydiard, R.B., Laraia, M., & Ballenger, J. (1991). Brain MRI in obsessive compulsive disorder. *Psychiatry Research*, 36:45–49.

Kendler, K.S. (1980). The nosologic validity of paranois (simple delusional disorder). *Arch. Gen. Psychiat.*, 37:699–706.

Kendler, K.S. (1985). Diagnostic approaches to schizotypal personality disorder: A historical perspective. *Schiz. Bull.*, 11:538–553.

Kendler, K.S. (1990). Familial risk factors and the familial aggregation of psychiatric disorders. *Psychol. Med.*, 20:311–319.

Kendler, K.S., & Gruenberg, A.M. (1982). Genetic relationship between paranoid personality disorder and the "schizophrenic spectrum" disorders. *Amer. J. Psychiat.*, 139:1185–1186.

Kendler, K.S., Gruenberg, A.M., & Tsuang, M.T. (1985). Psychiatric illness in first-degree relatives of schizophrenic and surgical control patients. *Arch. Gen. Psychiat.*, 42:770–779.

Kendler, K.S., & Hays, P. (1981). Paranoid psychosis (delusional disorder) and schizophrenia: A family history study. *Arch. Gen. Psychiat.*, 38:547–551.

Kendler, K.S., Masterson, C.C., & Davis, K.L. (1985). Psychiatric illness in first degree relatives of patients with paranoid psychosis, schizophrenia and medical illness. *Brit. J. Psychiat.*, 147:524–531.

Kendler, K.S., Ochs, A.L., Gorman, A.M., Hewitt, J.K., Ross, D.E., & Mirsky, A.F. (1991). The structure of schizotypy: A multitrait twin study. *Psychiatry Research*, 36:19–36.

Kernberg, O.F. (1967). Borderline personality organization. *J. Amer. Psychoan. Assoc.*, 15:641–685.

Kernberg, O.F. (1970). Factors in the psychoanalytic therapy of narcissistic patients. *J. Amer. Psychoan. Assoc.*, 18:51–85.

Kernberg, O.F. (1974). Further contributions to the treatment of narcissistic personalities. *Internat. J. Psychoan.*, 55:215–240.

Kernberg, O.F. (1975). *Borderline conditions and pathological narcissism*. New York: Aronson.

Kernberg, O.F. (1980). *Internal world and external reality*. New York: Aronson.

Kernberg, O.F. (1982). Paranoid regression, sadistic control and dishonesty in the transference. Unpublished manuscript.

Kernberg, O.F. (1982a). Psychoanalytische Objektbeziehungstheorie, Gruppenprozesse und klinische Institution. In H. Steinmetz-Schünemann (Ed.), *Psychologie der zwischenmenschlichen Beziehungen* (pp. 313–355). Darmstadt: Wissenschaftliche Buchgesellschaft.

Kernberg, O.F. (1984). *Severe personality disorders: Psychotherapeutic strategies*. New Haven: Yale University Press.

Kernberg, O.F. (1988). Clinical dimensions of masochism. *J. Amer. Psychoanal. Assoc.*, 36:1005–1029.

Kernberg, O.F. (1988a). Object relations theory in clinical practice. *Psychoanal. Q.*, 57:481–504.

Kernberg, O.F. (Ed.) (1989). *Narcissistic personality disorder. Psychiat. Clin. N. Amer.*, vol. 12(3).

Kernberg, O.F. (1989a). The narcissistic personality disorder and the differential diagnosis of antisocial behavior. In O.F. Kernberg (Ed.), *Narcissistic personality disorder* (pp. 553–570). *Psych. Clin. N. Amer.*, vol. 12.

Kernberg, O.F. (1992). *Aggression in personality disorders and perversions*. New Haven, CT: Yale University Press.

Kernberg, O.F., Selzer, M.A., Koenigsberg, H.W., Carr, A.C., & Appelbaum, A.H. (1989). *Psychodynamic psychotherapy of borderline patients*. New York: Basic Books.

Kestenbaum, C.J. (1979). Children at risk for manic-depressive illness: Possible predictors. *Amer. J. Psychiat.*, 136:1206–1208.

Kety, S.S., Rosenthal, D., Wender, P.H., & Schulsinger, F. (1968). Mental illness in the biological and adoptive families of adopted schizophrenics. In D. Rosenthal & S.S. Kety (Eds.), *Transmission of schizophrenia* (pp. 345–362). Oxford: Pergamon Press.

Kety, S.S., Rosenthal, D., Wender, P.H., Schulsinger, F., & Jacobsen, B. (1975). Mental illness in the biological and adoptive individuals who have become schizophrenic: A preliminary report based on psychiatric interview. In R. Fieve, D. Rosenthal, & H. Brill (Eds.), *Genetic research in psychiatry* (pp. 147–165). Baltimore: Johns Hopkins University Press.

al Khalil, S. (1989). *Republic of fear: The inside story of Saddam's Iraq*. New York: Pantheon.

Khan, M. Masud R. (1960). Clinical aspects of the schizoid personality, affects and technique. *Internat. J. Psychoanal.*, 41:430–437.

Klebanow, S. (Ed.) (1981). *Changing concepts in psychoanalysis*. New York: Gardner Press.

Kleiman, D. (1988). *A deadly silence: The ordeal of Cheryl Pierson: A case of incest and murder*. New York: The Atlantic Monthly Press.

Klein, D.F. (1977). Psychopharmacological treatment and delineation of borderline disorders. In P. Hartocollis (Ed.), *Borderline personality disorders* (pp. 365–383). New York: International Universities Press.

Klein, D.F. (1988). Cybernetics, activation and drug effects. *Acta Scand. Psychiat.*, Suppl. 341:126–137.

Klein, H.R., & Horwitz, W.A. (1949). Psychosexual factors in the paranoid phenomenon. *Amer. J. Psychiat.*, 105:697–701.

Klein, M. (1975). *Love, Guilt and Reparation & Other Works 1921–1945*. New York: Delta Books.

Klein, M. (1975a). *Envy, Gratitude & Other Works 1946–1963*. New York: Delta Books.

Kluft, R. (Ed.) (1985). *Childhood antecedants of multiple personality*. Washington, DC: American Psychiatric Press, Inc.

Knapp, P., Levin, S., McCarter, R.H., Werner, H., & Zetzel, E. (1960). Suitability for psychoanalysis: A review of one hundred supervised cases. *Psychoanal. Q.*, 29:459–477.

Knight, R.P. (1953). Borderline states in psychoanalytic psychiatry and psychology. *Bull. Menn. Clin.*, 17:1–12.

Knight, R.P., & Friedman, C.R. (Eds.) (1954). *Psychoanalytic psychiatry and psychology*. New York: International Universities Press.

Kocsis, J.H., Frances, A.J., & Mann, J.J. (1988). Imipramine treatment of chronic depression. *Arch. Gen. Psychiat.*, 45:253–257.

Kohlberg, L. (1976). Moral stages and moralization: The cognitive developmental approach. In T. Lickona (Ed.), *Moral development and behavior: Theory, research and social issues*. New York: Holt, Rinehart & Winston.

Kohlberg, L., Levine, C., & Hewer, A. (1983). *Moral stages: A current formulation and a response to critics*. Basel: S. Karger.

Kohut, H. (1971). *The analysis of the self*. New York: International Universities Press.

Kohut, H. (1977). *The restoration of the self*. New York: International Universities Press.

Kohut, H., & Wolf, E. (1978). The disorders of the self and their treatment: An outline. *Internat. J. Psychoan.*, 59:413–425.

Kolarik, G.-D., with Klatt, W. (1990). *Freed to kill: The true story of Larry Eyler*. Chicago: Chicago Review Press.

Kraepelin, E. (1909–1915). *Psychiatrie* (8th ed., vol. 4). Leipzig: J.A. Barth Verlag.

Kraepelin, E. (1921). *Manic-depressive insanity and paranoia*. Edinburgh: Livingstone.

Krafft-Ebing, R. von (1886). *Psychopathia sexualis*. Stuttgart: Enke.

Krafft-Ebing, R. von (1902). *Psychosis menstrualis*. Stuttgart: Ferdinand Enke.

Krämer, H., & Sprenger, J. (1496). *Malleus maleficarum*. Berlin: Jacob Springer.

Kraus, A. (1989). Der manisch-depressiv und sein Partner. *Daseinanalyse*, 6:102–120.

Kretschmer, E. (1922). *Körperbau und Charakter* (3rd ed.). Berlin: J. Springer.

Kroll, J. (1988). *The challenge of the borderline patient: Competency in diagnosis and treatment*. New York: W.W. Norton.

Kroll, J.L., Carey, K.S., & Sines, L.K. (1985). Twenty year follow-up of borderline personality disorder: A pilot study. In C. Shagass (Ed.), *IV World Congress of Biological Psychiatry* (vol. 7) (pp. 577–579). New York: Elsevier.

Kutcher, S.P., Blackwood, D.H., St. Clair, D., Gaskell, D., & Muir, W. (1987). Auditory P300 in borderline personality disorder and schizophrenia. *Arch. Gen. Psychiat.*, 44:645–650.

Kutchinsky, B. (1991). Pornography and rape: Theory and practice? Evidence from crime data in four countries where pornography is easily available. *Internat. J. Law & Psychiat.*, 14:47–64.

Kwawer, J.S., Lerner, H.D., Lerner, P.M., & Sugarman, A. (Eds.) (1980). *Borderline phenomena and the Rorschach Test*. New York: International Universities Press.

LaFrenière, P.J. (1988). The ontogeny of tactical deception in humans. In R. Byrne & A. Whiten (Eds.), *Machiavellian intelligence* (pp. 238–252). New York: Oxford University Press.

Langer, T.S., & Michael, S.T. (1963). *Life stress and mental health: The Midtown Manhattan Study*. London: Collier MacMillan.

Lasch, C. (1978). *The culture of narcissism*. New York: W.W. Norton.

LeBoit, J., & Capponi, A. (Eds.) (1979). *Advances in psychotherapy of the borderline patient*. New York: Aronson.

LeGrand de Saulle, H. (1891). *Les hystériques: État physique et état mental* (3rd ed.). Paris: J.-B. Baillière.

Leighton, A.H., Harding, J., & Macklin, D. (1963). *The character of danger*. New York: Basic Books.

Leith, R. (1983). *The torso killer: The shocking true crime account of Richard Cottingham, New York's deadliest serial murderer*. New York: Windsor.

Lenzenweger, M.F., & Loranger, A.W. (1989). Detection of familial schizophrenia using a psychometric measure of schizotypy. *Arch. Gen. Psychiat.*, 46:902–907.

LePois, C. (1618). *Selectiorum observationum*. Ponte ad Monticulum: C. Mercator.

Lerner, H.E. (1974). The hysterical personality: A "woman's disease." *Compr. Psychiat.*, 15:157–164.

Lessing, D. (1987). *Prisons we choose to live in*. New York: Perennial Books.

Leszcz, M. (1989). Group therapy. In T. Karasu (Ed.), *Treatments of psychiatric disorders* (pp. 2667–2678). Washington, DC: American Psychiatric Press, Inc.

Leszcz, M. (1992). Group therapy of the borderline patient. In D. Silver & M. Rosenbluth (Eds.), *Handbook of borderline conditions* (pp. 435–469). Madison, CT: International University Press.

Levin, J., & Fox, J.A. (1985). *Mass murder: America's growing menace*. New York: Plenum.

Levy, S. (1988). The unicorn's secret: Murder in the age of Aquarius. New York: Prentice Hall.

Lewis, C.E. (1991). Neurochemical mechanisms of chronic antisocial behavior (psychopathy). *J. Nerv. & Ment. Dis.*, 179:720–727.

Lewis, D.O., & Bard, J.S. (1991). Multiple personality and forensic issues. *Psych. Clin. N. Amer.*, 14:741–756.

Lewis, G., & Appleby, L. (1988). Personality disorder: The patients psychiatrists dislike. *Brit. J. Psychiat.*, 153:44–49.

Leyton, E. (1986). *Compulsive killers: The story of modern multiple murder*. New York: Washington News/New York University Press.

Liberman, D. (1957). Interpretacion correlativa entre relato y repeticion: Su Applicacion en una paciente con personalidad esquizoido. *Rev. de Psicoan.*, 14:55–62.

Lidberg, L. (1992, September 10). Platelet monoamine oxidase activity in the mentally disordered violent offender. Presented at the First European Symposium on Aggression in Clinical Psychiatric Practice. Stockholm.

Liebowitz, M.R., & Klein, D.F. (1981). Interrelationship of hysteroid dysphoria and borderline personality disorder. *Psych. Clin. N. Amer.*, 4(1):67–87.

Liebowitz, M.R., Stone, M.H., & Turkat, I.D. (1986). Treatment of personality disorders. *Annual Reviews of Psychiatry*, V (pp. 356–393). Washington, DC: American Psychiatric Press, Inc.

Lilienfeld, S.O. (1989). Comment on psychopathy. (Letter to Editor). *Brit. J. Psychiat.*, 154:568–569.

Linehan, M.M. (1987). Dialectical behavior therapy for borderline patients. *Bull. Menn. Clin.*, 51:261–276.

Linehan, M.M. (1992). Behavior therapy, dialectics, and the treatment of borderline personality disorder. In D. Silver & M. Rosenbluth (Eds.), *Handbook of borderline disorders* (pp. 415–434). Madison, CT: International University Press.

Links, P.S. (Ed.) (1990). *Family environment and borderline personality disorder.* Washington, DC: American Psychiatric Press, Inc.

Links, P., Mitton, J.E., & Steiner, M. (1990). Predicting outcome for borderline personality disorder. *Compr. Psychiat.*, 31:490–498.

Lion, J.R. (1992). The intermittent explosive disorder. *Psychiat. Annals*, 22(2):64–66.

Little, M.I. (1981). *Transference neurosis and transference psychosis.* New York: Aronson.

Livesley, W.J. (1986). Trait and behavioral prototypes of personality disorder. *Amer. J. Psychiat.*, 143:728–732.

Livesley, W.J. (1987). A systematic approach to the delineation of personality disorders. *Amer. J. Psychiat.*, 144:772–777.

Livesley, W.J., Reiffer, L.I., Sheldon, A.E.R., & West, M. (1987). Prototypicality ratings of DSM-III criteria for a personality disorder. *J. Nerv. & Ment. Dis.*, 175:395–401.

Livesley, W.J., & Schroeder, M.L. (1990). Dimensions of personality disorder: The DSM-III Cluster-A diagnoses. *J. Nerv. & Ment. Dis.*, 178:627–635.

Livesley, W.J., Schroeder, M.L., & Jackson, D.N. (1990). Dependent personality disorder and attachments. *J. Personal. Dis.*, 4:131–140.

Lombroso, C. (1878). *L'Uomo delinquents.* Torino: Bocca.

Lombroso, C. (1887). *L'Homme criminel: Criminel-né, fou moral, épileptique.* Paris: F. Alcan.

Loranger, A.W., Oldham, J.M., & Tulis, E.H. (1982). Familial transmission of DSM-III borderline personality disorder. *Arch. Gen. Psychiat.*, 39:795–799.

Lorenz, K. (1963). *On aggression.* New York: Harcourt, Brace.

Lourie, R. (1993). *Hunting the devil: The pursuit, capture and confession of the most savage serial killer in history.* New York: HarperCollins.

Louyer-Villermay, C. (1816). *Triaté des maladies nerveuses ou vapeurs et particulièrement de l'hystérie et de l'hypochondrie.* Paris: Méquignon.

Lowry, B. (1992). *Crossing over: A murder, a memoir.* New York: Knopf.

Luborsky, L. (1984). *Principles of psychoanalytic psychotherapy: A manual for supportive/expressive treatment.* New York: Basic Books.

Lucas, P.B., Gardner, D.L., Cowdry, R.W., & Pickar, D. (1989). Cerebral structure in borderline personality disorder. *Psychiat. Res.*, 27:111–115.

Lunde, D.T., & Morgan, J. (1980). *The lie song: A journey into the mind of a mass murderer.* New York: W.W. Norton.

Macaulay, D. (1988). *The way things work.* Boston: Houghton Mifflin.

Machiavelli, N. (1977). *The prince* (R.M. Adams, Trans. & Ed.) New York: W.W. Norton.

Machiavelli, N. (1983). *The discourses* (L.J. Walker, S.J., Trans.; B. Crick, Ed.) London: Penguin Books.

MacLean, H. (1988). *In broad daylight: A murder in Skidmore, Missouri.* New York: Harper & Row.

Mack, J.E. (1975). *Borderline states in psychiatry.* New York: Grune & Stratton.

Maeder, A. (1910). Psychologische Untersuchungen an Dementia Praecox-kranken. *Jahrbuch für Psychoanalyse*, 2:234–245.

Maher, B.A. (1991). Deception, rational man, and other rocks on the road to a personality psychology of real people. In W.M. Grove & D. Cicchetti (Eds.), *Thinking clearly about psychology. Vol. 2: Personality and psychopathology* (pp. 72–88). Minneapolis: University of Minnesota Press.

Maier, G.J. (1990). Psychopathic disorders: Beyond counter-transference. *Curr. Opin. in Psychiat.*, 3:766–769.

Maltsberger, J.T., & Buie, D.H. (1974). Countertransference hate in the treatment of suicidal patients. *Arch. Gen. Psychiat.*, 30:625–633.

Mamet, D. (1982). *Glengary Glen Ross*. New York: Grove Press.

Mandeville, B. (1730). *A treatise on hypochondriack and hysterick diseases* (3rd ed.). London: J. Tonson.

Mann, J., & Goldman, R. (1982). *A casebook in time-limited psychotherapy*. New York: McGraw-Hill.

Marazziti, D. (1992, September 10). The role of serotonin in aggression abnormalities. Presented at the First European Symposium on Aggression in Clinical Psychiatric Practice, Stockholm.

Marcus, J., Auerbach, J., Wilkinson, L., & Burack, C.M. (1984). Infants at risk for schizophrenia: The Jerusalem Infant Development study. In N. Watt, E.J. Anthony, L.C. Wynne, & J.E. Rolf (Eds.), *Children at risk for schizophrenia: A longitudinal perspective* (pp. 440–464). Cambridge, England: Cambridge University Press.

Markowitz, I. (1968). Respect, disrespect and the schizoid individual. *Psychiat. Q.*, 42:452–478.

Marks, I.M. (1982). Anxiety disorders. In J. Greist, J. Jefferson, & R. Spitzer (Eds.), *Treatment of mental disorders* (pp. 234–265). New York: Oxford University Press.

Marks, I.M. (1986). Genetics of fear and anxiety disorders. *Brit. J. Psychiat.*, 149:406–418.

Marks, I.M. (1987). *Fears, phobias and rituals*. London: Oxford University Press.

Marks, I.M., & Marks, M. (1990). Exposure treatment of agoraphobia/panic. In R. Noyes, Jr., M. Roth, & G.D. Burrows (Eds.), *Handbook of anxiety. Vol. IV: The treatment of anxiety* (pp. 293–310). Amsterdam: Elsevier.

Marr, D. (1992). *Patrick White: A life*. New York: Knopf.

Marshall, B., & Williams, P. (1991). *Zero at the bone: The true story of Roland "Gene" Simmons Christmas family massacre*. New York: Star Books.

Masson, J. (1985). *The collected letters of Sigmund Freud to Wilhelm Fliess*. Cambridge, MA: Harvard University Press.

Masters, B. (1985). *Killing for company: The case of Dennis Nilsen*. New York: Stein & Day.

Masterson, J.F. (1981). *The narcissistic and borderline disorders*. New York: Brunner/Mazel.

Maugham, W.S. (1915). *Of human bondage*. New York: Doubleday.

Mauri, M., Sarno, N., Rossi, V.M., Armani, A., Zambotto, S., Cassano, G.B., & Akiskal, H.S. (1992). Personality disorders associated with generalized anxiety, panic, and recurrent depressive disorders. *J. Personal. Dis.*, 6:162–167.

Mavissakalian, M., Hamann, M.S., & Jones, B. (1990). A comparison of DSM-III personality disorders in panic-agoraphobia and obsessive-compulsive disorder. *Compr. Psychiat.*, 31:238–244.

Mavissakalian, M., Hamann, M.S., & Jones, B. (1990a). DSM-III personality disorders in obsessive compulsive disorder: Changes with treatment. *Compr. Psychiat.*, 31:432–437.

Maynard-Smith, M. (1988). *Games, sex and evolution*. New York: Harvester Wheatsheaf.

Maziade, M., Côté, R., Bernier, H., Boutin, P., & Thivierge, J. (1989). Significance of extreme temperament in infancy for clinical status in pre-school years. I: Value of extreme temperament at 4–8 months for predicting diagnosis at 4.7 years. *Brit. J. Psychiat.*, 154:535–543.

McClelland, J.L., & Rumelhart, D.E. (1986). *Parallel distributed processing. Vol. 2: Psychological and biological models*. Cambridge, MA: MIT Press.

McConaghy, N. (1989). Thought disorder or allusive thinking in the relatives of schizophrenics? *J. Nerv. & Ment. Dis.*, 177:729–734.

McCrae, R.R., & John, O.P. (1992). An introduction to the five-factor model and its applications. *J. Personality*, 60:175–215.

McDougall, J. (1989). The anti-analysand in analysis. In R.F. Lax (Ed.), *Essential papers on character neurosis and treatment* (pp. 363–384). New York: New York University Press.

McGinnis, J. (1983). *Fatal vision*. New York: G.P. Putnam.

McGinnis, J. (1989). *Blind faith*. New York: G.P. Putnam.

McGlashan, T.H. (Ed.) (1985). *The borderline: Current empirical research*. Washington, DC: American Psychiatric Press, Inc.

McGlashan, T.H. (1986). The Chestnut Lodge follow-up study. III. Long-term outcome of borderline patients. *Arch. Gen. Psychiat.*, 43:20–30.

McGlashan, T.H. (1986a). Chestnut Lodge Follow-Up Study. VI. Long-term follow-up perspectives. *Arch. Gen. Psychiat.*, 43:329–334.

McGlashan, T.H. (1987). Borderline personality disorder and unipolar affective disorder: Long-term effects of comorbidity. *J. Nerv. & Ment. Dis.*, 175:467–473.

McGlashan, T.H., & Heinssen, R.K. (1988). Hospital discharge status and long-term outcome for patients with schizophrenia, schizoaffective disorder, borderline personality disorder and unipolar affective disorder. *Arch. Gen. Psychiat.*, 45: 363–368.

McGlashan, T.H., & Heinssen, R.K. (1989). Narcissistic, antisocial and non-comorbid subgroups of borderline disorder—Are they distinct entities by long-term clinical profile? *Psych. Clin. N. Amer.*, 12:653–670.

McGrath, R.J. (1991). Sex-offender risk assessment and disposition planning: A review of empirical and clinical findings. *Internat. J. Offender Ther. and Comp. Criminol.*, 35:328–350.

McGuire, C., & Norton, C. (1988). *Perfect victim*. New York: Arbor House/ Morrow.

McKeon, P., & Murray, R. (1987). Familial aspects of obsessive-compulsive neuroses. *Brit. J. Psychiat.*, 151:528–534.

McLynn, F. (1989). *Crime and punishment in eighteenth-century England*. London: Routledge.

Mednick, S.A. (1992, June 17). Congenital determinants of violence. Presented at the symposium on the Roots of Violence, Mental Health Centre, Penetanguishene, Ontario, Canada.

Mednick, S.A., Brennan, P., & Kandel, E. (1988). Predisposition to violence. *Aggressive Behavior*, 14:25–33.

Mednick, S.A., Moffitt, T.E., & Stack, S.A. (Eds.) (1987). *The causes of crime: New biological approaches*. Cambridge: Cambridge University Press.

Mednick, S.A., & Schulsinger, F. (1968). Some premorbid characteristics related to breakdown in children with schizophrenic mothers. In D. Rosenthal & S.S.

Kety (Eds.), *Transmission of schizophrenia* (pp. 267–291). New York: Pergamon.

Meehl, P.E. (1962). Schizotaxia, schizotypy and schizophrenia. *Amer. Psychol.* 17: 827–838.

Meehl, P.E. (1989). Schizotaxia revisited. *Arch. Gen. Psychiat.*, 46:935–944.

Meehl, P.E. (1990). Toward an integrated theory of schizotaxia, schizotypy, and schizophrenia. *J. Pers. Dis.*, 4:1–99.

Mehlum, L., Friis, S., Irion, T., Karterud, S., Vaglum, P., & Vaglum, S. (1991). Personality disorders 2–5 years after treatment: A prospective follow-up study. *Acta Psychiat. Scand.*, 84:72–77.

Meijer, M., & Treffers, D.A. (1991). Borderline and schizotypal disorders in children and adolescents. *Brit. J. Psychiat.*, 158:205–212.

Meissner, W.W. (1976). Psychotherapeutic schema based on the paranoid process. *Internat. J. Psychoan. Psychother.*, 5:87–113.

Meissner, W.W. (1984). *The borderline spectrum: Differential diagnosis and developmental issues.* New York: Aronson.

Meissner, W.W. (1988). *Treatment of patients in the borderline spectrum.* Northvale, NJ: Aronson.

Melges, F.T., & Swartz, M.S. (1989). Oscillations of attachment in borderline personality disorder. *Amer. J. Psychiat.*, 146:1115–1120.

Meloy, J.R. (1989). Unrequited love and the wish to kill: Diagnosis and treatment of borderline erotomania. *Bull. Menn. Clin.*, 53:477–492.

Merikangas, J.R. (1981). The neurology of violence. In J.R. Merikangas (Ed.), *Brain-behavior relationships* (pp. 155–185). Lexington, MA: Lexington Books.

Merikangas, K.R., & Weissman, M.M. (1986). Epidemiology of DSM-III Axis II personality disorders. *Annual Review of Psychiatry, V* (pp. 258–278). Washington, DC: American Psychiatric Press, Inc.

Metzner, J.L. (1991). Applied criminology. *Curr. Opinions in Psychiat.*, 4:856–860.

Mewshaw, M. (1980). *Life and death.* New York: Doubleday.

Mezzich, J. (1988, August 18) Personality conditions and the International Classification of Diseases (ICD). Paper presented at the First International Congress of Personality Disorders, Copenhagen.

Michaud, S.C., & Aynesworth, H. (1987). *The only living witness.* New York: Simon & Schuster.

Michels, R. (1989, February 10). Personality disorders; Axis I/Axis II relationships. Lecture at New York State Psychiatric Institute.

Miller, A. (1957). A view from the bridge. In *Arthur Miller's Collected Plays.* New York: Vintage.

Miller, L. (1992). The primitive personality and the organic personality: A neuropsychodynamic model for evaluation and treatment. *Psychoanal. Psychol.*, 9:93–109.

Millon, T. (1981). *Disorders of personality: DSM-III, Axis II.* New York: Wiley Interscience.

Millon, T. (1988, August 19). Overview of personality disorders. Keynote address: First International Congress of Personality Disorders, Copenhagen.

Millon, T. (1990). The disorders of personality. In L. Pervin (Ed.), *Handbook of personality theory and research* (pp. 339–370). New York: Guilford.

Minichiello, W.E., Baer, L., & Jenike, M.A. (1987). Schizotypal personality disorder: A poor prognostic indicator for behavior therapy in the treatment of obsessive-compulsive disorder. *J. Anxiety Dis.*, 1:273–276.

Mishkin, M., Malamut, B., & Bachevalier, J. (1984). Memories and habits: The neural system. In G. Lynch, J. McGaugh, & N.M. Weinberger (Eds.), *Neurobiology of learning and memory* (pp. 65–77). New York: Guilford.

Modestin, J., & Bachmann, K.M. (1992). Is the diagnosis of hysterical psychosis justified? Clinical study of hysterical psychosis, reactive/psychogenic psychosis and schizophrenia. *Compr. Psychiat.*, 33:17–24.

Modestin, J., & Villiger, C. (1989). Follow-up study on borderline vs. non-borderline personality disorders. *Compr. Psychiat.*, 30:236–244.

Modlin, H.C. (1963). Psychodynamics and management on paranoid states of women. *Arch. Gen. Psychiat.*, 8:263–268.

Mogstad, T.-E. (1979). Personal communication.

Money, J. (1990). Paraphilic serial rape (biastophilia) and lust murder (erotophonophilia). *Amer. J. Psychother.*, 44:26–36.

Moore, K., & Reed, D. (1988). *Deadly medicine.* New York: St. Martin's.

Moran, C., & Andrews, G. (1985). The familial occurrence of agoraphobia. *Brit. J. Psychiat.*, 146:262–267.

Moravec, H. (1992). *Mind children: The future of robot and human intelligence.* Cambridge, MA: Harvard University Press.

Moreau de Tours, P. (1888). *La folie chez les enfants.* Paris: J.-B. Baillière et Fils.

Morrison, A.P. (1986). Shame, ideal self and narcissism. In A.P. Morrison (Ed.), *Essential papers on narcissism* (pp. 348–371). New York: New York University Press.

Mullen, P.E., & Maack, L.H. (1985). Jealousy, pathological jealousy and aggression. In D.P. Farrington & J. Gunn (Eds.), *Aggression and dangerousness* (pp. 103–126). New York: Wiley.

Myers, W.A. (1991). A case history of a man who made obscene telephone calls and practiced frotteurism. In G.I. Fogel & W.A. Myers (Eds.), *Perversions and near perversions in clinical practice* (pp. 109–123). New Haven: Yale University Press.

Nacht, S. (1963). The nonverbal relationship in psychoanalytic treatment. *Internat. J. Psychoan.*, 44:328–333.

Nahas, G.G. (1973). *Marijuana—Deceptive weed.* New York: Raven Press.

Nash, J.R. (1973/1982). *Bloodletters and bad men: A who's who of vile men (and women) wanted for every crime in the book* (3 vols.). New York: Warner Books.

Ngor, H. (1987). *A Cambodian odyssey.* New York: Macmillan.

Niederland, W.G. (1984). *The Schreber case: Psychoanalytic profile of a paranoid personality.* Hillsdale, NJ: Analytic Press.

Nilsson, V. (1899). *Sweden.* New York: Peter Fenelon Collier & Son.

Norman, W.T. (1963). Toward an adequate taxonomy of personality attributes: Replicated factor structure in peer nomination personality ratings. *J. Abnorm. & Social Psychol.*, 66:574–583.

Norton, R.N., & Morgan, M.Y. (1989). The role of alcohol in mortality and morbidity from interpersonal violence. *Alcohol*, 24:565–576.

O'Brien, D. (1989). *Murder in Little Egypt.* New York: Morrow.

Offord, D.R., & Reitsma-Street, M. (1983). Problems of studying antisocial behavior. *Psychiat. Developm.*, 1:207–224.

Oldham, J.M. (1988, December 6). Patterns of comorbidity in a population of 100 borderline in-patients. Paper presented at the First New York State Office of Mental Hygiene Research Conference, Albany.

Oldham, J.M., & Morris, L.B. (1990). *The personality self-portrait.* New York: Bantam.

Oldham, J.M., Skodol, A.E., Kellman, H.D., Hyler, S.E., Rosnick, L., & Davies,

M. (1992). Diagnosis of DSM-III-R personality disorders by two structured interviews: Patterns of comorbidity. *Amer. J. Psychiat.*, 149:213–220.

Olsen, J. (1972). *Son: A psychopath and his victims.* New York: Dell.

Olsen, J. (1987). *Cold kill.* New York: Atheneum.

Ongkosit, Ch. (1983). Personal communication.

O'Shaughnessy, E. (1990). Can a liar be psychoanalyzed? *Internat. J. Psychoan.*, 71:187–195.

Ovesey, L. (1965). Pseudohomosexuality and homosexuality in men: Psychodynamics as a guide to treatment. In J. Marmor (Ed.), *Sexual inversion* (pp. 211–233). New York: Basic Books.

Pacepa, I.M. (1987). *Red horizons: The true story of Nicolae and Elena Ceasescu's crimes, life-style and corruption.* New York: Regnery Gateway.

Pao, P.-N. (1969). The syndrome of delicate self-cutting. *Brit. J. Med. Psychol.*, 42:195–206.

Paris, J. (Ed.) (1993). *Borderline personality disorder: Etiology and treatment.* Washington, DC: American Psychiatric Press, Inc.

Paris, J., Brown, R., & Nowlis, D. (1987). Long-term follow-up of borderline patients in a general hospital. *Compr. Psychiat.*, 28:530–535.

Paris, J., Nowlis, D., & Brown, R. (1988). Developmental factors in the outcome of borderline personality disorder. *Compr. Psychiat.*, 29:147–150.

Parnas, J., & Jorgensen, A. (1989). Premorbid psychopathology in schizophrenia spectrum. *Brit. J. Psychiat.*, 155:623–627.

Partridge, B. (1955). *The Ainsley case: Taken from the records of the well-known country lawyer of upstate New York.* New York: Random House.

Pattison, E.M., & Kahan, J. (1983). The deliberate self-harm syndrome. *Amer. J. Psychiat.*, 140:867–872.

Pauls, D.L., Raymond, C.L., & Robertson, M. (1991). The genetics of obsessive-compulsive disorder: A review. In J. Zohar, T. Insel, & S. Rasmussen (Eds.), *The psychobiology of obsessive-compulsive disorder* (pp. 89–100). New York: Springer.

Peabody, D. (Ed.) (1985). *National characteristics.* New York: Cambridge University Press.

Perry, J.C. (1989). Passive aggressive personality disorder. In *Treatment of Psychiatric Disorders* (vol. 3) (pp. 2783–2789). Washington, DC: American Psychiatric Press, Inc.

Perry, J.C., & Flannery, R.B. (1982). Passive-aggressive personality disorder: Treatment implications of a clinical typology. *J. Nerv. & Ment. Dis.*, 170:164–173.

Perry, J.C., & Klerman, G.L. (1978). The borderline patient. *Arch. Gen. Psychiat.*, 35:141–150.

Perry, M.E. (1990). *Handbook of sexology.* New York: Elsevier.

Person, E. (1986). Manipulativeness in entrepreneurs and psychopaths. In W.H. Reid, D. Dorr, J.I. Walker, & J.W. Bonner, III (Eds.), *Unmasking the psychopath: Antisocial personality and related syndromes* (pp. 256–273). New York: W.W. Norton.

Pfeffer, A.Z. (1961). Single case report: Follow-up study of a satisfactory analysis. *J. Amer. Psychoanal. Assoc.*, 9:698–718.

Phillips, K.A., Gunderson, J.G., Hirschfeld, R.M.A., & Smith, L.E. (1990). A review of the depressive personality. *Amer. J. Psychiat.*, 147:830–837.

Philo of Alexander (1927). *On the birth of Abel and the sacrifices offered him and by his brother Cain* (F.H. Colson & G.H. Whitaker, Trans.). Cambridge, MA: Loeb Classical Library, vol. 2, pp. 88–195.

Pienciak, R.T. (1992). *Murder at 75 Birch: A true story of family betrayal.* New York: Dutton.

Pinel, P. (1799). *Nosographie philosophique.* Paris: Maradan.

Plakun, E.M. (1989). Narcissistic personality disorder. A validity study and comparison to borderline personality disorder. *Psychiat. Clin. N. Amer.*, 12:603–620.

Plakun, E.M., Burkhardt, P.E., & Muller, J.P. (1985). Fourteen year follow-up study of borderline and schizotypal personality disorders. *Compr. Psychiat.*, 26: 448–455.

Plomin, R., & Daniels, D. (1987). Why are children in the same family so different from one another? *Behav. & Brain Sciences*, 10:1–60.

Plomin, R., & McClearn, G.E. (1990). Human behavioral genetics of aging. In J.E. Birren & K.W. Schaie (Eds.), *Handbook of the psychology of aging* (3rd ed.) (pp. 67–78). New York: Academic Press.

Plomin, R., & Rende, R. (1991). Human behavioral genetics. *Ann. Rev. Psychol.*, 442:161–190.

Posner, G.L. (1991). *Hitler's children: Sons and daughters of leaders of the Third Reich talk about themselves and their fathers.* New York: Random House.

Pössl, J., & von Zerssen, D. (1990). A case history analysis of the "manic type" and the "melancholic type" of premorbid personality in affectively ill patients. *Eur. Arch. Psychiat. Neurol. Sci.*, 239:347–355.

Poznansky, A. (1991). *Tchaikovsky: The quest for the inner man.* New York: Schirmer.

Premack, D. (1988). 'Does the chimpanzee have a theory of mind?' revisited. In R. Byrne & A. Whiten (Eds.), *Machiavellian intelligence* (pp. 160–179). New York: Oxford University Press.

Prichard, J.C. (1835). *A treatise on insanity and other disorders affecting the mind.* London: Sherwood, Gilbert & Piper.

Pritchett, V.S. (1977). *The gentle barbarian: The life, and works of Turgenev.* New York: Random House.

Pryce-Jones, D. (1989). *The closed circle.* New York: Harper & Row.

Pulver, S. (1970). Narcissism: The term and the concept. *J. Amer. Psychoanal. Assoc.*, 18:319–341.

Purcell, J. (1707). *A treatise of vapours, or hysterick fits* (2nd ed.). London: Edw. Place.

Quinsey, V.L. (1986). Men who have sex with children. In D.N. Weisstub (Ed.), *Law and mental health: International perspectives* (vol. 2) (pp. 140–172). New York: Pergamon Press.

Raczek, S.W., True, P.K., & Friend, R.C. (1989). Suicidal behavior and personality traits. *J. Personal. Dis.*, 3:345–351.

Rado, S. (1956). *The psychoanalysis of behavior. Collected papers.* New York: Grune & Stratton.

Raine, A. (1989). Evoked potentials and psychopathy. *Int. J. Psychophysiol.*, 8:1–16.

Raine, A., & Venables, P.H. (1988). Enhanced P3 evoked potentials and longer P3 recovery tomes in psychopaths. *Psychophysiology*, 25:30–38.

Rainer, J. (1978, May 6). Heredity and character disorders. Presented at the 14th National Scientific Meeting of the Association for the Advancement of Psychotherapy, Atlanta.

Rangell, L. (1955). The borderline case: A panel report. *J. Amer. Psychoan. Assoc.*, 3:285–298.

Rangell, L. (1968). A point of view on acting out. *Internat. J. Psychoan.*, 49:196–201.

Rapaport, D. (1954). On the psychoanalytic theory of thinking. In R. Knight & C.R. Friedman (Eds.), *Psychoanalytic psychiatry and psychology* (pp. 259–273). New York: International Universities Press.

Rapaport, D. (1954). On the psychoanalytic theory of affects. In R. Knight & C.R. Friedman (Eds.), *Psychoanalytic psychiatry and psychology* (pp. 274–310). New York: International Universities Press.

Rapoport, J., Elkins, R., Langer, D., Sceery, W., Buchsbaum, M., Gillin, J.C., Murphy, D.L., Zahn, T., Lake, R., Ludlow, C., & Mendelson, W. (1981). Childhood obsessive-compulsive disorder. *Amer. J. Psychiat.*, 138:1545–1554.

Rasmussen, S.A., & Eisen, J.L. (1990). Epidemiology and clinical features of obsessive-compulsive disorder. In M.A. Jenike, L. Baer, & W.E. Minichiello (Eds.), *Obsessive-compulsive disorders: Theory and management* (2nd ed.) (pp. 10–27). Chicago: Yearbook Publishers.

Ray, I. (1839). *Medical jurisprudence of insanity*. London: G. Henderson.

Regier, D.A., Boyd, J.H., Burke, J.D., Jr., Rae, D.S., Myers, J.K., Kramer, M., Robins, L.N., George, L.K., Karno, M., & Locke, B.Z. (1988). One-month prevalence of mental disorders in the United States. *Arch. Gen. Psychiat.*, 45:977–986.

Reich, J. (1987). Prevalence of DSM-III-R self-defeating (masochistic) personality disorder in normal and outpatient populations. *J. Nerv. & Ment. Dis.*, 175:52–54.

Reich, J.H. (1989). Familiality of DSM-III Dramatic and Anxious personality clusters. *J. Nerv. Ment. Dis.*, 177:96–100.

Reich, W. (1929). *Character analysis*. New York: Farrar, Strauss and Giroux.

Reid, W.H., Dorr, D., Walker, J.I., & Bonner, J.W., III (1986). *Unmasking the psychopath*. New York: W.W. Norton.

Remsberg, B. (1992). *Mom, dad, Mike & Pattie: The true story of the Columbo murders*. New York: Bantam Books.

Ressler, R.K., Burgess, A.W., & Douglas, J.E. (1988). *Sexual homicide: Patterns and motives*. New York: Macmillan.

Ressler, R.K., & Shachtman, T. (1992). *Whoever fights monsters: My twenty years hunting serial killers for the F.B.I.* New York: St. Martin's.

Restak, R.M. (1982). *The self-seekers: Understanding manipulators, the predominant personalities of our age*. New York: Doubleday.

Reston, J., Jr. (1981). *Our father who art in hell*. New York: Times Books.

Reznikoff, M., & Honeyman, M.S. (1967). MMPI profiles of MZ and DZ twin pairs. *J. Consult. Clin. Psychol.*, 31:100.

Rice, M.E., Harris, G.T., & Quinsey, V.L. (1990). A follow-up of rapists assessed in a maximum-security psychiatric facility. *J. Interpers. Viol.*, 5:435–448.

Rice, M.E., Quinsey, V.L., & Harris, G.T. (1991). Sexual recidivism among child molesters released from a maximum security psychiatric institution. *J. Consult. & Clin. Psychol.*, 59:381–386.

Richer, P. (1885). *Études cliniques sur la grande hystérie ou hystéro-epilepsie* (2nd ed.). Paris: A. Delahaye & E. Lecrosnier.

Rinsley, D. (1982). *Borderline and other self disorders*. New York: Aronson.

Rivele, S.J. (1992). *The Mothershead case: One vicious murder, two conflicting confessions. The crime that shocked Los Angeles*. New York: Bantam.

Robbins, M. (1989). Primitive personality organization as an interpersonally adaptive modification of cognition and affect. *Internat. J. Psychoanal.*, 70:443–459.

Robins, L.N., & Regier, D.A. (Eds.) (1991). *Psychiatric disorders in America*. New York: Macmillan.

Robins, L.N., Tipp, J., & Przybeck, T. (1991). Antisocial personality. In L.N. Robins & D.A. Regier (Eds.), *Psychiatric Disorders in America* (pp. 258–290). New York: Macmillan.

Robinson, T.E., Becker, J.B., & Camp, D.M. (1983). Sex differences in behavioral and brain asymmetries. In M.S. Myslobodsky (Ed.), *Hemisyndromes: Psychobiology, neurology, psychiatry* (pp. 91–128). New York: Academic Press.

Robson, F. (1989, October 28/29). The colossus of Boggo Road. *The Australia Magazine*.

Robson, K.S. (Ed.) (1983). *The borderline child: Approaches to etiology, diagnosis and treatment*. New York: McGraw-Hill.

Rohde-Dachser, C. (1983). *Das Borderline-Syndrom*. Bern: Hans Huber.

Root, M.P., & Fallon, P. (1988). The incidence of victimization experiences in a bulimic sample. *J. Interpers. Viol.*, 3:161–173.

Rosenfeld, H. (1969). On the treatment of psychotic states by psychoanalysis. *Internat. J. Psychoanal.*, 50:615–631.

Rosenhan, D.L. (1973). On being sane in insane places. *Science*, 179:250–258.

Rosenthal, R.J., Rinzler, C., Walsh, R., & Klausner, E. (1972). Wrist-cutting syndrome. *Amer. J. Psychiat.*, 128:1363–1368.

Ross, C.A. (1991). Epidemiology of multiple personality disorder and dissociation. *Psychiat. Clin. N. Amer.*, 14:503–517.

Rosse, I.C. (1890). Clinical evidences of borderland insanity. *J. Nerv. & Ment. Dis.*, 17:669–683.

Rothchild, J. (1991). *Going for broke*. New York: Simon & Schuster.

Rounsaville, B.J., Dolinsky, Z.S., Babor, T.F., & Meyer, R.E. (1987). Psychopathology as a predictor of treatment outcome in alcoholics. *Arch. Gen. Psychiat.*, 44:505–513.

Ruitenbeek, H.M. (1973). *Freud as we knew him*. Detroit: Wayne University Press.

Rule, A. (1983). *Lust killer*. New York: New American Library/Signet.

Rule, A. (1983a). *The want-ad killer*. New York: New American Library.

Rumelhart, D.E., & McClelland, J.L. (1986). *Parallel distributed processing. Vol. I: Foundations*. Cambridge, MA: The MIT Press.

Rushton, J.P., Fulker, D.W., Neale, M.C., Nias, D.K.B., & Eysenck, H.J. (1986). Altruism and aggression: The heritability of individual differences. *J. Pers. & Soc. Psychol.*, 50:1192–1198.

Russell, D. (1986). *The secret trauma*. New York: Basic Books.

Rycroft, C. (1960). The analysis of a paranoid personality. *Internat. J. Psychoan.*, 41:59–69.

Sacher-Masoch, L. Ritter von (1901). *Venus im Pelz*. Dresden: Dohrn.

Salzman, L. (1960). Paranoid state: Theory and therapy. *Arch. Gen. Psychiat.*, 2:679–693.

Salzman, L. (1973). *The obsessive personality*. New York: Aronson.

Sandiford, K., & Burgess, A. (1984). *Shattered night*. New York: Warner Books.

Sandler, J. (1985). *The analysis of defense: The ego and the mechanisms of defense revisited*. New York: International Universities Press.

Sashin, J.I., Eldred, S.H., & van Amerongen, S.J. (1975). A search for predictive factors in institute-supervised cases: A retrospective study of 183 cases from

1959–1966 at the Boston Psychoanalytic Society and Institute. *Int. J. Psychoanal.*, 56:343–359.

Satel, S., Southwick, S., & Denton, C. (1988). Single case study: Use of imipramine for attention deficit disorder in a borderline patient. *J. Nerv. & Ment. Dis.*, 176: 305–307.

Satterfield, J.H., Cantwell, D.P., & Satterfield, B. (1974). Pathophysiology of the hyperactive child syndrome. *Arch. Gen. Psychiat.*, 34:839–844.

Sawyer-Lauçanno, C. (1989). *An invisible spectator: A biography of Paul Bowles.* New York: Ecco Press.

Scaramella, T.J., & Brown, W.A. (1978). Serum testosterone and aggressiveness in hockey players. *Psychosom. Med.*, 40:262–265.

Schlesinger, N., & Robbins, F. (1974). Assessment and follow-up in psychoanalysis. *J. Amer. Psychoanal. Assoc.*, 22:542–567.

Schmideberg, M. (1946). On querulance. *Psychoan. Q.*, 15:472–502.

Schmideberg, M. (1947). The treatment of psychopaths and borderline patients. *Amer. J. Psychother.*, 1:45–70.

Schmideberg, M. (1959). Psychiatric treatment of offenders. *Mental Hygiene*, 43: 407–411.

Schmideberg, M. (1961). Psychotherapy of the criminal psychopath. *Arch. Criminal Psychodynamics*, 4:724–735.

Schneider, K. (1923/1950). *Psychopathic personalities.* London: Cassell.

Schreiber, F.R. (1984). *The shoemaker: The anatomy of a psychotic.* New York: Signet Books.

Schroeder, M.L., Schroeder, K.G., & Hare, R.D. (1983). Generalizability of a checklist for assessment of psychopathy. *J. Consult. & Clin. Psychol.*, 51:511–516.

Schwartz, A.E. (1992). *The man who could not kill enough: The secret murders of Milwaukee's Jeffrey Dahmer.* New York: Carol Publishing Group.

Sciuto, G., Diafera, G., Battaglia, M., Perna, G., Gabriele, A., & Bellodi, L. (1991). DSM-III-R personality disorders in panic and obsessive-compulsive disorder: A comparison study. *Compr. Psychiat.*, 32:450–457.

Scott, E.M. (1989). Is there a criminal mind? *Internat. J. Offender Ther. & Compar. Criminol.*, 33:215–226.

Searle, J.R. (1990). Is the brain's mind a computer program? *Scientif. Amer.*, 262(1):26–31.

Searles, H.F. (1961). Anxiety concerning change as seen in psychotherapy of schizophrenic patients, with particular reference to their sense of personal identity. *Internat. J. Psychoanal.*, 42:74–85.

Searles, H.F. (1965). Concerning a psychodynamic function of perplexity, confusion, suspicion and related mental states. In H.F. Searles, *Collected papers on schizophrenia and related subjects* (pp. 70–113). New York: International Universities Press.

Searles, H.F. (1979). *Countertransference.* New York: International Universities Press.

Searles, H.F. (1979a). Violence in schizophrenia. In H.F. Searles, *Countertransference* (pp. 288–379). New York: International Universities Press.

Searles, H.F. (1986). *My work with borderline patients.* Northvale, NJ: Aronson.

Segal, J.H. (1989). Erotomania revisited: From Kraepelin to DSM-III-R. *Amer. J. Psychiat.*, 146:1261–1266.

Semrud-Clikeman, M., & Hynd, G.W. (1990). Right hemispheric dysfunction in nonverbal learning disabilities: Social, academic and adaptive functioning in adults and children. *Psychol. Bull.*, 107:196–209.

Serban, G., & Siegel, S. (1984). Response of borderline and schizotypal patients to small doses of thiothixene and haloperidol. *Amer. J. Psychiat.*, 141:1455–1458.

Servadio, E. (1956). "Condizionamento emozionale" e "complementarità" nel fenomeno telepatico. *Parapsicologica*, 2:188–192.

Shane, M., & Shane, E. (1992). Transference, countertransference, and the real relationship: A study and reassessment of Greenson's views of the patient/analyst dyad. In A. Sugarman, R.A. Nemiroff, & D.P. Greenson (Eds.), *The technique and practice of psychoanalysis. Vol. II: A memorial to Ralph Greenson* (pp. 285–303). Madison, CT: International Universities Press.

Sharkey, J. (1990). *Death sentence: The inside story of the John List murders.* New York: Signet Books.

Sharkey, J. (1991). *Deadly greed: The riveting true story of the Stuart murder case.* New York: Prentice Hall.

Sheldon, W.H. (1940). *The varieties of human physique: An introduction to constitutional psychology.* New York: Harper.

Sheldon, W.H. (1954). *Atlas of men: A guide for somatotyping the adult male at all ages.* New York: Harper.

Shengold, L. (1989). *Soul murder: The effects of child abuse and deprivation.* New Haven: Yale University Press.

Siever, L.J., Bernstein, D.P., & Silverman, J.M. (1989). Schizotypal, paranoid and schizoid personality disorders: A review of their current status. Unpublished manuscript.

Siever, L.J., Coursey, R.D., & Alterman, I.S. (1984). Impaired smooth pursuit eye movement: Vulnerability marker for schizotypal personality disorder in a normal volunteer population. *Amer. J. Psychiat.*, 141:1560–1566.

Siever, L.J., Klar, H., & Coccaro, E. (1985). Biological response styles: Clinical implications. In L.J. Siever & H. Klar (Eds.), *Psychobiological substrates of personality* (pp. 38–66). Washington, DC: American Psychiatric Press, Inc.

Silver, D., & Rosenbluth, M. (Eds.) (1992). *Handbook of borderline disorders.* Madison, CT: International Universities Press.

Simonton, D.K. (1990). Personality and politics. In L.A. Pervin (Ed.), *Handbook of personality: Theory and research* (pp. 670–692). New York: Guilford.

Sjöbring, H. (1914). *Den individualpsykologiska frageställningen inom psykiatrien.* Dissertation, Uppsala University.

Sjöbring, H. (1958). *Struktur och utveckling, en personlighetsteori.* Lund: Gleerups.

Sjöbring, H. (1973). Personality structure and development, a model and its application. *Acta Psychiat. Scand.*, Suppl. 244.

Slavinska-Holy, N. (Ed.) (1988). *Borderline and narcissistic patients in therapy.* Madison, CT: International Universities Press.

Slipp, S. (Ed.) (1982). *Curative factors in dynamic psychotherapy.* New York: McGraw-Hill.

Smith, M.L., Glass, G.V., & Miller, T.I. (1980). *The benefits of psychotherapy.* Baltimore: Johns Hopkins University Press.

Smith, S.S., & Newman, J.P. (1990). Alcohol and drug-abuse-dependence disorders in psychopathic and non-psychopathic criminal offenders. *J. Abnormal Psychol.*, 99:430–439.

Snyder, S. (1986). Pseudologia fantastica in the borderline patient. *Amer. J. Psychiat.*, 143:1287–1289.

Soloff, P.H., George, A., Nathan, S., Schulz, P.M., Ulrich, R.F., & Perel, J.M.

(1986). Progress in pharmacotherapy of borderline disorders. *Arch. Gen. Psychiat.*, 43:691–697.

Solomon, M.I., & Murphy, G.E. (1984). Cohort studies of suicide. In H.S. Sudak, A.B. Ford, & N.B. Rushforth (Eds.), *Suicide in the young* (pp. 1–14). Boston: John Wright.

Spillane, R. (1987). Rhetoric as comedy: Some philosophical antecedants of psychotherapeutic ethics. *Brit. J. Med. Psychol.*, 60:217–224.

Spitzer, R.L., Endicott, J., & Gibbon, M. (1979). Crossing the border into borderline personality and borderline schizophrenia. *Arch. Gen. Psychiat.*, 36:17–24.

Spungen, D. (1983). *And I don't want to live this life.* New York: Random House.

Squires-Wheeler, E., Skodol, A.E., Bassett, A., & Erlenmeyer-Kimling, L. (1989). DSM-III-R schizotypal personality traits in offspring of schizophrenic disorder, affective disorder, and normal control parents. *J. Psychiat. Res.*, 23:229–239.

Starr, R.H., Jr. (1988). Physical abuse of children. In V.B. van Hasselt, R.L. Morrison, A.S. Bellack, & M. Hersen (Eds.), *Handbook of family violence* (pp. 119–155). New York: Plenum.

Stein, D.J., Hollander, E., Anthony, D.T., Schneier, F.R., Fallon, B., Liebowitz, M.R., & Klein, D. (1992). Serotonergic medications for sexual obsessions, sexual addictions and paraphilias. *J. Clin. Psychiat.*, 53:267–271.

Stein, G. (1992). Drug treatment of the personality disorders. *Brit. J. Psychiat.*, 161:167–184.

Stein, J., with G. Plimpton (Ed.) (1982). *Edie: An American biography.* New York: Knopf.

Steiner, M., Links, P.S., & Korzekwa, M. (1988). Biological markers in borderline personality disorders: An overview. *Canad. J. Psychiat.*, 33:350–354.

Steiner, R. (1989). On narcissism: The Kleinian approach. *Psych. Clin. N. Amer.*, 12:741–770.

Steingart, I. (1983). *Pathological play in borderline and narcissistic personalities.* New York: Spectrum.

Stern, A. (1938). Psychoanalytic investigation of and therapy in the border land group of neuroses. *Psychoanal. Quart.*, 7:467–489.

Sternbach, O. (1983). Critical comments on Object-relations theory. *Psychoanalytic Rev.*, 70:403–433.

Stevens, J. (1993). *Three Zen masters: Ikkyū, Hakuin, Ryohkan.* New York: Kodansha International.

Stevenson, J., & Meares, R. (1992). An outcome study of psychotherapy for patients with borderline personality disorder. *Amer. J. Psychiat.*, 149:358–362.

Stevenson, R.L. (1886/1990). *The strange case of Dr. Jekyll & Mr. Hyde.* Lincoln, NE: University of Nebraska Press.

Stewart, J.B. (1991). *Den of thieves.* New York: Simon & Schuster.

Stolorow, R.D., Atwood, G.E., & Brandchaft, B. (1988). Masochism and its treatment. *Bull. Menn. Clin.*, 52:504–509.

Stone, A.A. (1985). The new legal standard of dangerousness: Fair in theory, unfair in practice. In C.D. Webster, M.H. Ben-Aron, & S.J. Hucker (Eds.), *Dangerousness: Probability and prediction, psychiatry and public policy* (pp. 13–24). Cambridge, England: Cambridge University Press.

Stone, L. (1961). *The psychoanalytic situation.* New York: International Universities Press.

Stone, M.H. (1972). Treating the wealthy and their children. *Internat. J. Child Psychother.*, 1:15–46.

Stone, M.H. (1976). Middle-class childhood between 1500 & 1800: Examples from the lives of artists, musicians and writers. *J. Amer. Acad. Psychoanal.*, 5: 545–574.

Stone, M.H. (1977). The borderline syndrome: Evolution of the term, genetic aspects and prognosis. *Amer. J. Psychother.*, 31:345–365.

Stone, M.H. (1978). A psychoanalytic approach to abnormalities of temperament. *Amer. J. Psychother.*, 33:263–280.

Stone, M.H. (1979). Dreams of fragmentation and death of the dreamer: A manifestation of vulnerability to psychosis. *Psychopharmacol. Bull.*, 15:12–14.

Stone, M.H. (1980). Modern concepts of emotion as prefigured in Descartes' *Passions of the Soul. J. Amer. Acad. Psychoanal.*, 8:473–495.

Stone, M.H. (1980a). *The borderline syndromes.* New York: McGraw-Hill.

Stone, M.H. (1980b). Traditional psychoanalytic characterology reexamined in the light of constitutional and cognitive differences between the sexes. *J. Amer. Acad. Psychoan.*, 8:381–401.

Stone, M.H. (Ed.) (1981). Symposium on borderline disorders. *Psych. Clin. N. Amer.*, 4(1).

Stone, M.H. (1981a). Borderline syndromes: A consideration of subtypes and an overview; directions for research. *Psych. Clin. N. Amer.*, 4:3–24.

Stone, M.H. (1982). Premenstrual tension in borderline and related disorders. In R.C. Friedman (Ed.), *Behavior and the menstrual cycle* (pp. 317–344). New York: Marcel Dekker.

Stone, M.H. (1982a). Intimacy and supervision. In M.N. Fisher & G. Stricker (Eds.), *Intimacy* (pp. 427–442). New York: Plenum.

Stone, M.H. (1985). Disturbances in sex and love in borderline patients. In Z. DeFries, R.C. Friedman, & R. Corn (Eds.), *Sexuality: New perspectives* (pp. 159–186). Westport, CT: Greenwood Press.

Stone, M.H. (Ed.) (1985a). *Essential papers on borderline disorders.* New York: New York University Press.

Stone, M.H. (1985b). Analytically oriented psychotherapy in schizotypal and borderline patients: At the border of treatability. *Yale J. Biol. & Med.*, 58:275–288.

Stone, M.H. (1985c). Genetische Faktoren in schizotypen Patienten. In G. Huber (Ed.), *Basisstudien endogener Psychosen und das Borderline-Problem* (pp. 225–237). Stuttgart: Schattauer.

Stone, M.H. (1988). The borderline domain: The "inner script" and other common psychodynamics. In J. Howells (Ed.), *Modern perspectives in psychiatry* (vol. 11) (pp. 200–230). New York: Brunner/Mazel.

Stone, M.H. (1988a). Toward a psychobiological theory of borderline conditions. *Dissociation*, 1:1–15.

Stone, M.H. (1989). Borderline personality disorder: Current views on nosology and psychobiologic theory. *Psychiat. Annals*, Jan.:8–10.

Stone, M.H. (1989a). Individual psychotherapy with victims of incest. *Psych. Clin. N. Amer.*, 12(2):237–256.

Stone, M.H. (1989b). Long-term follow-up of narcissistic and borderline patients. *Psych. Clin. N. Amer.*, 12(3):621–641.

Stone, M.H. (1989c). Murder. *Psych. Clin. N. Amer.*, 12(3):643–651.

Stone, M.H. (1989d). Pharmacotherapy and psychotherapy of borderline personality disorder in clinical practice. *Psychopharm. Bull.*, 25:564–571.

Stone, M.H. (1989e). Schizoid personality disorder. In T. Karasu (Ed.), *Treatments of psychiatric disorders* (pp. 2713–2718). Washington, DC: American Psychiatric Press, Inc.

Stone, M.H. (1989f). Schizotypal personality disorder. In T. Karasu (Ed.), *Treatments of psychiatric disorders* (pp. 2718–2727). Washington, DC: American Psychiatric Press, Inc.

Stone, M.H. (1989g). The course of borderline personality disorder. *Annual Review Psychiatry* (vol. 8) (pp. 103–122). Washington, DC: American Psychiatric Press, Inc.

Stone, M.H. (1990). *The fate of borderline patients*. New York: Guilford.

Stone, M.H. (1990a). Abuse and abusiveness in borderline personality disorder. In P.S. Links (Ed.), *Family environment and borderline personality disorder* (pp. 133–148). Washington, DC: American Psychiatric Press.

Stone, M.H. (1990b). Borderline personality disorder. In R. Michels (Ed.), *Psychiatry* (2nd ed.), vol. 1, chapter 17. Philadelphia: Lippincott.

Stone, M.H. (1990c). Treatment of borderline patients: A pragmatic approach. *Psych. Clin. N. Amer.*, 13(2):265–283.

Stone, M.H. (1990d). Borderline-no-okori: Chiryoh kanohsei-no-kyohkai: Follow-up data-to chiryoh kanohsei ni tsuite. (Borderline anger: The border of treatability; follow-up data concerning treatment). *Psychiatrica et Neurologia Japonica*, 92:824–830.

Stone, M.H. (1990e). Toward a comprehensive typology of personality. *J. Pers. Dis.*, 4:416–421.

Stone, M.H. (1991). Psychotherapy for the treatment of anxiety disorders. In R. Noyes, Jr., M. Roth, & G.D. Burrows (Eds.), *Handbook of anxiety* (vol. 4) (pp. 389–404). Amsterdam: Elsevier.

Stone, M.H. (1991a, May). Incest-murder: When incest leads to suicide and becomes murder. Presented at the meeting of the American Academy of Psychoanalysis, New Orleans.

Stone, M.H. (1992). The borderline patient: Diagnostic concepts and differential diagnosis. In D. Silver & M. Rosenbluth (Eds.), *Handbook of borderline disorders* (pp. 3–27). Madison, CT: International Universities Press.

Stone, M.H. (1992a). Aggression, rage and the "destructive" instinct, reconsidered from a psychobiological point of view. *J. Amer. Acad. Psychoan.*, 19:507–529.

Stone, M.H. (1992b). Incest, Freud's seduction theory and borderline personality. *J. Amer. Acad. Psychoanal.*, 20:167–181.

Stone, M.H. (1992c, June 19). Biographical data on famous murderers: The prelude to violence. Presented at the symposium: *The roots of violence*. Penetanguishene Mental Health Center, Ontario.

Stone, M.H. (1992d). Religious behavior in the Psychiatric Institute 500. In M. Finn & J. Gartner (Eds.), *Object relations theory and religion* (pp. 141–154). Westport, CT: Praeger.

Stone, M.H. (1993a). Etiology of borderline personality disorder: Psychobiological factors contributing to an underlying irritability. In J. Paris (Ed.), *Borderline personality disorder: Etiology and treatment* (pp. 87–101). Washington, DC: American Psychiatric Press, Inc.

Stone, M.H., Hurt, S.W., & Stone, D.K. (1987). The P.I.-500: Long-term follow-up of borderline in-patients meeting DSM-III criteria. I. Global outcome. *J. Pers. Dis.*, 1:291–298.

Stone, M.H., & Pine, D.S. (1993). History of childhood abuse in obsessive-compulsive disorder. (Unpublished manuscript)

Stone, M.H., Unwin, A., Beacham, B., & Swenson, C. (1988). Incest in female borderlines: Its frequency and impact. *Internat. J. Family Psychiat.*, 9:277–293.

Strasburger, L.H. (1986). The treatment of antisocial syndromes: The therapist's feelings. In W.H. Reid, D. Dorr, J.I. Walker, & J.W. Bonner, III (Eds.), *Unmasking the psychopath* (pp. 191–207). New York: W.W. Norton.

Straus, M.A., Gelles, R.J., & Steinmetz, S.K. (1980). *Behind closed doors: Violence in the American family*. Garden City, New York: Anchor Books.

Strelau, J., & Angleitner, A. (Eds.) (1991). *Explorations in temperament: International perspectives on theory and measurement*. New York: Plenum.

Suetonius, G. (1913). *De Vita Caesarum (The lives of the Caesars)* (vol. 1). (J.C. Rolfe, Trans.). Cambridge, MA: Harvard University Press.

Sullivan, A. (1992, March 22). The Nobel Prize in misanthropy. Review of *Patrick White: A life*, by David Marr. *New York Times*, Book Review, p. 1.

Sutherland, J.D. (1980). The British object-relations theorists: Balint, Winnicott, Fairbairn and Guntrip. *J. Amer. Psychoan. Assoc.*, 28:829–860.

Tarnopolsky, A. (1992). The validity of borderline personality disorder. In D. Silver & M. Rosenbluth (Eds.), *Handbook of borderline disorders* (pp. 29–52). Madison, CT: International Universities Press.

Tarnopolsky, A., & Berelowitz, M. (1987). Borderline personality: A review of recent research. *Brit. J. Psychiat.*, 151:724–734.

Tartakoff, H. (1966). The normal personality in our culture and the Nobel Prize complex. In R.M. Loewenstein, L.M. Newman, M. Schur, & A. Solnit (Eds.), *Psychoanalysis—A general psychology* (pp. 222–252). New York: International Universities Press.

Tate, G. (1831). *A treatise on hysteria*. Philadelphia: Corey & Hart.

Taubman, B. (1988). *The preppy murder trial*. New York: St. Martin's.

Taubman, B. (1992). *Hell hath no fury: A true story of wealth and passion, love and envy, and a woman driven to the ultimate act of revenge*. New York: St. Martin's.

Tellegen, A. (1991). Personality traits: Issues of definition, evidence and assessment. In W.M. Grove & D. Cicchetti (Eds.), *Thinking clearly about psychology. Vol. 2: Personality and psychopathology* (pp. 10–35). Minneapolis: University of Minnesota Press.

Tellegen, A., & Atkinson, G. (1974). Openness to absorbing and self-altering experiences ("absorption"), a trait related to hypnotic susceptibility. *J. Abnormal Psychol.*, 83:268–277.

Theophrastus (1947). *Charaktere*. (W. Plankl, Trans.). Vienna: Verlag der Ringbuchhandlung.

Thomas, A., & Chess, S. (1977). *Temperament and development*. New York: Brunner/Mazel.

Thompson, J.S., & Thompson, M.W. (1980). *Genetics in medicine*. Philadelphia: W.B. Saunders.

Tomkins, S.S. (1987). Script theory. In J. Aronoff, A.I. Rabin, & R.A. Zucker (Eds.), *The emergence of personality* (pp. 147–216). New York: Springer.

Tomkins, S.S. (1991). *Affect, imagery, consciousness. Vol. III: The negative affects: Anger and fear*. New York: Springer.

Torgersen, S. (1983). Genetic factors in anxiety disorders. *Arch. Gen. Psychiat.*, 40:1085–1089.

Torgersen, S. (1984). Genetic and nosological aspects of schizotypal and borderline personality disorders. *Arch. Gen. Psychiat.*, 41:546–554.

Torgersen, S. (1985). Temperamental differences in infants and 6-yr. old children: A follow-up study of twins. In J. Strelau, F.H. Farley, & A. Gale (Eds.), *The biological basis of personality and behavior.* Washington, DC: Hemisphere.

Toufexis, A. (1989, June 12). Our violent kids. *Time, 52–58.*

Träksman-Bendz, L., Åsberg, M., & Schalling, D. (1986). Serotonergic function and suicidal behavior in personality disorders. In J.J. Mann & M. Stanley (Eds.), *Psychobiology of suicidal behavior* (pp. 168–174). New York: New York Academy of Sciences.

Trull, T.J., Widiger, T.A., & Frances, A. (1987). Covariation of criteria sets for avoidant, schizoid and dependent personality disorders. *Amer. J. Psychiat.*, 144: 767–771.

Tupes, E.C., & Christal, R.E. (1961/1992). Recurrent personality factors based on trait ratings. US Air Force ASD Technical Reports (#61–97). Reprinted in *J. Personality*, 60:225–251.

Turkat, I.D., Keane, S.P., & Thompson-Pope, S.K. (1990). Social processing errors among paranoid personalities. *J. Psychopathol. & Behav. Assess.*, 12:263–269.

Tyrer, P., & Alexander, J. (1979). Classification of personality disorder. *Brit. J. Psychiatry*, 135:163–167.

Tyrer, P., & Alexander, J. (1988). Personality assessment schedule. In P. Tyrer (Ed.), *Personality disorders: Diagnosis, management and course* (pp. 43–62). London: Wright.

Tyrer, P., Casey, P., & Gall, J. (1983). Relationship between neurosis and personality disorder. *Brit. J. Psychiat.*, 142:404–408.

Unger, C. (1988). *Blue blood: The story of Rebekah Harkness and how one of the richest families in the world descended into drugs, madness, suicide and violence.* New York: Morrow.

Utley, R.M. (1989). *Billy the Kid: A short and violent life.* Lincoln, NE: University of Nebraska Press.

Vachss, A. (1993, January 5). Sex predators can't be saved. *New York Times*, Op. Ed.

Valzelli, L. (1981). *Psychobiology of aggression and violence.* New York: Raven Press.

Vandenberg, S.G. (1967). Hereditary factors in normal personality traits, as measured by inventories. In J. Wortis (Ed.), *Recent advances in biological psychiatry* (vol. 9) (chapter 6). New York: Plenum.

van der Kolk, B.A. (1989). Compulsion to repeat the trauma: Reenactment, revictimization and masochism. *Psych. Clin. N. Amer.*, 12(2):389–412.

Vanggaard, T. (1979). *Borderlands of sanity.* Copenhagen: Munksgaard.

Vanggaard, T. (1989). *Panic: The course of a psychoanalysis.* New York: W.W. Norton.

van Hasselt, V.B., Morrison, R.L., Bellack, A.S., & Hersen, M. (Eds.) (1988). *Handbook of family violence.* New York: Plenum.

Vaughn, C.E., & Leff, J.P. (1976). The influence of family and social factors on the course of psychiatric illness: A comparison of schizophrenia and depressed neurotic patients. *Brit. J. Psychiat.*, 129:125–137.

Vela, R., Gottlieb, H., & Gottlieb, E. (1983). Borderline syndromes in childhood: A critical review. In K.S. Robson (Ed.), *The borderline child* (pp. 31–48). New York: McGraw-Hill.

Voeller, K.K.S. (1991). Social-emotional learning disabilities. *Psychiat. Annals*, 21: 735–741.

Voisin, F. (1826). *Des causes morales et physiques des maladies mentales et de quelques autres affections nerveuses telles que l'hystérie, la nymphomanie et le satyriasis*. Paris: J.-B. Baillière.

Volkan, V. (1987). *Six steps in the treatment of borderline personality organization*. Northvale, NJ: Aronson.

von Bertalanffy, L. (1968). *General system theory: Foundations, development, applications*. New York: G. Braziller.

von Ohlsen, S. (1991). Killer angels: Kids without conscience. *The World & I*, 6(10):270–277.

Waldinger, R.J., & Gunderson, J.G. (1984). Completed psychotherapies with borderline patients. *Amer. J. Psychother.*, 38:190–202.

Waldinger, R.J., & Gunderson, J.G. (1987). *Effective psychotherapy with borderline patients*. New York: Macmillan.

Walker, N. (1991). Dangerous mistakes. *Brit. J. Psychiat.*, 158:752–757.

Wallerstein, R.S. (1986). *Forty-two lives in treatment: A study of psychoanalysis and psychotherapy*. New York: Guilford.

Ward, A.A. (1948). The anterior cingulate gyrus and personality. *Assoc. for Research in Nervous & Ment. Dis.*, 27:438–445.

Watson, D., & Clark, L.A. (1992). On traits and temperament: General and specific factors of emotional experience and their relation to the five-factor model. *J. Personality*, 60:441–476.

Weber, J.J., Bachrach, H.M., & Solomon, M. (1985). Factors associated with the outcome of psychoanalysis: Report of the Columbia Psychoanalytic Center Research Project: II, III. *Internat. Rev. Psychoanal.*, 12:127–141; 251–262.

Weber, J.J., Solomon, M., & Bachrach, H.M. (1985). Characteristics of psychoanalytic clinic patients: Report of the Columbia Psychoanalytic Center Research Project: I. *Internat. Rev. Psychoanal.*, 12:13–26.

Webster, C.D., Ben-Aron, M.H., & Hucker, S.J. (Eds.) (1985). *Dangerousness: Probability and prediction, psychiatry and public policy*. Cambridge, England: Cambridge University Press.

Weitz, J. (1992). *Hitler's diplomat: The life and times of Joachim von Ribbentrop*. New York: Ticknor & Fields.

Welner, A., Welner, Z., & Leonard, M.A. (1977). Bipolar manic-depressive disorder: A reassessment of course and outcome. *Compr. Psychiat.*, 18:327–332.

Weyer, J. (1564). *De Praestigiis Daemonum*. Basel: Oporinus.

Weyer, J. (1577). *De Ira Morbo (On the Disease of Anger)*. Basel: Oporinus.

White, G.L., & Mullen, P.E. (1989). *Jealousy: Theory, research, and clinical strategies*. New York: Guilford.

White, T.W., & Walters, G.D. (1989). Lifestyle criminality and the psychology of disresponsibility. *Internat. J. Offender Ther. and Compar. Criminol.*, 33:257–262.

Whiten, A., & Byrne, R. (1988). Taking Machiavellian intelligence apart. In R. Byrne & A. Whiten (Eds.), *Machiavellian intelligence* (pp. 50–65). New York: Oxford University Press.

Whitman, R., Torsman, H., & Koenig, R. (1954). Clinical assessment of passive aggressive personality. *Arch. Neurol. Psychiat.*, 72:540–549.

Whytt, R. (1765). *Observations on nature, causes and cure of those disorders which have been commonly called nervous, hypochondriac or hysteric*. Edinburgh: J. Balfour.

Widiger, T.A., & Frances, A. (1988). The personality disorders. In J. Talbot, R. Hale, & S. Yudofsky (Eds.), *Textbook of psychiatry* (pp. 621–648). Washington, DC: American Psychiatric Press, Inc.

Widiger, T.A., Miele, G.M., & Tilly, S.M. (1992). Alternative perspectives on the diagnosis of borderline personality disorder. In J.F. Clarkin, E. Marziali, & H. Munroe-Blum (Eds.), *Borderline personality disorder: Clinical and empirical perspectives* (pp. 89–115). New York: Guilford.

Widiger, T.A., & Rogers, J.H. (1989). Prevalence and comorbidity of personality disorders. *Psychiat. Annals*, 19:132–136.

Widiger, T.A., & Trull, T.J. (1992). Personality and psychopathology: An application of the Five-Factor Model. *J. Personality*, 60:363–393.

Wiggins, J. (1979). A psychological taxonomy of trait-descriptive terms: The interpersonal domain. *J. Personality & Social Psychol.*, 37:395–412.

Wiggins, J. (1982). Circumplex models of interpersonal behavior in clinical psychology. In P.C. Kendall & J.N. Butcher (Eds.), *Handbook of research methods in clinical psychology* (pp. 183–221). New York: Wiley.

Wiggins, J., & Pincus, A. (1989). Conceptions of personality disorders and dimensions of personality. *Psychol. Assessment*, 1:305–316.

Willi, J., & Grossman, S. (1983). Epidemiology of anorexia nervosa in a defined region of Switzerland. *Amer. J. Psychiat.*, 140:564–567.

Williams, A.H. (1960). A psychoanalytic approach to the treatment of the murderer. *Internat. J. Psychoan.*, 41:532–539.

Williams, E. (1968). *Beyond belief: A chronicle of murder and its detection*. New York: Random House.

Williamson, S., Hare, R.D., & Wong, S. (1987). Violence: Criminal psychopaths and their victims. *Canad. J. Behav. Sci.*, 19:454–462.

Willis, T. (1668). *Pathologiae cerebri et nervosi generis*. Amsterdam: D. Elzevir.

Wilson, A. (1962). Envy. In I. Fleming (Ed.), *The seven deadly sins* (pp. 2–11). New York: Morrow.

Wilson, C. (1984). *A criminal history of mankind*. New York: Putnam & Sons.

Wilson, C., & Seaman, D. (1992). *The serial killers: A study in the psychology of violence*. New York: Carol Publishing Group.

Wilson, J.Q., & Herrnstein, R.J. (1985). *Crime and human nature*. New York: Simon & Schuster.

Winchell, R. (1992). Trichotillomania: Presentation and treatment. *Psychiat. Annals*, 22(2):84–89.

Winnicott, D.W. (1949). Hate in the countertransference. *Internat. J. Psychoanal.*, 30:69–74.

Winnicott, D.W. (1965). *The maturational processes and the facilitating environment: Studies in the theory of emotional development*. New York: International Universities Press.

Wittels, F. (1938). The position of the psychopath in the psychoanalytic system. *Internat. J. Psychoanal.*, 19:471–488.

Wolberg, A.R. (1973). *The borderline patient*. New York: Intercontinental Medical Book Corp.

Wolff, S., & Chick, J. (1981). Schizoid personality in childhood: A controlled follow-up study. In S. Chess & A. Thomas (Eds.), *Annual progress in child psychiatry and child development* (pp. 550–580). New York: Brunner/Mazel.

Wolff, S., & Cull, A. (1986). 'Schizoid' personality and antisocial conduct: A retrospective case note study. *Psychol. Medicine*, 16:677–687.

Wolff, S., Townshend, R., McGuire, R.J., & Weeks, D.J. (1991). 'Schizoid' personality in childhood and adult life II: Adult adjustment and the continuity with schizotypal personality disorder. *Brit. J. Psychiat.*, 159:620–629.

Wolowitz, H.M. (1972). Hysterical character and feminine identity. In J.M. Bardwick (Ed.), *Readings on the psychology of women* (pp. 307–314). New York: Harper & Row.

Wong, N. (1988). Combined individual and group treatment of borderline and narcissistic patients. In N. Slavinska-Holy (Ed.), *Borderline and narcissistic patients in therapy* (pp. 17–45). Madison, CT: International Universities Press.

Woody, G.E., McLellan, T., Luborsky, L., & O'Brien, C.P. (1985). Sociopathy and psychotherapy outcome. *Arch. Gen. Psychiat.*, 42:1081–1086.

Woolcott, P., Jr. (1985). Prognostic indicators in the psychotherapy of borderline patients. *Amer. J. Psychother.*, 39:17–29.

Wulach, J.S. (1988). The criminal personality as a DSM-III-R antisocial, narcissistic, borderline and histrionic personality disorder. *Internat. J. Offender Ther. & Compar. Criminol.*, 32:185–199.

Wynn, T. (1988). Tools and the evolution of human intelligence. In R. Byrne & A. Whiten (Eds.), *Machiavellian intelligence* (pp. 271–284). New York: Oxford University Press.

Wyre, R. (1986). *Women, men and rape.* Oxford: Perry.

Yalom, I.D. (1985). *The theory and practice of group psychotherapy.* New York: Basic Books.

Yang, K.S., & Bond, M.H. (1990). Exploring implicit personality theories with indigenous or imported constructs: The Chinese case. *J. Pers. & Social Psychology*, 58:1087–1095.

Yang, K.S., & Lee, P.H. (1989). Likeability, meaningfulness and familiarity of 557 Chinese adjectives for personality trait description. *Acta Psychologica Taiwanica*, 13:36–37.

Yarvis, R.M. (1990). Axis I and Axis II parameters of homicide. *Bull. Am. Acad. Psychiat. Law*, 18:249–269.

Yeudall, L.T., Schoplocher, D., Sussman, P.S., Barabash, W., Warneke, L.B., Gill, D., Otto, W., & Termansen, P.E. (1983). Panic attack syndrome with and without agoraphobia: Neuropsychological and evoked potential correlates. In P. Flor-Henry & J. Gruzelier (Eds.), *Laterality and psychopathology* (pp. 195–216). Amsterdam: Elsevier.

Yglesias, H. (1981). *Sweetsir.* New York: Simon & Schuster.

Yochelson, S., & Samenow, S. (1976). *The criminal personality* (2 vols.). New York: Aronson.

Yudofsky, S., Hales, R.E., & Ferguson, T. (1991). *What you need to know about psychiatric drugs.* New York: Grove Weidenfeld.

Zanarini, M., & Gunderson, J.G. (1990). Childhood experiences of borderline patients. *Comprehen. Psychiat.*, 30:18–25.

Zenhausern, R., Notaro, J., Grosso, J., & Schiano, P. (1981). The interaction of hemispheric preference, laterality and sex in the perception of emotional tone and verbal content. *Internat. J. Neurosci.*, 13:121–126.

Zetzel, E.R. (1956). Current concepts of transference. *Internat. J. Psychoanal.*, 37: 369–376.

Zilber, N., Schufman, N., & Lerner, Y. (1989). Mortality among psychiatric patients—the groups at risk. *Acta Psychiat. Scand.*, 79:248–256.

Zilboorg, G. (1941). *A history of medical psychology.* New York: W.W. Norton.

Zimring, F.E. (1991). Firearms, violence and public policy. *Scientific Amer.*, 265(11):48–54.

Zuckerman, M. (1991). *Psychobiology of personality.* New York: Cambridge University Press.

Index

525

SUBJECTS